HUMAN ATTACHMENT

McGraw-Hill Series in Developmental Psychology
Consulting Editor, Ross A. Thompson

HUMAN ATTACHMENT

Virginia L. Colin

The McGraw-Hill Companies, Inc.
New York St. Louis San Francisco Auckland Bogotá Caracas
Lisbon London Madrid Mexico City Milan Montreal New Delhi
San Juan Singapore Sydney Tokyo Toronto

McGraw-Hill

A Division of The McGraw·Hill Companies

5 6 7 8 9 0   QSR QSR   0 9 8 7 6 5 4 3 2

ISBN 0-07-011839-6

This book was set in Garamond by The Clarinda Company.
The editors were Beth Kaufman and Fred H. Burns;
the production supervisor was Margaret Boylan.
The cover was designed by Karen K. Quigley.
The photo editor was Anne Manning.
R. R. Donnelley & Sons Company was printer and binder.

Cover art: Henry O. Tanner, *The Banjo Lesson* (1893), Hampton University Museum, Hampton, Virginia.

Library of Congress Cataloging-in-Publication Data

Colin, Virginia L.
    Human attachment / Virginia L. Colin.
        p.   cm.—(McGraw-Hill series in developmental psychology)
    Includes bibliographical references and indexes.
    ISBN 0-07-011839-6
    1. Attachment behavior.   2. Attachment behavior in children.
  3. Parent and child.   I. Title.   II. Series.
  BF575.A86C65   1996
  155.4'18—dc20   95-41030

ABOUT THE AUTHOR

Virginia L. Colin earned her degrees in psychology from Swarthmore, Columbia, and the University of Virginia, where Mary Ainsworth, co-founder of attachment theory, was her principal mentor. As a self-employed research consultant since 1986, Dr. Colin has studied hundreds of babies and parents, some in low-risk samples, and some at high risk for developmental delays and/or disturbances associated with medical problems, poverty, immaturity, abuse, and neglect. She has worked on projects for the National Institutes of Health, Research Triangle Institute, the University of Notre Dame, Columbia University, and others. In addition to conducting research, Dr. Colin has worked as an assistant professor, provided developmental counseling and psychotherapy services, and provided specialized foster care services for troubled adolescents.

To Rebecca, Daniel, David, and Julia—

May you draw strength from
secure attachments all your lives.

C O N T E N T S

FOREWORD

The emotional connections between people throughout the lifespan—whether between parents and offspring, partners in love, grandparents and grandchildren, or close friends—help constitute our humanity and provide resources for understanding, empathy, and love. Is it any wonder, therefore, that the earliest of these attachments, between infants and their parents, inspires such interest and reflection? Throughout the centuries, philosophers have commented on the emotional ties between mothers and their offspring, and the earliest psychologists perceived this relationship as the foundation of human relatedness. Freud, for example, portrayed the infant-mother relationship as "unique, without parallel, established unalterably for a whole lifetime as . . . the prototype of all later love relations." Erik Erikson, sounding a similar theme, argued that the first psychosocial crisis of "basic trust versus mistrust" was resolved initially in the sense of security and confidence achieved by the infant with her or his mother. Such affirmations are observed daily in everyday family experience, whether in a one-year-old's shadow-like pursuit of his mother at home, or in a toddler's anguished raised-arms "pick-me-up" gesture when seeing her father after a separation, or in a young child's comfortable settling in the arms of a trusted caregiver. Early in life, attachments form the core foundation of a sense of security.

In recent years, however, infant-parent attachment has also become the focus of public attention and concern. Beginning almost a decade ago, and continuing to the present, scholars and public policymakers have debated whether early day care experience threatens the integrity of the infant's first ties to parents, and how the quality of day care can enhance or hinder the security of attachment. In well-publicized tragedies or in unpublicized reports of child maltreatment, we ponder how the apparent absence of attachment, or disturbances in attachment, can help to account for a parent's failure to adequately care for young offspring, or to contribute actively to their death. With public concern about "deadbeat dads," absent fathers, and other indicators of an apparently diminishing paternal involvement with offspring, policymakers consider what incentives (and sanctions) can be used to enhance a father's emotional commitment to his children. And from counseling sessions to talk-radio, many people wonder about the intergenerational transmission of attachment: how feelings of security or mistrust seem to be shared by parents and offspring, and passed on to the next generation.

In the context of theoretical interest and public concern, the contributions of carefully designed research on human attachment are essential to clear thinking and responsible intervention. In *Human Attachment,* Virginia Colin provides an invaluable resource to scholars, practitioners, and policymakers by offering a comprehensive, introductory review of the research literature on attachment and its implications for development throughout the lifespan. This well-written volume presents a remarkably broad sweep of research findings—from studies of the early antecedents of attachment to research on attachment in diverse cultural contexts; from studies of adult attachment to research on early intervention into attachment disorders; from studies of the later behavior of securely—and insecurely—attached children to research on children's conceptual representations of attachment in their lives. Moreover, the author provides a careful description of major assessment procedures for evaluating the quality of attachment in infants, children, and adults, and profiles ongoing research controversies as well as emerging new developments in this exciting field of study. In addition to these strengths, Virginia Colin draws on her own research background as well as her substantial clinical experience to provide case studies that exemplify many of the complex interactional processes she discusses, whether of a child who is raised by an insensitive parent or a single adult who is striving to cope with parenting problems in the context of poverty and other stresses. The result is a comprehensive account of attachment processes throughout life, written with clarity, skill, and compassion.

As a contributor to the research literature on attachment with my own views on the controversial issues discussed in this volume, I am impressed with both the scope and balance of Virginia Colin's portrayal of the attachment literature. In some respects, her writing helps to foster the kind of understanding that I hoped to attain when, many years ago, I participated with my son in a Strange Situation assessment. I had used the Strange Situation on countless prior occasions in my own studies of the security of attachment, but when my younger son reached the age of twelve months, I decided that it was time to become involved in this research literature as a participant, rather than just a researcher. The purpose of doing so was not to determine whether Brian was securely or insecurely attached, but rather to capture the feeling of the Strange Situation when it is *your own* child—rather than a research subject—who is observed throughout each episode. It was an eye-opening insight to do so, and has forever changed my perception of this research procedure and of the research based on it. In many ways, this book gives readers the same kind of first-hand "feeling" for attachment theory and research that can otherwise only be accomplished by becoming involved in this field, as either a researcher or a research participant (or both). For this, we are in Virginia Colin's debt.

The *McGraw-Hill Series in Developmental Psychology*, of which this volume is a part, has been designed to enrich and expand our common knowledge of human development by providing a forum for theorists, researchers, and practitioners to present their insights to a broad audience. As a rapidly expanding scientific field, developmental psychology has important applications to parents, educators, students, clinicians, policymakers, and others who are concerned with promoting human welfare throughout the life course. Although the fruits of scholarly research into human development can be found on the pages of research journals, and students can become acquainted with this exciting field in introductory textbooks, this series of specialized, topical books is intended to provide insightful, in-depth examinations of selected issues in the field from which undergraduates, graduate students, and academic colleagues can each benefit. As forums for highlighting important new ideas, research insights, theoretical syntheses, and applications of knowledge to practical problems, I hope that these volumes will find many uses: as books that supplement standard general textbooks in undergraduate or graduate courses, as one of several specialized texts for advanced coursework, as tutorials for scholars interested in learning about current knowledge on a topic of interest, and as sourcebooks for practitioners who wish to traverse the gap between knowledge and application. The authors who contribute to this series are committed to providing a state-of-the-art, accurate, and readable interpretation of current knowledge that will be interesting and accessible to a broad audience with many different goals and interests. We hope, too, that these volumes will inspire the efforts to improve the lives of children, adolescents, and adults through research and practice that are much needed in our world.

As a core component of our humanity, human attachments deservedly inspire our interest and concern. *Human Attachment* helps us to understand why these attachments make us who we are.

Ross A. Thompson
Consulting Editor

P R E F A C E

Human Attachment provides a thorough introduction to attachment theory, research methods, and research results. It discusses both healthy and pathological development in infancy, childhood, adolescence, and the adult years.

Attachment theory is widely regarded as one of the most viable theories of personality development and intimate relationships ever proposed. Unlike any other similarly comprehensive theory, this theory has always been closely tied to objective observations of babies, children, and parents living their real lives in their natural social environments. Partly because it is so well grounded in scientific observations, and partly because it offers such a rich framework for understanding and solving problems in adults' personalities and intimate relationships, attachment theory is quietly replacing Freudian theory in the minds of researchers, clinical psychologists, psychiatrists, social workers, and other educated, interested people.

Most of this book should be easy to read, though some familiarity with psychology would be advantageous. Readers who have had one introductory psychology course and one developmental psychology course will get more from this book than readers with less training.

While this book can introduce attachment theory to readers not yet familiar with it, the book also raises many of the questions that are at the cutting edges of attachment research. Whether you are a young person curious about human beings, love, and child-rearing, or you are a graduate student interested in doing research related to attachment, this is a good place to start your reading.

Virginia L. Colin

ACKNOWLEDGMENTS

I have many people to thank for encouragement and assistance in bringing this book into being. In 1991, I wrote a review of the literature on attachment for a conference initiated by the United States Department of Health and Human Services. Afterwards, Patrick F. Fagan and Sharon McGroder of the D.H.H.S. encouraged me to expand that review into a full-fledged book to make information about this very important topic readily available to the public.

Mary Ainsworth, Jay Belsky, John Borkowski, Jude Cassidy, Deborah Cohn, Pat Crittenden, Alicia Lieberman, Karlen Lyons-Ruth, and Charlotte Patterson, all colleagues with backgrounds in research and/or clinical psychology, further encouraged and assisted me in obtaining a contract to enable me to spend some time writing. Without their confidence in my abilities and their willingness to voice that confidence to others, this book would never have come into being.

My thanks go also to the following reviewers for their excellent recommendations about improving various drafts of the manuscript: E. Mark Cummings, West Virginia University; Mona El-Sheikh, Auburn University; Richard Lanthier, Indiana University; Renee Leonard; Alicia Lieberman, University of California, San Francisco; and Sally Wall, College of Notre Dame of Maryland.

At McGraw-Hill, I have several editors to thank: Jane Vaicunas for entrusting the project to me; Zaza Ziemba for her wonderfully thorough copy-editing; Fred H. Burns for superb work pulling the pieces together; and Beth Kaufman and Mike Clark for tremendous patience and tact through my three years of writing and rewriting.

At home, I thank my children for the patience and support they so often mustered as they endured the numerous unwelcome periods of my dedicating my attention to research and writing.

Virginia L. Colin

1

OVERVIEW

Why do babies get attached to their parents? Why are their attachments intense and persistent even if the parents provide poor or abusive care? How do parents and other caregivers help children become secure and self-confident? What are the consequences of the nature or quality of a child's early attachments? How long-lasting are the consequences? If two parents work outside the home and leave their baby with a nanny, will the nanny become more important to the baby than the parents are? These are the sorts of questions attachment theory addresses.

The questions go on from infancy and childhood to adolescence and adulthood: Why do some individuals feel that they can trust others to protect them when they are frightened, while other individuals do not? Why do some take it for granted that they are lovable, while others feel unworthy? Why do only some feel that it is safe to let their anger show, safe to get close to someone, and safe to need someone? Why are some people so rigid and controlling? Why and how do prior experiences in attachment relationships influence these matters? How can a psychotherapist help an individual improve his or her relationships? Why and how do parents' attachment histories affect the way they care for their children?

In Europe, North America, and elsewhere, attachment theory is widely regarded as one of the most viable, most-promising theories of personality and social development. Unlike any prior theory of social behavior, personality development, and emotional bonds, this theory has been tied to direct observations and scientific analyses of data throughout its evolution. Many of its propositions have been stated as empirically testable hypotheses and have subsequently been tested.

When observations contradicted hypotheses, the theory was modified to fit the data. In short, the theory and the research have evolved together, hand in hand, each guiding the other. They remain dynamic, still evolving.

Attachment theory integrates insights and data from four domains, each of which I will introduce briefly here: ethology, control systems theory, cognitive psychology, and psychoanalysis. *Ethology* is the science of animal behavior in the natural habitat. *Control systems theory* focuses on how elements in a system influence each other, with hierarchies of goals and plans determining observable responses. *Cognitive psychology* is the study of how people think, how they mentally represent reality and organize their representations of it, how they screen, interpret, store, use, reorganize, and recall information. *Psychoanalysis* is the study of unconscious affective (emotional) and cognitive processes and their effects on personality and behavior. Drawing from all these roots, attachment theory speaks directly and meaningfully about intimate human relationships from infancy through adulthood.

This unit introduces the major concepts in attachment theory and describes some of the well-established findings from early research in the field. It describes what attachment theorists have learned or hypothesized to be true of virtually all human beings. Then it introduces the ways in which the study of attachment has contributed to an understanding of the development of individual differences in personality, social behavior, and psychopathology. Because these first two chapters introduce almost everything I will describe in more detail in the rest of the book, the explanations of some concepts and data are necessarily brief. Later chapters will fill in the outline presented here.

THE EARLY HISTORY
OF ATTACHMENT THEORY
AND RESEARCH

In the 1950s and 1960s, John Bowlby, a British psychoanalyst, developed attachment theory to account for phenomena in personality development and psychopathology that were not well-recognized or explained by other psychoanalytic theories. Working in a child guidance clinic before World War II, Bowlby was struck by how often the early histories of apparently incorrigible juvenile thieves included severe disruptions in their relationships with their mother figures. He therefore focused research on the effects of the temporary separation of a child from his or her primary caregiver during the first 5 years of life, especially separations during which the child had to stay in an unfamiliar place with unfamiliar people. (At the time, it was quite common for a toddler or preschooler to be placed in a residential nursery for a week or two while the mother stayed in a hospital for childbirth or other care.)

Many of Bowlby's colleagues scoffed at the notion that separation from or loss of the mother figure in early childhood could have long-lasting consequences. Although many clinicians did believe that experiences in the early years exerted great influence on personality development, they based their opinions about what affected development on speculation and on retrospective reconstructions from adults who sought psychotherapy, not on reliable data. Some of Bowlby's associates undertook direct observations of children in residential nurseries and hospitals. A series of films and journal articles by Joyce and James Robertson (e.g., Robertson & Robertson, 1971) documenting the observations was particularly influential. The direct observations showed that the separations generally caused intense and prolonged distress, particularly among children whose parents did not visit them. Furthermore, follow-up observations of the children at home revealed that the relationship with the mother remained seriously disturbed for weeks or longer after reunion.

These observations and reports raised questions. What made the relationship with the mother figure so special? Why did separation from or loss of the primary caregiver cause so much distress, anger, and anxiety among children? Most psychoanalysts and learning theorists thought the child's bond to the mother was based on the fact that she provided food. Bowlby found that hypothesis unconvincing. If food, or even tender care, were all that mattered, a child should be able to shift easily enough from one caregiver to another. Instead, children quite often actively rejected substitute caregivers and cried inconsolably for their own mothers.

Around this time, Konrad Lorenz's work on imprinting was becoming known in England. Imprinting is species-specific learning that occurs within a limited period of time (a "critical period") early in the life of each individual animal and resists modification thereafter. For example, Lorenz showed that ducklings and goslings persistently follow the first large moving object they see after hatching, and treat that object as the mother, even if it is an adult male human being. Bowlby hypothesized that humans, like birds, might be biologically predisposed to form long-lasting bonds to specific individuals. For humans, as for birds, the social bond might depend on instinctive *social* behavior, not on learning to associate food with the mother figure. He began to study ethology, the science of animal behavior. Ethology deeply influenced both the research methods and the inferences of attachment theory.

Ethology is unfamiliar to many readers. For that reason, I intend to give it some emphasis here. Ethologists consider it very important to observe the species under study in its natural environment. Even though researchers may learn much in an artificial environment or a controlled experiment, they can more easily discover the natural organization and function of behaviors and behavior sequences in a natural or nearly natural environment. Inspired by ethologists, Bowlby and his associates moved beyond retrospective reports from patients in psychoanalysis and beyond the contrived stimulus-response connections behaviorists studied. They demonstrated the enormous importance of observing subjects in their natural environments—human subjects, as well as animal subjects. They began to understand the nature and role of instinctive behavior in humans, not only in other species.

Students who are new to the field often think that "instinctive" means unlearned, automatic, and unmodifiable. Some instinctive behaviors in some species do have those characteristics. They are called "fixed action patterns"; a certain sort of stimulus activates the instinctive behavior, the behavior automatically appears, and the behavior pattern automatically runs its full course. The animal does not need to learn the behavior and reinforcement contingencies manipulated by a behavioral scientist cannot easily influence the behavior.

However, much instinctive behavior must be learned. A bird species provides an interesting example. All male chaffinches in their natural environments learn to sing the songs that characterize their species. However, experimentation in contrived environments reveals that they are not born knowing the melodies. They sing them during the second year and beyond only if they hear them during the first year (Bowlby, [1969] 1982). Similarly, an animal in a zoo who gives birth to her first baby may fail to show many components of instinctive maternal behavior. Having grown up in an abnormal environment, she has not had the opportunity to observe and learn behavior that characterizes all mothers in her species in their normal environment.

Instinctive behaviors vary in the amount of learning required for their emergence. Some will emerge in virtually every member of the species in virtually any environment; no learning is necessary. Others emerge in some individuals or in some environments, but not universally. Interested readers can find excellent explications of the biological bases of human social behavior and of instinctive behavior in other species in a text by Robert Hinde (1974).

What about human attachment behaviors? Are they stable, automatic, and rigid, like fixed action patterns? Or are they supported and modified by learning opportunities and even reinforcement contingencies? I will address these questions at some length in Chapters 2, 5, and 6. For now, I will simply note that there is reason to believe that the forces of evolution permit and even reward variability (within limits) in instinctive behavior. A species whose behavior is very fixed is adapted to a very specific ecological niche. That species may be unable to survive when the environment changes, as it does from time to time. Humans have adapted successfully to a wide range of physical and social environments, so it is likely that attachment and caregiving behavior systems include great (but not infinite) flexibility. The way an individual organizes and expresses his or her attachment behavior certainly reflects some learning.

Contributions from ethology did not exclude psychoanalytic insights from the theory Bowlby was developing. On the contrary, attachment theory continues to share many important views with psychoanalytic theories. First, early adaptations have profound and long-lasting effects on the individual's personality, social relationships, thoughts, feelings, and behavior. Second, much of human motivation is unconscious. Third, development reflects a coherent underlying organization, even when surface manifestations in behavior change with age, state, and situation. The focus is on whole people interacting in intimate and committed relationships, not on single variables. For example, a behaviorist might study how the frequency, intensity, and duration of smiling vary with rewards and punishments. An attachment theorist, like a psychoanalyst, would be more interested in what meaning the smiles have to the interactants, which smiles express pleasure or affection, which smiles mask tension or anger, and what other paths of communication affect the relationship he or she is observing.

Discoveries in the field of cognitive psychology also enriched attachment theory as it evolved. People are not mysterious black boxes that sense external stimuli and emit observable responses determined by their reinforcement histories. People think. They develop internal, mental models of external and internal phenomena. Attachment theorists generally refer to these mental models as "representational models" or "working models." As Piaget (1952, 1970), Vygotsky (1978), and many others demonstrated, what human beings are capable of understanding and how they organize their thinking changes with age. Consequently, their representational models of themselves, of their attachment figures, and of their relationships change with age.

When a representational model bears a close resemblance to reality, it makes insight and foresight possible. That is, it enables the individual to try out behavior plans mentally, not physically. A baby has to use trial and error to find out how to get a cookie that is initially out of reach. She may stretch her fingers toward it, fuss for it, say "cookie," or stamp her feet until something works or until she gives up. A 4-year-old can sit still and think about the problem. That is, he can manipulate mental representations of behavioral strategies to select one that is likely to work. If he has, for his age, an average level of sophistication about social cognition, he will be able to make a good guess about whether asking Mom to give him the cookie will work on this occasion, whether asking Mom won't work but asking Dad will, or whether he had better wait until both parents have left the room, and then push a chair over to the counter, and climb up and get the cookie himself. Being able to manipulate mental models to plan an effective strategy for obtaining a cookie has consequences for nutrition and pleasure. Being able to manipulate representational models of the self, the other, and their interactions has consequences for personality development and social relationships.

Welcoming insights and analogies from other sciences, Bowlby ([1969] 1982) also discovered the utility of control systems theory for describing human attachment behavior. I will describe the basics of control systems theory and how it applies to human attachments in Chapter 2. As a rule, theorists who think in terms of systems theory stress the importance of understanding the interrelationships among elements in a system. Examining the elements in isolation from one another will never enable you to understand them, because, in natural circumstances, they exist always in relation to each other. The infant's attachment behaviors can be understood only in the context of the adult's caregiving behaviors and in relation to the infant's exploratory behaviors, and vice versa. Interested readers can find an excellent and more detailed description of attachment in the language of general systems theory in Marvin and Stewart (1990).

John Bowlby's associate, Mary Ainsworth (1967, 1972, 1983), conducted close observations of infant development and maternal care in very two different cultural settings: Uganda and the United States. Together, Bowlby and Ainsworth defined and developed the propositions of attachment theory.

MAJOR PROPOSITIONS
OF ATTACHMENT THEORY

In this chapter, I will state and describe the major propositions of attachment theory. Some are already well-supported by data. Others remain speculative. Further clarification of the amount of support for each will appear in later chapters.

DEFINITIONS

As defined by Bowlby ([1969] 1982) and Ainsworth (1973), an *attachment* is an enduring affective bond characterized by a tendency to seek and maintain proximity to a specific figure, particularly when under stress. The most familiar example of an attachment is the bond that almost always develops between an infant and her primary caregiver (usually the mother). Each aspect of the definition of attachment is important. Attachment behaviors such as crying, reaching, approaching, and clinging contribute to and illustrate the attachment, but they do not constitute the attachment. The attachment is the *emotional bond,* not the behavior. Most of the same sorts of behavior can also serve other behavioral systems, such as exploration and affiliation. Approaching a babysitter or crying when a new playmate leaves does not necessarily indicate attachment to the babysitter or playmate. An attachment is a *long-lasting* relationship, not a transient enjoyment of another's company or seeking of assistance or comfort from another in the primary attachment. (The *attachment figure* is the person to whom an individual is attached.) The attachment is to a *specific person.* If that person is available when the child needs comfort or protection, that person will be preferred. If that person dies or for some other reason disappears from the child's life, he will be missed. Other relationships may also be valued, and grieving may be resolved; but no other individual can fully replace a lost attachment figure. The existence and nature of the attachment bond are indicated by *attachment behavior,* which may include any behavior that results in a person's attaining or keeping proximity to, or contact with, some specific, preferred individual. Children's obvious attachment behaviors include crying, smiling, calling, reaching, approaching, following, clinging, and protest-

.ing strongly when left alone or with strangers. The individual intermittently seeks *proximity or contact* with the attachment figure, and does so especially when frightened, ill, tired, or otherwise under stress and in need of care and protection.

When the attachment figure is accessible and responsive, attachment behavior may consist merely of glancing at the attachment figure or listening now and then to verify the attachment figure's location. The attachment bond endures; the behaviors that illustrate the bond are used only intermittently.

THE BIOLOGICAL FUNCTION
OF ATTACHMENT BEHAVIOR

Ordinarily, attachment behavior becomes focused on and organized in relation to a specific figure. That is, human beings are instinctively inclined (biologically predisposed) to form attachments. Virtually every member of the species in any normal or nearly normal environment becomes attached to her primary caregiver. (However, some environments differ so radically from the environments in which humans evolved that instinctive behaviors take deviant paths or fail to develop at all.) Hence, attachment behavior is *species-characteristic* behavior.

When ethologists find a behavioral tendency that characterizes virtually every member of a species, they assume that the behavior serves some biological function. That is, they assume there is a reason evolution has selected for the given behavior pattern, a reason individuals who lack the behavior have not survived and are no longer represented in the gene pool of the species. The biological function of a behavior is not just a predictable or desirable outcome of the behavior; it is the outcome that contributes to the survival of the individual and, thus, of the species.

Bowlby ([1969] 1982) proposed that the biological function of attachment behavior is protection. Over the course of human evolution, individuals were in danger from cold, hunger, drowning (and other accidents), and predators. The modern world includes new dangers, such as electric shock and rapid automobiles, as well as such old dangers as fire, water, and, occasionally, dangerous animals. It remains true that the instinctive tendency to maintain proximity to an attachment figure increases the individual's chances of surviving and reproducing. Again, the instinctive pattern includes both a species-characteristic, genetic predisposition to become attached to someone and individual learning about which figure to select and how to organize behavior in relation to that figure. Ordinarily, one of the first attachment figures is the primary caregiver. Ordinarily, too, that specific individual is indeed more likely than others to provide care and protection.

GOAL-CORRECTED BEHAVIORAL SYSTEMS

Early in life, behaviors become organized into *goal-corrected* behavioral systems. A *system* is a set of discrete behaviors that function in some centrally organized way to help the individual achieve some goal. To say that the system is "goal-corrected" is to say that it acts flexibly to attain some goal. Bowlby ([1969] 1982) offered as analogies thermostats and heat-seeking missiles. When you set the thermostat on your heating system to 68 degrees, the system does not burn fuel constantly. Instead, it monitors the temperature of the room. When the temperature dips below 68 degrees, fuel is ignited and air or water is thereby heated and then circulated. When the temperature rises above 68 degrees, the heating system shuts the burner off.

Similarly, a heat-seeking missile does not fly directly from its launching point to a predetermined point in space. Instead, it monitors the environment for feedback about the location of a large hot object, and then corrects its path to pursue the goal of hitting that moving target. An object in motion (a missile) monitors its spatial relationship to another object in motion (another missile) and continuously corrects its path with the goal of making contact with the second object. Its actions are goal-corrected. The two objects in this example are missiles. However, the principles of goal-corrected behavior can also characterize a baby's following her father from room to room or a lovestruck adolescent's pursuit of the woman he imagines to be the embodiment and fulfillment of his dreams.

Feeding behavior is organized into a homeostatic system that, like your heating system, is goal-corrected. That is, the feeding system monitors progress through the environment and monitors changes in the environment and in the body. The system uses the available array of information to set a goal appropriate to the organism's state and situation. It then selects behaviors, checks feedback about the effectiveness of the behaviors in getting closer to the goal, and, as needed, modifies behavior. If moving in one direction doesn't work, the organism changes direction. If one food-gathering behavior doesn't work, the organism tries another.

For example, if you are hungry right now, you might look in your backpack for the sandwich you prepared this morning. If you find that you forgot to put it into your backpack, you might walk to the cafeteria to buy lunch. If you arrive there 5 minutes after the cafeteria has stopped serving, you might go to a snack-vending machine, insert some coins, obtain a bag of popcorn, open the bag, put some popcorn into your mouth, chew, and swallow. In this example, many different behaviors served your feeding system, and your selection of which behaviors to use and which way to point them was goal-corrected. If one behavior did not accomplish the goal of getting food into your stomach, you tried another behavior.

Attachment behavior is also goal-corrected. If crying doesn't bring the attachment figure to the child, the child may crawl, or walk, or run to the attachment figure. The goal is to attain or maintain a sufficient degree of proximity or contact. The child does whatever will work to achieve the goal.

ACTIVATORS AND TERMINATORS

When are attachment behaviors needed? In the tradition of ethologists, Bowlby, Ainsworth, and their colleagues looked to see what conditions activated and terminated attachment behavior. An *activator* is a stimulus or condition that turns the system on or turns the system up. A *terminator* is a stimulus or condition that turns the system off or down.

Activators and terminators can be external stimulus conditions, internal conditions, or a combination of the two. They include specific environmental stimuli, the way the system is organized in the central nervous system, the individual's current hormonal state, the individual's general state of arousal, and the general background stimulation.

For example, the sight of a vaguely fishlike object painted red underneath may elicit aggressive behavior from a male stickleback fish. A similar fishlike object that is not painted red underneath, has a swollen underside, and is held at a certain angle in the water does not elicit aggressive behavior but may elicit courtship behavior (Hinde, 1974). As you may have guessed, male sticklebacks have red bellies and are inclined to fight each other over territory or females; female sticklebacks who are nearing readiness for mating have swollen bellies that are not red.

Eliciting stimuli may at times produce an immediate response and at other times have more gradual effects. Much depends on the organism's readiness to respond. For example, rat pups elicit immediate maternal responses from female rats with litters, but virgin females may begin to show maternal behavior only after prolonged exposure to a pup. With a low internal level of male hormone, a male rat will copulate only with a receptive female. If an experimenter injects a high dose of the same hormones into the rat, the rat will mount a crude dummy.

Just as specific stimuli can increase the level of activation of specific behavioral systems, specific stimuli can signal the system to shut down. Consider the example of a bird building a nest. When the nest is completed, the bird stops building. If, however, a natural storm or a curious ethologist removes the nest (the terminating stimulus), the bird will begin again to gather twigs and straw and weave them together.

Among the largely external conditions that activate attachment behavior in human infants and young children are strangeness, frightening stimuli or events, cold, distance or separation from the attachment figure, a lapse of time since contact with the attachment figure, rebuffs from children or adults, and the attachment figure's departing, being absent, or discouraging the infant from coming close. Among the largely internal conditions that activate attachment behavior are fatigue, illness, and pain. This list of activating conditions includes circumstances that do indeed put the child at greater than usual risk and so increase the likelihood that the attachment figure's protection will be needed. Note that the list prominently includes a variety of expressions of the physical or psychological unavailability of the attachment figure. When the attachment figure is unavailable, the child may be unprotected. If the biological function of attachment is protection, it makes sense that unavailability of the attachment figure activates attachment behavior.

The intensity of activation of attachment behavior varies with the intensity of the threat. When a stranger enters the room, baby Dmitri may simply look over to make sure that his dad is still sitting in the chair reading his newspaper. If the stranger sits and talks to the father, Dmitri may just keep playing with his blocks. If, however, the stranger walks directly to Dmitri, greets him loudly, picks him up, and tosses him into the air, Dmitri is likely to cry, to struggle to get away from the stranger, and to reach hard for his dad. Furthermore, Dmitri may not calm down (i.e., terminate his attachment behavior) until his dad holds him close and speaks reassuringly for a long moment. If Dad tries to put Dmitri down too soon, that action will prompt Dmitri to intensify his attachment behavior: the baby will cling.

In general, getting close to the attachment figure or getting enough physical contact with him or her terminates attachment behavior. How much proximity or contact is needed depends on the intensity of activation of the behavioral system, on the quality of the attachment, and on the developmental level of the individual.

MOTIVATION

Attachment behavior is a class of behavior with its own dynamic. It is distinct from feeding behavior and from sexual behavior; it is not derived from either. In fact, Bowlby argued consistently that attachment is as basic and as important in human life as food and sex are.

In other words, there is no need to explain why attachment behaviors appear or why human beings form the strong, lasting emotional bonds we call attachments. Babies cry when they have been alone too long for the same reason babies cry when they have gone without food for too long: it's just the way babies are. The baby's need for contact with a caregiver is as basic as his or her need for food. When Bowlby (1958) first stated this opinion, it was a radical departure from the opinions of the psychoanalysts and social-learning theorists of the time. The proposition has gained increasingly widespread acceptance in recent years.

OTHER BEHAVIORAL SYSTEMS

While the attachment behavioral system is of primary importance in human life, it is not the only important behavioral system. In addition to the feeding system and the reproductive system (to both of which psychoanalysts have given much attention), attachment theorists have called attention to the following behavioral systems: exploration-play, affiliation, fear-wariness, and caregiving.

Each of these systems is assumed to be biologically based, with motivation built into the system—not derived or developed from any other behavioral system. For example, people naturally tend to explore and so to learn about their physical and social environments; healthy human beings do not have to be threatened or bribed to explore, play with, and learn about the objects around them. Similarly, they are instinctively inclined to direct social (affiliative) behavior to other members of their species, regardless of whether those others are attachment figures.

The fear-wariness behavioral system helps the individual avoid or escape from alarming stimuli or events. Some conditions do not activate the fear-wariness system until the individual has learned from observation or experience that they imply danger. Other conditions or events apparently arouse fear or wariness in infants naturally, or automatically; there is no need to learn that they signify a risk of harm. The natural clues to danger that Bowlby ([1969] 1982) identified include sudden loud noises, darkness, and being alone.

The various behavioral systems interact with each other. Perhaps the most obvious example of interweaving of behavioral systems is the meshing of a baby's attachment system with a parent's caregiving system. Attachment behaviors have the predictable outcome of increasing or maintaining proximity to a specific other, who is usually older, wiser, and capable of providing protection. Caregiving behaviors give physical or emotional nurturance, support, or reassurance and have the predictable effect of maintaining or increasing the well-being of another, who is often younger or weaker.

In ordinary situations, the baby's characteristics and behavior elicit proximity, protection, contact, and care from the parent. The baby monitors her proximity to her attachment figure, but the caregiver also monitors proximity. If the baby strays to an unsafe distance, the caregiver calls her back, follows her, or retrieves her. If anything alarming happens, both child and caregiver move rapidly toward each other. Attachment theorists see these patterns as evidence that the infant's attachment system and the adult's caregiving system have evolved together and work together to maximize protection of the child.

The various behavioral systems also interact within one individual. Among them, the attachment system is primary in young children. That is, strong activation of the attachment system commonly overrides the activity of competing systems, such as exploration or affiliation. When the attachment system is at a low level of activation, the child actively explores, plays, or directs social behavior to others. Intermittently, the child checks on the attachment figure. The attachment system, like the thermostat on your heating system, is always on; the child always monitors the whereabouts of the attachment figure. If a threat from a barking dog or an aggressive playmate arises, the fear-wariness system is activated, and the attachment system shifts to a higher intensity. Exploration and play stop, and the child, in a goal-corrected fashion, seeks contact, not just proximity, with the attachment figure. When a threat arises, the attachment figure serves as a haven of safety.

THE SECURE BASE PHENOMENON

In safe circumstances, the level of activation of attachment behavior can remain low for long periods while exploration and play continue. Use of the attachment figure as a "secure base" from which to explore has been well-documented not only in humans but also in other primates (Jolly, 1972; Van Lawick-Goodall, 1968). By the time they become able to move away from the mother (at birth, in some species), baby monkeys, baboons, chimpanzees, and gorillas almost always take care not to move too far away from her. Like human infants, toddlers, and preschoolers, they intermittently return to the attachment figure and figuratively or literally "touch base" even when nothing in the environment occurs to activate the attachment system. Just being away from the attachment figure for too long is enough to activate attachment behavior. Being near the attachment figure is usually enough to support exploration, play, and, sometimes, affiliative behavior.

Note that the attachment figure is a secure base *from which to explore.* In the cultures most-studied to date, babies do not ordinarily seek to maintain contact or even very close proximity to their caregivers all the time. The physical world intrigues them and draws them toward exploration. The emerging capabilities of their own bodies intrigue them and prompt exercise and expansion of their abilities. The social world intrigues them; they naturally seek interaction with a variety of others, despite some periods of caution toward or even fear of strangers. Babies want to see and do and learn, not just to cling to their caregivers. However, they act as if they want to feel sure that the caregiver is staying physically and psychologically available while they are seeing, doing, and learning.

For example, Anderson (1972) observed children estimated to be 15 to 30 months old when they came to a secluded area of a public park in England with their mothers. While the mother sat quietly, the child played near her, with occasional little trips to explore other parts of the park. The child generally moved either directly away from the mother or directly toward her, with frequent stops interrupting the explorations. Returns to the mother tended to happen in larger segments and with fewer interruptions than movements away from her. Stops near the mother lasted relatively long. Stops at a distance from the mother were more frequent and much shorter. Hardly any of the returns were prompted by anything the mother or anyone else in the environment did; the motivation to touch base seemed to come from within the child.

In a laboratory playroom in the United States, Rheingold and Eckerman (1970) found the same thing. Infants explored contentedly if the mother was present but became distressed when separated from the mother. Furthermore, the babies could move calmly away from their mothers to explore the room and the toys, but they cried and stopped exploring when their mothers moved away from them. Similarly, Carr, Dabbs, and Carr (1975) found that babies played more when they could see their mothers than when they could not. The babies did not actually look toward their mothers more when the mothers were in range; just knowing the mother was near enough to see was sufficient to support involvement in play. Increased exploration, increased play, reduced wariness of strangers, increased sociability toward strangers—all of these are supported by the secure base, the attachment figure. (See Caruso, 1989, for a review of other studies of the secure base effect.)

EMOTIONS AND ATTACHMENTS

Bowlby ([1969] 1982) made two important propositions about emotions in relation to attachment theory. The first dramatizes one reason many people find the theory so fascinating. At heart, this unusually empirical, scientific theory is about what matters most in their own lives to many human beings: their feelings.

Intense feelings arise in connection with human attachments. The process of forming a new attachment bond is the thrill and delight of falling in love. Maintaining an attachment bond is loving someone; an attachment is love. If the continuation of the bond is unchallenged, the bond supports a feeling of security. The threat of losing an attachment figure arouses anxiety and anger. The reality of losing a partner, whether through death, long separation, or the ending of a relationship, ordinarily triggers the intense feelings associated with grief and mourning, which usually include anger as well as sorrow. The renewal of a bond is a source of joy.

In other words, our attachments are a major source of what makes our lives feel rich and wonderful or lonely, sad, and utterly wretched. They are not the only source of strong feelings, of course. Marked success or failure in school or on the job, the thrill of a new adventure or a new discovery, the pleasure of sailing or hiking, the threat of war, the trauma of an earthquake or hurricane—any of these can also trigger strong feelings. More often than not, however, these feelings are brought back to the attachment figure. Keiko's happiness about getting an excellent grade in her statistics class becomes magnified when she shares her joy with her boyfriend Kim. Greg's distress over his girlfriend's unplanned, unwelcome pregnancy is eased when he seeks comfort and assistance from his parents. Hiking in the mountains may delight you, but doing it with a companion to whom you are securely attached makes it even more wonderful.

Bowlby's second major proposition about emotions is harder to comprehend. According to Bowlby, feelings, or "affective processes," are involved in the process of appraising internal and external situations and selecting a response; but feelings are not, in themselves, motivations. They are "phases of an individual's intuitive appraisal of his own organic states and urges to act or of the succession of environmental situations in which he finds himself." (Bowlby, [1969] 1982, pp. 104–105). The scientist, he says, should direct her or his attention to the full set and sequence of appraising processes, not focus principally on the emotions that precede or accompany choices and actions (Bowlby, [1969] 1982).

In everyday life, people often say they did things "because" they were angry or "because" they were happy. Psychoanalysts and other clinical psychologists have also often referred to emotions as motivations or causes of actions. In Bowlby's opinion, this is an error. According to both Bowlby and Ainsworth, an emotion may often be *felt* in association with the activation of a behavioral system, but the emotion is not the *cause* of the behavior that ensues. Affective and cognitive appraising processes often operate below the level of conscious awareness. Knowing this helps to explain the concept of an "unconscious feeling," which psychologists have found meaningful.

Unlike other aspects of Bowlby's theorizing, his specific definitions of the terms "feeling" and "emotion" have not received much emphasis in the writings of the second generation of attachment theorists and researchers, so I will not say much about them here. Nevertheless, his argument that motivation springs from the array of activators and terminators, the internal organization of the behavioral system, the hormonal state, and other factors, not solely or principally from feelings, remains important.

INFANT PATTERNS

The propositions from attachment theory that I have discussed above describe normative development. That is, they describe what virtually all human beings are like, what all human beings need, and what factors influence the development of all human beings. Some of the propositions that follow address questions about the differences that emerge among individuals as they develop.

From an ethological perspective, both a propensity to form attachments and flexibility in organizing attachment behavior are adaptive as the species evolves; they increase the likelihood that the species will survive. That flexibility allows for considerable variation among individuals as each adapts to the specific physical, familial, and cultural environment in which he or she spends a single lifetime.

In her pioneering research in Uganda and in Baltimore, Maryland, Mary Ainsworth (1967, 1973) made lengthy observations of infants and their mothers in their natural environments. She found that babies with different experiences organized their attachment behavior in different ways. Ainsworth and Wittig (1969) developed a laboratory procedure, the "Strange Situation," that activated the infant's attachment system and highlighted individual differences in the organization of attachment behavior. The Strange Situation is moderately stressful, as it includes two brief (3- to 6-minute) separations from the attachment figure in an unfamiliar place. I will have much more to say about the Strange Situation in Chapters 3 and 8.

Ainsworth, Blehar, Waters, and Wall (1978) found that most of the first 106 American babies they studied responded to the laboratory procedure with behavior that fit one of three major groups: secure, avoidant, and resistant. (The labels are based on associations with behavior at other times and in other settings.)

When moderately stressful events occur, a *securely* attached baby approaches or signals to the attachment figure at reunion and soon achieves a degree of proximity or contact that suffices to terminate attachment behavior. A secure baby accomplishes this with little or no open or masked anger, and soon returns to exploration or play.

Babies in the other groups do not confidently use the attachment figure as a safe haven in times of stress and a secure base in ordinary circumstances. The love in their attachments is entangled with defensiveness, anger, and/or fear.

When the attachment figure returns to the laboratory room after a brief absence, the infant with an *avoidant* attachment fails to greet her, ignores her overtures, and acts as if she is of little importance. The evidence that the caregiver is indeed important, that the separation was stressful for the baby, and that the baby's behavior at reunion is defensive will be presented in Chapter 7.

In babies with *resistant* attachments, both anxiety and mixed feelings about the attachment figure are readily observable. At reunion after brief separations in an unfamiliar environment, these babies mingle openly angry behavior with their attachment behavior. They may cry and reach to be picked up but then push away from the caregiver. They are often difficult to soothe.

Later, Main and Solomon (1986, 1990) provided guidelines for identifying a fourth major group: disorganized-disoriented. Babies in this group show a variety of indices of insecurity. Some appear to be clinically depressed; some show mixtures of avoidant behavior, openly angry behavior, and attachment behavior; and some show odd behaviors and behavior sequences that leave observers with a sense of discomfort or disturbance.

THE IMPACT OF EARLY EXPERIENCE

Early experience with a caregiver is believed to be the principal determinant of the pattern of attachment a baby develops in relation to that caregiver. (Determinants of infants' attachment patterns will be discussed at length in Chapters 5 and 6).

The search to identify and explain differences among individuals brings attachment theory back to its roots in psychoanalysis. Like classical analysts, attachment theorists regard infancy as a very sensitive and important period of life, when the basic cognitive-affective foundation of the psyche forms. Both groups emphasize the continuing impact of the individual's first love relationships. Primary attachments influence a person's perceptions, his or her interpretation of those perceptions, and his or her behavior and feelings in later relationships.

Individuals have different sets of experiences in their first relationships. On the basis of their experiences, different individuals develop different representational models—different sets of beliefs about themselves, different expectations about others, and different sets of conscious and/or unconscious rules for organizing and accessing information about feelings, experiences, and ideas related to attachment. The models based on the child's actual early experiences are then carried into new situations and new relationships. Unknowingly, the child helps recreate the blessings or woes of his or her first relationships.

In a chapter Bowlby (1991) wrote very late in his life, he made some strong statements about the developmental trajectories set in motion by the individual's first attachments. Clinicians, he said, judge both avoidant and resistant patterns in infancy to be predictive of disturbed development. According to them, the anxious-resistant child is uncertain whether the caregiver will be available or helpful when called upon. The child therefore tends to be clingy and almost always anxious about separation; her anxiety about access to her attachment figure often prevents her from directing her energy and attention toward exploration and play. An anxious-avoidant child expects the caregiver to push him away if he seeks comfort or protection, so he tries to live without love or support from other people. Infant patterns may predict disturbed development, but what happens in infancy certainly does not fully determine later outcomes. Many individuals change course.

ATTACHMENT HIERARCHIES

Unless a baby is in an institutional environment where she has no regular caregiver, she becomes attached to her primary caregiver. In the ordinary course of events, most babies also become attached to one or more others with whom they frequently interact, even if the interaction never involves feeding or other physical care (Schaffer and Emerson, 1964).

In 1958 Bowlby proposed the "monotropy" hypothesis—that the human infant has a strong genetic bias to focus most of his or her attachment behavior on one figure, the principal caregiver, and to show a clear, consistent, strong preference for that figure whenever the infant is under stress. Bowlby expected other attachments to be clearly supplementary and subsidiary, with significantly less impact on personality development and later social relations. Other theorists have proposed that, in a child's hierarchy of attachment figures, the difference between the importance and influence of the first figure and the importance and influence of the second may be moderate or, in some family circumstances, negligible.

Evidence does suggest that, in early childhood, separations from other attachment figures are far less distressing and disruptive than separations from the principal caregiver. Nevertheless, there is evidence that a secure attachment to a secondary caregiver can buffer a child from some of the negative effects associated with an anxious attachment to the principal caregiver. Data relevant to hypotheses about attachment hierarchies will be discussed in Chapter 11.

DEVELOPMENTAL CHANGES

While the importance of attachments may be fairly stable from infancy to old age, the organization of attachment behavior and the nature of attachment relationships change with age. Protection and security are the hallmarks of attachment throughout the life span; but the conditions that activate higher intensity levels of the attachment system, the types of attachment behavior used, and the degree of proximity (or "contact") that terminates attachment behaviors change with age.

■ Childhood

After infancy, overt attachment behaviors such as crying and clinging decrease in frequency. As the child's physical abilities, social skills, and knowledge increase, she can safely be more self-reliant; she has less need of proximity to her attachment figure. As the child's knowledge increases and as the organization of her knowledge becomes increasingly symbolic and increasingly logical, fewer situations are frightening. Longer separations can be tolerated comfortably, without shaking the child's confidence in the attachment figure when needed. Distal forms of communication, such as a picture, a letter, or a voice on the phone, can be substituted for physical proximity and contact.

Sometime between the third and fifth birthdays, as the child journeys beyond sensorimotor intelligence further and further into the realms of symbolic thought, he begins to participate in what Bowlby called a *goal-corrected partnership* with his attachment figure. As a toddler, he could to some degree modify his behavior in response to the caregiver's behavior, and he could try directly to influence the caregiver's behavior. With his new cognitive skills, including a nascent ability to see things from another person's point of view, he can now attempt to influence the adult's plans and goals, not just the adult's overt behavior. If all goes well, the child and the caregiver become increasingly able to make and implement shared plans about proximity. They rely more and more on language and social cognition, not just behavior, to regulate the attachment relationship. A more detailed discussion of these developments is available in Unit 3 of this book.

■ Adolescence

Attachments in infancy have been the topic of hundreds of studies; the bibliography at the end of this book is far from exhaustive. In contrast, most research on attachments in childhood, adolescence, and adulthood is quite recent. To describe attachments after childhood, we must look beyond the mother, father, and other major caregivers. Older siblings, other relatives, teachers, coaches, youth leaders, clergy members, friends, mentors, and therapists may be available as additional attachment figures.

Ainsworth (1989) has proposed that hormonal, neurophysiological, and cognitive changes associated with adolescence, not just socioemotional experience, may underlie normative shifts in attachment processes. Evidence suggests that most young adults achieve a new level of autonomy from their parents but also remain attached to them for the rest of their lives—even after forming a durable attachment and a sexual bond with a new adult partner. While most adults still intermittently seek contact with their parents, particularly in times of stress, a newer attachment may become more important.

In childhood, attachments are asymmetrical. That is, one figure gives protection and care and the other receives them. Between adults, attachments are often reciprocal. Two partners provide care and protection for each other. The shift from the asymmetrical attachments of childhood to the reciprocal attachments of adulthood is not well-understood. However, the shift probably begins in adolescence.

■ Adulthood

Attachment behaviors and the affective bonds to which they lead are present and active throughout the life span. For an adult to be attached to a spouse, lover, friend, or parent is ordinary, normal, and healthy. It is not an indication of immaturity or inadequacy. Prior to the development of attachment theory and prior to widespread awareness of the data attachment research produced, both psychoanalysts and social-learning theorists usually regarded attachment behavior in adults as an indication of childish and unhealthy dependency. That opinion is not nearly as common as it once was. *Excesses* of attachment behavior in an adult may indicate anxious attachment, but interdependency, including reliance on the partner as a safe haven and as a secure base, is the norm. If an adult has no strong attachment relationship, longing for one and seeking one are healthy and normal feelings and actions. The fantasies of a deeply troubled individual about how the illusory relationship will magically solve all his or her problems are not likely to be fulfilled, but the yearning for a reliable attachment figure is a natural one.

Just as attachment behavior can be directed by one adult toward another adult, not only by a child toward a parent, so can the complement of attachment behavior—namely, caregiving behavior—be directed by one adult to another. Indeed, care and protection of a parent, spouse, lover, or adult friend are common in times of illness, stress, and old age.

Some marriages seem to function as healthy, mature, goal-corrected partnerships. In such marriages, each spouse serves as an effective secure base for the other; each at times takes on the role of the older or wiser partner who gives protection and care, and each at times takes on the role of the younger or weaker partner who accepts protection and care. Other marriages are characterized by power struggles, power imbalances, and a dearth of cooperation and nurturance. They surely reflect anxious attachments, not secure ones. However, the available data on qualities of marriages come mainly from other research and theoretical traditions and from clinical cases. There are very few studies of marriage that have been guided by attachment theory.

Research on adult friendships as attachment relationships is even harder to find than research on the attachment component of marriages. Nevertheless, it seems likely that friends, like spouses, often alternate in serving as the strong, wise figure who provides nurturance and protection to the other and acquires a special value as an irreplaceable attachment figure for the other.

REPRESENTATIONAL MODELS

It is possible to assess and describe a baby's attachments by observing, describing, and making inferences from the baby's behavior. After infancy, however, you cannot describe an attachment adequately without describing the individual's representational models of relationships. A representational model, or "working model," of an attachment relationship is a mental representation of the self, the other, and their relations. Representational models include feelings, beliefs, expectations, behavioral strategies, and rules for directing attention, interpreting information, and organizing memory.

For example, consider Doug's mental model of himself. Doug is 24 years old. He feels secure. He believes that he is lovable and competent. He expects to succeed in his endeavors. He ordinarily employs a strategy of communicating openly and directly with others when he needs practical assistance or emotional support. However, he recognizes that some of the people he knows cannot be trusted to respond helpfully, so he makes intelligent choices about where to seek assistance. He notices when things do not go as expected and enjoys analyzing feedback from others. His mental model includes a rule that encourages making comparisons of and contrasts between bits of data for the purpose of integrating them into an accurate, coherent understanding of reality. He can remember incidents and qualities of relationships from his childhood easily and accurately.

For the last 3 years, Doug has been living with John, who has become one of the major attachment figures in Doug's life. In times of stress, such as when he lost his job, Doug seeks support and care from John more often than he seeks it from his parents. Doug trusts John to treat him well. His representational model of their relationship includes the expectation that John will be available and responsive when called upon.

Now consider Bill's representational models. Bill is 24 years old and has been married for 3 years. He seldom acknowledges feeling anxious, but the people who know him well say he seems insecure and hostile. He thinks it is important to be able to handle himself "like a man" in any situation that comes up. He believes that he must rely on himself to accomplish his goals and meet life's challenges. His preferred strategy is to figure things out on his own. He does sometimes seek information from others, but he avoids emotional interactions, even with his wife. He hates needing support or care from anyone and does not expect support or care to be available if he ever does need it. He does not like to think about his own nature, about others' personalities, or about relationships. He finds such matters confusing and distasteful. Bill thinks his parents were wonderful but does not remember many specific experiences from his childhood. He does not think what happened when he was a child is very important anyway.

Bill is annoyed by his wife's wanting to talk about her feelings and his. He finds her unpleasantly intrusive and clingy. However, he is vigilant for signs of disloyalty or independence. He wants her to be home always when he gets there and not to get sexually or emotionally involved with anyone else. He is not sure he can trust her. Bill's representational model of what attachment relationships are generally like is anxious.

If your models do represent reality with a fair degree of accuracy, then being able to use memory, information, and cognitive skills to choose a course of action saves time and effort. However, representational models do not always match reality well. Instead, the mental models an individual has developed can constrict or distort information processing and decision making. Consider Bill's models, described above. It is quite likely that many of the people with whom Bill interacts would be willing to work with him cooperatively and even to provide emotional support if he would only permit it. His ingrained distrust of others and his compulsive self-reliance prevent him from discovering those aspects of reality. His avoidance of emotional intimacy prevents him from developing a secure, trusting relationship even with his wife. In Bill's case, the distortions that result from his representational models are systematic. In other cases, distortions may be chaotic. I will have much more to say about representational models in Chapters 13, 14 and 17.

HOW REPRESENTATIONAL MODELS PERPETUATE EARLY PATTERNS

Once formed, representational models tend to maintain their coherence and pattern of organization. The individual acquires some fairly stable personality tendencies. New social partners are selected on the basis of, and/or are assimilated to, old models of people and relationships. As defined by Piaget (1970) *assimilation* is the process of incorporating a new object into an existing mental representation.

Just when and how internal models form, consolidate, and become increasingly self-perpetuating are matters of some uncertainty. Recently, attachment theorists have been delving into new theoretical models developed by cognitive psychologists and studying the insights thus obtained. These matters will be discussed in Chapter 13.

According to attachment theory, the individual's representational models set the stage for interactions with new social partners and have long-lasting consequences for personality development and for the nature of close relationships. The pattern of attachment behavior and the associated representational models of attachment relationships are adaptive for the environment in which the young child develops them. Each child does the best she can to get the protection and care every child needs, but she does it with limited physical and cognitive abilities, and she does it in the context of the qualities of care her family provides or arranges. From her actual experiences, she develops representational models of herself and of attachment relationships. Formed unconsciously and early in childhood, these models may constrain flexibility later and preclude optimal adaptations to later circumstances and possibilities. For example, a child whose mother resents the burdens and constraints of caring for him and frequently rebuffs his approaches is likely to develop a representational model of attachment that includes the knowledge that being open and direct about his needs will not work. He may also infer that he is unlovable, unworthy, and incompetent. He is likely to remain emotionally needy and angry.

Consider this example. When a little boy showed his mother his drawing, she was too busy to look. When, 5 hours after breakfast, he pestered her for lunch, she ignored his pleading. When his little sister knocked down his block tower and threw up on his teddy bear, the mother offered him no comfort and made him help clean up the mess. When he cried for attention, she scolded him and sent him to his room alone. Only when he spoke softly to her, brought her a cookie, and caressed her cheek, did she finally let him sit for a moment in her lap and lean against her. These sorts of experiences were repeated day after day, month after month. (Almost all mothers have a bad day once in a while, and it doesn't ruin a child's life.)

For the boy in this example, the strategy that worked most often was appearing to meet the mother's needs as a way of getting her to meet his. The representational model derived from his childhood experiences will probably lead him to be distrustful, manipulative, and resentful in new attachment relationships. If he bases his perceptions and behavior in new relationships on the model developed in his first attachment relationship, he may never discover that some people are quite willing to give nurturance and protection when he simply asks for it.

MULTIPLE MODELS

One more proposition about representational models must be introduced here. Bowlby (1980) asserted that it is not uncommon for a person to hold two conflicting internal models of an important relationship. This can occur when what a child is told contradicts her actual experience or when the experience itself is simply too painful to bear remembering. One of the child's representational models develops, Bowlby suggested, largely from direct experience, encoded and stored in episodic memory. A second, contradictory model may develop largely from cognitive input if what the parents tell the child conflicts with her actual experience.

For example, a child may discover repeatedly that when he is frightened or hurt and seeks contact with one of his parents, the parent rebuffs his appeal and scolds him for crying. He is likely to learn to deny his distress, his need for comfort and protection, and his parent's rejection of him. "Denying" a feeling, an impulse, or a piece of information means blocking it from awareness, keeping it unconscious, fiercely pretending it does not exist and is not important. The suppression of such feelings and behavioral tendencies from conscious awareness may be fortified by the parent's statements that he loves the child, is proud of him, and gives him good care. Powerless to change the parent's behavior, the child can adapt to his circumstances best by suppressing awareness of some of the emotional realities of his situation. One mental model of the parent will include the awareness that the parent does not nurture or protect the child when he needs it. The emotions associated with that model will include fear and anger. That whole model and the associated feelings are likely to be repressed. A second representational model, the one that is likely to be conscious, will say that the child has a fine parent. Evidence of the repressed model is likely to appear in the child's behavior. When frightened by an unexpected separation from his parent, the child may seek to hide his anxiety and his anger even from himself, but may hit or kick another child without apparent provocation or redirect his aggressive impulses to objects in the environment and heave or break something.

A child may also develop multiple, contradictory models of an attachment figure and of the associated attachment relationship if what happens to her is too painful to keep in awareness. This occur often in cases of sexual abuse. For example, if the man to whom a child became attached in early childhood and on whom she still depends for some measure of protection, affection, and care uses her for his own sexual gratification, the child is likely to "split" her knowledge about her father into two isolated mental models. She will have one model of a more-or-less caring, protective father and another model of a sexual, demanding father who brings her terror and pain. Clinical evidence makes a persuasive case that the second model and the associated memories may be entirely repressed. The girl may have no conscious knowledge of them for years. Some event in later life may trigger their reemergence as conscious memory. Or, in other cases, access to memories of the traumatic experiences may remain blocked indefinitely. A 50-year-old incest survivor with a kind husband may have no idea why she often experiences a panic attack (rapid breathing, rapid heartbeat, a feeling of terror) when her husband initiates sexual foreplay. A male survivor of sexual abuse may have no idea why he feels himself floating away from his body and experiences no physical sensations when a woman he finds attractive behaves seductively.

The blocking of memories of painful past experiences may prompt a person, years after the traumatic events have stopped, also to block awareness and processing of cues relating to current, similar experiences. Sadly, this blocking may leave the victim unable to recognize and so to avoid victimization in a new relationship.

When an individual has conflicting models of a single relationship, he or she is likely to have limited access or even no conscious access to one or more of his representational models. As the examples above illustrate, the unconscious model(s) may nevertheless profoundly affect his or her personality and behavior.

VULNERABILITY TO PSYCHOPATHOLOGY

The American Psychiatric Association recognized disturbances of attachment in infancy that are severe enough to be viewed as psychopathology. Their *Diagnostic and Statistical Manual of Mental Disorders* (DSM-IV, 1994) lists criteria for identifying attachment disorders of infancy. These disorders are characterized by the absence, disruption, or distortion of the developmental sequences of attachment behaviors that normally occur and that orient and tie the baby to his or her caregivers. Discussion of attachment disorders in infancy appears in Chapter 12.

The attachment system is also central to some forms of psychopathology that emerge later in life. School refusal is clearly a symptom of a disturbance in an attachment relationship. School refusal is not just initial or periodic *reluctance* to go to school; many healthy children exhibit that much reluctance. School *refusal* is persistent, very anxious behavior that truly prevents a child from attending school regularly.

Attachment theory incorporates much of the concept of *transference* from classical psychoanalytic theory. Transference occurs when the individual assimilates new partners (spouse, friend, employer, therapist, and even, sometimes, a child) to existing, largely unconscious, representational models of relationships—models developed in childhood and never revised or updated since then. That is, people tend to perceive and act toward new partners as they perceived and acted toward former partners. People often overlook considerable evidence that the old representational model does not fit the new relationship.

People also tend to get involved with new partners who fit their old models. Sometimes this tendency may reflect an unconscious effort to rework an old relationship and give it a happy ending. Often, it is simply easiest to interact with people who respond to your existing behavioral strategies as you want or expect them to.

Traditionally, psychoanalysts have often ascribed adult psychopathology to fixation at, or regression to, an earlier stage of development. Bowlby (1980, 1988) argues that individuals continue to go through all the usual developmental stages as they grow older, but how they experience each stage and the degree to which and manner in which they are prepared for the next one depends on earlier adaptations. When circumstances in infancy or early childhood require deviant adaptations, development does not stop, but it is likely to continue along a deviant path. A depressed adult is not an adult who thinks and feels as a baby thinks and feels; he or she is an adult responding to adult issues while still anxious about the availability and responsiveness of attachment figures. Sroufe (e.g., 1986) has written with particular eloquence and clarity about how the individual's underlying coherence and continuity in experience and adaptation will be manifested in different behavior patterns at different stages of development. His writing integrates insights from Erik Erikson's (e.g., 1963) work with insights centered in attachment theory.

It seems likely that many cases of depression and certain personality disorders in the adult years stem from disturbances in early attachment relationships. However, the probable connections between symptoms in adulthood and early experiences with attachment figures often go unacknowledged and are neither well-understood nor well-demonstrated. We need systematic research to test inferences from clinical cases.

According to Bowlby (1984), when a child is brought in for psychotherapy because of some emotional or behavioral problem, the whole family often falsifies or omits critical facts about the child's experience; family members often attribute symptoms to the wrong cause. Adult patients often make the same sorts of omissions and errors. Bowlby (e.g., 1984) proposes that the rules (often unconscious) these people learned in their families require that they deny the rejection, threats of separation, or family violence they experienced or witnessed.

Despite Bowlby's strong statements that resistant and avoidant attachments may serve as predictors of disturbed development, few researchers appear to believe that an anxious attachment per se constitutes psychopathology. Attachment theorists expect anxious attachment to increase the risks of unhappiness, low self-esteem, maladaptive responses, and difficulties in interpersonal relationships. Nevertheless, researchers tend to assume that most anxiously attached individuals remain within the normal range, free from psychopathology.

Similarly, a secure attachment to the principal caregiver in infancy is expected to decrease the risk of maladaptive responses, but it does not make the individual invulnerable to subsequent personality problems or interpersonal difficulties. Secure attachment should lay a good foundation, enabling the person to form other secure relationships, to seek support when needed, and to draw strength from the support that is given. Attachment theorists believe that early secure attachment fosters an expectation of being loved and competent and so strengthens the ability to manage stress and to recover from setbacks. Securely attached children are expected to become self-confident, self-reliant adults who can vary their behavior to suit their situations.

In contrast, anxiously attached children may be at risk for experiencing or manifesting depression, compulsive caregiving, compulsive self-reliance, agoraphobia, chronic mourning, or persistent delinquency, or may experience milder problems handling anxiety, anger, and intimacy. Extreme avoidance may underlie the sociopath's extreme isolation from his own and others' feelings and needs, including the need for a close personal relationship.

Clinical case studies support the view that a history of anxious attachment often plays a role in psychological disorders. Such studies are, of course, *retrospective:* they look back on what happened earlier to try to explain current difficulties. A systematic prospective study would be a more convincing research method for assessing the role anxious attachment plays in the emergence or severity of various sorts of psychopathology. A *prospective study* starts with a sample of subjects who have not yet developed the outcome of interest, assesses them intermittently as they develop, and then tests for statistical associations between early experiences or characteristics and later outcomes.

Such studies are not yet available; few psychologists have the time or money to assess patterns of attachment early in life, assess their subjects' development often and in a variety of ways during childhood and adolescence, assess other factors that may influence outcomes of interest, and so clarify what role early attachments play in later psychological health or pathology.

While attachment relationships, particularly the earliest ones, probably do affect the risk of psychopathology, their impact should not be overstated. The weight of research evidence suggests that some psychiatric disorders, such as schizophrenia and bipolar (manic-depressive) disorder, largely reflect physiological and biochemical factors and should not be attributed primarily to disturbances in early attachments. Both depression and anxiety can stem from inherited chemical imbalances in neurotransmitters; their primary roots in some individuals are genetic, not experiential. The patterns of a person's first attachments probably do affect the risk of developing psychopathology, but so do biological factors, stressful events and circumstances, and other, later, attachment relationships.

CONTINUITY AND CHANGE

Although attachment patterns and representational models tend to maintain themselves, attachment theorists, as noted earlier, have often emphasized that development continues all through childhood, adolescence, and, according to some, adulthood. In all but the most severe cases of psychopathology, change remains possible. A childhood conflict or concern is likely to be retained as a theme in later development; but other events, relationships, and internal changes will influence whether the individual resolves it in a healthy or an unhealthy manner.

Changes in a child's attachment behavior and in her representational models of attachment relationships can evolve from developmental changes and/or from changes in experience. A child who can walk and talk needs comfort and protection less often than a younger child. In addition, she is better able to seek care from another available or potential attachment figure (perhaps an older sibling) if the care her primary parent provides is inadequate. The growing set of experiences with other attachment figures may change her models of who she is and of what is possible in relationships.

Developmental changes in the child can also either support improvements or increase tension in her relationships with her parents. For example, some parents adore cuddly babies, but get upset and disorganized when confronted with toddlers who can get into everything and are fighting to establish their autonomy. Other parents are impatient with or exhausted by an infant's demands, but respond well to the needs of an older child who sleeps through the night and uses words to communicate what she wants.

Changes in the quality of the child's attachment can also result from changes in the parent's behavior that result from changes in the family's circumstances (such as an economic setback or advance, a move to a new neighborhood, the birth of a sibling, a death, a divorce, a marriage, psychotherapy, or a child's entry into day care or school.)

In adolescence, children develop the capacity for what Piaget called formal operational thought. (For a thorough introduction to Piaget's theory of cognitive development, see Ginsberg and Opper, 1969). At this stage, individuals can apply logical rules to situations that are either real or hypothetical, solve problems by systematically testing hypotheses, make complex hypothetical deductions about abstract concepts, think about how whole systems function, place themselves within those systems, imagine possibilities not yet experienced, and even think about their own thinking. These new cognitive powers may contribute to major changes in the individual's models of attachment relationships. The adolescent's ability to think about how she perceives relationships makes it possible for her to examine herself, her current relationships, and her attachment history in new ways; she can revise her models on the basis of discussion and reflection. A younger child must rely largely on corrective experiences to change unfortunate models of self, others, and relationships. The formal operational adolescent or adult can observe, plan, experiment, and comprehend contradictions and ambiguities in ways not previously possible. She can use experience gained in relationships with people outside the family (for example, with a teacher or youth group leader) to enlarge or modify her understanding of what is possible in attachment relationships.

The only logical limitation on this mode of altering representational models, and so beginning to change the nature of your actual attachment relationships, is that you must have conscious access to the aspects of the model you wish to change. Unfortunately, aspects of maladaptive models most in need of change are most likely to be blocked from conscious processing. In such cases, assistance from a psychotherapist may be necessary to achieve conscious awareness and reevaluation of the models.

PSYCHOTHERAPY

Even though representational models of attachment relationships affect deeply important aspects of our lives, most people are not consciously aware of their models. One goal of psychotherapy is to make these models available for conscious examination and reevaluation.

Bowlby (e.g., 1988) specifically recommended that the psychotherapist be aware of his or her role as an attachment figure for the client. The therapist should act as a secure base who, by being supportive and predictably available and responsive, can foster trust and enable clients to explore and revise their internal models of attachment relationships and of themselves. Often, the therapist can help by drawing attention to the characteristics and tendencies the client attributes to the therapist. (This is similar to the psychoanalytic procedure of analyzing the transference). Unlike most traditional psychoanalysts, Bowlby did not advocate restricting oneself to being a "blank screen" onto which the patient might project whatever was in his mind. The relationship between client and therapist must be a real relationship between real human beings.

Of course, forming an increasingly secure attachment to the therapist does not constitute the client's work in psychotherapy. It is a part of the work, it reflects the progress of the work, and it helps make continued work possible. In the language of attachment theory, the client's work in psychotherapy is also likely to include gaining access to unconscious representational models and memories; experiencing or reexperiencing the feelings associated with previously repressed knowledge; reevaluating perceptions and beliefs; developing a mental model of the self as lovable, worthy, and competent; experimenting with new behaviors; modifying existing relationships; and, for many clients, selecting new sorts of people as partners in their principal affiliative, sexual, and attachment relationships.

COMMON MISPERCEPTIONS ABOUT ATTACHMENT THEORY

Some people have heard a little about attachment theory but have not read much about it. Misunderstandings about the propositions, empirically established facts, and implications of attachment theory are common.

Three inaccurate perceptions are particularly widespread and should be corrected here. The first is that babies are attached only to the primary caregiver or mother figure. In fact, within a month after giving clear evidence of having developed a specific attachment to the primary caregiver, most babies manifest attachment to at least one other familiar person.

The second misperception is that experiences in the first year of infancy fully determine the individual's psychological future. Attachment theorists think experiences in the first year set the child on a developmental trajectory, but life provides many experiences and opportunities that can modify or even radically alter this trajectory.

A third misperception is that attachment theorists think the separations associated with infant day care are terrible for babies and toddlers. That proposition will be considered in depth in Chapter 10. For now, I will simply note that most babies in day care do develop secure attachments to their mothers. As a group, day care babies are somewhat more likely than babies with little nonparental care to develop avoidant attachments, but the difference is modest, and neither its cause(s) nor its implications are known.

CHAPTER SUMMARY

Although this chapter comes, of necessity, near the start of this book, it is also a summary of the major contents of the whole book. You may want to reread it when you come to the end of the final chapter.

By now, you should have some sense of the major facets of attachment theory: an ethological-evolutionary perspective, a focus on the organization of behavior in context, the importance of the secure-base concept, the importance of representational models, and the continuing openness of the theory to modification in response to new data.

Attachment theory does not try to explain everything about human psychosocial development. It does, however, offer a rich, integrated, persuasive set of hypotheses about the development of security, self-image, and intimate relationships throughout the life span. Many of its propositions about infancy and childhood are already well-supported by research. In the coming decade, research on attachments in adolescence and in the adult years is likely to be thrilling.

UNIT

2

INFANCY AND EARLY CHILDHOOD

For the first decade of attachment research, almost all of the research focused on infancy. Consequently, this unit is by far the largest in this book. It begins with a discussion of research methods for infancy studies because, in the social sciences, figuring out how to measure the construct you want to know about is the first step. Next comes a chapter about the phases babies go through in developing attachments.

Chapter 5 discusses the influence of the caregiver's sensitive responsiveness on the pattern of the infant's attachment to her. Sensitive responsiveness is the variable first discovered, most studied, and most clearly demonstrated to be influential. The same chapter introduces five longitudinal studies that underscored the importance of the caregiver's responsiveness and also yielded findings about other variables (discussed in later chapters). Among the other possible influences on how the infant organizes attachment behavior in relation to any particular caregiver the best-researched variables are the caregiver's personality, the infant's temperament, and the social network within which the infant-caregiver dyad is embedded. Each of these topics is discussed in Chapter 6. Research about the impact of demographic factors, the caregiver's drug use, and the newborn's health status is also discussed.

To what degree do patterns of attachment in infancy cause or at least help predict aspects of family relationships, reactions to new adults, relations with peers, and cognitive development in the early years? These issues are discussed in Chapter 7. How cultures vary in infant care practices, whether or not the laboratory procedure used for assessing attachments in the United States is valid in diverse cultures, and what aspects of later development in non-Western cultures can be predicted by infant patterns of attachment are discussed in Chapter 8. The next two chapters in this unit move on to questions about attachments to fathers, to mothers who have jobs outside the home, and to hired caregivers. Whether one of the early attachments is more important to the infant than other attachments in infancy is the topic of Chapter 11. Early intervention to prevent maladaptive patterns of attachment or to alter the course of nonoptimal patterns of attachment is discussed in Chapter 12.

Despite the wealth of research on attachments in infancy, you will discover as you read through these chapters that there are many intriguing and important hypotheses that have not yet been adequately tested.

C H A P T E R

3

RESEARCH METHODS
FOR INFANCY

There are three major methods for assessing attachments in infancy: naturalistic observations, the Strange Situation, and the Attachment Q-set. I will describe each in this chapter. The chapter may include more detail than casual readers want. Because the issues are important, I have included comments about such matters as administering procedures correctly, coding results accurately, and properly interpreting data provided by parents. Measuring a psychological construct such as security or defensiveness is not as simple as measuring height or weight. Before we can have confidence in research conclusions, we need to know what sort of yardstick was used to measure the constructs under study. If the methodology of an experiment or observational study is flawed, the results are likely to be of little use.

For measuring attachment patterns, *naturalistic observations* have the greatest face validity. That is, it is most immediately obvious that observing a baby with her caregiver in their natural setting(s) can enable you to see whether the baby is attached to the caregiver and how effective the caregiver is as a secure base for the baby. However, naturalistic observations are time-consuming. When a 20-minute laboratory procedure, *the Strange Situation,* was developed and appeared to yield as much information about attachment patterns as many hours of home observations yielded, the short laboratory procedure was quickly adopted and put into widespread use.

The Strange Situation also had limitations as a research tool. It was sometimes difficult to persuade people to come to the laboratory, the procedure is somewhat upsetting to many babies, and a researcher cannot repeat the procedure soon or often to verify or add to his or her understanding of an individual baby. Partly for these reasons, a third measure of attachment was developed, a Q-sort that can be performed by a parent, another caregiver, or a research assistant who has observed the baby for a few hours and has talked with one of the parents.

All three methods of assessing security of attachment in infancy have made valuable contributions to our understanding of patterns of attachment, their determinants, and their consequences. Although naturalistic observations are, in most studies, too brief and too infrequent, all three of the methods discussed in this chapter continue in widespread use.

NATURALISTIC OBSERVATIONS

The importance of naturalistic observations in attachment research can hardly be overstated. The goal of attachment research is to recognize and understand patterns of behavior and their functions in real life. To do so, we must observe behavior sequences and their outcomes in real life. No shortcut will be adequate. There are also times when contrived experimentation and laboratory procedures are appropriate, but what we learn from such methods must be tested against observations in natural environments. Observations in natural settings have another advantage: they maximize the likelihood of discovering something of importance that was not anticipated or hypothesized.

In addition to being naturalistic, observations must be both *longitudinal* (spread over a period of months or years) and lengthy to be maximally useful. One reason is that researchers can best see how patterns of behavior and interaction at a given time develop into the patterns observed at a later time by watching these patterns evolve. A second reason is that the presence of an observer makes the observation situation unnatural. Babies react to the presence of a stranger in the room. Caregivers tend to make certain that their houses are unusually clean, to put on unusually good-looking clothes, and to be on their best behavior while they are being observed. If the observer stays long enough and visits often enough over a period of weeks or months, it may become possible for him or her to sink into the background. The situation in which the subjects act or interact may then become almost natural, and the subjects may then behave as they would in the absence of an observer.

A third reason for observing a subject, dyad, or family for long sessions and for sessions spread over several weeks or months is that behavior is variable. (A *dyad* is a pair of people, usually in an ongoing relationship.) A father who is relaxed and playful with his baby on Friday evening may be harsh and rejecting on Monday morning. A baby who seems energetic, interested in the world around him, and easy to care for at 10 o'clock in the morning may have 3-hour crying spells that exhaust his loving parents most evenings. A day care provider who is calm and friendly during a structured story time in the morning may be distracted and irritable when her own children come home from school, the children in her care are tired, and the phone keeps ringing. Naturalistic observations that occur on only one or two occasions and last only a couple of hours can easily give a biased or incomplete picture of an individual or a relationship.

In addition to observing the subjects in the natural setting and observing them long and often, the researcher must focus the observations. Behavior is complicated, and the features and events in the environment that influence behavior are numerous. A person cannot write down and a camera cannot record everything that could possibly be of importance. The researcher must begin with some ideas about which aspects of behavior and what features and events in the environment are likely to be important for the construct she wishes to study. Then she focuses her observations on the relevant aspects of the behavior and the environment she observes.

Happily, attachment research began with an awareness of the necessity of naturalistic observations. In the 1950s, guided by Bowlby's hypotheses about disturbances associated with separation from the mother, James and Joyce Robertson (e.g., 1971) made close observations of young children who lived apart from their mothers for a week, a couple of weeks, or a month—usually because of the mother's hospitalization for childbirth or surgery. On paper and on film, they recorded the children's initial distress, their subsequent slow, painful adaptations, and the consequent disturbances in their relationships with their mothers, disturbances that often lasted for weeks or even months after the child's return home. The Robertsons' findings helped change hospital and family practices throughout England and, later, the United States.

In the realm of longitudinal naturalistic observations, Mary Ainsworth's two early studies still shine as stellar examples of what can be done and what can be learned. The first took place in Uganda. Ainsworth (1967) originally intended to study weaning in a Ganda village where, she was told, mothers still often used an ancient weaning practice of sending the child to live with another relative so that he or she would "forget the breast." The separations she expected to observe turned out to be very uncommon, so she focused not on weaning but on infant-mother attachment, observing babies, toddlers, and their mothers in their homes. With the help of a translator, she also interviewed the mothers about their babies and their child-rearing practices. Although Ainsworth had previously done some work with Bowlby at the Tavistock Clinic in London, she was not convinced that his ethology-based hypotheses had much value in explaining and describing infant-mother attachment.

Ainsworth's sample included some families that continued to live according to the traditions of the Ganda culture and some that had moved far toward adopting practices imported from Europe and elsewhere. Some families were Muslim, some were Roman Catholic, and some were affiliated with the Church of England. In general, the Muslims seemed most faithful in keeping to old Ganda customs. Five of the households in the sample were polygynous: more than one wife was present. (Three of those households were Muslim and two were Church of England.) Together, the five homes held seven of the twenty-eight babies in the sample.

When Ainsworth began her observations, the babies in her sample ranged in age from 2 days to 80 weeks. Her research plan was to visit each family at home for about 2 hours once every 2 weeks. This proved to be impossible to arrange, so she made many short visits to build rapport with each family, to maintain rapport between long visits, and to gather additional bits of data as circumstances permitted. By the end of her stay in Africa, she had visited 26 of the 28 Ganda babies at least 10 times, with a median of 23 visits spaced over several months. Four long visits (2 hours or more) proved sufficient for her to pose a planned set of questions in an informal style. Ainsworth succeeded in conducting at least that many long visits with the mothers of 24 of the 28 babies.

Accompanied by an interpreter, Ainsworth visited the subjects in the family's living room, which is where Ganda women usually entertain in the afternoon. She recorded the occurrence and onset of specific behaviors related to attachment. She was able to distinguish three groups of babies: those who were securely attached, and cried less than others; those who were insecurely attached, and cried more than others; and those who were not yet attached, which is to say that they did not yet respond to the mother differently from the way they responded to other adults. Ainsworth was able not only to describe the phases in the development of attachments (the topic of Chapter 4), but also to relate the security of the infant's attachment to an indirect measure of the quality of care the mother gave. That measure was the mother's excellence as an informant about her baby, a rating based on the interviews that took place over the series of visits. The top score on Ainsworth's 7-point scale measuring excellence as an informant was given to the eight mothers who stuck to the topic, volunteered information, gave much spontaneous detail about the baby, and never seemed impatient during the interview. A middle score was given to mothers who answered the questions briefly, were cooperative, and stayed focused on talking about the baby, but did not volunteer much information. The four mothers who received the lowest scores either had little to say about the baby or were much more interested in conversing with their visitor about other topics. The mean score for mothers of babies who appeared to be securely attached was 5.87; for mothers of babies who appeared to be insecurely attached, it was 4.86.

As the months passed, Ainsworth's direct, naturalistic observations persuaded her that Bowlby was right about the importance of ethology in understanding human attachments. Interviews alone, laboratory observations, or retrospective reconstructions of early experiences could not have provided the wealth of data obtained or the depth of learning that grew from Aisworth's direct observations of interactions and developments in a natural environment.

Ainsworth's second naturalistic longitudinal study of infant attachment occurred in Baltimore in the 1960s. Much of what she and her associates learned is included in Ainsworth, Blehar, Waters, and Wall (1978). Ainsworth and her associates were interested in exploring both the normative patterns of interaction and development and the roots of individual differences in patterns of attachment. The subjects were twenty-six white middle-class babies and their mothers, almost all of whom were full-time homemakers. Guided by an ethological orientation, observers visited the subjects at home for 4 hours at a time once every 3 weeks during the first year. In all, they obtained about 72 hours of observations of each mother-baby dyad over the first year.

Ainsworth and her associates were not primarily testing any well-articulated hypotheses; they were observing their subjects much as an animal ethologist might observe another species. Like animal ethologists, they found that it was not always possible to prevent the observer's presence from affecting the subject's behavior. They compensated for this difficulty by observing each family for many hours during many visits so that the subjects became accustomed to the presence of the observer and eventually appeared to go about their daily business as usual. After a few visits, the mothers did not seem to be performing for the observers or inhibiting behaviors they thought undesirable.

Guided by attachment theory, the observers made special note of the behaviors and the activating and terminating conditions likely to be involved in the attachment system: cries, vocalizations, smiles, "reaches," "pick-ups," "put-downs," the child approaching or following the mother, the mother entering the room, the mother leaving the room, and so on. The mother's sensitivity, cooperation, acceptance of the child's behaviors, and accessibility were rated on four separate scales. Scores on the four scales turned out to be highly intercorrelated.

A baby's confident use of the mother as a secure base was the primary evidence of secure attachment. A child's protest at separation in the home, ambivalence about being picked up and being put down, and other indications of anxiety and anger were taken as evidence of anxious attachment.

About the time the babies in the Baltimore sample were approaching their first birthdays, Mary Ainsworth and Barbara Wittig (1969) developed the "Strange Situation" laboratory procedure (described in the next section of this chapter). The Strange Situation later became the primary means of assessing the quality of attachment and has now been used in hundreds of studies. When she first developed the procedure, however, Ainsworth did not articulate and test many specific hypotheses. She was exploring what patterns of behavior might emerge and what associations there might be between behavior at home and behavior in the laboratory. She wanted a laboratory situation that would activate the attachment system at a level not routinely observed in the home and perhaps dramatize individual differences in the organization of attachment behavior. At the age of 51 weeks, 23 of the 26 infants from the Baltimore sample were observed in the Strange Situation.

THE STRANGE SITUATION AND THE PATTERNS OF ATTACHMENT

Attachment theory discusses not only *normative phenomena* (i.e., that which is universal or nearly universal about attachments), but also individual differences. To describe such differences and their determinants and implications scientifically, we must have a means of assessing them. Lengthy naturalistic observations provide one means. The Strange Situation laboratory procedure provides a second, much faster method of assessment.

The *Strange Situation* is a semi-standardized laboratory procedure for examining attachment behavior, exploratory behavior, and affiliative behavior in 1-year-olds. The procedure has proved to be extraordinarily informative and has been used to assess attachment patterns in thousands of infants. It captures individual differences in ways of organizing behavior, and the differences have meaningful connections with the infant's prior experiences and subsequent adaptations.

Ainsworth, Blehar, Waters, and Wall (1978) described the laboratory procedure, instructions for coding the infant's behavior, and three major patterns of behavior often observed in the Strange Situation. Main and Solomon (1990) subsequently described a fourth major pattern or set of patterns and published instructions for deciding whether a baby's behavior fit the new category. To comprehend most of the discussions in this book, you need first to understand the classifications of Strange Situation behavior patterns.

Strange Situation assessments are appropriate for babies 11 to 18 months old. The Strange Situation procedure is carried out in a place that is unfamiliar to the infant subject, most often a laboratory room. The room has a chair for the familiar caregiver (usually the mother or father), a chair for an adult female stranger, an attractive collection of toys, and space for the baby to move about. When the procedure begins, the two chairs and the toys are on three points of an imaginary triangle, and are far enough apart from each other so that researchers can observe whether the baby is near or oriented toward the caregiver, the toys, or, later, the stranger.

In general, both adults sit quietly in their chairs if the baby is okay. They do not initiate interaction except as specified below. However, they respond normally if the baby initiates interaction, and they are always free to comfort the baby if he or she is upset.

The Strange Situation consists of eight episodes. By design, the series of episodes
gradually becomes somewhat stressful; the level of activation of the attachment system is
gradually increased. The attachment figure and a stranger take turns in the room, with the
baby remaining in the room. This enables observers to see how the baby organizes behavior in relation to each and to compare their effectiveness in soothing the baby if he or she
becomes upset.

Table 3.1 shows who is present for each episode of the Strange Situation. In the first,
very brief episode, the experimenter shows the parent and baby into the room, tells the
parent where to sit, and asks her or him to set the baby down by the toys and then to sit
quietly. The other seven episodes are scheduled to last 3 minutes each, but can be curtailed
or prolonged (depending on the nature of the episode) if the baby is very upset. In series,
the episodes do become increasingly stressful, so it is not uncommon for a parent to return
early after a separation episode or to stay extra long before the second separation. The
instructions for all eight episodes appear in Table 3.1.

Ainsworth and Wittig (1969) had two observers dictate running accounts of the
baby's behavior during the Strange Situation into tape recorders. Now, however, the vast
majority of Strange Situations are videotaped. On the basis of instructions provided in

Episode	People Present	Procedure
1	B, C, E	E shows C where to put B and where to sit, then leaves. If necessary, C gets B to start playing with toys.
2	B, C	C does not initiate interaction but may respond.
3	B, C, S	S enters, sits quietly for a minute, talks with C for a minute, and engages B in interaction or play for a minute.
4	B, S	C exits. S lets B play. If B needs comfort, S tries to provide it. If B cries hard, episode can be terminated early.
5	B, C	C calls to B from outside the door, enters, greets B, and pauses. If B needs comfort, C may provide it. When B is ready to play with toys, C sits in her chair. If B is very upset and needs extra time with C, episode can be prolonged.
6	B	C exits. B is left alone. If B cries hard, episode can be terminated early.
7	B, S	S enters, greets B, and pauses. If B is OK, S sits. If B needs comfort, S tries to provide it. If B cries hard, episode can be ended early.
8	B, C	C calls to B from outside the door, enters, pauses, picks B up, comforts B if necessary, and lets B return to play when ready.

TABLE 3.1 The Strange Situation

Note: B = baby, C = caregiver, E = experimenter, and S = stranger.

Ainsworth et al. (1978), coders use scales for rating intensity of interactive behavior in four categories: (1) proximity seeking and contact seeking, (2) contact maintaining, (3) resistance, and (4) avoidance.

Resistance is openly angry behavior, such as pushing away from the mother, rejecting toys she offers, or hitting. *Avoidance* often appears to be neutral in tone and refers specifically to the child's avoiding proximity to and interaction with the parents, even interaction across a distance, in circumstances that normally activate attachment behavior. Avoidance can be as subtle as low-key gaze aversion, or as obvious as turning away from the parent and walking to the other side of the room. (Scales are also available for rating intensity of interaction across a distance and intensity of search behavior during separation episodes, but those scales are seldom used now.)

Because different specific behaviors can serve the same goal, what is coded is the *meaning* of the baby's behavior, not simply the frequency of occurrence of some discrete behavior, such as smiles or approaches. The next step in coding is to assign the whole pattern of behavior to one of the categories defined by Ainsworth et al. (1978) or by Main and Solomon (1986, 1990).

Ainsworth et al. described eight subgroups into which infant patterns of attachment behavior in the Strange Situation could be classified. Each of the eight subgroups was included in one of three major categories, but Ainsworth maintained throughout her career that distinctions between subgroups—even within a category—were important. She also noted that, as research continued, other groups might be identified. Table 3.2 lists and summarizes the patterns of Strange Situation behavior developed by Ainsworth et al., as well as the later category identified by Main and Solomon.

Initially, the three categories were defined on the basis of behavior in the laboratory. They were labeled simply as group A, with two subgroups; group B, with four subgroups; and group C, with two subgroups. Much later, on the basis of correlated data in other settings, group A was labeled "avoidant," group B was labeled "secure," and group C was labeled "resistant." Both the letter labels and the descriptive labels are still used. The group B babies from the Baltimore study had shown a healthy balance of exploratory behavior and attachment behavior at home. For the Baltimore babies in group A or group C, both of which were later labeled "insecurely attached," the mother had been much less effective as a secure base for supporting exploratory behavior in the home.

■ The "A" Category: Avoidant Attachment

Babies who fall into group A show conspicuous avoidance of proximity to or interaction with the mother in the reunion episodes. Those in subgroup A1 ignore the mother almost entirely; those in subgroup A2 show moderate proximity-seeking behavior mixed with strong proximity-avoiding behavior.

Here is one example of how a baby classified as an A2 behaved in the Strange Situation. In episode 2, Indira, then 12 months old, approached the toys eagerly and manipulated 7 of the 10 that were available. She particularly liked an hourglass-shaped rattle that had beads that fell from one side to the other, much as the grains of sand fall from one side of an hourglass to the other. She interrupted her play twice to carry a toy to her mother. Each time, she returned quickly to the pile of toys.

TABLE 3.2 Patterns of Strange Situation Behavior

Group A: Avoidant

- Little or no active resistance to interaction
- Often little or no distress during separations
- Often affiliative toward stranger

Subgroup A1

- Little or no proximity seeking
- Very little or no contact maintaining
- Little affective sharing, little interaction across a distance
- Conspicuous avoidance in reunion episodes

Subgroup A2

- Mixed response to caregiver
- Some tendency to greet and approach caregiver
- Greater tendency to avoid caregiver

Group B: Secure

- Uses caregiver as secure base for exploration
- Communicates affects during play
- Actively seeks contact or interaction at reunion
- Shows little or no resistance to contact or interaction
- If distressed, seeks and maintains contact and is soothed by contact

Subgroup B1

- Shows strong initiative in interaction across a distance
- Shows little distress during separations
- Actively greets the caregiver at reunion
- Does not seek proximity or contact much
- May show some avoidance, especially at first reunion

Subgroup B2

- Seeks proximity or contact, especially at second reunion
- May show some avoidance, primarily at first reunion
- Tends to show little distress during separations
- Shows fewer signs of mixed feelings than A2 babies show

Subgroup B3

- Explores during preseparation episodes (i.e., is not preoccupied with the caregiver)
- Actively seeks contact at reunion
- Actively resists cessation of contact
- Shows little or no avoidance of the caregiver
- May or may not be distressed during separations

Subgroup R4: Borderline Secure? Dependent?

- Seeks contact, especially during reunion episodes
- Seems less active and less competent than other B babies seem

- Is very distressed during separations
- May fuss or cry a lot, even when the caregiver is present
- Strongly resists release
- May be hard to soothe
- Often shows moderate resistance to caregiver (but less than C babies do)
- May seem wholly preoccupied with the caregiver even in preseparation episodes
- May seem somewhat anxious throughout the procedure
- Usually shows little or no avoidance

Group C: Resistant

- Appears obviously ambivalent about the caregiver
- Seeks proximity or contact, or resists release
- Shows open resistance to contact or interaction
- Tends to be very distressed during separations
- Has difficulty settling down during reunion episodes
- Shows little or no avoidance
- May show generally maladaptive behavior

Subgroup C1

- Shows unmistakably angry behavior: hits, kicks, squirms, and/or rejects toys
- Actively seeks proximity, maintains contact, *and* actively resists contact or interaction
- Often shows angry, resistant behavior to the stranger as well as to the caregiver

Subgroup C2

- Is passive—shows limited exploratory behavior and lacks initiative in interaction
- Nevertheless signals desire for contact and/or protests against release in reunion episodes
- Appears unhappy and helpless
- Does not seem as conspicuously angry as a C1 baby seems

Group D: Anxious-Disorganized-Disoriented

Shows one or more of the following:

- Disordered sequences of behavior (e.g., approach, then dazed avoidance)
- Simultaneous contradictory behaviors (e.g., marked gaze aversion during approach or contact)
- Inappropriate, stereotyped, repetitive gestures or motions
- Freezing or stilling
- Open fear of the caregiver (usually very brief)
- Attachment behavior directed to the stranger when the caregiver returns
- High avoidance *and* high resistance in the same episode
- Depressed, dazed, disoriented, or affectless facial expressions

When the stranger entered, Indira (holding the rattle) greeted her with a smile, walked toward her with her arm outstretched as if she intended to give her the rattle, but then turned, sat down near the other toys, and resumed her independent play. Later she brought three toys to the stranger and one to her mother. When the stranger sat down by Indira and invited her to take turns using the hammer to pound shapes through the appropriate holes in a pegboard, Indira joined in readily. She glanced up when her mother passed by on her way out of the room. She appeared to be playing contentedly throughout her mother's 3-minute absence.

When the mother returned, Indira looked up with a neutral expression and then turned back to the toys. The mother sat down. Indira had the rattle in her hand, but she did not really seem to be interested in it. After 20 seconds, Indira got up, brought the rattle to her mother, and initiated a little give-and-take game that lasted 12 seconds. Then she returned to the toys. By the end of the episode, she had made six more trips to deliver toys to her mother. (When the mother had thus accumulated four toys in her lap, she set them down on the floor.) Although Indira made seven full approaches to her mother in that first reunion episode, she did not seek physical contact.

At the experimenter's signal, the mother left the room, and episode 6 began. Indira played with the toys for a while, then gravitated toward the door, and, after 2 1/2 minutes alone, began fussing unhappily. Soon the stranger entered. Indira brought her a toy right away and seemed content for the rest of episode 7. She approached the stranger four more times and sometimes stayed near her for friendly little interactions.

When Indira's mother returned, Indira looked up, took a step toward her, stopped, and looked down. The mother walked over, picked Indira up, tried briefly to coax a smile from her, and then set her down. Indira remained unresponsive while her mother held her. She looked around, as if interested in other things. When her mother set her down, she moved some toys around a bit but did not seem truly interested in them. After 70 seconds, she brought a toy to her mother, and subsequently delivered two more, again without seeking contact.

How would you interpret Indira's behavior? Some parents are very pleased to have babies who seem to be so independent. Others would find the baby's relative unresponsiveness disappointing. They would notice that Indira does not seem to treat the mother as anybody special. She seems to dislike being left alone, but her behavior with the stranger seems very much like her behavior with her mother.

Is Indira's mother really unimportant to her, or is Indira just pretending? Do the separations really not bother her? After much research, Ainsworth and her colleagues concluded that most babies who act like Indira are masking discomfort and blocking their impulses to seek comfort from their mothers. Even though they are so young, their behavior indicates that they are using a psychological defense mechanism. They are not demonstrating secure independence. In the months prior to their participation in the Strange Situation, the group A babies in the Baltimore sample were fussy and showed open discomfort about separation from the mother even in the very familiar environment of their own homes.

When first introduced to the Strange Situation, the corresponding classifications of infant behavior, and the interpretation of those classifications, people often question the

If it occurred in the first moments of reunion, the seemingly neutral, disinterested behavior of these children would be coded as avoidance.

description of avoidant behavior as defensive, not secure. Avoidant babies often appear to the naive observer simply to be independent. They may show no overt distress and little desire to search for the mother during her absence, or may appear content when left with a stranger, but not when left alone. Whether they are secure and independent or are instead defending themselves against anxiety and against activation of attachment behavior is an empirical question. The great weight of evidence, discussed throughout Chapters 5 through 10, supports the view that avoidant babies are insecurely attached. One of the interesting bits of data is that, when the mother leaves the laboratory room, group A babies do show the same sort of physiological arousal that group B and group C babies show (Sroufe and Waters, 1977b). Their observable behavior looks independent, but their physiological arousal suggests discomfort and an impulse to take action to regain comfort. However, group A babies actively inhibit the impulse to seek comfort.

In Germany, Spangler and Grossmann (1993) replicated the finding that cardiac measures indicate that avoidant infants are experiencing the same physiological arousal that secure infants experience in response to the events of the Strange Situation, even though the behavioral responses of the avoidant infants are inhibited.

■ The "B" Category: Secure Attachment

Now consider Muhamidi, also 12 months old, but representing subgroup B3. Like Indira, he plunged right into exploration of the toys in episode 2. He vocalized quite a bit, showed a couple of the toys to his mother, and especially enjoyed playing catch with her with a large, soft ball. He seldom succeeded in catching the ball, but he enjoyed chasing it across the room. He hadn't been walking long and fell twice, but the falls did not seem to trouble him.

When the stranger came in, Muhamidi looked at her soberly, carried the ball to his mother, leaned against her knee for 4 seconds, and then toddled after the ball again. He hesitated a bit when, 105 seconds later, the stranger approached him, but then he played with the hammer, shapes, and pegboard with her. When Muhamidi saw his mother leaving, he followed her to the door, reached for the knob, dropped the toy hammer, and then looked to the stranger while stretching his arm up toward the knob again. The stranger carried him back to the pegboard and got him to start hammering again. Then she returned to her chair. Muhamidi gave the shapes two unenthusiastic taps, then walked to the door again. He banged on it with the hammer. After 25 seconds, he started crying. The stranger picked him up and sat by the toys with him in her lap. He accepted the contact and stopped crying, but showed little interest in the toys. Intermittently, he looked back at the door.

When Muhamidi's mother called to him from outside the door, a big smile spread across his face. As his mother entered the room, he was already walking toward the door. He stopped at her feet and reached to be picked up. She lifted him, gave him a hug, set him down by the toys, and got him started using the bead rattle, which he had not previously investigated. She returned to her chair. Muhamidi explored the toys actively, vocalizing happily, and now and then holding a toy up for his mother to see.

When the mother left the room again, Muhamidi stopped playing immediately, crawled to the door, cried, stood up, and reached for the knob. His crying grew more intense, and he stayed right by the door. The experimenter terminated the episode 45 seconds after it began.

Getting the stranger into the room was a little tricky, because Muhamidi was right by the door. When he saw who was entering, his crying took on an angry quality. The stranger picked him up and walked around slowly. She patted his back and spoke soothingly to him. He twisted away from her, stretching toward the door. Then, still crying, he rested his head on her shoulder for 3 seconds, pushed away as if trying to get down, rested against her body again, and gradually stopped crying. He stayed quiet for the rest of the episode. The stranger sat him down by the toys, crouched beside him, picked up a little plastic cube and dropped it into a translucent plastic bottle, and offered another cube to Muhamidi. He crawled the short distance (4 inches) to the stranger. She sat down and took him into her lap. She demonstrated the use of the cubes and the bottle again, and Muhamidi took a turn.

When his mother called from outside the door this time, Muhamidi looked right up but did not smile. When she came in, he was still sitting in the stranger's lap. The stranger leaned back a bit with her hands on the floor behind her, leaving the baby free to move. He cried and reached hard toward his mother in a clear signal that he wanted to be picked up. Following the experimenter's earlier instructions, the mother continued to pause before approaching Muhamidi. He wiggled out of the stranger's lap and, crying, crawled toward his mother. The mother met him halfway, picked him up, and held him close. He stopped crying right away.

The mother sat down by the toys, handed her son a cube, held up the bottle, and rattled the two cubes in it. Muhamidi dropped the cube his mother had given him and turned toward her to make closer contact. She held him gently for 18 seconds, and then lifted him off her lap and set him on the floor beside her. He protested and climbed back into her lap. She held him and murmured to him for another 55 seconds, then set him beside her again. He leaned back toward her. With her right hand, she held him close, letting him rest against her thigh, while with her left hand she dumped the cubes out of the bottle and began stacking them one on top of another. Muhamidi watched her build a tower five blocks high, smiled, vocalized happily, and, keeping one hand on his mother's leg, reached out to take the top block. His action made three blocks fall off. His mother exclaimed in mock surprise. Muhamidi laughed, handed her a block, and watched her rebuild the tower. When it had six blocks, he slid away from her side and kicked the bottom block. Both players cheered for his success in tumbling the tower. The mother returned to her chair. Muhamidi crawled after her. She pointed at the toys and asked him to get the ball. He stood up, walked to the ball, picked it up, and tossed it into the middle of the room. He continued playing and vocalizing contentedly until the end of the episode.

At reunion, babies in Group B greet the caregiver and seek instruction, proximity, or contact.

Like Muhamidi, other babies in group B (secure) actively seek proximity to and contact with the mother, or at least interaction with her, especially in the reunion episodes. Babies in subgroup B1 show strong initiative in interaction across a distance. Babies in subgroup B2 seek proximity and contact with the mother more than B1 babies do, but less than B3 babies do. B1 and B2 babies sometimes show some avoidant behavior, but positive attachment behavior is stronger than avoidant behavior, especially in the second reunion. B3 babies, often regarded as the most securely attached, actively seek and maintain physical contact with the mother. Like Muhamidi, they show little or no resistance or avoidance.

B4 babies were initially defined as "wholly preoccupied with the mother throughout the Strange Situation," but they were rare in American samples, and Ainsworth remained open to clarification and partial redefinition of this subcategory. Main and Solomon (1986) proposed that babies who show moderate resistance but still seem secure should be included in the B4 subgroup, even if they are not preoccupied with the mother, and Ainsworth agreed. B4 babies tend to be very sensitive to separation, may show some resistance or avoidance, and generally seem to be less competent than B1, B2, and B3 babies. I will have more to say about B4 babies after I describe groups C and D.

■ The "C" Category: Resistant Attachment

Carlos's responses to the events of the Strange Situation differed noticeably from Indira's and Muhamidi's. Carlos, also 12 months old at the time of assessment, represents subgroup C1. His behavior in episodes 2 and 3 was unremarkable. He played with the toys, vocalized, and interacted with his mother and with the stranger. During his mother's first absence, Carlos cried angrily, rejected the toys the stranger offered him, and squirmed down when she picked him up. When his mother returned, he greeted her with a cry, a full approach, and a reach to be picked up. His mother picked him up, carried him to the toys, set him down by the pegboard, and handed him the hammer. He protested loudly, threw the hammer hard at the floor, and wrapped his arms around his mother's leg. She picked him up again. He seemed to want to be held, but he also pushed and kicked a little, and he cried again off and on for 50 seconds. Then his mother got him interested in the hourglass-shaped rattle, and he kept playing with it while she returned to sitting quietly in her chair.

The mother's second departure prompted immediate protest. Carlos cried angrily at the door and then threw himself onto the floor and kicked and thrashed in classic tantrum style. Twenty seconds after the mother's exit, the stranger came in and picked Carlos up. He screamed, pushed, kicked, and struggled hard against being held. Twenty seconds was enough to convince the experimenter that the stranger would not be able to comfort Carlos. He sent the mother back in.

Carlos went right to his mother and pulled on her skirt. She bent down and picked him up. Still crying, he pushed away as if he wanted to get down. The mother set him down. He screamed, clung to her leg again, and then hit her. She picked him up again. His crying began to shift from angry to simply distressed. His mother gave him the big, soft ball. He threw it down hard. She sat on the floor with Carlos in her lap, gave him a cube, held up the bottle, and, in a gentle voice, invited him to put the cube in. He threw

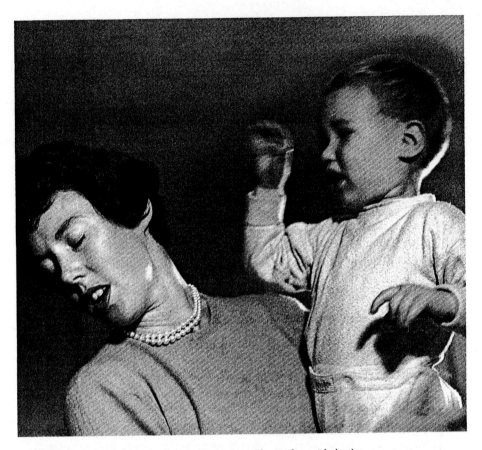

At reunion, babies in Group C mix angry behavior with attachment behavior.

the cube across the room. She gave him another. He dropped it, cried, and turned toward her for closer contact. She held him close. After a minute, the physical tension in his body relaxed visibly. As the 3-minute episode came to an end, he seemed ready to use the toys again.

Except for some B4 babies, babies in groups A and B show little or no resistance to the attachment figure—little or no hitting, pushing, kicking, cranky fussing, or rejecting contact or interaction with the parent. Evidence of high resistance to the parent is generally sufficient for classifying a baby's attachment pattern as C, anxious-resistant. Babies in subcategory C1 show strong proximity-seeking and contact-maintaining behavior, but they also show obvious resistance. Their anger is, like Carlos's, unmistakable.

Although babies in both subgroups of the C category show moderate or strong resistance to the attachment figure, those in subgroup C2 look very different from those in subgroup C1. The most conspicuous characteristic of C2 babies is their passivity. They are less active and seem less competent than other babies. They do not move around the room very much and do not use the toys as energetically as A, B, or C1 babies do. Under stress, they look sadly helpless. They do seek proximity in the reunion episodes, but they are more likely to cry and reach for their parents than to crawl rapidly to their parents. Their resistance often shows in persistent cranky fussing, rejection of toys, resistance to contact, and/or resistance to interference, but without the energetic fierceness many C1 babies show.

The full meaning of any behavior depends on the context in which it occurs. Securely attached infants may at times stage dramatic tantrums. However, the events of the Strange Situation do not provoke tantrums in babies categorized in groups A and B. Furthermore, those babies who have had tantrums in the Strange Situation and who have also been studied at home have been classified as insecurely attached on the basis of behavior at home, as well.

When Ainsworth and her colleagues first assigned a word label to group C babies, the term they selected was "anxious-ambivalent." Over the years, however, many published reports referred to such babies as "resistant" rather than "ambivalent." I have chosen the term "resistant" to refer to group C infants in this book because "resistant" specifies the defining characteristic of C1 babies and a usual characteristic of C2 babies. All anxiously attached infants are ambivalent. Consequently, that term does not differentiate group C infants from other insecure infants.

■ Misfits, Anomalies, and the Emergence of the "D" Category

Some of the first studies of attachment patterns in infants who had been abused and/or neglected (e.g., Crittenden, 1988c; Egeland and Sroufe, 1981) found surprisingly high percentages of infants who, on the basis of existing criteria, had to be classified as group B babies. Group B classification was by then known to indicate secure attachment. Doubting that many maltreated babies could be securely attached, researchers examined their Strange Situation videotapes very carefully. Closer inspection of the videotapes revealed abnormalities in the behaviors of many infants initially classified into group B. For example, some showed both avoidance and resistance; some kept the head or front of the body averted while approaching the mother; some froze in place in odd postures for a few seconds; some showed other odd behaviors.

Crittenden (e.g., 1985, 1988c) found that maltreated children often showed behavior that at first resembled normal behavior, but, on closer inspection, appeared to be an anxious approximation of normal interaction. For example, a child might repeatedly approach the mother and hand toys to her without ever looking at her or touching her. Crittenden modified the definitions of resistance and avoidance somewhat and identified an *avoidant-resistant* (A-C) pattern in her samples of maltreated children. About the same time, Radke-Yarrow, Cummings, Kuczynski, and Chapman (1985) described an A-C pattern of attachment behavior in toddlers whose mothers suffered from major unipolar depression or from bipolar disorder (formerly known as "manic-depressive disorder").

Most studies that have found *many* babies whose Strange Situation behavior did not fit Ainsworth's A-B-C classification system have focused on high-risk samples. However, the first report of babies whose Strange Situation behavior did not fit the description of any of those three patterns was based on an upper-middle-class sample. Main and Weston (1981) reported that 14 percent of their Strange Situation videotapes (each a separate session) were "unclassifiable" using the criteria for the A, B, and C categories. Behavior was considered unclassifiable when, for example, a baby demonstrated both extreme avoidance and extreme distress throughout the Strange Situation, or when the baby showed the approaching and clinging behavior that might characterize a securely attached baby, but appeared affectless and depressed. Furthermore, Main and Weston said, forced classification of such infants into one of the A, B, or C categories would very often result in misclassification of an insecure infant as secure; 13 of their 19 unclassifiable subjects would have been placed in the B category if coders were forced to choose one of the three major groups defined by Ainsworth et al. (1978).

Intrigued by their own data and by reports of anomalous Strange Situation behavior in many babies in high-risk samples, Main and her colleagues gathered and studied Strange Situation videotapes from many projects. Eventually, Main and Solomon (1986, 1990) published criteria for classifying Strange Situation behavior in a newly defined category D, anxious-disorganized-disoriented. The shorter term "disorganized" is often used as the label for babies in group D.

Like many others, Mary Ainsworth (1990) believes that the data now available warrant revision of the classification system she published in 1978: too many babies do not fit the A, B, or C categories. Ainsworth (1991b) definitely recommends inclusion of Main and Solomon's D category in *all* Strange Situation studies to avoid misclassifications. Obviously, our understanding of paths of development will be limited and confused by the inclusion of inaccurate classifications.

■ The "D" Category: Anxious-Disorganized-Disoriented Attachment

Infants in Group D, said Main and Solomon (1986, 1990), appear to have no coherent strategy for handling separations and reunions. Group B babies have coherent strategies for using the attachment figure as a secure base. In the Strange Situation, which is moderately stressful, group A babies use a defensive strategy of diverting their attention from anything that would activate attachment behavior. This strategy includes diverting attention away from the attachment figure herself. Group C babies, according to Main and Solomon, employ a strategy of exhibiting extreme dependence on the attachment figure. The group D babies do not consistently employ any one of those behavioral strategies. Consequently, their behavior appears at times to be disorganized or disoriented.

Main and Solomon (1990) list a variety of criteria for classifying an infant into group D. Some patterns of behavior preclude classifying the baby into group A, group B, or group C, and so prompt the coder to place the baby in group D. In such cases, the baby often indicates disorganization or disorientation indirectly. For example, the baby may show some disordering of expected temporal sequences: she may first approach the caregiver and then show dazed avoidance, or she may suddenly cry out after having appeared to settle down. Or, the baby may show contradictory behaviors simultaneously, such as approaching the parent while taking great care not to look at him. Other behaviors are taken as direct indices of disorganization and disorientation (see Table 3.2). These include (1) freezing for 10 seconds or longer in a posture that requires active resistance to gravity, (2) directly showing fear or apprehension of the caregiver, (3) responding to the caregiver's return by directing attachment behavior to the stranger, and (4) showing dazed, disoriented, affectless, or depressed facial expressions.

Crittenden (1988a, 1994) has argued that some of the A-C attachments that Main and Solomon would code as D's are disturbed but organized responses to disturbed patterns of caregiving. If so, calling such responses "disorganized" is mislabeling them. For example, a baby's behavioral stilling as the caregiver reenters the room may not indicate a lack of a strategy for responding to separation. Instead, it may reflect an adaptive strategy of pausing to take a reading of the mother's apparent mood and her behavioral tendencies before selecting a response. When a baby has an inconsistent, sometimes abusive mother, there is no sense in seeking care when the mother's facial expression shows that she is not in the mood for providing comfort right now. In fact, getting too close and displaying a need for contact might provoke a hostile response. On the other hand, the baby's attachment system *has* been activated. If comfort is available this time, she will not want to miss the opportunity to receive it. Freezing for a moment to take a reading before initiating approach behavior, avoidant behavior, or other behavior may be an indication that the baby has a complex, organized strategy.

In a paper about infants reared in circumstances of abuse and neglect, Crittenden and Ainsworth (1989) noted that a maltreated child has the same instinctive need for proximity and contact after separation that other children have. In fact, his prior experiences of maltreatment may intensify his distress during the brief separations of the Strange Situation, thus intensifying the need for contact. However, he has learned that the mother is likely to ignore, rebuff, or even punish his bids for contact. When a maltreated child maintains avoidance after separation, limits her open anger to aggression against objects in the room—not against the parent—and employs indirect means of achieving proximity, such as keeping her back to the parent while moving closer to her, this suggests not disorganization, but a highly controlled pattern of behavior. It reflects a coherent strategy for managing the conflict between the child's need for proximity and her expectations concerning the parent's responses.

Main and Solomon described three possible subgroups within the D category: *depressed, apprehensive,* and *avoidant-resistant.* They offered their descriptions as tentative ones and noted that many group D babies do not fit any of the three tentative subgroups. Main and others are continuing work on clarifying the D category and defining subgroups within it. As presently defined, group D includes many severely disorganized, very disturbed, and/or depressed babies, but I have also seen group D babies who seem no more insecure than a typical A2 baby. Group D includes most, but not all, of the babies who were classified A-C in earlier studies, and many babies who do not fit the criteria for A-C classifications. Most babies who cannot be classified as A, B, or C do fit into group D, but a few remain unclassifiable even when the fourth category is available.

Why an abused or neglected infant might react to the events in the Strange Situation with group D behavior is clear. However, about 10 percent to 15 percent of babies in low-risk samples also show group D behavior. Why? The best answer is that we do not know. We have almost no data about what sorts of day-to-day experiences in the natural environment precede group D classification in the Strange Situation. We urgently need extensive home observations of babies classified as anxious-disorganized-disoriented in the Strange Situation.

■ Redefinition of the B4 Subgroup

Questions about B4's have been with us since the development of the classification system. In low-risk samples in the United States, B4's are observed rather infrequently, so it has been hard to get a picture of the precursors, meaning, and implications of this pattern of attachment. Several investigators (e.g., Sagi et al., 1985) have wondered whether B4's really belong in group B at all. In the process of defining the D category, Main and Solomon (1986) also offered a revised definition of the B4 subcategory.

Naturalistic observations show that B1, B2, and B3 babies are securely attached. Group B is now considered to be the category for securely attached infants. Whether B4's are securely attached is uncertain. Many babies who have been classified as B4's seem somewhat ambivalent and are not well able to use the mother as a secure base in the Strange Situation. Instead of exploring the toys in an alert, involved way, these B4's show strong proximity-seeking behavior, are somewhat resistant, and are difficult to soothe. Of course, they do not show as much resistance as group C babies do.

Van IJzendoorn, Goossens, Kroononberg, and Tavecchio (1985) had 22 B4's in a sample of 136 Dutch children and so were able to examine the subgroup in more detail. They confirmed that it appears to be a borderline or hybrid group, as the B4 infants' behavior was in many ways similar to the behavior of group C infants, but the B4's showed less resistance. They proposed the label "dependent attachment" for the B4 subgroup.

Main and Solomon proposed a two-part solution to the classification difficulties regarding B4's. Their first recommendation is to restrict use of the B4 category to babies who *do* seem to be securely attached. Babies whose behavior includes stereotypies (odd, awkward, dysfunctional bits of behavior), marked gaze aversion during contact, or other signs of disturbance are probably not securely attached. They should be coded D, anxious-disorganized-disoriented, not B4. Ainsworth (1990) agreed with this revision in the specifications for classifying a baby as a B4. It will be easiest to learn more about the precursors and effects of secure attachments if we include in the B category only secure, not disorganized, attachments.

The second change in the criteria for B4 classification that Main and Solomon proposed is the inclusion of infants who, while showing a noticeable amount of resistance, are not preoccupied with the attachment figure and do seem to be securely attached. Ainsworth et al. (1978) provided two categories (B1 and B2) that accommodated babies who showed noticeable avoidance but nevertheless appeared to be securely attached. Unless we follow Main's lead, we do not have a category for babies who show noticeable *resistance* but nevertheless appear to be securely attached. Ainsworth has also endorsed this change in classification criteria (personal communication, May 12, 1989).

If Main and Solomon's revisions to the criteria for classifying an infant as a B4 are widely adopted, an infant in the Strange Situation who appears to be securely attached but also shows (1) a noticeable amount of resistance, (2) preoccupation with the attachment figure, perhaps even in preseparation episodes, or (3) both, will be classified as a B4.

The precursors and consequences of showing some open anger in the Strange Situation within the context of a secure attachment may differ from the precursors and consequences of preoccupation with the mother. We will need extensive home observations to clarify what each path to B4 classification reflects about real life.

■ Interim Summary: Subgroups in the Strange Situation

Now that all of the subgroups for classifying patterns of behavior in the Strange Situation have been introduced, a summary of the principal characteristics of each subgroup may be helpful. Table 3.2 provides such a summary.

It is time to explain my departure from the usual way of printing the numbers that label subgroups. Most published reports about Strange Situation classifications have shown the subgroup number as a subscript. This practice makes the subgroup classification look considerably less important than the larger group classification. Nevertheless, Ainsworth always treated subgroup differences as matters of importance. Recent studies have raised a lot of questions about differences among subgroups. In this book, I want to emphasize that these differences may be very important. For example, the difference between a C1 and a C2 may be as great as the difference between a C1 and a B4. In each case, the two subgroups may differ in kind as apples and oranges differ in kind, not only in the relative degree of some shared characteristic(s). To emphasize the importance of subgroup classifications, their numbers are printed in this book in type that is as large as the letter labels for the categories. A C2 is a C2, not a C_2.

■ Administration of the Strange Situation

A surprising number of researchers have modified the Strange Situation procedure for a variety of reasons and then hoped to be able to interpret their results as if they had used the complete, standardized procedure. As Sroufe (1990) has argued, this just doesn't make sense. A standardized assessment is a standardized assessment. If you change the procedure, say, by lengthening episode 3 to 15 minutes, using only one separation instead of two, or by telling the caregiver to play with the baby instead of telling her to sit quietly in her chair, then you cannot be sure your assessment of attachment is valid. However, if you administer the assessment the same way it was administered in other studies and code results the same way results were coded in other studies, you can safely use the huge body of data associated with Strange Situation experiments to aid in interpreting the results you obtain. If you change the procedure (or rely on inadequately trained coders), you cannot be sure what your results mean.

One important reason for following the instructions for conducting the Strange Situation is that the stress level that develops during the procedure must be comparable from baby to baby and from study to study. Brief separations from the mother in an unfamiliar place are somewhat stressful for babies and activate the attachment system. However, the stresses associated with coming to a new place, being in the presence of a female stranger, and having the mother leave the room for two brief periods are the *only* stresses the experimenter should include. Consequently, the Strange Situation should be scheduled for a time when the baby is likely to be reasonably well-rested and recently fed. It should not occur when the family circumstances differ much from whatever is normal for that family. For example, it should not occur in the evening after the baby's first 9-hour day with a new babysitter.

Another way to make a Strange Situation too stressful, and therefore invalid, is to conduct it too soon after a previous Strange Situation. Ainsworth et al. (1978) found that, in a second Strange Situation session 2 weeks after the first, infants who were 12 months old showed greater distress and more proximity-seeking and contact-maintaining behavior than they had in the first Strange Situation experiment. All group A babies were classified as group B babies in the second Strange Situation. (They might now be reclassified as group D babies if the data were available on videotape.) Apparently, recall of the first laboratory visit increased the stress level of the second one, and avoidant defenses broke down. In the second assessment, some group B babies were shifted to group C, and some group C babies moved into group B. With too little time between Strange Situations, the results of the second were contaminated by the babies' memories of the first.

Just how much time between Strange Situations is enough? Several investigators (e.g., Belsky, Rovine, and Taylor, 1984; Chase-Lansdale and Owen, 1987; Sagi et al., 1985) have observed infants in a first Strange Situation with one caregiver and in a second Strange Situation with another caregiver 3, 4, or 6 weeks later. They found no order effects on the distribution of attachment classifications. That is, avoidant attachments were not significantly more common in the first experiment than in the second. This suggests that the interval was long enough in most cases to allow avoidance to appear in the second assessment.

In a study of 39 infants in the Netherlands, Goossens, Van IJzendoorn, Tavecchio, and Kroonenberg (1986) also found evidence that 1 month between Strange Situation assessments is sufficient. At the same time, they illustrated the importance of conducting the procedure in an unfamiliar place. They arranged for some Strange Situations to occur in a laboratory playroom, as is usual, while other, "Not-So-Strange" Situations (my label, not theirs) followed the usual sequence of episodes, but were conducted in the child's own living room with his or her own toys. There were four groups in the study; each group was assessed on two occasions. One group participated in two Strange Situations in the laboratory. One group had both assessments occur in the home. The third group had the first assessment in the laboratory and the second at home. The fourth group, of course, had the first assessment at home and the second in the laboratory.

Both the scores on interactive behavior scales (proximity seeking, contact maintaining, resistance, and avoidance) and pattern classifications (avoidant, secure, or resistant) showed high test-retest reliability when both assessments occurred in the same setting. That is, with 1 month between assessments, most subjects got about the same interactive behavior scores and the same pattern classifications for each Strange Situation. However, this was *not* the case when one assessment occurred at home and the other in the laboratory. Children's responses to a procedure developed for use in the laboratory were not directly comparable to their responses to the same procedure at home. The mother's departure from the family living room evidently had a different meaning from her departure from an unfamiliar room. Even so, her departure from the living room did activate attachment behavior in most subjects.

The available studies show that 2 weeks is clearly not enough time between Strange Situations. A 4-week interval does appear to be sufficient, as noted above, but 6 weeks may be preferable. With older babies (15 to 18 months), a longer interval between assessments may be needed, because the baby may remember the discomfort of the first assessment longer than a 12-month-old would remember it.

To avoid raising the stress level of the Strange Situation itself, it is best for experimenters to conduct the Strange Situation as the first assessment in any laboratory visit.

If any long procedure precedes the Strange Situation, it will tire the baby. If a stressful procedure precedes the Strange Situation, it will add to the subject's stress and distress levels and may affect behavior in ways that change classification of the infant's attachment.

For example, Sagi et al. (1986) conducted sociability assessments right before conducting Strange Situations. For 10 to 15 minutes, babies were observed reacting first to one stranger and then to another of the opposite gender. The subjects were Israeli kibbutz (commune) babies. (Kibbutz child rearing will be described in Chapter 8.) The sociability assessment incapacitated many of the kibbutz babies, as evidenced by their behavior in the Strange Situation, and raised questions about the validity of their Strange Situation classifications.

In studies in the United States (Thompson and Lamb, 1983) and in Sweden (Lamb et al., 1982), conducting the same assessment of sociability right before the Strange Situation procedure did not cause any obvious problems. Nevertheless, Sroufe (1990) does recommend that the Strange Situation should never be preceded by any other assessment in any given laboratory visit.

I have given several examples of problems that can make the Strange Situation too stressful and therefore invalid. An experimenter can also err in the other direction. In administering the Strange Situation, the researcher must take care that it is stressful enough. If the baby's attachment behavior is not activated, the researcher cannot assess the pattern of attachment. Some investigators have attempted to assess attachment after allowing the subject a rather long period of familiarization with the laboratory setting—15 or 20 minutes instead of 3 minutes. Investigators have also attempted to assess attachment after a single brief separation. In those circumstances, coders cannot get enough information to describe the infant's attachment pattern. D'Angelo (1986) provided a specific illustration of the fact that abbreviating the Strange Situation yields false positives for secure attachment. Forty-five infant-mother dyads were observed in Strange Situations. One observer classified patterns of attachment (A, B, or C) from the infant's behavior during the complete procedure; the other based classifications only on behavior in the introductory episodes, the first separation, and the first reunion. The second observer, working with insufficient data, reported a significantly higher number of secure attachments than the first observer did.

The Strange Situation does appear to be a robust research tool, often yielding meaningful results even when experimenters tinker with the procedure. However, you cannot change its rules and procedures a little and still be entirely confident that your results will have the same meaning they would have if you had followed the standard procedure.

■ Coding Strange Situations

In most cases, administering the Strange Situation correctly is not unduly difficult. The next set of problems to consider involves issues about coding the videotapes. For results of Strange Situation studies to be useful, you need reason to be confident that classification criteria used reliably within one laboratory very closely match the classification criteria used in other laboratories. The coders in each research project must have training from an experienced, trained coder. Their training is not complete until their classifications match the classifications assigned by someone who can trace his or her expertise to agreement with someone Ainsworth fully trained.

The first step in accurate coding is to assign scores for proximity and contact seeking, contact maintaining, resistance, and avoidance. Performing this step is usually not a problem. Learning to recognize avoidance and resistance is not too difficult for most trainees. Most can learn to assign scores from all of the interactive scales described by Ainsworth et al. (1978) easily enough. Even experienced researchers do, however, need training from an experienced Strange Situation coder. Relying on the written instructions Ainsworth et al. (1978) provided is not usually enough. Exactly how hard it is to teach people to recognize indices of disorganization (Main and Solomon, 1990) is not yet clear.

The next step in coding is to classify the pattern of the Strange Situation behavior as secure, avoidant, resistant, or disorganized. Learning to do this requires guided observation of examples of the various subcategories. It also requires an ability to make a clinical judgment about how the baby's behavior fits together and what it indicates. Obviously, it would be nice if the need for this step, and the training time it requires, could be eliminated. According to Sroufe, most new coders need a few weeks of training. If clinical judgment were not necessary, training would be much faster and coding would be faster, cheaper, and more objective.

Richters, Waters, and Vaughn (1988) addressed the challenges of coding by conducting a multiple discriminant function analysis with data from 255 Strange Situations. That is, they used fairly sophisticated mathematical procedures to develop a way a programmed computer could serve in the place of a trained human coder. They obtained discriminant functions and classification weights that permitted the assignment of A, B, and C classifications directly from scores on interactive behaviors and on crying during reunion episodes. Agreement between classifications assigned by trained coders and those assigned by the discriminant functions was 90.6 percent for B versus non-B classification and 94.3 percent for A versus C classification. Unfortunately, group D, which had only very recently been defined, was not used, and classification into subcategories was not attempted. Van Dam and Van IJzendoorn (1988) used the Richters et al. (1988) discriminant functions to assess a sample of 39 Dutch toddlers and obtained 85 percent agreement with the judgments of trained coders using the A, B, or C classifications.

These results from computerized scoring are initially promising. Formulas developed in a large sample in one country worked with a small sample in a different country. Agreement between the mathematics-based computer coding and trained human coding was as high as agreement between two trained humans normally is: about 85 to 90 percent. That is, two trained coders usually agree about which category (avoidant, secure, resistant, or disorganized) 85 to 90 percent of the videotaped infants belong in, but will initially disagree about a few tapes. What people can do that discriminant function analysis cannot yet do is recognize indications of disorganization or disorientation, assign tapes to subgroups (e.g., B3 versus B4, not just B versus non-B), and judge the close cases accurately (e.g., A2 versus B1).

As Speiker and Booth (1988) have noted, some babies in Strange Situations are frankly hard to code. Routine use of two coders for each Strange Situation and coding by consensus when the two coders' initial codings disagree might increase the accuracy of coding and so advance our efforts to understand the determinants and implications of different patterns of attachment. Speiker and Booth also suggest that, when testing hypotheses about relationships between attachment patterns and other variables, using only the clear cases may be most informative. That is, they suggest analyzing results only for babies whose Strange Situation behavior clearly fits within a category's boundaries. Data from babies whose Strange Situation behavior is borderline or ambiguous can be excluded from the analyses.

■ Validity of the Strange Situation

A psychological measure is said to be *valid* if it truly measures what it is supposed to measure, and if the score a subject gets on the measure accurately reflects his or her ability or characteristics in terms of the construct the method is designed to measure. To be valid, the Strange Situation must accurately assess the pattern of a baby's attachment behavior, and the pattern observed in the laboratory must have a meaningful relation to the pattern of the baby's behavior in natural settings.

As the numerous studies cited in this book will illustrate, the Strange Situation does appear to have convincing levels of *construct validity*. That is, it accurately measures what it is supposed to measure—namely, the quality of an infant's attachment to a caregiver. In studies in which both naturalistic and Strange Situation observations have been conducted, the Strange Situation classifications have been related in meaningful, consistent ways to the home behavior. The procedure also has convincing *external validity*, both concurrent and predictive. That is, Strange Situation categories are related in meaningful ways to measures of constructs other than attachment, including measures of how the baby is doing around the time of the Strange Situation assessment (*concurrent validity*) and measures of how the child is developing later in life (*predictive validity*).

For many years, Michael Lamb and his colleagues took great care to maintain a skeptical, scientific stance toward attachment research. If anyone was going to prove that the Strange Situation was not valid, they were the people to do it. In a detailed review of all the evidence available at the time (Lamb, Thompson, Gardner, and Charnov, 1985), they concluded:

> It is clear that the infant's prior experiential history outside of the Strange Situation does relate in a predictable and consistent fashion to Strange Situation behavior. Overall, there is good reason to believe that mothers who behave in a fashion considered sensitive or socially-desirable by Americans tend to have infants who later exhibit B-type behavior in the Strange Situation. . . . Further, the studies conducted on maltreated infants, those on the differences between mother- and father-infant attachments, . . . and those on the effects of changing caretaking arrangements . . . all suggest that variations in the infant's experiential history with a specific caretaker do influence Strange Situation behavior in a consistent and predictable fashion.

A discordant note about the validity of Strange Situation assessments appeared in Field (1987). Field concluded that mother-infant interaction patterns are more sensitive indicators of the mother-infant relationship and are more responsive to intervention than Strange Situation classifications of attachment behavior are. Her review relied on evidence from atypical populations (premature babies, abused and neglected infants, and babies with depressed mothers), and she noted that many of the subjects in these studies may have been misclassified because the D category had not yet been defined. Regular use of that category in new studies and perhaps in reanalyses of old data may change Field's conclusions. Most researchers are confident that the Strange Situation is a valid method for assessing the pattern of a baby's attachment to the primary caregiver.

Some words of caution are appropriate, however. The Strange Situation was developed and validated as a research tool, not as a clinical test. In studies of many babies, group B babies differ in consistent, meaningful ways from group A and group C babies. However, there is a potential for error in almost any psychological measure. One source of measurement error is the difficulty of coding. Well-trained coders may disagree about classifying 10 percent to 15 percent of videotapes. Another source of measurement error can occur when, unbeknownst to the experimenter, any individual baby behaves in a way that is unusual for that baby just when he or she participates in the Strange Situation. For example, a baby who has an upsetting experience just before the assessment may be less avoidant or more clingy than is usual for him, but his caregiver may not mention the experience when they arrive at the laboratory. Similarly, a secure baby who has an undiagnosed ear infection is likely to be unusually irritable and may therefore appear to be resistant. However, the experimenter, the coders, and, at the time of the assessment, the caregiver, will probably not be aware that there is such a simple explanation for the baby's resistance.

Such problems—confusing, uninterpretable sources of error—add "noise" to the assessment. Despite the noise, when *groups* of infants are compared, similarities and differences among them can still be seen. The differences among groups are strong enough to show up despite misclassification of a few babies. The presence of differences among *groups* does not justify using the Strange Situation by itself to make decisions about an *individual* infant's custody, foster care placement, or psychotherapeutic treatment. The Strange Situation may be an appropriate measure to include among other measures in a clinical assessment of a baby's development, but it was not designed for clinical uses and has not been validated for them.

As noted earlier, the Strange Situation was initially validated in studies of white middle-class babies and their mothers, almost all of whom stayed home full-time taking care of their babies. Extensive home observations from Ainsworth's small Baltimore sample provide the primary basis for ascribing real-life meaning to the pattern of the baby's behavior during the laboratory procedure. Other major and minor studies, including many studies of poor families, have further validated the Strange Situation as a measure of security of attachment to a white American mother who is a full-time homemaker.

When researchers began using the Strange Situation with familiar caregivers who were not unemployed white American mothers, they assumed the burden of accumulating evidence that the procedure was valid for assessing attachments to those figures. Strange Situation assessments of attachments to employed white fathers raised no protest, despite the evidence that father-infant interaction differs qualitatively from mother-infant interaction and that fathers interact with their babies far less than mothers do. Some results from the first uses of the Strange Situation outside the United States made people uncomfortable and prompted much careful thinking. Results of studies that used the Strange Situation to assess babies' attachments to employed white mothers had political implications and triggered vivid debates.

Is the Strange Situation a valid assessment of security of attachment to the father? There is no particular reason to doubt that it is, but surprisingly few studies have specifically addressed the question. (See Chapter 9.) Does the procedure provide a valid measure of attachment to the day care provider? Probably so, but few studies have tested the likelihood. Is the Strange Situation a valid procedure for assessing attachment to the mother in babies with considerable day care experience? I think so, but there are well-respected psychologists who remain skeptical. I will describe the research and perspectives on these questions in Chapter 10.

When the Strange Situation was first exported to Germany, Israel, and then Japan, results raised questions about whether the procedure was valid in countries where infants' experiences and adults' child-rearing goals differed markedly from experiences and goals in the United States. These issues will be discussed in Chapter 8.

■ Distribution of Attachment Patterns

In most samples drawn from ordinary middle-class or working-class families in the United States, about 60 to 65 percent of babies are classified as securely attached (group B), about 20 to 25 percent as avoidant (group A), and about 10 percent as resistant (group C). Now that the D category (anxious-disorganized-disoriented) has been defined and described, it appears that about 10 to 15 percent of the babies in nonclinical middle-class and working-class samples fit the group D criteria (Cicchetti, 1987). In studies of maltreatment, psychiatric patient, and other high-risk sample populations, group D attachments appear to occur with very high frequencies, often greater than 50 percent of cases. In one high-risk sample, all of the subjects were classified into group D.

■ A Continuum of Security?

Rather recently, several investigators (Crittenden, 1985; Cummings, 1990; Main et al., 1985; Waters and Deane, 1985) have proposed ways to rate degrees of security of attachment along a continuum, in addition to or even instead of classifying patterns of attachment. Both for clinical work and for research, having a security scale available would be valuable. The construct of security is a meaningful one. If you say that one person is more secure than another, people understand what you are talking about. From a scientific perspective, however, the term must be precisely defined, and the means of measuring it must be empirically validated.

The simplest and most common method for rating degree of security when Strange Situation classifications are available is to translate them into scores on a quasi-interval scale. (On a true interval scale, such as an accurate yardstick, the distance between each point on the scale and the next point is equal; there is a consistent unit of measurement, such as an inch. On a quasi-interval scale, the ordering of points is consistent, but the degree of difference between each point and the next is inconsistent and usually uncertain.) When translating Strange Situation classifications into security scores, Main et al. (1985) proposed regarding B3's as very secure (score = 3); B1's, B2's, and B4's as secure (score = 2); and A's, C's, and D's as insecure (score = 1). There may be a problem with this approach.

Suppose you were inventing a system for classifying fruits. You might develop scales for rating how tough the skin is, how firm the flesh is, how juicy the fruit is, what size it is, and so on. Using the scalable information, you might identify criteria for classifying some fruits as berries, some as citrus fruits, some as firm fruits (e.g., apples and pears), and some as soft fruits (e.g., peaches, kiwis, plums, apricots). Cherries and grapes might be hard to classify. Could you then arrange your categories (berry, citrus, firm fruit, soft fruit) along a scale that measures overall appeal of a fruit? Would you have any justification to give berries a 6 on the scale, give firm fruits a 5, and give citrus fruits a 4? Blueberries, oranges, apples, and plums are all appealing fruits. One may be more subjectively appealing than another, but their classification as berries or citrus fruits does not tell you how appealing they are. Lemons, tangerines, grapefruits, and oranges are all citrus fruits, but they are not all equally appealing. Strawberries and blueberries are more appealing than huckleberries and cranberries. As a group, are berries more appealing than citrus fruits, or vice versa? Or should they get the same score? The whole idea just does not work. Hence, you cannot treat classifications as points along a continuum.

The same difficulty may arise when people try to treat Strange Situation groups A, B, C, and D as points along a continuum of security. The groups were defined by recognizing sets of infants whose behavior in the Strange Situation was similar to each other's but differed from the behavior of other groups. By analogy, infants were classified as berries, citrus fruits, or firm fruits. No scale for rating security was used, and, in the beginning, no such scale was implied. The labels emerged long after the groups were identified.

My own impression is that, on the average, degrees of security do differ between groups, but also vary quite a bit within groups and even within subgroups. For example, A1's look more insecure than A2's—A1's are more powerfully and more rigidly defended. C2's look more insecure than C1's: the C2's look sad and helpless, while the C1's are still fighting to get the caregiver to meet their needs. Some B2's look as secure as the average B3, but some do not. As previously noted, babies coded D vary widely in apparent degree of security.

Despite these reasons for caution in translating Strange Situation classifications into security scores, Cummings (1990) reports that Ainsworth agreed that it was reasonable to do so. She thought B3's would generally be most secure. As distance or avoidance increased, the subgroups, in descending order of degree of security, would be B2, B1, A2, and A1. As resistance and anxiety increased, the subgroups, in descending order of security, would be B4, C1, and C2. Infants who showed high levels of both avoidance and resistance or showed other strong indicators of insecurity, such as open fear of the parent or visible depression, would get even lower security scores than A1's and C2's.

At present, the unit of measurement for degree of security has no operational definition. There is no empirical basis for saying that a B3 is 5 units more secure than a B2, or that a C1 has just as few units of security as an A2. However, what Crittenden (1985), Cummings (1990), and Main et al. (1985) have each proposed is not an interval scale but a quasi-interval scale. Many statistical tests developed for use with variables measured on interval scales work well even if the available data are arranged on quasi-interval scales.

Even though investigators are working with a system that classifies patterns, not a system initially designed to rate degrees of security, we clearly have data that justify giving group B babies higher security scores than other babies. The analytical advantages of being able to rate degrees of security on a more detailed scale, even an imperfect quasi-interval scale, are attractive. They certainly justify continued efforts to define and validate a security scale for Strange Situation behavior. Cummings (1990) has offered some useful ideas about rating an infant's degree of security on a scale designed for that purpose, using a variety of behavioral indices that can be observed in the Strange Situation. This direct approach to rating degrees of security may eventually prove more fruitful than translating Strange Situation classifications into security scores.

THE ATTACHMENT Q-SET

■ The Emergence and Evolution of the Attachment Q-set

For about 15 years after Ainsworth and Wittig developed the Strange Situation, naturalistic observations and the Strange Situation were the only methods available for assessing patterns of attachment. Eventually, the need for another method of assessment became clear. Naturalistic observations lengthy enough to reveal an infant's pattern of attachment were almost never conducted, because of the expense. The coding system Ainsworth et al. (1978) developed for Strange Situations is valid only for a very limited age range (11 to 18 or maybe 20 months). The procedure cannot be repeated soon or often without compromising the validity of the assessment. There is also a problem of convenience: it is sometimes difficult to persuade parents and other caregivers to come to the laboratory. Persuading subjects to contribute a moderate amount of time for research while remaining in their own environments is less difficult.

For all these reasons, researchers needed to have an additional standardized means of assessing attachment in infancy, preferably one that did not require a trip to the laboratory. Such a tool is exactly what Waters and Deane (1985) attempted to provide in their Attachment Q-set. I cannot improve on their own introduction to the importance of their effort (Waters and Deane, pp. 41–42):

> At times, it seems as if attachment research could fall victim to its own success. In the span of barely 15 years, we have come to accept Freud's view that attachment in infancy constitutes a genuine love relationship. We have recognized that this relationship is closely tracked by patterns of behavior toward caregivers and that this behavior is complexly organized, goal-corrected, and sensitive to environmental input. We have also adapted observational techniques employed by behavioral biologists and learned to examine infant behavior in detail and in context. . . .
>
> In the midst of these and other advances . . . , it is easy to lose sight of the fact that there have been very few nonlaboratory observations of attachment behavior during the last ten years. Reports on attachment behavior outside the 12–18 month range have also been few and far between. Questions about . . . individual differences beyond security and anxiety have received surprisingly little attention. . . . In fact, most of the recent data on the correlates of secure versus anxious attachments are simply being assimilated to the general hypothesis that "all good things go together." This . . . introduces the risk that the attachment construct will lose its definition

and once again fall in among the feckless personality trait variables from which it was only recently rescued.

When designing their new measure, Waters and Deane tied it closely to Bowlby's control systems model of attachment. They wanted their method to measure the degree to which and the manner in which a young child (12 to 36 months) used the attachment figure as a secure base across time and across situations. Their goals for developing a valid method of assessment were well-thought-out. They wanted the measure to (1) refer to observable behavior in context, (2) permit evaluation of relationships among affect, cognition, and behavior, (3) allow for qualitative developmental change (i.e., change in kind, not change in amount), (4) detect coherence in development over time despite changes in behavior, (5) discriminate security of attachment from similar constructs associated with other theoretical perspectives (namely, dependency and sociability), and (6) minimize the impact of observer bias.

The first published version of the Attachment Q-set consisted of 100 statements. Each descriptive statement refers to some specific behavior and taps one of the following constructs: security, dependency, detachment, self-efficacy, aspects of object orientation, communication skills, predominant mood, response to physical comforting, fearfulness, anger, and trust. To reduce the risk of observer bias, Waters and Deane took care to state the items in nonevaluative terms. Each item says something specific and observable about how a child ordinarily behaves in a given sort of situation. For example, one item says the child actively solicits comforting from the adult when distressed. Another says the child remains fearful of moving toys or animals. A list of some items from the current Q-set appears in Table 3.3.

To begin, an observer sorts the items into three piles and then subdivides those three into nine piles, ranging from least characteristic of the child to most characteristic of the child, in each case. Then, working from the outer piles toward the center, the observer adjusts each pile so that the final result is a unimodal, symmetrical array of items. When the sorting is done, each pile has a predetermined number of behavioral items in it. When 100 items were in the Q-set, the nine piles consisted of 5, 8, 12, 16, 18, 16, 12, 8, and 5 items, respectively.

Each item then gets a score based on its placement. That is, each of the 5 items in the first pile (the pile of statements that are least characteristic of the child), gets a score of 1. Each of the 8 items in the next pile gets a score of 2, and so on. The 5 items in the last pile each get a score of 9. When two or more observers use the Q-set to describe the same child, the investigator can form a composite description of the child by averaging the scores each observer gave to the same item. In general, the reliability of any Q-sort description of a subject increases when several sorts are averaged to obtain a composite Q-sort.

The observers, who are either trained research assistants or the child's usual caregivers, do not need to know what constructs will be extracted from the data they provide. They also do not need to know norms for the behaviors mentioned on the Q-set items. To prepare a caregiver to use the Q-set, the researcher explains the procedure and then asks the caregiver to familiarize himself or herself with the items by sorting them into three piles: characteristic, neither characteristic nor uncharacteristic, and uncharacteristic. The researcher encourages the caregiver to ask about the items and about the sorting proce-

TABLE 3.3 Example Items from the Revised Attachment Q-set

Items with High Scores in Criterion Sort for Security

1. Child readily shares with mother or lets her hold things if she asks to.*
18. Child follows mother's suggestions readily, even when they are clearly suggestions rather than orders.*
36. Child clearly shows a pattern of using mother as a base from which to explore.*†
41. When mother says to follow her, child does so.†
42. Child recognizes when mother is upset.*†
53. Child puts his arms around mother or puts his hand on her shoulder when she picks him up.*
60. If mother reassures him by saying "It's OK" or "It won't hurt you," child will approach or play with things that initially made him cautious or afraid.*
71. If held in mother's arms, child stops crying and quickly recovers after being frightened or upset.*
80. Child uses mother's facial expressions as a good source of information when something looks risky or threatening.*

Items with Low Scores in Criterion Sort for Security

2. When child returns to mother after playing, he is sometimes fussy for no clear reason.*
33. Child sometimes signals mother (or gives the impression) that he wants to be put down, and then fusses or wants to be picked right back up.*
38. Child is demanding and impatient with mother. Fusses and persists unless she does what he wants right away.
54. Child acts like he expects mother to interfere with his activities when she is simply trying to help him with something.*
61. Plays roughly with mother. Bumps, scratches, or bites during active play.*
65. Child is easily upset when mother makes him change from one activity to another.†
75. At home, child gets upset or cries when mother walks out of the room.*†
79. Child easily becomes angry at mother.*
81. Child cries as a way of getting mother to do what he wants.*
88. When something upsets the child, he stays where he is and cries.*

*The Q-set card defines behavior warranting low and/or middle placement of this item.

†The Q-set card gives one or more examples or further definition of this behavior.

Source: Waters, Vaughn, Posada, and Kondo-Ikemura, in press.

dure. The purpose of this three-pile sort is simply to acquaint the caregiver with the items; no data are recorded. Then the caregiver observes the child for a week with the expectation of completing the full nine-pile Q-sort at the end of the week. After completing that Q-sort, the caregiver observes for another week and provides another sort. The two sorts are averaged to yield a composite description of the child.

Any Q-sort is a forced-choice procedure. If almost all of the items that reflect secure attachment wind up in the three piles that yield high scores, that result is likely to reflect something about the child. It is not likely to occur by chance, because a fixed number of items must be in each pile when the sorting is done. Half of the items will be in the three piles that yield middling scores, and one-quarter of the items will be in the piles that yield low scores.

■ Criterion Sorts

According to their purposes, researchers can choose among many different ways of "reducing" (organizing and summarizing) and analyzing the data from a Q-sort. One of the methods Waters and Deane (1985) recommend is comparing the Q-set description of each subject with a *criterion sort* provided by experts. A criterion sort is an operational definition of a construct. It is a profile, a set of scores for items in the Q-set, that specifies the criteria that define a construct.

Waters and Deane asked 43 Ph.D. psychologists familiar with developmental theories of those constructs to use the items in the Attachment Q-set to define security, dependency, and sociability. These experts represented a wide range of theoretical perspectives and included behaviorally oriented child clinicians, eclectic cognitive social-learning theorists, and psychodynamically trained personality researchers. [See Waters and Deane (1985) for the impressive roster.] From these various experts working independently, Waters and Deane collected eight sortings for each construct as it would appear in the behavior of a 12-month-old infant and eight for each construct as it would appear in the behavior of a 3-year-old child. There was exceptionally good agreement among experts with different theoretical backgrounds about the Q-sort definition of each construct at each age. In addition, eight Ph.D. students in developmental psychology sorted the Q-set items into nine piles ranging from most socially desirable to least socially desirable for each age.

One goal of this research was to test whether the constructs of security and dependency differed from each other. At the time, many psychologists were using the two terms as if they referred to the same construct in babies or as if they were opposites of each other in 3-year-olds. As I have already explained, attachment theorists hold that an attachment can be either secure or insecure, and that some behaviors that psychoanalysts and social-learning theorists have labeled as immature and/or dependent may be healthy expressions of secure attachment. Attachment theorists also recognize the unhealthy nature of excessive dependency. The point is, they treat dependency and attachment as different constructs, not different terms for the same characteristic.

The correlation between Q-set criterion sorts of security and dependency indicated that the constructs were indeed unrelated to each other in 12-month-olds. That is, the array of Q-set item scores that indicated security was not in any systematic way the same as or different from the array of scores that indicated dependency. A correlation is a measure of the degree of association between two variables. Correlations can range from −1.00 to +1.00. A correlation of zero indicates no systematic linear relationship between the two variables. The higher the absolute value of the correlation is, the greater the degree of association between the two variables is. When the correlation is positive, high scores on one variable are associated with high scores on the other variable. When the correlation is negative, high scores on one variable are associated with *low* scores on the other variable. As experts used the Q-set to define security and dependency in 3-year-olds, the two constructs were moderately negatively correlated ($r = -.36$). That is consistent with the view that excessive dependent behavior in a 36-month-old child implies a degree of insecurity. However, security and dependency remain separate concepts.

The criterion sorts indicated that security and sociability were conceptualized in very similar ways ($r = .82$ for 12-month-olds; $r = .88$ for 36-month-olds). This casts some doubt on the accuracy of one or both of the measures. In theory, there is no strong reason to expect securely attached young children to be more sociable than insecurely attached young children are. In the Strange Situation, for example, securely attached babies vary greatly in their sociability with the caregiver and with the stranger. I would expect the same to be true in other settings. Some insecurely attached infants (especially those in group A) are quite outgoing and sociable. Recent research lends strong support to the view that there is a powerful genetic influence on how shy or how sociable a child will be. On theoretical grounds, the correlations between sociability and security that Waters and Deane obtained should not happen. The authors did not elaborate on the problem. Also, they did not report on the degree to which security correlated with social desirability. A significant correlation between measures of those two constructs, while not surprising, would present some challenge to interpreters of the data.

To use the criterion sort for security as a reference point for assessing the security of a child's attachment, a researcher can correlate the child's item scores with those of a prototypically secure infant (as defined by the experts' criterion sort) to obtain the child's security score. Correlations with other expert sorts provide scores for the child's sociability and dependency and for the social desirability of the description of the child's behavior.

Soon after its invention, the Attachment Q-set was used in several studies. Waters and his colleagues found some difficulties with it and made appropriate revisions. Some items were hard for caregivers to understand, so the researchers simplified the wording. In the first version of the Q-set, each item stated one characteristic type of observable behavior but did not say what the opposite or absence of that sort of behavior would look like. The current version specifies the meaning of low placement as well as the meaning of high placement on most items. On some items in the initial set, observer-observer or observer-parent agreement was not reliable. Those items were eliminated, reducing the number of items from 100 to 90. Using the revised set of items, another set of experts provided sorts to create new criterion definitions of security, dependency, and sociability.

■ Measurement Reliability

The Attachment Q-set has several advantages the Strange Situation lacks. It rates degree of security on a scale; it can be repeated almost as soon and as often as an investigator wishes; it can be administered almost anywhere; and natural caregivers, not just trained observers, can provide the data. If it proves to be a valid method of assessing security of attachments, it will be a tremendously valuable research tool.

A first step in establishing the validity of the measure is demonstrating that observers can provide reliable data. Mothers, fathers, and other regular caregivers are the obvious "observers" to involve; they know the most about the children under study. However, they may be inclined to say the children they love are healthier and more wonderful than the children really are. Research assistants are less likely to be biased, but they have less opportunity to observe the range of the child's behavior in everyday life.

If two different observers, whether caregivers or trained research assistants, can use the Q-set to provide accurate descriptions of young children's usual behavior, then there should be a high correlation between the item scores from one observer's sort and the item scores from the other observer's sort. The strength of the correlation does vary somewhat from child to child and from observer pair to observer pair. However, when two trained observers perform the Q-sort, the correlation between the two arrays of item scores generally is high enough to support confidence in the reliability of the assessment.

Do mothers' sorts match trained observers' sorts? When Waters and Deane introduced the Q-set, they had research assistants make two long (3- to 4-hour) visits to observe the child in the natural setting. Each observer then sorted the Q-set independently, and the two sets of scores were averaged. The correlations between the mother's Q-set description of her child and the observers' averaged description ranged from .59 to .93, with a mean of .80. These high positive correlations were certainly encouraging. The authors did suggest that three long visits might be better than two, but their results indicated that both trained observers and mothers could provide reliable data.

Of course, mothers' sorts and researchers' sorts were not identical. Which type of observer is more likely to provide valid data? Waters and Deane suggested that many differences between descriptions from mothers and descriptions from research assistants arose from the fact that mothers knew more about their children's behavior. To the extent that this is true, mothers would be in a better position to provide valid data. However, there are at least two other reasons that mothers' Q-set descriptions may differ from objective observers' descriptions. First, as noted above, mothers may tend to say that their children's behavior is more desirable than it really is. Second, some mothers may have defense mechanisms or preoccupations that prevent them from perceiving their children's behavior accurately. Recall the discussion of representational models in Chapter 2. Perceptual biases resulting from distorted representational models would make some parents less likely than objective observers to provide valid data.

■ Construct Validity

The first step along the path in demonstrating the validity of the Attachment Q-set was to establish that caregivers, trained observers, or both could use the Q-set to provide reliable data about a child. The next step is for researchers to show that children who get higher scores for security on the Q-set also get scored as more secure on some other, adequately validated measure of security of attachment.

The ultimate criterion is, of course, the quality and consistency of secure-base behavior as verified by lengthy naturalistic observations. Are 6 to 8 hours of observations by trained observers and the sorting of the Q-set sufficient to reflect the pattern of behavior researchers would observe over a period of months? Do parents' and other caregivers' Q-set descriptions of a child match what an objective observer would see in periodic, long observations? Neither question has been empirically addressed.

The other validated measure of security of attachment is the Strange Situation. If the Q-set is similarly valid, then group B infants should get significantly higher Q-set security scores than group A, C, or D infants get. Actual results have been mixed.

For example, in a study of 94 firstborn 1-year-olds (Belsky and Rovine, 1990), security scores and social desirability scores from mothers' Q-set descriptions of their children were very highly correlated ($r = .85$). This correlation should make us wonder. Did the Q-set assess the security of the baby's attachment or merely the strength of the mother's tendency to give socially desirable responses? The Q-set security scores did not correspond to Strange Situation classifications. This suggests that the mothers' Q-sorts did not yield valid assessments of security of attachment.

Fortunately, statistical methods are available to separate the portion of the variability in security scores attributable to the tendency to give socially desirable responses from the portion attributable to some other factor or factors. After adjusting statistically for social desirability, the security scores from the mothers' Q-sorts *were* associated with Strange Situation classifications: Group B infants obtained the highest scores, group C babies, significantly lower scores, and group A babies, the lowest scores. Further, the mothers' adjusted Q-sorts differentiated avoidant babies from other infants on dependency and sociability, but they did not differentiate securely attached infants from resistant infants on those variables. (The D category was not used in this study.)

In the Netherlands, Van Dam and Van IJzendoorn (1988) obtained similar results in a study of 39 toddlers (average age, 18 months) in the Strange Situation and in a period of free play with their mothers. The information reported suggests that this was a white middle-class sample, but does not clearly say so. Using Deane's early 75-item parental version of the Q-set (translated into Dutch), the mothers made two sortings, about 10 days apart. Test-retest reliability scores for security, dependency, sociability, and social desirability from the Q-set were good: .75, .86, .78, and .82, respectively.

In the interim between the first and second sortings, the Strange Situation was conducted. As in Belsky and Rovine's study (1990), Strange Situation codings and Q-set assessments failed to converge. Q-set security scores were not related to A-B-C classifications or to scores for proximity seeking, contact maintaining, resistance, or avoidance in the Strange Situation. If Strange Situation classifications were valid in this sample, we must conclude that mothers' Q-set sorts did not provide valid assessments of security.

In contrast, Vaughn and Waters (1990) found significant associations between Strange Situation classifications and observers' Q-set descriptions. They observed fifty-eight 1-year-olds in the Strange Situation and in the home and completed Q-set descriptions of their behavior within 4 weeks of the Strange Situation assessment. Almost all of the subjects were from white middle-class families in the Chicago area. Fourteen different observers participated, and Q-set descriptions for most babies represented the consensus of two different observers. Compared to babies classified as anxiously attached, babies who were classified as secure in the Strange Situation got higher Q-set scores for security and sociability, but did not differ significantly on dependency. Vaughn and Waters suggested two reasons their results might differ from those of Van Dam and Van IJzendoorn (1988). First, the Dutch investigators used an earlier, abbreviated version of the Q-set. Second, they had mothers, not trained research assistants, sort the Q-set items.

Vaughn and Waters (1990) also suggested that the association between Strange Situation classifications and home behavior as described in Q-set descriptions may differ in different cultures. The correlation may be highest in cultures that allow infants considerable floor freedom, encourage infants' independence, and encourage raising infants at home. The association may be lowest, or nonexistent, in those that set a high value on the child's connection to the mother and a low value on independence.

Given those reservations, researchers might doubt whether the Q-set should work well with subjects living in poverty in Chile. However, using just such a sample, Valenzuela and Lara (1987, cited in Main, 1990) found that the Q-set *did* reliably distinguish between secure and anxious attachments as assessed in the Strange Situation.

Another sound approach to exploring the validity of the Q-set as a measure of attachment security is to test its concurrent and predictive validity in a variety of ways. Do children who get high security scores on the Q-set behave on other measures as theorists expect secure children to behave? Do they enjoy the developmental advantages theorists expect secure children to enjoy? If so, that would support the view that the Q-set does provide a valid measure of security.

Unfortunately, early results on such measures of validity are, like early results on association with Strange Situation classifications, mixed. Enough of the results accord with expectations to warrant continued exploration of the measure. However, discordant results are common enough to warrant continued skepticism.

■ Use of the Q-Set for Classifying Patterns of Attachment

One of the goals Waters and Deane had in mind was to create a valid method for assessing *degrees* of security, to develop an interval scale for security of attachment. Perhaps for that reason, they did not attempt to use the Q-set to classify children into groups A, B, and C. A few years later, however, other investigators did propose a method for using Q-set profiles to classify attachments as avoidant, secure, or resistant. Whether their system has any validity is entirely unknown, but the effort was interesting and the goal seems worth pursuing. If the method interests you, you can read about it in an article about a large sample of children in day care (Howes and Hamilton, 1992a).

In short, the Attachment Q-set is both an attractive research tool and a work in progress. Further clarification of the Q-set's construct validity and its relation to other measures of attachment and social development should prove interesting. Such studies are ongoing. In fact, as this book goes to press, one monograph (Waters, Vaughn, Posada, and Kondo-Ikemura, in press) and one collection of Q-set studies (Waters and Vaughn, in preparation) should also be going to press. The new research may clarify much.

You will find studies that used one version of the Attachment Q-set or another here and there throughout this book. One of the best uses of the Q-set seems to be in conjunction with Strange Situation data. The combination of measures usually yields more information about the infants under study than either measure can yield by itself. By including both in studies that also use other measures, we learn more about what each assessment method measures and predicts.

CHAPTER SUMMARY

Three methods are available for assessing attachments in infancy. Observing the baby in his or her usual environment in naturalistic longitudinal studies is for many purposes and reasons the best method. Unfortunately, such studies are expensive and time-consuming and, therefore, rare.

The Strange Situation provides a well-validated, brief laboratory procedure for classifying the way a baby organizes his or her behavior in relation to his or her attachment figure. It is appropriate for infants who are 11 to 20 months old.

The Attachment Q-set attempts to rate the degree of security of attachment in children who are 12 to 36 months old. It also attempts to differentiate attachment from constructs such as sociability and dependency. The data obtained can be analyzed in a variety of ways. Although the validity of the method has not yet been established, the method is intriguing and promising.

PHASES IN THE DEVELOPMENT OF ATTACHMENTS IN INFANCY

Some of the basic normative phenomena in the emergence of attachments in infancy are now well known. Based on her observations of babies in Uganda and in Baltimore, Ainsworth (1972) described four phases in the development of attachment in early childhood. The two cultural settings differed considerably. The Ganda babies rarely saw strangers. Their houses and villages were small. Their mothers were seldom out of sight for brief periods; when the mother departed, she was likely to be gone for a few hours to work in her garden. Several of the households were polygynous. In contrast, the American babies often saw strangers in stores and elsewhere. Their houses and suburban towns were large. Their mothers were often out of sight, in another room, for a few minutes, but were seldom gone for long stretches of time. (Only one of the mothers was employed outside the home.) None of the households included a second mother with small children. Despite these differences in family and cultural circumstances, the general nature of maternal care, the congenital behavioral characteristics of the babies, and the sequence of developments in the babies' attachment behavioral systems were very similar across the two cultures.

Cultures do vary in breast-feeding and weaning practices, amount of carrying, amount of floor freedom, early behavioral training, involvement of others besides the mother in care for the infant, exposure of infants to a variety of settings, and exposure to strangers. Despite the many cultural variations in child-rearing practices throughout the world, the phases Ainsworth described have not been contradicted in any research on infants raised in family environments anywhere. However, surprisingly little research has been designed to test, in other cultures, the accuracy of Ainsworth's descriptions of the phases.

PHASE 1: THE PREATTACHMENT PHASE

The first phase, which comprises the first few weeks of life, is the *preattachment phase*. It is a phase of nondiscriminative orientation and signaling to figures. That is, very young babies tend to orient their sensory receptors toward people, and they emit signals that people tend to respond to, but the babies do not discriminate among people. A very young baby appears to like to look at or listen to almost any person, and gives little evidence of preferring her primary caregiver to any other person. In fact, although newborns react to stimulus characteristics that people have, there is no evidence that they know these stimulus characteristics are connected to each other and emanate from individuals who are members of the same species as the newborn. They do not even know that the various parts of their own bodies are connected to each other.

Although the range of a newborn's visual field is limited, he or she can see and can direct his or her eyes toward a selected stimulus. Even in the early weeks, babies prefer to look at visual arrays that have contrasts of light parts and dark parts rather than at less vivid, more uniform visual arrays. They also prefer visual arrays that move to those that stay still. The motion should be slow enough so that (1) it is not startling and frightening and (2) the baby can keep the moving object in his visual field. It should be frequent enough so that the stimulus does not become boring. With eyes and mouths that move, and eyes, mouths, and hair that contrast with the shade of the skin, human faces are very attractive visual stimuli for young babies.

Similarly, tests have shown that babies are more responsive to human voices than to other sounds. Initially, babies just look and listen more to people than to other available sensory stimuli. When, around the age of 4 to 6 weeks, social smiling emerges, babies smile more in response to people than in response to other phenomena.

Just as babies are drawn to human stimuli, they naturally tend to emit signals that are likely to elicit attention and care from their parents and from others. A newborn's behavioral repertoire is rather limited, and many behaviors are *reflexive,* not voluntary. Crying, grasping, and smiling are all initially reflexive, although they come under voluntary control as the baby matures. That is, little babies cry because they feel bad or need something, not because they are trying to get your attention or assistance. They don't even know you exist. The same rule applies in the modality of physical contact. If you press a baby's palm gently with your finger, the baby's hand will close tightly around your finger. This is the *grasping reflex.* The baby has no conscious intention of keeping you close. She doesn't even know that your finger is part of you. If you press her palm with a rattle instead of your finger, she will close her hand around the rattle as automatically as she closed it around your finger. Fortunately, this scientific fact seldom discourages parents from feeling warmed and gratified by the baby's grasp.

All of these reflexes—crying, grasping, and, later, smiling—tend to draw caregivers near or keep them close. Ethological observations of children and adults show that many have strong tendencies to take action to soothe a crying baby—even if misguided scientists have told them not to reinforce crying. Crying is a noxious stimulus. That people want to terminate it or escape from it requires no explanation. That they often terminate it by comforting or feeding the crying child, not by abandoning him, suggests a biological predisposition toward caregiving. Ethological observations also show that a baby's smile is a powerful social stimulus and reinforcer. Children and adults are drawn toward smiling babies and tend to stay and to interact with them.

The rooting and sucking reflexes also play a role in the formation of attachment and the eliciting of care. If you touch a baby's cheek softly, he will turn his face toward the touch, open his mouth, and search around with his mouth for a little while. That is the *rooting reflex.* If his mouth comes across something it can latch onto, such as a thumb or a nipple, the mouth will close around it. The feel of something against the roof of his mouth will then trigger the *sucking reflex.* Together, these reflexes obviously help the baby obtain food. However, whether the food comes from a breast or a bottle, it is almost invariably given by a human being, and, more often than not, the very young baby is held in someone's arm or lap while he drinks. Even the *feeding reflexes* thus draw the caregiver into behavioral involvement with the infant.

The reflexes enumerated above are *species-specific* universals. That is, they are common to virtually all members of the species. In the ways noted above, the behaviors of a baby who is too young to be able to do much more than exercise his reflexes serve as *precursor attachment* behaviors. They draw caregivers toward the baby and trigger interaction sequences. In time, one (or more) of the caregivers becomes an attachment figure.

PHASE 2: ATTACHMENT-IN-THE-MAKING

As the early weeks and months pass, the baby gradually orients himself and directs signals to familiar people more often than to others. This shift characterizes phase 2, *attachment-in-the-making.* It is hard to say just when this phase begins, because figure differentiation happens earlier in some sensory modalities than in others. A baby as young as 2 days old can demonstrate a preference for the smell of his own mother's milk over the smell of another mother's milk. A baby who is only 3 or 4 weeks old may be soothed more easily by the smell and feel of a familiar caregiver than by the smell and feel of a stranger. When he is a little older, the baby reacts differently to familiar voices than to unfamiliar ones.

Differential responding to visual cues associated with a familiar caregiver emerges later than differential responding to his or her smell, feel, and sound. When social smiling first emerges, any adult can elicit smiles from a baby by holding his face at an optimal distance in front of the baby (12 to 20 inches), so the baby can see him well. Add a voice that is not too loud and motion that is not too fast to follow, and you will almost always be able to elicit smiles from a baby who is 1 to 4 months old. After 4 months, smiles to strangers decrease in frequency, intensity, and ease of elicitation. At the same time, smiles to familiar figures increase in frequency, intensity, and ease of elicitation. The mother, father, big brother, or other familiar person may not need to talk, rock, tickle, or even smile. Just presenting the familiar face where the baby can see it may be enough to get a smile from him.

Reaching is a skill that babies practice and develop in the early months of life. When they first discover that objects that can be seen can also be grasped, babies tend to reach for any person or thing that looks interesting. As the weeks pass, reaching, too, becomes better controlled and more selectively directed. By the age of 5 or 6 months, it is common for babies to reach more readily for contact with their caregivers than for contact with strangers. As the attachment-in-the-making phase draws to a close, we might reasonably say that discriminative smiling and reaching nearly demonstrate the existence of attachments to familiar people. In addition, babies who are 5 or 6 months old can usually be soothed more easily by familiar caregivers than by others.

Despite the evidence that babies have some preference for a familiar caregiver by the age of 5 or 6 months, we do not say that so young a baby has developed a full-fledged attachment (phase 3). At that age, "out of sight" is still "out of mind." It does not make sense to say that a baby is attached to her father if she is not capable of thinking about him in his absence. She may recognize him and react to him with a delight not shown in response to strangers, but she cannot have developed an enduring affective bond to a specific individual. In fact, her primary caregiver can be replaced by a hospital nurse or an adoptive parent with relatively little disruption in the baby's social and emotional life.

THE TURNING POINT: EVIDENCE FROM SEPARATION STUDIES

All this changes rather abruptly around the age of 7 months. Studies of babies who had to be hospitalized and studies of babies in foster care consistently show that babies under the age of 7 months usually adjust to the new place and the new caregiver relatively easily. Family-reared babies over 7 months old definitely do not.

Extensive research in the 1960s (e.g., Heinicke and Westheimer, 1966; Robertson and Robertson, 1971) closely examined how babies and toddlers reacted when separated from the mother for a period of from 1 to 3 weeks. The separation usually occurred when the mother went to a hospital to give birth and sometimes occurred when the mother or child needed surgery. The reactions were remarkably similar to other primates' responses to separation (e.g., Spencer-Booth and Hinde, 1967, 1971). When separated, the infant cried and showed intense and prolonged behavioral distress. He or she searched for the lost attachment figure and often resisted others' efforts to give comfort. After some hours (the time varies with the species, with the individual, and with the circumstances of substitute care), the infant sank into a period of despair, a state of passivity and obvious sadness, which was sometimes interrupted by renewed outbursts of overt distress.

After some days, the infant began to reorganize and remobilize behavior and appeared to be functioning normally again. During this period, of prolonged separation, human infants evidenced a third response to separation. Called "detachment," it is a period of active ignoring and avoidance of the attachment figure when she or he returns. The behavior appears to be defensive. The child treats the returning caregiver as a child would normally treat an unimportant, or even unwelcome, stranger. When reunited with their mothers, infant primates generally show greatly intensified attachment behavior. When reunited with a "lost" attachment figure, a young human being often maintains detachment for some hours or even days, and then clings to the caregiver and protests even minor separations for days or weeks. The intensity of the attachment behavior when it reemerges suggests that its earlier suppression was active and defensive.

This sequence of responses to separation (protest, despair, detachment, and then intensified attachment behavior) first occurs when the baby enters the phase of clear-cut attachment. Although some unhappiness and disorganization of behavior appear when babies under the age of 7 months are removed from their mothers, the changes in mood and behavior appear to be related to changes in circumstances and interactions. After the age of 7 months, family-reared infants react specifically to disruption of the relationship with the attachment figure.

The children in these studies were 6 months to 5 years old and often spent the period of separation from the mother in a residential nursery. Sometimes the father visited, but the child was cared for primarily by strangers in an unfamiliar institution. The Robertsons (e.g., 1971) demonstrated that care from a single figure in a home (not from a series of shift workers in an institution) mitigated the severity of the child's reactions. Use of photographs of the mother and reminders of home also eased the child's distress. Heinicke and Westheimer (1966) found that the presence of a sibling, even a younger one, also reduced distress in residential nurseries.

PHASE 3: CLEAR-CUT ATTACHMENT

Babies who do not suffer the misfortune of separation from the attachment figure also show evidence of entering the phase of *clear-cut attachment* around the age of 7 months. In the home and in the community, the baby now shows active, "goal-corrected" maintenance of proximity to a specific figure by locomotion as well as by signaling. The repertoire of attachment behaviors now includes not only crying, smiling, and reaching, but also following, approaching, and clinging to the attachment figure, and protesting separations.

By no coincidence, this is the age at which cognitive psychologists have found that infants first search for objects hidden from view, thereby showing an ability to recall that an object continues to exist even when the baby cannot see, hear, feel, smell, or taste it. At about the same age, babies first differentiate means from ends. That is, they become able to use the same behavior intentionally for different purposes, and they can keep trying different behaviors until one succeeds in accomplishing a single goal (Piaget, 1952).

These milestones in cognitive development are necessary for the demonstration of clear-cut attachment. If a baby cannot use his behaviors flexibly in a sustained effort to achieve a predetermined goal, he is not likely to switch from vocalizing to crying to following the mother when his first behaviors fail to keep his mother close to him. If he does not know that his mother still exists when he cannot see her, he is not likely to follow her around the corner from the dining room into the kitchen.

Obviously, when a baby is old enough to crawl, a behavioral system that keeps the baby near an attachment figure who can protect him serves an adaptive function. From an ethological-evolutionary perspective, it seems no coincidence that the cognitive leaps that occur around the age of 6 to 8 months emerge just as the ability to crawl is developing. Babies cannot recognize and avoid all the dangers that might exist in their environments. Caregivers usually have other things to do besides watch and restrain their babies constantly. Once a baby is physically capable of wandering off, being inclined to keep himself near a protector helps him to stay alive while he explores and learns about the world. He benefits greatly from being able to remember who his attachment figure is and to use a variety of behaviors to stay near the attachment figure and to keep him or her nearby.

Having developed an attachment does not mean that the baby will seek contact or interaction with the attachment figure all the time. On the contrary, babies have other things to do, such as exploring and discovering. The degree of proximity or contact that the baby seeks varies with the situation. When all is well, the baby is likely to turn her attention to exploration or play, with just occasional visual, auditory, or physical reconnecting with her secure base. Should something alarm her, however, she is very likely to seek full contact.

Bowlby always deemphasized the significance of feeding in attachment relationships. He wanted to differentiate attachment theory from orthodox psychoanalytic theories, which assert that the baby's bond to the mother develops *because* she provides food. Stimulus-response secondary-drive theories and social-learning theories also treat the bond to the mother as a secondary effect of learning to associate the mother with reduction of a primary drive (hunger) or with provision of a primary reinforcer (food). Bowlby (e.g., [1969] 1982) wanted to emphasize that the tendency to form an attachment is a *primary,* biologically based tendency, not a secondary effect of some more fundamental drive or need.

Although feeding a baby is neither necessary nor sufficient to produce an attachment to a social partner (Schaffer and Emerson, 1964), breast feeding can become an attachment behavior. It can become another way of clinging to the mother, a way that is more intimate and more soothing than any other sort of physical contact. Konner (1972) reported that breast feeding was an important component of infant-mother attachment among the !Kung San Bushmen, who live a hunter-gatherer lifestyle in Africa. Ainsworth found that the same was true for traditionally reared Ganda babies, who were breast-fed on demand and not weaned before the attachment to the mother was established. "Under these circumstances, feeding behavior is so enmeshed in the organization of the attachment relationship that weaning may threaten the whole relationship," she reported (Ainsworth, 1977, p. 128, cited in LeVine and Miller, 1990).

Studies of separation protest and other attachment behaviors indicate that most babies in family environments also become attached to at least one other person within weeks or months of the emergence of the first clear-cut attachment (Schaffer and Emerson, 1964). However, babies do not become attached to all available figures. A critical factor in determining whether a baby will become attached to a person seems to be whether and how that person responds to the baby's social behavior. The extent to which one figure is preferred over others and the implications of that preference are topics for Chapter 11.

PHASE 4: THE GOAL-CORRECTED PARTNERSHIP

Around the age of 4 years, the nature of a child's attachment relationship changes significantly. A toddler (age 12 to 24 months) must accommodate himself or herself to the caregiver's current behavior or seek directly to change it. Preschoolers become sufficiently advanced cognitively to understand that the caregiver has feelings and plans that may differ from their own. The extent to which they can now understand or make inferences about the other person's feelings and thoughts, although limited, is adequate to enable them to try to change the caregiver's behavior by trying to change the latter's plans and short-term goals. Bowlby ([1969] 1982) described this new type of relationship as a "goal-corrected partnership"; the child becomes a partner in planning how the dyad will handle separations.

Because this unit is primarily about infancy, I will defer detailed discussion of phase 4 until Chapter 13. Phase 4 is, of course, not the end of the story. Later developments will be described in Units 1 and 4.

ABNORMAL ENVIRONMENTS: BABIES IN INSTITUTIONS

The first four phases in the development of attachment have been described as they occur in infants who are raised in families. The normal environment for a human infant is a family, and the normal environment for the family includes a social group. In a family, there is almost always at least one caregiver who responds to the baby in ways that are influenced by the baby's signals and behavior; there is almost always at least one person who reacts to the baby's actions. What happens to babies who have little opportunity to experience contingent responsiveness from others?

Answers to that question are available from studies of babies reared in abnormal environments—namely, institutions where no specific, individual caregiver is regularly available to the baby (e.g., Goldfarb, 1955; Spitz, 1945; Yarrow, 1964). In the 1930s and 1940s, orphaned babies were commonly housed in institutions that were kept very clean and provided good food (delivered from propped-up bottles) and medical care. However, the infants received little individual attention, had few or no toys, and had few opportunities for interaction with other babies, children, or adults. A startling percentage of the babies sickened and died despite the good physical care. Among those who stayed alive, development of motor skills and cognitive abilities lagged far behind those of family-reared infants. Social developments relevant to forming attachments were not only delayed but also tended to take deviant paths. The fundamental importance of meeting an infant's attachment needs was illustrated well.

Among the babies who spent much of infancy in an institution, two patterns of disturbance in social relations were common. Some children became *socially indifferent:* they showed little interest in forming attachments to *any* caretakers or peers and little ability to do so. Others showed a pattern that Spitz (1945) called "affect hunger"; they seemed to want social attention and affection all the time and could never get enough of it. Like the socially indifferent children, these affect-hungry children did not discriminate among social partners. They wanted attention and affection from everyone, not from anyone in particular. Their ability to form meaningful attachments was severely impaired.

The vast majority of the institutionalized babies in these studies in the 1930s and 1940s showed serious delays in cognitive development, motor development, and social development. Spitz (1945) believed such developmental delays resulted from the lack of opportunity to form an emotional bond with a frequently present, long-term caregiver. In the absence of such a relationship, the infant showed little interest in his or her physical environment.

Later, critics argued persuasively that the infants suffered from lack of cognitive stimulation, not just lack of affective care. It now appears that the damage from early institutionalization that does provide adequate physical and cognitive stimulation, but no regular caregiver, occurs mainly in the areas of personality development and social relations. (Physical and cognitive development can progress normally.) Prolonged early institutionalization may result in gross and permanent impairment of the ability to form deep personal relationships. Impulse control and emotionality may also be lastingly impaired.

NONATTACHMENT

One of the recognized disorders of attachment in infancy is *nonattachment* —the failure to form an enduring bond to a specific individual. Such a disorder is likely to develop only when the infant has no opportunity to form an enduring bond because no major caregiver stays involved in his or her life. Evidence suggests that there may be a critical period for forming a first attachment. If the child stays too long in circumstances that do not allow her to become attached to some specific individual, her ability to become involved in intimate relationships may be permanently impaired. The child is also at risk for distortions of social behavior in a variety of contexts, not only in potentially intimate relationships.

In England, Tizard and Rees (1975) conducted a prospective study of 26 children who were placed in residential care before they were 4 months old and stayed there until they were at least 4½ years old. The institution gave good physical care, rich cognitive stimulation and opportunities for exercise and play, but did not encourage close, enduring caregiver-child relationships. In fact, by the time they were 2 years old, the children had had an average of 24 different nurses who had taken care of them for at least 1 week. One child had been taken care of by only 4 nurses. Another child had already had 45 nurses. By age 4½, the children had had an average of 50 different caretakers. According to the staff, by that age, 18 of the 26 children did not care deeply about anyone.

When the children were 8 years old, Tizard and Hodges (1978) found that many of them had been adopted or restored to their natural parents. Some of the mothers believed the children were closely attached to them. Teachers, however, reported that most of the children evidenced severe problems. They showed excessive attention seeking, restlessness, and disobedience, and were antisocial and unpopular. This was true even of the children who were adopted into good homes if the adoption occurred after the child's fourth birthday.

A replication of Tizard and Hodge's London findings is cited in Smith (1980). In research conducted by Dixon, children reared in institutions with many caretakers (sometimes as many as 50 to 80 per child) were unlikely to develop secure attachments or harmonious social behavior. Their development in the domains of cognition and language was approximately normal, but their behavior was not. Both teachers and objective observers found the children to be disruptive and to show high levels of attention-seeking behavior. Outcomes were different for a comparison group of children who spent their early years in personal foster care, not in an institution. These children were much less likely to develop emotional and social problems. The characteristics of the biological parents of the two groups of children were similar, so the later differences in the children did seem to be the result of their early environments, not of any preexisting advantages in the foster care group.

In short, research suggests that children who have no opportunity to form a first attachment in their first 4 years may have difficulty *ever* forming deep personal bonds. They are likely to show disruptive, attention-seeking behavior for years, perhaps all through childhood. The critical period may be much shorter than 4 years.

CHAPTER SUMMARY

Phase 1 in the development of attachments in infancy is the preattachment phase of orienting and signaling to human beings without discriminating among them. In phase 2, the phase of attachment-in-the-making, the baby gradually orients himself and directs signals more to familiar people than to others. Around the age of 7 months, the baby rather abruptly enters phase 3, the phase of clear-cut attachment. She now shows active, goal-corrected maintenance of proximity to a specific figure, accomplished by locomotion as well as by signaling. She is likely soon to demonstrate attachment not only to the principal caregiver but also to others who respond to her socially.

As far as we know, these three phases emerge at around the same ages in virtually all babies raised in families in every human culture. For babies raised for too long in an abnormal environment where there is no caregiver to whom the baby can become attached, social development is likely to be delayed and distorted, with consequences that can be long-lasting or permanent.

C H A P T E R

5

SENSITIVE RESPONSIVENESS

In infancy, what factors or variables determine how individual babies organize their attachment behavior? That single question is the topic of the next two chapters. The discussion will begin with the variable first discovered, most studied, and best demonstrated: the quality of care the attachment figure provides. Based on her exploratory, naturalistic research in Uganda and in Baltimore, Ainsworth (e.g., 1967, 1973) inferred that what mattered most was the caregiver's *sensitive responsiveness*. Sensitive responsiveness includes noticing signals from the baby, interpreting them accurately, and responding appropriately and fairly promptly. "Insensitivity," as Ainsworth defined it, is not necessarily hostile or actively unpleasant behavior on the part of the caregiver. It exists when the caregiver fails to read the baby's states or goals or fails to respond supportively, and thereby fails to help the baby attain a positive state or achieve his goal. The insensitive caregiver thus teaches the baby that his signals are ineffective—or even counterproductive. After Ainsworth articulated the "sensitivity hypothesis"—the hypothesis that sensitively responsive care fosters secure attachment—it was explicitly tested and supported in a number of longitudinal studies.

THE BALTIMORE STUDY

In Baltimore, Ainsworth and her colleagues observed 26 white middle-class mother-infant dyads at home for about 72 hours spaced over the first year. Ainsworth et al. (1978) judged most of the babies to be securely attached (on the basis of behavior in natural settings) and to belong to group B (on the basis of Strange Situation assessments). Some others showed insecure attachments in naturalistic observations and avoidant behavior (group A) in the laboratory. Some were insecurely attached at home and resistant (group C) in the laboratory.

What enabled the group B babies to develop secure attachments? The mothers of securely attached babies received high scores for sensitive responsiveness during the home observations. When the baby cried, the mother came soon, figured out what the baby needed, and helped her get it. When the baby was hungry, the mother fed her. When she needed a little longer to chew and swallow, the mother waited before offering the next spoonful of food. When the baby wanted social interaction or contact comfort, the mother provided it. When the baby wanted to explore, the mother did not interfere. When the mother's or family's schedule required that the baby shift to a different place or activity, the mother was tactful about guiding the baby through the transition. When the baby was tired, the mother helped her settle down to sleep. When the baby was able to crawl, the mother, without harshness, enforced appropriate limits to keep the baby safe while allowing the baby to exercise her increasing motor skills and explore her enlarging world.

On separate but highly intercorrelated 9-point scales for measuring sensitivity, acceptance, cooperation, and accessibility, the mothers of the anxiously attached babies scored significantly lower than the mothers of securely attached babies did. The deficiencies and problems in the care of the avoidant and resistant infants were not in the quantity of interaction, but in its nature and timing. The mothers of anxiously attached babies did not hold their babies less or interact with them less than mothers of securely attached babies, but their interactions lacked emotional harmony and ease of communication. Many of these mothers were slow to respond to crying. Some abruptly swooped in on the baby for playful, overstimulating interaction when he was contentedly exploring something, but refused to pick the baby up when he cried for contact comfort. Some carried the baby from place to place without any tender, close contact. Some shoveled spoonfuls of food into the baby's mouth faster than he could handle them; others had their attention on a visitor or another child or elsewhere and left the baby waiting and waiting between bites. Some mothers were just very inconsistent and unpredictable: sometimes warm and wonderful, but sometimes inattentive, inaccessible, irritable, and/or rejecting.

■ Comforting, Feeding, Interacting, and Holding

Differences in the behavior of mothers whose babies developed secure attachments and mothers whose babies developed anxious attachments were already evident in the first 3 months and were relatively consistent to the end of the first year. In the first 3 months of the first year, there were huge differences in mothers' responses to crying. At the extremes, one mother ignored 96 percent of her baby's episodes of crying, while another ignored only 4 percent. There were also sizable differences in how long mothers took to respond to the baby's crying. The average latency for most mothers in the first quarter was 2 to 9 minutes. In the fourth quarter, the mothers of the anxiously attached babies were still much slower to respond to the baby's crying than the group B mothers were.

In behavior relevant to feeding during the first quarter, the group B mothers were more sensitive to the infant's signals with regard to timing of initiation, timing of termination, dealing with the baby's food preferences, and adjusting the rate of feeding to the baby's rate of intake. Ainsworth (e.g., 1983) has argued that the caregiver's sensitive responding helps the baby achieve her goals and so helps her experience and develop a sense of confidence, both about the trustworthiness of others and about her own effectiveness.

When the babies were only 6 to 15 weeks old, the mothers of group B babies showed skill in pacing and modifying their social behavior in response to the baby's cues. This resulted in longer bouts of interaction than other dyads sustained. The babies who experi-

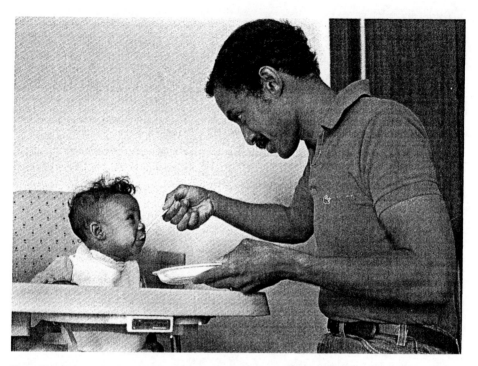

Harmonious timing during the little interactions of everyday life is associated with the development of secure attachments.

enced many harmonious and happy face-to-face interactions began to respond to the mother differently from the way they responded to the observer by the time they were 3 months old.

Mothers of group B babies were also tender and careful for a much higher percentage of time when holding their babies and inept for a much lower percentage of time than the group A and C mothers were. In face-to-face interaction, they paced their behavior according to the baby's more than the group A and group C mothers did. They used a routine manner (just feeding, diapering, or otherwise physically tending the baby, without much affective involvement) less than other mothers and they were more likely to greet the baby when entering the room.

In contrast, the mothers of anxiously attached babies (groups A and C) were more likely to pick the baby up in an abrupt, interfering manner—particularly in the case of group A. When holding the baby, they were less likely to behave affectionately and more likely to behave ineptly. During the last quarter, the mothers of group C (resistant) babies devoted a much higher percentage of the time spent holding their babies to routines, especially feeding the baby, than mothers of secure babies did. This observation gains meaning from the fact that many of the babies were by then eager to feed themselves or at least to sit by themselves while being spoon-fed. The mother's behavior was not well-tuned to the baby's needs and desires.

■ Avoidant Attachment as an Adaptation to Insensitive Care

In their summary of the aspects of maternal behavior most associated with the development of infant avoidance (group A in the Strange Situation), Ainsworth et al. (1978) list rejection, aversion to close bodily contact, covert anger, and a generally compulsive kind of adjustment. The mothers of avoidant babies appeared to have rigid, compulsive personalities. Compared to other mothers, they were especially rejecting toward their infants. Several lines of evidence suggest that they chronically gave frustrating responses when their babies sought proximity and contact. In the first quarter, they showed more aversion to physical contact than other mothers did, and provided the baby with a greater number of unpleasant, even painful, experiences associated with close contact. However, they did not hold their babies significantly less than other mothers did. They believed that babies needed to be held, especially during feedings when very young, and they acted accordingly—even though they appeared not to enjoy holding their babies. However, they were especially likely to refuse contact when the baby most needed it—that is, when the baby's attachment system was activated at high intensity. Ainsworth et al. (1978) proposed that the result for the infant is an approach-avoidance conflict. In circumstances that ordinarily activate instinctive attachment behavior, the infant defends himself from rebuff by diverting his attention away from anything that might activate his attachment behavior, including the attachment figure herself. These patterns of infant behavior, caregiver behavior, and the associations between them were not specifically anticipated or predicted; they emerged from ethological observations conducted by people with some clinical training.

■ Resistant Attachment as a Response to Insensitive Care

The mothers of the four resistant infants (group C) in the sample intermittently demonstrated the ability to respond sensitively to their infants. However, they could not be relied upon to do so. They were at times psychologically inaccessible and at other times intrusive, interfering with the baby's activity. Even though there were so few group C infants, a consistent picture of what was going wrong emerged. These mothers differed from mothers of secure babies on 9 of 11 aspects of behavior coded from narrative records of the home observations during the first year. They were less affectionate when picking their babies up, less tender and careful when holding them, more inept when handling them, less responsive to crying, less sensitive to infant signals, less likely to greet or otherwise acknowledge the baby when entering the room, less accessible, less cooperative, and less accepting. However, they showed no aversion to close bodily contact. The baby's mixture of attachment behavior and angry behavior in the Strange Situation seemed a logical consequence of the unpredictable mixture of responses the baby had experienced in interaction with his mother.

The difficulty for the group C babies, as for the group A babies, was not that their mothers interacted with them too little or too much but that the nature and timing of the interaction did not consistently meet the infant's attachment needs well. Crittenden and Ainsworth (1989) later summarized the dilemma anxious-resistant babies face as follows. Bids for proximity and contact are often frustrated, so attachment behavior persists and anger mingles with it. Then, when the caregiver does respond, the baby behaves ambivalently and is hard to soothe. Unable to rely on the caregiver to be accessible, the baby stays near the caregiver, becomes vigilant for signs of decreased proximity, and shows more distress at and anger about little everyday separations or threats of separation than secure babies do.

LIMITATIONS OF THE BALTIMORE STUDY AND ITS REPLICATIONS

A great tower of understanding and belief about the determinants of secure, avoidant, and resistant infant attachment has been built on the data obtained from the Baltimore study. No other study of a low-risk sample has duplicated the length and frequency of naturalistic observations spread over 11 or 12 months. Consequently, many aspects and factors may still require further study.

Lamb, Thompson, Gardner, and Charnov (1985, pp. 60–66) have provided a thorough listing of the methodological limitations of the Baltimore study. They remind us that it should be viewed as an exploratory, hypothesis-generating study, not a hypothesis-testing study. As Ainsworth herself has pointed out, 23 babies constitute a very small sample on which to base major inferences about universal relationships among variables in infant development.

Despite the importance another major naturalistic study would have, no full-scale replication of Ainsworth's Baltimore study has been attempted. Although several partial replications with large samples have been conducted, these have generally included only two or three home visits prior to the Strange Situation assessment, and the visits have seldom been as long as the visits in the Baltimore study. Even good caregivers have bad days, and caregivers who are generally quite insensitive can manage to look good for an hour or two at a time and are likely to try to do so in the presence of an observer. By having the same observer visit a family for long sessions many times during the first year, Ainsworth and her associates maximized their ability to get a true picture of the variability of the interactions an infant experienced. Later researchers have not done so. Consequently, you might expect that they would have difficulty replicating Ainsworth's findings even if the patterns she observed were true for the population at large. Despite this methodological problem, ratings of maternal sensitivity in interaction at home in the first year have quite consistently distinguished between infants who developed secure attachments and infants who developed anxious ones. Each replication, albeit partial, did find evidence to support the sensitivity hypothesis. Later in this book, discussions of variables other than maternal sensitivity and discussions of follow-up studies later in childhood will refer back to these four longitudinal studies. For that reason, each is introduced in some detail here.

THE MINNEAPOLIS STUDY

The first partial replication of the Baltimore study with a very large sample was the Minneapolis study of babies in disadvantaged families (Egeland and Farber, 1984). It began in 1975 with 267 firstborns and their mothers. Many of the families were poor, and

62 percent of the mothers were single. The mean age of the mothers was 20.5 years, and 41 percent of them had not graduated from high school. Eighty percent of them were white, thirteen percent were black, and seven percent were Hispanic or Native American. Children in this sample grew up in circumstances that changed much more, and much more often, in early life than is the case in most middle-class samples. Families moved to different apartments; couples joined or split up; parents found, lost, or changed jobs; illnesses came and went; alternate caregivers came and went; people joined and left the living group; some parents increased or decreased drug use.

In the Minneapolis study, the babies were observed at home at 3 months old and 6 months old, and in the Strange Situation at 12 and/or 18 months. (At 12 months, 212 infants participated in the Strange Situation assessment; at 18 months, 197 did.) Two of Ainsworth's scales (cooperation and sensitivity) were used to rate the mother's behavior during the home observations of play and feeding when the babies were 6 months old. As expected, mothers of group B infants got higher scores for sensitivity and cooperation than other mothers got when the classifications from Strange Situations at 12 months were used. This was true for the sample as a whole and for the subsample of boys, but not for the subsample of girls. I will have more to say about these mixed results in a moment.

The babies later classified as resistant (group C) in the Minneapolis sample were a little slow developmentally and did not solicit responsive care as much as the other babies did. Mothers of the infants later classified as avoidant (group A) tended to have negative feelings about motherhood, to be tense and irritable, and to treat their babies in a perfunctory manner. Unlike the resistant babies, however, the avoidant babies remained active, not helpless. In the Baltimore sample, the mothers of group A infants showed covert (hidden, suppressed) anger and rejection of their babies. In the Minneapolis sample, with its lower levels of income and education and its much more stressful circumstances, the anger and rejection from the mothers of avoidant babies may often have been open and obvious.

On the whole, the Minneapolis study supported the sensitivity hypothesis: that is, sensitively responsive mothers tended to have securely attached babies. However, not all available measures of the mother's sensitivity were good predictors of security of attachment. Observations of the differences in quality of physical contact, facility in caretaking, and positive regard for the infant in feeding at 3 months and at 6 months failed to distinguish between infants who developed secure attachments and those who did not. As noted above, the sensitivity and cooperation ratings at 6 months had the predicted relation to Strange Situation classifications for the whole group, but not for the subgroup of girls.

Why did some measures of sensitivity predict security while others did not? Why were some results significant for boys but not for girls? There are a number of possible explanations. One is that the relation between sensitivity and security just was not pervasive; other determinants of security overwhelmed the influence of sensitive responsiveness for some babies. A second explanatory hypothesis is that some measures of sensitivity, being based on brief observations that did not accurately reflect the dyads' everyday lives, were inadequate and invalid.

A third factor that may have limited the power and clarity of this ambitious study is that it occurred before the D category of Strange Situation behavior had been defined.

High-risk samples are now believed usually to include many group D (anxious-disorganized-disoriented) attachments. Consequently, it seems likely that many infants in the Minneapolis sample were misclassified (by current standards, not by the information available at the time). Inclusion of misclassified babies would weaken all findings.

THE BIELEFELD STUDY

The second large, partial replication of Ainsworth's Baltimore study took place in Bielefeld, in the northern part of Germany (Grossmann, Grossmann, Spangler, Suess, and Unzner, 1985). The subjects were 49 infants and their mothers in families with varied economic and educational backgrounds but stable living conditions. They were observed in the hospital shortly after birth and in the home at 2, 6, and 10 months of age.

Each 2-hour home visit included an interview and 45 to 60 minutes of intensive observation by two observers. On the basis of a transcript of the whole observation session, one observer assigned a score on Ainsworth's sensitivity scale and the other assigned a score on Ainsworth's cooperation scale. As in Baltimore, the two ratings were highly correlated ($r = .76$), and mothers who never ignored the baby's crying during the visit at 10 months (twenty-two of the forty-nine mothers) had babies who cried significantly less often and for shorter periods than the other babies. Individual differences in sensitivity scores were quite stable across the three home visits, although the average score in Bielefeld (but not in Baltimore) declined at the 10-month visit. Infants of sensitive mothers quieted more readily when picked up and protested less when put down.

When they were 1 year old, the 49 Bielefeld babies were observed in the Strange Situation with their mothers. Avoidant attachments were far more common in the Bielefeld sample than in Baltimore (49 percent versus 26 percent), and secure attachments were less common (33 percent versus 57 percent). The frequencies of resistant attachments were not strikingly different (12 percent in Bielefeld versus 17 percent in Baltimore).

As in Baltimore, higher scores for maternal sensitivity were associated with infant security. However, that was true only for the sensitivity ratings from the 2-month and 6-month visits, not from the visit closest in time to the Strange Situation. One likely interpretation of this finding is that the baby's behavior in the Strange Situation reflected the expectations about the mother's responsiveness that the baby had developed throughout the entire first year; it was not based solely on the most recent interactions.

Other conspicuous differences between the Baltimore sample and the Bielefeld sample shed further light on the relation between sensitive responsiveness and secure attachment. In Baltimore, two-thirds of the securely attached babies were in subgroup B3 (little or no resistant or avoidant behavior). In Bielefeld, only one-third of the securely attached babies were in subgroup B3. The largest subgroup in Bielefeld was B2, a pattern that often reflects the appearance of some avoidant behavior prior to the activation of proximity seeking and contact maintaining in the reunion episodes.

Differences between the two groups also emerged in the sensitivity ratings based on home observations. In Bielefeld, the average sensitivity score was about 1 point lower than in Baltimore on the 9-point scale. In Baltimore, the average sensitivity score for group B mothers in the fourth quarter of the first year was about 4 points higher than the average scores for A and C mothers. In Bielefeld, group B mothers were only 1 or 2 points above group A mothers at 2 and 6 months, and were not significantly different from them at 10 months. The mean for group B mothers was lower at the 10-month home visit ($M = 5.1$) than at the earlier visits ($M = 5.8$). The mean sensitivity ratings of the A mothers were about halfway between the ratings of the B and C mothers in Bielefeld; in Baltimore, A and C mothers got similarly low scores.

What does this pattern of results mean? The differences in average sensitivity ratings, in distributions of avoidant and secure attachments, and in associations between sensitivity ratings and attachment classifications of the two samples all make sense in the context of the Bielefeld mothers' culture-specific caregiving models. According to Grossmann et al. (1985), most mothers in Bielefeld (and northern Germany in general), unlike the mothers in the Baltimore sample, believed that infants should be weaned from close bodily contact as soon as they were mobile. They felt that carrying a baby who could move on her own would spoil her, as would responding to every cry by picking the baby up. Their goal was to have a self-sufficient baby who did not cling or make demands, but who unquestioningly obeyed the parent's commands.

In the Baltimore sample, mothers of avoidant infants tended to have rigid personalities and appeared to be uncomfortable with close bodily contact; their behavior could accurately be described as rejecting. In Bielefeld, most of the mothers were trying to train their babies to comply with cultural norms about independence and interpersonal distance. Even when their behavior was insensitive, it may not have indicated rejection of the infant. As the child developed and was better able to be self-reliant, maternal sensitivity to his signals and needs might reemerge. Can infants differentiate between insensitivity that expresses personal rejection and insensitivity in the service of independence training? Perhaps not. By the age of 12 months, many babies adapted to insensitive interaction by developing avoidant defenses, both in Baltimore and in Bielefeld.

THE BLOOMINGTON STUDY

In Bloomington, Bates, Maslin, and Frankel (1985) conducted another longitudinal study of the determinants and sequelae of infants' attachment patterns with a large sample. *Sequelae* means "phenomena that follow after the events and attachment patterns of the first year." Which associated sequelae are effects of attachment patterns and which are correlates but not effects is often unclear. (Throughout this book, I use the term "sequelae," not "consequences," because the former is accurate and the latter may not be.)

The Bloomington study began with 168 infants, mostly from middle-class families, and their mothers. When the babies were 6 months old, they were observed at home for two 3-hour sessions. In addition, mothers filled out some questionnaires. Bayley Developmental Assessments were done at the laboratory; mothers were interviewed about family adjustments since the baby's birth; and 9-minute sessions of face-to-face play were videotaped, with the mother instructed to be unresponsive in the middle 3 minutes of interaction. When the babies were 13 months old, one 3-hour home observation occurred, mothers completed two questionnaires, Bayley assessments were repeated, and 74 of the subjects were observed in the Strange Situation (but only 68 were classified with confidence).

In Bloomington, as in Baltimore, the mothers of infants later classified as secure responded faster to their infants' cries and bids for social interaction than the mothers of anxiously attached infants did. They appeared to be more involved and more responsive. In addition, they organized the home environment better. Furthermore, in the home observations at 13 months, mothers of securely attached babies were more affectionate and were better teachers than mothers of anxiously attached babies were.

Other measures in the Bloomington study also indicated greater harmony and warmth between securely attached infants and their mothers than between anxiously attached infants and their mothers. Affectionate maternal contact at 6 months was associated with secure attachment at 13 months. There were no differences between mothers of secure infants and mothers of anxious infants in the type or degree of stimulation of their infants or the amount of nonaffective communication with the babies. At the age of 6 months, infants who later developed secure attachments to their mothers showed more mutually positive face-to-face interaction with them than the infants who developed anxious attachments showed.

THE PENNSYLVANIA INFANT AND FAMILY DEVELOPMENT PROJECT

The Pennsylvania Infant and Family Development Project, which eventually included more than 200 mother-infant dyads, was another partial replication of the Baltimore study. Most of the families were middle class. Naturalistic observations were conducted in the home at 1, 3, and 9 months of age. The subjects were brought to the laboratory for Strange Situations when they were 12 or 13 months old.

The method of testing the sensitivity hypothesis in the Pennsylvania project differed from earlier research. Belsky, Rovine, and Taylor (1984) reported on 60 mother-infant dyads from the project's first cohort. Instead of using Ainsworth's scales for rating maternal behavior at home, they recorded specific details of the mother's behavior and the infant's behavior and based many of their data analyses on a measure they called *reciprocal interaction.* The measure appears to reflect mainly the quantity of interaction, not necessarily its quality.

Belsky et al. (1984) hypothesized that intermediate levels of reciprocal interaction would reflect sensitive care and would be associated with secure attachment, that high levels would reflect overstimulation and would be associated with avoidant attachments, and that low levels would reflect understimulation and would be associated with resistant attachments. Their hypotheses were unusual, given that attachment theorists had generally emphasized quality of interaction, not quantity. Furthermore, quantity of mother-infant interaction varies greatly with the child's birth order and with the family's culture, but neither factor seems to significantly affect development of secure attachment.

The Pennsylvania hypotheses may have been based on an inference that differences observed in high-risk samples would also help explain outcomes within the low-risk range. In high-risk samples, other investigators had found associations between quantity of interaction during brief observations and security of attachment. For example, in samples of neglected infants, Crittenden (1988c) and Egeland and Sroufe (1981) found very low levels of mother-baby interaction, and those low levels were associated with anxious-resistant attachments, particularly the passive C2 subgroup. In samples of abused infants, Crittenden (1985) had found excesses of intrusive, controlling, demanding maternal behavior while the mother was aware of being observed. The overstimulation during very brief videotaped interactions was associated with avoidance in the Strange Situation and with Group A or A-C classification. It appears that Belsky et al. (1984) were testing whether a relation discovered in studies of developmental psychopathology also appears within the normal range.

In the first cohort of 60 mother-infant dyads in the Pennsylvania project, the predicted relationship between quantity of interaction and attachment pattern appeared only in the third home visit (Belsky et al., 1984). It was the mother's behavior at the 9-month visit, not the infant's, that differentiated among the three attachment groups.

Belsky et al. (1984) also found that mothers of resistant infants were significantly less responsive to distress at 3 and 9 months than other mothers were, and they were significantly less responsive to vocalizations at 9 months. The score for being "responsive" was actually the result of dividing the frequency of the relevant maternal behavior by the frequency of the relevant infant behavior; it may or may not have been a good measure of the mother's contingent, appropriate behavior in direct response to the infant's signals.

QUALITY AND QUANTITY OF INTERACTION

Is *quantity* of interaction an appropriate operational definition for "*quality* of sensitive responsiveness." Given that caregivers' behavior when being observed may not match their usual behavior, did the amount of interaction the Pennsylvania researchers observed during 45 minutes of close observation at 9 months reflect the babies' usual experiences? Or were the mothers of the avoidant infants "performing" for the two obviously present observers? Mothers of avoidant babies may have differed from other mothers in (1) their concept of the best sort of maternal behavior to display while observed and/or (2) their inclination to stage a display for the observers. Indeed, the two individual categories of maternal behavior that differentiated among mothers of avoidant, secure, and resistant infants at 9 months were "undivided attention" and "stimulate-arouse." If the mothers were "performing," whether for conscious or unconscious reasons, their behavior during the home observations cannot be taken as representative of their usual behavior. This has important implications for interpreting the data.

In a later cohort from the Pennsylvania study, Isabella and Belsky (1991) again found an association between avoidant attachments and high levels of intrusive, overstimulating maternal behavior, especially verbal behavior, during brief home observations. They also reported an association between resistant attachments and observations of unresponsive and, indeed, uninvolved mothering. At 3 months and at 9 months, the dyads in which secure attachments developed showed well-timed, mutually rewarding interactions.

Other researchers have also found, in low-risk samples, associations between (1) quantity of interaction during brief observations and (2) pattern of attachment. Smith and Pederson (1988) assessed forty-eight 12-month-old infants with their mothers in Strange Situations. They also videotaped the dyads for 3 minutes in a situation designed to make things a bit difficult for the mother, as she was likely to have to manage the competing demands of the experimenter and of the baby. The mother was asked to complete a questionnaire. While she worked on it, her baby was left to explore the room, which held no toys. The mother's responses to infant cues in this situation were coded as "appropriate," "insufficient," and/or "intrusive." Summary measures of the mother's sensitivity in this very brief observation period showed a strong relationship with the infant's security of attachment. As in the Pennsylvania samples, mothers of avoidant infants responded intensely, perhaps excessively, to their babies, and the mothers of the resistant infants were less responsive and less involved than were other mothers. Malatesta, Culver, Tesman, and Shepard (1989) also found that mothers of avoidant infants were intrusive and overstimulating during brief, structured face-to-face interactions.

■ Does Overstimulation Cause Avoidance?

Given this association between high rates of maternal interactive behavior during brief observations (often overstimulating, intrusive, and/or noncontingent behavior) and avoidant attachments, it is reasonable to ask whether overstimulation causes avoidance. Caution in inferring a causal relationship is warranted. Behaviors that occur rather infrequently can be observed only if observations are long. Behaviors that the subject regards as undesirable are likely to be suppressed or masked during brief observations, but may be revealed in lengthy ones. Behaviors that the subject regards as desirable, but seldom exercises in everyday life, may be enacted at high rates when she is aware of being observed.

As noted earlier, Ainsworth and her colleagues visited the subjects in the Baltimore study for 3 or 4 hours at a time every 3 weeks during the first year. They emphasized (Ainsworth et al., 1978) that the group A mothers' strong aversion to physical contact with their babies was rarely expressed openly and might have been overlooked if the visits had not been long enough and frequent enough to encourage the mothers to behave naturally. Furthermore, even the group A mothers did show tenderness and affection at times. In everyday life, after the subjects had become accustomed to the presence of an observer, the critical differences between group B mothers and other mothers were in the affective tone and timing of the mother's behavior, not in the quantity of it.

The association between pattern of attachment and quantity of mother-infant interaction during a brief observation sometimes contradicts the hypotheses Belsky and his colleagues articulated. For example, Zaslow et al. (1988) observed 40 middle-class, firstborn 12-month-olds at home for 1 hour with just their mothers (dyadic context) and for 2 separate hours with both parents present (triadic context). At 14½ months, the mothers and infants participated in the Strange Situation procedure. In the presence of the father, mothers of securely attached toddlers and mothers of avoidant toddlers behaved similarly. In the father's absence, mothers of secure babies increased their playful interaction with their infants, but mothers of avoidant babies stayed at the same low level of playful involvement. This is the exact opposite of the contrast Belsky et al. (1984), Isabella and Belsky (1991), and Malatesta et al. (1989) found in brief observations.

In a Swedish study, Bohlin, Hagekull, Germer, and Andersson (1989) also obtained results opposite to those of the Pennsylvania researchers. When the babies were 4 months old, Bohlin et al. observed mother-infant dyads at home in face-to-face interaction and during a diaper change. The study measured maternal intrusiveness, operationally defined as overwhelming the baby with stimulation, interfering with his activity, or unduly hindering or interrupting his behavior. When the subjects were 12 months old, home visitors conducted a brief (less than 5 minutes) observation of sociability toward a stranger and then observed the baby's behavior during four 3-minute episodes: separation, reunion, separation, and reunion. Bohlin et al. (1989) did not attempt to classify the infants' attachment patterns. However, they did code resistance toward and avoidance of the mother in the reunion episodes. Low scores for maternal responsiveness and physical contact when the baby was 4 months old predicted avoidance when the baby was 12 months old; maternal intrusiveness and global insensitivity predicted resistance—exactly the opposite of the relations observed by Isabella and Belsky (1991). Nonetheless, the mother's sensitive responsiveness remained a good predictor of the baby's confident, unambivalent reunion behavior (Bohlin et al., 1989).

Thus, in different samples with different investigators, results have been contradictory. There are also simple failures to replicate. For example, working with naturalistic observations at 1, 4, and 9 months of age, Isabella (1993) found almost no support for the hypothesis that overstimulation in the natural environment fosters avoidance in the Strange Situation. When the association between overstimulation and avoidance has been found, the overstimulation has been recorded during relatively brief and very infrequent observations. In these cases, were the mothers of infants who developed avoidant attachments consistently overstimulating their infants in real life? Or did overstimulation occur mainly when they were trying to look good to observers? Were they insensitive, rejecting, and covertly angry in their usual interactions, as the mothers of avoidant babies in the Baltimore sample were? Nothing less than very lengthy naturalistic observations is likely to clarify the ordinary causes of avoidance.

DIVERGING RESEARCH APPROACHES, CONVERGING RESULTS

The major studies discussed above—the studies in Baltimore, Minneapolis, Bielefeld, Bloomington, and Pennsylvania—were all unusually ambitious research undertakings. Each was a longitudinal, multimethod investigation. Three of these studies had very large samples (over 100 infants). The Baltimore subjects were studied through ethological observations more extensively than any other human infants in a nonclinical sample have ever been studied in their natural environments. Children from the Bloomington sample, the Bielefeld sample, and the Minneapolis sample are now adolescents, and follow-up research continues in all three samples.

Because each of these studies included the standardized Strange Situation, their contributions to attachment research are especially easy to tie together. Each of these studies found evidence that the mother's sensitive responsiveness made a significant contribution to the infant's developing a secure attachment to her. Many shorter studies have also addressed the sensitivity hypothesis.

For example, Gaensbauer et al. (1985) observed 107 babies at home at intervals through the first year. Then, at the age of 12 months, the babies experienced a 43-minute laboratory sequence of free play, responding to a stranger, responding to the mother's instructed behavior, and then testing of the babies' developmental levels. The developmental testing included mild frustrations. After all of this, there were two separations from the mother and two reunions with her.

Obviously, assessment of attachments based on this procedure are not directly comparable to assessments from Strange Situations. To make use of their data, the investigators chose to rate the baby's attachment behavior in the laboratory as "optimal" or "problematic." *Optimal attachment behavior* was defined as (1) use of the mother as a secure base during the low-stress period of free play and (2) unambivalent proximity seeking, contact seeking, and contact maintaining when distressed. *Problematic behavior* included avoidance, resistance, or other indications of mixed feelings about the mother or a lack of confidence about seeking comfort from her.

In this assessment situation, some babies consistently and unambiguously showed optimal attachment behavior; some consistently and unambiguously showed problematic attachment behavior; and some showed inconsistent or ambiguous attachment behavior. When the pattern of behavior in the laboratory was consistent and unambiguous, it reflected the quality of caretaking that had been observed in the home, and the sensitivity hypothesis was supported. When the attachment behavior in the laboratory was inconsistent or ambiguous, it could not be used to make inferences about the history of caretaking.

Israeli kibbutzim (communal villages) have provided another way of gauging the effect of sensitive responsiveness on security of attachment. On some kibbutzim, all of the babies stay all night in the infant house, with one caretaker available and responsible for all of the infants in the house. On other kibbutzim, each baby stays all night in the family's home. (The decision about where an individual baby will sleep is made by the collective, not by the baby or by the baby's family.) In other respects, kibbutz child care arrangements are similar. Beginning very early in life, infants spend most of their time in group day care. The difference in sleeping arrangements among kibbutzim therefore provides a natural experiment.

Sagi, Van IJzendoorn, Aviezer, Donnell, and Mayseless (1994) offered two ways of analyzing their Strange Situation data from kibbutz samples. Whether they used the D category or forced their data into the traditional A-B-C classification system, they found that babies who slept at home were much more likely to develop secure attachments to their mothers than babies who slept in infant houses were. The two groups (those who slept at home and those who slept in an infant house) did not differ on measures of infant temperament, early life events, mother-infant interaction in a brief observation of the mother's effort to teach the baby a new skill in a play setting, quality of the infant's daytime environment, the mother's origin (kibbutz or elsewhere), the mother's job satisfaction, or the mother's anxiety about separation from her infant.

Using forced classifications, 11 of 23 infants (48 percent) in communal sleeping arrangements were securely attached, while 20 of 25 (80 percent) who slept at home were. All the rest were classified as resistant. With the D category available, babies were shifted from the B and C categories to category D with similar frequencies. Disorganized attachments were more common on kibbutzim than they are in middle-class, family-reared North American samples. The results are presented in Table 5.1.

A likely interpretation of these kibbutz results is as follows. Having the baby stay with the family all night made it possible for the mother to respond sensitively to the

TABLE 5.1 Attachment Patterns of Kibbutz Infants According to Sleeping Locations				
Sleeping Location	A	B	C	D
Infant house	0%	26%	30%	44%
Family	0%	60%	8%	32%

Source: Adapted from Sagi et al., 1994.

baby's needs during the night. The added time together may even have helped the mother learn to respond more sensitively to him during his waking hours as well. The time may also have helped the baby to develop trust in the mother's responsiveness. However, other aspects of kibbutz child care (described in more detail in Chapter 8) apparently rendered secure attachment less common and both resistance and disorganization more common than they are in other circumstances. It appears that kibbutz infant care nearly erases avoidance from the vocabulary of infant attachment behavior.

The results of this natural experiment support the sensitivity hypothesis by inference. True experiments, in which subjects are randomly assigned to treatment conditions, are rare in attachment research. However, two direct experimental tests of the sensitivity hypothesis are available. Both strongly support the hypothesis that sensitive responsiveness contributes to secure attachment.

Anisfeld et al. (1990) managed to design and conduct a true experiment intended to influence maternal sensitivity and infant security. Low-income inner-city mothers of newborns were randomly assigned to groups. The mothers in the experimental group were given soft baby carriers with the expectation that this would increase physical contact between mother and child and so promote greater maternal responsiveness and more secure attachment. The mothers in the control group were given infant seats.

In a play session when the babies were 3½ months old, mothers in the experimental group did show more contingent responding to their babies' vocalizations than mothers in the control group did. This supports the view that the experimental manipulation of close bodily contact had the expected effect of increasing maternal sensitivity. At the age of 13 months, the babies participated in Strange Situations. Results supported the sensitivity hypothesis. Of the 23 babies in the experimental group, 19 (83 percent) were securely attached. Of the 26 babies in the control group, only 10 (39 percent) were securely attached to their mothers.

Another true experiment comes from the Netherlands. Working with a lower-class sample there, van den Boom (1990) found that experimental manipulation of the mother's sensitive responsiveness dramatically altered attachment outcomes. Using the Neonatal Behavioral Assessment Scales (NBAS, described in Chapter 6), which measure a newborn's behavioral capabilities, van den Boom identified 100 babies who showed irritability in an initial assessment some time between the tenth to thirteenth days of life and also in a second NBAS assessment 5 days later. Believing that she had identified a group of babies who would be difficult to care for, van dem Boom then assigned the 100 babies, at random, to an experimental group or to a control group. When the babies were 6 to 9 months old, mothers in the experimental group received three very individualized sessions focusing solely on maternal responsiveness. Through guided observation of their babies and themselves on videotape, the mothers were taught how to read their babies' cues and respond sensitively to them. The control group received no intervention.

The results of this brief, focused intervention were impressive. In the experimental group, 68 percent of the babies were securely attached at 1 year. In the control group, only 28 percent of the babies were securely attached. In the absence of intervention, infant irritability apparently contributed to a chain of events that raised the frequency of anxious attachments far above the level we usually see. In the context of that risk factor, just three lessons in sensitive responsiveness sufficed to bring the frequency of anxious attachment back to the frequency that characterizes randomly selected groups of infants.

Recently, Isabella (1993) has replicated the findings that mothers of infants later classified as secure got higher scores for sensitive responsiveness during naturalistic observations (at 1 and 4 months) and were less rejecting (at 1 and 9 months) than mothers of insecurely attached infants. Furthermore, how old the baby was when the mother showed a high level of rejecting behavior helped to explain which babies developed resistant attachment and which babies developed avoidant attachments. The mothers of the babies who became resistant were the least sensitively responsive and the most rejecting in the observations at 1 month but became less rejecting as the months passed. At 1 month, many babies need help from their caregivers to regulate their own physiological states. These babies did not get the help they needed. The mothers of babies who became avoidant were most rejecting in the observations at 9 months. At that age, infants are mobile and relatively competent; they can express emotions, anticipate the caregiver's behavior, and pursue their own objectives in a goal-corrected fashion. The mother's negative, physically controlling, interfering behavior was greatest when the baby was old enough to be involved in behavioral conflicts about pursuing her own goals.

The studies I have described here reflect many different research approaches. They converge in support for the sensitivity hypothesis. The mother's sensitive responsiveness to the baby clearly contributes to the baby's development of a secure attachment to the mother.

MALTREATMENT STUDIES

Another cluster of studies, maltreatment studies, also supports the sensitivity hypothesis. Abuse and neglect are extremes of insensitive care. The sensitivity hypothesis clearly predicts that maltreated babies will develop anxious attachments, not secure ones. Neglected babies experience extreme unresponsiveness. Abused babies experience harsh, interfering, controlling, and otherwise negative care. Some babies, both abused and neglected, experience fluctuations between those two extremes (Crittenden, 1981, 1988c; Crittenden and Ainsworth, 1989).

The data from studies of maltreated babies support the sensitivity hypothesis unambiguously. Even before the D category was defined, two studies (Egeland and Sroufe, 1981; Gaensbauer and Harmon, 1982) found that anxious attachments were significantly more common among maltreated infants and toddlers than they were in comparison groups. Also using very well matched, low-income comparison groups, other investigators have consistently found that maltreated infants develop anxious attachments to their primary caregivers significantly more often than adequately reared infants do (Crittenden, 1985, 1988c; Schneider-Rosen, Braunwald, Carlson, and Cicchetti, 1985; Schneider-Rosen and Cicchetti, 1984). In fact, estimates of the frequencies of anxious attachments in maltreated children have ranged from 70 to 100 percent. This contrasts with about 35 percent in low-risk samples, regardless of socioeconomic class.

In addition—and as expected—maltreated babies show clearly disturbed patterns of attachment much more often than other babies do. They often show one of the very disorganized, disturbed, or depressed D patterns or the combined avoidant-resistant (A-C) pattern Crittenden defined.

The usual association between maltreatment and anxious, often disorganized attachments appears in a study by Carlson, Cicchetti, Barnett, and Braunwald (1989a). They studied 22 mother-infant dyads from families receiving protective services because of maltreatment and 21 dyads from comparison families with similar demographic characteristics. In the maltreatment group, 82 percent of the infants' attachments were anxious-disorganized-disoriented; in the comparison group, only 19 percent were. The researchers were unable to avoid one flaw in matching the characteristics of the two subsamples. On the average, comparison families had 3 adults for every 2 children in the household. There were only 2 adults for every 3 children in the maltreatment group. The ratio in the comparison families was less likely to strain the caregiver's abilities. However, the adult-to-child ratio did not account for the difference in distributions of attachment patterns. Maltreated children were significantly more likely than comparison children to have anxious attachments even after the investigators controlled statistically for effects of adult-to-child ratio and birth order.

Using her own avoidant-resistant (A-C) category, instead of the D category, Crittenden (1988c) found that different patterns of anxious attachment were associated with different problems in caregiving. Her sample of 121 mother-child dyads from low-income families included abused, neglected, abused-and-neglected, marginally maltreated, and adequately reared children. Determinations by local welfare departments were used to classify quality of child rearing. The children ranged in age from newborns to 48-month-olds ($M = 24$ months), so it was necessary for Strange Situation coders to make age-related modifications in scoring the meanings of some children's behaviors. Attachments were classified as avoidant-resistant (A-C) if the child showed (1) moderate or high proximity seeking or contact maintaining, (2) moderate or high resistance, *and* (3) moderate or high avoidance.

The distributions of patterns of attachment are displayed in Table 5.2. The main point is that there are significant and meaningful associations between specific patterns of maternal care and specific patterns of attachment. Among the adequately reared children, frequencies of secure (59 percent) and avoidant (31 percent) attachments were similar to those usually obtained in nonclinical samples. Most of the marginally maltreated children were either secure (36 percent) or avoidant (41 percent). Children in this subsample experienced intermittent periods of harshness bordering on abuse and/or periods of neglect that was not severe enough to be life-threatening. They were less likely than adequately reared children to form secure attachments, but they could handle their difficulties with a defensive strategy often observed in low-risk samples. Few of them developed disturbed or deviant ways of coping.

TABLE 5.2 Percentages of Children in Each Child-Rearing Group Showing Each Pattern of Attachment				
	Attachment Pattern			
Family Care Provided	Secure	Avoidant	Resistant	Avoidant-Resistant
Adequate	59%	31%	3%	7%
Marginal maltreatment	36%	41%	14%	9%
Neglect	10%	50%	20%	20%
Abuse	5%	36%	9%	50%
Abuse and neglect	13%	26%	3%	58%

Source: Adapted from Crittenden, 1988c.

Secure Strange Situation behavior was extremely rare in children believed to have been abused or neglected. Avoidance was the most common response to neglect, but was not uncommon in any of the five categories of care. Avoidant-resistant (A-C) behavior was very rare in the adequately reared and marginally maltreated children, but very common among children who had been abused, whether or not they had also been neglected.

The avoidant-resistant children included some whose attachment behavior, resistant behavior, and exploratory behavior resembled C1's, and some whose passivity and help-lessness warranted classification as A-C2, not A-C1. Of the A-C2's (both avoidant and helpless), 87 percent had experienced serious neglect. Like the A-C category, the C category was split. The openly angry C1 subcategory was associated with marginal maltreatment, while the passive C2 category, like the A-C2 category, was associated with neglect. There is a clear suggestion here that C2's are in an important way quite different from C1's. The C2 histories and behaviors imply that they are at risk for learned helplessness and depression.

Zeanah and Zeanah (1989) have provided a fine analysis and review of the evidence on how a maltreating parent's representational models produce distorted perceptions and interpretations of the baby's behavior and lead to insensitive and sometimes abusive responses to the baby. The anxiety and disturbances in the children's attachment patterns follow predictably from the behavior to which they must struggle to adapt. I will have more to say about this transmission of attachment patterns from generation to generation in Unit 4.

MEASURING SENSITIVITY

A researcher's ability to detect the impact of any explanatory variable is always limited by her ability to measure the variable accurately. Both in major longitudinal studies and in less ambitious research with low-risk and high-risk samples, we find significant but usually modest correlations between the mother's sensitivity and the infant's security. Do the correlations accurately reflect the limit of the mother's influence on attachment security? Or would the correlations be higher if we were better able to measure sensitivity, security, or both? A part of the answer to the second question lies in knowing whether we are getting the most reliable, valid measures of the mother's sensitive responsiveness to the baby's behavior.

Among the measures of sensitivity most often used and least often questioned, Ainsworth's four 9-point rating scales for the mother's accessibility, cooperation, acceptance, and sensitivity are prominent. Each of the four scales provides a long description of the construct to be assessed and a paragraph to anchor each of the odd points on a 9-point scale. Using the scales requires the observer to develop a good understanding of the mother's psychological processes and the infant's needs.

Recently, a Canadian team (Pederson, Moran, Sitko, Campbell, Ghesquire, and Acton, 1990) developed a promising new measure of the caregiver's sensitivity. The *Maternal Behavior Q-sort* is designed to rely on clinical judgments less than Ainsworth's scales do. Like Ainsworth's scales, the new Q-sort requires that the coder observe the caregiver's responsiveness in a situation that tests his or her ability to divide his or her attention between the demands of the baby and other tasks. When there are no competing demands on the caregiver's attention, his or her ability and willingness to notice and respond to the baby's signals are not well tested.

The Maternal Behavior Q-sort has 90 items that focus on maternal behavior. The items encourage observers to direct their attention to aspects of mother-infant interaction that are relevant to attachment. The Q-sort is designed to yield a detailed description of the caregiver's behavior and a summary assessment of maternal sensitivity. The latter goal is achieved by comparing the Q-sort description of the observed mother's behavior with the Q-sort description of a prototypically sensitive mother.

For the first published report about the Maternal Behavior Q-sort (Pederson et al., 1990), observers watched each of 40 mothers and their 12-month-old babies at home for 2 hours on two occasions. Then they used both their new measure and Ainsworth's rating scales to describe maternal sensitivity. The observers used Waters's and Deane's (1985) Attachment Behavior Q-set to describe the infant. Maternal sensitivity was unrelated to age and income, but correlated positively with maternal education. There was a strong relation between infant attachment and maternal sensitivity, whether the latter was measured by the Ainsworth scales or by the new Maternal Behavior Q-sort. The Maternal Behavior Q-sort may prove to be a valuable research instrument. Whether this Q-sort is also appropriate for assessing a father's or babysitter's sensitivity is a question for later research.

For assessing sensitivity accurately, having a measure that is valid for the period observed is necessary but not sufficient. A scientist also needs evidence that the behavior during the period observed accurately reflects the caregiver's behavior in everyday life. The possibility that a caregiver's sensitivity varies quite a bit from time to time or from situation to situation must be considered.

Six studies, summarized in Crockenberg and McCluskey (1986), have found statistically significant, but modest, correlations between sensitivity at one time and sensitivity at another. Overall, the weight of evidence is consistent with the view that levels of maternal sensitivity tend to be stable over time, but that maternal responsiveness varies somewhat from hour to hour and from day to day, and that its modal level may change as the months pass.

In the Baltimore sample (Ainsworth, personal communication), ratings of maternal sensitivity during long home visits bounced up and down quite a bit from month to month for some mothers; they were consistently high for other mothers and consistently rather low for still others. Measuring a caregiver's sensitive responsiveness reliably may require making repeated, long visits. Two or three glimpses at contingent responsiveness sometime during the first year may not be sufficient to tell us what we need to know about the average level or the range of a caregiver's sensitivity to the baby's signals and behavior.

In the existing research, it is likely that some of the mothers were assessed during brief periods that were among their best while others were assessed during brief periods that were among their worst. More-reliable measures of a caregiver's usual level(s) of sensitivity in the usual settings for interaction with the baby may yield even stronger support for the sensitivity hypothesis than we already have.

CRITIQUES OF STUDIES OF MATERNAL SENSITIVITY

In a series of critiques, Michael Lamb and his colleagues (e.g., Lamb, Thompson, Gardner, and Charnov, 1985) have called attention to the methodological limitations of the research on infant attachment. Several studies have used a large number of measures and reported results only for those with statistically significant associations among variables, not for all that were expected to show associations. If we have 10 ways of measuring maternal sensitivity, only 3 of them are associated with infant security, and those are the only 3 we report, we can make it appear that maternal sensitivity plays a clearer or more powerful role than it does play.

Many measures in attachment research do depend on clinical ratings, not on highly specific, measurable behavior sequences. Given the goal of assessing the underlying meaning of the behavior, not just recording the surface display of behavior, some degree of clinical inference is often necessary. Even after agreement among trained observers is established, some scientists remain uncomfortable with the degree of subjectivity involved in any clinical rating. Lamb et al. have also suggested that some techniques labeled as measures of maternal sensitivity measures, may actually reflect harmony in mother-infant interaction, and the harmony may stem as much from the infant's contribution as from the mother's.

While the association between measures of maternal sensitivity and secure attachment as assessed in the Strange Situation is fairly consistent, it is, according to Lamb and colleagues, not as strong or as well-demonstrated as attachment researchers sometimes make it seem. Lamb et al. (1985) concluded that the impact of maternal sensitivity had not been adequately demonstrated. The great majority of attachment researchers disagreed. However, Lamb and his colleagues were not alone in their skepticism. Temperament researchers (e.g., Goldsmith and Alansky, 1987) and people whose primary work lies outside attachment theory (e.g., Field, 1987; Kagan, 1982) were also unconvinced of the influence of maternal sensitivity on the organization of the infant's attachment behavior.

Given the hour-to-hour variability in maternal behavior, the fact that people do not act the same way in the presence of an observer as in the absence of one, and the typical brevity of observations of "normal" interaction at home, it strikes me as almost extraordinary that researchers *have* found a relationship between the caregiver's sensitivity and the infant's pattern of attachment. Many different studies conducted by different investigators with different populations (middle-class, poor, American, German, etc.) have demonstrated the existence of this relationship. The relationship between sensitivity and security must be quite strong, or it would not show up so consistently in such different and often minimal observation situations.

It is true that some proposed measures of the caregiver's responsiveness have sometimes failed to predict security of attachment. However, no association between sensitive responsiveness and anxious attachment has ever been reported. That is, there have been partial failures to support the sensitivity hypothesis, but it has never been contradicted by data.

CHAPTER SUMMARY

Within the normal range, Bowlby (e.g., 1991) and Ainsworth (e.g., 1973) argue that one of the most important aspects of caregiving is the willingness and ability to recognize, respect, and meet the child's need for a secure base. One of the most common sources of anger in children, they say, is frustration of the need for supportive, protective care. One of the most common sources of anxiety is uncertainty about the psychological availability of the attachment figure. To support optimal development, the caregiver should also respect and support the child's need to explore. If attachment theory is correct, a caregiver who is reliably available to the baby and is reliable about responding sensitively to the baby's needs lays the foundation for secure attachment, which is the foundation for exploration of the physical and social environment, for self-reliance, and for self-esteem.

The weight of evidence from studies encompassing a wide variety of research approaches, investigators, and countries clearly supports the sensitivity hypothesis. Caregivers who are accessible and responsive generally have securely attached babies. Caregivers who are unpredictable (sometimes sensitive, sometimes inaccessible, and sometimes intrusive) generally have anxious-resistant babies. Caregivers who are covertly or overtly angry and rejecting generally have avoidant babies, particularly if rejection takes the form of rebuffing the infants' bids for contact. In addition, avoidance may be the usual adaptation to prolonged, severe unresponsiveness, such as the dearth of care neglected infants experience.

Even so, individual variations in the caregiver's sensitive responsiveness to infant signals account for only a modest proportion of the variability in infants' attachments. There is plenty of room for additional explanatory variables, such as infant characteristics and social support for the caregiver. Evidence about those and other possible factors is the topic of the next chapter.

MORE INFLUENCES ON ATTACHMENT PATTERNS

As attachment-based research increased, investigators considered many factors that they thought might influence the type of pattern of attachment an infant develops: demographic factors; the primary caregiver's personality and drug use; the infant's temperament, premature birth and early illness; and the amount and quality of social support the primary caregiver receives. This chapter discusses the evidence about each of those variables.

THE CAREGIVER'S PERSONALITY

Is there any reason to think the primary caregiver's personality should determine or influence the infant's attachment pattern? In some cases, yes. A caregiver who suffers from a mental illness or from a personality disorder may care for and respond to an infant in limited and/or deviant ways. The infant would then develop a guarded, distorted, or deviant pattern of attachment behavior.

In the absence of psychiatric problems in the caregiver should we expect associations between measures of the caregiver's personality and classification of the infant's attachment pattern? Maybe. Unfortunately, the overall picture that emerges from studies that have assessed maternal personality in low-risk samples is fuzzy. In some studies, maternal personality variables do not help to predict patterns of attachment at all. Specific personality variables that do predict patterns of attachment in one study do not predict them in another. However, when relationships between such variables are found, it is almost always the case that positive maternal characteristics, such as autonomy, flexibility, and nurturance, are associated with secure infant attachments.

Part of the difficulty in demonstrating associations between the mother's personality and the baby's attachment pattern may stem from the difficulty of developing good measures of personality variables. Many personality tests are available, but none has unquestioned validity. In addition, the relationship between a caregiver's personality structure or strengths and his or her responsiveness to a baby is probably very complex. What directly affects the baby is surely the caregiver's behavior in response to that baby, not the caregiver's internal personality structure.

■ Mental Illness

Let's consider first the most extreme cases: those in which the caregiver is known to suffer from a severe psychiatric problem: unipolar clinical depression, schizophrenia, or bipolar disorder. According to Radke-Yarrow et al. (1985) and Teti et al. (1991), about half of the babies and toddlers whose mothers suffer from unipolar depression are anxiously attached. This is, of course, a higher frequency of insecure attachments than we find in low-risk samples. When unipolar depression appears in the context of poverty, the rate of anxious attachment rises to about 80 percent (Lyons-Ruth, 1988). For most patients, depression is episodic. Evidently, their behavior during periods of effective treatment or spontaneous remission, in which they feel energetic and hopeful, can be sufficient to support the development of secure attachments in their infants. The more severe and chronic the parent's depression is, the more likely it is that the baby's attachment to that parent will be insecure.

Why do most babies with depressed mothers develop anxious attachments? The available data suggest that infants of depressed mothers experience a dearth of rewarding, contingent responsiveness. Lyons-Ruth (1991) reported observations of depressed, low-income mothers and their babies at home when the babies were 6 months old. Observers found very little eye contact and smiling between the mother and baby, even in specially structured, face-to-face situations. Instead, they saw subtle but systematic gaze aversion by both partners. The mutual delight and synchronized, harmonious responsiveness that characterizes normal face-to-face interactions between American mothers and babies at this age was rarely observed. In Strange Situations at 18 months, most of these babies showed anxious patterns of attachment, especially the disorganized-disoriented patterns.

According to Gelfand and Teti (1991), care from depressed mothers is often detached and unresponsive, but it is also often hostile and intrusive. Teti and Gelfand (1991) found that *self-efficacy*—the mother's belief in her own ability to be effective—helped to predict the mother's interaction with her baby even after controlling statistically for the mother's depression. Mothers who believed they could be effective with their babies had more-positive, more-harmonious interactions with them.

In the case of mothers with bipolar disorder (once known as "manic-depressive psychosis"), Radke-Yarrow et al. (1985) found that about 80 percent of the babies developed anxious attachments, many of which would now be classified as D's. Näslund, Persson-Blennow, McNeil, Kaij, and Malmquist-Larsson (1984) cite evidence that babies of schizophrenic mothers are also more likely than babies of normal mothers to be anxiously attached. D'Angelo (1986) reported that most of the firstborn babies of fifteen schizophrenic mothers were avoidant in Strange Situations at 12½ months, most of the firstborns of the fifteen depressed mothers were resistant, and most of the firstborns of the fifteen mothers in the control group were secure. It does seem that some mothers with psychotic illnesses can support secure attachments in their infants. What roles medication, psychotherapy, and support from the spouse or others play in caring for these dyads is not yet known.

■ Personality Disorders

Unipolar depression, bipolar disorder, and schizophrenia are serious psychiatric conditions that seem likely to cause at least intermittent inadequacies or distortions in caregiving. What about a less severe class of psychological problems? The Diagnostic and Statistical Manual of the American Psychiatric Association specifies criteria for identifying 11 different *personality disorders.* When personality traits are inflexible and maladaptive and either cause significant impairment in social and occupational functioning or cause significant subjective distress, the individual has a personality disorder. Such a diagnosis is made only when the traits in question have characterized the individual for a long time, not just during a discrete period of illness or a period of adjustment to stressful events.

Without labeling the mothers' difficulties as personality disorders, Ainsworth et al. (1978) did report that mothers of very avoidant infants in the Baltimore study had rigid, compulsive personalities. In ratings of behavior throughout the year, the mothers of avoidant infants were more rigid, compulsive, and perfectionistic than other mothers, not just toward the baby, but in general. In face, voice, or bodily movements, they appeared overcontrolled or mechanical. Compared to other mothers, they showed little emotional expression.

Unfortunately, no hypotheses about specific relationships between personality disorders and infant attachment patterns have received direct research attention. Most personality disorders go undiagnosed and untreated. Consequently, it is quite likely that samples selected more or less randomly from low-risk populations include parents with personality disorders. Is inclusion of such parents in a study enough to demonstrate a connection between inflexible, maladaptive personality traits in the parent and insecure attachment in the child? In a word, no. There are several reasons.

The principal explanation is that researchers seldom find what they do not systematically look for. Even when focusing on personality variables, infant attachment researchers have almost never tried to determine whether a parent has any specific personality disorder. They ordinarily use sets of scales that measure nurturance, antisocial tendencies, self-esteem, dominance, and other such constructs as *continuous variables.* They do not classify parents into *categories* such as "mentally healthy" and "personality disordered."

Within the mentally healthy range, there are wide variations in personality characteristics and scale scores. Almost any personality disorder probably causes lapses in and/or deviations from giving good care to a baby. However, some such disorders may not show up as extreme scores on the sorts of personality scales that are used in research. Also, different personality disorders probably produce extreme scores on different scales. When the researcher tests the hypothesis that, across the whole sample, parents who get high scores on a certain variable tend to have babies who are securely attached, the qualitative differences between individuals are likely to get lost in the quantitative analyses of scores. Also, there might not be enough caregivers with one particular sort of personality disorder in the sample to make them stand out as a group from the widely varied array of other individuals in the sample.

In real life, a borderline personality disorder in the parent may almost always produce a disorganized or avoidant-resistant attachment in the child. In real life, a passive aggressive personality disorder in the parent may almost always produce an avoidant attachment in the child. Either because these hypotheses are wrong or because researchers have never systematically tested them, no such connections have been demonstrated.

■ Mentally Healthy Subjects

Apart from studies that have specifically included mothers who suffer from depression or some other psychiatric problem, most studies have not directly assessed the mental health of the parents. When researchers do include personality variables, they usually assess the degree to which a parent has some characteristic such as nurturance or aggressiveness. The difficulties in measuring such personality characteristics, conceptualized as *behavioral tendencies,* are beyond the scope of this book. Most people do vary their behavior greatly depending on what situation they are in, who is involved in the interaction, and who else is present. Because of the great flexibility and variability of an individual's behavior, some psychologists have argued that it is not reasonable to describe most people in terms of enduring traits.

In the absence of mental illness, no specific maternal personality variable has consistently, across a number of studies, shown a relation to the infant's attachment pattern. In one study, Ricks (1985) found that mothers of secure babies had higher self-esteem than mothers of anxiously attached babies, but the finding was not specifically replicated in later research. Maslin and Bates (1983) used a series of personality tests and found that, compared to other mothers, mothers of securely attached babies were likely to be more nurturant, more autonomous, less aggressive, more inquisitive, less dominating, and less self-centered. Efforts to replicate these findings were also largely unsuccessful.

The association between desirable maternal personality characteristics and secure infant attachment was not well replicated in the Minneapolis high-risk sample or the Pennsylvania low-risk sample. In the former, measures of aggressiveness, suspiciousness, impulsiveness, succor, and social desirability in the mother's responses to personality tests before the baby's birth and at 3 months postpartum failed to predict which babies would be securely attached (Egeland and Farber, 1984). Only the mother's maturity and the complexity of her thinking helped to predict secure attachment. In the Pennsylvania sample, Belsky and Isabella (1988) also considered many measures of the mother's personality and found few to help predict attachment status. Mothers of secure infants did get better scores on interpersonal affection than other mothers, and mothers of avoidant babies showed less ego strength than other mothers. Neither nurturance nor self-esteem differentiated the groups of mothers. Statistical analyses indicated that the mother's personality had both direct and indirect effects on the infant's attachment. For example, mothers with poor prenatal scores on ego strength and interpersonal affection tended to experience the greatest declines in marital quality after the baby's birth, and deterioration in the marriage was associated with an increased likelihood of insecure attachment.

Within low-risk samples, levels of optimism and tendencies toward self-blame vary from parent to parent. (A parent's belief that he or she has a lot of influence on the baby's development is not exactly a personality trait, but research about it seems to belong in this section anyway.) Donovan and Leavitt (1989) thought the mother's expectations about her influence might affect her baby's actual development. To test their hypothesis, they asked 40 mothers of 5-month-old babies to estimate their ability to bring an end to a baby's cry in a contrived laboratory simulation of a child care task. The mother had to push one of two buttons in an effort to terminate a recording of a baby's cry. In fact, each button terminated the cry exactly 50 percent of the time. The mother's actual control over the cry was zero. Nevertheless, mothers' estimates of their levels of control varied considerably. Compared to other mothers, those who greatly overestimated their control over the baby's crying also showed evidence of a depressed mood state (but were not clinically depressed).

Only 7 of the 40 babies (18 percent) in this study were judged to be insecurely attached. Insecure attachments, as assessed in Strange Situations at 16 months, were associated with overestimation of maternal control and with a depressed mood in the mother. In other words, the mothers who thought they could do much more than they really could do to stop a baby's cry tended toward depression and tended to have babies who became anxiously attached.

These results present an intriguing contrast to the implications of Teti and Gelfand's (1991) finding about the apparent effect of self-efficacy in a sample of depressed mothers. Among mothers who suffered from clinical depression, the mother's belief that she could influence the infant interaction outcomes that mattered to her improved the quality of parent-infant interaction and so probably decreased the risk of anxious attachment. Among mothers who were not clinically depressed, a similar belief was associated with an increased risk of anxious attachment and with a somewhat depressed mood. The difference in results may reflect a real difference between depressed and nondepressed mothers in the importance of self-efficacy. However, the difference in outcomes may instead reflect the difference in how the mother's beliefs about her effectiveness were measured. Teti and Gelfand used a questionnaire measure of self-efficacy. Nine of their ten items asked about the mother's feelings of self-efficacy in relation to specific aspects of infant care: soothing, understanding what the baby wants, getting the baby to understand the mother's wishes, maintaining joint attention and interaction, amusing the baby, knowing what the baby enjoys, disengaging from the baby, performing routine tasks (feeding, changing, etc.), and getting the baby to show off for visitors. The tenth item tapped the mother's global feelings of self-efficacy in her role as a mother.

The depressed mothers who got relatively high scores on feelings of self-efficacy as mothers may have been making accurate estimates about how effective they were. Their greater faith in their ability to influence outcomes was associated with observable benefits for the baby during interactions. The mothers in the nonclinical sample who got high scores for believing they could influence crying were clearly overestimating their power. Although the two studies at first seem to be measuring the same construct, a closer look makes it hard to tell how the different results should be interpreted. This is often the case when we try to compare studies of how the parent's personality or expectations affect the baby's attachment.

DEMOGRAPHIC FACTORS

Does the baby's gender, birth order, or social class influence the pattern of attachment that develops in infancy? Socioeconomic status helps to predict patterns of attachment to the mother only when it is very low. In the case of very poor families, anxious attachments to the mother are more common than they are at more favorable economic levels. Families in poverty are often coping with multiple problems. Distributions of secure, avoidant, resistant, and disorganized attachments to the mother appear to be about the same among working-class, lower-middle-class and upper-middle-class families, among firstborns and later-borns, and among boys and girls.

What about the mother's age? Very young mothers may be less likely to foster secure attachments than other mothers are. Lamb, Hopps, and Elster (1987) observed 40 babies and their adolescent mothers at home when the babies were 6 months old and in Strange Situations when the babies were 14 months old. Avoidant attachments were more common in this group (45 percent, not the usual 20 or 25 percent) than they are in studies of American mothers who are over 20 years old. At 6 months, mutual engagement and level of infant vocalizing were lower in the avoidant dyads than in the secure dyads. The mothers of future secure babies provided more care for them at 6 months than the mothers of future avoidant babies did. When the mother is very young, the grandmother is often the baby's primary caregiver. The teenage mother's quantity of involvement at 6 months may have reflected the quality of her investment in the relationship. In short, when neither poverty not maternal immaturity is a factor, demographic variables appear to have no influence on the pattern of attachment to the mother.

DRUG USE

In recent years in the United States, the use of legal and illegal drugs during pregnancy has been a topic of considerable concern among doctors and psychologists. It is now clear that prenatal exposure to alcohol, cocaine, heroin, and other psychoactive substances can have long-lasting or even irreversible effects on a baby. In addition, the low quality of care often provided in families in which one or more adults are addicted to such drugs probably has many undesirable effects on a child, including increasing the likelihood of anxious attachment.

To study effects of alcohol use during pregnancy, O'Conner, Sigman, and Brill (1987) studied 46 firstborns whose mothers were over 30. In fact, almost all of the mothers were white, highly educated, middle-class, married women over the age of 35. Mothers reported on their own drug use during pregnancy. All denied using heroin, amphetamines, PCP, LSD, cocaine, morphine, and mescaline. Five said they used marijuana regularly. On the average, the women drank less alcohol during pregnancy than before it, but light drinkers remained light drinkers and heavy drinkers remained comparatively heavy drinkers. According to their own reports, the mothers who had decreased their alcohol consumption during pregnancy did not increase it again after pregnancy. The investigators suspected that these well-educated mothers may have been reluctant to report alcohol use during and after pregnancy. The alcohol-use groups did not differ significantly in use of caffeine or tobacco.

As you can see from Table 6.1, there was a clear association between alcohol use and anxious attachment. Only 22 percent of the babies whose mothers drank little or no alcohol during pregnancy developed anxious attachments; 48 percent of those whose mothers

TABLE 6.1 Alcohol Consumption during Pregnancy and Security of Attachment		
	Attachment	
Alcohol Use	Secure	Anxious
Light	7	2
Moderate	13	12
Heavy	2	10

Source: Adapted from O'Conner, Sigman, and Brill (1987). Copyright © 1987 by the American Psychological Association. Adapted with permission.

were moderate drinkers developed anxious attachments; and 83 percent of those whose mothers were heavy drinkers developed anxious attachments. Four of the five infants whose mothers admitted using marijuana during pregnancy were anxiously attached. (In the sample as a whole, 48 percent of the infants were secure, 13 percent were avoidant, 4 percent were resistant, and 35 percent were disorganized.)

O'Connor, Sigman, and Kasari (1992) used a statistical procedure called "structural equation modeling" to test ideas about how a mother's (self-reported) alcohol consumption might contribute to the development of anxious attachment in her baby. The measures in their study of 44 firstborns of women over 30 included 8 minutes of interaction in a laboratory playroom at the age of 12 months. They found evidence that the mother's drinking *during* pregnancy was related to negative affect in the infant, which led the mother to be less positive in interactions with the infant, thus increasing the risk of anxious attachment. However, in the range included in this study, the mother's alcohol consumption *after* pregnancy did not significantly influence either her interaction with her baby or the baby's attachment behavior.

Rodning, Beckwith, and Howard (1991) studied 39 babies with prenatal drug exposure. The presence of phencyclidine (PCP) in the infant's urine after birth was the selection criterion. Many of the babies also had evidence of cocaine exposure, but mothers who used heroin were excluded from the study. Mothers selected for the comparison group had the same very low economic status as the PCP group and lived in the same area of Los Angeles. In addition, they were matched to the PCP mothers on the variable of ethnicity. Mothers in the comparison group showed no signs of PCP, cocaine, or heroin use at the time of the infant's birth or in repeated contacts over the course of the study. In Strange Situations at 15 months, the anxious-disorganized-disoriented (D) category was both necessary and meaningful for describing the overwhelming majority of children in the group prenatally exposed to drugs. Only a small percentage of the children in the comparison group had disorganized attachments.

In short, the mother's PCP use or heavy alcohol use during pregnancy clearly predicts anxious attachment. In the case of PCP use, it predicts disorganized attachment. The attachment outcome may stem partly from neurophysiological effects on the baby's mood and responsiveness and partly from deficits in maternal care associated with continued drug abuse.

THE INFANT'S TEMPERAMENT

Among developmental psychologists, temperament was a hot topic in the 1980s. Consensus on a definition of "temperament" proved hard to reach. In general, however, temperament dimensions are expected to reflect biological origins, to be fairly stable across situations, to be fairly stable over time (at least within major developmental periods), and to be related to early personality (Goldsmith, Bradshaw, and Rieser-Danner, 1986). Temperament traits that various investigators have proposed include activity level, attention span, proneness to distress, sociability, fearfulness, emotional reactivity, soothability, and persistence.

Whether, how, and how much an infant's temperament might influence the pattern of attachment behavior she develops has been a topic of heated debate and quite a bit of research. For example, Kagan (1982) proposed that a congenitally fearful baby might chronically have the attachment system activated and so appear to be anxiously attached. At the opposite extreme, a baby who was, by temperament, unlikely to be stressed by novelty, might be disinclined to go to the mother at reunion in the Strange Situation and so would be erroneously classified as less securely attached than a baby who was distressed by novelty. Other temperament researchers proposed that a baby with an irritable temperament who showed anxious-resistant Strange Situation behavior might just be showing his or her temperamental reactivity (intense, easily triggered emotionality).

■ Evidence from the Baltimore and Pennsylvania Studies

To the extent that crying reflects fear, irritability, or reactivity, the data from the Baltimore study were not consistent with the strong hypothesis that temperament determines attachment pattern. Bell and Ainsworth (1972) divided the first year of life into four quarters, scored frequency and duration of crying in each quarter, and calculated correlations between scores for a baby's crying and for his mother's responsiveness to crying. The frequency and duration of the infant's crying changed over the first year much more than the mother's responsiveness to crying changed. The mother's responsiveness in one quarter predicted the infant's crying in a subsequent quarter significantly better than the infant's crying in one quarter predicted the mother's responsiveness to crying in a subsequent quarter. In short, it appeared that the mother influenced the infant's crying much more than the infant influenced the mother's responses to crying. Crying patterns in the first quarter did not predict those in the fourth quarter, but maternal responsiveness in the first quarter did. Ainsworth et al. (1978) conducted further analyses of related data and found that mothers who responded promptly to crying signals in the early months had babies who became securely attached.

Similarly, Belsky, Rovine, and Taylor (1984) found that infants in their Pennsylvania sample who developed secure attachments did fuss and cry less than the other infants at the 3-month and 9-month visits, but not at the 1-month visit. Quantity of maternal involvement was consistently stronger as a predictor of later infant fussiness than infant fussiness was as a predictor of the quantity of subsequent maternal involvement. However,

Hubbard and Van IJzendoorn (1987) were unable to replicate Bell and Ainsworth's findings about maternal unresponsiveness and infant crying.

Some years before temperament researchers threw themselves into the debate, Ainsworth et al. did consider the possibility that infant characteristics, not maternal sensitivity, might underlie security of attachment. However, they were unable to identify any individual differences among infants that helped to predict security of attachment. Nevertheless, Ainsworth (1983) later speculated that the influence of a baby's temperament on the mother might be masked by maternal sensitivity. The sort of behavior that constitutes sensitive, responsive care to a baby who is initially irritable is different from the sort of behavior that constitutes sensitive care for an "easy" baby. Consequently, rating the sensitivity of the mother's responses to the particular infant in her care might mask intriguing differences in how mothers respond to irritable babies and to "easy" babies. The infant's temperament might influence the mother's behavior a great deal without predicting the infant's pattern of attachment.

■ The Debate

Working from the perspective of temperament researchers, Goldsmith et al. (1986) proposed a subset of babies for whom the Strange Situation would not provide a valid assessment of attachment. For an infant who is, by temperament, highly sociable with strangers, active in exploration, and low in fearfulness, the Strange Situation would not, they thought, activate the attachment system at sufficient intensity to provide a valid assessment of security. Bowlby thought that fearfulness and the tendency to explore reflected the infant's confidence in the caregiver's availability, which, in turn, reflected his actual experience with that caregiver. The proposition that fearfulness, sociability, and inclination to explore are heritable traits represents a real challenge to the attachment theory perspective.

For over a decade, many researchers addressed the hypothesis that characteristics of infants' temperaments would influence their attachment patterns and/or their Strange Situation classifications. Some also considered the possibility that an infant's attachment pattern would influence the development of his temperamental characteristics. Some noted that temperaments are malleable and that aspects of the developing relationship between a parent and baby may affect both temperament and attachment.

The research was difficult to do, as temperament researchers could not agree on dimensions of behavior that might be influenced by a child's temperament or on valid ways of measuring temperament variables. (Goldsmith and Alansky, 1987; Goldsmith, Bradshaw, and Reiser-Danner, 1986). The mother's reports on temperament questionnaires often failed to match objective observations of the infant's behavior, and questions about the reliability of observations of temperament dimensions arose. For example, Seifer, Sameroff, Barrett, and Krafchuk (1994) found only modest week-to-week correlations on temperament dimensions as rated by mothers and by observers once a week for eight weeks. (However, they found that ratings based on aggregates of the eight observation sessions had high reliability both for observers and for mothers.) Using a questionnaire that mirrored the researchers' system for scoring the videotaped observation sessions, each of the fifty mothers rated her baby's behavior during the observation period. In addition, the mothers filled out four widely used temperament questionnaires. Neither set of maternal ratings matched well with observers' ratings.

Many studies failed to find any relations between temperament variables and attachment patterns. However, several studies did find some associations between temperament and attachment—most often between (1) irritability, proneness-to-distress, or negative affectivity either across situations or early in infancy and (2) resistant behavior in the Strange Situation at 12 to 18 months. However, the directions of such effects were seldom clear.

Attachment theorists have noted that classification of Strange Situation behavior is never a direct reflection of temperament variables. An "easy" baby can approach the mother and be coded B2 (secure) or avoid her and be coded A1 (avoidant). An irritable baby who is very distressed by the stranger or by the separations in the Strange Situation can settle down and quiet well when the father holds him and be coded B3 (secure), or cry and push away from the father and be coded C1 (resistant).

■ Evidence

When babies are assessed in Strange Situations at 12 months and again at 18 months, their discrete behaviors, which might be presumed to reflect temperament, are not indices of attachment and are not stable over time (Sroufe and Waters, 1982). The attachment classifications, however, are highly stable for babies in stable family and socioeconomic circumstances. Secure 12-month-olds often cry at separation and cling at reunion. Six months later, the same babies greet and show toys to the caregiver and need less contact at reunion. What stays constant is the ability to use the caregiver as a secure base.

Babies who participate in one Strange Situation with one parent, and later participate in another Strange Situation with the other parent, often show a different pattern of attachment to each parent. If the baby's temperament characteristics determined his Strange Situation classification, this could not happen.

One baby from my dissertation sample vividly dramatized the inadequacy of interpreting Strange Situation behavior as an expression of temperament traits. The laboratory procedure was a sequence of 3-minute episodes in which the baby was introduced to the laboratory playroom and to a female stranger and then underwent a series of separation and reunion episodes. Specifically, the baby was, in sequence, with both parents, then also a female stranger, then only the stranger, then only the first parent, then the stranger, then only the second parent, then no adult, then only the first parent, then no adult, and then both parents again. The baby in question showed moderate to high resistance and avoidance in each reunion with one parent but, in each reunion with the other parent, approached, nestled in, and rested for a long time in that parent's arms.

If the term "temperament" includes fairly stable reaction tendencies, we must hold that the baby had the same temperament throughout the entire sequence of separations and reunions. His reunion behavior, however, changed from disorganized to secure to disorganized to secure depending on which parent was present. The parent toward whom the baby's behavior was disorganized said he had been a difficult baby who cried a lot for the first 5 or 6 months. The other parent did not think the baby had cried excessively and thought there was a reason for it when he did cry. Both parents had had the opportunity to get to know the baby very well. They both had full-time jobs, and each had cared for the baby in the other parent's absence for many hours a week for many months.

Sroufe and Waters (1982) also offered two other compelling types of evidence that the Strange Situation assesses attachment, not temperament, and reflects history of care, not predetermined characteristics of the infant. In the Minneapolis poverty sample, a shift in the infant's attachment from anxious to secure often reflected a decrease in the stress in the mother's life. A shift from secure to anxious often reflected an increase in stress in the mother's life. From the temperament proponent perspective, there is no reason changes in the mother's circumstances should produce corresponding changes in the baby's Strange Situation behavior. From the attachment perspective, the changes are easy to understand. A decrease in stress enables the mother to give better care to her child; an increase has the opposite effect.

As Sroufe and Waters (1982) pointed out, many findings from follow-up studies of the Minneapolis sample make no sense from a temperament perspective. For example, children who were avoidant with their mothers in the Strange Situation tended to be highly dependent on their teachers a couple of years later. In nursery school, they sought much physical contact, showed much negative affect, and showed much aggression. If temperament were driving their behavior, the contrasts would make no sense. If avoidance of the mother is a mask for anger and a defense against expressing unmet attachment needs, the later behavior in nursery school becomes easy to understand.

■ A Meta-Analysis

In 1987, Goldsmith and Alansky published a meta-analysis of data from many other studies to weigh evidence about both maternal sensitivity and infant temperament as determinants of the infant's attachment pattern (Goldsmith and Alansky, 1987). They concluded that the mother's sensitive responsiveness did predict attachment security in the Strange Situation, but not as powerfully as other reviews had suggested. One temperament variable, the infant's proneness-to-distress, made a significant, albeit low, contribution to predicting resistance in the Strange Situation. While the ability to predict one category of interactive behavior is not the same as the ability to predict attachment classification, it is important.

As Goldsmith and Alansky (1987) noted, proneness-to-distress is not a genetically determined, unchanging characteristic of an infant. When it is measured at 3, 6, 9, 12, or 13 months, as it was in many of the studies, it may reflect the infant's history of care. When it is measured by maternal report, as it often is, it may say as much about the mother's perceptions as about the infant's behavior. Indeed, Vaughn, Joffe, Bradley, Seifer, and Barglow (1987) found that prepartum measures of the mother's characteristics, taken *before her baby was born,* predicted the degree of difficulty that she would perceive in her infant and report on the Carey (1970) Infant Temperament Questionnaire (a widely-used measure) several months later. Frodi, Bridges, and Shonk (1989) also found that mothers' ratings of infant temperament at 4 months were related to prenatal measures of the mother's child-rearing attitudes and of her physiological responses to recorded infant cries. In their study, ratings on Carey's Revised Infant Temperament Questionnaire (Carey and McDevitt, 1978) were significantly related to quality of attachment at 1 year.

Building on the hypothesized connection between infant proneness-to-distress and anxious attachment (Goldsmith and Alansky, 1987), Vaughn, Lefever, Seifer, and Barglow (1989) asked 119 mothers to fill out temperament questionnaires in the middle of the infant's first year. Babies who were rated as difficult at about 6 months did show more distress than other babies showed in Strange Situations at 12 to 14 months but only during separation episodes, not during reunion episodes. Temperament classifications (e.g., "easy" versus "difficult") simply were not related to attachment classifications.

■ The Goodness-of-Fit Hypothesis

Mangelsdorf et al. (1990) assessed proneness-to-distress through an observational procedure at 9 months and through a Carey questionnaire, filled out by the mother, at 13 months. Strange Situations were conducted at 13 months. Neither proneness-to-distress measure predicted whether the attachment would be secure or anxious. Each also failed to predict whether the attachment pattern would be "distal" or "proximal." *Distal attachment patterns* are those in which infant and mother interact across a distance or do not interact much at all. Distal patterns can be avoidant (A1 or A2) or secure (B1 or B2). *Proximal attachment patterns* include interaction during contact or in close physical proximity. They can be resistant (C1 or C2) or secure (B3 or B4). This study of 66 infant-mother pairs failed to find any direct association between temperament and attachment. However, infant temperament was associated with maternal behavior and personality, and the statistical interaction between maternal personality and infant proneness-to-distress did make a significant contribution to predicting security of attachment. These data suggest that infant temperament and maternal personality are each less important than how well a given dyad "fits together."

This proposition is called the "goodness-of-fit hypothesis." If it is correct, then you need to know something about the baby's temperament and something about the mother's personality—how well they "fit"—in order to predict the attachment outcome.

In a recent paper on emotion regulation, Cassidy (1991) concluded that converging studies suggest that infants have temperamentally based tendencies toward patterns of regulating their own emotions, and that these tendencies appear early and are stable over time. Thus, the baby's responses to the care the parent provides will probably fall within a range influenced by the baby's temperament. Also, influences between parent and child travel a two-way street: infants respond to parental care, but variations in infant temperament contribute to the quality of care a particular parent gives. According to Cassidy, the goodness-of-fit hypothesis may help predict security of attachment. For example an energetic, curious, active baby may fit well with the preferences of her father and develop a secure attachment to him. However, the same baby's mother may feel disappointed or even rejected by the dearth of cuddliness in her baby, and the lack of fit between the two may contribute to the development of an anxious attachment.

■ Interaction of Variables

Like others searching for an effect of temperament on attachment, Belsky and Isabella (1988) found that neither temperament scores from Brazelton's (1973) NBAS (described below) nor objective observations of behaviors that might reflect temperament factors at 1, 3, and 9 months differentiated among babies who became secure, avoidant, or resistant in their Pennsylvania sample. However, there was an interesting statistical interaction between maternal reports of temperament and later attachment status. Mothers of secure infants perceived their babies as becoming more predictable and more adaptable over time, while mothers of insecure babies perceived them as becoming less predictable and less adaptable over time. Meanwhile, objective observers found no temperament differences between the two groups.

Unambivalent comfort seeking when distressed in infancy indicates secure attachment and is clearly related to positive developmental outcomes. According to evidence summarized by Lyons-Ruth (1991), neither separation distress nor the lack of it shows a consistent relation to developmental outcomes. Distress that occurs in response to separation may be partly accounted for by a heritable temperament tendency. Whether the baby seeks comfort when distressed and does so without ambivalence probably reflects experience, not temperament.

The research I have discussed so far provides little evidence that inherited aspects of temperament have much impact on the pattern of attachment the baby develops. The hypothesis that retains some credibility is that a "negative" temperament may in some cases increase the risk of anxious attachment. Nevertheless, many mothers and fathers appear to be well able to respond sensitively even to an irritable, difficult baby and so to support the development of secure attachments.

■ Neonatal Measures of Temperament

Because so many researchers have used the Brazelton (1973) Neonatal Behavioral Assessment Scale (NBAS) to try to assess temperament in newborns, a few words about the instrument are in order. Brazelton, a pediatrician, designed the NBAS to assess individual differences in the behavior of newborns. It has 20 items that assess neurological development and 27 items that assess behaviors. The neurological items on the NBAS include measures of reflexes such as the Moro, plantar, rooting, and sucking reflexes. The behavioral items include measures of the baby's ability to orient to various visual and auditory stimuli (e.g., a light, a ball, and a rattle), and measures for activity level, motor abilities, irritability, response to stress, response to comforting, and ability to control state. Each item must be administered at the state specified for it (e.g., drowsy, alert, active, crying), so the baby's behavior partly determines the order in which items are administered.

As noted above, many researchers have hoped to find early indices of an infant's temperament in her responses to items on the NBAS. Other researchers have argued that the NBAS is better described as an assessment of a neonate's current capability for interaction with a caregiver. The choice of emphasis may be important. Assessing temperament implies that you are assessing heritable, fairly stable characteristics. Demonstrating that you have a valid means of assessing current capabilities is easier than demonstrating that you have a valid means of assessing temperament.

Data now show only a weak relationship between NBAS scores and later behavior. According to R. Q. Bell (1988–89), individual differences among newborns are not at all stable from day to day and seldom help to predict the later characteristics, interactions, or relationships of the babies. Very rapid maturation and organization of the central nervous system occur in the first 2 months after birth. Consequently, unless the baby's physical condition or the mother's characteristics lie outside the normal range, the newborn's characteristics may have little impact on how the relationship with the mother develops. Many studies, both published and unpublished, have sought and failed to find a link between NBAS scores and later attachment patterns. Nevertheless, in combination with other measures, irritability on the NBAS has shown interpretable links to attachment in some studies.

Another useful measure of an aspect of temperament in the newborn period is response to interruption of nonnutritive sucking. A newborn who reacts quickly and cries for a long time when someone pulls a pacifier out of his mouth is likely to show low levels of smiling and positive affect in laboratory and home observations at 3 and 8 months and a low level of exuberance in play in the early preschool period (Bell, 1988–89). Miyake, Chen, and Campos (1985) found that, among newborns, a slow increase in crying after the initial outburst in response to abrupt removal of the pacifier was associated with later development of insecure attachments in their sample of 19 Japanese babies. Ultimately, responses to interruption of nonnutritive sucking may prove to be more stable and more informative than variables from the NBAS.

■ Temperament and Social Support

One relatively early study shed more light than usual on the manner in which and degree to which infant irritability might influence attachment. Crockenberg (1981) studied 46 middle- and lower-class babies. Brazelton's NBAS was administered to the infants on the fifth day and again on the tenth day after birth to assess irritability. When the babies were 3 months old, one 4-hour home visit took place. Its maternal responsiveness was then measured with promptness in responding to distress as the criterion. During the same visit, mothers were interviewed about their sources of support and stress and given scores. The mother's score for social support depended on the amount of affective and material support she reported receiving in her role as a mother, relative to the stresses she experienced. Crockenberg deliberately relied on the mother's subjective perceptions of what was stressful and what was supportive.

In Crockenberg's study, high irritability on the NBAS was associated with anxious attachment only when social support was low. Similarly, low social support was associated with anxious attachment only when infant irritability was high. In other words, the only babies *not* likely to become securely attached were those who were irritable as newborns *and* who had mothers who reported low social support when the babies were 3 months old. If the baby was relatively undemanding and easy to comfort, the mother could provide responsive care even in the absence of good social support. If the baby was difficult, then emotional and material support from others could make a critical difference in the mother's ability to provide responsive care.

When studies do, like Crockenberg's, find evidence of some association between infant irritability and attachment outcome, they usually link irritability with an increased risk of resistant attachment. However, the literature includes one striking exception. In van den Boom (1990) (which I described in Chapter 5), infant irritability, as measured on the NBAS, was associated not with anxious-*resistant* attachment, but with a greatly increased risk of anxious-*avoidant* attachment. It is not clear why the path of development set in motion by the newborn's irritability differed in this Dutch sample from the path most often reported in other studies.

■ Proximal and Distal Attachments

By now, it should be obvious that aspects of temperament are difficult to define and measure at any age. They may be more difficult to define and measure in newborns than in older infants. However, the older the baby is, the more likely it is that we are measuring tendencies influenced by experience, not purely inherited or congenital tendencies. The challenges to researchers are considerable and continue to attract many scientists.

Belsky and Rovine (1987) have proposed a specific model of how temperament factors might affect not whether an emerging attachment is secure, but what pattern of secure or insecure behavior develops. They began with an insight first reported in a study by Frodi and Thompson (1985). In that study, significant early differences in emotional expression were associated with later Strange Situation classifications. However, infant emotionality did not predict whether infants would be secure or insecure. Instead, it was associated with the attachment's categorization as distal (A1, A2, B1, or B2) or as proximal (B3, B4, C1, or C2).

Belsky and Rovine (1987) presented evidence that newborns in their samples (two cohorts from the Pennsylvania study) who showed more tremors and startles and less motor maturity on the NBAS were more likely to develop proximal attachments than newborns with greater autonomic stability were. In one sample, the infants who were more alert and positively responsive as newborns were more likely to develop distal attachments. In both samples, the mothers of babies with distal attachments described their babies as easier to care for at 3 months of age than the infants who developed proximal attachments. In addition, infant-mother attachment was not associated with infant-father attachment on the traditional A-B-C division of categories, but there was significant concordance between infant-mother and infant-father attachment when the distal-proximal division of categories was used. This again suggests that the infant's temperament may have influenced whether the attachments he developed were proximal or distal, while the quality of care from each parent influenced whether the attachment was secure or anxious.

In a meta-analysis of data on 710 babies from 11 studies, Fox, Kimmerly, and Schafer (1991) also found that most babies who were distal with one parent in Strange Situation classifications were also distal with the other, and most babies who were proximal with one parent were also proximal with the other. Within those clusters, being secure-distal with one parent did not increase the likelihood that the baby was secure-distal, not avoidant, with the other parent; and being secure-proximal with one parent did not increase the likelihood that the baby was secure-proximal, not resistant, with the other parent. These data are certainly consistent with the Belsky and Rovine (1987) hypothesis, which warrants further study.

■ Overlapping Domains?

Vaughn et al. (1992) proposed a different way of thinking about temperament and attachment. Initially, people tended to view the two as unrelated constructs competing to explain some of the same aspects of infant-mother interaction, especially the variability in infant behavior during Strange Situation assessments. Vaughn et al. (1992) proposed that attachment and temperament may more usefully be conceptualized as *overlapping domains,* because child behavior and affect regulation occur and are measured in a social context. They analyzed data from six samples that had used either the original Waters and Deane Attachment Q-set or a revised version. Five different temperament questionnaires were used for the six studies, but four of the five were developed by Carey and his colleagues (e.g., Carey and McDevitt, 1978). Temperament assessments occurred as early as 5 months in one study and as late as 42 months in another study. A factor called "emotional reactivity" was statistically extracted from the temperament data from each of the samples. Attachment assessments occurred between 12 and 45 months.

When researchers relied on the mother's description of the child on a temperament questionnaire and on the mother's description of the child on the Q-set, they found a significant negative correlation between emotional reactivity and attachment security at each age of assessment. That is, high scores for emotional reactivity were associated with low scores for attachment security, and vice versa. However, the results were different when the mother filled out the temperament questionnaire and someone else sorted the Attachment Q-set. With the mother's insights, broad database, and personal biases affecting only one of the two measures, emotional reactivity and attachment security were unrelated in infancy. However, correlations between emotional reactivity and attachment security were significant, albeit modest, for children over 24 months old.

Among the older children, the correlation remained merely modest even when researchers used the data that made it appear strongest—namely, maternal reports both on a temperament questionnaire and on the Attachment Q-set; less than 25 percent of the variance in attachment scores was shared with temperament dimensions. Across informants (mothers, fathers, and trained observers), the negative correlation was stronger for older children than for infants or young toddlers.

The pattern of results from these six samples lends very little support to the view that differences in temperament are primary causes of differences in attachment security. But why would temperament and attachment show increasing overlap as the first years pass? One possibility is that, by the time children are 3 years old, their patterns of attachment are affecting their emerging traits, which temperament questionnaires assess. Another possibility is that, over time, certain aspects of temperament become increasingly stable and heritable for reasons related to maturation, not experience. In that case, the lack of association between temperament and attachment in the first year would reflect the instability of temperament variables early in life.

Vaughn et al. (1992) point out that the Q-set describes attachment behavior in the context of a range of observational data wider than the range available in Strange Situation assessments. Consequently, Q-set security scores are more likely to covary with other domains, including temperament scores, than Strange Situation classifications are.

■ Physiological Measures

What if we use a physiological measure of temperament instead of a questionnaire? Observable motor behaviors that might reflect individual differences in temperament appear also to reflect responses to the individual's experiences. A possibility worth considering is that physiological responses might more directly reflect inherited aspects of temperament. Human beings, even very young ones, can learn to smile when they feel sad or to appear to go on with their ordinary activities instead of crying in fear, trying to escape a feared stimulus, or approaching a caregiver for comfort and protection. People bring much of their overt, readily observable behavior under conscious control. However, their physiological reactions may be less likely to be inhibited or exaggerated in response to experience; they may provide a better measure of temperament.

One possible measure of individual differences in temperament at the physiological level is *cortisol levels.* When stressful events or circumstances arise, the nervous system and the endocrine system work together to ready the body for coping with the problem. The activation of this neuroendocrine system produces increases in the level of the hormone cortisol circulating through the body. In nonhuman primate infants, separation from the mother triggers large, long-lasting elevations in cortisol levels. Furthermore, nonhuman primate infants with balanced, harmonious attachment relationships show greater increases in cortisol at separation than do similar infants having less harmonious relationships. In a study of 66 human infants, Gunnar, Mangelsdorf, Larson, and Hertsgard (1989) sampled adrenocortical activity at 9 months and at 13 months and conducted Strange Situations at 13 months. Emotional temperament at 9 months, as indexed by cortisol levels, was strongly correlated with emotional temperament at 13 months, but it was not associated with attachment classifications.

Another possible physiological measure of other aspects of temperament is *heart-rate variability.* Izard, Simons, Haynes, Hyde, Parisi, Porges, and Cohen (1991) proposed that greater heart-rate variability may be linked to greater irritability and/or to greater emotional expressivity; heart-rate patterns do ordinarily reflect homeostatic physiological processes regulated by brain stem structures, not by conscious control. Using an experimental method for deriving security scores from the Strange Situation data, they found that measures of heart-rate variability taken at 3, 6, and 9 months did help in accounting for security scores at 13 months. Measures of heart-rate variability were significantly higher in anxiously attached infants than in securely attached infants.

Another promising hypothesis about a specific way temperament might affect attachment comes from van den Daele, a researcher who is also a psychoanalyst. He reports that quick rocking is an extremely effective way of quieting the vast majority of crying infants (about 93 or 94 percent), regardless of age, sex, developmental quotient, or history of rocking.

Van den Daele's study (1986) of identical and fraternal twins led him to believe that the failure to quiet in response to rocking was a heritable trait in the baby, not an effect of deficient care. His work as a psychoanalyst led him to the conclusion that mothers often react in one of two extreme ways to a baby who cannot be soothed. Some mothers become very resentful and rejecting. Others take the baby's behavior as evidence of their own utter inadequacy in the maternal role. Either response may have pervasive and long-lasting repercussions in mother-child interaction, affecting attachment and other aspects of the relationship. There are also mothers and fathers who acknowledge that their babies are difficult, don't blame themselves for that, and remain accessible to their babies while waiting for them to outgrow or learn to manage their proneness-to-distress or low soothability. These parents presumably foster secure attachments and don't show up in the psychoanalyst's office. Nevertheless, van den Daele's case studies do illustrate how a characteristic of the baby may draw the trajectory of interaction toward a path that leads to anxious attachment to a parent who could probably foster secure attachment in a less difficult child.

■ Integrating Perspectives

Joan Stevenson-Hinde (1991) proposed a way to integrate information about attachment and temperament, using fearfulness as an example. Kagan (1982) and many others have offered evidence that *fearfulness,* defined as the tendency toward behavioral inhibition as the initial reaction to unfamiliar or challenging events, is an aspect of temperament on which some babies show early and long-lasting differences with measurable physiological correlates. However, Bowlby (e.g., [1969] 1982) argued that a secure attachment should dissipate fear and support exploration, while an insecure attachment should intensify fearfulness. So which has more impact or is more important, temperament or attachment?

According to Stevenson-Hinde (1991), the question is not very useful. We will learn more if we ask, How does fearful behavior develop in relation to attachment behavior? As Kagan (1982) has pointed out, early measures of the physiological pattern associated with behavioral inhibition (high heart rate, low heart rate variability, high cortisol levels) serve, at best, as modest predictors of future behavioral inhibition. Add relevant early behavior to the physiological measures, and you improve your ability to predict later fearfulness significantly.

Social influences are clearly a factor. Uninhibited children rarely become fearful. Behaviorally inhibited (fearful) children do sometimes become uninhibited. Parents can help them do so by structuring the environment so that a highly reactive child will not be overstimulated and by teaching the child cognitive strategies for coping with high emotional arousal.

According to Stevenson-Hinde (1991), there is no reason to regard one of these two behavioral systems—wary-fearful and attachment—as more biological or more primary than the other. For each class of behavior, researchers can specify the contexts in which it occurs; variations in the intensity, quality, and patterning of the behavior; and the outcomes of the behavior.

Considerable overlap exists among the circumstances and events that activate wary-fearful behavior and those that activate attachment behavior. Each of the two classes of behavior is more likely when an infant is in an unfamiliar place than when the infant is at home. Each may be triggered by the appearance of a stranger or of any other stimulus that is novel and potentially harmful. The ordinary outcome of fearful behavior, as well as attachment behavior, is avoidance of (and protection from) the feared stimulus, or at least a decrease in proximity to it. Like attachment behavior, fearful behavior has the biological function of protection from harm.

Developmental changes occur both in the wary-fearful behavior system and in the attachment system. For example, when a stranger approaches, a baby may cry, a toddler may move away or look frightened, and a preschooler may just look down for a while and be reluctant to speak to the stranger. Both attachment behavior and wary-fearful behavior can at first be elicited by a wide range of stimuli. As time passes, both become focused, or tuned to a narrower range of stimuli. Among humans and other primates, infants learn what to fear and what not to fear by observing adults, especially their primary caregivers. In addition, Stevenson-Hinde (1991) cites evidence that initial, genetically influenced levels of fearfulness are subject to sex-typed social influences. For example, shyness is tolerated or even welcomed in girls much more often than it is in boys, and outright fearfulness is less vigorously discouraged in girls.

The emerging consensus in the field is as follows. Infants certainly differ from each other at birth and in the early weeks because of genetic and prenatal factors. Differences such as irritability, sociability, fearfulness, proneness-to-distress, and being "easy" or "difficult" may certainly affect the tone of parent-infant interactions. Such differences are subject to change with maturation and with social experience and are unlikely by themselves to determine the security of the infant's emerging attachment. However, in interaction with other factors, such as the parent's responsiveness and the social support available to the parent, congenital differences in temperament may influence either (1) security of attachment or (2) whether the attachment is proximal or distal. Biological and social influences intertwine in complex ways very early in life.

PREMATURE BIRTH AND EARLY ILLNESS

Another set of infant characteristics likely to affect early interactions with caregivers comprises qualities associated with premature birth. As Frodi and Thompson (1985) noted, preterm babies tend to be less alert at birth, to show poorer motor coordination, to have an aversive cry, and to be more irritable, more difficult to feed, and more difficult to comfort than full-term babies. In the early weeks, their mothers are less likely than mothers of full-term babies to pace interactions according to infant cues; they tend to be more active and intrusive. Interaction with their babies is less rewarding, since their babies fuss more, avert their gazes more, smile less, and laugh less than full-term babies.

All of this might set the stage for a continuing series of frustrating and insensitive interactions if the mother stays highly involved, or might lead the mother to give up and become somewhat rejecting. Happily, that is not what usually happens. At least, it is not what has happened in most of the middle-class samples studied to date. Premature babies with no prolonged health problems appear to be as likely as full-term babies to be securely attached at 1 year. Field (1987) cited evidence from several studies showing that, compared to mothers of full-term babies, mothers of premature babies are more sensitive to cues for proximity and contact, more responsive and encouraging in early face-to-face interactions, more affectionate and gentle, and more positive in their vocalizations. Apparently, these mothers perceive their babies as being vulnerable and needing extra care, and they respond accordingly. As time passes, they are as likely as other mothers to foster secure attachments, despite the special challenges of the early weeks.

The review of the literature on premature babies offered in Macey, Harmon, and East-erbrooks (1987) supported Field's findings. Even studies that followed babies as far as the second birthday have also reported less positive affect, less physical activity, less explo-ration and play, closer proximity to the mother, less verbal interaction, and more frequent distress behavior in preterm babies than in full-term babies. Nevertheless, the first six studies of healthy premature babies found no differences between their Strange Situation behavior and that of full-term babies (Macey et al., 1987). These studies did not use the D category.

The picture changes when researchers include sick premature babies as well as healthy ones. Plunkett, Meisels, Stiefel, Pasick, and Roloff (1986) studied 62 premature babies with respiratory distress syndrome (RDS)—either transient or chonic—and tested the hypothesis that medical risk level might affect the infant's pattern of attachment, presum-ably by influencing the nature of the care the baby elicited. The distribution of attachment patterns for preterm babies without RDS replicated the usual distribution for full-term infants: 27 percent avoidant, 64 percent secure, and 9 percent resistant. For the babies with transient RDS, the distribution was 18 percent avoidant, 53 percent secure, and 29 percent resistant. For the infants with chronic RDS, the high frequency of resistant attach-ments was even more striking: 6 percent avoidant, 53 percent secure, 41 percent resistant. The reason for the unusual percentage of resistant attachments is not clear. One possibil-ity is that the extra care needed by the babies with chronic or even transient RDS may have exhausted some parents, leaving them feeling covertly resentful and guilty and likely to respond to their babies in inconsistent and unpredictable ways.

Goldberg, Perotta, and Minde (1986) initially thought their findings contradicted those of Plunkett et al. (1986). In their premature, low birth-weight sample, worse neona-tal illnesses were associated with secure attachment, not anxious attachment. Later, the Strange Situation videotapes were reviewed and reclassified, this time using the D category (Goldberg, 1990). Some infants previously classified as secure (group B) were reclassified as disorganized-disoriented (group D). In the reanalysis of data, secure attachments were significantly less common among infants born prematurely (54 percent secure) than among infants in a healthy, full-term control group (74 percent secure). In studies done before the D category was used, several investigators had noted that babies born prematurely were often difficult to classify. Widespread use of the D category in new studies may modify the current view that premature babies—despite the challenges they present to their care-givers—are as likely as others to become securely attached.

The results from one recent study of babies in low-income families contrast vividly with the usual findings in studies of attachment in middle-class babies born prematurely. Wille (1991) studied 18 babies in each of three groups: (1) full-term, (2) healthy prema-ture, and (3) ill premature. Babies in the third group required oxygen for more than 48 hours after birth or had intraventricular hemorrhages. In Strange Situations at 12 months, 15 of the 18 full-term babies (83 percent) were judged to be securely attached. Only 44 percent of the preterm babies were securely attached. In both the healthy preterm group and the ill preterm group, five babies (28 percent) were avoidant and five (28 percent) were resistant.

As a whole, the research on premature infants is inconclusive. It appears that, as attachment theorists expect, parents have great flexibility in selecting behavioral strategies and are often able to cope successfully with the special challenges involved in caring for a premature baby. It may be that premature birth increases the risk of anxious attachment only when it is associated with another risk factor, such as a lasting illness or economic stress. However, increasing use of the D category, which increases the validity of Strange Situation assessments, may change the picture.

Premature birth is not the only condition associated with difficult characteristics or medical needs that might increase the risk of anxious attachment. Goldberg, Simmons, Newman, Campbell, and Fowler (1991) observed 42 infants with congenital heart disease and 46 healthy infants in Strange Situations. Those with congenital heart disease were significantly less likely than the controls to have secure attachments to their mothers. Within the heart disease sample, the parents' reports of their own stress and psychological well-being did not help predict which babies would become securely attached.

Infant deafness constitutes another medical condition that might affect parent-child interactions and so might affect attachment patterns. Evidence so far suggests that it has no systematic effect on attachment. Lederberg and Mobley (1990) observed 41 hearing toddlers and 41 hearing-impaired toddlers (mean age for the sample, 22 months) with their hearing mothers in a 15-minute free play session in a laboratory playroom and, a week later, in the Strange Situation. During the play session, the hearing-impaired toddlers and their mothers spent less time interacting than the comparison dyads did. However, ratings of the mothers' affect, sensitivity, control, and teaching behavior were similar across the two groups. So were ratings of the toddlers' initiative, compliance, affect, attention spans, and pride in mastery. Hearing-impaired toddlers were as likely as hearing toddlers to be securely attached. They were not more difficult to classify and were not more likely to be classified in the D category. Regardless of hearing status, in comparison to anxiously attached toddlers, securely attached toddlers were happier, were more socially interactive and more compliant, had longer attention spans, and showed more pride in mastery.

INTENSITIES OF EFFECTS OF PARENT FACTORS AND INFANT FACTORS

The data discussed in Chapter 5 indicate that the parent's sensitive responsiveness to the baby has a significant influence on the baby's pattern of attachment but that sensitive responsiveness does not account for even half of the variance in security of attachment. People sometimes wonder about the comparative impact of parent factors and infant factors such as those discussed above in influencing attachment outcomes. One way to address the question is to look at extreme cases.

Curious about the relative impact of parent and child on attachment, Van IJzendoorn and his colleagues (1992) conducted a meta-analysis of data from 34 clinical studies on attachment and a similar analysis of data from 21 studies with low-risk North American samples. Samples of infants selected because of problems or risk factors in the mother (maltreatment, mental illness, alcohol abuse, drug exposure, adolescent motherhood) showed attachment pattern distributions that differed greatly from the distributions observed in low-risk samples. Anxious attachments were more common; and the D (anxious-disorganized-disoriented) and/or the A-C (avoidant-resistant) categories (when used), were much more common in the clinical samples (41 percent) than in the normal samples (15 percent). When the clinical sample was based on a child problem (such as premature birth, Down's syndrome, autism, or deafness), not a maternal problem, the distribution of attachment patterns was quite similar to the distributions observed in low-risk samples. Studies that used the D or A-C categories did find these categories to be more common in child-problem samples than in normal samples, but the resulting distribution was still much closer to a usual one than the distributions in mother-problem samples were. This suggests again that mothers are often able to make whatever adjustments are necessary to foster secure attachment in infants with special needs, but infants who must cope with deviant parental behavior tend to develop anxious, and often deviant, patterns of attachment behavior.

As noted above, this approach to gauging the relative impact of mother and child on security of attachment relies on extreme cases. Within the normal range, the relative impacts of the partners might differ. Each may also be influenced by the larger social context within which the dyad interacts.

THE SOCIAL NETWORK

As noted above, Crockenberg (1981) found evidence that the mother's social support network can make an important contribution to the quality of her baby's attachment to her. Specifically, mothers who reported receiving high levels of social support generally were able to handle their irritable babies well enough to foster secure attachments; mothers receiving little social support often were not. The social support available to the mother was also directly available to the baby in many cases. Grandparents, fathers, and older siblings were providing loving, responsive care for the babies, perhaps filling the gaps the mother might have left, and buffering the child from the negative effects the mother's intermittent unresponsiveness might otherwise have caused.

Does the mother's having some adult partner in the home increase the likelihood that her baby will be securely attached to her? Does the quality of the mother's relationship with her partner affect or help predict the infant's attachment security? Does support for the mother from other relatives and friends make much difference in the baby's life?

■ Presence of a Partner

One aspect of the social network that seems likely to have a great impact on the mother's ability to care well for her baby is whether she has a partner to help provide economic support and physical and emotional care for the family. Although the partner could be the mother's friend, relative, or lesbian lover, researchers usually look for a husband or boyfriend. In the disadvantaged Minneapolis sample as a whole (described in Chapter 5), the mere presence of a husband or boyfriend in the home did not contribute significantly to the likelihood of secure attachment to the mother at 12 months (Egeland and Farber, 1984). In this sample, the majority of babies in all living-arrangement groups ("living with," "not living with," and "no relationship") were securely attached. However, boys may have been affected by the presence of a father in the home. Most boys in two-parent intact families were securely attached to the mother; most boys living with single mothers were anxiously attached to them. A high percentage of the mothers who were involved with a man but not living with him had sons who were anxious-avoidant.

At least two interpretations of these results suggest themselves. Both interpretations are consistent with attachment theory, and the two are not mutually exclusive. One possibility is that the father's presence in the home helped the mother to provide better care for her son and so to foster a secure attachment. The second explanation is that a common factor—the mother's representational model of attachment relationships with males—underlaid both the mother's relationship with her adult male partner and the quality of care she gave her male child. Mothers with secure models would have an advantage both in maintaining lasting, positive bonds with their men and in providing sensitive care for their sons. An insecure representational model would increase the likelihood that the mother's relationships with men would be anxious and unstable, and it would interfere with her noticing and responding sensitively to her son's signals.

The fact that the father's presence in the home had an impact on sons but not on daughters suggests that the father's direct interaction with the baby may also have been a factor. There is reason to believe that fathers take more interest in their infant sons than in their infant daughters (Bornstein and Lamb, 1992). Fathers of sons, when present in the home, may have been more inclined than fathers of daughters to play with and even care for their babies, thus easing the mother's burden and enhancing her ability to provide good care. All this speculation, however, does not explain why most daughters were securely attached to their mothers, whether or not there was a father in the home. Perhaps many of the mothers had more ambivalence about males, including their sons, than about females, including their daughters.

The social ecology of the home environment, including the presence of a man and the quality of his relationship with the mother, was associated with infants' attachments in other interesting and sometimes complicated ways. For example, babies whose secure attachments at 12 months were still secure at 18 months were compared with babies whose attachment classifications changed from secure at 12 months to insecure at 18 months. Mothers of the babies who stayed secure were more likely to have resident partners than were mothers of babies who shifted from secure to anxious. In some families, the parents split up during the course of the study. Most of the mother-boyfriend relationships in these cases had been chaotic and disruptive, and many had been violent. The breakup improved the home situation. By 18 months, all of the boys whose parents had split up were securely attached to their mothers.

The results about the impact of the father on the baby's attachment to the mother in the Minneapolis sample are somewhat confusing and contradictory. If the D category had been available, the results might have been easier to interpret.

Working with a different sort of high-risk sample, depressed mothers, Radke-Yarrow et al. (1985) found that depression in the father did not increase the risk of anxious attachment to the mother. However, not having any male partner in the household did increase the risk of anxious attachment to the mother if she suffered from either bipolar disorder or major unipolar depression.

So far, main effects of single motherhood on infant attachment have been reported only in these two samples, one at risk because of the stresses associated with poverty, and the other at risk because of the mother's mental illness. Few other samples have included many single mothers. Aggregation of data from several samples for meta-analysis may later reveal a statistical association between single parenthood and increased risk of anxious attachment, either in high-risk samples or in the population at large. The critical question may not be whether a mother is married or whether she has a resident boyfriend, but whether she has any sort of resident partner to assist in caring for the baby. As noted above, the partner in child rearing might be any supportive relative or friend. A mother who must take care of a baby all by herself 24 hours a day every day is likely to have a difficult time, even if she does not have to earn a living at the same time.

■ Marriage Quality

Does the quality of a marriage (often labelled "marital adjustment") help predict the security of the infant's attachment to either parent? Does the amount or quality of support or assistance the father gives the mother affect how secure the baby will be? So far, it is hard to say.

Goldberg and Easterbrooks (1984) did find an association between security of attachment at 20 months and marital adjustment. When the latter was high, the toddlers were likely to be securely attached. When it was low, anxious attachments to one or both parents were more common. However, Levitt, Weber, and Clark (1986) found no relationship between security of the infant's attachment to the mother and the emotional and caretaking support she reported receiving from her husband.

In another such study, Lewis, Owen, and Cox (1988) rated marital quality during the second trimester of pregnancy and conducted Strange Situations at 12 months. Baby girls of mothers from highly competent marriages were more likely to be securely attached to their mothers than were baby girls from dysfunctional marriages. The same was not true for boys. For both sexes of children, there was a trend toward positive correlation of security of attachment to the father and the quality of the marriage, but the trend did not quite reach statistical significance.

Howes and Markman (1989) assessed qualities of 20 heterosexual relationships both before marriage and after the birth of the first child (3 to 5 years after the premarital assessment). Thirty-nine parents completed measures of marital satisfaction, conflict, and communication at each time period. When the children were 1 to 3 years old, each of the parents completed Attachment Q-set descriptions of them. Correlations between the mother's sort and the father's were significant and fairly high (mean $r = .54$), indicating both similarities and differences in the two parents' reports of a given child's behavior.

For mothers, high marital satisfaction, low conflict in the marriage, and high communication quality in the marriage, both before marriage and after the child's birth, were related to the child's security of attachment and dependency scores from the Attachment Q-set. The marriage variables were not related to sociability scores from the Q-set. The premarital measures of satisfaction, conflict, and communication in the adult-adult relationship had the same association with child Q-set variables as the postmarital measures did. For fathers, higher levels of premarital conflict and lower levels of communication quality were positively related to the child's dependency. Children of fathers who were relatively dissatisfied with their marriages tended to be dependent, while children of mothers who were relatively dissatisfied with their marriages tended to be insecure and unsociable (Howes and Markham, 1989).

Howes and Markham emphasized that the couple's communication skills and ability to manage conflict before marriage predicted the child's well-being almost as well as concurrent ratings of the marriage did. This suggests that the parents' abilities to handle negative affect have important effects not only on the quality of their marriage but also on their child's functioning.

In their comparison of Pennsylvania families (discussed earlier) Belsky and Isabella (1988) found no differences in marital adjustment between mothers of secure babies and mothers of anxious babies prior to the baby's birth or even in the first quarter of the baby's first year. In this sample, most mothers reported declines in positive activities and feelings and increases in negative activities and feelings in their marriages after their babies were born. However, marital adjustment at 9 months postpartum was no worse than at 3 months postpartum in the families in which infants developed secure attachments, but showed a further decline in the families in which babies developed anxious attachments.

When studies do find an association between marital adjustment and secure infant attachment, the direction of causality is seldom clear. Because all of the relevant research has used samples in which the mother was the primary caregiver for the baby, most of the explanations that can be offered have a sexist undertone. It may be that having a supportive husband enables a mother to provide better care for her child and so contributes to secure attachment. It may be that securely attached infants, being more cooperative, less fussy, less demanding, and less angry than anxiously attached infants, put less strain on a marriage. It may be that, because of underlying representational models, the same women who can trust and care for their husbands, thereby contributing to good marital adjustment, can care sensitively for their babies, thereby contributing to secure attachment. It may be that, when there is a baby in the home, the husband must provide emotional and/or physical support for the caregiving mother if good marital adjustment is to be maintained. Again, this list of possible explanations is not exhaustive, nor are the possibilities mutually exclusive.

Overall, the research on associations between marriage quality and infant attachment remains inconclusive. Babies of single mothers may or may not be at risk for anxious attachment. Positive marital adjustment is probably correlated with secure infant attachment, but the relationship between variables is not strong enough to show up consistently. (The opposite, an association between poor marital adjustment and secure infant attachment, has never been reported.) When the correlation is found, the reason for it is not clear.

■ The Larger Social Network

What about the influence of support from other relatives and friends? In the Crockenberg (1981) sample, it did not appear to matter whether social and material support for the mother came from the father, a grandparent, a friend, or even a child. Parents of secure babies in the Belsky and Isabella (1988) sample did report prenatally that they found their neighbors more friendly and helpful than parents of insecure babies did. However, there was no association between the infant's attachment classification and the mother's reports of frequency of supportive contacts with friends, neighbors, and other relatives during the first year. Belsky and Isabella (1988) concluded that frequency of contacts was a crude measure that overlooked the quality of support from the social network, as well as the possibility that contact with some of its members could increase stresses and difficulties for the mother.

Rutter (1985) cited evidence that the mother's satisfaction with her relationships, not the frequency of her social contacts or the number of people in her social network, is what supports good parenting even in difficult circumstances. Of course, the quality of those relationships may reflect the subject's interpersonal skills and representational models, not just the availability of supportive people among relatives and neighbors.

What happens when researchers directly manipulate social support for the mother? Jacobson and Frye (1991) studied 46 mothers and their firstborn infants. Each family was receiving WIC (Women, Infants, and Children) food supplements, which indicates that their incomes were low. The mothers were randomly assigned to experimental and control conditions. At the beginning of the study, the two groups did not differ on perceived social support, as indexed by the number of people in their social networks. Most of the mothers were rather isolated, with less access to or contact with neighbors, community groups, professionals, or even a telephone than most people want. Female volunteers who were trained to provide support and information for mothers met with the mothers in the experimental group during their pregnancies and during the first year postpartum.

When the babies were 14 months old, one of three observers visited the mother and baby at home for 3 to 4 hours and then used the Attachment Q-set to describe the baby's behavior. The usual correlation with the expert criterion sort for the hypothetically "most secure child" was calculated as one security score. In addition, the investigators calculated an "attachment ratings score" based on the 21 Q-sort items intended to index response to comforting, differential responsiveness to the attachment figure, and attachment-exploration balance. Babies from the experimental group were rated as significantly more secure than babies in the control group on the attachment ratings score but did not differ from controls on the usual criterion-sort security score. The study thus provided equivocal evidence that giving social support to low-income mothers increases the degree of security in their babies' attachments to them, even when there is no reason to think the mothers will have any unusual difficulty in giving good care to their babies. Compared to the usual security score, the attachment ratings score was at least as sensitive to variations in maternal affect, perceived support, and the HOME (Caldwell and Bradley, 1979), a well-validated measure of the quality of stimulation provided in the home. This suggests that the alternative way of analyzing data from the Attachment Q-set might be useful in other studies, too.

As in the case of marital quality, broader social support appears to have some association with secure attachment, but not a strong enough influence to show up in every study. Subjective evaluations of the *quality* of emotional and practical support appear to be much more useful than *quantitative* measures of numbers of friends and relatives or frequency of contact with them. The opposite of the expected association has never been reported; no one finds that low social support is associated with secure attachment. When a correlation between social support and secure attachment is found, the reasons for it are not always clear. Nevertheless, it seems likely that positive social support for the primary caregiver contributes to secure attachment. In the correlational study that most clearly showed a relationship between social support and infant attachment (Crockenberg, 1981), the support was not just friendship. It often included direct, practical assistance in caring for the baby.

NEXT STEPS IN RESEARCH

At least two improvements in methodology are warranted on the basis of what we have learned so far. First, we need to use the rather recently defined anxious-disorganized-disoriented (Group D) category in all new studies. Where possible, we should reanalyze data from old studies after recoding Strange Situation tapes with the D category available to rectify earlier (inevitable) misclassification of some attachments.

Second, we need to visit babies more often and for longer periods, so that the naturalistic observations will include closer approximations of the interactions occurring in the absence of an observer. We need a full-scale replication of the Baltimore study, guided this time by the hypotheses that emerged from that study, and expanded to include variables that other research suggests may also be important, such as infant temperament and quality of social support for the primary caregiver. In addition, we need improved measures of temperament, marital quality, social support, and other variables of interest.

Third, an increase in the number of controlled experiments now seems desirable. In one study, the investigator (van den Boom, 1990) directly manipulated sensitive responsiveness and found that brief, individualized training in it produced a huge effect. In another study, a direct manipulation of social support produced a clear effect (Jacobson and Frye, 1991). Ethological observations are necessary and wonderful, but there is also a place for experiments. Two or three well-designed experimental tests of the impact of a specific factor can demonstrate a causal relationship more convincingly than converging findings from 10 correlational studies.

BLAMING THE VICTIM:
A POLEMICAL INTERLUDE

The research to date leads me to believe that, when a baby develops an anxious attachment rather than a secure one, the explanation usually lies more in the caregiver's behavior than in the baby's characteristics. This conclusion raises the risk that readers may be inclined, inappropriately, to blame the parent or other caregiver for the baby's difficulties. Much more often than not, I think, this would be an example of "blaming the victim." Because most of this book takes a scientific perspective, it is important to say here that this section is based on unsystematic observations, not on systematic research. My clinical experience persuades me that these unscientific observations warrant inclusion here.

Although I cannot cite research to support my conviction, I am persuaded that most parents try to nurture and raise their children well. Often, known or unacknowledged psychological wounds from their own childhood experiences interfere with their abilities to foster secure attachments in their offspring. Too often, current circumstances impair their abilities to care for their children well.

Consider the case of Janie and Arthur. Janie was born 10 months after her young parents' marriage, which both sets of Janie's grandparents had opposed. Arthur was born 18 months later, despite the couple's use of a birth control method that is 90 percent effective. The mother stayed home to care for the two children. Three weeks before Arthur's birth, his father lost his construction job. He couldn't find steady employment for the next 2 years. The mother got a part-time job in a local restaurant, but the father, whose own father had been quite distant from his children, just didn't know what to do when his babies cried, fought, pulled all the books off the bookshelf, spilled lunch all over the floor, or resisted falling asleep at nap time. There was never enough money in the household, the parents fought a lot, the husband was depressed about his failure as an economic provider, and the wife felt increasingly isolated and emotionally depleted. Relatives offered almost no help.

Janie and Arthur couldn't read their parents' minds. They were, in fact, too young to understand that their parents—or they themselves—had minds. They had no way of knowing that their parents loved them deeply but were preoccupied with financial worries and marital distress. What they did know was that their signals were ineffective and their needs unmet. Janie, who had experienced adequate care from her mother during her early months, became anxious-resistant as the family circumstances deteriorated. Her attachment to her father was avoidant. Born into a distressed family and raised by parents who felt increasingly overwhelmed and inadequate, Arthur developed avoidant attachments to both parents. The children's nonoptimal patterns of attachment resulted from the quality of care they experienced, not from any defects they brought into the world, but condemning the parents for failing to provide better care would make no sense at all.

The difficulties faced by the family in this example are not unusual. Some families, including many headed by single parents, struggle to provide good care for their children in circumstances worse than those surrounding Janie and Arthur. American middle-class society tends to blame, and even to punish, families that are not self-sufficient. Pressures about whether a mother should stay home to care for her baby herself or should get out and contribute to the family's income vary greatly in the various subsystems of American society. When I say that research shows that caregivers influence infants' attachment outcomes more than the infants themselves do, my purpose is not to add to the burden of blame and guilt too many parents already carry. Instead of blaming parents for their children's insecurities, our society could encourage the development of strong systems of emotional and practical support for parents of young children. Paired with effective encouragement of thoughtful family planning, generous social and material support for parents of young children would be a wise investment in America's future.

CHAPTER SUMMARY

Within the normal range of parent behavior, insensitive caregiving is the only variable that has consistently been demonstrated to predict anxious attachment. Major affective disorders in the caregivers increase the risk of anxious attachment, presumably because they increase the risk of inadequate caregiving. Whether some specific personality disorders also increase the risk of anxious attachment has never been tested. Within the normal range and with the personality measures currently available to researchers, no associations between maternal personality variables and infant attachment outcomes have consistently emerged.

The available evidence supports the view that the mother's use of alcohol, PCP, and other psychoactive substances also increases the risk of anxious attachment. However, it is not clear how much of the risk stems from long-lasting physiological effects on the baby and how much stems from deficiencies in maternal care that are correlated with substance abuse.

Within the normal range, infant characteristics appear to have less impact on attachment security than caregiver variables have. An extensive search for associations between infant temperament variables and attachment outcomes yielded several useful hypotheses, a mixed array of evidence, and some very good thinking about how both temperament traits and attachment patterns develop. There is increasing agreement that heritable differences in irritability, soothability, sociability, fearfulness, or other behavioral tendencies can affect the tone of parent-infant interactions and may, in combination with other factors, influence either (1) security of attachment or (2) whether the attachment pattern is proximal or distal.

Research about whether premature birth increases the risk of anxious attachment is inconclusive. Early studies of healthy preterm babies in comfortable economic circumstances found distributions of attachment patterns very similar to those found in low-risk samples of full-term babies. However, these studies did not use the D category. The available evidence (of which there is only a little) suggests that premature babies who are sick or are born into families with low incomes develop anxious attachments more often than babies in low-risk circumstances do. Increasing use of the D (insecure-disorganized-disoriented) category may reveal that, even in the absence of other risk factors, premature birth is a risk factor.

A variety of hypotheses about effects of the social network on infant attachment outcomes have been offered. In low-risk samples, whether the mother's having some partner to help her care and/or provide for her family affects security of infant-mother attachment has not been tested. In the Minneapolis poverty sample, findings about correlates of having a husband or boyfriend in the home were somewhat confusing, and differed according to the gender of the child. In a sample of mothers with mental illnesses, the presence of a male partner in the home was associated with a decreased risk of anxious attachment.

Some but not all studies of low-risk samples have found an association between positive or high quality marital adjustment and secure infant attachment. When the correlation is found, several different, mutually compatible explanations for it are available.

When researchers look beyond the mother's husband or boyfriend to the larger social network, they find that, if there is a risk that the mother will have difficulty giving good care to her baby, the support she gets from relatives and/or friends can make a critical difference. Neither the number of people in the mother's social network nor the frequency of contacts with them helps to predict infant attachment outcomes. The mother's subjective evaluation of how supportive her network is does.

Real poverty is associated with unusually high frequencies of anxious attachment to the mother. The mother's being very young may also be a risk factor. With those two exceptions, demographic variables seem to be of little or no importance in determining infant attachment patterns. Frequencies of secure, avoidant, and resistant attachments to mothers appear to be quite similar in middle-class and working-class samples. The gender and birth order of the baby do not generally seem to affect the likelihood of secure attachment.

Whether the various risk factors affect attachment outcomes (1) because they influence or help predict the primary caregiver's sensitive responsiveness to the baby or (2) for some other reason is not clear. In many cases, the presence of a single risk factor, such as an unstable living situation or infant irritability, seems to have little effect on attachment outcomes, but the co-occurrence of two or more risk factors greatly increases frequencies of anxious attachment. To learn more about the relative influences of the various factors that may affect attachment outcomes, we need to make some improvements in methodology. First, the D category should be used in all new Strange Situation studies. Second, we need to make naturalistic observations of infants longer and more often; just two or three glimpses at interaction sometime in the first year do not tell us enough. Third, we need improved measures of temperament, marriage quality, and social support. Fourth, we need some well-designed experiments to test whether relations between variables are causal or merely correlational.

7

EARLY CORRELATES
AND SEQUELAE OF
ATTACHMENT PATTERNS

In the preceding chapter, I reviewed hypotheses and data about the factors that influence a baby to develop one pattern of attachment behavior rather than another. This chapter is about the early correlates and sequelae of infants' attachment patterns. I have chosen the terms "correlates" and "sequelae" carefully, to emphasize that inferences about causality often rest on shaky ground. Even where data justify confidence that some set of character-istics or behaviors appears more often among children who were securely attached in infancy, we seldom have evidence that the characteristics or behaviors were directly *caused* by the child's secure attachment. They may be other effects of the factors that produced secure attachment, or they may be correlated with secure attachment for some other reason.

Most of the discussions in this chapter are restricted to correlates and sequelae of infant attachment patterns in toddlers and preschoolers. Later correlates and sequelae of infant patterns will be discussed in Chapter 15.

STABILITY OF ATTACHMENT
PATTERNS IN INFANCY

Before we can consider what other variables or later outcomes are associated with, caused by, or predicted by early attachment patterns, we need to know whether early attachment patterns show enough stability to be likely to predict anything. Do patterns of attachment, once formed, tend to persist? If so, why? How early in life do representational models begin to guide attention and behavior in ways that make the models resistant to change?

■ Pattern Stability in Middle-Class Families

In stable middle-class homes, most studies find very high stability of attachment patterns in infancy. For example, Connell (1976) found 81 percent stability of attachment to the mother over a 6-month period. That is, 81 percent of the infants in the sample were classified the same way (group A, B, or C) at 12 months and at 18 months. Waters (1978) found even more impressive pattern consistency. He assessed 50 middle-class babies in the Strange Situation with their mothers at 12 months and again at 18 months and found that 48 of them (96 percent) had the same major group classification (A, B, or C) at each session. Main and Weston (1981) reported that 13 of 15 babies (87 percent) assessed with their fathers in the Strange Situation showed the same attachment pattern at 20 months as at 12 months.

Given that there is at least a little measurement error with almost any assessment procedure, these rates of stability in independently coded assessments are almost astonishing. In most of the families in these early studies, the mother was the primary caregiver and the father had a full-time job.

One study of a middle-class sample (Thompson, Lamb, and Estes, 1982) found only 53 percent stability in Strange Situation classifications (using groups A, B, and C) over 6 months. That anomaly has never been replicated. The norm for middle-class samples remains about 80 percent stability; that outcome has been replicated several times. Changes in attachment classification in the Thompson et al. (1982) sample were associated with maternal employment and the onset of regular nonmaternal care. When the mother was employed, changes from anxious to secure attachment were about as frequent as changes from secure to anxious attachment. Data about how long the mother worked each week and how long she had been working before the Strange Situation assessment were not gathered. There was also a possibility that the father's loss of a job was associated with the mother's acquisition of one.

With or without a concomitant change in the father's employment status, the "social ecology" of the family could be expected to change quite a bit with a change in the mother's employment status. Recently, Marvin and Stewart (1990) have proposed that transitional periods of instability in infants' attachments can reasonably be expected when the family undergoes a "normal crisis," such as the birth of a new baby. The parent's change in job status might also prompt changes in the parents' roles, accessibility, and responsiveness. After the family situation restabilizes, infants' attachments might revert to what they had been or might reflect substantial reorganization in response to changed patterns of interaction. Transitional disorganization and reorganization may have been factors in the unusually low attachment pattern stability in the Thompson et al. (1982) study.

Addressing the question of whether the mother's employment status affected the stability of the infant's attachment patterns, Owen, Easterbrooks, Chase-Lansdale, and Goldberg (1984) found one result that was even harder to explain: a change in the mother's employment status was associated with a decrease in the stability of the pattern of attachment to the father but did not decrease the stability of the pattern of attachment to the mother. The subjects, middle-class firstborns, participated in the Strange Situation with one parent when they were 12 months old and with the other parent 3 to 6 weeks later. At 20 months old, the subjects returned for another Strange Situation assessment with one of their parents and, 3 to 6 weeks later, a Strange Situation with the other. Some mothers did acquire or leave jobs during the course of the study, but, in each case, the mother's employment status had been stable for some months before each assessment, so the transient changes in attachment patterns could not have confounded the data.

In this study, 59 babies completed both Strange Situations with the mother; 78 percent of them were in the same attachment category (A, B, or C) at each visit. Fifty-three of the fathers came for two separate Strange Situations; 62 percent of their babies were in the same attachment category at each visit. Infants' attachments to their mothers were actually more stable when the mother increased or decreased her work hours than when her job status (full-time, part-time, or unemployed) was stable.

However, stability of attachment to the father was significantly lower for the group in which the mother's job status changed in any way between 12 and 20 months ($N = 13$) than for the groups in which the mother's job status was stable. In response to evidence that, in their sample, stability of the infant's attachment pattern was highest for the mother and lowest for the father when the mother changed job status, Owen et al. (1984) offered the interpretation that these middle-class mothers planned carefully for the family life changes that would result from their job changes, while the fathers did not prepare themselves as well for changes in their roles, routines, and responsibilities.

None of the studies mentioned above used the D category. How using it will affect our understanding of the degree of stability in attachment patterns and the reasons for stability and for change remains to be seen.

Does the high stability in infants' attachment patterns over a period of 6 to 8 months, as evidenced above, stem from stability in the attachment figure's contribution to their interactions, or from a tendency for the infant's pattern to maintain itself even when circumstances and interactions begin to change? In the absence of observations of interaction patterns both before the first Strange Situation and between the first and the second, it is not possible to say. Naturalistic observations before, during, and after changes that seem likely to affect patterns of interaction would be especially informative. So far, such data are not available.

■ Pattern Stability in High-Risk Samples

We do have evidence that, when living situations are persistently unstable, infant attachment patterns are also less stable than in the generally stable middle-class samples described above. Using Strange Situation classifications of 189 babies from the Minneapolis poverty sample at both 12 and 18 months, Egeland and Farber (1984) found only 60 percent stability of major category (A, B, or C). There was evidence that secure attachments were more stable than anxious attachments: 74 percent of the secure babies remained secure, 45 percent of the avoidant babies remained avoidant, and 37 percent of the resistant babies remained resistant.

The data available in this study offer some hints and possible explanations about why some infants retained their patterns of attachment and why other infants changed theirs. Babies who changed from secure to anxious attachment tended to have mothers who had higher prenatal and postnatal scores on aggressiveness and suspiciousness and lower prenatal scores on giving socially desirable responses than mothers whose babies remained securely attached. They also had less education. Mothers whose babies changed from secure to resistant experienced an increase in life stress in the 6 months between assessments. Seventy percent of them were single mothers who were not living with their boyfriends. The rest of them were single parents for the first 6 months of the baby's life but married or had a boyfriend move in before the baby's first birthday. Perhaps coping with the adjustments of including a new family member was as difficult for this group as coping with the difficulties of caring for a baby alone.

Mothers whose babies remained securely attached reported a decrease in life stress during the 6 months between Strange Situations. All but 15 percent of them had resident husbands or boyfriends. Changes from insecure to secure attachment often reflected growth and increasing competence of young mothers. In short, both the frequency and the direction of changes in attachment patterns in this high-risk sample were interpretable. However, they were not predicted, so the proposed explanations require systematic testing in other samples. Including the D category is likely to provide more valid findings, and more accurate information about rates of stability, and so to lead us to better explanations for stability and change.

In a sample of infants known to have suffered serious abuse or neglect, stability of attachment patterns was even lower than it was in the Minneapolis sample. In this sample, stability of A-B-C classifications was only 47 percent (Egeland and Sroufe, 1981). That figure is difficult to interpret, because the D category was not available at the time. Anxious-disorganized-disoriented attachments might, particularly in the context of maltreatment, be quite stable.

PREDICTIONS FROM THEORY

What outcomes should follow from secure attachment in infancy? Why? If Isaac shows a secure pattern of attachment to each of his parents at 12 months while Igor has avoidant attachments to each of his parents at the same age, how should we expect them to differ 1 year or 2 years or 4 years later?

As described in Chapter 2, attachment theorists have proposed that a child whose caregiver is insensitive is likely to develop an image of himself as unworthy, perhaps even unlovable. He is not likely to expect others to treat him well, and his interpersonal strategies are likely to be constrained and maladaptive. He may be delayed in learning the communication skills that would lead to harmonious, satisfying interactions with a more responsive partner. In severe cases, he may even be at risk for behavior problems.

In contrast, a child who has received sensitive care and developed secure attachments knows that he is lovable and worthy of love. He knows this at the deep level of inner awareness that develops before language. He is free to learn and grow by exploring his physical and social environment and his own emerging abilities. His natural expectation is that others will treat him well. His self-image and social skills are likely to be positive; his behavior is likely to be flexible, readily adapted to the situations he finds himself in and the social partners available.

Attachment theorists certainly expect security of attachment in infancy to affect social behavior in other, later relationships, especially in intimate relationships. Should it also affect anything else, such as developing physical and cognitive skills? As noted earlier, some have thought so. The argument is that, having a secure base from which to explore, the securely attached infant or child can learn more or faster, and is likely to be ahead of her insecurely attached peers in skills such as talking, hopping on one foot, counting to 20, bouncing a ball, or persuading a playmate to trade sandwiches or to play the game of the secure child's choosing.

Although the explanations for associations between infant attachment and later cognitive, affective, and behavioral outcomes are often unclear, some of the associations have been demonstrated very convincingly. Many studies have included measures both of cognitive development and of interpersonal behavior with adults and/or peers. For the most part, I have attempted to group them in this chapter according to the major focus of the study.

DEVELOPMENTS IN FAMILY RELATIONSHIPS

After the age of 12 months, what is the natural course of development of the relationship between a securely attached child and his primary attachment figure? How does it differ from that between an anxiously attached child and her primary attachment figure? Several investigators (e.g., Londerville and Main, 1981; Matas et al., 1978; Waters, Wippman, and Sroufe, 1979) have brought toddlers back to the laboratory for a variety of assessments some months after Strange Situations conducted in infancy. Those who were securely attached in infancy often appear to carry advantages into the toddler and preschool years. Because the results from the various studies were all very consistent with each other, I am not providing a long list of methodological details and specific citations here.

In response to separation from the parent in an unfamiliar place, securely attached infants often show distress. At age 2, many of them are still distressed by such separations. However, in the presence of the parent, they show more autonomy and social confidence than toddlers with anxious attachment histories show. They show more flexibility and more persistence in their efforts to handle a frustrating task, but they are also more likely to ask for help from their mothers if the task is too difficult for them. Like toddlers with anxious histories, securely attached toddlers show rather high rates of noncompliance with parental requests. However, securely attached toddlers are more likely to be cooperative and affectionate with their mothers than other toddlers are.

Unfortunately, most of these ideas about developments in attachments in the second year of life, when autonomy and discipline are big issues for many children and parents, are based on two or three glimpses at a dyad's behavior. Sometimes the brief observations occur in a standardized situation in a laboratory, and sometimes they occur in the home, but surprisingly few studies have more than 3 or 4 hours of any sort of observations of a toddler's behavior. To the best of my knowledge, no one has yet attempted the study that is, from an ethological perspective, the obvious next step: an extension of Ainsworth's Baltimore methodology through the second year of life. Such a study would provide data that would constitute a huge contribution to the field. Standardized laboratory assessments

when the children were 2 years old could then be tied to well-info᷍
experiences had brought the infants to their strategies and feelings a

As stated earlier, in Strange Situation assessments, avoidant infa᷍
appear to be most autonomous. This remains the case in laboratory
months: they separate from their attachment figures easily and witho᷍
them are friendly to strangers, and they readily explore their surroundin᷍ ᵔᵒ᷍ However, compared to secure toddlers, they ignore their mothers more, smile at them less, and get lower
scores for quality of affective sharing with the mother. They direct more anger, aggression,
and noncompliance toward their mothers. They do not use their mothers effectively for
help with difficult tasks.

Which outcomes are most desirable? What sets of strengths and associated limitations will best serve a developing child? People of different cultures; people in different
family, societal, and economic situations; and people with different attachment histories
will give different answers to those questions. The consensus among attachment theorists,
well-stated by Lyons-Ruth (1991), is that desirable strengths in the toddler years include
an ability to express affection unambivalently, an ability to use the parent as a source of
help and guidance, an ability to seek comforting contact vigorously when under stress, and
an ability to initiate activities in pursuit of the child's own goals and to oppose the parent
without fear of rejection. It is the balance of attachment behavior and exploratory behavior that matters, not independence or closeness alone. When all is going well in a toddler's
development, the child is learning to integrate her initiatives into the flow of social behavior while maintaining a warm connection to the parent or other caregiver. Lyons-Ruth
(1991) proposed that "assertive relatedness," not "autonomy," describes adaptive behavior
in toddlerhood well. Researchers observe assertive relatedness more often in young children with histories of secure attachment than in young children with histories of anxious
attachment.

INTERACTIONS WITH TEACHERS

Among the variables that are, according to theory, likely to be affected by the early
attachment pattern are (1) the child's basic trust, (2) the child's capabilities and tendencies
in social interaction, (3) the child's openness to involving himself in new relationships,
rather than being preoccupied with anxieties in the primary attachment relationship, and
(4) the child's ability to adapt his behavior flexibly to the various partners and circumstances he experiences. Consequently, we might expect to find a significant effect of early
attachment patterns in lasting relationships with new adults or children.

With similar expectations, the research team studying the Minneapolis poverty sample
invited children who had shown stable attachment patterns in infancy to attend a special
nursery school program when they were 4 to 5 years old (Sroufe, Fox, and Pancake, 1983).
Forty children attended. Sroufe et al. used a variety of measures to assess *over*dependency in
the preschool: observer ratings, teacher ratings, teacher Q-sorts, frequency of sitting in the
teacher's lap at circle time, and contact initiations. The results were dramatic.

Children who had been anxiously attached in infancy, including those who showed
avoidance and might appear to an uneducated observer to be showing precocious indepen-

In preschool, children with anxious attachments to their mothers shows more dependency on the teacher than secure children show.

dence in the Strange Situation, were much more dependent than the secure children were on every measure. They required comparatively high levels of contact, guidance, and discipline. Among the preschoolers who had had resistant attachments in infancy, the high levels of attention-seeking behavior were mixed with observable neediness, tenseness, impulsivity, frustration, passivity, and helplessness.

Even though children with secure attachment histories were less dependent on their teachers than the other children were, the secure children were more likely to call on the teacher when doing so was clearly appropriate and advantageous—that is, when they faced challenges they could not manage alone. Avoidant children were less likely to do so.

The teachers reacted differently to children with different attachment histories. Without knowing the children's histories, the teachers demanded more mature behavior from those who had been securely attached than from others. They showed higher and more positive expectations of the secure children, and showed less tendency to control them.

RELATIONS WITH PEERS

Does the quality of attachment in infancy help predict how a child will interact with peers in the ensuing months and years? Clearly, yes. From infancy onward, studies using concurrent and longitudinal measures have found correlations between a secure attachment history and positive skills with peers and responses from peers. The relevant studies have used a wide variety of outcome measures and a variety of methods for assessing attachments: Strange Situations, the Attachment Q-set, and assorted separation-reunion procedures. Despite this methodological diversity, the results of the studies converge easily. Securely attached infants and toddlers interact with peers more than anxiously attached children do (Pierrehumbert, Iannotti, and Cummings, 1985; Pierrehumbert, Iannotti, Cummings, and Zahn-Waxler, 1989; Vandell, Owen, Wilson, and Henderson, 1988). In addition, infants and preschoolers with secure attachment histories show more advanced and more positive social skills with peers and elicit more positive responses from peers.

Based on Strange Situation behavior at the age of 18 months, Jacobson and Wille (1986) selected eight secure, eight avoidant, and eight resistant focal children. Each focal child was then paired with an unfamiliar securely attached playmate of the same age for observation in play sessions from age 2 to age 3. In this small sample, the hypothesis that attachment patterns would predict differences in the focal children's sociability or responsiveness to peers was not supported. However, the initial differences in attachment patterns did account for variations in how the (secure) peers responded to the focal children. By age 3, the secure focal children were receiving the greatest number of positive responses. Among the anxiously attached children, the resistant ones were receiving more positive responses than the avoidant ones, but they were also receiving more disruptive responses, more agonistic initiations, and more resistance from their playmates. These mixed responses were likely to perpetuate their ambivalent feelings and expectations about relationships in a new category of relationships: the peers were playmates, not attachment figures. This is an exciting piece of evidence about how early attachment patterns may instigate chains of interactions that influence social relations long after infancy.

Based on observations in nursery schools or day care centers, several studies (e.g., Arend, Gove, and Sroufe, 1979; Waters, Wippman, and Sroufe, 1979) have found preschoolers with secure attachment histories to show more competence than children with anxious attachment histories show in interactions with peers. Analyzing data from the Minneapolis poverty sample, Sroufe (1983) found that, compared to children with anxious attachment histories, children who had been securely attached in infancy were more affectively positive toward others: they were ranked higher on social competence, number of friends, popularity with peers, compliance, and empathy. Sroufe (1983) also found different types of subclinical behavior problems associated with the two major categories of anxious attachment. In preschool, the group C children were more disorganized than the other groups and group A children were more devious.

Similar results have been observed in low-risk samples. Among children in day care in California, securely attached children showed higher levels of social pretend play with peers and showed less conflict during play (Howes and Rodning, 1992). In Germany, Grossmann and Grossmann (1991) found that peers included children with secure attachment histories in group activities more readily than they included children with insecure attachment histories.

Additional evidence of social advantages for securely attached children comes from a study of preschoolers playing with their best friends (Park and Waters, 1989). Forty children who were 3½ or just barely 4 years old were selected as the first set of subjects. Their mothers listed the two best friends of each of those children. Each mother then completed a revised version of the Attachment Q-set. Each pair of friends was observed for one hour of free play in a laboratory. A female experimenter was present but intervened only if a child did something dangerous or became distressed. Secure-secure pairs were more harmonious, less controlling, more responsive, and happier than pairs that included one insecurely attached child. A year later, at age 5, 18 of the same pairs of white, middle-class friends were again videotaped during one hour of free play (Kerns, 1994). Again, the 10 secure-secure dyads showed more positive social interaction, harmony, and responsiveness and less negative control of each other than the eight dyads that included one child with an insecure attachment to the mother showed. In addition, at age 5, the secure-secure friends were better at maintaining coordinated interaction sequences than the secure-insecure dyads were.

Troy and Sroufe (1987) studied pairs of preschoolers from the Minneapolis high-risk sample playing with each other. These pairs were not necessarily good friends. After the children had been in nursery school for at least 6 weeks, the experimenters assigned them to same-gender pairs so that all possible combinations of attachment histories would be represented in the pairings. The subjects, now 4 to 5 years old, had participated in Strange Situations at 12 and 18 months of age.

An adult aide was present during the sessions but interacted with the children only to stop potentially dangerous or destructive actions and to prevent the children from leaving the room. The dyads were rated for the presence or absence of a pattern of victimization in their interaction. *Victimization* was defined as a relationship characterized by a sustained pattern of exploitation and manipulation.

Coders could reliably identify victimization, and it was clearly associated with attachment history. In the nine dyads that included a securely attached child, victimization never occurred. Children with secure attachment histories were neither victims nor bullies. In contrast, all five pairs in which an avoidant child was paired with an avoidant or resistant child showed victimization. (Only one dyad had two children who both had resistant attachment histories. Neither child persistently victimized the other in that pair.)

As described in this study, victimization always went beyond control of resources; it included verbal hostility, physical aggression, or both. Victims often played active roles in perpetuating their victimization. With histories of physical abuse, rejection, or emotional unavailability from their mothers, avoidant children were found to be victims as well as victimizers. Troy and Sroufe (1987) interpreted this to mean that these children could organize their behavior with peers either around their anger, making them victimizers, or around their sense of unworthiness, making them victims.

The early relationships of children with resistant attachments were marked by disorganization, inconsistency, and unmet needs. The children remained motivated to make contact but were not skilled at forming smooth relationships. Like their caregivers, they kept trying, and so were easily victimized. With early relationships characterized by consistency, warmth, and respect, the securely attached children were not motivated to victimize others and were able to fend off aggression or withdraw from interaction with potential victimizers.

Although the weight of evidence is clear, some studies fail to find that children with histories of anxious attachment show less desirable social behavior than secure children show. For example, Fagot and Kavanaugh (1990) studied 81 white children of varied socioeconomic status who, at 18 months, had been unequivocally classified as secure (B1, B2, or B3, but not B4) or avoidant. Using several methods, the children's parents reported on problem behaviors at 24, 27, 30, and 48 months. At 18 and 30 months, researchers observed the children both at home with their families and in play groups. The only significant effect of attachment category was that teachers and observers of the play group said avoidant girls were more difficult to deal with and had more difficulty with peers than secure girls did. That is, of course, the sort of difference that people usually find, but it showed up in this sample only for girls, not for boys; only in play groups, not in family observations; and only at 30 and 48 months, not at 24 or 27 months. Neither parent reports nor home observations revealed any significant difference between the groups.

Despite this exception, there is great consistency in most studies of attachment and peer relations. As infants, toddlers, or preschoolers, children who were securely attached to their mothers in infancy interact with peers more often than anxiously attached children do; during the preschool years, they show more competence and less conflict in interaction with peers, interact more positively, and are unlikely to be either bullies or victims.

COGNITIVE DEVELOPMENT

Are securely attached children more advanced cognitively than anxiously attached children? Having a reliable secure base may enable the child to involve himself more attentively and for longer periods in exploring his environment, and learning about it. In addition, mothers who are sensitive to a child's attachment signals may also be sensitive and responsive to their child's developing cognitive interests and abilities. However, it is also possible that early cognitive development is highly *canalized.* That is, the biologically based tendency to exercise and expand physical and cognitive abilities may be so powerful in infancy that any normal environment will support good cognitive development. A secure attachment cannot give much of a boost to something that will surely happen anyway. According to this viewpoint, only a severely depriving or anxiety-provoking environment would prevent the child from having sufficient opportunities to practice and expand cognitive abilities.

What do the data say? Most studies (e.g., Egeland and Farber, 1984; Pastor, 1981; Waters, Wippman, and Sroufe, 1979) have not found differences between securely attached and anxiously attached infants on developmental quotients. A *developmental quotient,* or DQ, is a summary measure of an infant's scores on scales of early mental and motor abilities. It is somewhat analogous to an IQ score, or "intelligence quotient," but DQs, unless they are very low or very high, do not predict much about the child's later IQ. They simply measure the child's current status.

As the examples below will show, several studies have found that secure children show advanced cognitive abilities somewhat earlier or more often than anxiously attached children do. However, this tendency is not strong enough to make differences appear in all studies or even on all the cognitive measures within a study. In the Baltimore study, the group B babies got higher scores than the other babies on the Griffiths Scale of

Infant Intelligence, but the difference was not statistically significant (Ainsworth et al., 1978).

When a group difference in cognitive abilities does emerge, the group with lower scores is sometimes the whole group of anxiously attached children, sometimes just the group C children, and sometimes just the group A children. For example, Harmon, Suwalsky, and Klein (1979) found that avoidant infants spent the most time playing with objects, but they played in ways that were less advanced than those of other babies the same age.

Whether researchers find differences between attachment groups in cognitive development may depend on what they measure and on when and how they measure it. Pipp, Easterbrooks, and Harmon (1992) used Strange Situation assessments, including the D category, with age-appropriate modifications for scoring behaviors, to classify forty 12-month-olds, forty-three 24-month-olds, and thirty-nine 36-month-olds as securely or anxiously attached to the mother. They found that the two groups of 12-month-olds showed similar abilities to point to someone's nose, point to a named person, and find some correct way to answer simple questions that began with "where," "who," or "whose." Secure two-year-olds, however, gave correct answers to the same questions and additional questions about gender more often than anxiously attached two-year-olds did, and the difference between secure and anxious children was even greater in three-year-olds. At all three ages, children with secure attachments acted on themselves and on the mother with greater complexity than insecurely attached children did.

Even in the absence of differences in cognitive abilities, many studies have found differences between secure and anxious children in how they pursue challenging cognitive tasks. Differences in socioemotional variables that affect cognitive performance, such as persistence and cooperation, emerge more often than differences in cognitive achievement do.

Working with a middle-class sample, Matas, Arend, and Sroufe (1978) used Strange Situation assessments at 18 months and then gave the same subjects challenging tool problems and observed them at play and during a clean-up period at 2 years old. The secure children were more enthusiastic, persistent, cooperative, and effective in solving the problems than their anxiously attached peers were. They showed less frustration, less negative affect, less crying or whining, and less aggression toward the mother. Mothers were available to help, and the mothers of the securely attached subjects were better helpers.

The two groups also differed on one measure of cognitive development: the secure children showed more symbolic play than the anxious children did. *Symbolic play,* or pretending, is one marker of the transition from Piaget's first stage, sensorimotor intelligence, to his second stage, preoperational intelligence. On a standardized DQ measure, however, there was no significant difference between the secure group and the anxiously attached group.

Slade (1987) observed 15 toddlers in the Strange Situation at 16½ to 18 months of age. Seven were securely attached and eight were anxiously attached. Afterwards, the subjects were videotaped during free play sessions at regular intervals from 20 to 28 months of age. The secure babies showed more high-level symbolic play than their anxious peers. When the mother participated actively in the child's play, the secure children showed higher-level play and longer episodes of it than they showed on their own. The mother's involvement did not facilitate similar advances in the play of anxiously attached toddlers.

As a set, these results suggest that secure toddlers move into representational thought earlier than anxious toddlers do because group B mothers support advances in cognitive development through direct, well-tuned interaction, not because the secure babies have more energy for exploring and experimenting with objects in their environments.

In a sample in which 12 of the 38 subjects (32 percent) changed Strange Situation classifications between 12 months and 20 months, Frodi, Bridges, and Grolnick (1985) tested some specific hypotheses about relations between the mother's control style, the infant's attachment classification, and the child's mastery-related behavior. They presented the children with quite challenging toys and observed their play. Mothers who supported autonomy had toddlers who were more persistent and more competent than the children of more controlling mothers. As in other studies, anxious-resistant babies showed less persistence and more negative affect than secure or avoidant babies. Anxious-avoidant babies were as persistent as secure babies, but were less competent. However, those associations were *concurrent,* not predictive. That is, the child's attachment category at 12 months was related to her persistence, competence, and negative affect in the mastery observations at 12 months, and attachment at 20 months was related to the other variables at 20 months, but attachment at 12 months did not predict outcomes for the other variables at 20 months.

Working with somewhat older subjects from the Minneapolis poverty sample, Erickson and Farber (1983) also found that securely attached children handled cognitive tasks better than children with resistant attachments did. The children selected for this follow-up research had all shown stable Strange Situation classifications at 12 and 18 months. At 42 months of age, the preschoolers from group C were less persistent, less enthusiastic, and less compliant than the secure children, expressed more anger and frustration, and relied on the mother for support more. The children from Group A did not differ from the secure children on the measures used in this study.

Focusing on an unusual at-risk group, Brinich, Drotar, and Brinich (1989) studied children with early histories of *nonorganic failure to thrive* (NOFT). When an infant is underweight for his age and is extremely slow to gain weight and no organic condition that would interfere with appetite or digestion can be found, a doctor makes the NOFT diagnosis. Intermittent hospitalization is not uncommon for NOFT babies; many gain weight faster in the hospital than at home. In this NOFT sample, security of attachment was assessed at 12 months. Despite their medical difficulties, some of the children appeared to be securely attached. At 42 months, these children were less rigid under stress, set higher standards for their own performances, and were rated as more competent, skillful, and creative than the anxiously attached children. Infant patterns of attachment did not predict physical growth status 2½ years later, nor did they predict frequency of accidents, but anxiously attached children were rehospitalized nearly twice as often as the securely attached children. There is a hint in this that the parents of the anxiously attached children may have been more anxious than the other parents and so turned to the hospital for help more often than the parents of the secure children did.

In a cross-sectional study of 1½-year-olds, 3½-year-olds, and 5½-year-olds, Bus and Van IJzendoorn (1988) assessed children's attachments, mother's teaching styles, and children's emergent-literacy skills. All three age groups were observed interacting with their mothers while watching a segment from "Sesame Street," while reading a picture book, and while looking through an alphabet book with letters and corresponding words and pictures. The 3½- and 5½-year-olds also took emergent-literacy tests. Strange Situations were used to assess attachment in the toddlers, and classifications were translated into a scale for degree of security. Categories A and C were assigned scores of 1 (anxious); B1, B2, and B4 were scored 2 (secure), and B3 was scored 3 (very secure). Subjects in the two older groups were separated from their mothers in the laboratory for about an hour, during the last 3 minutes of which the child was left entirely alone. Behavior at reunion with the mother was used to evaluate attachment on a 3-point scale. A score of 1 was assigned if the child appeared very anxious after separation and avoided the mother or resisted her. A score of 2 was assigned if the child was somewhat distressed and out of step with the mother, or seemingly somewhat indifferent, but readily accepted the mother's invitation to play or explore the environment together. A score of 3 was assigned if the child greeted the mother very positively, did not avoid or resist her, and was eager to share experiences. During the teaching interactions, securely attached children were observed to be less easily distracted than anxiously attached children, and there was less need to discipline them. The secure dyads paid more attention to reading instruction and did more proto-reading. Children who received more reading instruction (as opposed to narration) got higher scores on measures of emerging literacy.

Another intriguing instance of finding an association between attachment classification and cognitive development comes from a study of children in Holland and Israel (Van IJzendoorn, Sagi, and Lambermon (in press). Because of the parents' jobs, each infant had a third primary caregiver. To calculate a summary score for the quality of the whole attachment network in infancy, the investigators added the security scores for the attachments to the mother, the father, and the third caregiver. This score for the quality of the whole attachment network in infancy bore a significant relationship to IQ scores 3 or 4 years later, when the subjects were 5 years old. Greater security was associated with higher IQ scores.

The picture of securely attached children that emerges from all this research is a very positive one. They appear to be curious, self-confident about managing cognitive tasks, persistent in the face of frustration, and cooperative. On the average, avoidant children often perform as well as secure children on measures of cognitive development, but their responses to frustration and challenge are less adaptive. Resistant children also tend to show maladaptive responses when faced with cognitive challenges. The pattern of results is quite convincing. The same sorts of differences among groups with differing attachment histories show up in studies in Germany, Holland, Israel, and the United States.

THE CORRELATES AND IMPLICATIONS OF AVOIDANCE

In attachment research, in most U.S. samples, about 20 to 25 percent of the subjects are classified as avoidant. Consequently, a large number of avoidant children have been studied. It has become possible to develop an integrated set of propositions about their development. (Because resistant attachments are less common than avoidant attachments, no analogous description of later development in resistant children has been developed.)

As noted earlier, Mary Main (1981) argued that avoidant children systematically exclude from awareness information that might activate attachment behavior. Cassidy and Kobak (1988) have presented a good summary of evidence that children with avoidant attachments often develop generalized strategies of restricting awareness and expression, not just of feelings about attachment, but of negative affect in general. The defensive process that is an effective adaptation to the insensitive, rejecting care they often received in infancy gets carried into other situations and interactions, where it is maladaptive. The specific socioemotional difficulties an avoidant child experiences with the first attachment figure and carries into interactions with others limit the child's ability to request and use assistance from others in learning about the environment. In his summaries, Alan Sroufe (1988a and 1988b) has also noted that avoidant attachment in infancy has been associated with emotional insulation, a lack of empathy, and hostile or antisocial behavior in the preschool years.

Grossmann, Grossmann, and Schwan (1986) compared aspects of the communicative behavior of secure and avoidant babies in the low-stress introductory episode and the two high-stress reunion episodes of the Strange Situation. *Direct communication* could occur through eye contact, facial expression, vocalization, and/or showing or giving objects. Direct communication with the mother was more common in secure infants than in avoidant ones. Furthermore, as stress increased, direct communication with the mother increased in secure babies but decreased in avoidant babies. Some avoidant infants did engage in direct communication, but they did so only when they were not distressed or angry. They did not seek bodily contact. In contrast, no secure infant stayed away from the mother when the infant's mood was negative. In Strange Situation reunion episodes with fathers, too, a high proportion of securely attached infants communicated directly, but only a few avoidant infants did so.

Grossmann and Grossmann (1991) extended such explorations of dyadic communication and interaction in the Strange Situation (at 12 or 18 months). Among infants who had avoidant attachments, the more the infant's mood and play were impaired by the two separations in the Strange Situation, the less the infant communicated directly to the parent being observed. Avoidant infants most in need of communication or contact with the parent to alleviate distress were least likely to seek it. The opposite was true of most babies who had secure attachments. How free the affective communications in a dyad were depended on the specific infant-parent relationship; it was not a stable characteristic of the baby. That is, in cases in which a baby had a secure attachment to one parent and an avoidant attachment to the other, the baby communicated directly to the first parent when distressed but not to the second parent.

How might avoidant babies have learned such behavioral strategies? A clue is available from an earlier German study. Escher-Graub and Grossmann (1983, cited in Grossmann and Grossmann, 1991) studied parents and babies in a play situation at 12 and 18 months. The parents were aware of being observed. Parents of avoidant infants joined in when their babies were already engrossed in play and withdrew when their babies showed signs of negative feelings. Parents of securely attached infants engaged in mutual play when their babies appeared to be at a loss for what to do next, but watched quietly when the infants did not need them. Parents of securely attached infants ignored only 4 percent of their babies' signals during play, while parents of avoidant infants ignored 18 percent. Elaborating on similar analyses, Grossmann and Grossmann (1991) reported that parents of avoidant infants stayed away from the babies and rarely offered toys when the baby was in a low interest state or a poor mood. When the baby was already playing with high interest, the parent initiated many play activities. The observed effect was that the parent was interfering, and joint play ceased abruptly. The infants showed many gestures and expressions of uncertainty.

Grossmann and Grossmann (1991) also reported contrasts in the behavior of secure and avoidant infants in an assessment of the child's emotional responses in the clown paradigm developed by Main and Weston (1981). In the presence of one parent, a female stranger with her face painted like a clown's appears happy, invites the infant to interact playfully, and finally cries. Infants with secure attachments to the parent who was present reflected the clown's affective states more promptly and more accurately than did infants with avoidant attachments to the parent who was present. The same baby reacted differently in his two clown sessions if the qualities of his attachments to his two parents differed.

According to the Grossmanns (1991, p. 109), "Avoidant strategies negate negative emotions in order to maintain personal integrity at the expense of reality." That is, the avoidant child guards against letting herself be aware of her own or others' anger, fear, and need for comfort. She thus manages to keep her behavior organized and to preserve a false self-image of feeling alright, being able to handle things, and maybe even being adequately loved. She protects herself from approaching her attachment figure and getting rebuffed or rejected. Earlier, Main (1981) called such defensive exclusion a "second-best strategy." Blocking awareness of needs and information related to attachment has the disadvantage of preventing the child from recognizing some very important aspects of reality, but it does allow the child to continue to get as much protection as the caregiver is willing and able to give.

Lütkenhaus, Grossmann, and Grossmann (1985) observed 3-year-olds in interaction with an adult stranger who involved them in a competitive tower-building game. When it appeared that the stranger would win the game, those who had been securely attached at age 1 tried harder, while those who had had avoidant attachments reduced their efforts. The secure preschoolers felt sad about losing and showed it when the game was over. The children who had been avoidant in infancy also felt sad about losing, but the sadness showed only while there was no eye contact between the new adult and the child. When the game was over, the avoidant children masked their sadness and sometimes even replaced it with smiles. The tendency to mask feelings was apparently transferred from the relationship with the parent to interaction with a new social partner.

One unusual measure from a study of 6-year-olds in the Berkeley Social Development Project literally illustrates the defensive restriction of emotions that characterizes avoidant children (Kaplan and Main, 1985). Each child was asked to draw a picture of his or her family. Those who had been classified as avoidant with their mothers in infancy generally drew tense, rigid figures with no individuality. The figures were separate and often lacked arms—a vivid depiction of the fact that they could not reach out to each other. The faces often had very big, stereotyped smiles, not unlike the tense, polite smiles with which these avoidant 6-year-olds masked their anxiety and anger in reunions with their mothers.

In a study of 52 white middle-class 6-year-olds, Cassidy (1988) found analogous differences between avoidant children and secure children. On a story completion task, secure children made up endings that presented the mother as important and supportive; avoidant children did not. In response to an interview from a puppet, seven of the eight avoidant children (88 percent) insisted that they were perfect. A few of the secure children also glorified themselves in this playful interview setting, but fourteen of the twenty-two (64 percent) ascribed positive but not flawless attributes to themselves; they were not defensively idealizing their self-images. (As you can read in detail in Chapters 17 and 18, there is some evidence that avoidance continues to distort perceptions and interfere with interactions and relationships in adolescence and adulthood.)

ARE SEQUELAE EFFECTS?

Why are so many positive outcomes associated with a history of secure attachment in infancy? Are the various outcomes direct effects of early attachment strategies? Or do many of the sequelae follow from continuities in the social environment? Do the same parents who foster secure attachments in the first year or two of life tend ordinarily to remain sensitive to their children's signals and needs and supportive of their development in the ensuing years? Is it this continuity in care, not the early pattern of adaptation, that causes the positive outcomes associated with early security? In most cases, we cannot answer these questions.

Both theory and data suggest that there is very often continuity in quality of care. Attachment theory, psychodynamic theories, and social-learning theories all agree that children interact with both familiar people and new people on the basis of their previous adaptations, thereby helping to maintain self-perpetuating adaptive or maladaptive cycles.

When attachment status in infancy and an outcome variable measured later in childhood are associated, at least two explanations are possible. One is that the early attachment pattern contributes directly or indirectly to developments reflected in the later measure. Another is that an associated third variable influences both the early attachment pattern and the later outcome variable. The different sorts of explanations and the need for distinguishing between them may be clearer if we consider a specific example. Suppose that an investigator assesses security of attachment at 12 months and enthusiasm for exploration at 36 months, and finds that secure attachment is associated with enthusiasm for exploration. One possibility is that having a secure attachment directly enables the child to devote high levels of attention and energy to exploration. A second possibility is that both attachment patterns and enthusiasm for exploration develop from parent-child interactions. The parents who provide warm, accessible secure bases for their babies may be the same parents who are especially likely to delight in and encourage their offspring's natural enthusiasm for exploration. If so, it would be the parent-child interaction pattern, not the baby's attachment strategy, that explains the 3-year-old's level of enthusiasm for exploration.

In fact, several studies have found explicit evidence of continuity in the quality of maternal care (e.g., Bates et al., 1988; Bus and Van IJzendoorn, 1988; Frankel and Bates, 1990; Londerville and Main, 1981; Main, Tomasini, and Tolan, 1979; Matas, Arend, and Sroufe, 1978; and Pierrehumbert et al., 1985). Is the mother's continuing sensitivity and supportiveness sufficient to explain correlations between early security of attachment and later outcomes? In a word, no. In one study, Renken, Egeland, Marvinney, Sroufe, and Manglesdorf (1989) looked at a number of factors that might help explain how much aggression a child displayed. Even when they subtracted all of the variability in aggression that could be statistically accounted for by the variability in experiences that occurred after infancy, early attachment history still helped to explain later aggression scores. Similar results emerged from a longitudinal study that never assessed attachment directly. In this case, Bradley et al. (1988, cited in Belsky and Cassidy, 1994) found that the acceptance and responsivity shown by the mother to her child in infancy (factors which ordinarily help predict security of attachment) predicted the child's considerateness at age 10. The mother's responsiveness in infancy helped to account for individual differences in this positive quality in the 10-year-old even after the investigators controlled statistically for what could be explained by the mother's behavior when the child was 10. These bits of evidence support the view that quality of care and security of attachment in infancy contribute to long-lasting effects that cannot be ascribed to continuities in the environment or to later care.

While the direct effects of early attachment patterns are likely to be difficult to separate from the effects of correlated aspects of early and later experience under any circumstances, an improvement in research methodology might be helpful. Most studies to date have used *incomplete panel designs:* attachment is assessed in infancy and some outcome is assessed later in life, but there is no measure of the outcome variable in infancy, and no assessment of attachment at the later time. Assessment of both variables at both points in time should shed more light on patterns of causality and continuity.

LIMITATIONS ON THE PREDICTIVE POWER OF EARLY ADAPTATIONS

In much of this chapter, I have called attention to research evidence that early experiences relevant to attachment and early security of attachment are statistically associated with various later outcomes in ways that attachment theory predicts or easily comprehends. It seems important now to emphasize that these statistically significant associations are rarely very strong. Generally, they are modest, but consistent from study to study. Some individual children may change radically for better or for worse. When we compare groups, however, children with early histories of secure attachment turn out to be in better shape than children with early histories of anxious attachment.

Why are the cross-time associations not stronger? At least three answers are plausible. First, our ways of measuring attachment itself and the outcomes of interest are limited.

Perhaps if we could measure each more precisely, we would discover stronger or clearer associations between attachment patterns and other concurrent or later outcomes. Second, early attachments may truly have only limited effects on later development. We may be finding modest associations between early attachment and some later outcomes because the associations are in fact modest. Third, there may be lawful processes of discontinuity. That is, there may be identifiable reasons why certain later experiences would divert a child from the path her first attachment(s) set her on. These three answers are not mutually exclusive. There may be elements of the truth in each of them.

Some investigators have attempted to make sense of both continuity and change, using data from a single large sample. Over the years, Sroufe, Egeland, and their colleagues have conducted an impressive series of follow-up studies of children from the Minneapolis poverty sample (e.g., Sroufe, 1983). In a recent paper, Sroufe, Egeland, and Kreutzer (1990) reported on the later progress of 190 children who showed poor functioning in the preschool period: they got comparatively low scores for flexible problem solving, self-management, and curiosity. The investigators divided these children into two groups: those who had shown secure attachment in infancy and movement toward harmonious autonomy in the toddler period and those who had shown anxious attachment in infancy and conflict, over-dependency, or other problems in the toddler period. In this group of children who were all doing poorly in preschool, the children who looked good in the infant and toddler assessments showed greater rebounding into positive functioning in the elementary school years than the other children did. Negative behavioral change in the preschool years did not erase all benefits of the supportive care these children had experienced in their first 2 years. Unfortunately, no measure of parent-child interaction during the elementary school years was available. That contribution to current functioning was not assessed.

Sroufe et al. (1990) interpreted these findings as support for Bowlby's view that development is always a product of both the individual's history *and* the individual's current circumstances. The individual's history includes genes, experiences, and the series of adaptations she has previously constructed. Furthermore, once the child acquires a set of characteristics and habits, she contributes something to constructing her own social environment. When searching for lawful patterns of continuity and change, it is important to remember that effects may be manifest in some contexts but not in others. Patterns that have not been apparent for a long time may reemerge when the environment changes or when the child faces a critical developmental issue.

CHAPTER SUMMARY

Once formed, patterns of attachment in infancy tend to be stable when the family circumstances are stable. In high-risk samples, with their frequent changes in residence, job, household membership, and health status, patterns of attachment are less stable. It may be possible to explain changes from secure to anxious and from anxious to secure attachment on the basis of changes in interactions and experiences, but too few data are available to justify certainty about this explanation.

Children who were securely attached to the mother in infancy have some advantages in a variety of arenas as toddlers, preschoolers, and kindergartners. They show more cooperation and less anger, aggression, and dependency than children with histories of anxious attachment show. They sometimes do better than anxiously attached children do on tests of cognitive development. When faced with difficult problems to solve, they are more persistent. When the problem is too difficult for the child to solve, secure children are more likely to request assistance from their mothers or teachers. Securely attached children have more-harmonious interactions with their peers than anxiously attached children do, and their peers and teachers like them better. Compared to avoidant preschoolers, secure children are less likely to be victims or victimizers. There is suggestive evidence that these positive outcomes are to some degree effects of secure attachment in infancy, not just effects of correlated aspects of more recent care.

CULTURAL VARIATIONS IN ATTACHMENT RELATIONSHIPS

In outline, the content of this chapter seems simple: What variations in human cultures exist? How should these variations affect attachment patterns in diverse cultures? Does the Strange Situation, which works so well for assessing infants' patterns of attachment in the United States, measure the security of attachment and the nature of an infant's defenses, ambivalence, or behavioral disorganization equally well in other cultures?

Efforts to answer these simple questions become complex. Across the cultures in which Strange Situation studies have been conducted, most babies are classified in group B. Whether that indicates that the babies are securely attached is not entirely clear, however. In some cultures, most of the babies who are not in group B are in group A. The increase in avoidance generally makes sense in light of the pressure toward early independence these babies experience, but the rarity of openly resistant attachments has not been well explained. In other cultures, most of the babies who are not in group B are in group C. The meaning of their Strange Situation behavior and its implications for later development are subject to debate.

Trying to understand what we should expect and what we are observing soon leads into speculation about what patterns of caregiving behavior and what patterns of attachment behavior are most adaptive in different cultures and in different individual circumstances. Eventually, we must consider that behavior patterns that perpetuate the species and perpetuate the particular culture may in some cases be detrimental to the individual's mental health or even to the individual's survival.

BASIC CONSIDERATIONS

Attachment theory was proposed as a universal theory of human development. If attachment is biologically based and adaptive in the evolutionary sense, as Bowlby ([1969] 1982) asserted, then the major propositions in attachment theory should apply to all human beings in all times and places. The theory need not describe all aspects of develop-

The physical and social context of infant care in this !Kung San family contrasts with European traditions.

ment and does not claim to do so, but what it does say should apply in all cultures, races, and ethnic groups.

It is also true that child-rearing goals and caregiving patterns vary greatly from culture to culture. If attachment theory is on target, the repertoire of attachment behaviors and defense mechanisms available to human beings should be universal, but the selection and patterning of behaviors is very likely to vary according to culture (or subculture).

There are about 1300 human cultures on earth. The point of cross-cultural research on attachment should be to gain insight into both the universal and the culture-specific aspects of attachment.

Within the range of secure attachments, there is evidence that infants in different cultures tend to organize their attachment behavior in different ways. For example, Van IJzendoorn (1986) reported that the B1 pattern is modal in Strange Situation research in the Netherlands. This pattern reflects confident reliance on the attachment figure as a secure base through interaction across a distance, not through close physical contact. In the United States, the B3 pattern, with its high levels of contact seeking and contact maintaining in reunion episodes, is modal and, in many theorists' opinion, optimal. Van IJzendoorn proposed that, in the context of the Dutch culture's emphasis on independence, the B1 pattern may be more adaptive than the B3 pattern.

Furthermore, even if the same subpattern of Strange Situation behavior reflected optimal adaptation in all cultures within the period of infancy, the later sequelae of a given pattern of infant attachment might vary greatly from one culture to another. The consequences of an avoidant, secure, resistant, or disorganized-disoriented pattern of attachment may vary with the goals and methods of subsequent child rearing in different cultures. They may also vary according to a child's or family's physical, economic, and social situation.

In a multicultural society such as ours, subcultural differences in the implications of a given pattern of attachment for later development may be quite important. For example, some of the usual sequelae of avoidance for inner-city black children may be quite different from the usual sequelae of avoidance for suburban white children. Similarly, the consequences of a C1 (openly angry) pattern of attachment in infancy in a Mexican American family may differ greatly from the consequences of the same pattern in infancy in a Chinese American family. Research into such possibilities has barely begun.

DIFFERENCES AMONG CULTURES

One of the best ways to test the universality of a theory is, of course, to observe relevant behaviors in a diverse set of sociocultural environments. Attachment researchers have done exactly that. Indeed, Ainsworth's early work in Baltimore was preceded by extensive naturalistic observations among the Ganda in Africa. She found many similarities in attachment behavior in the two cultures (Ainsworth, 1973). The phases in the development of an attachment, the powerful tendency to form an attachment to the primary caregiver, and the retreat to the attachment figure when frightened or merely away for too long were the same. Nevertheless, some normative patterns were far more dramatic in the Ganda sample than in the American one. For example, the Ganda babies showed much more distress in response to brief separations from the mother in a familiar environment. In their experience, *brief* separations from the mother were infrequent. When the mother left, she was likely to be gone for 3 or more hours of working in her garden. (During that time, someone else, usually the grandmother or a female child, looked after the baby.) When the mother left the room, Ganda babies protested as if she would be gone for hours. The Baltimore babies generally retained their composure as the mother went from room to room. In their everyday experience, most mothers went from room to room often. When the mother disappeared from sight, the baby could still expect that she would return soon, that she would come if called, and perhaps that the baby himself could follow the mother and so regain proximity.

The Ganda babies also showed more fear of strangers than the Baltimore babies did. The Ganda babies seldom encountered strangers in their village. Most American babies move among strangers in stores and other public places very often. Differences in infants' behavior patterns made sense in light of cultural differences in experience and resulting differences in infants' expectations. Use of the mother as a secure base from which to explore, even in ordinary environments, was also more pronounced among the Ganda than in the Baltimore sample. Despite such differences in specific attachment behaviors, Ainsworth (1967; Ainsworth et al., 1978) concluded that, in each of the two cultures, about two-thirds of the babies who were old enough to have formed attachments were securely attached.

In many human cultures, babies are held or carried almost all day and sleep next to the mother all night.

The differences in ordinary experiences of the babies in Ainsworth's two longitudinal samples provide one illustration of differing cultural patterns that are likely to influence attachment patterns. Other illustrations are readily available. For example, among the Gusil of Kenya, when babies are 12 months old, they are still being held about half of the daytime, they are rarely in the mother's presence without being held by her or someone else, and they are given no toys (LeVine and Miller, 1990). All this contrasts markedly with American norms. In the United States, most 12-month-old infants are encouraged to play with their many toys, to exercise their motor skills, and to nap alone, not to rest or ride on the mother's back half of their waking time. Cultural contrasts in nighttime sleeping arrangements are also huge. In the United States, pediatricians generally advise against letting an infant or young child sleep in the parents' bed, and middle- to upper-class families usually arrange for the infant to sleep not only in a separate bed, but also in a separate room, often by the time the baby is 6 months old. In many other parts of the world, almost all babies sleep in the same bed with the mother for at least the first year (Morelli, Rogoff, Oppenheim, and Goldsmith, 1992).

Cultures also differ in the types of roles mothers and fathers take in relation to their infants. Across cultures, parents may at times be playmates, teachers, or disciplinarians, not just caregivers or attachment figures. In the United States, parents do often play with their babies. Among Mayan Indians in Mexico, mothers rarely play with their babies, but they are clearly available and responsive as caregivers (Bretherton, 1985).

Without leaving the United States, it is easy to find profound cultural differences in methods and goals for raising children. Compared to the Puerto Rican mothers in the United States, Anglo-American mothers placed greater stress on qualities associated with personal development and self-control of negative impulses (Harwood, 1992). They described an active yet related toddler as most desirable and a clingy, distressed toddler as least desirable. Compared to the Anglo mothers, the Puerto Rican mothers focused more on qualities associated with respectfulness and lovingness. They described as most desirable a quiet, responsive toddler whose behavior leans more toward maintaining proximity than toward exploring actively. To them, an active, avoidant toddler was least desirable.

In the Strange Situation, the two A patterns express high autonomy and low relatedness. The two C patterns express high relatedness and low autonomy. The four B patterns reflect differing balances between the two. Both Anglo-American and Puerto Rican American mothers reported, in response to descriptions, that they would prefer group B over group A and group C patterns of Strange Situation behavior. Within the B group, however, Anglo-American mothers gave the distal B1 and B2 patterns higher ratings than the Puerto Rican mothers gave them, and the Puerto Rican mothers gave the proximal, dependent B4 pattern higher ratings than the Anglo-American mothers did. Contrary to Harwood's prediction, there were no cultural differences in the reported desirability of the B3 toddlers and undesirability of the C1 toddlers. However, it appeared that the mothers had different, culturally relevant reasons for the desirability ratings. Anglo-Americans disliked the C1 toddler's inability to function autonomously; Puerto Rican Americans disliked his inability to maintain a calm, respectful demeanor. Both sets of mothers approved of the B3 infant's ability to behave well, but one group emphasized autonomy while the other emphasized calmness and respect.

CULTURAL CONTRASTS

Of the countries in which a substantial amount of attachment research has been done, at least two care for infants in ways that differ greatly from the practices of white middle-class parents in the United States and northern Europe. The two cultures are first, Japan, and second, the kibbutzim (communes) found in Israel.

■ Japan

Japan offers intriguing opportunities to study human development. Although it is now a fully industrialized country, it retains traditions that were, until 100 years ago, entirely isolated from western influences. It is a culture that values children and the mothering role very highly. It encourages the development and continuation of very close ties between mother and child throughout life (Bradshaw, 1985–86). Children are expected to rely on their mothers for help and emotional support in a wide variety of situations throughout childhood. Very high levels of physical closeness characterize mother-infant dyads in Japan; babies are not often separated from their mothers, and are very rarely left with strangers.

According to Takahashi (1990), traditional Japanese methods of raising children seek to protect the baby from experiencing any sort of stress. (Note the contrast with Anglo-American methods, which encourage the infant to learn to handle moderate stress on her own.) In Japan, a caregiver is always near the infant. The baby usually sleeps in the same bed with the mother, bathes with the mother, and is carried on the mother's back. Some modern Japanese authors still recommend these traditional methods. Even after infancy, Japanese children usually sleep in the same room as their parents, and young mothers do not hesitate to take a baby into the parents' bed when the baby cries or asks to be fed. In one study Takahashi cited, only 10 of 300 kindergarten children slept alone in a separate room. Even in urban middle-class Japanese families, 62 percent of 1- to 2-year-old children slept in the same room with one or both parents. Carrying a baby on the parent's back and bathing together are also still common practices.

Where physical contact with a caregiver is so nearly continuous, contact may not acquire the meaning it has for American middle-class babies. A mother who holds her baby almost all the time can seldom use holding him as a means of increasing the comfort she gives to him when he is distressed. A baby who is held almost all the time without even asking for contact may not make active efforts to gain contact when distressed and may not be comforted by contact to the degree that American babies generally are.

In Japan, babies are left with hired caregivers far less often than is customary in the United States. In a longitudinal study, Takahashi (1990) asked 60 Japanese mothers how often they had left their babies in someone else's care during the twelfth month of the baby's life. The average of their responses was only 2.2 times—about once every 2 weeks. The other caregiver was always the child's father or grandmother. When asked to participate in Strange Situations for research purposes, some Japanese mothers would not consent to leave the baby alone in an unfamiliar place—they were unwilling to subject their babies to so much stress. Other Japanese mothers did consent to having their babies participate in Strange Situations. Before I discuss the data that emerged from such studies, I will discuss child-rearing practices of one more culture.

■ Israeli Kibbutzim

Infant care practices on Israeli kibbutzim differ from American practices even more radically than Japanese practices do. Indeed, as Abraham Sagi (1990) has pointed out, kibbutzim present natural laboratories for the study of attachment. While they do not deviate from the caregiving environment in which human behavior evolved as much as orphanages often do, they present some interesting challenges to infants' capacities to adapt. On kibbutzim, infants are cared for primarily by hired caregivers called *metaplot*. ("Metaplot" is the plural form of "metapelet.") The metaplot often lack motivation for caring for infants. They do not choose their jobs as caregivers; they are assigned to them. They admit to spending much of the time chatting with other metaplot and mothers, not interacting with the babies in their care. Each metapelet has responsibility for three infants, which may make it difficult to respond sensitively to any of them, even if the metapelet's motivation to do so is high. The babies spend only a few hours a day in their parents' care, mostly around suppertime. If a baby is distressed and needs care at night, the care on many kibbutzim may be very slow in coming and will come not from a parent or from the daytime metapelet, but from a night watchwoman. That is because many kib-butzim maintain communal sleeping arrangements for infants and have one night watch-woman monitoring all of the babies in the building.

What effect do these infant care practices have on kibbutz babies' attachments? Before I describe the data on that topic, let's consider some general questions about the cross-cultural validity of the Strange Situation.

VALIDITY OF THE STRANGE SITUATION ACROSS CULTURES

By definition, it should be possible in any culture to index an infant's secure attach-ment by his or her confident use of the caregiver as a secure base in the natural environ-ment. But can we take a shortcut? Is the Strange Situation a suitable method for assessing quality of attachment in cultures with infant care practices that differ substantially from infant care practices in the United States? That has been the subject of much debate.

■ Stress Level

Much of the debate focuses on the level of stress the procedure produces in different cul-tures. Because infants' experiences vary with culture, the meanings they attribute to the events in the Strange Situation may also vary with culture. Therefore, the validity of the Strange Situation for assessing attachments in such vastly different cultures is certainly open to question.

Ainsworth and Wittig (1969) originally developed the Strange Situation as a culture-specific laboratory procedure. They were curious about eliciting from the Baltimore babies certain attachment behaviors that had occurred more intensely and more frequently in the natural environment of the Ganda babies. The sequence of episodes in the Strange Situa-tion was designed to increase the level of stress gradually. The progressive increase in stress levels of the same series of episodes might be very different for babies from a different cul-ture. As noted above, separation protest, fear of strangers, and obvious use of the mother as a secure base were more vivid in naturalistic observations in Uganda than in the United States. The Strange Situation, which proved so useful in the United States, might have been much too distressing for the Ganda babies.

■ Socialization of Reunion Behaviors

Just as babies from different cultures may experience different degrees of stress in the Strange Situation, babies from different cultures may acquire different reunion behaviors. This could present a problem in interpreting data, because Strange Situation classifications are determined primarily by the infant's behavior in the reunion episodes.

The reunion behaviors that mothers encourage in their babies do vary with culture. In the United States, many middle-class mothers appear to enjoy, solicit, and reward excited greetings from their babies upon reunion. In many African cultures, quiet holding and breast feeding are the usual reunion behaviors.

Would cultural variations in reunion behavior compromise the validity of the Strange Situation in other cultures? Until we have more data from several contrasting cultures, we will not really know. It does seem unlikely that there are many cultures in which parents actively encourage their babies to show resistance or to turn away instead of greeting or approaching at moments of reunion. However, cultures may differ in the degree to which they tolerate resistance. Data from Japan, which I will discuss later in this chapter, suggest that some cultures leave very little room for a baby to show avoidance.

■ Approaches to Testing the Cross-Cultural Validity of the Strange Situation

Several approaches to evaluating the validity of the Strange Situation in a new culture are possible. One approach is to examine the culture's infant care practices, predict from those practices what patterns of attachment should be most common, and see whether the predicted distribution of patterns does emerge in Strange Situation studies in that culture. A second approach is to test whether the sequelae of each Strange Situation pattern are consistent across cultures. If the later course of a child's development can be predicted from the infant's Strange Situation pattern in the same way and with the same accuracy across different cultures, that may be evidence that the Strange Situation does provide a valid assessment of patterns of attachment across cultures.

A third, most convincing approach to evaluating the validity of the Strange Situation requires lengthy naturalistic observations of certain infant-caregiver dyads. With a sound ethological basis for confidence in data regarding the quality of each attachment, the researcher could then see whether Strange Situation classifications of the attachment patterns match observation-based classifications of the attachments. This worthwhile but time-consuming approach has not yet been attempted.

DISTRIBUTIONS OF STRANGE SITUATION CLASSIFICATIONS IN CONTRASTING CULTURES

One way of evaluating whether the Strange Situation is a valid research tool in other cultures is to ask whether frequencies of A, B, and C classifications vary across cultures in ways that attachment theory can predict or explain. (The D category has not been used much yet in other countries.)

Exporting the Strange Situation to northern Europe was not a problem. Infants' experiences there seem fairly similar to infants' experiences in the United States. It was and is reasonable to expect that the laboratory procedure there would be only moderately stressful for most babies, as it is in the United States. Nevertheless, there are modest variations from country to country in infant care practices. Those variations appear to be reflected in the distribution of Strange Situation classifications in specific cultures.

On the average, northern European cultures (those of Germany, Sweden, and the Netherlands) stress the importance of early independence somewhat more than Americans do. Many parents press babies to behave independently and rebuff their infants' bids for contact even in the first year. What distribution of attachment patterns would attachment theory predict for such cultures? An increase in the frequency of avoidant attachments would seem likely. That is exactly what has been observed. Avoidant attachments are more common and resistant attachments are less common in Germany and Sweden than in the United States. In addition, a shift among securely attached babies towards B1 and B2 classifications, which reflect distal interaction and often include moderate initial avoidance, would seem likely on theoretical grounds and, in fact, has been reported (Grossmann et al., 1981; Van IJzendoorn, 1986).

What about Israeli kibbutzim? What about Japan? Do patterns of responding to the events of the Strange Situation in those cultures have the same meanings they have in the United States? Can the Strange Situation serve as a valid means of assessment in a culture that does not normally expect or require babies to stay with strangers even for a few minutes? Maybe not. In studies of babies on kibbutzim and in Japan, the infant's reactions to separation are more intense than the reactions observed in babies in the United States. Many kibbutz babies were so distressed that the Strange Situation procedure could not be completed. Some theorists have argued that the stress level of the Strange Situation for babies from such cultures is so high that classifications are not likely to be valid. Others have disagreed. Let's look at some data.

■ Data from Japan

In the study mentioned earlier in this chapter, Takahashi (1990) assessed 60 Japanese babies in Strange Situations at the age of 12 months. (For a review of the sequence of episodes in the Strange Situation, see Table 3.1.) All of the mothers were full-time, primary caregivers in nuclear families. For these Japanese babies, the stress produced by the laboratory procedure, especially the baby-alone episode, was much more than moderate. An unusually high number of babies showed a group C pattern of behavior; not one baby showed a group A pattern. About half of the group C babies showed a high level of resistance only in the second reunion. To Takahashi, it appeared that the mounting stress of the procedure pushed these babies from type B behavior into type C behavior. On the basis of behavior through the first reunion, only 17 percent of the babies were classified as type C babies. That percentage is only a little higher than the percentage researchers find in most American samples. After the baby-alone episode and the second reunion, twice as many (32 percent) of the Japanese babies were classified as type C. Similar results had been reported by Miyake, Chen, and Campos (1985).

Table 8.1 illustrates the cultural differences in U.S. and Japanese babies' responses to the Strange Situation; the table was adapted from Takahashi's own vivid listing of behavioral differences between 106 American babies and 60 Japanese ones. None of the cultural differences were significant in the first reunion. All of the listed differences between the two groups of babies in episodes 6 and 8 were statistically significant. Some are striking.

Takahashi's research team repeated Strange Situations with the same babies at the age of 23 months. She reasoned that the stress the procedure caused for 23-month-old Japanese babies would be similar to the stress it produces for 12-month-old American babies. As predicted, being left alone was less stressful for babies who were almost 2 years old than it had been for the same babies near their first birthdays. This time, 81 percent were classified into group B and only 19 percent into group C. (The comparable figures at 12

TABLE 8.1 Behavior of Japanese and American 12-month-olds and Their Mothers in the Strange Situation

Episode	Behavior	Percent Showing Behavior U.S.	Japan
5 (first reunion)	Baby cried when mother returned.	42	37
	Baby stopped crying within 15 seconds.	Most	45
	Baby showed some initial avoidance.	30	32
	Mother went to her chair directly.	41	41
	Mother held baby.	34	52
	Mother held baby over 120 seconds.	7	20
6 (baby alone)	Baby cried at some time in episode.	78	96
	The episode was curtailed.	53	90
	The episode was skipped.	0	10
	Baby cried immediately when mother left.	45	93
	Baby was crying at end of episode.	58	91
	Baby engaged in exploration.	62	9
8 (second reunion)	Baby achieved contact within 15 seconds.	78	100
	Baby showed some avoidance.	47	17
	Baby was crying at start of episode.	53	79
	Mother held baby.	89	100
	Holding failed to soothe baby.	9	33
	Baby was in contact over 120 seconds.	24	51
	Baby manipulated toys.	82	44

Note: $N = 106$ in the United States; $N = 60$ in Japan.

Source: Adapted from K. Takahashi, (1990). Are the key assumptions of the "Strange Situation" procedure universal? A view from Japanese research. *Human Development, 30,* 23–30. Reprinted by permission of S. Karger, AG, Basel, Switzerland.

months were 68 percent into group B and 32 percent into group C.) Avoidance of the mother was still rare and, if present, brief; there were still no group A babies. Fourteen subjects shifted from group C to group B, and five from group B to group C. In all, 32 percent of the babies were classified into two different categories at their two Strange Situations, 11 months apart.

For stable nuclear families in which the mother is a full-time homemaker, that is an unusually high rate of instability in Strange Situation classifications. If some assessments were invalid, that would help explain the inconsistency of classifications. Takahashi (1990) argued that some of the assessments at 12 months may have been invalid because the separations, especially being left alone, caused too much stress for these babies. Some of the assessments at 23 months may have been invalid because of developmental changes in the babies' physical and cognitive abilities. (The coding instructions, as you may recall, were intended for babies 12 to 18 months old.)

Why is avoidance so rarely observed in Strange Situations in Japan? From infancy on, Japanese children are socialized to maintain harmonious interpersonal interactions. Japanese citizens are expected to be very sensitive to others and to try to maintain harmony in personal relationships. Avoidant behavior would be, at any age, considered rude. In preparing their children to live in a culture that values sensitivity and harmony, parents probably discourage their babies from ignoring caregivers or even turning the face away from a social partner. Ignoring the adult is certainly not likely to be interpreted or encouraged as a sign of healthy independence.

In the second reunion in the Strange Situation, most mothers in Takahashi's sample rushed to pick the baby up before the baby showed any sign that he wanted contact. It appeared that it never occurred to the mothers that the baby might want to avoid the mother. They assumed that separations were stressful and that the baby would want comfort, and rushed to provide it. If such assumptions and actions are, as seems likely, an ordinary part of Japanese care of infants, avoidance as it is practiced (and, sometimes, valued) in the United States and Germany would not easily emerge.

In traditional Japanese society, it was very rare for a baby to be separated from the mother. In *some* modern Japanese families, such separations are no longer uncommon. For these babies, the Strange Situation may not be as stressful as it is when separation from the mother is almost entirely foreign to the infant's experience. Would Japanese babies who are accustomed to separations respond differently in Strange Situations than the babies in Takahashi's sample did? If so, would the differences be great enough to affect Strange Situation classifications? Would the resulting classifications reflect the quality of interaction over the preceding months? Would they have predictive validity? We have almost no data with which to address these questions. However, one study of 36 city babies in Japan did find 5 avoidant attachments (Durrett et al., 1984, cited in Van IJzendoorn, 1990). This result suggests that further research is well worth doing.

■ Data from Kibbutzim

What about attachments on Israeli kibbutzim? Sagi (1990) has proposed that kibbutz babies may be confused by the "multiple mothering" they experience and anxious because of the inconsistency and unpredictability of responsiveness from their assigned metaplot. Neither frequent rejection of contact behavior nor pressure to act independently has been reported for kibbutz samples. Consequently, the kibbutz babies' attachments, when anxious, seem likely to be resistant, not avoidant. That is, in fact, what has been reported (Sagi, 1990). Group A Strange Situation classifications are uncommon in kibbutz samples. The occurrence of enough resistant behavior to produce group C classification is much more common on kibbutzim than it is in the United States. Compared to global distributions, group A classifications are more rare and group C classifications are more common on kibbutzim, whether the attachment figure is the mother, the father, or the metapelet.

Given the kibbutz patterns of caregiving, even secure attachments might be expected often to be tinged with resistance and/or preoccupation with the caregiver, who may often have been unavailable. In Strange Situation assessments, such resistance and preoccupation produce B4 classifications. Subgroup B4 classifications, like group C classifications, are decidedly more common among kibbutz babies than they are in most American, German, or Swedish samples.

Even though kibbutz babies find the Strange Situation much more distressing than their American counterparts find it to be, the distribution of attachment classifications derived from such assessments of kibbutz babies accords with predictions from attachment theory. Avoidance in the Strange Situation is rare, and moderate or high resistance is comparatively common. (Unusually high frequencies of disorganized-disoriented attachments might also be expected. The D category has rarely been used with a kibbutz sample, so it is too early to say how common such attachments are.)

IS THE STRANGE SITUATION TOO STRESSFUL?

Does the Strange Situation procedure—which is much more distressing for Japanese babies and for kibbutz babies than it is for American babies—produce valid assessments of security of attachment in cultures in which infant care practices differ greatly from those of the middle class in the United States?

If the experimenter does nothing to relieve the baby's distress about being left with the stranger or being left alone, then yes, the stress level is too high, and the assessment is invalid. However, several researchers who have paid close attention to cross-cultural data on attachment (Main, 1990; Sagi, 1990; Van IJzendoorn, 1990) have argued that the procedure is likely to produce valid classifications across cultures *if the experimenter shortens separation episodes for highly distressed babies.* Curtailing episode 6, the "baby alone" episode, is common even in the United States. In the sample that provided data for Table 8.1, episode 6 was curtailed for slightly more than half of the American babies. Main (1990) says that, in research at Berkeley, experimenters do not let a separation exceed 30 seconds if a baby cries persistently. When necessary, they cut episode 6 to 10 seconds.

If the Strange Situation were just too stressful for infants of some culture under study, we might expect a clear majority of infants to be inconsolably distressed by it. That is not what has been reported. Even in Japan and on kibbutzim, about 67 percent of subjects are classified as type B—secure, if the pattern has the same meaning there as in the United States and in northern Europe. Group B attachments appear to be as common in those two cultures as they are in the United States. The increased frequency of group C classifications is associated with a huge decrease in the frequency of group A classifications, not with any decrease in the frequency of the behavior patterns associated with secure attachment.

However, the predominance of group B classifications in all cultures studied to date is not sufficient evidence that group B classification reflects secure attachment in all those cultures or that the majority of babies in all those cultures are securely attached. For one thing, the D category has not been used in non-Western cultures. Many of the babies who have been classified into group B may not belong there. In addition, there is the possibility that, in cultures where being left with a stranger or being left alone is rare, the stress in the Strange Situation rises to a level that overwhelms avoidant defenses the same infant might use in an assessment procedure better-suited to her culture. As you may recall, when Ainsworth and her colleagues (1978) reassessed American infants in a second Strange

Situation 2 weeks after the first, most of the babies showed more distress. All of the babies who had been classified into group A in the first Strange Situation were classified into group B at the second assessment. The researchers did not infer from this that the attachments had shifted from avoidant to secure in the intervening 2 weeks. Rather, they concluded that, when an avoidant baby is overly distressed, the avoidant defense breaks down. A possibility researchers cannot yet rule out is that, despite the high level of physical contact and the cultural pressure toward polite, harmonious interactions, some Japanese babies may develop avoidant strategies that would be observable in a culturally appropriate assessment procedure.

META-ANALYSES

Do distributions of attachment patterns vary with culture in ways that attachment theory can predict or account for? Van IJzendoorn and Kroonenberg (1988) addressed that question through a meta-analysis of data from Strange Situation studies in the United States, Germany, Israel, Japan, Sweden, and the Netherlands. Group B attachments were modal in all of the countries. Also, the A-B-C distribution from the original Baltimore sample and from the aggregated sample of babies in the United States each resembled the "world" distribution of Strange Situation classifications. However, there was great variation from sample to sample both within and between countries. In northern Europe, A's are more common and C's are less common than elsewhere. In Japan and Israel, C's are more common and A's are less common than elsewhere.

Using different statistical procedures, Van IJzendoorn and Kroonenberg (1990) later checked data sets from seven investigators in six countries (Germany, Sweden, the Netherlands, Japan, Israel, and the United States). Except when scoring the subject's interactions across a distance, coders in all countries appeared to be using the interactive scales for reunion episodes in the same ways and scoring behaviors according to the original (Ainsworth et al., 1978) instructions. Discriminant functions developed by Richters et al. (1988) showed that classification groups resembled each other across cultures more than cultures resembled each other across classification groups. That is, group A babies acted like other group A babies whether they came from the United States, northern Europe, or, in less common cases, Japan or Israel. Group C babies acted like other group C babies regardless of what country they came from, and so on. However, group A babies were more common in some cultures than in other cultures, and group C babies were more common in some cultures than in others.

In general, it appears that distal patterns of caregiving and attachment characterize northern European cultures, proximal patterns of caregiving and attachment characterize Japan, and inconsistent, sometimes inattentive caregiving may characterize Israeli kibbutzim. So far, however, it appears that there are, across cultures, similar associations between the caregiver's behavior and the infant's attachment pattern. Where proximal or inconsistent modes of interaction predominate, infants under stress seek or maintain proximity and physical contact with their attachment figures. Some mingle resistance with their attachment behavior, and some do not. Very few show avoidance. Where distal modes of interaction and pressure toward early independence predominate, many infants develop avoidance, and babies who appear to be securely attached generally fall into sub-group B1 or B2, not subgroup B3, in the Strange Situation.

UNANSWERED QUESTIONS

It should be emphasized that the associations and contrasts mentioned in this chapter have been demonstrated by comparing cultural groups, not by conducting longitudinal observations of different infant-caregiver dyads in Japan or on a kibbutz. We need etho-logical observations of infants' use of the caregiver as a secure base and as a haven of safety in the natural social environments of non-Western cultures. Until such data are available, it is not possible to know with certainty whether, for example, group C classification in the Strange Situation truly reflects anxious attachment in Japan or Israel.

Inclusion of the D category in studies on kibbutzim and in Japan may change our understanding of patterns of attachment in those cultures. It is also possible that defining one or more new classifications of Strange Situation behavior will be necessary as cross-cultural research expands. Some pattern of attachment behavior that has rarely or never been captured on videotape in the United States may be fairly common in another culture. Until naturalistic longitudinal data on the development of individual attachment rela-tionships in other cultures are available, the *meanings* of Strange Situation classifications for babies in those cultures must remain unknown.

In addition to testing the validity of the Strange Situation in a different culture, something close to a replication of the Baltimore study in a non-Western culture would test the sensitivity hypothesis across a range of normal interactions that differs from the range sampled in the white middle-class suburbs of Baltimore. Support for the sensitivity hypothesis would be much more powerful if we found that, in Tanzania, Argentina, Japan, Israel, or a Puerto Rican community in New York City, just as in the little sample from Baltimore, (1) sensitively responsive care fosters secure attachment, (2) unpredictable, unreliable care fosters anxious-resistant attachment, and (3) rejection of the infant and rebuffing of bids for contact foster avoidant attachment. An unending stream of immi-grants consciously or unconsciously seeking to perpetuate a wide variety of cultural histo-ries, values, and practices makes it easy to do respectful cross-cultural research without leaving the United States.

SEQUELAE OF STRANGE SITUATION
CLASSIFICATIONS IN OTHER CULTURES

A different way of asking whether the Strange Situation is a valid research method in other cultures is to ask whether the sequelae of the various classifications accord with attachment-theory predictions, even for other cultures. However, it may be easy to fall into error in making cross-cultural predictions. That is so because even if the determinants of an infant's attachment pattern are the same all over the world, the consequences of the pat-tern may differ in different cultural, familial, and individual circumstances. For example, the clingy dependency associated with group C classification may be irritating to adults in one culture, while adults in another culture interpret it as an ordinary, almost inevitable aspect of infant behavior. An avoidant infant's seemingly independent behavior may be valued in some cultures and regarded as an appalling lack of affection, courtesy, or connection in others.

In cultures much different from our own, will we still find that avoidant and resistant attachments in infancy frequently lead to psychologically maladaptive patterns of interaction later in life? Cultural and individual differences in what children will later be required or expected to do and in what they will be punished for doing make it difficult to offer broad predictions about the sequelae of infant attachment patterns. Even so, one possibility worth considering is that group B classification reflects security and bodes well for subsequent adaptation in almost any culture. Any other behavior pattern may imply distorted or constricted emotional responses and constrained perceptions and behavioral strategies. If the Strange Situation assessment proves valid across cultures, then infants in groups A, C, and D should be much more likely than group B infants to experience difficulties later in life. Across cultures, their personalities should more often be characterized by mistrust, brittleness, anger, anxiety, helplessness, dissociations, and/or unhappiness. In particular, problems in emotional, intimate relationships should be more common among them than among individuals with group B attachment histories.

In the United States, the Strange Situation so far appears to have good predictive validity across subcultures and socioeconomic groups. As the data discussed earlier show, the procedure also has some predictive validity on Israeli kibbutzim, where infant care comes mostly in a group setting, not in a family home.

While helpful, these bits of evidence do not constitute demonstrations of the cross-cultural predictive validity of the Strange Situation. We need more data. Even if we focus exclusively on subcultures within the United States, we cannot be confident that Strange Situation classifications predict the same outcomes across groups. For example, we have very few studies in which the majority of subjects are African American, and little explicit testing of whether the precursors or sequelae of Strange Situation classifications are the same in the African American subsamples as they are in the white subsamples. And what about other subcultures in the United States? So few published Strange Situation studies have used Hispanic, Asian, Native American, Middle Eastern, or other non-European American samples, we have almost no data about whether the procedure is valid for these subcultures.

■ Group C

The great distress Japanese babies show at separation and the rarity of avoidance at reunion are exactly what Bowlby and Ainsworth would have predicted on the basis of what is known about Japanese practices in caring for infants. Across samples in Japan, about 30 percent of babies are classified into group C. In the United States, group C behavior in the Strange Situation is regarded as maladaptive. In Japan, however, it may be that the events of the Strange Situation are so deviant that a baby's resistant or passive behavior does *not* reflect any representational model built from the mother's unpredictability. *Does* group C classification reflect or predict maladaptive development in Japan?

A first set of answers is available from Takahashi's (1990) longitudinal project. She followed the 60 Japanese babies for 2½ years after they participated in Strange Situa–

tions at the age of 12 months. As in the United States, the Japanese B babies behaved more adaptively than the C babies during the second year of life. At 16 months and at 23 months, the B babies complied more readily with the mother's directions. At 23 months, they showed more curiosity about unfamiliar objects, were more competent socially, and formed more-effective relationships when paired with unfamiliar peers than group C babies did. However, the Japanese group C babies overcame their disadvantages by the time they were 2½ years old. At 32 months, the former B babies had no advantage over the former C babies on the Peabody Picture Vocabulary Test (a widely used estimator of intelligence) or on compliance with the mother. At 36 months, they had no advantage in social relationships in everyday situations. At 42 months, they had no advantage in peer interactions. In short, classification into group B or group C at 12 months had limited predictive validity in this Japanese sample.

In Japan, group C classification in this study predicted behavior in experimental situations for very young children, but had no predictive value later. In a culture that does not value social independence or self-reliance, Takahashi (1990) suggested the B and C Strange Situation patterns may not predict future adaptation well at all. In fact, her skepticism about the implications of group C classification extends to findings from other countries. In several studies in the United States, Germany, and Israel, children who had anxious attachments in infancy, whether resistant or avoidant, continued to show disadvantages in preschool and kindergarten. Ordinarily, there are too few A's or too few C's in any one study to support statistical analyses of differences between the two insecurely attached groups. Takahashi (1990) suggested that the differences between secure and anxious children in most research may be carried mainly by the avoidant children. She thinks we may know less than we thought we knew about the long-term implications of group C attachments in infancy, even in the United States.

■ Group A

In the United States, it appears that the surest way to foster sturdy independence in a child is to lay a secure foundation for its development by responding sensitively to the child's signals in infancy. Children whose babyish, dependent behavior is rebuffed too early in life tend to be actually more dependent than others and to have poorer relations with peers and teachers later.

In the first attachment research in Bielefeld in northern Germany, about half of the infant-mother and infant-father attachments were avoidant. When Grossmann et al. (1985) first discovered this, they suggested that the sequelae of avoidance in Germany might differ from its sequelae in the United States. To cope with the pressure toward early independence, a substantial number of German children developed avoidant defenses that were observable in Strange Situations. However, the German researchers thought the northern European cultures that consider early independence so important might have developed methods of supporting secure independence in later childhood even in the children who showed avoidance at 12 months. Data they collected later did not support that hope (Grossmann and Grossman, 1991).

Sagi (1990) cited three studies from Germany in which the sequelae of Strange Situation classifications were the same as they are in the United States. The Grossmanns

(1990) now believe that individuals with secure attachment histories can tolerate conflicting emotions and can pay attention to the full range of external causes for such emotions. At any given time, individuals with avoidant attachment histories pay attention only to selected fractions of their own emotional reactions, and they tend to lose sight of some of the external causes for potentially conflicting emotions. As an appraisal system, emotions can direct one's attention to the real events that triggered them. In Germany, as in the United States, according to the Grossmanns, people with anxious attachment histories selectively ignore or dramatically misperceive real events. In both countries, avoidant attachments have maladaptive implications.

As an example, the Grossmanns (1990) described contrasts between group B subjects and group A subjects (classified in Strange Situations in infancy) from their Regensburg sample. The children, now 5 years old, were revisited in their assorted preschools. The group B children were better able to concentrate on their play and were less easily disturbed than the group A children. More B's than A's showed behavior that was planful and organized. The motor movements of A's were comparatively uncoordinated and aimless. On the basis of observation of their facial expressions and gestures, more B's than A's appeared to be relaxed. In their social contacts, more B's tended toward friendliness; more A's were sober or were frequently dissatisfied and in poor moods during social exchanges. More A's showed a tendency to get involved in frequent conflicts.

When several of the Regensburg preschool observation variables were combined to create a "competent" versus "incompetent" classification system, 14 of the 21 group B children were identified as competent (67 percent), but only 3 of the 11 group A children were (27 percent). All of the children in this low-risk sample were from ordinary families. A search for evidence of even marginal behavior problems—aggression, hostility, or isolation—uncovered no problem in 75 percent of the group B children, but found some problem in the social behavior of 82 percent of the group A children (Grossmann and Grossmann, 1990).

All of the above differences between B's and A's in Germany are analogous to the sorts of differences between B's and A's found in the United States. In a culture in which investigators thought that avoidance in the Strange Situation in infancy might have few negative or long-lasting implications, data led them to a less optimistic conclusion.

ADAPTIVE BEHAVIOR FROM A BIOLOGICAL PERSPECTIVE

What does it mean when we call a pattern "maladaptive"? Some clarification is necessary. *As ethologists,* attachment theorists often speak of what is adaptive in a biological or evolutionary sense: What behaviors help an individual survive, reproduce, and assist his or her offspring or genetic group to survive and reproduce? *As clinicians and developmental psychologists,* attachment theorists often speak of what is adaptive in supporting the individual's mental health. That is, what cognitive, affective, and behavioral patterns help an individual build, maintain, or regain abilities to perceive and appraise reality accurately and to select and enact behavioral responses flexibly and appropriately? *In some circumstances, what is adaptive from a biological perspective is maladaptive from a mental health perspective.*

What behavior patterns *are* adaptive in the evolutionary sense? Hinde (1982), who is an ethologist, argued that natural selection probably would not produce *one* best way of mothering or *one* best pattern of attachment. Instead, it might produce a flexible range of behaviors, so that individuals, families, and perhaps whole cultures could adapt to different environmental circumstances.

Are avoidant or resistant patterns of attachment truly maladaptive in the biological sense? This seems unlikely. Behavior patterns that interfered with the survival of the species would not be likely to become common. About 1 of every 3 babies in the countries studied to date have avoidant or resistant attachments, so we know these patterns are common.

Furthermore, it is easy to understand how a social group of genetically related individuals would have a biological advantage if individuals with anxious attachments, not only individuals with secure attachments, had a good chance of surviving and reproducing. Throughout recorded history, circumstances and events that would cause anxious attachment have been very common even in the lives of individuals who received good care in a safe environment in infancy. Through illness, accident, or war, many parents have died when their children were too young to bear the loss. A parent's struggle to get enough food and shelter for the family in adverse circumstances has often meant he or she could not provide sensitive care for a baby or young child. Political rulers, employers, and slave owners have often disrupted attachments by removing parents from their children temporarily or permanently. If infants and children were not able to survive such adversities, there would be far fewer human beings on the planet today.

Like individuals in other social species, parents and babies have conditional strategies for dealing with different circumstances. Economic, demographic, and cultural variables affect (1) the individual's decision about how many offspring to produce, (2) how and whether the individual cares for or provides for his or her offspring, and (3) whether efforts are made to raise any particular infant to maturity. At one extreme, educated parents in secure economic circumstances often choose to have only one or two children. At the opposite economic extreme, in regions where rates of infant mortality remain high, rates of reproduction generally also remain high, and adults sometimes cope by building up emotional defenses to distance themselves from their children. In some cultures, infanticide is still practiced as a reproductive or economic strategy. If a family has insufficient economic resources to support another child or if the new baby is deformed or weak, the baby may be sacrificed to increase the chances that other offspring will survive to reproductive maturity.

If evolution selects for altruistically, cooperatively behaving *groups* (over internally competitive groups), not just for such *individuals,* then selection of sensitive-secure dyads over rejecting-avoidant dyads seems likely. However, among biologists, the theory of *group selection* has been largely replaced by a theory of *kin selection.* This theory proposes that individuals act to increase the reproductive success of themselves and/or their kin. An infant's biological interest may be only in his own survival. His mother, however, can maximize her reproductive success by considering not only that baby's need's but also her own needs, the needs of her other offspring, and, in many cases, the needs of the mate or other partner(s) who contribute to the protection and support of the whole family. The father can maximize his reproductive success by helping to protect and provide for all of his offspring and their mother(s). Consequently, the baby's interests may at times conflict with the mother's and/or the father's. It may not always be in the parent's interest (still from an evolutionary perspective, not a psychological one) to be maximally sensitive and responsive to any given infant. If the parent is often rejecting and the baby becomes avoidant, the baby's strategy is, from a biological perspective, adaptive. By learning not to demand what he cannot have, the baby is making an active, strategic contribution to his own survival in the face of parental rejection.

Hinde (1982, p. 72) argued the case for the biological adaptiveness of a variety of attachment patterns most vigorously: "Optimal mothering (and attachment) behavior will differ according to the sex of the infant, its ordinal position in the family, the mother's social status, caregiving contributions from other family members, the state of physical resources, and so on . . . a mother-child relationship which produces successful adults in one situation may not do so in another." Recall, however, that the measure of biological success is simply effectiveness in reproducing. A person or group can be very successful biologically without being either happy or healthy psychologically.

Rather recently, Hinde and Stevenson-Hinde (1991) expanded the discussion of the implications of natural selection regarding attachment and adaptation. As they pointed out, much of an individual's behavior has a goal other than surviving, reproducing, or assisting his or her close relatives to survive and reproduce. Indeed, some goal-directed behavior has the predictable outcome of *reducing* the individual's reproductive success. Often, such behavior is encouraged by the norms and values of the society.

As an extreme example, self-sacrifice for the benefit of others in the tribe in a war or an emergency may be culturally mandated even though it clearly reduces an individual's reproductive success. In everyday life, many individuals pursue learning that will never be of any economic or other survival-enhancing benefit. Many pursue artistic and spiritual goals that are unlikely to increase their reproductive success. These activities are often encouraged by cultural norms and values. In short, cultural imperatives may either coincide with or contradict biological ones.

However, societies and cultures themselves are as natural to humankind as attachment and sexual bonding are. Humans survive in groups and must be adapted to living in complex societies. The tendencies that give rise to culture—the tendencies to learn from others, to copy, to conform, to teach, and to maintain an affiliation with the tribe—all of these are themselves products of natural selection. In many circumstances, individuals not only increase their reproductive success but also benefit in other ways from being guided by tradition. Arguments about what patterns of caregiving behavior and attachment behavior are most adaptive from the biological perspective can become quite complex.

ADAPTIVE ADVANTAGES FROM THE MENTAL HEALTH PERSPECTIVE

Let's move now to the issue of what is adaptive in terms of individual mental health. Here we must make yet another differentiation. What is adaptive very early in life, when the infant's survival depends on a specific caregiver who may have regrettable psychological and behavioral tendencies, may be maladaptive later. If your nanny always rebuffs you when you are frightened, cry, and approach her for comfort, learning to repress your fear and your need for comfort is adaptive. The defenses help you survive with minimal conscious discomfort while you are in your nanny's care. Later, however, your repressed anger and your expectation that attachment figures will not comfort or protect you may interfere greatly with your ability to form a trusting, close relationship with someone you might marry.

Bowlby (1973) hypothesized that an insecure attachment would often give rise to an inflexible, untrusting personality and produce difficulties in the areas of sympathy and sensitivity, particularly in building, experiencing, and sustaining loving relationships. Bowlby's hypothesis was not restricted to British society; he expected it to hold true around the world.

Main (1990) has elaborated an explanation of why insecure attachments, even if adaptive when they first emerge, are maladaptive later in the individual's life. Babies with secure attachments can and do safely employ *primary strategies*. Primary strategies are those that directly serve a goal of a major behavioral system. For example, seeking proximity to or contact with the attachment figure when under stress is a primary strategy. Even if primary strategies are overridden, they cannot be completely deactivated, Main says.

Secondary strategies, such as avoiding the attachment figure in stressful circumstances, require overriding a primary strategy and therefore result in complex experiences and distorted perceptions and may decrease psychological well-being. Memories that are inconsistent with that pretense are likely to be dissociated from their affective implications or repressed altogether. These primary and secondary strategies are not assumed to be conscious. According to Main (1990), the psychological and behavioral adaptations required of an avoidant or resistant baby are more complex than the adaptations required of a securely attached baby. When frightened or distressed, "the secure infant faces the problem of alerting the parent to its condition, while the insecure infant must deal simultaneously with the environment and with the parent" (Main, 1990, p. 58).

While continuing to believe that the ability to develop a variety of caregiving patterns and attachment patterns is biologically advantageous, Hinde and Stevenson-Hinde (1991) have concluded that sensitive responsiveness is likely to be a precursor to secure attachment across cultures. Secure attachment is, in turn, likely to be associated with later ego resilience, social competence, positive affect, empathy, persistence, and compliance across cultures. According to Hinde and Stevenson-Hinde (1991), insecure attachment patterns lead to increased vulnerability, both biological and psychological, and to decreased resilience.

Across many aspects of belief and behavior, what is considered "positive" in one culture may not be so in another. Even so, say Hinde and Stevenson-Hinde (1991), if psychological well-being is the ability to appraise and express emotions and to rely on close social relationships for support in times of stress, behavioral flexibility may be positive in any culture. They have concluded that it is reasonable to assume that security of attachment may promote psychological well-being in all cultures. However, psychological well-being will not always walk hand-in-hand with cultural values and norms and will not always augment reproductive success. For example, concerned about straining the earth's capacity to support its ever-increasing human population, some cultures now discourage high rates of reproduction. It is entirely possible that, in these cultures, individuals who are secure and psychologically healthy are overrepresented among the individuals who respect the reasons for reducing the human birthrate and have sufficient self-discipline and relationship skills to act accordingly. In other cultural or religious groups, secure individuals would be at least as likely as anyone else to produce several children.

All things considered, Hinde and Stevenson-Hinde (1990, 1991) have concluded that biological, cultural, and psychological desiderata probably overlap well in nonindustrialized cultures but have diverged and are sometimes in conflict in modern industrialized societies. Few simple, globally valid statements about what should be true of people with secure attachment histories are likely to hold up. Unfortunately, discussions of the degree to which group A or group C behavior patterns may be maladaptive and of the ways in which they may be maladaptive in non-Western cultures remain largely speculative. So far, relatively few data are available.

CHAPTER SUMMARY

If attachment theory is correct, then the instinctive tendency to form attachments and many of the short-term effects of factors that influence the patterning of attachment behavior in infancy should be universal. Because of the survival and reproductive advantages of belonging to a tribe, versus living alone or in a very small group, the forces of natural selection favor individuals who learn from and perpetuate the traditions of their cultures.

Preliminary evidence suggests that distributions of infant attachment patterns vary across cultures. In cultures in which distal modes of interaction and encouragement of early independence predominate, Strange Situation classifications A, B1, and B2 are more common than they are elsewhere. In cultures in which infants are typically near to or in contact with their caregivers, seldom see strangers, and/or are seldom left alone, Strange Situation classifications C and B4 are more common than they are elsewhere. In all cultures studied to date, most infants (usually 65 to 70 percent) show group B Strange Situation behavior.

The Strange Situation was developed as a culture-specific assessment procedure. Whether it is a valid method for assessing infants' attachments in other cultures has been the subject of much debate. What meaning the classification groups and subgroups have in various cultures cannot be known until we have more data from those cultures. Naturalistic longitudinal observations of infant-caregiver dyads with intermittent standardized assessments would be especially valuable. We need data about both the precursors and the sequelae of the various Strange Situation patterns in other cultures. We may also find that very different culture-specific procedures would be more useful for assessing attachment patterns in cultures that differ from white middle-class U.S. samples.

There has been a good bit of debate about what pattern of attachment behavior is most adaptive within or across cultures. What is most adaptive from the individual, biological perspective (maximizing reproduction) can easily differ from what is most adaptive from the individual mental health perspective (maximizing the individual's psychological well-being) and from what is most adaptive for the culture (sacrificing some individuals to perpetuate the strength of the tribe and its traditions). It is likely that the individual's ability to respond to his or her experiences with one of several attachment patterns is adaptive for the species. In the context of the individual's mental health, forming an insecure attachment has been called a "second-best" strategy. It is more complicated than forming a secure attachment and often it appears to have disadvantageous consequences later in life, but it is the best way for some infants to adapt to their immediate circumstances in the short run. In the long run, forming secure attachments early in life—staying free from excessive anxiety, anger, and psychological defensiveness—is probably most adaptive for individual mental health in any culture.

C H A P T E R

FATHERS

In most primate species, individuals live in groups, infants are clearly attached to their mothers, and the males of the group protect the whole group from external threats. Play between youngsters and adult males has been observed among chimpanzees and other apes, but caregiving by males and infant attachment to males in nonhuman mammals are rarely reported; infants are almost always with their mothers. West and Konner (1976) have argued that something similar was probably true of the way human beings lived for almost all of the time their behavior patterns were evolving. They proposed that the nomadic hunter-gatherer lifestyle of Africa's !Kung San (Bushmen) approximates the subsistence adaptation which characterized at least 98 percent of human and protohuman history. The habits of the !Kung San show striking similarities to the relations among mothers, infants, juveniles, and the rest of the group in chimpanzees (van Lawick-Goodall, 1968) and many other primates (Jolly, 1972). Adult human males, however, are generally believed to be unlike many other primates in that they tend to form lasting bonds with individual females and often demonstrate enduring social bonds with individual children, usually their own. This raises the possibility that interlocked mother-infant-father behavioral systems may have evolved into something quite different from the isolated mother-infant systems of other primate species.

Among the !Kung San, Konner (1972) observed that mothers interacted with their infants during almost all of the infants' waking time. The comparable figure for fathers was 13.7 percent of the time. The !Kung San were at the top of the range for father-infant closeness among the 80 historically separate, nonindustrial subsistence cultures West and Konner (1976) surveyed; close relationships between fathers and infants were common in only 3 of the 80 cultures.

These data must be interpreted in light of the presence and necessity of breast feeding throughout most of human evolution, and in light of gender role socialization. For all but the last few decades of human evolution, most infants had to be near their mothers frequently, or they would die of malnutrition. If the practices of existing subsistence cultures reflect those of earlier cultures, we can surmise that mothers have always worked—gathering plant foods, hunting small animals, preparing food, carrying water, gathering firewood, making clothing, and making household tools, as well as tending children. Prior to the introduction of agriculture, and even when gardening began, most of a mother's work could be done with an infant tied to the mother's back or side or playing nearby. Fathers, who could not feed young babies, could be spared for long group hunts for large animals and for other tasks that took them away from their small children.

How the roles of men and women differed in the past may not be a good guide to what their capabilities were and are. An example from a nonprimate species provides a good illustration of the difference between what is usual and what is possible. A male rat will emit caregiving behavior after about 5 days if an experimenter gives him a fresh litter of newborn rat pups each day (Rosenblatt, 1969). In their natural environments, the mother never leaves her pups alone with a male long enough for them to elicit caregiving behavior from him. The sight, sound, smell, and feel of rat pups elicit caregiving behavior much faster from a female rat than from a male rat, particularly if the female rat has recently been pregnant.

Both everyday observations and scientific research show that male humans are capable of doing all the things female humans do to care for babies, except for breast feeding. Hormonal differences between the sexes, especially after delivery of an infant and during the period of breast feeding, may prime the mother for caregiving. The stimulus threshold for eliciting caregiving may be lower for mothers than it is for fathers. On the other hand, traditional gender role socialization clearly pushes females toward caregiving more than it encourages males in the same direction. Minor biological differences may be much exaggerated by cultural traditions. Given the opportunity, fathers might be as well able as mothers and as strongly inclined as mothers to give care to babies, with the single exception of breast feeding.

In the United States today, as in ancient and modern preindustrial cultures, fathers spend far less time interacting with their babies than mothers do. The amount of time the father-baby dyad interacts varies greatly from family to family and probably varies with socioeconomic and subcultural differences. Pederson and Robson (1969) found that, based on the mothers' reports, individual fathers in their sample spent anywhere from 45 minutes to 26 hours per week interacting with their babies, who were 8 to 9½ months old. The average was 8 hours a week—slightly more than 1 hour a day. In another study, the average was much lower: only 15 or 20 minutes a day, based on the *father's* report (Lewis and Weinraub, 1974). The father's involvement does increase as the baby gets older. Clarke-Stewart (1978) found that mothers played with their babies at 15 months more than fathers did, but both parents participated in similar amounts of play when the same babies were 20 months old, and the fathers were playing with them more than the mothers were when the children were 30 months old.

THE FATHER'S ROLE

What role does a father usually take when his son or daughter is just a baby? To what extent is he a playmate, a physical caregiver, an emotional caregiver, a protector, a disciplinarian, or a teacher? These considerations matter, because many of the same behaviors serve different behavioral systems at different times in the same infant. For example, a baby may smile with delight when an object she is exploring does something a little surprising and interesting. In that case, the smile is not even a social signal. A baby may also smile at a new adult who comes to visit her family. This is affiliative behavior, inviting social interaction with a new partner, but not seeking care or protection from the visitor. The same baby may also smile with delight when her father enters the room after his daily 9-hour absence. This greeting smile may be attachment behavior, or it may be delight at the reappearance of a familiar and entertaining playmate.

To assess an attachment relationship, we must be able to differentiate attachment behavior from affiliative behavior. We cannot just count smiles or approaches or minutes of physical contact to determine whether an attachment bond exists. We must look at the behaviors in context and attend to the meaning of and motivation for the behaviors. Does the infant use the father as a secure base, monitoring and maintaining proximity to him when they are away from home? When frightened, does the infant cry for the father or rush to him? Does contact with the father soothe the infant? Does the baby protest when the father leaves the house? These behaviors would indicate attachment.

In some cultures, neither fathers nor mothers play with their babies much. Babies play with objects around them, and with other children, but not usually with adults. In such circumstances, the existence of an attachment bond might be easy to observe. In infancy, the alternative to an attachment bond to the father might be no bond at all. In the United States, fathers often interact as playmates, not protectors or comforters (Bornstein and Lamb, 1992); many fathers let the mother take over when the baby's attachment system is activated at a high level (Lamb, 1978). Under these circumstances, testing whether an infant-father attachment bond exists requires careful thought.

When you look at a baby interacting with his father, is most of what you see attachment behavior, or is it affiliative behavior? Bridges and Connell (1991) took an imaginative tack in addressing that question. They studied babies at 12 months with one parent and at 13 months with the other. At each age, they assessed the baby's emotional behavior in a free play setting and in the Strange Situation. Emotion was more consistent across the two settings with fathers than with mothers. The investigators took this to imply that interactions with the father primarily reflected affiliative aspects of the relationship, not the attachment component of it.

A BASIC QUESTION

The cross-cultural evidence discussed briefly above reveals that many babies have very little interaction with their fathers. In U.S. samples, when a baby is interacting with his father, the father is often in the role of playmate, not in the role of attachment figure. Do babies normally develop attachments to their fathers anyway? It seems very likely that most do.

In everyday life, babies often protest when the father departs from the room or from the house, just as they often protest when the mother departs. They often greet their fathers at reunion, just as they generally greet their mothers at reunion. If the father is away for a week or a month, the baby is not likely to exhibit prolonged protest or sink into despair while he is in the mother's care, but a measure of detachment at reunion with the father, followed by intensified attachment behavior, sometimes occurs. If the mother is away for a week or a month, the baby's protest, despair, and detachment are all likely to be less severe if the baby is in the father's care rather than in a stranger's. All this suggests that the father is valued as an attachment figure in his own right.

The same conclusion follows from an experiment in which the Strange Situation was modified to include separations from and reunions with the father as well as, in other episodes, the mother. During separations, the baby was never alone; a stranger stayed in the room with him. Using this laboratory procedure, Kotelchuck (1976) observed the responses of infants ranging in age from 12 to 21 months. On the average, the father's presence had the same sorts of effects as the mother's, but they were less intense. For example, babies cried the most when the mother left the room; they cried, but not as much, when the father left the room; and they did not cry when the stranger left the room. Exploration and play dropped to their lowest levels during the mother's absences; decreased, but not as much, during the father's absences; and continued undiminished during the stranger's absences. Clinging to the adult when he or she returned was most intense and longest for reunions with mothers; occurred, but less intensely, with fathers; and was infrequent with strangers. Although some babies drew some comfort from the stranger when no parent was available, they did not treat the stranger as an attachment figure. The babies clearly treated their fathers as attachment figures who were able to serve as secure bases.

Several other investigators have also presented evidence that, by the age of 12 months, most babies do treat the father as an attachment figure—as a more-or-less secure base (Cohen and Campos, 1974; Feldman and Ingham, 1975; Grossmann et al., 1981; Lamb, 1978; Main and Weston, 1981, and Willemsen et al., 1981). All found that infants in an unfamiliar place, such as a laboratory playroom, move around and explore or play with the available toys when either parent is present. If the only adult present is a stranger, babies move less, play less, cry more, and search for the missing parent(s). When both a parent and a stranger are present, babies approach, stay near, and touch the parent far more than the stranger. In Strange Situation studies in the United States, Germany, Sweden, and Israel, babies' behavior with their fathers can be coded and classified according to the criteria developed for assessing attachments to mothers. It is rare for an infant to take so little notice of the father's comings and goings in the Strange Situation that the infant is regarded as nonattached. The father may or may not be a major attachment figure in infancy, but he does seem to be at least a subordinate attachment figure.

DISTRIBUTION OF PATTERNS OF ATTACHMENT TO FATHERS

Are babies as likely to develop secure attachments to their fathers as to their mothers? It seems so. Results of the studies discussed below converge on the finding that the distribution of infants' patterns of attachment to their fathers is about the same as the distribution of infants' patterns of attachment to their mothers: approximately 65 percent secure, 25 percent avoidant, and 10 percent resistant. (Most of this research was done prior to the definition of the D category.)

DETERMINANTS OF SECURITY

Does the amount of time a father spends in interaction with his baby help predict whether the baby will be securely attached to him? Research results are mixed. Bass (1982) found evidence that quantity of interaction did help predict security of attachment. She defined low interaction, for fathers, as 14.5 or fewer hours per week and high interaction as 22 or more hours. The interaction could be play or caretaking, with or without the mother's presence. Using parents' responses on questionnaires about amount of interaction in an average week, she identified 18 one-year-olds for each of the two groups. Only 44 percent of the babies who had low levels of interaction with their fathers were securely attached to them. Of the 18 babies who experienced high levels of interaction with their fathers, 72 percent were securely attached. Resistance to the father in the Strange Situation was higher in the low-interaction group, but avoidance was not. The babies most likely to be securely attached to their fathers had high levels of interaction with both parents.

Did more interaction actually help a baby develop trust in her father as a reliable secure base? Maybe. Did fathers who were inclined to respond in ways that foster security choose to spend more time with their babies? Probably. Bass (1982) inferred that how much time the fathers in this sample spent with their babies reflected the fathers' or parents' choices, not any external factor. The two groups of fathers spent similar amounts of time at work, and so did their wives. All of the families were middle class. There were five insecure babies in the high-interaction group and eight securely attached babies in the low-interaction group, so amount of interaction clearly was not the only factor that contributed to security of attachment.

In a Swedish study, Frodi, Lamb, Hwang, and Frodi (1983) also considered this hypothesis about quantity of interaction. They located a sample of fathers who spent more than 1 month out of the first 9 as the primary caregiver for the baby and compared those nontraditional fathers with fathers who had traditional, less-involved relationships with their babies. Regardless of the father's involvement in infant care, the 51 babies in the study directed more affiliative behavior and more attachment behavior to their mothers than to their fathers. Within the range sampled in this study, there was no relationship between the amount of the father's time with the baby and the security of attachment to the father. In short, results in this study differed from Bass's results about quantity of interaction.

Another way to approach the question of whether quantity of interaction affects quality of attachment is to look for sex differences in quality of infant-father attachment. Fathers spend more time with their infant sons than with their infant daughters. This has been shown in a series of studies in the United States, in one study on Israeli kibbutzim, and among the nomadic !Kung San Bushmen in Africa, according to evidence cited by Lamb and Stevenson (1978). Given that fathers get more involved with their infant sons than with their infant daughters, are boys more likely than girls to be securely attached to their fathers? Bass (1982) found no significant sex differences in her small sample, but few researchers have tested for sex differences in attachments to fathers.

If attachment relationships with fathers are anything like attachment relationships with mothers, quality of interaction, not quantity (or not *just* quantity), should predict security of attachment. Surprisingly few studies have explicitly tested that hypothesis. There was some support for it in the Bielefeld study (Grossmann et al., 1981). Recently, Cox, Owen, Henderson, and Margand (1992) observed 38 fathers interacting with their firstborn 3-month-olds and interviewed the fathers. Each dyad was observed in the Strange Situation when the baby was 12 months old. The quality of interaction at 3 months and the father's early attitudes about the infant and about the paternal role each helped to predict the infant's later security of attachment to the father. Despite the fact that hundreds of babies have participated in Strange Situations with their fathers, we have few data on their prior interactions with their fathers in other settings, natural or contrived. We cannot say with confidence what the precursors of secure attachment to the father are.

CONCORDANCE IN INFANT-MOTHER AND INFANT-FATHER ATTACHMENTS

Is an infant who is securely attached to the mother likely also to be securely attached to the father? Does the pattern of attachment generalize from the relationship with the mother into the relationship with the father, or does the pattern of attachment to the father result specifically from interactions with the father? Most of the early studies of concordance between an infant's Strange Situation classification with his mother and his Strange Situation classification with his father failed to find any significant association between the two (e.g., Grossmann, Grossmann, Huber, and Wartner, 1981; Main and Weston, 1981; Sagi, Lamb, Lewkowicz, Shoham, Dvir, and Estes, 1985). The early conclusion was therefore that Strange Situation behavior reflected the history and organization of independent attachment relationships. How the baby acted with his mother in the Strange Situation depended on what sort of interaction he had experienced with her; how the baby acted with his father depended on what sort of interaction he had experienced with him. There was apparently no association between the way his mother interacted with him and the way his father interacted with him.

However, the early studies all used small samples. Most babies show secure attachments to their mothers and most show secure attachments to their fathers. Consequently, the likelihood of finding that babies were securely attached to both parents would be high, even in the presence of random associations between the two attachment patterns. To demonstrate an association between patterns of attachment to the two parents even greater than the association that might easily occur by chance would be difficult. Either there would have to be very strong concordance between the two attachment patterns, or there would have to be a very large sample. Very strong concordance between the two attachment patterns evidently does not exist. Many years passed before a team of investigators (Fox, Kimmerly, and Schafer, 1991) amassed data on a very large sample (discussed in the next section).

There are, I believe, several reasons why we should expect *some* concordance between the pattern of attachment to the mother and the pattern of attachment to the father. First, the individual's representational models of attachment relationships probably influence both (1) whom a person marries and (2) the quality of care he or she gives to babies. Adults with secure representational models are more likely than other adults are to notice whatever rigidities or distortions often arise in an insecure partner's contributions to inter- action. They are therefore less likely to tolerate unsatisfactory interactions and less likely to develop enduring, close relationships with unrewarding partners. With this advantage in screening out less satisfying partners, secure adults should be somewhat more likely to marry secure partners than other adults are. Being relatively free from maladaptive defenses and distortions in perception and interpretation, they are also more likely to respond sensitively to their babies. Similarly, adults who defend against attachment needs or remain locked into angry struggles to get their own needs met are more likely than secure adults to tolerate and choose each other. They are likely to have difficulty giving sensitive care to their babies.

A second reason to expect some degree of match in a baby's pattern of attachment to the mother and the same baby's pattern of attachment to the father is that it seems likely that a sensitive spouse often provides both modeling and "scaffolding" for a less sensitive spouse's interaction with their baby. *Modeling* is simply demonstrating a response or a pat- tern of responding; it need not entail any conscious attempt to teach the observer. *Scaf- folding* is behavior that props up or supports new behavior the partner is learning. Through modeling and scaffolding, the sensitive parent increases the likelihood that the second par- ent will also respond sensitively to the baby. This increases the probability that the baby will develop confidence in both parents, even if one in the absence of influence from the other would have behaved insensitively and so fostered an anxious attachment.

Third, a sensitive parent may simply take over when an inconsistent second parent is unresponsive. The sensitive parent would thereby protect the baby from experiencing much of the second parent's ignoring, interfering, or rejecting behavior. For example, a mother who is sensitive to her baby's signals and wants her baby to have a close, positive relationship with her husband may facilitate his sensitive involvement with the baby and step in to provide good care of the baby during the father's lapses. The baby would rarely experience poor care from her father; she would be left to interact with the father only when the father was available for positive interaction. Unaware of indirect, triadic effects, she would develop confidence in both parents' responsiveness.

In short, I am proposing three hypotheses. The first is that people who will later be parents tend to choose partners whose attachment models and caregiving behavior are sim- ilar to their own. The second is that parents generally support the partner's tendency to act as they act toward the baby. The third is that sensitive parents tend to buffer their babies from deficiencies and distortions in the other parent's care. If these hypotheses are correct, there should be some association between security of attachment to one parent and secu- rity of attachment to the other. How the infant acts in the Strange Situation with his father presumably reflects the baby's expectations about his father's responses, based on his history of interaction with the father. How he acts in the Strange Situation with his mother reflects his expectations about his mother's responses, based on his history of inter- action with her. What I am proposing is that there are reasons to expect (1) similar histo- ries of interaction between each parent and the child and (2) concordant patterns in the child's attachments to the two parents.

I am not arguing that there should always be perfect matching between an infant's patterns of attachment to his two parents. Many factors besides the three listed above affect how people select spouses and how they interact with their babies. For example, sexual attraction can easily override dissatisfaction with other aspects of interaction. Physical exhaustion or chronic illness can undermine a potentially wonderful parent's ability to give sensitive care to a baby. What I *am* proposing is that the degree of matching between the attachment to one parent and the attachment to the other should be even greater than the substantial degree of matching that would occur by chance.

As noted above, we have evidence that, in many families, fathers interact very little with their babies. In such cases, the baby's attachment pattern with the father during the mother's (infrequent) absences could conceivably be a direct carryover from the way he has learned to organize his attachment behavior in relation to his primary caregiver (i.e., the mother). This possibility should also contribute to some concordance between Strange Situation classifications with the two parents.

A META-ANALYSIS

Recently, Fox, Kimmerly, and Schafer (1991) conducted a meta-analysis of data from 11 studies of concordance of infant-mother and infant-father attachment. The scope of the meta-analysis is impressive: 710 babies were included. Unfortunately, most of the studies occurred before the D category was defined, and all of the data were forced into the A-B-C classification system. In one study (32 babies), the Strange Situation with the second parent was conducted only 1 week after the first, so some of the classifications were probably invalid. In three other samples (189 babies), the second Strange Situation occurred only 1 month after the first, so some assessments may have been contaminated. Despite these limitations, the results of the meta-analysis are persuasive.

There were significant associations between security of attachment to one parent and security of attachment to the other, between type of insecurity (avoidant or resistant) with one parent and type of insecurity with the other, and between subcategory of security (B1 or B2 versus B3 or B4) with one parent and subcategory of security with the other. In other words, babies who were secure with one parent tended also to be secure with the other, more often than we would expect to occur by chance. Specifically, 65 percent of the babies were secure with the mother, and 66 percent were secure with the father. However, 76 percent of babies who were secure with one parent were also secure with the other. If there were no association between security with one parent and security with the other, we would expect to find only 66 percent of the babies who were secure with the mother also to be secure with the father. With so large a sample, the difference between 76 percent and 66 percent is both statistically significant and persuasive. Of the babies who were anxiously attached to one parent, 55 percent were anxiously attached to the other, and 55 percent is obviously significantly greater than 34 or 35 percent that would appear in a random distribution.

When a baby was secure with one parent but insecure with the other, the insecure attachment was about equally likely to be avoidant or resistant. In contrast, the meta-analysis revealed that babies who were avoidant with one parent were likely to be avoidant or secure (rarely resistant) with the other. Similarly, a baby with a resistant attachment to one parent was very unlikely to have an avoidant attachment to the second parent.

A number of explanations of the observed associations are possible. One set of explanations is provided by the hypotheses I stated above. However, as Fox et al. (1991) pointed out, infant temperament may also be a factor. Proneness to cry or emotional reactivity might affect the developing relationships in general or the Strange Situation behavior in particular, with both parents. High sociability in the baby might elicit high responsiveness from both parents and so contribute to the development of secure attachments to both.

Obviously, infants' patterns of attachment to their two parents did often differ. About 1 out of every 4 babies in the meta-analysis had a secure attachment to one parent but an anxious attachment to the other. It certainly still appears that behavior in the Strange Situation reflects experience with the specific caregiver participating in it, not a general model derived from one relationship and transferred automatically to all others.

CHAPTER SUMMARY

Although most fathers interact with their babies much less than mothers do, it appears that, in the cultures where infant-father attachments have been studied, most infants do become attached to their fathers. Whether the Strange Situation is a valid procedure for assessing patterns of attachment to fathers has seldom been tested explicitly, but, after observing hundreds of babies with their fathers in the Strange Situation, researchers have not noticed anything that leads them to question the validity of the procedure.

Almost all of the published research on infant-father attachments has used Strange Situation classifications A, B, and C, but not D. Each of those three patterns has been observed as often with fathers as with mothers.

Theorists expect the pattern of attachment to the father to reflect the baby's history with and expectations about the father; they do not think the attachment to the father is copied from the relationship with the mother. Unfortunately, very few researchers have made direct observations of infant-father interaction in the first 12 months of life and tied them to Strange Situation assessments. The available data are consistent with predictions from theory, but are not sufficient to show what aspects of interaction with the father contribute to the development of the different patterns of attachment.

When data from small samples were aggregated into a very large sample, the pattern of attachment to the father matched the pattern of attachment to the mother more often than would have occurred by chance.

MATERNAL EMPLOYMENT AND INFANT DAY CARE

Biological mothers are usually the primary caregivers for infants and toddlers in this and most other cultures. Partly for that reason, attachment research, like other research on child development, has focused primarily on mothers. For reasons that may be less scientific, child development research for many years focused on mothers who stayed at home with their babies most of the time. Eventually, however, developmental psychologists began paying attention to mothers whose jobs, studies, or volunteer activities took them away from their babies for hours at a time on a regular basis. Routine nonparental care of infants and toddlers has become common in the United States. As a result, we now have some data and many interesting questions and hypotheses about employed mothers, hired caregivers, and their effects on infant attachment and its sequelae. These matters are the topics of this chapter.

MATERNAL EMPLOYMENT

Early in his career, Bowlby argued that separations from the mother should be kept to a minimum. Later, however, in response to persuasive data, Bowlby (1984) changed his opinion. A subsidiary attachment figure, he wrote, can meet a baby's needs adequately in the primary figure's absence.

Whether and how a mother's employment might affect her children was a topic of great interest in the 1980s. Many scientists, politicians, and parents were worried that children, especially infants, would suffer if anyone but the mother cared for them most of the time. Others argued that such worries were based on oppressive sexist prejudices, not on data.

Moderately long, depriving separations, such as those that occur when an infant stays in a hospital or temporary residential care institution for many days, are known to have negative and sometimes long-lasting effects on attachments (e.g., Heinicke and West-heimer, 1966; Robertson and Robertson, 1971). However, brief separations during the mother's volunteer activities, shopping, exercise classes, and recreational activities are common in our culture for babies whose mothers are their primary caregivers. We have no evidence to suggest that these separations are deleterious.

Do the one-day-at-a-time separations associated with working outside the home provoke anxiety and anger in infants as separations of 2 weeks do? Are job-related separations from the mother more distressing than job-related separations from the father? In the presence of the primary caregiver, babies tolerate long daily separations from their employed fathers with no apparent decrease in the frequency of secure attachments. In the presence of a familiar hired caregiver, might babies not tolerate long daily separations from their employed mothers with similar equanimity?

What frequency and duration of separations can an infant tolerate comfortably? At what age can a baby who is old enough to form attachments comfortably manage a 9-hour period of separation from the primary caregiver? To what extent do the effects of separation depend on the quality of care from the primary caregiver? To what extent do they depend on the quality of care during the separation? Is the size of the day care group or the caregiver-to-child ratio important? Are continuity and stability of alternate care arrangements important? What do babies need from the social environment? What infant day care arrangement are compatible with their needs? Do infants benefit from having more than one major caregiver in infancy, more than one relationship laying the foundation for the child's representational models of the self and of relationships?

Suwalsky, Klein, Zaslow, Rabinovich, and Gist (1987) identified six types of naturally occurring separations and called attention to the possible importance of predictable patterning of separations. They defined separations as *patterned* if (1) there was at least one separation per week for 4 consecutive weeks, (2) the timing and duration of the separations was the same from week to week, and (3) the caregivers and care setting were the same each time. Their hypothesis that patterned care would contribute to the infant's comfort and sense of security during separations from the primary caregiver has seldom been investigated.

■ Correlates of Maternal Employment

How does maternal employment affect family dynamics? According to a thorough summary in Schachere (1990), research suggests the mother's employment is sometimes associated with regrettable changes in the quality of the marriage or in the relationship between the father and the baby. In one study of working-class families, husbands did not object to their wives' holding jobs outside the home, and they often did increase their participation in child care, but they were then more dissatisfied with their marriages. In a study of middle-class families, husbands of employed women found their toddlers more annoying than husbands of unemployed women did. In addition, husbands of women with full-time jobs were less sensitive to their children in an assessment using a problem-solving task than husbands of women with part-time or no jobs were. Observational studies have also revealed that women with full-time jobs take up a lot of the baby's evening time with play and talk, while women with part-time or no jobs tend to step back and leave time in the evenings for the father to spend with the baby. The mother's employment may often affect the baby's relationship with the father.

Owen and Cox (1988) found that, by 3 months after birth, employed mothers were less invested in parenthood than unemployed mothers were, and mothers who were employed more than 40 hours a week had high levels of anxiety. High anxiety can get in the way of giving good care to a baby.

The available research suggests that, when the mother works outside the home, links between the father's involvement with the baby and the quality of the marriage seem quite strong. Of course, this correlation provides no evidence about direction(s) of effects. Fathers in harmonious marriages may be more inclined than fathers in unhappy marriages to get involved with their babies. Or, fathers who get involved with their babies may thereby directly contribute to the harmony and happiness of their marriages.

Schachere (1990) studied employed mothers and their toddlers, all of whom entered nonmaternal care in the first year of life. In this sample, she concluded, the quality of the marriage had a direct effect on the mother's attitudes about parenting, and the mother's attitudes had a direct effect on the quality of the baby's attachment to her.

Chase-Lansdale and Owen (1987) considered the possibility that the mother's holding a job might affect not only her relationship with her child, but also her husband's relationship with their child. They observed firstborns from intact, two-parent, middle-class families in two Strange Situation assessments, the first with one parent when the infants were 12 months old and the second with the other parent 3 to 6 weeks later. The sample included 40 babies whose mothers had returned to full-time jobs when the baby was between 2 weeks and 6 months old, and the babies were cared for in relatively stable home settings. There was no relation between maternal employment status and the quality of the infant's attachment to the mother. However, for boys (but not for girls), anxious attachment to the father was more common in the employed mother group than in the unemployed mother group. The anxious attachments to the fathers tended to be openly resistant, not defensively avoidant. Chase-Lansdale and Owen (1987) proposed that the employed mothers might be making up for lost time with their babies in the evenings and so getting in the way of the sorts of father-infant interaction that would foster the baby's confidence in the father's sensitive responsiveness.

Owen, Easterbrooks, Chase-Lansdale, and Goldberg (1984) observed 59 of the babies from the Chase-Lansdale and Owen (1987) study again when the babies were about 20 months old. Fifty-three of them were seen in separate Strange Situations with each parent, with 3 to 6 weeks between the laboratory visits. Six were seen only with the mother. If, during the 12 to 20 month age period of the infant's life, the mother's employment status (full-time, part-time, or unemployed) was stable, it did not help predict whether the infant's attachment pattern to the mother or to the father would also be stable over those 8 months. When the mother's employment status changed in any way during the period of study, there was still no effect on stability in the infant's attachment to the mother, but changes in the infant's attachment *to the father* were unusually frequent (46 percent). The change was more often from secure to insecure than from insecure to secure.

In contrast, Thompson, Lamb, and Estes (1982) found that changes in the mother's employment status between the time the baby was 12 months old and the time he was 19 months old were associated with changes in the infant's pattern of attachment *to the mother*. Neither study provided much information about why the mother did or did not have a job outside the home or about how the employed mothers or their husbands felt about the mother's employment. Without more information, the data from the two studies are hard to interpret.

Picking up the thread of research on whether the mother's employment affects the infant's attachment to the father, Belsky and Rovine (1988) observed 82 infants in the Strange Situation at the age of 12 or 13 months. For boys (but not for girls), they replicated the Owen and Cox (1988) finding that infants whose mothers had full-time jobs (more than 35 hours per week) were more likely to be insecurely attached to their fathers than infants whose mothers were unemployed or held part-time jobs. In addition, in this sample, the infants who had more than 20 hours per week of nonmaternal care showed more avoidance of the mother at reunion and were more likely to be classified as insecurely attached than infants with fewer than 20 hours per week of nonmaternal care (Belsky and Rovine, 1988).

All these bits of evidence put together are consistent with the hypothesis that the mother's full-time employment in the baby's first year increases the risk of some undesirable outcomes. Of course, the financial consequences of a mother's lack of employment can also be associated with undesirable outcomes. There are hints that the quality of the marriage may be extra important but may also be extra hard to maintain when the mother has a full-time job and the family has a baby under 1 year old. The baby's relationships with both parents may be affected. All of this, of course, remains to be proven or disproven. Much more research—well-planned, carefully conducted research—must be done before we can speak with confidence about how the mother's employment early in the baby's life reflects or affects family dynamics.

■ The Great Debate

As the 1980s came to an end, the possibility that leaving the baby's care to a nonparental caregiver for many hours each week might affect the baby's attachment to the mother was the topic of heated debate and several reviews (Belsky, 1988; Clarke-Stewart, 1988; Gamble and Zigler, 1986; McCartney and Galanopoulos, 1988; Richters, 1988; Schachere, 1990; Sroufe, 1988; and Thompson, 1988). Except for one dissenting voice (Thompson, 1988), the reviewers agreed on two major points. First, a majority of babies whose mothers hold full-time jobs become securely attached to the mother, even if the baby is less than 6 months old when the mother returns to her job. Second, avoidant attachments are significantly but not vastly more common in that group than they are among babies who receive little nonparental care in the first year.

The extent of the increase in the frequency of anxious attachments is unclear. In her summary of information from several samples, Clarke-Stewart (1988) reported that avoidant attachments were only 8 percent more common when the mother had a full-time job than when she was a full-time homemaker. Six years later, Belsky and Cassidy (1994) estimated that the rate of anxious attachment to the mother across studies is about 40 percent for babies with early and extensive day care experience. They cited three specific studies in which the rates of anxious attachment were 24 percent, 65 percent, and 83 percent higher for babies with more than 20 hours a week of nonparental care in the first year than for the respective comparison babies.

In studies of maternal employment and infant attachment, most of the research samples have been white and middle class. However, studies with working-class samples also found increased avoidance when the mother had a full-time job that started early in the baby's life. The association between early, full-time, nonparental care and increased frequency of avoidant attachment appeared even when the quality of nonparental care was known to be good. It appeared when child care was in a home as well as when it was in a day care center. There was a little evidence that boys might be more at risk than girls. Most reviewers concluded that part-time day care did not appear to be a risk factor. They also agreed that day care that began after the baby's first birthday did not appear to jeopardize the quality of the infant's attachment to the primary caregiver.

In Australia, Barnett et al. (1987) found no relation between maternal employment and infant attachment. In the United States, however, evidence converged on the conclusion that avoidant attachments to mothers were more common in families in which the mother returned to a full-time job early in the baby's life than they were in other families. In the context of general agreement about that, the debate was about the causes, meaning, and implications of the higher frequency of avoidance.

In a controversial paper, Belsky (1988) called attention to evidence that extensive nonmaternal care in the first year was associated with avoidant attachment, and to the fact that avoidant attachment had been, in separate studies, associated with aggression and noncompliance in the preschool and the early school years. He expressed concern that early full-time employment of the mother might contribute to increased aggression and noncompliance in the child. Clarke-Stewart (1988) responded with a declaration that Belsky's worry was premature, unfounded, and likely to be harmful to many families. The practical difficulties of one family's managing two jobs plus care for one or more small children are considerable, and many employed mothers also experience stressful levels of doubt and guilt. No direct association between maternal employment and child aggression or noncompliance had been demonstrated (Clarke-Stewart, 1988).

Clarke-Stewart proposed that the entire connection between maternal employment and avoidant attachment might be specious. Infants with extensive day care experience might simply be accustomed to separation and so might not find it upsetting. For them, the brief separations involved in the Strange Situation might not be sufficiently stressful to activate attachment behavior. The infant's ignoring the mother at reunion might mean that he really was not troubled by her absence, not that he was guarding against expressing attachment needs because he anticipated rebuff.

While this argument must appeal to those who wish to reassure mothers that separations associated with employment will not harm a baby, it rests on shaky ground. Blind to background information about the infants in Strange Situations I was coding for other investigators' research projects, I have watched videotapes of many babies whose mothers worked outside the home. Like other babies, most of these subjects did react to separation in an unfamiliar place and did show attachment behavior. Even babies who are not troubled by brief separations from the mother are still likely, if securely attached, to greet their mothers at reunion, not ignore or avoid them. Positive greetings at reunion are a major factor in differentiating secure (subgroup B1 or B2) babies from avoidant babies. For a baby or toddler to act as if the mother is of no importance when all available data suggest that she is of great importance is surely an indication of a defensive process.

To address Clarke-Stewart's challenge, Belsky and Braungart (1991) compared two groups of 12-month-olds with avoidant attachments. One group ($N = 9$) had experienced less than 20 hours per week of nonparental care, and the other ($N = 11$) had received more than 20 hours per week of nonparental care. The group with more nonparental care fussed and cried more and played with objects less in the reunion episodes than the other group did. In this small sample of avoidant babies, those who had had extensive nonparental care certainly seemed to be actually insecure, not misclassified.

■ A Meta-Analysis

Recently, Lamb, Sternberg, and Prodromidis (1992) conducted a meta-analysis of data from 13 U.S. studies of nonmaternal care and infant-mother attachment. Together, the studies included 897 babies (493 boys and 404 girls) assessed in the Strange Situation when the baby was between 11 and 24 months old. Sixty-six percent of the babies were firstborns. Almost all of the families were white, middle-class, two-parent families, so it was not possible to test for effects of socioeconomic or cultural status. Mothers of children receiving regular nonmaternal care were employed for an average of 32.6 hours per week. Some infants were in day care centers; some were in family day care in the care provider's home; some were cared for by relatives; and some were cared for by hired babysitters in the family home.

Half of the babies in the aggregated sample received fewer than 5 hours per week of regular nonmaternal care. They were treated as the "exclusive maternal care" group. The mother's age, mother's education, father's age, and father's education were highly similar in the two sets of families (those using child care regularly and those not doing so). Initial testing revealed no significant differences between groups of babies who spent 21 to 30, 30 to 40, or more than 40 hours per week in care. Consequently, those groups were combined for subsequent analyses.

At one point in the day care debate, Belsky (1988) had reminded the research community that the timing of recruiting a family for research can affect the results of the research. To be specific, employed mothers who agree to participate in a study of the effects of maternal employment on children may be the ones who are already pretty sure its effects are positive or neutral. Mothers who are recruited for research before they have decided whether to return to a job may constitute a less-biased sample. However, in the meta-analysis, differences in the timing of recruitment were not associated with any differences in proportions of securely attached infants in the exclusive maternal care groups or the nonmaternal care groups.

The meta-analysis confirmed that secure attachments were significantly more common among babies who were almost always in the mother's care than among babies whose mothers held full-time jobs. Unlike earlier studies, the meta-analysis also found that part-time maternal employment was associated with an increase in avoidance.

Although the mean difference between groups was statistically significant, it was less than half of a point on Ainsworth's 7-point avoidance scale. Resistance scores were also slightly but significantly higher among the infants receiving regular nonmaternal care than among the other infants. This was especially true for babies who entered nonmaternal care early in the first year. The increases were, in many cases, not enough to affect Strange Situation classification: 65 percent of the infants in regular nonmaternal care and 71 percent of those in exclusive maternal care were classified as securely attached to the mother. (Only one study included in the meta-analysis had used the D category.)

In most cases, the quality of nonmaternal care was not known, so its effects could not be assessed. However, anxious attachments to the mother were significantly more common among infants in day care centers than among those in family day care homes or in their own home in the care of hired babysitters.

One finding from the meta-analysis is hard to interpret. Anxious attachments were more common among babies assessed after 15 months of age than among younger babies. The authors did not say how many babies were over 20 months old at the time of the Strange Situation assessment and what, if any, age-related modifications of coding were used for them.

Among the babies who were in nonmaternal care, those who entered it before they were 7 months old were more likely to be securely attached to the mother than those who entered it between the ages of 7 and 12 months. Earlier reviewers had proposed that the mother's waiting at least 6 months before taking a job might reduce the risk of anxious attachment. The meta-analysis suggested instead that the risk of disturbing the security of infant-mother attachment may be greatest if nonmaternal care begins during the period when the first attachment is consolidating.

In this meta-analysis, as noted earlier, 12 of the 13 studies did not use the anxious-disorganized-disoriented category (often because they took place before it was defined), so it is probable that some anxious attachments were misclassified as secure. Such misclassifications may have been more common in one group than another. In addition, an unspecified number of infants were assessed in Strange Situations when they were over 20 months old—perhaps too old for the traditional coding criteria to be valid.

Despite these limitations, the results of the meta-analysis should certainly be considered seriously. What is striking about the results is the number of variables that made no significant difference or were associated with a difference that was, although statistically significant, slight. For white, middle-class, educated families, there is little evidence here that maternal employment per se has much effect on security of attachment to the mother, whether the employment is part-time or full-time, or whether it begins early in the infant's life or after the first year. A sizable majority of the infants in every subgroup were securely attached to the mother.

Nevertheless, the meta-analysis did find an association between maternal employment and a small increase in the frequency of anxious attachments to the mother. The individual studies on which the meta-analysis was based often specified that the increase was in avoidant attachments, not resistant attachments.

■ Interpretations

What might explain the small statistical association between maternal employment and infant avoidance?* We do not have the sort of data that would enable us to answer that question. Is the avoidance a means of coping with anxiety and anger that result from frequent, long separations? Do employed mothers, as Belsky (1988) suggested, try to make

---

*The ideas in this section appeared earlier in V. Colin (1993), Public policy, attachment, and science, in the *Journal of Social Behavior and Personality, 8,* 21–23, and are published here with permission.

up for lost interaction time and so overstimulate their babies when they are together? Are the mothers also struggling to manage dinner, errands, household chores, and at least a little communication with their husbands during the little time they have with their babies each day? If so, that might limit their availability and responsiveness and so encourage the baby to develop avoidant defenses. Are the babies tired and therefore showing quite a bit of attachment behavior most of time the mother and baby have together on job days? If attachment behavior is high while the mother is trying to manage competing demands on her attention, the baby might often feel rebuffed.

Are the mothers who would behave insensitively to their infants under any circumstances precisely the mothers most likely to accept full-time jobs even if doing so is not an economic necessity? That seems very possible. As research I will describe in Chapter 17 has shown, mothers who dismiss the importance of attachments are the most likely to rebuff their infants' attachment behavior. They are probably also the most likely, in a culture that still doubts whether anyone but the mother can give optimal care to an infant, to conclude nonetheless that it will be fine to have a full-time job. In that case, maternal employment would regularly be correlated with infant avoidance, but it would not actually be causing it.

If maternal employment does directly or indirectly increase the frequency of infant avoidance, what are the consequences? How long-lasting are they? Is the avoidance a fairly transient response to managing separations when a baby is too young to handle them comfortably? Does it give way to secure expressions of attachment behavior when the child gets a little older, can handle daily separations more easily, and develops confidence in the mother's predictable and reliable return? Or does the avoidance represent a pattern of anger and defensiveness that will linger and hamper both the primary attachment relationship and other relationships?

We don't know. We need observations of employed mothers' and of alternate caregivers' interactions with babies in the course of everyday life and of fathers' interactions with the babies and the mothers. We need to see what percentage of babies of employed mothers are showing healthy secure-base behavior at home and in their day care settings. We need naturalistic, longitudinal observations of how mother-baby interactions or mother-baby-father interactions change when the mother accepts or returns to a job.

Would avoidance of the employed mother be less common if good-quality nonmaternal care were easier to obtain? The possibility that quality and stability of alternate care influence whether the mother's employment is associated with anxiety in the infant's attachment to her has often been mentioned. For example, several studies of employed mothers whose babies were in stable, patterned, high-quality care during the mother's absence (e.g., Chase-Lansdale and Owen, 1987; Field, Masi, Goldstein, Perry, and Parl, 1988; Suwalsky and Klein, 1980) have found no evidence of any association between maternal employment and anxious attachment.

Recently, Roggman, Langlois, Hubbs-Tait, and Rieser-Danner (1994) have argued that *many* other studies may also have failed to find any increase in anxious attachment associated with nonmaternal care. The problem is that journals rarely publish nonsignificant results. No one can tell how many file drawers are filled with unpublished studies that found no correlation between nonmaternal care and attachment outcomes.

Even with unstable, nonoptimal alternate care, most babies of employed mothers are securely attached. For example, Vaughn, Gove, and Egeland (1980) drew 104 white subjects from the Minneapolis study of disadvantaged families and compared attachment classifications at 12 and at 18 months. They called mothers who returned to jobs by the time the baby was 12 months old their "early work" group ($N = 34$). Mothers who began jobs when their babies were 12 to 18 months old were the "late work" group ($N = 18$). Mothers who remained unemployed through the child's eighteenth month were in the inaccurately labeled "no work" group ($N = 52$). Infants in each of the three groups were about equally likely to be securely attached, but there were disproportionate numbers of avoidant infants in the "early work" group (but not the "late work" group) at both 12 and 18 months. The findings are difficult to interpret, because employment status was confounded with marital status. Inspection of the data suggests that the heightened frequency of avoidant attachment in the "early work" group appeared mainly in the infants of single mothers. Despite the high frequencies of four possible risk factors in this sample (poverty, single parenthood, early employment, and unstable alternate care arrangements), the majority of infants were classified as securely attached.

SECTION SUMMARY

Because actions based on conclusions about maternal employment and infant day care can have quick and harmful effects on public policy and on parents' peace of mind, great care in drawing them is certainly warranted. We have much evidence that most babies whose mothers hold jobs are securely attached to them. However, there appears to be a small increase in the frequency of avoidant attachments when the mother is employed full-time early in the infant's life. We do not know whether the increase is an effect or just a correlate of maternal employment.

The interpretations mentioned here are only a few of the many offered in the current debate on maternal employment and infant attachment. As noted earlier, we need lengthy naturalistic observations.

INFANT DAY CARE

How common is it for someone other than the mother to take care of a baby? In most modern industrialized countries, it is quite common. However, in 90 percent of the subsistence cultures West and Konner (1976) surveyed, the mother was the infant's principal caregiver; she took care of the baby for more than half of the baby's waking hours. In the remaining 10 percent, the mother often provided half or less than half of the infant's care. In 54 percent of the cultures, however, someone besides the mother was also important in providing care for the infant. Often, the care came from another female relative, ranging, in different families and cultures, from young girls to grandmothers. It appears that human babies can adapt quite successfully to receiving care from a secondary attachment figure.

In our culture, as many as half of the mothers of babies under 1 year old are now employed; many babies are spending most of their waking time, 5 days a week, in day care. The questions to be asked about attachments to alternate caregivers are numerous and important. Do babies almost always become attached to their hired caregivers? What is the normative distribution of patterns of attachment to hired day care providers? Are babies in family day care settings more or less likely than babies in institutional day care to form secure attachments to their caregivers? Is the pattern of attachment to the mother a good predictor of the pattern of attachment to the hired caregiver? Does a given day care provider tend to foster the same pattern of attachment (secure, avoidant, resistant, or disorganized-disoriented) in each of the babies he or she cares for? How much do interactions with the alternate caregiver influence the formation of the infant's representational models of self, others, and relationships? Can a secure attachment to another caregiver buffer the infant from the negative effects associated with an anxious attachment to the primary caregiver? How does the high rate of turnover among day care providers affect babies? Does an infant mourn the loss of a significant attachment figure when a hired caregiver disappears from his life? Does a young child who has experienced repeated losses of caregivers develop defense mechanisms to guard against forming new attachments? Might such defenses continue to operate when they are no longer adaptive?

Research has barely begun to address most of these important questions.

■ A Basic Question

Do babies get attached to hired caregivers at all? If so, they should actively and selectively seek proximity to and contact with their day care providers when they are frightened, tired, or sick, and they should show secure-base behavior in everyday situations. Do they? Probably so, but few specific observations to prove it have been reported.

One relevant study comes from East Africa, where Liederman and Liederman (1973) identified a group of babies for whom the mother was the principal caregiver in less than half of the naturalistic observations scattered through everyday life. Even so, the babies had been in almost constant contact with their mothers for the first 4 months of their lives. By the age of 5 or 6 months, the infant might be left with another caregiver for up to half of each day. This caregiver was usually a 7- to 12-year-old girl who took her responsibility seriously but also had other chores and peer playmates. The babies showed neutral or mildly positive responses when a stranger walked out of sight and showed very negative responses when the mother walked out of sight. At the age of 7 to 9 months, the babies reacted to the alternate caregiver's departure as they reacted to the stranger's departure. At 10 to 12 months, however, they reacted to the alternate caregiver's departure as they reacted to the mother's. Distress at separation indicated that they had become attached to their alternate caregivers.

In the United States, Barnas and Cummings (1994) observed forty toddlers (11 to 27 months old) during routine activities in day care centers. They classified caregivers as "stable" if they had been in attendance with the child at the center for at least twice as long as the "unstable" caregiver who was also under study. The stable caregivers had been present with the toddler for an average of 10.6 months; the unstable caregivers, for 1.8 months. When distressed, toddlers directed attachment behavior toward stable caregivers more often than they did to unstable caregivers, and the stable caregivers were more effective in soothing them. When not distressed, there were indications of using the stable caregivers more often than less familiar ones as secure bases. Like the Liederman's study in Africa, all this suggests that infants do become attached to day care providers, and that the attachments take some months to form.

By definition, if a baby becomes attached to a caregiver, a lasting emotional bond has formed. When, as often occurs in the case of a hired caregiver, the relationship ends, there should be some indication that the baby misses the attachment figure. There is anecdotal evidence suggesting that a baby who has been in a specific person's care for many months may look sad and ask for the person when she or he disappears from his life, but I know of no systematic research indicating that babies grieve for lost day care providers. It is possible that a baby who stays in a certain person's care for hours each day, 5 days a week, soon enough organizes her attachment behavior in relation to that person, but it may take months before the baby develops any important emotional bond to the caregiver—or the baby may never become attached to him or her at all. This possibility has generally been overlooked in the attachment research on day care. Too often, it is just assumed that babies get attached to their day care providers and that the attachment measures validated with mothers will work with day care providers.

An early study that used Kotelchuck's (1972) variation of the Strange Situation found evidence that babies do organize their attachment behavior differently in relation to different caregivers. Fox (1977) studied 122 children who were born and raised on Israeli kibbutzim. About one-third of the children were in each of the following age groupings: 8 to 10 months, 12 to 15 months, and 21 to 24 months. As the mother, the metapelet who cared for the baby all day, and a stranger came and went from the room, responses to separation from and reunion with mother and metapelet were recorded. The baby was never left alone. When left with a stranger, these babies, who rarely interacted with strangers in everyday life, protested equally hard against separation from the mother and from the metapelet. This indicates that both the mother and the metapelet were attachment figures. The infants' responses to separation showed no differentiation between mother and metapelet. Reunion behaviors, however, did in many cases differ with respect to the two different caregivers. The two sets of reunion responses from the same baby in the same half-hour often did not fall into one single pattern. If most babies showed the same pattern with both caregivers, we might assume that the one pattern was based on the infant's temperament or was generalized from one relationship to the other. Instead, the data from this sample suggested that the baby's responses at reunion reflected the infant's history with and expectations about each specific caregiver.

■ Assessment with Day Care Providers

Assuming that babies do get attached to hired caregivers, how can we assess the quality of the attachment? Is the Strange Situation a valid method? Is the Attachment Q-set a valid measure? Validation of either procedure for nonparental infant-caregiver attachments is still in its very early stages.

If most babies do get attached to their hired caregivers, then their Strange Situation behavior should be classifiable by the usual criteria. If unclassifiable cases are extremely common, this would be reason to question whether babies ordinarily do develop coherent strategies for organizing attachment behavior directed toward the caregiver. Unfortunately, the available studies that have used Strange Situation assessments with day care providers have forced classifications into the traditional A, B, and C categories, so we don't know whether D patterns or unclassifiable cases are common. Obviously, however, researchers were able to fit behavior with hired caregivers into the same three categories discovered in studies of mother-baby dyads. No one reported any great difficulty doing so.

If the Strange Situation or the Q-set is a valid method for assessing attachment to the nonparental caregiver, the caregiver's sensitive responsiveness should probably help predict the baby's classification. Further, if the child stays long enough in that person's care, the pattern of her attachment to the caregiver should probably help predict the quality of her later attachment relationships, and should perhaps also help predict more-general aspects of her later socioemotional functioning.

■ Determinants of Security

If babies do get attached to their hired caregivers, what determines the pattern of attachment? Is the caregiver's sensitivity an important factor, as the mother's is? Two studies, one in the Netherlands and one in the United States, have found direct evidence that the hired caregiver's sensitivity to the child is indeed related to the quality of the child's attachment to the caregiver. Toddlers whose caregivers were more sensitive, responsive, and available were more likely than others to develop secure attachments.

In the Netherlands, 75 babies who stayed in day care centers while their parents were at work came to a laboratory for Strange Situation assessments at 12 months, 15 months, and 18 months, once with each parent and once with the professional caregiver (Goossens and Van IJzendoorn, 1990). Unfortunately, each Strange Situation was directly preceded by 15 minutes of free play with the parent or caregiver.

In this study, the A-B-C distribution of attachments to paid caregivers was about the same as the distribution of attachments to either parent (Goossens and Van IJzendoorn, 1990). Fourteen of the professional caregivers were observed with two or more babies. In all such cases except one, one of the babies had a secure attachment and another had an anxious attachment to the same caregiver. These results fly in the face of the expectation that an adult tends to give similar quality care to different infants and that the quality of care predicts security of attachment. What can we make of these unexpected data? The possibilities are numerous. One is that, in general, the Strange Situation may not be appropriate for assessing the pattern of attachment to the day care provider. Another possibility is that, in this study, some classifications were thrown off by the failure to use the anxious-disorganized-disoriented category. Another very real possibility is that professional caregivers do in fact provide care differently for different babies. They may respond to each child according to the baby's temperament and according to the social habits the baby brings from earlier social relationships into the new relationship. Some babies are better than others at eliciting attention and responsiveness from a new caregiver. For those and other idiosyncratic reasons, day care providers may have favorites among their wards and give warmer, more responsive care to some than to others.

Yet another possibility is that some of the babies had not been with the provider long enough for behavior with that provider to be based primarily on experience with that provider. The study required that the baby had been in that provider's care for at least 3 months. That does sound like enough time for the babies to have modified or discarded models carried forward from the relationship with a prior caregiver, but we have no direct evidence that it is.

Goosens and Van IJzendoorn (1990) also searched for factors that could help explain why some babies had secure attachments to their professional caregivers and others did not. Neither the set of attachments to the parents (two secure, one secure, or two anxious), the sex of the baby, nor the caregiver's years of experience made a significant contribution to predicting security of attachment to the caregiver. However, the number of hours per week a baby spent in day care was positively correlated with security of attachment to the caregiver, and babies who were securely attached to their caregivers came mostly from middle-class homes. Their caregivers tended to be younger and to show more sensitivity during the free play period than the caregivers of anxiously attached babies did.

Of the 14 babies who had anxious attachments to both parents, 7 (50 percent) showed secure attachment to the hired caregiver. If the assessments were valid, that is an impressive bit of evidence that the baby's trust in the hired caregiver's responsiveness can reflect positive experience with him or her even when the expectations based on experience with the parents are anxious and angry. On the average, the professional caregivers got higher scores than either mothers or fathers for sensitivity during the free play period. However, as noted earlier, sensitivity during 15 minutes of free play in a psychologist's observation chamber may not be a good index of sensitivity to attachment behavior in everyday life.

In the United States, Howes and Hamilton (1992a) observed 403 infants, toddlers, and preschool children with their day care center teachers or family day care providers. After dropping Attachment Q-set items they seldom observed in day care settings, they used their modified, 65-item version of the Waters and Deane Attachment Q-set to assess attachments to day care providers. They also used a 75-item version of the Q-set to describe observations of 110 of the children with their mothers on arrival at and departure from the child care setting. The mean security score with mothers was .51; with teachers, .30—a highly significant difference. Neither security score was correlated with the child's age, gender, or duration of acquaintance with the teacher.

Instead of just scoring degree of security, Howes and Hamilton (1992a) developed profiles for using the Q-set to differentiate secure, avoidant, and resistant attachments. By these yet-to-be-validated criteria, 76 percent of the attachments to the mothers were secure, 10 percent were avoidant, and 14 percent were resistant. For teachers, the distribution of classifications was highly similar: 73 percent secure, 14 percent avoidant, and 13 percent resistant. Children whose interactions with their teachers placed them in the avoidant and resistant categories were more likely than secure children to have teachers who were rated as comparatively high in harshness and detachment and low in responsiveness and involvement. Teachers of children in the avoidant category were rated as more harsh and detached than teachers of resistant children. If this use of the Q-set proves valid, these data may serve as further evidence that the way the child organizes her attachment behavior in relation to a hired caregiver reflects the quality of care the child experiences from that individual.

■ Quality of Care

Because quality of care is related to many outcomes of importance, a few words about it are in order here. According to Howes' summary, three readily measurable factors indicate good-quality child care in the United States (Howes, 1990). First, the relationship with the caregiver should be stable over time. Second, the employed caregiver should have formal training in child development. Third, there should be a good caregiver-to-child ratio—not too many children per adult. Sensitive and appropriate care comes most reliably from trained caregivers who have lasting relationships with the children in their care and do not have too many children in their care. By these standards, many infants and toddlers in the United States are not getting good care.

Which children are most likely to get good care from the hired caregiver? Probably those who also get good care at home. Child care quality and family characteristics are related. In Howes' own study, more complex lives and less desirable socialization practices characterized families that later enrolled their children in low-quality child care (Howes, 1990). It is also possible that high-quality child care reduces family stress, thereby enhancing the parents' ability to provide good care at home.

As noted above, some American researchers have expressed great concern that early entry into full-time day care increases the risk of anxious attachment to the parent and increases the risk of undesirable social behavior later in childhood. Some data suggest that this concern is misplaced. In Sweden, where very good child care is readily available for almost all families, Andersson (1989) found that 8-year-olds who began day care in the first year were in some respects more competent than those whose nonfamilial care began later. In the United States, where quality of nonfamilial child care is quite variable, Howes (1990) found that quality of care when a child was a toddler was a much better predictor of toddler, preschool, and kindergarten functioning than age of entry into day care was. Together, these studies suggest that Americans might be wise to give more attention to quality of care and less attention to age of entry into nonparental care.

■ Concordance of Attachment Patterns

Should we expect the pattern of attachment to the hired caregiver to match the pattern of attachment to the mother or father? As in the cases of infant-mother and infant-father attachments, there are some reasons to expect more than a chance level of concordance. For one thing, it seems likely that, when a number of day care choices and sufficient information are available, parents choose alternate caregivers who have child-rearing styles similar to their own. Similarity in care should foster similarity in the baby's organization of attachment behavior in relation to each adult. For another thing, the relationship with a day care provider often begins after the pattern of attachment to the parent has jelled. It seems likely that the toddler would carry expectations and behavioral tendencies from the relationship with one or both parents into the new relationship. Over time, contrasting experience with the new caregiver might change the toddler's behavior pattern around that caregiver, but it might take powerful contrasting experiences or a large number of contrasting experiences before the toddler's pattern would change. Meanwhile, the pattern the child brought into the relationship might be influencing the new caregiver's responses. For example, a child who masks his need for contact and acts independently is likely to be left on his own a lot; he may never discover that his new teacher is quite willing to be more nurturant than his mother and father are. As another example, a child who is resistant—clingy, angry, hard to soothe, and probably upset about his parent's departure—may not get affectionate, responsive care as readily as a secure child would.

These two reasons—parent selection of hired caregivers who act as they act, and carryover from the parent relationship into the new relationship—have led me to think there should be some concordance between infant-parent attachments and other infant-caregiver attachments. In fact, that is what I did find in my dissertation research (Colin, 1985). My procedure was a much-modified version of the Strange Situation, assessing the hired caregiver, the mother, and the baby. (The validity of the procedure is uncertain, just as the validity of every modification of the Strange Situation is uncertain.) The procedure included four brief separations, two solo reunions with one familiar caregiver, one solo reunion with the other, and, at the end, a joint reunion with both caregivers. The preseparation episodes and the two solo reunions with the first figure were used to classify the pattern of attachment to that caregiver as A, B, C, or D. For half of the babies, the mother was in the role of first attachment figure during the first laboratory visit; for the other half, the hired caregiver was in that role. Three months later, when the infant, mother, and hired caregiver returned to the laboratory, the two adults reversed roles for the assessment procedure.

In this small sample ($N = 22$), there was very high concordance of security of attachment to the two figures. On the basis of assessments separated by 3 months, 86 percent of the babies were classified as securely attached to both figures or as anxiously attached to both figures.

The other available studies, however, have not found such concordance. Three studies used the Strange Situation, which is probably the best procedure available for assessing security of attachment to the hired caregiver. Unfortunately, none of them used the D category. In the Goossens and Van IJzendoorn (1990) Dutch study (described above), there *was* significant concordance between attachment to the mother and attachment to the father: 67 percent of the babies fell into the same group (avoidant, secure, or resistant) with both parents. However, there was no association between the pattern of attachment to the professional caregiver and the pattern of attachment to either parent. The other two Strange Situation studies of attachments to day care providers, one in the United States (Owen and Chase-Lansdale, 1982) and one on Israeli kibbutzim (Sagi et al., 1985), also found little or no concordance between attachment to the mother and attachment to a hired caregiver.

Using the original Attachment Q-set, Howes, Rodning, Galluzo, and Myers (1988) also failed to find concordance in infant-mother and infant-caregiver attachments. They reported on two studies of infants in day care. In one sample, babies were seen in Strange Situations with their mothers at 12 months and observed in child care when they averaged 21.5 months, after a minimum of 2 months in the observed, out-of-home child care setting. The babies averaged 23 hours a week in child care, but the range was 3 to 55 hours. Based on very brief observations in child care, researchers used the Attachment Q-set to describe security of attachment to the caregiver. Because the security score is a correlation with a criterion sort for a maximally secure child, it can range from −1.0 to

+1.0. In fact, it ranged from −.01 to .67. Based on a suggestion from Waters, children with security scores of .33 and higher were classified as securely attached, and those with lower scores were classified as anxiously attached. Of the 42 toddlers, 27 (64 percent) were classified as securely attached and 15 (36 percent) as anxiously attached to the hired caregiver.

Nineteen (45 percent) of the children had concordant attachments with mother and caregiver: 14 were secure with both, and 5 were insecure with both. Those who were secure with both adults were in child care settings with relatively few children per adult, while those who were insecure with both adults were in settings with relatively many children per caregiver.

The other 23 children (55 percent of the sample) were, of course, secure with either the mother *or* the hired caregiver and insecure with the other attachment figure. The secure attachment was about as likely to be with the mother (10 children) as with the caregiver (13 children). Obviously, there was no evidence in this study that security of attachment to the mother contributed to or in any way predicted security of attachment to the caregiver.

In the second sample, 60 toddlers were observed in child care when they were around 18½ months old, and security of attachment to the parent was assessed through the original Attachment Q-set, based on observations during arrivals at and departures from child care. Limiting observations to times of separation and reunion constitutes basing the Q-set descriptions on a much more limited set of observations than the set it was designed to draw from. This may or may not turn out to be an especially informative way to use it to assess attachment security. In a pilot study that used the Q-set this way, 15 of 23 children (65 percent) at a mean age of 19.7 months were given the same classifications with the Q-set (secure or insecure) that they were given based on Strange Situation assessments at 12 months. Because some children do shift classification over a period of 8 months, the authors thought this level of agreement between the two methods was satisfactory (Howes et al., 1988). Most scientists will want more-convincing evidence that the Q-set as used in these studies provides valid assessments of security of attachment to the parent and to the hired caregiver.

In this sample of 60 toddlers, 40 (67 percent) were classified as securely attached to the caregiver and 46 (77 percent) were classified as securely attached to the parent who dropped the child off and picked him or her up. (In five cases, that parent was the father.) If security of attachment to the hired caregiver is unrelated to security of attachment to the parent, we should expect to find concordant attachments in about 60 percent of the children in this sample (52 percent secure with both adults and 8 percent insecure with both). Classifications from Q-set security scores indicated that 34 toddlers (57 percent) were secure with both adults and 8 (13 percent) were insecure with both. These figures are slightly higher than predicted from the null hypothesis, but they certainly do not indicate any strong association between security with the parent and security with the other caregiver. Of the 18 toddlers who were secure with one adult but not the other, 12 were secure with the parent and 6 were secure with the caregiver. Obviously, the weight of evidence so far contradicts my expectations. If there is significant concordance between infant-mother or infant-parent attachments and other infant-caregiver attachments, it certainly does not appear to be very high.

As was the case with infant-father attachments, however, concordance may be hard to find until we have both a valid measure and a very large sample. It appears that, across samples, about two-thirds of attachments to employed caregivers are classifiable as secure when researchers use the A-B-C coding system for Strange Situations, just as two-thirds of attachments to mothers and two-thirds of attachments to fathers are classified as secure when researchers use only those three categories. Consequently, even if there is no association between security of attachment to the mother and security of attachment to the day care provider, many infants (45 percent) will have secure attachments to both caregivers and some (11 percent) will have anxious attachments to both. To find a statistically significant level of concordance, we must find even more matches of attachment patterns than the 56 percent that would result from random distributions of the two sets of attachments. In samples of 42, 60, or even 86 children, investigators generally have not found significant concordance. However, use of the anxious-disorganized-disoriented category and/or aggregation of data from small samples for meta-analysis may change our picture of associations between attachment to the mother and attachment to a hired caregiver.

CHAPTER SUMMARY

Like most babies who are in the mother's care almost all of the time, babies whose mothers work outside the home usually develop secure attachments to them. However, babies who begin full-time day care before they are 6 months old are somewhat more likely to have avoidant attachments to their mothers than other babies are. Many explanations for the increase in avoidance have been offered, and none have been well tested. It may be just a correlate of the mother's employment, not an effect of it. Political preferences have clearly played a major role in the scientific debates about the extent of avoidance and about the implications of avoidance in attachments to mothers who have full-time jobs.

Very few studies have directly addressed attachments to hired caregivers. We suspect that most babies do become attached to every major caregiver, but there are many questions we cannot begin to answer. Researchers have barely begun to learn what procedures are valid for assessing the pattern of attachment to a hired caregiver and what factors influence the pattern.

ATTACHMENT HIERARCHIES

What happens when a baby has two highly involved parents and also spends 25 to 50 hours a week with a hired caregiver? Are babies, as Bowlby (1958, [1969] 1982) proposed, *monotropic*—genetically biased to direct most of their attachment behavior toward one particular person and to become strongly possessive of that person?

METHODOLOGICAL ISSUES

How can a researcher measure a child's attachment hierarchy? We have no reliable way of measuring the *absolute* intensity of the attachment bond in any relationship. Consequently, proposed measures of a child's attachment hierarchy must focus on the *relative* importance of each attachment figure. At least two approaches to measuring the attachment hierarchy are possible: preference under stress, and the adequacy of one figure as a substitute for others.

The clearest, least debatable measure of an attachment figure's place in a child's hierarchy is the child's preference under stress. There must be some stress, so that attachment behavior will be activated. In addition, the child must be in a situation that allows her to choose which attachment figure to approach or signal to. Surprisingly little research to date has satisfied these minimal conditions for assessing attachment hierarchies.

Data about preferences between parents in low-stress situations, such as playing at home, are not directly relevant. The attachment system is at very low intensity of activation, so any observed preference may be a preference for the parent as a playmate, not as an attachment figure.

Data about the intensity of attachment behavior directed toward each of the attachment figures in the other's absence are also not sufficient for assessing the relative importance of the two figures to the baby. Because the quality of an attachment clearly affects the intensity of attachment behavior, that intensity cannot be interpreted as a measure of the intensity or importance of the relationship. For example, consider the case of a baby who has a secure, independent attachment (Strange Situation subgroup B1) to the father and a resistant attachment (subgroup C1) to the mother. Under similar levels of stress with one parent at a time, the baby would direct more proximity-seeking and contact-maintaining behavior (as well as more resistance) to the mother than to the father. This would be true even if the intensity of the attachment bond to the father was greater than the intensity of the attachment bond to the mother.

A second plausible measure of the attachment hierarchy is each figure's relative adequacy as a substitute for the other (or others). If a baby misses and asks for both parents while in a nanny's care but never seeks the opportunity to stay with the nanny when a parent is available, it seems safe to assume that the parents have higher places in the hierarchy than the nanny does. Here, too, caution against misinterpretation is warranted. A child may be very fond of playing with his nanny or going to the park with her. Asking for a presumed attachment figure is not always motivated by the attachment bond.

A third proposed measure of a figure's place in the hierarchy is the predictive power of the attachment to that caregiver. There is certainly some logic to the argument that the quality of the most important early attachment relationship(s) should have more impact on later ego strengths and social behaviors than the qualities of other attachments. However, it is also reasonable to expect that anyone who has a child in his or her care for a long portion of the child's early life will have a big impact, even if the child never becomes very attached to that caregiver.

DETERMINANTS OF THE ATTACHMENT HIERARCHY

What factors determine which figure will be at the top of the attachment hierarchy and how great the difference in the intensities of a child's two or more attachments will be? Several factors may be influential: (1) how much time the child spends in each figure's care, (2) the quality of care each provides, (3) each adult's emotional investment in the child, and (4) social cues. Mothers, fathers, and hired caregivers may usually cue the child to treat the mother as the principal attachment figure. Fathers do often take the role of playmate and step back to let the mother respond to distress signals. Nannies and day care providers must ordinarily expect the baby to be more attached to the mother than to themselves, and act accordingly.

NATURALISTIC OBSERVATIONS

Some empirical data support Bowlby's (1958) monotropy hypothesis. In naturalistic observations among the Ganda, Ainsworth (1967) observed that babies did tend to focus most of their attachment behavior on one special person. Particularly when hungry, tired, ill, or alarmed, the baby would turn to that specific person if she was available. In this sample, the intensity of the preference for the mother among babies who regularly had more than one caregiver seemed about the same as the intensity of the preference for the mother among babies who were also accustomed to someone else's care.

In many societies, most people expect one person (usually the mother) to be of greatest importance to a baby, and most people behave accordingly. What happens in a society in which two or more mothers live together and share in raising all their children? Marvin, VanDevender, Iwanaga, LeVine, and LeVine (1977) studied 15 mobile Hausa infants in their natural polymatric settings in Nigeria. Each baby's mother played the major role in feeding her. In all other forms of interaction, however, the mother played the major role for only 7 of the 15 infants. In 14 of the 15 cases, the baby was most attached to the caregiver who held her and otherwise interacted with her the most: in 8 of these 14 cases (57 percent), that person was *not* the mother. For human beings, as for Harlow's (1958) monkeys, feeding (even breast feeding) may be less important than social interaction and physical contact when it comes to forming social attachments.

More data supporting the monotropy hypothesis are available from Morelli and Tronick's (1991) observations of Efe (pygmy) infants. Although Efe babies ordinarily experience sensitive caregiving from multiple others, they develop primary attachments to their mothers by the time they are 12 months old. In Efe culture, only the mother takes care of the baby during the night, and sleep is interrupted by interludes of social interaction (and breast feeding) involving only the mother and baby. The times when a baby is falling asleep may be times when the bond to the caregiver is especially likely to grow.

EXPERIMENTS

Some laboratory research in the United States has created the conditions for clearly assessing an attachment hierarchy: moderate stress and the opportunity to choose between two or more available caregivers. In such research, Cummings (1980) and Farran and Ramey (1977) found clear, strong preferences for the mother over a familiar day care provider.

I once observed 39 infants in a laboratory procedure that involved four brief separations (Colin, 1985). At the start of the final episode, the baby was alone in a room with the stranger, who held the infant. The mother and a second caregiver returned through separate doors and paused to let the infant make the first response. The stranger then set the baby down at a point that was equally far from the two caregivers. In each case, the second caregiver was someone who had taken care of the baby in the mother's absence for at least 20 hours per week for at least 4 months. The laboratory procedure was repeated 3 months later. Most babies showed clear preferences between attachment figures, and the preferences tended to be stable over time.

Later (Colin, 1987), I videotaped 50 babies, aged 12 to 19 months, in a laboratory playroom with both parents coming and going. The sequence of 3-minute episodes was as follows: (1) baby with both parents, (2) baby and parents joined by a stranger, (3) baby alone with the stranger, (4) baby reunited with both parents, (5) baby all alone, and (6) baby reunited with the parents again. Interviews with mothers included questions about the nature and extent of the father's involvement with the baby. Trained coders who were blind to interview information scored the direction and intensity of preferential attachment behavior in episodes in which both parents were present. The strength and clarity of infants' preferences between their parents increased as the episodes progressed and the level of stress rose. Most infants directed more attachment behavior and stronger attachment behavior toward the mother, especially as stress increased. However, in the final reunion, 12 of the babies (24 percent) directed more or stronger attachment behavior to the father than to the mother, and 6 (12 percent) showed no clear preference for either of the two attachment figures.

In almost every family in this sample, the mother was the primary caregiver. Preferences for the father and reductions in the intensity of preference for the mother were associated with the father's having spent a substantial amount of time with his baby and having participated in the baby's care, not just in play with the baby. Something about the nature of the interaction with each parent, not just the quantity of time spent in each parent's care, apparently contributed to the formation of the attachment hierarchy.

Babies whose mothers held full-time jobs outside the home were as likely as babies with unemployed mothers to treat the mother as the preferred attachment figure. This, too, indicated that something in the *nature* of the interactions the baby experienced, not just the amount of time he spent in someone's care, influenced the attachment hierarchy.

The same conclusion follows from kibbutz research. Kaffman, Elizur, and Sivan-Sher (1984) developed a projective test for assessing children's preferences among attachment figures in situations of distress and joy. They studied children from 18 kibbutzim, including some on which children slept in the family home and some on which children slept in the children's houses. The sample included every child who had been born and raised on each of the 18 kibbutzim and was 3 to 8 years old at the time of the study. This produced a sample of 918 children.

A psychologist showed each subject, one at a time, a picture of a crying child (of the same gender as the subject). The psychologist said that the child was crying so loudly you could hear him all over the kibbutz, and that everyone wanted to help him. Then the child was asked to draw a line or to point to the pictured figures the child wanted to go to. The available choices were (1) the two parents, pictured together, (2) the child's peers playing in front of the children's house or the school, (3) the child's siblings playing in front of the parent's home, and (4) two caregivers together (either two metaplot, or one metapelet and one teacher, depending on the subject's age). Then the subject was given a different picture and a story of a child who was very happy about something and was asked to show which figures that child wanted to go to.

When the child in the picture was distressed, 71 percent of the subjects indicated that he wanted to go to the parents. When he was very happy, 57 percent said he wanted to go to the parents. These numbers are, of course, highly significant. Children in all age groups selected the parents more often than they selected caretakers, peers, or siblings. This was true regardless of the sex of the child and regardless of the sleeping arrangements on the kibbutz. Although the metapelet is clearly an important agent of socialization, this evidence indicates that the emotional intensity of the bond with the parents is greater and may increase with age, even for children who spend very few hours per day and no time at night with their families.

THE ATTACHMENT NETWORK

Secondary attachment figures may have considerable importance for at least two reasons. First, they mitigate the discomfort and ill effects that might otherwise follow from the principal attachment figure's absence. Second, if they are sensitive caregivers, secondary attachment figures can compensate in some degree for the difficulties a child often experiences when the principal attachment is an anxious one.

Several studies now have found that infants with two secure attachments function best. In each available study, children with no secure attachments function worst. Main and Weston (1981) were the first to report this result. When they observed toddlers in play sessions, they found inappropriate affect, "odd" behavior, or otherwise disturbed behavior in almost every baby who was classified as avoidant with each parent in separate Strange Situations. They found no evidence of disturbances in babies who were securely attached to *either* parent. When a child has one secure attachment and one anxious attachment, she behaves more competently if the secure relationship is with the mother than if it is with the father or another caregiver (Belsky, Rovine, and Taylor, 1984; Easterbrooks and Goldberg, 1987; Howes et al., 1988; Main, Kaplan, and Cassidy, 1985).

CHAPTER SUMMARY

Research on attachment hierarchies is in its infancy. The best way to assess the attachment hierarchy is to observe the infant in a moderately stressful situation where he has equal access to two or more attachment figures. Both naturalistic observations and laboratory experiments usually find the mother at the top of the attachment hierarchy in infancy. Nevertheless, some infants seek the father or another familiar caregiver in preference to the mother, even in times of stress, and even when the mother has been the primary caregiver. Theory and preliminary data suggest that the following factors may each influence an infant's attachment hierarchy: amount of time spent with each caregiver, quality of interaction with each caregiver, and each caregiver's emotional investment in the relationship.

It does appear that secondary attachments influence the developing child's representational models and social behavior. When data about the qualities of two or more attachments in infancy are available, the children who seem to be doing best on cognitive and social outcomes are those who have two (or more) secure attachments. Infants with one secure and one insecure attachment fall in the middle, and infants with no secure attachments show the least desirable, least adaptive behavior.

All of these inferences must remain tentative until we have much more research on attachment hierarchies.

EARLY INTERVENTION

Data already presented show that 35 or 40 percent of infants in an ordinary low-risk sample are classified as anxiously attached. On the average, children who are anxiously attached in infancy show less competence in handling a variety of developmentally appropriate tasks over the next few years. Some are at risk for behavior problems or psychopathology. In high-risk samples, as many as 70 to 100 percent of infants are classified as anxiously attached. That is a frightening figure.

Can preventive interventions in the first year reduce the likelihood that attachments will be anxious? When a young child has formed an anxious attachment, how difficult is it to change the child's representational models and behavior patterns? What sorts of interventions have been attempted, and which are the most promising?

DISORDERS OF ATTACHMENT IN INFANCY

According to Lieberman and Pawl (1988) there are three major categories of attachment disorders in infancy: *nonattachment, disrupted attachment,* and *anxious attachment.* The first disorder, nonattachment, occurs when a baby has no opportunity to form emotional connections with other human beings. Development is likely to be impaired in the areas of impulse control (particularly aggression) and interpersonal relationships. Whether caregivers who are very unavailable emotionally (due to mental illness, drug abuse, or some other difficulty) provide so little human responsiveness that their babies, like babies raised by a series of caregivers in an institution, often remain nonattached is doubtful. The care sufficient to maintain life appears almost always to be sufficient to elicit attachment when no better potential attachment figure is available—as long as the caregivers are not many and transient. The biological propensity for an infant to form an attachment is powerful. Clear cases of nonattachment are almost never reported in samples of noninstitutionalized babies.

The second disorder, disrupted attachment, involves separation and loss and their effects. Disrupted attachments result from the premature and prolonged (or permanent) separation of a child from the attachment figure. When the child is old enough and in manageable circumstances, a few days of separation from the principal attachment figure can encourage psychological growth. From the time when clear-cut attachments first emerge (age 7 months) until the goal-corrected partnership develops (when the child is 4 or 5 years old), however, separations even as short as a week or two are often painful and distressing. Loss of the principal attachment figure or repeated long separations from him or her may trigger anxiety intense enough to overwhelm the child's coping mechanisms. Loss or repeated separations may cause long-lasting impairments in the child's ability to form enduring, trusting bonds.

Fortunately, nonattachment and disrupted attachments are not overly common. Anxious attachments, however, are very common. Indeed, the validity of classifying anxious attachment as a disorder, as Lieberman and Pawl (1988) proposed, seems debatable. Secure attachment is happier and more adaptive than anxious attachment, but "disorder" is a strong word. In some cases of anxious attachments, the defenses, angers, or disorganization may not warrant so strong a label. We do not yet have good measures of the degree of insecurity, defensiveness, incoherence, ambivalence, or resistance to healthy changes in any particular anxious attachment.

Some attachments, even in infancy, are so extremely anxious and maladaptive that the label "attachment disorder" clearly does describe them well. Working as clinicians providing psychotherapy to *severely* disturbed infants and their mothers, Lieberman and Pawl (1988) repeatedly observed three major patterns of distortion in secure-base behavior. Each pattern could be viewed as a defensive adaptation, an effort to ward off the child's anxiety about the parent's unavailability as a secure base. The first was *recklessness and accident proneness:* the child would wander away from the mother for prolonged periods, show no distress, and make no effort to restore proximity. The mother, in a panic, would belatedly start a search for the child. In other cases, the child would repeatedly cut himself while playing with sharp objects, fall while climbing, or bang into things while running. In both sorts of recklessness, there is a deficiency of the attachment behavior that normally keeps exploration within safe limits. (The caregiving behavior seems clearly deficient, too.)

The second distortion of secure-base behavior Lieberman and Pawl reported was the opposite: *inhibition of exploration.* Children showing this pattern hesitated to approach, touch, and manipulate objects; withdrew from unfamiliar people; were often immobile in unfamiliar situations, even in the presence of the mother; and showed marked constriction of affect. (The last characteristic clearly distinguished this group from children who are simply slow to warm up around new people or in new places.) Some of these children clung to the mother for prolonged periods; their mothers seemed to be gratified by their dependency and either withdrew or became punitive when the child moved toward exploration and autonomy. Other children avoided both the mother and exploration. Their mothers repeatedly and unpredictably punished their children for actions that displeased them. The children seemed to be keeping their distance in an effort to avoid both the dangers from the mother and the dangers from the environment.

A third group showed *precocious competence* in self-protection. They often reversed normal child-parent roles and gave care to the parent. Secure-base behavior was distorted because the child could not rely on the parent as the primary protector. Instead, the child incorporated into her own behavior substantial portions of the parent's role. Crittenden (1988b, 1988c) has also reported role reversals and compulsive caregiving in very young maltreated children.

SUCCESSES IN TREATING ATTACHMENT DISORDERS

Thorough descriptions of the behavior of babies who clearly do have attachment disorders can be heartbreaking. That a child who is so young can be so depressed, so anxious, or so disturbed was a surprise to many clinicians and researchers. Psychoanalysts once believed that the ego (the adaptive, reality-testing part of the self) did not even emerge until a baby had been in the world for many months. The baby had to discover that reality was often frustrating—that desires for food, for something to suck, for warmth, and for other gratifications did not always produce the desired experience. Only then would the baby be motivated to invest some of his or her psychic energy in learning about reality. More months of experience would be necessary before the nascent ego could develop defense mechanisms such as repression and denial. Selma Fraiberg, a psychoanalyst, discovered otherwise. After treating many infants who already showed serious to severe affective disorders, she called attention to infants' abilities to use pathological defenses long before the ego and ego defense mechanisms were thought to have emerged (Fraiberg, 1982).

Many of the babies Fraiberg treated had been neglected or abused. Their parents were largely unable to nurture them. Many of the parents had grave personality disorders or were severely depressed. In a complete reversal of normal social patterns, the babies avoided their mothers through every available system of contact. Even when hunger, solitude, a sudden noise, or some other stimulus triggered disorganized screaming and flailing to the point of exhaustion, some of these babies did not turn to their mothers for protection or comfort. Such extreme avoidance goes far beyond the avoidance that is often observed in the Strange Situation. In addition to showing more-extreme avoidance, Fraiberg's clinical sample (Fraiberg, 1982) showed avoidance earlier (sometimes by 3 months of age), more consistently, and more pervasively than the avoidant infants in Ainsworth's low-risk Baltimore sample did.

In addition to extreme avoidance, Fraiberg (1982) observed a variety of symptoms that, in milder forms, would suffice to classify a baby's attachment as anxious-disorganized-disoriented or anxious-avoidant-resistant. *Freezing*—remaining immobile and glassy-eyed for as long as 20 minutes—occurred in babies as young as 5 months of age. Some of the older babies (12 to 18 months) used fighting as a way of warding off anxiety and disorganization. Some showed giddy, almost manic behavior in response to frightening stimuli. Some recklessly banged their heads and limbs against furniture, walls, and floors but showed no sign of pain. Some substituted actions such as rubbing the eyes for normal reactions to conflicts, because the child could not resolve or safely acknowledge the conflict.

In every case, Fraiberg and her colleagues found repetitions from the mother's past as stumbling blocks in the current mother-infant relationship (Fraiberg, Adelson, and Shapiro, 1975). Distresses, disturbances, and conflicts from the mother's early relationships wrote the script for her baby's life. Painful old dramas replayed themselves with a new actor in an unwelcome but familiar role. The therapists sought to disengage the children from the mothers' old conflicts. They included infants in psychotherapy sessions when the mother wished to do so or had difficulty making other arrangements. This allowed them to see exactly how the interactions were going and to intervene directly in the new relationship while continuing to work on issues from the mother's old relationships.

With these very disturbed mothers, explaining how and why the mother should change her behavior was never enough. To change her caregiving behavior, the mother had to exorcise the "ghosts in the nursery." She had to change her working model of herself as an attachment figure. To change her internal model, she had to rediscover and relive the emotions appropriate to her own early experiences of abandonment, neglect, and/or abuse. To do that, she needed to let herself be drawn into a relationship with the therapist, who served as a secure base for exploring defensively excluded information and affect. In the language of attachment theory, the disturbed mother had to reexamine and revise the dysfunctional, distorted representational models of attachment relationships that she had acquired in childhood.

Despite the extreme disturbances in the parents and infants referred to their clinic, Fraiberg and the therapists working with her had great success in strengthening the children's ties to their mothers and fathers, educating the parents about their children's needs and feelings, enabling the parents to act as their children's protectors, alleviating the children's anxiety, and healing the parent-child relationships. The picture of hope for change that emerges from their work is one of great optimism.

The available clinical literature includes other accounts of great therapeutic success with very impaired mother-infant dyads. For example, Lieberman and Pawl (1988) described a baby referred to them for intervention at the age of 6 weeks because of nonorganic failure to thrive (NOFT). The baby's mother came from a deprived, emotionally empty background and was unable to recognize and respond to the infant's hunger signals and social signals. The intervention consisted of helping her to recognize her long-buried feelings of being empty, worthless, and unwanted and then helping her to see the links between those feelings and her difficulty feeding her baby and enjoying interacting with him. She became more aware of her own needs and more responsive to her baby's signals. He gained weight and, within the first year, developed a secure attachment to his mother.

A CASE STUDY: TANYA

Other reports reflect more cause for concern about the persistence of the effects of early troubles in attachment relationships. In some cases, the difficulties clearly stem from the parent's inability to change. For example, Lieberman and Pawl (1984) describe the case of Tanya and her mother Jody. Despite some real love for her daughter, Jody (age 30) was often preoccupied with her own needs and feelings and was unaware of and unresponsive to her child. When Lieberman and Pawl met the dyad, Tanya (then 2 years old), was already accustomed to taking care of herself much of the time. She monitored her mother's moods closely and did what she could to make her mother feel better. For example, when Jody cried, Tanya often stopped playing and gently dried her mother's tears. Tanya stayed close to Jody and watched for her opportunities to elicit warmth and playfulness. It was Tanya who usually began the dyad's social exchanges. She knew how to be an engaging companion. When her timing was right, she could elicit very affectionate, sensitive responses from her troubled mother. Her awareness of her mother's moods was unusually advanced for her age, but her language skills and her representational play showed developmental delays. Maintaining proximity was mostly Tanya's job. For example, Jody often marched heedlessly down a long hall without glancing back at Tanya, who trotted laboriously after her.

Treatment for Tanya in her relationship with her mother began inauspiciously. Despite extensive involvement with the local Department of Social Services and with therapeutic services, Jody had abused her 5-year-old son while she was still on probation for an earlier incident of abuse. An outraged judge placed the son in long-term foster care, ordered Tanya's father, who was abusive to Jody, out of the home, and, in hopes of protecting Tanya and keeping her in her mother's care, ordered treatment for the dyad. As far as the various professionals involved with the family knew, Tanya herself had not been abused.

For Jody, the price of keeping her daughter was losing her lover. She voiced very mixed feelings about this. She believed she had no problems with her daughter and felt very resentful about the court's orders. Motivation to explore her feelings and actions toward Tanya was largely missing. Such motivation is generally considered necessary if treatment is to be successful. A second basic condition of treatment, confidentiality, was also compromised from the beginning. A social worker was monitoring Jody's compliance with treatment, and the therapist was expected eventually to write a report for the court.

The therapists began with an extended assessment to gather information about whether intervention was feasible. The assessment, which took several weeks, included home visits, office visits, use of a standardized test of developmental abilities, and videotaping of the dyad during a period of free play together. Despite Jody's periods of inattention, it was obvious that the tie between child and mother was strong. Jody was afraid that she would abuse Tanya. "As Jody told her story, her responses quickly changed from convulsive crying to intense anger and then to a tough, devil-may-care attitude punctuated by shrill laughter" (Lieberman and Pawl, 1984, p. 532). Jody had never known her father. Her mother had been intermittently psychotic, with many periods of absence from the home and many episodes of violent abuse of her two children. Jody and her brother lived in 10 foster homes, in some of which they were physically abused and sexually harassed. When Jody was 3 years old, neighborhood children raped her. On her own at age 18, Jody got involved with a series of abusive men, several of whom were pimps. When she was 25, she met the man who became the father of her two children. An immigrant from Europe, he spoke almost no English and had a violent temper. In the next 5 years, he went to jail twice for theft, and Jody was jailed once for prostitution and once for abusing her son. In the same period, the children were in shelter care three times, and they were in foster care once for 3 months.

Jody's inability to find stable, nurturant relationships for herself and her child seemed to be a permanent effect of the disturbances and disruptions in her own attachment history. This mother had never been, as a child or as an adult, able to choose what people would be closely involved with her or to control how they would treat her. There were many people who deserved blame for her troubles, and she blamed them ragefully. She appeared to be unable to see her own role in perpetuating her victimization and her daughter's suffering, even though she did at times want to change.

Persuaded that intervention was warranted and that Jody was willing to participate in treatment, Alicia Lieberman continued the work begun during the assessment period. Jody, Tanya, and Alicia met once a week for 5 months. With difficulty, some therapeutic progress was made. When Jody screamed with rage about being exploited by a sexual partner and Tanya watched in frozen horror, Alicia told Tanya, "Mommy is not angry with you, Tanya. She is angry at a bad man who was not nice to her" (Lieberman and Pawl, 1984, p. 535). After repeated reassurances, Tanya relaxed and returned to playing. Jody had not previously noticed how her anger affected Tanya. With support and guidance from the therapist, she made some progress in acknowledging her own role in abusing her son. She voiced her wish to be different from her violent, crazy mother and voiced her doubts about her ability to change. She said that she felt drained by Tanya and impatient toward her. Then, to everyone's surprise, she confessed to heroin addiction, which no one had suspected, and willingly entered a drug treatment program.

Therapy went well for 2 months, but then a problem about enrolling Tanya in preschool precipitated a rapid reversal of almost everything that had been accomplished. Abusive men, alcohol, other drugs, rage, prostitution, sexual assault, loss of food and money because of theft—chaos and violence once again permeated the home. Tanya's physical health deteriorated, and Jody barely spoke to her except to scold her. Worst of all, in the therapist's opinion, Jody lost all willingness to examine her own role in everything that was going wrong. She attributed all of her problems to abusive men exploiting her. No amount of support or interpretation helped her see how there was anything she could do differently to improve things for herself and her child.

Prompted by a recommendation from Tanya's pediatrician, the social worker removed Tanya from Jody's care. For 2 months, Jody made no effort to see her daughter. Then, having used drugs again, Jody was sent to jail for violating the terms of her probation. The judge ordered Jody to attend a residential drug treatment program for 18 months. Tanya was to be in foster care for that period, and treatment for both mother and child was to continue. However, it seemed unlikely that the mother would ever learn to choose companions well or to behave in ways likely to end the chaos and deprivation of her own life. It seemed unlikely that she would ever stabilize her ability to care for her child.

Tanya's predicament was further complicated by the laws of her state. The law required that all involved attempt to reunite Tanya and her mother after the 18 months of court-ordered treatment, instead of permitting that Tanya be permanently placed in a stable home.

Tanya's first attachment was to an inadequate, unstable, rageful mother. The child was placed in foster care at the age of 2. Her mother was to be in jail and in treatment for 18 months. Tanya could not use that time to make a permanent place for herself in a healthier family. No one could say with whom she would live when she was 4.

A CASE STUDY: SARAH

Even in optimal later circumstances, the effects of early disruptions can be surprisingly long-lasting. Lieberman and Pawl (1988) described the case of Sarah, who was referred to their clinic for evaluation at the age of 21 months. She had experienced a series of disruptions in her first 12 months but had been with a stable, loving couple since then.

Sarah was conceived in a mental hospital; both parents were diagnosed as paranoid schizophrenics. They were released from the hospital before Sarah's birth and had refused to accept social services of any kind. Sarah was hospitalized for an illness at 1 month. Not long after she returned home, her mother left. When Sarah was 3 months old, her father also abandoned her. She stayed in shelter care for 2 weeks, then in a foster home for 3 weeks, and then in a second foster home, where she stayed from 4½ to 10½ months of age. The care there turned out to be minimal, and Sarah was moved to an excellent foster home. Unexpected circumstances disrupted that placement, too, and, at the age of 12 months, after at least seven major changes of caregivers, Sarah was placed with excellent foster parents who hoped to adopt her.

Nine months later, Sarah was referred for evaluation because she showed indiscriminate friendliness and a lack of differential responsiveness to her foster parents, who were, in the assessment team's opinion, excellent. The foster parents wondered whether Sarah was attached to them at all. The assessment team concluded that she was, but anxiously so, despite the excellence of their care. Her indiscriminate friendliness seemed to be counterphobic. Still unconsciously expecting that any stranger might take her away from her new home and family and place her in another, she coped by moving toward the new relationship before it could be imposed on her. Even though she was much too young to be able to analyze her experiences and feelings and make conscious plans about preventing recurrences of past anguish, she was trying to exert some control over her situation and so to master the anxiety and pain associated with anticipated loss.

The intervention team assured the foster parents that Sarah's apparent preference for interacting with strangers was defensive and indicated anxiety about losing her foster parents, not a lack of attachment to them. The parents needed some help to remain emotionally available to Sarah and not to feel unloved and betrayed. By the age of 30 months, Sarah was relating to her foster parents in much more positive ways, but still showed her counterphobic tendency to move toward strangers. She had been in an excellent, stable situation for 19 months—for three-fifths of her life—but the inadequacies and disruptions of her first year had not been erased; her attachments were still anxious.

IDENTIFYING FAMILIES IN NEED OF INTERVENTION

When and with whom should intervention be undertaken? As Greenspan and Lieberman (1988) pointed out, difficulties in dyadic interaction can be recognized very early in life. By the age of 3 or 4 months at the latest, healthy babies can participate in complex, joyful relationships. They respond to their caregivers' faces, smiles, and voices with alertness and brightening and often with smiles and reciprocal vocalizations.

Greenspan and Lieberman (1988) briefly described the cognitive and behavioral capabilities that normally emerge and the socioemotional tasks that infants normally accomplish in the first 2 years. Using those norms, they developed a system for identifying and classifying attachment problems throughout infancy. Two sorts of problems relevant to attachments-in-the-making can occur as infants move or fail to move through the normal series of socio-emotional tasks. First, there may be defects in achieving a new organizational level. Second, the baby's affective range at the new level may be constricted. Greenspan and Lieberman's system appears likely to be very useful in identifying, while the infant is very young, the infant-parent dyads who are at risk of or are already experiencing problems.

Also relying on observation of social behavior, Crittenden (e.g., 1981) has used videotapes of brief dyadic interactions early in life to differentiate among infant-caregiver dyads from families characterized by abusive, neglectful, problematic, and adequate child rearing. Crittenden's scales for coding dyadic interaction were developed as research instruments and are not intended for use as clinical assessment tools (Crittenden, 1981). However, she succeeded in finding in very brief, easily obtained videotapes good clues about the nature and severity of any difficulties a dyad is experiencing. Her approach may provide a quick, easy way to identify dyads who may be in trouble or headed for trouble and should undergo further assessment.

A much different "red flag" about attachment difficulties has been proposed by Harris, Weston, and Lieberman (1989): high cumulative use of nonroutine medical care services during the first year of life may identify infant-mother dyads experiencing strained relationships. These investigators examined pediatric records for the first 12 months of life for frequency and type of visit, symptoms, diagnoses, and treatment. At 12 months of age, the 56 babies participated in Strange Situations. Anxiously attached babies ($N = 39$) had used acute care services (walk-in and emergency room services) significantly earlier and more often than securely attached babies had ($N = 17$). There were no differences between groups in prenatal difficulties, birth complications, or use of well-baby care.

Another proposed method for identifying infants who are at risk and in need of preventive intervention is by paying attention to the sort of care their parents have given to the children's older siblings. For many years, it was believed that maltreating families often chose a single child as the target of abuse or neglect, a scapegoat for the family's difficulties. However, Jean-Gilles and Crittenden (1990) presented evidence that family dysfunctions tend to be pervasive. In families reported to have abused one child, the siblings' histories are similar to that of the abused child in the areas of stressful life experiences, quality of home environment, reported behavior problems, and experience of maltreatment. A logical implication is that all the children in a maltreating family should receive preventive or protective intervention.

Early recognition of the risk of attachment difficulties or actual maltreatment would provide opportunities for early comprehensive assessment and, where warranted, early intervention. However, validation of the screening or flagging procedures introduced here awaits further research.

BEGINNING INTERVENTION WITH HIGH-RISK FAMILIES

Having identified a family in need of intervention to support the infant's emotional well-being, what approach should a social worker or psychologist take? Emde (1988) reviewed preliminary evidence from several studies of intervention with infants and their families. He found that the effectiveness of intervention depended on the quality of the relationship between the subject and the intervener. He also pointed out that interventions that focus on cognitive development may have little or no influence on attachment. This fact had long been familiar to clinical psychologists, but it was not initially obvious to researchers.

Establishing a good relationship between the subject and the intervener is not an easy matter. Lyons-Ruth et al. (1987) briefly described the great difficulty home visitors had in winning the trust of the low-income, high-risk parents they sought to assist. The home visitors had to be very persistent and very gentle. Crittenden (1990) argued that the representational models of parents in maltreating families anticipate rejection, lack of care, and other negative behaviors from potential attachment figures. These parents' ability to use the intervener as a secure base to support the client's growth and adaptive behavior is severely impaired. The histories of parents who are at risk for abusing or neglecting their children generally include a preponderance of figures who failed to comfort and protect the individual who is now a parent. Why should a person who rarely got comfort or protection from his or her parents trust a stranger to be caring and reliable? The family may be all too well aware that the stranger's purpose is to change the course of events in the family. There must be a strong tendency to perceive the intervener as a messenger delivering the judgment that what the parent is doing now is wrong.

The difficulty of establishing a therapeutic alliance with a high-risk parent increases when the parent's racial or ethnic heritage differs from the intervener's. In such circumstances, according to Lieberman (1990), it is important to be aware of and respectful of subcultural differences. How adults receive a baby into the world, how they perceive the baby, and how they care for the baby are all shaped by the survival needs, philosophical outlook, and moral beliefs of their culture or subculture. For example, a white American social worker who tries to get nonwhite immigrants from El Salvador to encourage their babies' independence is likely to encounter considerable resistance and a lack of respect or credibility. In Central America, as in Japan, mothers are expected to give close care to their babies, and babies are expected to need such care.

THE COMPLEXITY OF EFFECTIVE INTERVENTION

Social service agencies are seldom fortunate enough to have the resources to identify families who are at risk and provide supportive, protective services before things go awry. More often, the family does not come to the attention of potential interveners until abuse, neglect, and/or a serious disturbance of patterns of socioemotional interaction has already occurred. The problem then is not to support secure or minimally anxious attachment, but to change an attachment that is already disturbed.

If a very young child's expectations about relationships are to change from anxious to secure, the child must directly experience a supportive relationship. The best thing to do is change the behavior of the primary attachment figures. To do this successfully, the intervener must structure treatment from the parent's point of view. If you tell a parent she is not giving good care to her child, you are likely to trigger antagonism and defensiveness. If you tell a parent truthfully that you can understand some of the difficulties he has caring for the child in his current situation, he is more likely to accept your help. The help must be for the parent, not only for the child. The intervener must treat the parent as someone who is valuable in his or her own right; the parent is not just a tool for the therapist to use for the baby's benefit. The intervener can help the parent find ways to change the baby's behavior so that the relationship will be easier and more rewarding for the parent.

Establishing enough trust to allow the intervention to occur is only the first step. For babies in situations of potential or actual abuse, neglect, or disorders of attachment or socioemotional functioning, the risk factors are many and the intervention must be multifaceted.

A model Infant-Parent Program is being conducted by Lieberman and her colleagues in San Francisco. Having incorporated and extended Fraiberg's methods, they offer a flexible integration of developmental guidance (modeling and direct teaching), infant-parent psychotherapy, emotional support (from a counselor or a parent group), and practical assistance for the families referred to them (Lieberman, 1985).

Some families need to learn what the reasonable expectations for a baby at a given age are, what babies need, and what their behaviors mean. Some families need assistance finding adequate housing and obtaining food. Some need emotional support, some need psychotherapy, and many need more than one sort of assistance. Many of the parents referred to the Infant-Parent Program are not only poor but also unskilled, untrusting, and isolated. Often the care they provide is so inadequate that the children have been removed to temporary or permanent foster homes. The children must be treated in the context of great social and psychological instability.

Of all the intervention programs that have been reported to improve attachment relationships and the child's socioemotional functioning in very troubled families, none has relied primarily on didactic parent training. Explaining to parents how babies of different ages act and react and what sort of care is therefore appropriate does not appear to be sufficient. All of the programs that have been effective have included psychotherapy to help the parent become able to receive and give nurturant, protective care (Lieberman 1985, 1991; Lyons-Ruth, Connell, Gruenbaum, and Botein, 1984, 1990).

DAY CARE AS A
COMPONENT OF INTERVENTION

To protect children from abusive or negligent parents, social service agencies sometimes recommend temporary or permanent removal of the child from the home. When the dangers to the child do not necessitate foster care, day care is sometimes recommended. The hope is that having a break from child care responsibilities for several hours a day will ease the strain on the parents and so improve the quality of care they provide when the children *are* with them. In addition, day care can, in many cases, give the child an environment that stimulates and supports cognitive, physical, and social development better than the child's family does.

To see whether protective day care was really helpful, Crittenden (1983) studied 22 children for whom mandatory protective day care was sought because of abuse, neglect, or a high risk of maltreatment in the home. Fully random assignments to treatment groups were not possible, but quasi-random assignments were accomplished because day care placements were available for only 13 of the 22 children.

In addition to easing stresses on the family, day care was intended to give the family time to learn adequate caregiving skills. The short-term effect of day care was the opposite of what was intended. In this high-risk sample, the daily separations appeared to exacerbate processes of anger and rejection in both child and parent, and so made the home less safe for the child. The children for whom day care had been found were removed from the family and placed in foster care earlier than the children for whom day care had been recommended but not available. One year after the decision to seek day care, none of the day care children were living with their families. Seven (54 percent) had been permanently removed, and six (46 percent) were in temporary foster care. In contrast, only one (11 percent) of the children who couldn't be placed in day care was permanently removed from the family. Five (56 percent) were in temporary foster care, and three (33 percent) were at home.

Examination of placements 3 years later suggested that day care had not affected long-term outcomes about whether a child would stay with her family; it had apparently just speeded up changes that were going to happen anyway (Crittenden, 1983). Four years after the decision to seek protective day care, the outcomes for the two groups were similar. Just over half of the children in each group had been permanently removed from the family of origin, and three from each group were at home. Three of the day care children (23 percent) and one (11 percent) of the non-day care children were in temporary foster care.

Permanent removal of a child from a family is an extreme outcome. Social service agencies almost always try first to help a family provide adequate care for the child. Removal merely because of anxious attachment never happens; anxious attachment is a common condition. Removal because of emotional abuse is extremely rare; emotional abuse is too hard for courts to recognize and measure. Physical abuse, sexual abuse, and physical neglect are much easier for social workers to recognize and demonstrate to the court. Consequently, removal of a child from the family reflects both maltreatment that lasted or recurred over a long period of time and the failure of whatever efforts were made to help the family do better and stay together.

Given those facts, whether protective day care helped these children *in regard to attachment issues* is unclear. If speeding up the process of removal led to early, long-lasting placements with foster parents or adoptive parents who gave good care, a lessening of anxiety, anger, and disturbances in self-image and social behavior is likely. If early removal simply meant early severance of contact with one or two attachment figures and repeated disruptions of subsequent attachments, then protective day care may have intensified attachment disorders. Further study of the whole set of questions is needed.

THE EFFECTIVENESS OF INTERVENTION

We do have reason to believe that intervention is, in many cases, effective. Fraiberg's clinical reports of success with extremely distressed infant-mother dyads are certainly encouraging (e.g., Fraiberg, Adelson, and Shapiro, 1975). Controlled studies have also found evidence that intervention can work.

One such recent intervention study [described in Lieberman, Weston, and Pawl, 1991, and in Lieberman (1991)] focused on a sample of mothers who were at high risk for depression and emotional unavailability to their infants because they were recent immigrants coping with poverty, unemployment, and cultural uprootedness. One hundred mother-infant dyads were recruited from well-baby clinics. The mothers were Spanish-speaking immigrants from Mexico and Central America who had been in the United States for less than 5 years. The father was present in 80 percent of the households. The babies were 11 to 14 months old when they entered the study; 44 percent were male and 52 percent were firstborns. In Strange Situations conducted at the beginning of the study, 63.4 percent of the babies were classified as anxiously attached (group A, C, or D).

Anxiously attached babies were assigned at random to the intervention group or the control group. The securely attached babies constituted a second comparison group. The intervention began right after group assignment and lasted until the baby's second birthday. It consisted of infant-mother psychotherapy tailored to the specific needs of the dyad, conducted in weekly sessions in either the home or the office, whichever the mother preferred. Each session lasted 1½ hours. Each dyad had the same intervener for the whole study. There were four interveners, all bicultural, bilingual women with master's degrees in psychology or social work. They were asked to focus especially on (1) the mother's empathic responsiveness to the child and contingent responsiveness to signals, (2) the availability of developmentally appropriate opportunities for exploration, (3) protection from danger, and (4) the tactful negotiation of conflict and competing agendas between mother and child. As is usual in infant-parent psychotherapy, all of this was done in the context of trying to give the mother a *corrective attachment experience* in her relationship to the intervener. That is, the intervener tried to be caring and reliable, to deserve and elicit trust, to serve as a secure base from which the parent could explore painful past experiences and current conflicts.

When the infants were 18 months old, Strange Situation assessments were repeated. Most of the avoidant infants in the anxious control group remained avoidant. In the intervention group, however, most of the avoidant babies had become secure, anxious-resistant, or anxious-disorganized-disoriented. It appeared that intervention had helped to break down distancing defenses, but that some babies had replaced these defenses with direct expressions of anger or with confusion in behavioral strategies. These toddlers had not yet developed confidence in the mother; they could not yet use the mother as a secure base and a haven of safety.

After another 6 months, the toddlers in the intervention group were clearly doing better than the toddlers in the control group. The assessment at 24 months was modeled after the Strange Situation, but with much longer episodes. The child had 20 minutes of free play with the mother, 20 minutes of free play with the stranger, 20 minutes of child-directed play while the mother and the stranger conversed, 10 minutes of separation from the mother while the stranger stayed in the room, and then 5 minutes of reunion with the mother, at the beginning of which the stranger left. The mother's behavior during free play was scored for empathic responsiveness and for initiation of interaction. The toddler's behavior during the period of free play with the mother was scored for restriction of affect and for angry behavior. In the reunion episode, the Ainsworth et al. (1978) 7-point scales for scoring resistance and avoidance were applied. In addition, a 9-point scale was developed and used for rating the degree to which the dyad evidenced a goal-corrected partnership upon reunion (Lieberman, Weston, and Paul, 1991).

Eighteen families dropped out of the study. At the end of the study, there were 29 in the intervention group, 23 in the anxious control group, and 30 in the secure comparison group. The validity of these three measures could not be fully established within one study. As predicted, mothers in the intervention group got higher scores for empathic responsiveness and initiation of interaction than mothers in the anxious control group got, and infants in the intervention group showed less angry behavior, less avoidance, and less resistance than infants in the untreated control group. Intervention dyads also got higher scores for partnership during the reunion episode. As hoped, the intervention group did not differ significantly from the secure comparison group on any measure.

Despite the success of this program, intervention results are not always as we would wish. Egeland and Erickson (1993) described an intervention program that sounded wonderful. While pregnant for the first time, women who were at high risk because of various social and economic factors were recruited for the study. Of the 154 subjects, 74 were randomly assigned to the intervention program and 80 were randomly assigned to the comparison group. A "facilitator" was assigned to each mother-to-be in the intervention group. Taking care not to imply criticism or rejection of the subject, the facilitator visited her repeatedly at home. If necessary, she demonstrated just by coming again and again that she would not give up on a mother-to-be who had requested that she visit. If possible, she also visited the subject in the hospital at the time of the baby's birth.

After several weeks of trying to build trust through home visits, the facilitator invited the mother-to-be to join a group of 7 to 9 other clients with due dates near her own. The same facilitator led the group sessions, which occurred once every 2 weeks for 3 hours at a time. A young mother provided van transportation to the group sessions and helped as a facilitator. The group sessions had mother-centered and baby-centered activities. The goal was to help mothers recall and understand what they had experienced in their earlier attachment relationships, see its influence on their present relationships, and become free to give their babies better care than they had received. Each group had at least one mother who spoke readily of the pain of an abusive past, and that almost always helped others begin to face and discuss their own stories.

Home visits continued on the weeks when there was no group meeting. Unfortunately, much of the home visit time, instead of building a corrective attachment experience, was spent helping a mother manage one crisis or another and deal with stress; it was often hard, in the circumstances of their lives, for these mothers to focus on learning parenting skills. However, the facilitator and mother did often watch videotapes of the mother interacting with the baby, and the facilitator used a nonjudgmental approach to help the mother understand the baby's perspective, the baby's cues, and the developing relationship. Group sessions and home visits continued until the baby was 12 months old.

Mothers in the treatment group did come to understand their babies and their relationships with their babies better than mothers in the control group did. They also had lower depression and anxiety scores, and provided more-stimulating and better-organized home environments. However, the positive effects of the intervention did not show up in assessments of patterns of attachment.

The babies participated in Strange Situations at 13 months and again at 19 months. At 13 months, significantly more babies in the *control* group were securely attached: 67 percent versus 46 percent. Almost all of the difference lay in the frequency of category D attachments: 41 percent of the intervention group versus 19 percent of the control group. The authors offered the interpretation that the mothers in the intervention group were indeed learning to be more sensitive and responsive, but were not yet sufficiently consistent about it to support secure attachments (Egeland and Erickson, 1993). Their relationships were in transition and so appeared disorganized.

When attachments were reassessed at 19 months, the frequency of secure attachments in the control group had dropped from 67 to 48 percent, but the frequency of secure attachments in the intervention group was still only 47 percent, and the frequency of disorganized attachments was still 39 percent. Frequencies of both avoidant and disorganized attachments had increased in the control group.

The target group for this study was a challenging one to work with. There was evidence of personality disorders, drug and alcohol abuse, histories of antisocial behavior during childhood and adolescence, histories of abuse, hostility in relationships, and difficulty controlling anger. Many of the mothers who had boyfriends had a lot of conflict and tension, including physical violence, in these relationships. Many of the mothers who did not have boyfriends were preoccupied with finding a man. The changes in mothers' thoughts, feelings, and behaviors were not large enough or did not occur soon enough to increase frequencies of secure attachments within the period of study.

In both of these controlled experiments, intervenors worked with very high risk mother-infant dyads and offered extensive and varied therapy, education, and support services. Both found an increase in the frequency of disorganized attachment patterns while relationships were in transition. One study found evidence that the multifaceted intervention changed some anxious attachments to secure ones within a year or so (Lieberman, Weston, and Pawl, 1991). The second study did not find evidence of similar success (Egeland and Erickson, 1993). Why the results differ is not clear. Future intervention experiments should prove very interesting.

SOCIETAL INTERVENTION: A POLEMICAL INTERLUDE

Attachment theory and research generally focus on the infant-parent dyad or the family unit. In the context of a discussion of intervening to increase security of attachment in high-risk infants, however, it seems appropriate to mention variables that affect whole communities, not just the individuals and families in the communities.

When an infant is abused and/or neglected, the parent's behavior often appears to be the proximal cause of the infant's anxious attachment. This can lead us to overlook background factors that influence the parent. Some maltreating parents are psychologically deviant or even mentally ill, but many would not stand out in a group of nonabusive parents of the same subcultural background.

With or without psychopathology in the parent, there is evidence that child maltreatment often reflects social, economic, and cultural influences, not only parent characteristics. Among the societal variables research has shown to be associated with child abuse, Crittenden and Ainsworth (1989) listed unemployment, job dissatisfaction, single parenthood, and social isolation of low-income, multiproblem families. The common theme is that stressful circumstances can so strain a parent, a pair of parents, or a family that both child abuse and anxious attachment may result.

A likely implication is that intervention at the societal level, not only at the family level, might reduce the frequency and severity of disturbances in primary attachment relationships. Provision of safe, stable housing and prevention of social isolation of stressed parents might assist many families in fostering healthy attachment patterns in the next generation. Good-quality, affordable day care; parent support groups; and good access to transportation could be part of the solution. Encouraging family planning, so that parents' psychic resources do not get spread too thin, might reduce child neglect and reduce the incidences of physical and emotional abuse that stem from stress and exhaustion. Discouraging the acceptance and widespread use of physical punishment in our culture might reduce the frequency of abusive excesses.

Research relevant to hypotheses about the community's influence on the risk of maltreatment (and anxious attachment) is beyond the scope of this book. I mention these factors here so that I will not contribute to the erroneous opinion that problems in child rearing have all their roots inside the parents who hurt their children. Too many people want to judge and punish parents who do poorly with their children. Too few are willing to work to change their societies or cultures so that more parents will be able to care for and guide their children well.

ASSISTANCE TO FAMILIES IN LOW-RISK CIRCUMSTANCES

Even in families not initially believed to be at high risk for fostering insecure attachments and raising children poorly, about one-third of infants develop anxious attachments. Intervention to improve their situations and their security is surprisingly difficult. For example, Nezworski, Tolan, and Belsky (1988) offered brief psychotherapy (12 weeks, maximum) to some of the parents of anxiously attached babies (eight A's and six C's; the D category was not used) in their Pennsylvania longitudinal sample. The families were mostly in the middle class and not believed to be at risk for maltreatment or serious psychopathology. Although no comparison group was involved and the outcome measures were limited, the discussion of the therapy is insightful.

All of the mothers said their husbands made little effort to help with the additional work created by the birth of a child, and all of them felt resentful. Many felt overwhelmed with the housework and child care work, and many were disorganized in handling these duties. These mothers seemed to be almost always coping with the most pressing demand or crisis in the situation; they could not often enjoy playing with their babies. Several of the mothers were disorganized not only about household work but also about mealtimes, sleep schedules, and babysitters' schedules. Their children's worlds were surprisingly chaotic. At the time of intervention, the babies were in their second year. The mothers had little patience for the messiness their toddlers' explorations created and were ineffective in their efforts to train the children to behave properly. They gave little support to the child's cognitive development, differentiation of self from mother, and budding autonomy.

Many of the mothers in the Nezworski et al. (1988) sample were experiencing great marital difficulty. Conflicts arose easily, husbands were described as unavailable, and the women found it very difficult to share emotional needs and ask for support from their husbands. They expected their husbands to ignore them, ridicule them, reject them, leave them, or become physically abusive. Several of the women complained about not having sex often enough but appeared reluctant to do anything to solve the problem, and some suspected their husbands were having affairs but were unwilling to talk with their husbands about their fears.

None of the mothers in this sample appeared to have had happy childhoods; they did not feel that they had been nurtured adequately. Most of them recalled specific events that suggested that their early years were troubled and painful. They had low self-esteem and little insight into themselves.

What is most striking about the Nezworski et al. (1988) study is that the subjects came from an ordinary, largely middle-class sample. They were selected from the larger group and invited to receive brief psychotherapy because their babies were anxiously attached. Classification of a baby as avoidant or resistant was, in this particular low-risk sample, sufficient to identify the mother as one who really did appear to need psychotherapy for herself and, in many cases, counseling for the marriage.

Initially, the research team doubted that families of insecure infants really had any need of psychotherapy. However, all of the mothers who accepted the researchers' invitation and participated in the clinical treatment program appeared to have substantial personality problems that had been with them for a very long time. They were chronically stressed but afraid to reach out for help. In about half of the subjects, the problems were so severe that there were signs of clinical pathology such as depression, anxiety problems, psychosomatic disorders, or abuse of alcohol or another drug.

This is not meant to imply that the Strange Situation assessment is sufficient for identifying families in need of intervention. It does, however, suggest that insecure attachment in the Strange Situation is a good indicator that further assessment may be appropriate and that psychotherapy may be acceptable and beneficial to the parents and the child. Marvin and Stewart (1990) made a good argument for viewing the infant-parent dyad not as an isolated unit, but as a part of a whole family in need of assistance.

Twelve weeks was not nearly enough time to resolve the problems these mothers faced. The therapists thought their clients had just begun to form working alliances with them when it was time to terminate the therapy. Little attention had been given to the stressed marriages and the basic maladaptive parenting styles, so it was likely that the children would remain insecure. However, most of the mothers reported feeling safer about their therapists and about the possibility of continuing or later reentering therapy with someone else, which suggested that positive changes had begun. Apart from therapists' and clients' reports, there was no formal assessment of therapy outcomes.

A much more systematic effort to influence attachment outcomes in a middle-class sample also uncovered unexpected difficulty. In a nonclinical Australian sample of primiparous mothers, Barnett, Blignault, Holmes, Payne, and Parker (1987) identified a group who got high scores on trait anxiety scales on the third or fourth day postpartum. As the label implies, *trait anxiety* is chronic anxiety—anxiety the subject reports having experienced over a long period of time across a variety of situations. It differs from *state anxiety*— the amount of anxiety the subject is experiencing at a particular time.

The mothers with high trait anxiety were divided into three groups. Some received no intervention, some received 12 months of nonprofessional intervention from an experienced mother, and some received 12 months of professional intervention from experienced female social workers. The social workers offered general support, promoted self-esteem, encouraged responsiveness to infant signals, encouraged husbands to be more involved with their babies and more supportive of their wives, and used specific antianxiety measures. State anxiety levels decreased by 19 percent for the mothers receiving professional intervention. They did not decrease significantly for the other two groups of anxious mothers.

The authors expected that, in the absence of intervention, anxious attachments would be much more common among the babies raised by these highly anxious mothers than they are in ordinary, low-risk samples. They also expected that lowering the mother's state anxiety level would increase the likelihood of secure attachment. Neither hypothesis was supported. If the results of this study are replicated, then it can be concluded that chronically anxious mothers are about as likely as anyone else to foster secure attachments in their babies; they are not a high-risk group, per se, and diminishing their state anxiety will not improve the already good attachment outcomes most of their babies experience. In an effort to find out what else they could learn from their data, the authors conducted some post hoc analyses (Barnett et al., 1987). These exploratory analyses suggested a cycle of intergenerational transmission of difficulties in interpersonal relationships. Specifically, mothers who considered their relationships with their parents to have been unsatisfactory tended to have anxiously attached infants; other mothers generally had securely attached babies.

Not all interventions to increase attachment security have such limited success. As noted in Chapter 5, Van den Boom (1990) identified 100 newborns who showed high physiological irritability on Brazelton's NBAS. She then assigned them at random to one of four groups in a 2 × 2 design: with and without pretest observations at 6 months, and with and without intervention between 6 and 9 months of age. The control group that received pretest observations also received observation visits at the times when subjects in the experimental group received intervention visits. This excellent research design made it possible to separate effects of mere attention from effects of actual intervention.

The intervention consisted of three visits, at 3-week intervals. From the Van den Boom (1990) report, neither the duration nor the location of the visits is clear, except that the environment was a natural one. When these initially irritable babies were 6 months old, many of the mothers appeared to be uninvolved or ineffective with them. The sole focus of intervention was sensitive responsiveness, and intervention was highly individualized. The intervener watched the baby and the mother in a setting that allowed natural interaction and coached the mother in personal detail about how to respond effectively to her baby.

The effects of this very limited, focused intervention were impressive. Mothers in the intervention group were significantly more responsive, more stimulating, and more visually attentive to their babies at 9 months than mothers in the control group were. Intervention directed toward the mother had measurable effects on the baby. The babies in the treatment group showed more positive social behavior, showed less negative emotionality during interaction, explored more, and showed higher qualitative levels of exploration than the control babies.

Further, the impact of intervention on attachment itself was startling. In the control groups (with and without pretest observations), only 28 percent of these irritable, lower-class babies were classified as secure at 12 months. Fifty-six percent were avoidant, and sixteen percent were resistant. In the experimental groups, 68 percent were securely attached at 12 months, despite having been irritable as newborns, and, in many cases, despite having mothers who appeared uninvolved or ineffective when the babies were 6 months old.

Until this study is replicated, some of its implications must remain uncertain. All of the intervention was done by a single person. While the researcher's explicit focus was on individualized parent education designed to increase sensitive responsiveness, other aspects of her behavior may have contributed to her therapeutic impact. Even so, the possibility of profound benefits from minimal intervention has now been demonstrated. When the risk factor lies in the infant, not in the mother's attachment history or current mental health, as few as three focused, individualized intervention visits can produce a huge increase in the frequency of secure attachments (Van den Boom, 1990).

CHAPTER SUMMARY

The picture that emerges from all of these studies is a fairly coherent one. Difficulties in primary relationships and risk factors can be identified very early in life. With tact and persistence, further assessment and intervention (where warranted) may be accepted. Both in low-risk samples and in high-risk samples, difficulties in providing responsive care for the baby very often reflect difficulties or disturbances in the parent's attachment history. Some parents are so impaired that they may never be able to care adequately for their children, but many families do benefit from treatment, and some benefit enormously.

When the primary challenge to developing secure attachment is infant irritability, as few as three intervention visits with a very specific focus on teaching the mother to respond sensitively to her infant's signals and to develop enjoyable interactions with him or her may have a profound positive impact. When the primary impediment to the development of secure attachment rests in the mother's personality, treatment can still be successful but is likely to require much more time, effort, depth, and scope. In high-risk families, interventions that are brief or simple, such as parent education, are not effective. Successful programs for such families include psychotherapy (often infant-parent or family therapy), practical assistance, social support, modeling, and instruction; successful programs generally continue to provide clients with services for a year or more. However, even programs that do include all of those components are not always successful.

3

CHILDHOOD

Because both continuous and stagelike changes in physical, cognitive, and linguistic abilities tumble rapidly forward, how a child organizes attachment behavior and how a child can organize representational models of relationships change greatly around age 4 and, in the next 2 or 3 years, change again.

While the child is only 2 or 3 years old, the parent or other caregiver probably does much more than half of the cognitive and behavioral work that makes the dyadic interaction look as if it comes from a goal-corrected partnership. After enough experience in an emerging partnership, the child learns, probably around the age of 4 or 5, to participate in a true partnership.

Like Units 2 and 4, this unit begins by exploring aspects of attachment theory that are particularly relevant to the age period under discussion. The focus in Chapter 13 is on representational models: what they can include, what they cannot comprehend, how they change, and how different experiences in attachment relationships in the early years affect the child's processing of information, emotion, and memories. There are implications for variations in normal development and for psychopathology. Under specifiable circumstances, children are expected to develop multiple, conflicting, incompatible representational models of their attachment relationships.

The most widely used approaches to assessing patterns of attachment in preschoolers and in children who are about 6 years old rely on separation-reunion paradigms. Two different systems for interpreting and coding preschoolers' behavior have been offered; which will prove most useful is not yet clear. The only available system for coding 6-

year-olds' reunion behaviors shows great promise but does not have the level of reliability and validity associated with the Strange Situation. The researchers who developed the system recommend supplementing reunion data with another source of information about the security and pattern of the child's attachment. These and other methods of assessing security of attachment in preschoolers and in somewhat older children are introduced in Chapter 14.

Ideas that are fascinating and important have proliferated faster than research can test them. The available data do suggest high consistency in patterns of attachment to the mother from infancy to age 6 in stable family circumstances. Children with secure attachments appear to have more positive interactions with parents, siblings, peers, and even strangers. Children with anxious attachments appear to have subclinical behavioral problems more often than secure children. What the various patterns of attachment predict about developmental trajectories for boys may be quite different from what they predict for girls. These issues are discussed in Chapter 15.

REPRESENTATIONAL MODELS

Most of this chapter is about theory, and much of the theory I will describe here is new and relatively untested. This new theorizing is important for at least two reasons. First, it stands on its own as a meaningful, plausible way of understanding some very important aspects of psychological development. Second, it provides the framework within which attachment research moves forward. Theory and research continue to evolve together, each informing the other, just as they did throughout Bowlby's and Ainsworth's careers.

Virtually all children raised in families move from exercising goal-corrected attachment *behavior* in infancy to participating in a goal-corrected *partnership* with the attachment figure by the age of 5 or 6. Often, my specification of ages in this chapter will be broad, and at times vague. The age ranges stated are broad because individuals with different genetic makeup and different life experiences progress through normative stages at different rates. The ranges are sometimes vague because so little research has been done about normative development in attachments after infancy. Some changes in representational models are associated not with normative trends but with individual differences.

There is widespread agreement that secure attachment is associated with representational models that are effective for assessing current social circumstances, possibilities, and probable responses from others and so for choosing a behavioral strategy that serves the child's goals effectively. Theorists believe that different specifiable sets of distortions and constrictions in representational models are associated with different and specifiable behavioral strategies. In this chapter, I will introduce ideas about (1) how to interpret and label the attachment patterns of young children and (2) how the various types of representational models may differ from each other in structure, in content, and in rules of operation.

FEATURES OF REPRESENTATIONAL MODELS

Attachment theory is, at one level, a biological theory about physical protection and survival of the infant and the species. Representational models move attachment theory into the realms clinical psychologists address: individual differences in understanding the self, in readiness to trust others, in abilities to perceive and to express emotions, in abilities to recognize and use available information, and in the desire and tolerance for intimacy.

Bowlby certainly introduced a number of important ideas about representational models. He defined a representational model or working model as an individual's conscious and unconscious mental representation of the world and of himself in it. The biological function of representational models, Bowlby ([1969] 1982, 1973, 1980) asserted, is to help the individual perceive events, forecast the future, and construct plans. From an evolutionary perspective, the reason humans can and do develop representational models is that, by making insight and foresight possible, mental models yield a survival advantage. The models include both affective and cognitive components. In fact, Bowlby described affects (emotions) as an appraisal system, a guide to understanding the meaning of an event and selecting a response.

Bowlby's own theorizing about the construction of representational models in childhood was sketchy. It was based largely on clinical work with children and adults and on what was then known about developments in cognitive and memory abilities in childhood. The next generation of attachment theorists, including especially Bretherton (1985, 1987, 1991), Crittenden (1990, 1992a, 1992b, 1993, 1994), and Main (1991; Main, Kaplan, and Cassidy, 1985) has added considerable detail to the theory of the development and effects of representational models. Much of the material presented in this chapter is drawn from the writings of these three theorists. All three have argued that secure attachment, open communication, and adequate representational models tend to go together in human development. Indeed, that view is shared by almost everyone currently doing much research or theory development in the field of attachment.

In contrast, as noted earlier, many insecure children develop dual (or multiple) models of themselves and of their relationships—models whose contents and rules are often contradictory and incompatible with each other. The models cannot both be true. Often, according to Bowlby, the child consciously recognizes and believes one model while the other is highly influential but relatively or completely unconscious.

Some representational models work better than others. A model that works well enables the child or adult to manipulate images and *cognitively* (either consciously or, more often, unconsciously) select an effective strategy. Thus, behavioral trial and error, with its frequently risky or painful consequences, may not be necessary. To be functional, the model need not be perfectly accurate or highly detailed, but it must be consistent with the reality it represents.

Among the representational models the child constructs for understanding her physical and social world, models of the self and of principal caregiving figures are, according to Bowlby (1973), particularly important. Key features of the model of the self are how acceptable, lovable, worthy, and competent the self is. Key aspects of the model of the attachment figure include his or her accessibility and emotional supportiveness. Both models are, of course, based on actual experience.

Models are necessarily simpler than the realities they represent. From a large number of somewhat variable experiences, the child extracts, encodes, and stores in memory the recurring patterns. Some simplification of incoming information is inevitable and, indeed, adaptive. Simplifying information increases the efficiency with which the child can recognize a recurring type of situation and choose a course of action. The price of the gain in efficiency is the loss of some detail. Ordinarily, this is not important.

The processes of forming and using representational models of interactions and then of the self, specific others, and relationships are exactly analogous to the Piagetian processes of forming, expanding, and modifying schemes. As Piaget (1952, 1970) used the term, a "scheme" is a mental structure. A *sensorimotor* scheme coordinates sensory and motor information in order to produce the same end, such as thumb-sucking, in a variety of situations. (Getting the thumb to the mouth requires different movements when the baby is lying on his stomach on a mattress, for example, than it requires when he is being carried upright on his father's chest.) An *operational* scheme, such as determining what class an item belongs in and whether that class is a subclass of another class, can be exercised at an entirely representational level, without any motor action. In either case (sensorimotor schemes or operational schemes), new events or interactions are, when possible, assimilated to existing schemes: the individual interprets and responds to what is happening now on the basis of what he or she already knows. Sometimes what happens next is so different from what was expected that the individual notices the difference, but not so different that the individual cannot comprehend it at all. Then *accommodation*—the modifying of the mental scheme or the updating of the representational model—begins.

The existence and nature of representational models cannot be directly observed. We observe behavior and make inferences about what is going on in the individual's mind. Because the concept of a working model is a hypothetical construct, there is a risk that we may *reify* the construct. That is, we may regard representational models as things that have been proven to exist in reality, not as concepts developed to help explain observable phenomena. While it is clear that cognitive processing happens, detailed hypotheses about working models are too new and too little tested to justify treating them as facts.

Whether attachment theorists are right about representational models is of some importance. Bowlby (1980) asserted that, once organized, representational models tend to operate outside of conscious awareness and tend to resist dramatic change. If that were not the case, then just teaching children different behavioral skills might be enough to reduce the developmental risks they face as a result of unfavorable experiences in early attachment relationships. If, as attachment theorists argue, representational models are influential, largely unconscious, and resistant to change, then helping children who are traveling down maladaptive developmental pathways to change their courses will be difficult. It will be necessary to change the child's expectations and his rules for attending to and processing information. Understanding how representational models are organized at different stages of development and how they are modified at different stages of development may be very useful to people who work with troubled children (see Crittenden, 1992b).

THE GOAL-CORRECTED PARTNERSHIP

Some of the best theory development about the preschool shift from phase 3, the phase of specific attachment, to phase 4, the phase of the goal-corrected partnership, is in Marvin (1977). In the later development of theory and of research methods, some of Marvin's early insights seem to have been left behind, unexamined and forgotten. As attachment researchers give increasing attention to normative changes and individual differences in childhood attachments, his ideas deserve consideration.

As described in Chapter 4, around the age of 7 months, rather abruptly, a baby's attachment behavior becomes goal-corrected. The baby seeks to maintain proximity to a specific figure. An attachment has formed. At any given moment, the attached baby has a *set-goal*, an internal, cognitive representation of a specific degree of proximity or contact he seeks to attain or maintain. He has at least a few different behavioral plans he can activate in pursuit of that goal.

Later, as the conceptual and communicative skills of the young preschooler develop, it becomes possible for parent and child to communicate their goals and plans to one another and so to share common goals and plans. In addition, the child becomes increasingly skilled at inhibiting his own behavior. This allows his plans for achieving any particular goal to become increasingly complex. He becomes able intentionally and consciously to consider the parent's probable behavior before starting an action or activity of his own. He can treat the parent's plans or behavior as an element in his own plan. He can inhibit his attachment behavior until the circumstances fit the plans and goals of both the child and the parent. He can participate in a partnership. A *partnership* is defined as an enduring relationship between two individuals that is characterized by mutual adjustments of goals and plans. Over time, an integration and balancing of the two individuals' hierarchies of goals and plans evolves, and an integration of how they control behavior in the relationship evolves.

Marvin (1977) developed a direct procedure for assessing a child's ability to inhibit her goal-directed behavior and incorporate the mother's plan into her own. While being videotaped at home, the mother showed the child a cookie, told her she could have it when the mother had finished writing a letter, laid the cookie in sight but out of reach, tried to write for 3 minutes, and then gave the cookie to the child. Very few 2-year-olds (19 percent) could accept the mother's plan and wait for the cookie. Most 3- and 4-year-olds, however, accepted the situation easily. Only 25 percent of the 3-year-olds, and none of the 4-year-olds, did the things that most of the 2-year-olds did: crying, trying to reach the cookie, pushing the mother's hand away from the paper, grabbing the pen, and the like.

Marvin's cookie test provides an example of a simple context in which the child is asked to fit his plans into the mother's plans. The same sort of skill (inhibiting an impulse until the parent is ready for the child to enact it) is probably harder to exercise in the context of three siblings tumbling over each other to greet the mother when she comes home from her job.

Although a 2- or 3-year-old child can insert her father's plan into her own, she cannot conceive of his plan as a set of thoughts in his mind. She can agree to wait until Daddy has finished cooking the spaghetti sauce before they go swimming together, but she cannot picture Daddy thinking about how he will also manage to fit in all his evening tasks: paying the bills, buying the lumber he needs for building a doghouse, and phoning the teenagers on the family's child care list until he finds one who is available for Saturday evening. To recognize that the parent's plan is a set of thoughts in his mind, the child must outgrow her cognitive egocentrism. When she becomes able to see things from another person's point of view, her ability to cooperate in general and her partnership with her attachment figure in particular will become more sophisticated.

Both autonomy and connection are salient developmental issues for toddlers and preschoolers. It is consistent with evolutionary theory that *behavior* that maintains proximity to the principal attachment figure should decrease as the child develops skills to protect herself. These include motor skills, cognitive skills, and communicative skills: running, making appeasement gestures, foreseeing and so avoiding dangers, fighting, and gaining a place in a peer group where there is safety in numbers.

Little evidence of an ability to participate in a goal-corrected partnership has been found in 1- or 2-year-olds. In fact, 2-year-olds tend to maintain as much proximity to the mother as 1-year-olds do. When separated from the mother (at the mother's initiative), 2-year-olds protest less than 1-year-olds, but they are generally not willing to be left with a stranger.

Marvin (1977) proposed that the phase of the true goal-corrected partnership is often preceded by a phase in which there is an emergent partnership. During that phase, the parent provides the "scaffolding" for negotiating and forming joint plans. At first, the parent might tell the child where or why she is going, when she will return, what the child can do while the parent is gone, and what they can do together when the parent returns. If she is a sensitive caregiver, she gives voice to the child's desires and goals and incorporates them into her planning. The child learns to label and discuss feelings. Gradually, the child learns to carry out his part by saying how he feels and what he wants to do, recognizing how the parent feels and what the parent wants to do, and having input in the decision process.

Marvin's (1977) particular contribution to theory in this area is the controversial hypothesis that the basis or definition of the attachment relationship changes, in most children, sometime around the age of 4 or 5. The set-goal for a young child—at least, through age 3—is always some degree of physical proximity or contact. The set-goal for a school-age child, Marvin proposed, is a matching of the internal perspectives of the two partners and a sharing of control of the relationship. Interaction in proximity becomes less and less important. The child now knows that the parent-child relationship continues even when the two are not near each other. Sharing ideas, values, attitudes, goals, and plans becomes increasingly important. The child's goal, Marvin argued, is not to achieve physical proximity, but to achieve mutual regulation of the relationship, which entails bringing the attachment figure's perspective and the child's perspective into balance with each other. (Two perspectives can be in harmony either by being the same or by being complementary.)

As Marvin acknowledged, interaction in proximity and physical contact continue to be important parts of all close emotional relationships. A child whose principal goal in an attachment relationship is a matching of internal perspectives is still likely to fall back on the security of physical proximity when the balance in the relationship is upset. Marvin's hypothesis is not that the child abandons the goal of intermittent proximity or contact, but that this goal is transformed by or subordinated to the goal of integrating perspectives.

By age 4 or 5, the child's skills and interests are developing steadily, and he is probably initiating separations that last for hours so that he can play with his friends. As the degree and frequency of proximity to the principal attachment figure decrease, does the essence of the relationship change? What *is* the internal set-goal of the attachment system in a child who is 4, 5, or 6 years old? Intermittent proximity? Felt security? Attention and nurturance? Shared perspectives? Mutually regulated goals and other internal states? To the end of her career, Ainsworth maintained that the set-goal of the attachment system at any age is access to the attachment figure, with physical proximity or contact being pursued at least once in a while. Much more theory development and data gathering will be necessary before we can evaluate Marvin's proposition that the goal of proximity gets subordinated to the goal of integrating perspectives in the partnership.

DEVELOPMENTAL PSYCHOPATHOLOGY

Clinical psychologists working from many different theoretical perspectives often regard the earliest years of childhood as a "sensitive period" for determining both the individual's personality and the sorts of relationships the individual will participate in as an adult. Considering early childhood a sensitive period has two implications. First, it means that if certain phenomena do not emerge in this period, then either it will be difficult or impossible to induce them later, or they may never take a normal form. An extreme example appears in children who spend all their early years in institutions with no regular personal caregiver available and later seem unable to form normal attachments to foster parents. Second, it implies that the traits that develop and the qualities of the relationships that develop in those years have effects that are, compared to traits and relationships that come later, disproportionately enduring and influential.

Attachment theorists generally agree that early childhood is a sensitive developmental period for personality and intimate social relations. Even so, their views are generally much less deterministic than Freud's and much more optimistic about resiliency as a normal characteristic of human development.

The human infant comes into the world with a compelling propensity "to establish and preserve emotional ties to preferred caregivers at all costs, while simultaneously attempting to find a place within these relationships for his or her own goals and initiatives" (Lyons-Ruth, 1991, p. 10). As Lyons-Ruth (1991) noted, past theories about the normal development of social relations have been based on patterns seen primarily in adult or child pathological states. This is especially true of psychoanalytic theories. It is now clear that we need a theory of normal development that is based on normal childhood patterns. We also need theories of psychopathology that do not rely on notions of fixation at early normal stages of development.

Attachment theory addresses both needs. It is a theory of development, both healthy and pathological. In the realm of abnormal psychology, attachment theory offers the hypothesis that psychopathology consists of traveling along a deviant developmental pathway. This is different from prior hypotheses about the nature of psychopathology. For example, Freud and most other psychoanalysts based their clinical work on the hypothesis that psychopathology resulted from (1) being fixated at an early stage of normal psychosexual or psychosocial development or (2) regressing to a normal early stage. Bowlby's (1988) proposition that psychopathology is deviant but continuing development, not fixation or regression, invited other psychoanalysts to revolutionize their thinking. According to Bowlby, whether the developments are healthy or pathological, the individual does continue to develop, integrating constitutional, maturational, and experiential factors.

The caregivers who become attachment figures not only protect infants from harm but also provide the interpersonal context in which children learn to use their minds. Very early in childhood, individual differences in representational models contribute to individual differences in self-image, personality, social behavior, and openness to change. Early representational models differ not only in the content of what the child learns about himself and his attachment figures, but also in the rules the child learns or constructs about what to pay attention to, how to interpret perceptions, and what to remember.

DEFENSIVE EXCLUSION

Humans are always surrounded by much more information than they can attend to, think about, and put to good use. Consequently, they are always selective about what they attend to, process, and store in memory. The ability to be selective is clearly adaptive. Without selective exclusion of unimportant information, we would all be like computers with overloaded circuits all the time. Instead, we routinely ignore a vast amount of unimportant perceptual information, such as the colors of the clothes of the people on the last bus you rode. In general, the unimportant information simply never reaches conscious awareness. At some preconscious level of cognitive appraisal, we decide it does not warrant further processing.

When an event or a recurring sequence of interactions does seem important, we tend to abstract, encode, and store only the essential properties of the event or sequence. Such simplifying and generalizing enables us to make sense of our physical and social worlds and to recall critical information.

In some cases, however, the loss of specific, detailed information from a representational model can be maladaptive. Some working models call for the selective exclusion of certain information from conscious awareness. Repression, denial, and other defense mechanisms identified by psychoanalysts can be understood as special cases of the selective exclusion of information. Such *defensive exclusion* from awareness once seemed to be a preposterous hypothesis. How could a person exclude aspects of internal or external reality from further processing without first becoming aware of them? Research conducted by cognitive psychologists has now made it clear that information undergoes many stages of selective processing before it reaches awareness, and there are opportunities for exclusion from further processing at each level.

Defensive exclusion is believed to occur when awareness of what is excluded would cause great psychological pain or conflict. Information from the treatment of clients in psychotherapy suggests that such conflict commonly occurs when the attachment figure repeatedly punishes, rejects, or disavows the anxious, angry, or needy feelings the child communicates to the attachment figure. Specific examples include the caregiver's ridiculing a child's security-seeking behavior and labeling his own rejection of a child as an expression of love. Keeping his longing for closeness to the parent, his anxiety, and his anger out of awareness protects the child from mental pain, conflict, and confusion. However, the defensive exclusion of feelings and information limits the representational model to a distorted correspondence to reality. The defenses help the child adapt to a painful reality with a minimum of suffering, but they leave him poorly prepared to recognize and enjoy the benefits of more-supportive possibilities in other relationships.

For example, consider the case of a child whose parents, for whatever reasons, consistently ridiculed and condemned her for acting like a baby when she got hurt and needed comfort. The child coped by excluding from awareness her pain and her longing for contact comfort. When the child was 2 years old, her parents separated. When she was 5, her father remarried. His new wife is a responsive, caring stepmother. The child, however, learned long ago that only babies cry and seek help when they are hurt, and that it's bad to be a baby. Now, when she falls and skins her knee, she does not allow herself to notice that she wants comfort. She feels angry but does not know that her anger has its roots in the unconscious belief that no comfort is available. The child never discovers that her stepmother would wash the wound gently and cradle the child in her lap until the child feels better.

To the extent that the individual's representational model screens out important information about reality, it interferes with effective coping and with optimal development. When a bully taunts and shoves the child described in the example above, the child does her best to exclude from awareness her fear and her need for protection. Instead of seeking help to cope with a problem that is too big for her to handle alone, she withdraws from involvement with peers. Defensively excluding awareness of needing comfort and protection, the child does not tell her father or stepmother about the incident with the bully. She does not ask them for help. Not knowing how to tell which playmates are dangerous and which are not, she withdraws from them all.

This example is, like most examples, oversimplified. Nevertheless, it illustrates the sorts of hypotheses attachment theorists are developing about how early representational models affect later perceptions, interpretations, actions, self-images, and relationships.

What a child's working models can include increases as the child's cognitive, linguistic, and behavioral abilities continue to develop. In addition, the working models of the self, the attachment figure, and the attachment relationship may change in nature as the child moves from one level of cognitive development to another. As Piaget (1970), Vygotsky (1978), Werner ([1940] 1980), and many others have vividly illustrated, children do not just come to know more and more; they also develop new ways of knowing. They increase both the differentiations encoded in mental structures and the integrated, hierarchical organization of mental structures.

Much of what we can infer about what a working model can include and how it can operate depends on such changing cognitive abilities as how a child's memory works and on how a child processes information.

MEMORY SYSTEMS AND INFORMATION PROCESSING

When Bowlby (e.g., 1980) wrote about representational models, he based his theorizing partly on Tulving's (1972) theory of memory. Tulving, at that time, was arguing that people have two largely separate sorts of memory: episodic and semantic. *Episodic mem-*

ory stores recall of specific events or episodes. It holds chronologically organized experiences. For example, "When I was 5 years old, I had a birthday party, and six friends came, and I wore a yellow dress with a big collar, and my brother bumped into my mother and made her drop the cake on the floor, and she yelled at him for making it fall and yelled at me for crying about it."

In contrast to episodic memory, *semantic memory* stores generalizations or summaries of the *meanings* of recurring patterns. For example, "My mother always made sure our house and our clothes were clean and beautiful." The information in episodic memory can contradict the information in semantic memory. For example, a child's episodic memory store may include recall of many times when the child longed for his father to play with him, but the father was busy watching TV, reading the newspaper, talking with his wife, or working in his garden or workshop, where children were not welcome. However, the father often tells the child that he loves playing with him, it's just that right now he is busy, or he is too tired, or he has to work, or he needs to talk to Mommy about something. Based on what the father says and on the child's recall of the few times when the father did play with him, the child's semantic memory store may include the generalization "Daddy loves playing with me. It's his favorite thing to do." The child does not notice that this generalization contradicts his experience of how his father chooses to spend his time. Evidence I will introduce in Chapter 17 indicates that many individuals, adults as well as children, apparently do little cross-checking between the two hypothesized memory stores; they do not try to make episodic and semantic memories consistent with each other.

More-recent research and theorizing by cognitive psychologists have revealed that information-processing and memory systems are much more complex than Tulving (1972) first proposed. Crittenden (1990, 1992a, 1993, 1994) draws on Tulving (1985), which demonstrated that there are *at least* three different memory systems that appear in childhood and continue to operate all through the adult years. In addition to episodic memory and semantic memory, human beings have *procedural memory*, which begins in infancy and is based on sensorimotor representations. For much of the first year of life, the only memory system available is procedural memory.

Procedural memory consists of recall of repeatedly enacted and experienced patterns of behavior that become generalized. After the same sort of interaction has happened over and over again, the baby comes to expect the caregiver's and his own familiar pattern of behavior. However, the infant expects the pattern *behaviorally*, not consciously. A simple example can be observed when someone dresses a baby or toddler. When her own mother is dressing her, the child seems to know when to lift an arm so that a sleeve can go on, when to hold relatively still so that the mother can push the buttons through the buttonholes, when to lean forward and rest her forehead on her mother's chest so that the mother can tuck her shirt into her pants, and so on. All the little details of the often-repeated sequence flow smoothly. The child's body anticipates the mother's next action and works easily with it. The body knows the large and small movements to make; there is no need for or evidence of conscious mental processing.

That the baby does remember the movements and participate actively in the smooth repetition of the sequence becomes obvious when someone new tries to dress her. She starts to lie back, expecting the pants to come next, when the caregiver is picking up her shirt; or she fails to lift her arm when the caregiver starts trying to wiggle it into the sleeve; or she leans forward when the caregiver was not planning to tuck her shirt in. The timing of the interaction is off. Sometimes the caregiver can feel the resistance in the child's movements when she moves differently from the way the mother moves, but an observer could not see the subtle mistiming of small movements.

. Although procedural memory begins in infancy, its importance does not end there. Quite the contrary. Tulving (1985) concluded that preconscious, procedural "thinking" guides most of our daily behavior across the life span. Once you have learned how to walk, ride a bike, wash your face, or walk to the corner store, your body enacts the motions with no need for thinking about what you are doing. Your mental processes become conscious only when you notice a discrepancy between what you expected and what you are experiencing.

Crittenden's new theorizing about how children construct and update representational models draws from Tulving's recent work on memory systems and information processing. Another attachment theorist, Bretherton (1987, 1991), bases her ideas on a different set of propositions about mental structures. Bretherton found that Schank's (1982) theory about memory systems and scripts is particularly useful for understanding how individuals build, use, and modify representational models.

Schank (1982) hypothesized that most mental structures simulate events in the world and preserve representations of space, time, and causality as they are understood to exist in the world. Schank argued that perceptual, semantic, and affective information from episodic memories is reprocessed, cross-indexed, and summarized in a variety of ways. He deliberately blurred Tulving's categorical distinctions between episodic and semantic memory. He proposed instead that memories exist in a multiply interconnected hierarchy of schemes. The schemes range along a continuum from those that are very near some actual experience to those that are very general. On the basis of continuing input, the individual constructs and continually reconstructs and revises the hierarchy of schemes.

Determining whether Tulving's model, Schank's model, or some other model best fits all that we know about memory and information processing is beyond the scope of this book. So far, the two theories about memory systems seem to have similar implications for the continuing development of attachment theory.

Both Bretherton and Crittenden have found the mental structure called a "script," or an "event scheme," to be a useful concept. A *script* summarizes skeletal information about similar events that have been repeated many times in the individual's experience. It differs from a procedural memory in that it is a symbolic representation: you can recall it without enacting it. A script differs from an episodic memory in that it represents abstracted, generalized information, not a single specific instance. The script stores recurring information about who does what to whom, and perhaps where and how. For example, a script memory might represent the information that, at dinnertime, Daddy "always" scolds all the kids for everything they did wrong that day; another script memory might store the information that, a little before bedtime, Daddy cradles the child in his lap and reads him a fascinating, magical story.

Whatever a child experiences frequently and routinely is likely to be encoded as a script. If attachment theorists are right, it is not likely to be questioned: *the information encoded in a script is received and stored as a basic fact about relationships.* Memories of the specific experiences that led to the generalized script may be hard to recover. The same sort of information may not even be represented in any stored autobiographical episodes. In that case, the child will not be able to retrieve any episodic memories; there are no occasion-specific memories to retrieve. If the child's experiences have been benign, this is likely to be unimportant. When the experiences stored in scripts include pervasive unresponsiveness from a clinically depressed parent, routine incestuous molestation, or recurring family violence, the damage these scripts can do to the child can be painfully serious, and retrieving any occasion-specific memories for reinterpretation in psychotherapy can be painfully difficult.

Current theories of memory agree that some mental structures store brief scripts, such as playing peekaboo or listening to a bedtime story. According to Schank, other mental structures organize brief scripts into longer sequences of coordinated events. What is represented is not just the experience of sitting with the parent and brother for a bedtime story, for example, but the entire sequence of bathing, putting pajamas on, choosing clothes for the morning, brushing teeth, listening to a story, praying, and getting tucked in. Other mental structures generalize about events related in other ways. For example, one mental structure might store generalizations about feeding situations regardless of context. Another mental structure might abstract commonalities from a wide variety of caregiving routines.

Brief scripts or event schemes result from processing autobiographical memories and storing them in summary form. *Existing schemes then guide how the individual processes new information.* This is a critical point for understanding how early experiences and relationships set the child on a developmental trajectory in which she is likely to actively recreate the same sorts of experiences and relationships later. What she already knows on the basis of her personal experience and limited cognitive abilities determines how she interprets and responds to new experiences. In the ordinary course of events, attachment theorists believe, the child very often *is* father to the man. Luckily for people who had anxiety-provoking, angry childhoods, early history does not fully determine destiny. To change the course of personal history, however, many interconnected mental schemes or scripts may need to be changed.

When one unexpected turn of events occurs, the child is likely either to ignore the novel event or to encode it as an exception to the familiar script. If the formerly unexpected event recurs many times, the child will encode it in a new scheme. So far, this is only a restatement of Piaget's (1970) propositions about assimilation and accommodation. What Schank added is that information from the once-unexpected episode will also be fed into many other mental structures, structures that represent generalized, summarized information about agents, actions, intentions, and emotions.

Schank's model of how memories work is a complex one. What implications does this model have for hypotheses about how a growing child's working models relevant to attachment relationships develop and change? The answer to that question is not yet clear. Before I can say much more about developmental changes in children's representational models, I must discuss developmental changes in memory, cognition, emotion, and social interaction.

DEVELOPMENTAL CHANGES

How complex a representational model can be depends upon how complex a child's knowledge, information processing, and memory processes can be. In the beginning, of course, there are no representational models.

Obviously, knowledge, information processing, memory processes, linguistic skills, emotions, and social interaction all increase in complexity as the child gains age and experience. A detailed review of studies of emerging abilities is beyond the scope of this chapter. Here, I will offer only a brief summary of data about developmental changes that are relevant to making inferences about representational models early in childhood. Most of the data I will mention here are cited in theoretical papers presented by Bretherton (1987, 1991), Crittenden (1990, 1994), Main (1991), and Marvin (1977).

■ Memory

As noted above, procedural memory develops in the first months of life. Most theorists and researchers currently believe that children rely mainly on procedural memory throughout infancy. Semantic memory abilities start to develop in infancy, but the child is not yet adept in using them.

According to Crittenden (1993), infants (even older infants) have another important limitation on their ability to form working models. Specifically, they may be able to classify knowledge into only two categories, not several points along a continuum. In reality, hardly any caregivers are all good or all bad. Almost all caregivers are at least a little inconsistent in terms of how sensitive, accessible, and responsive they are, and some caregivers are very inconsistent. Crittenden (1993) argues that infants who have very inconsistent primary caregivers may have no way to comprehend and encode such complexity. They may be able to classify their caregivers only as good or bad; warm or cold; predictable or unpredictable; not as usually good, very confusing, or usually bad.

The beginnings of *semantic* memory may emerge as early as the eleventh or twelfth month. Avoidance upon reunion in the Strange Situation could conceivably be guided by procedural memory, without the involvement of symbolic, representational skills. However, many avoidant babies also distract themselves from cues that would activate attachment behavior even during the brief period of separation. These 1-year-olds have clearly moved beyond just adjusting to a partner who is present.

Supported by the child's developing ability to use words, semantic memory clearly emerges in most children before the second birthday. In their pretend play, toddlers show that information about everyday events is available to them in schematic form. When a child using a doll and a toy car pretends that the doll is Mommy and she is saying bye-bye to her little girl and getting into the car to drive to work, the child is demonstrating that she has drawn and can draw upon symbolic representations of familiar events. Memory is no longer just in her body; it is also in her mind.

A number of studies have shown that 3-year-olds have semantic representations, not just procedural memories, of the orders of the action sequences of routine, everyday events, especially when the events are causally related. They do not have to observe an event very many times to construct a scheme of it. When asked to produce specific memories of routine events, however, such as eating dinner last night, they tend to produce scripts—abstracted, generalized versions of the event. That is, when asked for episodic memories, they tend to produce semantic memories. Only extraordinary events are likely to be recalled as episodic memories.

Episodic memory may not emerge until after the child's second birthday. In the preschool years, interpretation of these "memories" is difficult, because the reports that seem to be episodic memories may not be. There is evidence that some are wishes, some are night dreams, some are made up, some are stories told by parents, and some are revised versions of actual events, as "corrected" or reinterpreted by a parent or other caregiver. While they are still preschoolers, children do not always know whether what they "remember" is something that really happened or something they have imagined.

■ Language

Once a child understands words, others can tell him how to construe certain interpersonal events. Words can correct childish misinterpretations and can either usefully or harmfully guide the child's interpretation of ambiguous events. For a child who has supportive caregivers, new linguistic skills help him fine-tune his interactions with other people and with the environment more rapidly than he previously could. For children whose experiences have been painful, new linguistic and cognitive skills may make it possible to change relationships and representational models in constructive ways. Unfortunately, for such children, Crittenden (1992a, 1994) argued, the new skills are likely instead to be used to solidify distortions that developed in procedural memory.

Different social partners can offer widely different labels and meanings for themselves, others, and events. Consider what happens when a 2-year-old spills half a cup of juice. One father may say "Uh-oh, what a mess," and hand the child a sponge to clean it up. Another father may bristle "You stupid brat," and bring the child's meal to an abrupt end. Another may smack the child's hand or bottom without saying anything. The consequences for the child's formation of scripts and representations of the self would obviously be quite different in these three scenarios.

As the child gradually develops some understanding of causality (usually around age 3 or 4), scripts may include information about why, as well as who, where, and how. Depending on the source of the information, on how advanced the child's inferential, deductive, and hypothesis-testing skills are, and on how free the child is to recognize and explore emotions and motivations, the script's summary of why people interact in recurring patterns may or may not be fairly accurate. In addition, what parents tell their children can have a major impact on what the children encode as fact.

Consider this example. About 5:45 p.m. each day, the mother gets home from work. Her job usually makes her tense, and the drive home in rush hour traffic usually makes things worse. The father, whose job is just as stressful, usually gets home 10 or 15 minutes later. The parents have repeatedly instructed their 19-year-old nanny to get the children (ages 3 and 4) to pick up their things so that the house is orderly, if not calm, when the two parents return from their jobs, but art supplies, books, puzzle pieces, building bricks, and other toys are often scattered all over. The previous nanny was a strict disciplinarian but made the children seem insecure and unhappy, so, despite their frustration, the parents tolerate this affectionate nanny's inability or unwillingness to maintain order.

One evening, when the mother gets home, the children are watching TV and the nanny is on the phone with a girlfriend. The mother starts screaming about what a horrible mess the place is, how selfish and sloppy the children are, and how she works hard all day so she'll have enough money to give them what they want, and the least they could do is clean up their mess before she gets home. Frozen with fear, the children stare at her silently. The mother turns the noisy television off and marches to the kitchen to get a cool drink. The nanny quietly hangs up the phone and softly directs the children to help her gather up the puzzle pieces. By the time Daddy gets home, the living room is looking less lived-in, and Mommy is looking less angry. But the next day, order starts to slip again, and the job-related pressures on mother and father do not decrease.

A similar scenario recurs at least once a week. What effect does this have on the children? Obviously, there is likely to be some negative effect when a scenario like this is repeated over and over. The amount of lasting fear, anger, shame, and damage to the children's self-images that results from these periods of distress will depend on what else also happens in the family relationships. The point I want to emphasize here is that language may be one important factor. How and how much these frightening scenes affect the children will depend partly on what the caregivers say to the children about what happened and why. What the caregivers communicate about the mother's little explosions of frustration can affect what the children come to believe about themselves and about attachment figures. What they say can affect what the children remember and, years later, how accessible to recall and open to interpretation their memories are.

One possibility is that the father verbally reinforces the mother's message about how bad the children are, sends the children to their rooms in disgrace, and also scolds and criticizes the nanny for her negligence. Still frustrated and unapologetic, the mother does nothing to lessen the impact of her first angry words. The next day, wishing to reassure the children, the nanny tells them that she is sure their mommy didn't mean it. But a few days later, the scene is repeated, and the mother certainly sounds as if she means it, so the nanny's words are not very convincing. Without being aware of how it is happening, the children come to believe that they are selfish, lazy, ungrateful, bad people. They learn that it is not safe to turn to an attachment figure for comfort or protection when they are frightened—it is an attachment figure who is frightening them. The gentler nanny does not dare to comfort the children when they most need it, right after the mother's outbursts, because her doing so would appear to be a criticism of her employer, and she might lose her job. If this scenario is a typical example of what happens in this pressured family, the children may have no model of a relationship in which a powerful attachment figure provides the protection and comfort they need.

An alternative, more favorable course of events is as follows. After a few minutes, the mother apologizes for her outburst. She tells the children that, even though she is angry about the mess, she understands that little kids are often messy; they will learn how to clean up better when they are a little older. She knows that they are good children and she loves them very much. She was just very grouchy because she had a bad day at work, and she is very sorry she yelled so loud and frightened them. She suggests watching *Sesame Street* or looking at a book together so she can have a rest time with the children before she starts her evening chores. The children relax and snuggle up with Mommy on the couch. They begin to tell her about one or two things that happened during the day, and she listens with interest. Later the 4-year-old tells the father that Mommy was angry because she and her little brother made a big mess, and then *she* (the child) was angry because Mommy yelled at her, but now everybody is fine. The father says he is glad they solved the problem. At dinnertime, the whole family, nanny included, feels friendly, and no one gets unduly upset when the 3-year-old spills some squash as he is trying to serve himself.

If this sort of sequel usually follows the outbursts of frustration, the outbursts may cause no serious problems for the children. The children learn labels for emotions. They learn that it is safe to talk about emotions, even "bad" feelings. Really understanding that good people sometimes do bad things may be beyond their current cognitive abilities, but they have a solid basis in experience for later recognizing that important truth. They can take it for granted that they are still good people and that they are loved and valued even if they are sometimes messy. They learn that, despite occasional bad moments, they can generally count on their attachment figures to comfort and protect them.

Direct evidence of an effect of language skills on the child's ability to participate in a goal-corrected partnership comes from studies of deaf children (Greenberg and Marvin, 1979; Greenberg and Speltz, 1988). Some children of hearing parents receive very poor early training in communication, because the parents do not know sign language and the children cannot hear spoken language. Even with psychologically healthy, responsive parents, these children experience developmental delays in learning to label emotions and to converse and negotiate to form joint plans. The deaf children who could not yet communicate with their parents about feelings and plans could accept the parent's plan but could not participate in forming a joint plan. The emergence of the goal-corrected *partnership* was therefore delayed. In addition, the lack of communication about emotions during early childhood is related to impulsiveness and higher-than-usual frequencies of behavior problems later in childhood.

■ Emotion

By the age of 18 months, most toddlers move from just experiencing different emotions to being able to label basic feelings such as happy, sad, angry, or scared. Soon enough, they can not only use words to name their own feelings, but they can also make inferences about another person's feelings by noting the other's facial expressions, words, and actions, and can label how the other person feels.

Before they are 2 years old, many children can pretend to have a feeling and can talk about having that feeling. Most children exercise this ability in the context of play, but, for some, it is a survival skill. Before they are 2 years old, infants in abusive families learn to give false displays of emotions; they learn to hide their true feelings of anger at the parent and to smile brightly when the parent demands a display of affection or appreciation.

By age 3, most children can participate in conversations about their own feelings, others' feelings, and the causes and consequences of feelings. The opportunities for caregivers to influence children's beliefs and memories about emotions increase enormously. Caregivers can teach their children accurate labels and interpretations about how individuals feel and why, or they can foster distorted representations of affective experiences and communications.

■ Social Interaction

When they are still preverbal, infants give evidence of anticipating a partner's behavior in context. Around the age of 7 to 9 months, a maturational, neurological shift occurs. Several interrelated affective and cognitive developments occur. Specific attachments and, in many infants, fear of strangers emerge. In addition, infants soon become able to associate their own feelings with other people's behavior. For example, they become able to associate their anger or distress with something a caregiver did or failed to do. This can lead to focused anger and directed aggression in place of the undirected distress or rage of a younger infant.

Bowlby (e.g., 1973) argued that this directed anger may serve the biological function of increasing the availability of an unresponsive caregiver. If a parent is ignoring a little child, the child's screaming and hitting the parent is very likely to elicit the parent's attention. If repeated at appropriate intervals, it may even help train the parent not to tune the child out so often. Similarly, if the directed anger occurs in response to an unacceptably long period of separation, it may discourage the parent from being gone for so long in the future.

As the months and years pass, infants and children become increasingly able to recognize associations among perceptions, feelings, and behavior. The nature of the experiences an individual has as maturational developments unfold can have huge effects on what new emotions, new cognitions, and new ways of integrating cognition and affect she develops.

Experience ordinarily includes extensive interaction with other human beings. Behavior is the means of communication between the infant and any other. Because the caregiver has considerably more-advanced and -sophisticated cognitive and physical abilities, it is primarily the caregiver who interprets the behavior of both parties and gives dyadic meaning to the behavior. If the caregiver misconstrues the infant's behavior or gets enmeshed in the infant's affective states, she will have difficulty helping the infant learn to understand himself and his world and to moderate his own affective states.

Changes in cognitive, linguistic, and memory abilities are accompanied by other developmental changes that affect relations with the parent and affect what a parent must do. The child becomes larger and stronger and develops new motor skills. For 1 or 2 critical years, she is likely to be impulsive and invested in establishing her autonomy. As the toddler begins to realize that she is a separate individual, she begins to want to exercise power and control.

To fulfill his role as well as is possible, the parent must now not only nurture the child, as in infancy, but also become skillful at setting limits. The 2-year-old child has been described by many as a willful bundle of impulses with a separate sense of self who needs both acceptance and guidance. In healthy families, the parents may let the child express emotions fully, but they also teach desirable behavior and set appropriate limits. It may be okay to yell and stamp your feet when you're angry, but you still have to give your big brother a turn to use the new toys, and no, you can't have an ice cream cone right now. If all goes well, the child soon enough develops a respectable level of self-control.

All children experience fear, anger, and sadness. Some caregivers respond with empathy and correctly label the child's feelings but do not get overwhelmed by them. This helps the child learn that her feelings will not overwhelm her or others; they can be communicated and tolerated. However, if the caregiver systematically misinterprets and denies the child's emotions and needs, the child must develop a false self. That is, she must learn to mask her true feelings and pretend to feel the way her caregivers communicate (verbally and/or behaviorally) that she should or does feel. She may lose almost all awareness of her true feelings and, at the conscious level, believe that the false self she has constructed is her whole, true self. If the caregiver recognizes and labels the child's emotions accurately but does not tolerate strong negative emotions well, the dyad's interaction is likely to be angry and coercive. That is, both the child and the caregiver are likely to feel upset and angry much of the time, and both are likely to be enmeshed in a struggle to get the responses they want from the partner.

As previously noted, all children have some mixed feelings about the individuals who are both their attachment figures and their disciplinarians. As the attachment relationship evolves, the *parent's* ability to tolerate separations and ambivalence (both his own and the child's) influences how he responds to the child's conflicting emotions about the parent and to the child's struggle to become a separate individual. The parent's ability and willingness to mesh his goals and plans with the child's is important in helping the preschooler acquire the ability and willingness to mesh her goals and plans with the parent's.

Just when a child develops the ability to resist attractive rewards and to fit his plans into his partner's plans obviously depends partly on maturational processes. Within the range determined by inherited factors, the characteristics of the interactions the child experiences evidently also play a role. Cicchetti et al. (1990) reported that security of attachment was associated with the ability to wait for an attractive reward both in Marvin's cookie test and in another laboratory waiting task.

■ Coy Behavior

Most of the theorists and researchers who have sought to elaborate on Bowlby's propositions about the preschool years have assumed that they would find in preschoolers the same patterns of attachment Ainsworth and her colleagues (1978) discovered in their studies of babies. An exception appears in Crittenden's (1992a, 1992b, 1993, 1994) work. To understand Crittenden's ideas about how preschoolers reorganize their representational models and their patterns of attachment behavior, we must consider not only the new cognitive abilities preschoolers develop, but also a new type of social behavior they develop—namely, *coy behavior.*

In children and adults, coy behavior is behavior that is shy but subtly inviting, suggestive of both interest in and fear of another person. Coy behavior in human children relies on the same sorts of behavioral signals that other mammals use to disarm aggressive behavior. For example, when two dogs or cats or monkeys are fighting, they rarely fight to the death. Instead, the one who is, after a while, clearly losing displays a set of submissive behaviors that acknowledges the dominance of the other animal. Quite often, this set of behaviors also serves a second function: it maintains a social relationship. The specific behaviors include displaying the belly, offering the bared neck, opening the mouth while covering the teeth, and glancing sideways toward the victor. Offering the belly and the bared neck makes the loser vulnerable to the winner; the winner could easily kill the loser. In contrast to bared teeth, which signal aggressive intent, a wide-open mouth with covered teeth is an exaggerated signal of the absence of aggressive intent. An animal who is only submissive may be destroyed or forced out of the social group. The sideways glances signal the desire to maintain contact but also constitute an unmistakable contrast to an aggressive stare. The combination of signals establishes the winner's victory and begs the winner not only to let the loser stay alive, but also to let him stay in the group. The places of the two animals in the dominance hierarchy are established, and the group maintains a social order without sacrificing a member who may be an asset to the group's survival on another occasion.

Among humans, coy behavior uses a similar set of signals: wide smiles, sideways glances, and exaggerated signals of vulnerability. For example, when a stranger meets a family, the preschool-age child will often hide behind the parent and peek out with shy smiles. If the stranger's eyes meet the child's, the child's smile broadens, but his eyes dart quickly away, and he may hide his whole body behind his attachment figure for a moment, before peeking out again. The behavior combines elements of invitation and elements of submission. Children who are acting coy are cute, like defenseless babies. They concede that the other is more powerful and so disarm aggression and elicit nurturance.

According to Crittenden (1993, 1994), this set of coy behaviors may be important to the child's survival. Babies begin to show aggression by the end of the first year of life. However, they cannot do any real harm to their caregivers or older playmates, so their aggression can be ignored. Two-year-olds are big enough to cause some real pain when they make directed attacks. As their desires often bring them into conflict with their caregivers and playmates and the toddlers sometimes do display their resulting anger, 2-year-olds (and 3-year-olds) sometimes provoke very angry responses from people who are much bigger and more powerful than they. They need ways to disarm aggression.

Virtually all children discover how to behave coyly. As their social networks expand to include many adults and children outside the family, coy behavior serves an adaptive function. It lets the child signal both interest and vulnerability. The normal response is a slowing of the newcomer's approach; the interactions evolve at a pace that does not frighten and overwhelm the child. The preschool years are also a time when most parents expect increasing self-regulation from their children. When the child breaks a rule, coy behavior signals submission and requests mercy; it often appeases the angry parent.

■ The Limits of Preschoolers' Abilities

What 3-year-olds cannot do is think about thought—their own or anyone else's. They know that some things are "pretend" and some things are "real," but they do not know that what they understand about the real world is, like what they understand about the pretend world, representational. They do not know that what they believe about the real world may be exactly wrong, simply contrary to fact. They cannot really understand that some people believe things that are not true and that they themselves may have believed or may currently believe things that were not or are not true.

Preschoolers have mental representations of experiences, but they cannot think about whether their representations are true or where their representations came from. They do not know which of their memories come from direct observation, which from inference, and which from what others have told them. In one well-designed study (cited in Bretherton, 1991), 4-year-olds at first remembered where a piece of information came from, but soon forgot the source while remembering the information.

In addition, there is a limit to the number of propositions a young child can consider simultaneously. Multiple representations that involve conflicting emotions are especially hard to hold in working memory. Young children have difficulty understanding that the same person can be both "nice" and "mean." The great majority of 4-year-olds use all-or-nothing thinking about emotions. They cannot integrate sets of positive and negative emotions.

Another limitation is that very young children are cognitively egocentric. It has not yet occurred to them that other people have knowledge, thoughts, and feelings different from their own. By the age of 3 or 4, children can, in simple situations, recognize that another person's *perceptual* perspective is different from the child's own. For example, if the child and the other person are sitting on opposite sides of a table with one green tower near the child and one red tower near the other, the child can tell that the other sees the red tower in the foreground of his visual field. If the other is wearing a stereo headset, the child can tell that the other hears music the child does not hear. It is more difficult to recognize that the other's *conceptual* perspective differs from the child's own. For example, few 3-year-olds but most 4-year-olds know that, for her birthday, their mother would probably like a new dress or a picture to hang on the wall, not a new doll or toy truck (Marvin, 1977). Very few 3-year-olds but most 4-year-olds know that, when they choose an item to be the "secret item," a person whose eyes were covered when the choice was made does not know which item is the secret one. Two-year-olds don't understand how to play such a game, and most three-year-olds think everyone knows the secret (Marvin, 1977).

WORKING MODELS IN INFANCY

Using the sorts of data about memory, language, emotion, and interaction introduced above, Crittenden (1993, 1994) offered detailed theoretical descriptions of infants' representational models of their attachment figures, of each attachment relationship, and of themselves. Her ideas are sufficiently coherent and persuasive to guide the next steps in gathering relevant data.

According to Crittenden, the experiences of a baby whose caregiver is sensitively responsive stay within the realm the baby can comprehend. She can recognize her own feeling states, communicate them openly, interpret her caregiver's signals, and explore extensively with the caregiver as an effective secure base. In contrast, some parents tend to intrude with overly bright affective signals when the baby is involved in his own activity. This behavior suggests a desire for close involvement. However, when the baby signals a desire for closeness and comfort, the same parent rebuffs him. The parent creates a situation in which the baby cannot learn what affective signals really mean. Behaviorally, the baby becomes avoidant. The working model encoded in his procedural memory system guides him to keep his attention on objects in the environment; to block awareness of anxiety, anger, and the desire for loving care; and to tune out environmental cues that might trigger conscious awareness of the denied affective experiences.

Another set of babies—those who show group C (resistant) behavior in the Strange Situation—have parents who communicate their feelings clearly but are inconsistent about responding to the baby. When the parent feels calm and content, she responds in a sensitive way to the child's signals. When the parent is angry, she doesn't hide the anger under a sweet, polite mask; she yells and bangs things and maybe hits people. The baby can easily enough learn the meanings of various sets of emotional behaviors. The difficulty is that he cannot predict or control what set of emotional responses will surround him. When he does elicit the parent's attention, the parent's behavior may be either supportive or hostile. Even when the baby moves from reliance on procedural memory into use of primitive representational abilities, he cannot predict such a parent's responses, so he cannot organize his behavior around them. (In some home observations, even a trained psychologist cannot predict the parent's responses.) The infant remains anxious and angry much of the time.

In short, Crittenden (1993, 1994) proposed that the baby's experiences in the relationship are too inconsistent for him to be able to comprehend them. Cognition fails him. In contrast, highly emotional communication is sometimes effective; intense displays of affect, including anger, sometimes do elicit caregiving. Even if such displays are also sometimes punished, they are, in the language of social-learning theory, being reinforced on a variable, intermittent schedule. The predictable result is that they will be maintained at a high frequency. The baby remains aroused and angry, but attachment behavior is, according to Crittenden, unorganized.

Main and Solomon (1990) suggested that group C babies employ the strategy of exhibiting extreme dependency. Group C babies do often appear to be very dependent, and directing angry behavior at the attachment figure upon reunion can be interpreted as part of a behavioral strategy that dramatizes dependency; it punishes the parent for leaving the child, even briefly. In Main and Solomon's view, group D babies have no consistent strategy for handling separations and reunions.

In contrast, Crittenden (1993, 1994) argues that group C babies are the ones who are unorganized. Making sense of the caregiver's inconsistent behavior is beyond their cognitive abilities, so they cannot organize their attachment behavior or their angry behavior. Many of the babies in subgroup C1 display dramatically unorganized, conflicted behavior. Many of the babies in subgroup C2 appear to have given up trying to find a way to elicit the responses they want from the parent; they are passively, helplessly unorganized.

Behaviorally, different infants classified into group D differ greatly from each other. Crittenden (1992a) argued that some group D infants have an intelligent, well-organized strategy for interacting with an abusive caregiver: they pause for a moment to read the available signals about what the caregiver wants and how she is likely to respond at this particular moment. The child's *behavior* may look abrupt, inconsistent, or temporarily frozen, but the *strategy* is organized and adaptive in the context of dysfunctional caregiving.

Other group D babies may have been assessed during a period of change, a period of reorganizing their representational models and attachment strategies in response to changes in the family (such as the birth of a sibling). Both behaviors and strategies are likely to look disorganized for a while as the individual leaves an old representational model behind and gradually forms a coherent new model. Still other group D babies, in Crittenden's view, do seem truly unorganized; they have not yet developed a plan for when to seek comfort, when to act angry, when to act falsely independent, when to act helpless, and so on.

By the time they reach their first birthdays, most babies have rudimentary working models of their attachment relationships. If Crittenden's interpretations are correct, securely attached infants show age-related competence both with affective communication and with cognitive organization. Even as they approach the end of infancy, however, they are too young to be able to recognize and make sense of the small or moderate inconsistencies in the parent's behavior, so they have oversimplified, unduly positive working models. Avoidant infants are, within the limits set by maturational factors, competent with cognitive organization, but they mask and distrust affective communication. They have oversimplified, unduly negative models. They have learned how to avoid rejection and punishment, but not how to elicit the loving care they naturally desire. Resistant infants are competent in expressing and perhaps in recognizing affective communications, but, in Crittenden's (1990, 1992b, 1993, 1994) view, they cannot organize representational models to make sense of their inconsistent experiences and to guide their subsequent behavior. They have not found effective strategies for predicting the parent's behavior or influencing it. Although Crittenden's hypotheses about the varied content and organization of the working models of 1-year-olds with group D attachments are plausible, we need more data to evaluate them.

WORKING MODELS IN THE PRESCHOOL YEARS

Abilities to use language and semantic memory and to manipulate mental representations—the hallmarks of preoperational intelligence—expand rapidly from age 3 to age 5. They increase the child's ability to organize and reorganize representational models. They make it possible for children to form increasingly accurate, detailed models of attachment relationships and to develop increasingly effective behavioral strategies for managing them. They also make it possible for children to develop increasingly subtle psychological defenses. Bretherton, Crittenden, and Main have all argued that caregivers influence not only the content of the interactions the child experiences, but also the rules the child develops for deciding what information to store in generalized form, what information to keep as accurately as possible, and what information to discount altogether.

Throughout the preschool years, both assimilation and accommodation continue. The mind looks for regularities, for patterns. With preoperational intelligence, however, children learn to recognize some shades of gray, not just "good" and "bad" caregivers. They are better able to notice discrepancies between what they expected and what occurred. They can then incorporate newly recognized information into their representational models. Both secure and avoidant infants have discovered patterns and can assimilate new experiences to existing schemes or scripts. Preschoolers with resistant attachment histories can, perhaps for the first time, organize a coherent working model of the attachment relationship.

In a supportive environment, the child's perceptions and interpretations of the caregiver's behavior become more accurate, and the working models become more differentiated, more complex, and more accurate. However, when communication in the attachment relationship is constricted, distorted, overwhelming, unorganized, or otherwise dysfunctional, the attachment will be insecure and the working model is likely to omit uninterpretable aspects of experience and to deny painful aspects of reality.

As their minds develop, securely attached children can use their growing cognitive abilities smoothly and integrate the new information they discover into their old working models, gradually updating the models. Elaborating and updating working models will not go as smoothly for preschoolers with avoidant attachment histories. They have affective reasons to discard information that is inconsistent with their old models, so they have less experience in integrating new information into old models.

Within this general framework for understanding how representational models are organized and how they guide behavior in the preschool years, it is possible to describe differences among the models of children with different attachment histories. Crittenden (1992a, 1993, 1994) has offered the most elaborate set of propositions. Her ideas inform the descriptions presented below.

■ Group B: Secure or Balanced

Throughout childhood, children still need a secure base. Toddlers and preschoolers need a caregiver who supports emerging skills and also respectfully but clearly sets boundaries on dangerous exploration and on behavior that antagonizes the caregiver. In the preschool years, sensitive caregivers pay attention and allow or encourage open communication of their children's thoughts and feelings. They validate their children's perceptions and tolerate negative affects, even when the anger or momentary hatred is directed at the caregiver. They help children tie experiences to generalizations. They participate in meaningful negotiations with their children; they talk with the children to construct joint plans that the caregiver will honor. They make it easy and natural for children to learn to participate in smoothly functioning goal-corrected partnerships. The children will probably observe and experiment with tantrums, refusals, threats, and other coercive behaviors, but the sensitive caregiver is not likely to reward such behavior. Soon enough, group B children will conclude that the secure strategy of open and direct communication works best.

Securely attached preschoolers have good access to both cognition and emotion and can integrate both sorts of information. They can use information from all of their memory systems (procedural, episodic, and semantic).

■ Group A: Avoidant or Defended

Babies who are classified as avoidant in the Strange Situation have learned to deny their anger and their need for nurturance. Having learned that open contact seeking and comfort seeking will be rebuffed, they stay close enough to derive some physical protection from the proximity of the attachment figure, but not close enough to suggest to either themselves or the caregiver that intimacy is sought.

The reasons for developing such a behavioral strategy may differ in different families. Some mothers of group A babies are interfering when the baby is involved in her own activity and rejecting when the baby seeks closeness. Studies of troubled families have found that some mothers of avoidant babies are openly hostile, while others are withdrawn and unresponsive. Crittenden's opinion is that both the causes of the initial avoidance and the nature of the child's continuing experience influence what kinds of changes occur during the preschool years in the child's working models of the attachment and of the self. She therefore refers to group A attachments as "defended," not "avoidant."

By the time a child is 4 years old, adults may regard open avoidance or ignoring of the attachment figure as rude and unacceptable. With their new skills at manipulating mental representations, preoperational children can internally inhibit perception of their need for nurturance and their anger at the figure who fails to provide it. They no longer need to turn their eyes away or move their bodies away, which would offend the attachment figure. They can now look at and speak to the caregiver without giving any signals that suggest a desire for closeness. Interactions look cool and proper. In the context of a well-structured activity, a defended preschooler can stand very close to her attachment figure, but will still subtly seek to evade hugs and other intimate, emotional interchanges (Crittenden, 1993). Group A parents tend to be most comfortable with cognitive tasks and are proud of their children's achievements, so many defended children learn that cognitive activities bring rewarding outcomes. Affect, however, misleads and cannot be trusted. Defended children use cognition to moderate affect.

How, then, is the child to obtain the closeness and nurturance he naturally desires? In ordinary cases, the child gets by on whatever amount and type of affection or support the attachment figure does at times give. The child defensively excludes almost all awareness of a desire for anything more, and builds up a working model that says everything is all right just as it is. In the levels of the working model that are readily accessible to consciousness, the relationship is affectively neutral, and that is fine. At another level, defensively excluded from awareness, episodic memories or perhaps a semantic representational model encode the incompatible, painful knowledge that the child longs inarticulately for intimate loving care and that the attachment figure is insensitive, rejecting, or hostile.

From studies of children in very troubled families, Crittenden (1992a, 1993, 1994) concluded that defended children who have withdrawn, depressed parents often learn not only to inhibit expression of their own feelings, but actually to put on a show of artificially bright affect. These *compulsively caregiving* children appear to be reassuring the parent that everything is all right, everything is happy; the parent can give attention to the child without worrying that the child will make any demands of her. Again, there are at least two models of the relationship, and the two are incompatible with each other. One model says that the dyad acts happy and feels happy. The other says that something profoundly important (something the child cannot identify unless he experiences it in another relationship), is missing from this relationship.

Another set of defended preschoolers have caregivers who are often openly hostile and demanding. These children learn not only to inhibit their own desires and affects but also to do exactly what their caregivers demand. Knowing that their social environment is dangerous, they monitor their caregivers vigilantly, anticipate their desires, and comply promptly with them (Crittenden, 1993). Often, these *compulsively compliant* children are overachievers, especially if their parents value evidence of the child's obedience and performance. Being overly compliant may be as unhealthy as being aggressive and defiant.

For all of these defended children, the child's underlying strategy includes inhibiting awareness and expression of her own true feelings and substituting the behavior and feelings the parent wants or needs the child to show. Defended children rely on cognition to regulate behavior and defend against affect. When they do show their true feelings, their insensitive parents are likely to tell them that they should be ashamed of themselves. Most of what defended children do know about their own feelings is apparently kept in memory fragments blocked from conscious processing and isolated from the dominant representational model of the attachment relationship.

Because much information, particularly affective information, is discarded as unreliable or unbearably painful, defended children fail to notice discrepancies between their mental models and the realities the models represent. Accommodation in the Piagetian sense does not happen. Having no conscious awareness of any discrepancy between the expected and the real, the child has no reason to integrate new information into the old representational model and no reason to reorganize the model. In cases that may not be at all uncommon, a defended child may bury her true feelings far underground and construct and present to the world a false self that shows only the feelings her parents and teachers want her to have.

■ Group C: Resistant or Unorganized, Then Coercive

Now consider group C, the set of children labeled as resistant in Strange Situations. According to Main (1991), they are likely to construct multiple, incompatible models of the attachment figure, because the attachment figure has strong and unpredictable changes in mood or responsiveness. Given the child's cognitive limitations, the child cannot integrate all the contradictory experiences into a single model.

Crittenden (1992a, 1993, 1994) interpreted the same set of behaviors differently. She proposed that *infants* in group C have learned to display affects but have not yet found any way to organize attachment-related cognitions and behaviors; they have no strategy for regulating themselves or their interactions. As they mature, preoperational intelligence and coy behavior give them a way to organize a strategy that will force their inconsistent, preoccupied caregivers to respond to them.

The strategy is to judiciously alternate dramatic displays of affect: first anger, then coy fear and neediness. The angry behavior may succeed in forcing the caregiver to comply with the child's wishes. The coy, vulnerable behavior is likely to disarm any counteraggression that might otherwise occur and is likely to elicit nurturance, which is what the child wishes. The coy behavior may continue until the caregiver gets exasperated with the feigned helplessness and unending demands and grows angry again. Then the child switches back to threatening behavior. The two partners are enmeshed in a cycle of angry and soothing interactions that rarely meet the child's need for an attentive, accessible secure base from which she can move away to explore the world. The child is likely to miss many opportunities to develop self-reliance and many opportunities to acquire new information, new cognitive skills, and new social skills. She is particularly likely to learn little about balancing her feelings and desires with the feelings and desires of others.

In a paper about emotion regulation, Cassidy and Berlin (1994) came to similar conclusions about children with resistant attachments. In their review of the literature, the most frequent precursors of group C attachments appeared to be (1) relatively low or inconsistent psychological availability of the mother and (2) biological vulnerability of the infant. Subsequently, infants with resistant attachments tended to show limited exploratory competence. In short, Cassidy and Berlin (1994) inferred, the resistant infant tends to become an incompetent, overdependent preschooler whose attachment system is frequently activated at high intensity.

Let's consider an example of a coercive preschooler in action. Suppose Emily, age 2½, asks her mother to build block towers with her. Mom is on the phone, and is not paying attention to Emily. Emily asks again, asks louder, then screams and throws a block at her mother. Mom finally notices. How will she respond? Emily doesn't know. Mom may yell at Emily or smack her, or she may apologize for being inattentive, hang up the phone, and take Emily into her lap. If she responds sympathetically, she is rewarding Emily for angry, aggressive behavior, and so helping to maintain it. If she responds angrily, she is still partly reinforcing the behavior by giving her attention. She is also partly punishing it, because the attention she gives is hostile. However, Emily can then look coy, cute, sweet, and vulnerable. This is very likely to bring the mother's aggressive behavior to an end and elicit nurturance. Now it is safe for Emily to express her anger again. She fusses and makes new demands, and the cycle goes on.

What Emily learns is a coercive pattern of behavior that maximizes the attention she gets from her mother. She now has an attachment strategy that doesn't make her happy but does accomplish a purpose. The strategy is to read the mother's affective state and respond selectively with angry demands or a coy show of fear and desire for nurturance. By alternating the two behavior patterns and escalating their intensity when the mother's responsiveness lags, Emily keeps her inattentive, inconsistent mother highly involved with her.

The mother is likely to feel frustrated and victimized by this coercive, manipulative behavior. In an effort to gain control of the relationship, she may resort to threats, bribes, and dishonest tricks. If she follows through with threatened consequences and promised rewards and learns not to give in to Emily's threats and not to let her escape the unpleasant logical consequences of her behavior by acting coy, the relationship will remain mutually coercive for a long while, but a foundation for healthy change will be built. Unfortunately, parents who have been sufficiently preoccupied or distracted to let the child's coercive behavior become habitual in the first place are likely to have a hard time tolerating the negative emotions in the relationship, ignoring other demands on their attention, and building new, constructive, consistent reinforcement contingencies into the relationship. If the parent does resort to dishonest tricks, such as offering a bribe and failing to deliver it, she will make the child's problem worse. The child will learn not to be fooled by cognitive and verbal arguments. The tendency to rely on intense displays of affect will be augmented.

Of course, very few preschoolers are as calculating or manipulative as this simplified example may seem to imply. They do not deliberately think about what they want and how to get it from their unresponsive parents. They simply learn from experience what behaviors work and what behaviors get punished.

Although all or almost all children discover and try out coy behavior and aggressive behavior, they are unlikely to maintain a coercive strategy unless the partner participates in it (Patterson, 1976, 1991). Crittenden reported that, in the Strange Situation when the child is 3 or 4 years old, parents of coercive children comply with unreasonable demands in an effort to appease their pouty, disruptive children. In response to disarming behavior, they begin by offering nurturant assistance. If that fails to satisfy the child's demands, they get frustrated and then angry, but finally give in and do what the child appears to want. The mutual anger and struggle continue. Some coercive children go on to discover the power of blaming the parent for provoking the child's bad behavior.

Coercive preschoolers have learned, in Crittenden's view, the opposite of what defended preschoolers have learned. Coercive children find that attention to affect produces a predictable and desired outcome: at least some attention, and sometimes some affection or nurturance. Many coercive preschoolers probably disregard, distrust, or defend against cognition. Because they get what they want through intense displays of affect, they may learn little about modulating their own emotions and regulating their own behavior in relatively calm, cooperative ways. They are likely to have difficulty constructing a single, coherent model of the self. They have strayed far from the developmental paths that lead naturally to self-reliant, responsible behavior.

■ Traumatic Events and Lies

Eventually, both avoidant-defended and resistant-coercive children probably develop multiple, contradictory, incompatible representational models of their attachment relationships. An additional source of conflicting models, one that interested Bowlby (1980, 1984, 1988) greatly, was the parent's denial or distortion of traumatic events the child experienced or witnessed. For example, parents who hit the spouse and/or the children commonly lie about how injuries were caused and lie about who was most at fault. They pressure their children to believe and repeat the parent's version of the story, even though it contradicts what the child saw, heard, and felt. They also say that they love their children (which may indeed be true). The child, Bowlby (1984) said, copes by developing two separate sets of models of the attachment figure, the self, and the relationship. One set of working models reflects the child's real experience. The other contains what the child has been told and needs to believe, so that he can minimize further emotional and physical pain. At a level of cognitive processing that may never become conscious, the child keeps the two sets of mental models largely isolated from each other, but each at times influences the child's behavior.

SCHOOL-AGE CHILDREN

As the years pass, the child gains in knowledge, in perspective-taking abilities, in memory abilities, and in information-processing abilities. By the fifth birthday, most children know quite a lot about the attachment figure's interests, moods, and intentions, and are able to use that knowledge to guide their interactions with him or her. The child can easily plan longer and more-complex sequences of behavior than she could before. She can discuss and consider events not present, communicate about her own internal states, and talk to herself (out loud or even internally) to control her impulses.

Most 5-year-olds know that a person can deliberately tell a lie. By age 5 or 6, many children are very good at displaying emotions they do not feel. Many also understand, in some circumstances, that another person may actually be feeling a different emotion than the one he is expressing. Such basic metacognitive abilities may make it possible for most 5- or 6-year-old children to do something 3-year-olds cannot do: to consider the possibility that what the attachment figure says about the child may not be true.

By age 6, most children can think, at least a little, about their own thoughts. They can even, to some degree, regulate their own thinking. They may be able to integrate information from the three (or more) memory systems.

By age 6 or 7, a child can be consciously aware of herself; self-reflection becomes possible. If her experiences have generally been favorable, she may be able to draw together information encoded in different ways or in different memory systems and build a single, increasingly coherent, hierarchically organized model of herself that includes opposite qualities, such as being naughty at times and "good" at other times. She can represent and simultaneously consider two different points of view (e.g., her own and her attachment figure's) and evaluate how well they match.

According to Main (1991), as noted earlier, the mental processes of secure children differ from those of insecure children in two important ways. First, of course, they differ in content. What a secure child believes about himself and about his attachment figure differs greatly from what an insecure child believes about himself and his attachment figure. Second, secure children have mental processes that are more flexible and more open to self-examination than those of insecure children are.

Crittenden's (1994) ideas about defended or avoidant children elaborate on themes Main (1991) introduced. Given the sorts of experiences these children have had, they are likely to develop two isolated, unintegrated models of the self. In one model, the child is idealized; she is represented as she acts, polite and pleasant to adults. In the second model, the self is bad, the way the child feels, full of anger and, judging by how the parent treats her, unworthy of tender loving care. Virtually all of the child's attachment-relevant memories are likely to be connected to conflicting emotions. Because the memories are painful, the child is likely to have little desire to explore her own personal history. The old models guide perception, interpretation, and behavior, so new experiences tend to be like her old ones, or the differences go unnoticed. The defended child is unlikely to question, reevaluate, complicate, integrate, and update her representational models.

According to Main (1991), resistant children are also likely to develop multiple, incompatible models of the self. Crittenden (1994) thinks it more likely that coercive children develop one incoherent self who is either good or bad at the whim of the unpredictable accuser. If the child perceives discrepancies between her multiple models of herself or between contradictory aspects of her incoherent model of herself and describes her puzzlement to a supportive adult, she may be able to sort things out. If the attachment figure is offended or hurt by the child's real feelings, she may ignore, criticize, or "correct" the child's words and stories, and the child will continue to have great difficulty developing a coherent, integrated model of herself.

PSYCHOPATHOLOGY

If current attachment theories are correct, then, in the ordinary course of events, children with secure attachments develop balanced representational models that can recognize and integrate affective and cognitive information. Their behavior remains flexible, appropriately responsive to the various situations they find themselves in and the various partners they interact with. If no grave challenge throws them off course, they are likely to be psychologically healthy. Anxiously attached children, whether their working models are defended, coercive, or otherwise organized, may be locked into skewed patterns of perception, interpretation, and action. This increases the risk that actual psychopathology will develop.

So far, we have hardly any systematic research that identifies children's patterns of attachment in infancy, in the preschool years, or even in first or second grade and then looks for evidence of concurrent or later psychopathology. Most of the theory that I will describe in the rest of this section is recently articulated and untested.

According to Crittenden (1993), most of the young children who are referred for psychological services have coercive-threatening patterns of attachment and representational models. These children are more likely than other children to be loud, demanding, and disruptive. They attend to affect and downplay cognition. They often fail to regulate their own emotions or to control their own behavior. They remain anxious about relationships and hence demanding of attention. If they are also unable or unwilling to focus on teacher-assigned activities for long periods, they may appear to have attention deficit disorders and learning disabilities when there is no neurological basis for such diagnoses. Some coercive-threatening children may so antagonize others with their emotional outbursts and irrational demands and arguments that they become victims of violence, or they themselves may become bullies.

Coercive children who enact the disarming part of the coercive strategy much more often than the threatening part of the strategy also have representational and interpersonal problems, but they are less disruptive and more appealing. They are likely to be overlooked or babied, not referred to agencies for psychological services.

In the school years, the intelligent coercive child can become skillfully irrational—good at using logic as well as emotional displays to manipulate others into doing what the coercive child wants. In extreme cases, psychopathology may emerge from the representations of self and relationships that threatening-disarming coercive children develop. The sorts of psychopathology that seem most likely are conduct disorders, anxiety disorders, and borderline, narcissistic, and histrionic personality disorders.

Many defended children are likely to have their problems overlooked in the preschool and elementary school years. They inhibit their own negative affects, display positive affect even if it is artificial, make few demands, and try to comply with adults' demands. Parents and teachers tend to be quite pleased with them. Some very defended children, unconsciously angry at their attachment figures, redirect their aggressive impulses toward others (especially when they think no adults are watching) and are later identified as bullies. A few defended children may be recognized as troubled, withdrawn children, but most, Crittenden thinks, are probably overlooked until adolescence.

In adolescence, the pressure to develop intimate peer relationships is likely to bring the fears and inadequacies of defended individuals to the fore. Some, with the help of teachers, friends, youth leaders, relatives, therapists, or their own parents, who have themselves changed as their children have grown, will reclaim access to affect, live through the necessary pain, and develop satisfying relationships and balanced representational models. Some will use promiscuous sexuality to obtain physical intimacy without psychological closeness. Some will continue to focus on cognition, not affect, and hide their loneliness behind overachievement. Some may find enough success and social reinforcement in sports or performing arts to distract them from the pain of their inability to form intimate relationships. Some will fall into depression, substance abuse, or suicide. Some will develop schizoid, narcissistic, or avoidant personality disorders. Bowlby's (1944) early clinical work with juvenile thieves suggests that teenagers who are very angry and have representational models that we would now call avoidant or defended may often redirect their repressed rage and neediness into vandalism, theft, and even assault.

In the face of such unhappy predictions, it is important to remember that attachment theorists have never suggested that a majority of children with anxious attachments will develop psychological disorders. Children can be very resilient. What attachment theorists do propose is that anxious attachment is one of the many factors that increase the risk of psychopathology. Furthermore, what sort of psychopathology emerges, when it emerges, and when adults first notice that there is a problem may all be influenced in predictable ways by the particular type of anxious representational models the child has developed early in life. The hypothesized developmental trajectory for avoidant or defended children is quite different from the hypothesized developmental trajectory for coercive-threatening children, and both differ from the hypothesized developmental trajectory for coercive-charming children.

Even if these hypotheses about relations between anxious attachment and psychopathology are all eventually supported by hard evidence, the unwelcome outcomes discussed above need not be inevitable or unalterable. Some children who have defended or coercive primary attachments may draw protection, more positive self-images, and better-balanced models of how attachment relationships can work from secondary or later attachments. Some children who travel rather far down a deviant developmental pathway eventually find a way to change course.

CHAPTER SUMMARY

This was a chapter primarily about theory. I have described hypotheses about how age-related changes in cognition, memory, language, and social interaction may affect representational models as the child develops. Some of the changes are normative. Presumably, virtually all children move from goal-corrected attachment behavior in infancy to an emerging partnership supported primarily by the parent's behavior at age 2 or 3 and then to a true goal-corrected partnership at age 4 or 5. Other changes are associated with individual differences. The representational models of secure, defended, and coercive children are believed to differ from each other in content and in rules of operation.

Most of the ideas I have presented in this chapter are speculative, not yet well-supported by empirical research. This is especially true of the hypothesized associations between later psychopathology and different maladaptive representational models in childhood.

ASSESSMENT IN CHILDHOOD

This chapter is about how to assess patterns of attachment and degrees of security in children who are 3 to 7 years old. In childhood, as in infancy, we must rely on behavior to make inferences about security of attachment, but behavior becomes more complicated and more subtle with age. For example, 12-month-olds do not use language to negotiate whether a separation from the parent will happen or how it will be handled; preschoolers do. Unlike many infants and some preschoolers, most 6-year-olds do not greet a returning parent with a request to be picked up and held for a while. Similarly, ignoring or avoiding a parent is more subtle at age 3 or 4 than in infancy, and still more subtle at age 6. A baby can turn his body entirely away from a returning attachment figure or even move away. When a child is 6 years old, completely ignoring the parent or turning away from the parent is less likely to be tolerated; it is too rude.

Following the lead of Sroufe and Waters (1977a), some attachment theorists and researchers appear to have adopted the idea that, after infancy, the set-goal of the attachment system is not proximity to the attachment figure, but felt security. According to Ainsworth, this is a serious error. Security, she wrote, is the feeling associated with an evaluation that "all is OK; there is no basis for wariness, alarm, hesitation, or reserve" (Ainsworth, 1990, p. 473). Certainly a child's confidence that he can rely on his attachment figure is one source of felt security. However, it is not the *only* source of feeling secure. When an individual has sufficient experience in an environment to know how to interpret and respond to the events and people there with confidence that all will go well, she may enjoy a comfortable feeling of security based directly on self-reliance, not on access to the attachment figure.

Furthermore, Ainsworth (1990) pointed out, an avoidant or defended individual may *feel* secure to the extent that his defense is working effectively and so keeping anxiety unconscious. The unconscious feelings of insecurity may betray themselves by influencing behavior or physiological processes and may under stress become obvious, but the conscious level of felt security in familiar settings may ordinarily be high. To assess patterns of attachment at any age, we must be alert for evidence of defensive processes.

To assess attachment, we must measure something that reflects how the child organizes behavior toward the adult when the attachment system is activated at high intensity and the adult is or should be in a protective, caregiving role. Interactions during periods of play, teaching, or discipline may be correlated with patterns of attachment, but they cannot be taken as direct assessments of patterns of attachment, as noted earlier.

After much experimentation with a variety of separation-reunion paradigms, most of the researchers investigating possible methods of assessment have concluded that Ainsworth's Strange Situation procedure, with minor modifications because of the preschoolers' increased language skills, works well for assessing 3- and 4-year-olds. However, two different systems, the Cassidy-Marvin system and the Miami system (discussed later), have been developed for interpreting, coding, and classifying the behavioral data from the assessment.

Another method for assessing preschoolers' attachments does not require the participation of the attachment figure. It relies instead on an evaluation of the child's use of language and imagination. An examiner tells the child beginnings of stories that involve attachment issues, and the child makes up endings for the stories. The child's creations are then coded for evidence of confidence in the attachment figure, anxiety, anger, and defense mechanisms.

The first effort to assess patterns of attachment in somewhat older children (age 6) also used separation to activate the attachment system at high intensity and analyzed behavior at reunion to reveal levels of security, mixed feelings, and defense mechanisms (Main, Kaplan, and Cassidy, 1985). In the same laboratory session, the investigators also experimented with two other methods: (1) a projective test in which the subjects were asked to tell how a hypothetical child in a picture might feel and what he or she could do in the face of brief or long separations from the parents and (2) observation and coding of the child's response when given a very recent photograph of himself with his parents. All three methods look promising; none has been fully validated yet. Use of a fairly simple reunion behavior checklist instead of the quasi-clinical evaluation ordinarily involved in coding reunion behavior has also been proposed.

PRESCHOOLERS: SEPARATION-REUNION PARADIGMS

For some years, researchers thought that the brief separations in the Strange Situation (designed initially for 1-year-olds) would be easy for 3- and 4-year-olds to tolerate. Consequently, they experimented with quite a variety of separation-reunion paradigms for assessing attachment in preschoolers. One conclusion drawn from this large body of work was that the Strange Situation does indeed present enough stress to make assessment of preschoolers' attachment patterns possible. The *coding* manuals for scoring and interpreting the behavior of preschoolers differ noticeably from the instructions Ainsworth et al. (1978) wrote for scoring the behaviors and classifying the patterns of 1-year-olds, but the assessment *procedure* can be almost identical.

■ Marvin's Early Work

Robert Marvin (1977) published the first systematic study of preschoolers in a modified Strange Situation. His subjects were 16 children at each of three ages: 2, 3, and 4 years old. The modification of the Strange Situation consisted of adding to the procedure an explanation of the mother's departure and assurance of her return. Before leaving the child alone at the end of episode 5, the mother said, "I have to make a phone call; I'll be back."

Even brief separations in an unfamiliar place clearly did activate attachment behavior for most of the subjects. In fact, about half of them cried when the mother left them alone in an unfamiliar place (56 percent at age 2, 56 percent at age 3, and 44 percent at age 4).

When the stranger came in, thereby ending the child-alone episode, 89 percent of the 2-year-olds who had been crying continued to cry, rejected the stranger, and continued to try to get to the mother. They were unable to inhibit their attachment behavior. Of the 2-year-olds who did not cry when they were alone, all but one played happily with the stranger. When the mother returned in episode 8, 63 percent of the 2-year-olds approached her (67 percent of those who had cried when alone, and 57 percent of those who had not).

The company of the stranger alleviated distress much more effectively for children who were 3 or 4 years old than for children who were only 2 years old. Specifically, 67 percent of the 3-year-olds and 86 percent of the 4-year-olds who cried when alone stopped crying and played with the stranger in episode 7. Most of the 3-year-olds (75 percent) in this sample did approach the mother in the final reunion episode, and approaching was as common among children who did not cry when alone as among children who did.

One of Marvin's explicit goals was to gather evidence about children's abilities to participate in goal-corrected partnerships (Marvin, 1977). There was no evidence that the 2-year-olds could participate as partners in planning how to manage the brief period of separation; the child could not accept the mother's explanation and insert her plan into his own. In fact, 2-year-olds did not look very much different from 1-year-olds in the Strange Situation.

Among the 3-year-olds, there was still not much evidence that the attachment relationship had progressed to the phase of a goal-corrected partnership. Only 4 of the 16 three-year-olds either tried to construct a plan regarding the separation or explicitly agreed to the mother's plan.

In contrast, the issue of being included in the process of planning seemed particularly important to many of the 4-year-olds. In fact, 12 of the 16 four-year-olds in this sample fell into one of two very different groups. When the mother said she was leaving to make a phone call, seven of the children said "OK" or an equivalent thereof. None of these children cried when alone, and all but one played happily with the stranger. When the mother returned, one child gave her a quick hug and then returned to the toys. The others greeted their mothers but did not approach. Each of the seven then continued playing, occasionally talking to the mother in a relaxed, happy way. In short, all of these 4-year-olds appeared to be securely attached and to be more comfortable with separations and more self-reliant than younger children.

Five of the sixteen 4-year-olds displayed a radically different and thoroughly unexpected pattern of behavior. When the mother said she was leaving, the child rushed to the door and begged to go with her. When the mother refused to take the child and departed, the child cried. No systematic analyses were undertaken, but observers reported that the crying of the 4-year-olds seemed more controlled and angry than apprehensive, and sounded quite different from the crying of most of the 2- and 3-year-olds. When the stranger came in, all five protesting 4-year-olds immediately stopped crying. Four played well with the stranger. When the mother returned, four of the five children approached her and stayed near her for some time. All five made demands that seemed out of context and repeated them insistently, fussing and whining all the time, even though the mother explained that she could not fulfill the demand at the moment. For example, one girl demanded a glass of water, insisted four times that she needed it immediately, then demanded to be taken up onto the mother's lap, and, when the mother helped her reach that goal, returned to demanding water, and then demanded beer! In short, these five children displayed the pattern of behavior much later labeled "coercive" by Crittenden (e.g., 1992a) or "controlling-punitive" by Main et al. (1985).

Four of the sixteen 4-year-olds did not fit either of the two predominant patterns Marvin (1977) observed. Two begged to go with the mother but accepted the stranger, stayed near the mother for a few moments when she returned, and then went back to playing happily with the toys. They did not show coercive or punitive behavior. Two completely ignored the mother's departure and return. With no other information about them, it is not possible to say whether they had solidly avoidant attachments or were both secure enough and mature enough not to have their attachment behavior activated by brief separations in a safe playroom with intriguing toys.

■ Scientific Competition: Two Classification Systems

After Marvin's early work, there was a long lull in research on attachment in the preschool years. Then came a surge of interest in which two competing classification systems were developed independently and were picked up by other researchers around the same time. One classification system for preschoolers, the "Miami system," was developed by Crittenden (1991), who had begun videotaping preschoolers in the original Strange Situation procedure as part of her series of studies of children in adequate and maltreating families.

The other system for classifying preschoolers' patterns of attachment was developed by Cassidy, Marvin, and the MacArthur Working Group on Attachment (1992). Initially, the MacArthur Group worked with videotaped data from a wide variety of separation-reunion paradigms. Some researchers had used brief separations, and some had used separations that exceeded 30 minutes. Some procedures called for two separations and two reunions; some had only one episode of each type. How long the child had for becoming familiar with the laboratory setting before the first separation also varied from sample to sample.

Despite the variety of observation procedures, it was clear to all involved that the individual differences in reunion behaviors were informative. Even so, finding what aspects of behavior to tune in to and how to interpret them proved to be very challenging. Eventually, Cassidy, Marvin, and the MacArthur Attachment Group (e.g., 1992) prepared and periodically updated manuscripts that described coding procedures and classification criteria. Their method is generally called the "Cassidy-Marvin system."

Neither the Cassidy-Marvin system nor the Miami system treats 3-year-olds differently than it treats 4-year-olds. Few 3-year-olds but most 4-year-olds appear to have all the communication skills, memory skills, information-processing skills, and social perspective-taking skills they need to participate in a goal-corrected *partnership,* not just a goal-corrected *attachment*. Consequently, it seems likely that the criteria that are appropriate for assessing 4-year-olds' attachments may differ greatly from those that are appropriate for assessing 3-year-olds' attachments. The use of the same coding system at both ages seems especially surprising in the Cassidy-Marvin system, as it was Marvin's (1977) own work that so clearly illustrated the differences in how 3-year-olds and 4-year-olds organize attachments. Why was the leap from one qualitative level to another overlooked? Perhaps because the hypothesized "leap" happens gradually, with dyadic behavior in the substage that precedes the transformation looking very much like dyadic behavior after the transformation. Whatever the reason, both assessment systems do use the same scales and behavioral definitions for both 4- and 3-year-olds, and preliminary evidence suggests that this works.

■ The Strange Situation for Preschoolers

To be effective as an assessment procedure for preschoolers, the Strange Situation must (1) activate the child's attachment behavior, (2) permit the caregiver to function as an attachment figure (not just as a playmate, teacher, or disciplinarian), and (3) let the child reveal her strategies for coping with stress, seeking protection, and exploring the environment (Crittenden, 1992a).

Many 3- and 4-year-olds attend preschool or day care and have, with their parents, developed behavior patterns for handling routine separations. Consequently, to activate the attachment system at high intensity, the impending separations in the Strange Situation should be, from the child's perspective, unexpected. This enables observers to gain information about the child's attachment that may be masked when the dyad activates routine patterns for handling separations.

In addition, the experimenter must not tell the attachment figure what to say or what not to say when departing. Letting the dyad decide how and how much to negotiate about the impending separation gives the observer useful information. The separation itself is less important than the two partners' ability to plan together about how to handle it. *Whether* the child and the adult come to agreement about a plan is not a sufficient indicator of the security of the child's attachment. *How* they form the plan and how the child behaves at reunion are also indicators. For example, a child's acceptance of a plan could result either from a fear of displeasing the parent or from a sense of secure trust in the parent. A child's resistance to a plan could reflect either secure assertiveness or anxiety about how hard it will be to regain access to the parent after he leaves the room. Both secure and insecure children want to have a voice in regulating access to the parent.

The need for retaining the stranger in the Strange Situation for preschoolers was for a while debated. Including the stranger provides information about how the child handles her feelings. Children who are distressed can use the stranger for distraction, comfort, information, or assistance in regaining the attachment figure. The Miami coding system makes use of this information. The stranger must not give the child any information the attachment figure did not provide about the separation. She must not say, "Don't worry, she's just in the next room; she'll be back in a minute," if the mother did not give the child that information. She can, however, comfort a distressed child with conversation, play, or physical contact, and she can ask about the child's feelings.

In short, the only modifications of the Strange Situation researchers must consider when they use the procedure with preschoolers are those necessitated by the older child's greater cognitive and linguistic skills. When soothing an infant, whoever is taking the role of the stranger often murmurs, "Don't worry, Mama will be right back." This may not be optimal with older infants, but it does not seem to interfere with valid assessment. When working with a preschooler, who understands a good bit more than a baby understands about time and distance, the stranger's providing the same words of reassurance when the parent failed to do so may alleviate anxiety the parent routinely fails to alleviate, and so may produce an invalid assessment. Similarly, explaining a departure or conferring about a separation are not ordinary parts of a parent's behavior with a 12-month-old. They *are* ordinary parts of many parents' behavior with 3- and 4-year-olds, and different parent-child dyads handle such interactions in very different ways.

■ The Cassidy-Marvin System

The Cassidy-Marvin system for coding preschoolers' attachments appears to be designed to identify the same four major patterns of attachment that are currently identified in 1-year-olds and in 6-year-olds. (You can read about the system for 6-year-olds in a later section of this chapter.) Cassidy et al. (1992) reported that the preschool coding system uses "age-appropriate manifestations" of proximity seeking, contact maintaining, resistance, and avoidance—the same four types of behavior that are coded when 1-year-olds are observed in the Strange Situation. Like the Main and Cassidy system for 6-year-olds, the Cassidy-Marvin system for preschoolers uses a 7-point avoidance scale and a 9-point security scale.

On the 9-point security scale, a score of 1 indicates that the child's attachment is very insecure. The behavior may be avoidant, dependent, controlling, disorganized, or some combination thereof. A security score of 5 indicates that the attachment shows indications of both security and insecurity but, on balance, the child seems secure. A score of 9 indicates that the child is highly secure. At reunion, the child initiates interaction, proximity, or contact with complete ease and no ambivalence; the child is particularly calm but at the same time particularly pleased to see the attachment figure.

This classification system produces four categories that are almost the same as those used in infancy: secure, avoidant, resistant, and "disorganized-controlling." "Disorganized" appears to me to be a misnomer: both the behavior and the underlying strategy sound well-organized. There are two very different styles of "controlling" the interaction at reunion: the child's behavior is either (1) hostile and punitive or (2) caregiving.

With the Cassidy-Marvin coding system, 3- and 4-year-olds are classified as securely attached if their behavior at reunion suggests a warm and intimate relationship with the mother. Some orient toward the mother, approach her, or stay physically close to her. Some converse freely and smoothly with the mother or invite her to join in their play.

Children are classified as insecure-avoidant if their behavior suggests distance and coolness in the relationship. They respond minimally when the mother speaks to them and do not initiate or expand conversation. They also turn away or move away from the mother. Children are classified as insecure-resistant if they show dependent, resistant, and/or immature behavior, such as wriggling and whining. (Actually, Cassidy and Marvin used the term "insecure-ambivalent," but I prefer the term "insecure-resistant," as explained earlier.)

Children are classified as "insecure-disorganized-controlling" if they take charge of the interaction with the mother. There are two contrasting styles of "controlling" behavior. Some children are openly hostile and punitive. The child from Marvin's sample who demanded over and over to have a drink of water or beer right away provides a good example. Other "disorganized-controlling" children reverse usual child-parent roles and "control" the mother through caregiving behavior. For example, the child reassures the mother that everything is okay.

■ Assumptions and Outcomes

The first three categories in the Cassidy-Marvin system are obviously closely analogous to the secure, avoidant, and resistant classifications for infants in the Strange Situation. The fourth category, "insecure-disorganized-controlling," matches a classification Main and Cassidy (1988) developed for the reunion behavior of 6-year-olds, many of whom had been classified as anxious-disorganized-disoriented in infancy.

Having chosen to describe assessment procedures for preschoolers before describing assessment procedures for school-age children, I have described the system that was developed second before saying very much about the system on which it was partly based. One point, however, must be mentioned here.

The Main and Cassidy (1988) system for classifying 6-year-olds' patterns of attachment was initially validated through the association of classifications of 6-year-olds with classifications of the same children in the Strange Situation in infancy. The method of validation might not have worked if Main and Cassidy had not found ways of interpreting 6-year-olds' behavior as indicative of four categories that were analogous to the four categories that had been used to classify the subjects' attachments in infancy. To develop their system for coding and classifying the attachments of children who are 2½ to 4½ years old, Cassidy, Marvin, and the MacArthur Working Group on Attachment (1992) then drew ideas from the coding procedures for infants and for 6-year-olds. The system they developed closely resembles the Main and Cassidy (1988) system for children who are 5 to 7 years old. In fact, this system for classifying preschoolers' attachments was initially validated with reference to the system for classifying 5- to 7-year-olds, which was validated with reference to infant Strange Situation categories.

This chain of efforts represents one reasonable scientific approach to developing and beginning to validate assessment systems for different ages. There may be an advantage in having systems that all result in the same four classification categories: they make it easy to study continuity and change over time. However, the whole approach is based on the untested, and possibly incorrect, assumption that the same four categories are in fact useful and appropriate for classifying the organization of attachments at each age. To test this assumption, researchers will have to obtain data about whether this system for classifying preschoolers' attachments produces classifications that reflect the child's history, correlate with the child's current functioning, and predict the child's future functioning in ways that are specified by or congruent with attachment theory.

The researchers' expectation of finding age-appropriate cues that coders could use to identify Group A, B, C, and D attachments in 6-year-olds and then in preschoolers may have prevented them from finding that a different set of categories would be more appropriate for classifying the ways preschoolers organize their attachments. If you are looking for how differences among types of butterflies resemble differences among the types of caterpillars they used to be, it may take you a long time to discover that what is important and meaningful in the survival and behavior of a butterfly is quite different from what is important and meaningful in the survival and behavior of a caterpillar.

■ The Miami System

Working separately on the same research problem—how to describe and assess preschoolers' attachments—Crittenden (1991, 1992a) began with a different perspective. She had observed many infants and preschoolers and their parents in a variety of natural and contrived semistandardized situations. Her samples often included families known to have abused or neglected their children, so she had observed common adaptations to maltreatment. With this background in developmental psychopathology as well as normal development, Crittenden gradually developed both the theoretical ideas presented in Chapter 13 and the Miami Preschool Attachment Classificatory System (Crittenden, 1991) for assessing patterns of attachment in 3- and 4-year-olds.

In the Miami system, children are classified as secure (type B) if they show open and direct communication, negotiation, and affective exchange with the attachment figure. Securely attached preschoolers derive comfort and pleasure from being psychologically and at times physically close to their attachment figures.

Children are classified as defended (type A) if they show inhibition of communication and affect. They may tolerate moderate physical proximity, but without psychological intimacy. If they inhibit communication and affective displays primarily through straightforward avoidance, they are classified as A1 or A2. When they use caregiving to mask their true feelings of anxiety and anger, they are classified as A3. When they show compulsive compliance to the attachment figure's directions instead of communicating freely and affectively, they are classified as A4.

In the Miami system, children are classified as coercive (type C) if they show "leveraged communication," which is defined as (1) partial displays of feelings, and (2) attempts to coerce the attachment figure through threatening and/or disarming behavior. They generally show high levels of physical proximity with partial psychological intimacy. They may show their anger and deny their hurt and fear, or they may show considerable vulnerability and hide their anger. The four subtypes emphasize resistance (C1), coyness (C2), punitiveness (C3), and helplessness (C4).

Strange Situation classifications in infancy are based almost entirely on the infant's behavior. To classify a preschooler's pattern of attachments, the Miami system uses not only the child's behavior, but also the regulation of feeling states, the regulation of displays of affect, the underlying strategy, the attachment figure's behavior, and the dyad's pattern of negotiation.

Preliminary validation of the Miami system came from associations between attachment classifications based on this system and concurrent data about the same dyad in other settings. Both the mother's sensitivity to the child during dyadic interaction and the overall quality of child rearing (normal, abusive, neglecting, etc.) were related to attachment classifications.

■ Contrasts between the Two Classification Systems

The Cassidy-Marvin system and the Miami system obviously tap into many of the same dimensions of preschoolers' behavior. However, they use somewhat different classification criteria, make different inferences about underlying representational models, and group subtypes of behavior patterns differently. If a trained coder used the Cassidy-Marvin system to classify 100 preschoolers' attachments and a different trained coder used the Miami system to classify the same children's attachments from the same videotapes, the two sets of classifications would not match. I suspect that there would be good agreement about which children were securely attached, but sizable differences in the interpretation and labeling of anxious patterns. In addition, Crittenden (1994) has argued that, having grown old enough to discover strategies that include coy behaviors and coercive behaviors, some children who had secure attachments (group B) and some who had avoidant attachments (group A) in infancy shift into one of the coercive patterns (group C) in the preschool years. The Cassidy-Marvin system appears to anticipate that the distribution of the various attachment patterns in the preschool years will closely resemble the distribution of A, B, C, and D patterns in infancy.

Each system's coding and classification procedures have been used in a number of studies now. Each has produced results that were meaningfully related to other data (from prior, concurrent, or later assessments) in at least a few studies. I will describe one example later in this chapter. Efforts to validate and/or improve each system are ongoing in several laboratories. Neither system has yet been thoroughly validated in the most convincing way possible—namely, by showing that it produces results that are reliably associated with the way the attachment relationship plays out in everyday life.

PRESCHOOLERS: STORY COMPLETION

By the time children are 3 or 4 years old, most are, in a suitable setting, willing and able to use language to communicate quite a lot of information to researchers. What they cannot say well in words, they will often act out with play materials. Consequently, preschoolers' beliefs and feelings about attachments can be assessed without enacting a separation-reunion sequence. In fact, it may be possible to assess the child's attachment in the absence of the attachment figure. One method for doing so is by inviting the child to tell stories about issues relevant to attachment.

Bretherton, Ridgeway, and Cassidy (1990) attempted to access 3-year-olds' representational models by giving them a set of stories to complete. The experimenter told the beginning of each story and asked the child to "show me and tell me what happens next." The child had small family figures with which to act out an ending to the story.

In the first story, the child spills juice and the mother exclaims. In the second, the child falls and hurts her knee. In the third, the child is sent upstairs to bed and then cries out about a monster in the bedroom. In the fourth, the parents depart for an overnight trip, leaving a grandmother to look after the two children. In the final story, the grandmother looks out the window the next morning and tells the children the parents are coming back.

As a set, the stories provide opportunities for the child to reveal expectations about the attachment figure as an authority figure and as a source of comfort and protection in times of pain or fear. The last two stories raise the issues of separation anxiety, coping ability, and reunion behavior. Most 3-year-olds were able to produce resolutions to the stories. Most depicted the parents as protective, empathic, and remarkably nonpunitive. The story endings the children made up often expressed separation anxiety and reunion pleasure.

Children who resolved the story issues fluently and appropriately were classified as secure. Those who avoided the story issues were classified as avoidant. Sometimes they just said "I don't know" or "I want another story," even after a couple of prompts. Odd and disorganized responses—for example, violently throwing the child figure onto the floor or enacting a car wreck after the family reunion—were regarded as indicating a different sort of insecurity. Just giving answers that did not make sense within the story was also interpreted as indicating insecurity.

For twenty-eight 37-month-olds, classifications based on the story completions were compared with classifications of reunion behavior using the Cassidy-Marvin criteria. Twenty-one (75 percent) of the children received concordant classifications, either secure or insecure, from both procedures. That is certainly a significant level of agreement, but perhaps not an inspiring one. The two measures appear to tap the same construct, but cannot be treated as equivalents of each other. Classification of the type of insecurity was not consistent across procedures. When translated into security scores, the classifications from the story completion test were only marginally correlated with security scores from the Attachment Q-set, sorted by the mother. If both the story completions and the Q-sorts were valid measures of attachment, the security scores from the two measures should have been highly correlated.

Use of story completion data to assess attachments is still new and experimental. Within the entirely normal range of differences among individual 3-year-olds, there is enormous variability in language skills and developmental quotients. We will need careful research to find out how much such differences affect story completions in ways that interfere with accurate assessment of attachment patterns.

For the particular sample described above, observations of interactions between the children and their parents in their natural settings were not available. Bretherton et al. (1990) suggested that extensive naturalistic observations would be valuable for validating *any* method of assessing security of attachment in preschoolers.

ASSESSMENT AROUND AGE 6

When children in the Berkeley Social Development Project were near their sixth birthdays (M = 69.5 months), Main, Kaplan, and Cassidy (1985) did a follow-up study of their attachments. The subjects were 40 children whose attachments to both parents had been studied in infancy. Both parents participated with the child in the follow-up assessment session. Before venturing into the uncharted territory of attachments in 6-year-olds, Main and her colleagues developed several measures that they thought, based on theory, would reflect patterns of attachment. Of the measures I will describe in this section, almost all were developed for this sample. Some have since been used with other samples.

■ Reunion Behavior

How the child behaves when reunited with the parent after a brief separation is the principal source of evidence about patterns of attachment in infants in the Strange Situation. It seemed likely to the Berkeley researchers that behavior at reunion would also reveal aspects of a 6-year-old's representational model of his or her attachment relationships. Anticipating that a separation of only a few minutes might not activate attachment behavior in 6-year-olds, Main and her colleagues planned a 1-hour separation and used some of the time during the separation to focus the child's attention on matters related to attachment.

When a child and his or her two parents arrived at the laboratory, a member of the project staff took an instant picture of them. Next, the family watched a film about changes in a 2-year-old's behavior as he underwent a 10-day separation from his mother. Then the parents left for separate offices.

For the first 15 to 20 minutes after the parents left, a female examiner interacted with the child in a warm-up session. Next, she administered the Klagsbrun-Bowlby (1976) version of the Hansburg Separation Anxiety Test (HSAT), which I will describe in the next section. Then she presented the family photograph, and the child's reaction was noted. The child then had a period of free play until the parents returned.

The principal measure of security of attachment was based on the child's response to reunion with the parent. The project staff did not give the parents any instructions for the reunion episode and did not place any special emphasis on it. They simply told each parent in turn that he or she was essentially finished with the study and could return to the playroom. One parent returned, 3 minutes of the reunion were videotaped, and then, with the first parent still present, the second parent returned and 3 minutes of that reunion were videotaped. For half of the subjects, the father returned before the mother.

The next step in developing the coding system was to figure out what aspects of reunion behavior illustrated the quality of each attachment and to develop clear descriptions that could be used for identifying patterns of attachment from the same sort of data in another sample.

After viewing the videotapes of the reunions repeatedly, the project staff developed a 7-point avoidance scale and a 9-point security scale for coding the child's reunion behavior (Main and Cassidy, 1988). They had a working definition of what "security" meant: confidence that the attachment figure was accessible and would show warm interest in the child. They also had a working definition of "avoidance": the masking of anger, affection, discomfort, distress, and the desire for closeness. With those a priori notions, they searched the reunion tapes for specific behavioral indicators of security and of avoidance. Blind to the Strange Situation classifications of the subjects, Cassidy did most of this viewing and re-viewing, searching for ways to define points on the two scales.

On the resulting 7-point avoidance scale, high scores are given to children who ignore the parent or greet the parent coolly, do not initiate conversation, respond only minimally when addressed, and perhaps move (but not abruptly) to a distance from the parent. Scores above 5.5 on the avoidance scale cannot be given if the child shows open annoyance, clear pleasure in the parent's return, or hurt. Children who get a score of 6 to 7 on the 7-point avoidance scale are automatically classified as avoidant. Children with intermediate scores for avoidance can fall into another category.

Obviously, a high score for avoidance necessitates a low score for security. However, many insecure children lack avoidant defenses, so security must be defined by something more than the absence of much avoidant behavior. On the 9-point security scale, children are rated as very secure if they affectionately and confidently initiate conversation, interaction, or contact with the parent and/or show eager responsiveness to the parent's remarks. A score of 5 on the 9-point security scale is used to indicate that the rater's "best guess" is that the child is secure with that parent. This score is used when the child shows no marked signs of security or insecurity but seems sufficiently at ease with the parent and sufficiently free from anxiety in the parent's presence to justify the inference that the attachment is probably a secure one. This score is also assigned when a child shows signs of security that would justify a higher rating but also shows some difficulty. For example, a child might be reserved with the parent for quite a while before brightening and showing the warm responsiveness that characterizes more-secure children.

A low score (2 to 4.5) on the security scale is given when the child shows avoidant, ambivalent, or controlling-caregiving behavior, but also shows some signs of security in the relationship or in himself or herself. A score of 1 indicates that the child is extremely avoidant, extremely punitive, extremely ambivalent, or shows a combination of indices of insecurity *and* shows no signs of security.

In general, children classified as secure greeted the parent warmly, shared recent experiences freely, seemed pleased by the parent's return, and eventually gravitated toward the parent. (Physical contact with the parent at reunion is rare in 6-year-old children, even in secure relationships.) Some seemed secure in a straightforward, affectionate way. Some showed some initial reserve or some initial uncertainty about what to do but soon warmed to the parent. Some were feisty, even to the point of showing some good-natured, confident bossiness toward the parent. For example, one child who was classified as secure insisted, "*No* Daddy, that's my castle, we're playing Separate Castles." Children who are classified as secure-feisty stick up for themselves, but they do not behave in a nasty or scornful way or seek to embarrass the parent.

In the Berkeley follow-up sample (Main et al., 1985), two patterns of insecure attachment were common. The first, avoidance, was common among children who had been judged avoidant in the Strange Situation in infancy. The second insecure pattern had two distinct subtypes. Main and Cassidy grouped these subtypes as one pattern because they perceived both as strategies for controlling the parent. Some children showed directly hostile or punitive behavior. What they said or did seemed intended to keep the parent puzzled or quiet or even to embarrass him or her in front of observers. The specific examples of things "controlling-punitive" children said to their parents would shock many parents. For example, "Don't bother me!" or "I am *not* going—Why don't you leave?!" or "You're really clumsy, ha-ha. . . . I told you, keep quiet!" Prolonged silence can also be punitive,

Secure 6-year-olds show relaxed, engaged behavior when reunited with their parents.

not avoidant. For example, when the father asks, "What are you doing, honey?" and the child either gives no answer or waits a long time before saying flatly or sullenly, "Playing," the father is likely to feel humiliated.

Other children judged to be insecure-controlling "controlled" the parent through anxious, overly bright caregiving behavior. In some cases, the coder had to give careful attention to the nuances of behavior to distinguish artificially cheerful, helpfully directive behavior from securely affectionate behavior. For example, one child asked, "Want to play with me, Mommy, in the sandbox? . . . It's fun, isn't it, Mommy?" Most of the children who showed controlling (either punitive or caregiving) patterns at age 6 had been classified as anxious-disorganized-disoriented in infancy.

Having found patterns of reunion behavior at age 6 that were meaningfully associated with the anxious-avoidant (group A), secure (group B), and anxious-disorganized-disoriented (group D) patterns of Strange Situation behavior in infancy, Main and her colleagues expected that there would also be a childhood pattern associated with infant anxious-resistant (group C) attachment. There were not enough examples of such a pattern in the Berkeley follow-up sample to define it with any confidence. However, examination of videotapes of other 5- and 6-year-olds at reunion with the parent did yield evidence of such a pattern. Children who showed mixed feelings of avoidance, responsiveness, sadness, subtle fear, and/or subtle or open hostility at reunion were thereafter classified as "insecure-ambivalent," analogous to group C. Main and Cassidy (1988) described the behavior of children in this group as confusing or incoherent. Like group

C infants, these 6-year-olds show mixed behaviors, both seeking and resisting interaction, proximity, and contact. These children often show immature behavior (such as "cute" whininess, "cute" affectionateness, or "cute" proximity seeking or contact seeking) in which physical ambivalence about proximity to the parent is striking. For example, one girl initially moved away from the mother, then lay on her stomach beside her mother, wriggling uncomfortably and talking in a "cute," breathy voice. When she sat up to speak to her mother, she tipped her head to one side, creating a "cute" posture that would not be necessary in a secure relationship. Then she put her arms carefully around her mother's shoulders while at the same time pulling away and attempting to point out various things in the room.

Coding reunion behavior in 6-year-olds takes considerable training. The observed differences among attachment groups in greeting behavior, understandable engrossment in play, and subtle ways of ending or minimizing conversation almost always fall within the range of acceptable or even polite social behavior. The classification system remains open to revision.

In another study, Cassidy (1988) used a 1-hour separation and the reunion coding system described above with a new sample of 5- and 6-year-olds. She then brought the subjects back to the laboratory for a second assessment 1 month after the first. Test-retest reliability was 64 percent. That is, the classification from the second assessment matched the classification from the first assessment for 64 percent of the subjects. That is much better than the chance rate for matching classifications would be, but it is not high enough to justify relying on this method as the sole index of a child's pattern of attachment. Main and Cassidy (1988) recommended using more than one method of assessment when studying attachments in children who are 5 to 7 years old.

■ The Hansburg Separation Anxiety Test (HSAT)

Hansburg (1972) developed a separation anxiety test for adolescents. Klagsbrun and Bowlby (1976) adapted it for use with younger children, especially ages 4 to 7. Main, Kaplan, and Cassidy (1985) further modified it when they used it with the Berkeley sample of 6-year-olds.

In all its variations, the Hansburg Separation Anxiety Test (HSAT) is a projective test. That is, an examiner asks the subject to respond to a stimulus that allows a wide variety of responses, and the psychologist who scores the subject's responses assumes that they are a projection of the subject's unconscious and/or conscious feelings and expectations about the issue the stimulus brings to mind. The issue in this particular projective test is parent-child separation; the stimuli are photographs.

In the Klagsbrun-Bowlby adaptation of the HSAT, the examiner presents six photographs of young children experiencing separations from their parents, one photograph at a time. In the mildest example, the parents are saying goodnight. In three others, the parents (1) ask the child to play while they talk, (2) bring the child to the first day at school, and (3) leave for the weekend. In the most intense, the parents are leaving for a 2-week trip. The children in the pictures are approximately 4 to 7 years old. In the photographs used for testing girls, the protagonist is a girl. In the photographs used for testing boys, the protagonist is a boy.

The examiner tells the child, "Parents worry sometimes what children think when they have to go away for a while" and asks the child, "Tell me what you think a child your age would feel and what a child your age would do when parents go away for a little while." After showing each picture, the examiner asks the subject what the child in the picture would feel and then what the child in the picture would do. If a child says, "I don't know," or otherwise resists answering the examiner probes gently until it seems clear that the child is finished answering or just does not want to answer. In the Berkeley study, the test was curtailed if the child seemed to be disturbed by the questions.

The children's verbal and affective responses are scored for "emotional openness." A high score indicates that the subject could imagine the pictured child experiencing appropriate negative affects (loneliness, sadness, fear, anger) and could give reasons why the child might feel that way. Children who get high scores complete the test with minimal resistance, withdrawal, or stress. Low scores reflect a variety of insecure responses, including silence, inability to express feelings, denial, overt depression, irrational responses, and marked disorganization. An example of irrational, disorganized responding comes from the Berkeley sample. One child insisted that the child in the picture would "feel good" or "feel *nothing*." At the same time, she became increasingly hysterical and began hitting a stuffed animal, saying "Bad lion! Bad lion!" (Main et al., 1985, p. 88).

It was predicted that emotional openness would reflect security of attachment. A child who is confident of his parent's acceptance and support can tolerate his own ambivalent feelings; he can manage them without having to deny them. As expected, in the Berkeley sample, the child's emotional openness on this test at age 6 was strongly correlated with security of attachment to the mother in infancy ($r = .59$). However, it showed no relation to security of attachment to the father in infancy.

In addition to scoring emotional openness, Main et al. (1985) developed a scale for coding the child's expressed strategies for coping constructively in response to the picture of parents leaving for a 2-week vacation—the most stressful scenario. The highest score is given for actively persuading the parents not to go or for preventing the separation by another means, such as hiding in the trunk of the car. High scores are also given for expressing disappointment, anger, or distress directly to the parents or with the implication that this might end the separation, and for finding another attachment figure to stay with and seeming satisfied with that solution to the problem of managing the separation. Children who answer that they can distract themselves by playing get middle scores. Children who say "I don't know," remain silent, or say something that would actually decrease the availability of the attachment figure get low scores for their coping strategies. Examples of the last of these included giving story completions in which the child killed himself, killed the parents, or locked himself away.

The strategic coping score for the response to this single question was as strongly correlated with security of attachment to the mother in infancy in the Berkeley sample ($r = .59$) as the overall rating for emotional openness was. It was not at all related to security of attachment to the father in infancy.

Children from the Bielefeld sample in Germany also took the Klagsbrun-Bowlby adaptation of the HSAT. Those who had been securely attached to their mothers in infancy got high scores for emotional openness and had ideas about how to cope constructively with the imagined separation, including seeking social support from others. Their nonverbal behavior was mostly relaxed during the test. However, many of the children with avoidant attachment histories seemed strained and tense during the HSAT. Some denied that the child in the picture had any feelings of vulnerability. Some were overly pessimistic. A few even said that the parents might never come back. Most of the coping behaviors these defended children suggested were unrelated to the reported feelings or were plainly unrealistic (Grossmann and Grossmann, 1991).

If the same representational model influences responses both to the HSAT and to actual separations and reunions with the mother, scores on the two procedures should be related. To test whether they were, Shouldice and Stevenson-Hinde (1992) used the Klagsbrun-Bowlby adaptation of the HSAT and a 1989 version of the Cassidy-Marvin reunion coding guidelines. In scoring answers to the HSAT, the authors scored specific aspects of discrete responses, not overall emotional openness. The 74 subjects, all second-borns, were seen at the age of 4½ years. After getting acquainted with the laboratory room, taking a picture vocabulary test administered by a stranger in the mother's presence, and completing a joint task with the mother, the child was left alone for 1 minute. Next, the stranger returned to administer the HSAT, which took about 10 minutes. Then the mother returned, and the reunion was videotaped.

Scores on the two measures of security were indeed related. Children who were classified as secure on the basis of reunion behavior were, compared to insecure children, more open to appropriate negative feelings and better able to tolerate the discomfort aroused by the separation pictures of the HSAT. As expected, the resistant preschoolers expressed more anger during the HSAT than other groups did. Some secure children as well as some insecure children expressed anger, but the secure children did it in a more moderate and reasonable way. None of the avoidant or secure children interrupted the administration of the HSAT, but 5 of the 6 resistant children did, often in babyish ways. As you would expect if the defenses of the avoidant children were working, none of them expressed separation anxiety or anger during the HSAT. One did express overly sad affect.

As in infancy, behavior *during* separation did not differentiate between securely attached and insecurely attached children. A few secure children and a few insecure children asked for or tried to regain the mother during the HSAT. There were no sex differences in the attachment category distribution.

Despite the significant associations between the two measures of security, agreement was far from perfect. Knowing everything about a child's responses to the HSAT was not enough to predict the child's reunion classification. For example, while 75 percent of the avoidant (in reunion) preschoolers gave avoidant responses on the HSAT, half of the secure and resistant preschoolers also gave avoidant responses on the HSAT.

■ Response to a Family Photo

In the Berkeley study, after administering the HSAT, the examiner held up the photograph of the child and his or her parents and said, "But here is a photograph of yourself and your family, and you see, you are all together." (Main et al., 1985, p. 89). If the child did not take the photograph, the examiner laid it near the child and waited for the child's response. She did not press the child further. Using the videotapes, judges were asked to estimate the security of the child's feelings about his or her family. The ratings were based mainly on repeated slow-motion examination of the child's nonverbal behavior.

Children were rated as secure if they readily accepted the photograph, smiled, inspected it for a few seconds or made a few positive comments, and then let go of it casually. They were considered insecure if they refused to accept the picture, actively turning from it or turning it away when the examiner placed it near. They were also considered insecure if they became depressed or disorganized when the picture was presented.

There was a strong correlation between response to the family photograph at age 6 and security of attachment to the mother in infancy ($r = .74$). Even though the father was also in the picture, there was no relationship between the security of attachment to him in infancy and the response to the photograph at age 6.

■ Validity of Measures in the Berkeley Study

The rating of emotional openness in response to the HSAT was validated before it was used in the Berkeley study. The other two measures described in this section (reunion behavior and responses to family photos) were developed during and for the Berkeley study. Main et al. (1985) offered the correlations between each of these measures and security of attachment to the mother in infancy as evidence (1) that the new measures are valid measures of security at age 6 and (2) that security of attachment is highly stable from infancy to age 6 in stable middle-class families. Both propositions require replication in other samples before we can gauge their accuracy with any confidence. Each has received support in at least one other study.

If the various measures of security are all valid, children should get similar scores on each method. The rating of security with the mother based on reunion behavior was, as hoped, highly correlated with concurrent but independent measures of security in the Berkeley study: emotional openness in the HSAT ($r = .68$) and response to the family photograph ($r = .50$). However, the rating of security with the father showed little or no relationship to the other two measures of security. This pattern of correlations can be interpreted as evidence that, in stable middle-class families in which the mother is the primary caregiver, the attachment to the mother has much more impact on the child's overall security than the attachment to the father does.

A little evidence supporting the validity of the reunion coding and classification system comes from other studies that connect it to other aspects of the child's concurrent development (see Chapter 15). The ultimate validation of the method, tying reunion codings to more-or-less recent attachment-relevant interactions in everyday life, has not yet been attempted.

In Germany, 40 children from the Regensburg sample were brought back to the laboratory at age 6 for a separation-reunion procedure like the one used in Berkeley (Grossmann and Grossmann, 1991). For the three traditional classifications (A, B, and C), prediction from the Strange Situation pattern in infancy to the reunion pattern at age 6 was accurate for 35 of the 40 children (87 percent). Avoidance ratings on a 7-point scale in infancy were highly correlated with avoidance ratings at age 6 (Grossmann and Grossmann, 1991). If attachment patterns were stable over time in both samples, it seems likely that the reunion codings were measuring what they were intended to measure, the 6-year-old child's attachment pattern. The Regensburg data shed no light on the Berkeley association of group D Strange Situation behavior in infancy with disorganized-controlling behavior at age 6.

The German study did find indirect evidence of the validity of the reunion classifications of security of attachment. Children who showed secure reunion behavior at age 6 had scored higher in play quality, had handled conflicts more competently, and had been more skilled or well-meaning in their perception of others when assessed in kindergarten at age 5.

From a variety of sources, there is preliminary evidence that the Main and Cassidy system for coding reunion behavior has substantial validity. It appears to be fairly successful in measuring what it is intended to measure and in assigning accurate classifications to most children. Main and Cassidy (1988) reported that classifications of reunion behavior at age 6 were not only predictable from infant attachment patterns but also stable over 1 month. Nevertheless, the measure is relatively new and may require modification.

Two aspects of the Main and Cassidy reunion coding system as used in the Berkeley study seem open to question. In Berkeley, one parent returned after the child had been alone with an examiner for an hour, but the second parent returned when the child had already had 3 minutes to regain comfort and/or to cope with the tensions aroused by the first parent's return. In short, the reunion with the second parent occurred in a set of interpersonal circumstances much different from the circumstances of the reunion with the first parent. Should we assume that the continuing presence of the first parent did not influence the child's behavior toward the second? Without making such an assumption, we cannot expect the coding system to be equally valid for both reunions. Future research may demonstrate that it does indeed work well anyway, or may reveal that predictions from prior assessments and associations with current and later behavior are stronger for reunions with the parent who reappears first. The available research does consistently find that mothers' interactions with their children differ in the father's presence from their interactions in his absence. It may also be true that fathers interact with their children differently in the mother's presence than in her absence. Children may act differently with either parent alone than with both parents together. In future research on coding reunion behavior, these possibilities will have to be considered.

The other obvious limitation of the Main and Cassidy coding system is that it relies solely on the child's behavior to assess a pattern of attachment that is almost certainly a goal-corrected *partnership*. By the time the child is 5 to 7 years old, the dyad, not the individual, maintains the stability of interaction patterns in the relationship. When one partner makes a change, the other makes a complementary change that maintains homeostasis. Consequently, directly coding the *dyad's* behavior—not just the child's behavior in context—may eventually prove to be more informative and accurate than the current system.

■ The Parent-Child Reunion Inventory

The Main and Cassidy method for assessing security of attachment requires a lot of time, equipment, and training. Hoping to find a faster, easier way to accomplish the same goal, Marcus (1990) developed a paper-and-pencil measure of reunion behavior, based on parents' assessments. He called it the *Parent-Child Reunion Inventory*. It describes hypothetical everyday separations that last at least an hour. The parent is asked to rate each item on a list of behaviors a child might show at the time of reunion. The parent rates each behavior as usually, occasionally, or never occurring. The inventory lists 20 behaviors Main and Cassidy (1987) used in their coding system. Items such as "Child seems relaxed throughout reunion" and "Child initiates positive interaction with the parents (e.g., invites the parent to see what they are doing)" reflect secure attachment (Marcus, 1990). Items such as "Child moves away from parent" and "Child rejects the parent by asking parent to leave the room or saying 'Don't bother me'" reflect anxious attachment (Marcus, 1990).

At first glance, it seems unlikely that such a measure would work. Simple behavior checklists have seldom proved informative in attachment research. Parents whose children are anxiously attached might be reluctant to report the child's negative behavior. Defended parents might not even consciously acknowledge some of the behavior. However, when Marcus (1991) asked foster parents to fill out his Parent-Child Reunion Inventory to describe their foster children, he got results that were meaningfully related to other measures in his study, which included interviews with the foster children, assessments of the children from their social workers, and the widely used Achenbach Behavior Problem Checklist (1978).

This one study certainly is not sufficient to establish the validity of the Parent-Child Reunion Inventory. However, it does suggest that such a checklist may indeed be useful. I remain skeptical about parents using it to describe their natural children. Nonetheless, trained observers might use it to describe ordinary reunions such as those that occur when a child comes home from school and when a parent comes home from work. Such a procedure would be faster and easier than getting the dyad or family to come to the laboratory, and an observer in the background might not provoke any more self-consciousness than the known presence of a video camera would. The Parent-Child Reunion Inventory may in time prove to be a useful tool for focusing and summarizing naturalistic observations.

NEXT STEPS IN METHODOLOGY

Obviously, theorists and researchers have taken major steps toward developing reliable, valid ways to study attachment in children who are 3 to 7 years old. Obviously, too, no measure has yet acquired the convincingly demonstrated validity and robustness the Strange Situation has for infants. As noted earlier, Main and Cassidy (1988) strongly recommended aggregating information from multiple methods of assessment. Their recommendation remains sound—at least until one method is very well validated.

Both the *pattern* of attachment, however assessed, and the *degree of security*, measured along a continuum, can be informative. The pattern might best predict what forms problems are likely to take (if any emerge); the degree of insecurity might best predict the degree of risk for difficulties in development or the severity of problems that may emerge.

Very innovative ways of assessing attachment may yet emerge. What is needed is some way of gathering information about self-reliance, defensiveness, anger, the child's confidence about the parent's availability and supportiveness, the parent's provision of comfort and support, dyadic communication patterns, and other clues about cognitive, affective, and behavioral strategies and representational models of the attachment relationship.

To activate the attachment system at high intensity, stressors other than separation could be used. Almost any situation that causes emotional conflict for the child in the presence of an attachment figure should yield information about the dyad's style of diverting attention or acknowledging and responding to the child's need for a secure base. For example, asking the child and the parent to work near each other on separate, frustrating, difficult tasks might yield much information. When two children in the same family are studied (which is, unfortunately, seldom), a situation that provokes competition for the parent's attention might prompt attachment behavior. Such a procedure would, like separation-reunion procedures, have the advantage of being ecologically valid.

CHAPTER SUMMARY

Several promising approaches to assessing level of security and/or pattern of attachment in preschoolers and in children who are 5 to 7 years old have been offered.

The Strange Situation procedure, with slight modifications because of the preschool child's cognitive and linguistic skills, works well for illuminating patterns of attachment behavior and the underlying representational models. Two systems, the Miami System (Crittenden, 1991) and the Cassidy-Marvin System (Cassidy et al., 1992), have been developed for coding and classifying Strange Situation data from 3- and 4-year-olds. There are interesting commonalities and contrasts between the two systems. In addition, Bretherton et al. (1990) offered a system for drawing inferences about representational models of attachment from preschoolers' completions of a set of stories about separations from the parents.

The Klagsbrun-Bowlby (1976) adaptation of the Hansburg Separation Anxiety Test is a more direct projective test of strategies for handling separation, which are believed to reflect the child's representational model of the attachment relationship. This test can be used for children 4 to 7 years old.

For children who are 5 to 7 years old, Main and Cassidy (1987) have developed a system for scoring the child's levels of security and avoidance and for classifying the pattern of attachment from a videotape of the first 3 minutes of reunion after the parent has been away from the child for an hour in the laboratory. Marcus (1990) drew from their system to develop a Parent-Child Reunion Inventory that can be used to rate the degree to which each of twenty behaviors commonly occur at reunion. From those ratings, a score for security of attachment can be derived. Main, Kaplan, and Cassidy (1985) also used the child's response to a family photograph presented under specified conditions as an index of the security of the child's attachment.

None of these methods for assessing security or pattern of attachment has been fully validated yet. Studies to explore the reliability and validity of the systems for coding and classifying reunion behavior are ongoing in several psychological laboratories. A few researchers also continue to explore the other methods described in this chapter, and new approaches to assessment may yet emerge.

C H A P T E R

15

CHILDHOOD CORRELATES
OF ATTACHMENT PATTERNS

In Chapter 7, I listed the evidence that patterns of attachment show very high stability from the age of 12 months to the age of 18 or 20 months if the family's circumstances are stable. When the circumstances are unstable, patterns of attachment in infancy still show a tendency toward stability, but they do sometimes change in ways that appear to reflect changes in the infant's experiences. Now we move our inquiry further into childhood. Are patterns of attachment generally stable from infancy to childhood? Under what circumstances are they especially likely to be stable, and under what circumstances are they likely to change? Are the changes predictable or at least explainable? When patterns of attachments change over time, what best predicts other aspects of development: the early pattern of attachment to the principal caregiver, the degree of security in current attachments, or a combination of the two?

Beyond stability and change in attachment patterns themselves, what do we know about associations between infant attachment patterns and later behavior with parents, peers, and others? The Minnesota high-risk sample and the Bielefeld and Regensburg samples have been followed from infancy to age 10. (Actually, both they and the Bloomington sample have been followed into adolescence, but many of the most recent data have not been analyzed and published yet.) Children from these and other longitudinal samples have participated in observations and assessments as 3- to 6-year-olds, so the database for this chapter is broad.

From a theoretical perspective, what concurrent or later characteristics or behaviors *should* be correlated with security of attachment in childhood? Should all good things go together, or are there only some specific outcomes that should be associated with early attachment patterns? Do research findings match predictions from theory?

In general, attachment theorists predict continuity in the child's developmental pathway both because of the self-maintaining aspects of the early representational models and because of the tendency toward continuity in the quality of parental care. Theory predicts that children with secure early attachments will manage the stresses associated with the birth of a sibling, a parent's illness, the parents' divorce, or other difficulties more successfully than children with anxious early attachments will. However, as noted previously, neither biology nor experience in infancy determines the child's destiny. Early attachment patterns help predict certain later outcomes, but they do not come close to accounting for all of the rich variability in later behaviors, thoughts, and affects.

Although children do, within the first year of life, start along developmental pathways that lead in different directions, the pathways can later branch and even arrive by different routes at similar points. According to Greenberg and Speltz (1988), early quality of attachment may not *directly* affect later security, insecurity, mental well-being, or psychopathology (e.g., Fraiberg et al., 1975; Greenspan, 1981; Harmon et al., 1990). Sensitively responsive care, they suggest, is critical throughout early childhood, but what a caregiver must do to be sensitive changes with a child's age. The clinical literature includes cases of mothers who gave good care in infancy but sought to maintain symbiosis and so interfered with the child's healthy individuation and self-reliance in childhood. There are also many case studies of mothers who had grave difficulty with their infants but became able to give good care during the child's preschool years. Both biological factors (e.g., temperament variables) and psychological factors (e.g., the child's early representational models) may affect later representational models and security.

Further, Carlson et al. (1989b) espoused a transactional model of compensatory and potentiating factors. There are, they reported, multiple pathways to adaptive and maladaptive outcomes. There may be qualitatively different precursors underlying apparently similar current outcomes. To understand what has happened, one must consider long-term vulnerabilities, enduring protective factors, short-term challenges, and buffers. Long-term vulnerabilities might include variables such as poor parenting skills in the caregiver; a difficult temperament in the child; chronic illness, poverty, alcoholism or other drug dependency in the family environment; and a history of family violence. Enduring protective factors might include variables such as good parenting skills in the caregiver; an "easy" temperament in the child; intelligence; a strong, stable support network; and a safe neighborhood. Short-term challenges might be nonchronic illnesses, the caregiver's loss of a job, the death of a grandparent, or the birth of a sibling. Buffers might include good care from a second parent or other relative, availability of good-quality day care, or financial assistance from wealthy grandparents.

STABILITY AND CHANGE

■ Predictions from Theory

How early in life do representational models begin to resist change? The years from birth to age 7 are a time of rapid expansion and reorganization of the child's cognitive abilities. In addition to serving as a secure base for exploration and a haven of safety in times of perceived threat, the parent must set limits on the child's dangerous physical behaviors and culturally unacceptable social behaviors and must encourage a culturally appropriate level of self-reliance. Patterns of behavioral interaction gradually change. The child's representational models of relationships may continue forming and reorganizing all through the early years. However, some aspects of these models may become self-maintaining quite early in life.

As you may recall from the discussion in Chapter 13, information encoded in scripts may be received and stored as given fact by the child. In the ordinary course of events, the child's early scripts may go unquestioned for many years, and conscious recall of the specific episodes of experience from which they developed may be impossible. It may be very difficult and rare for a child to reevaluate his earliest beliefs about himself and about his attachments. It cannot occur before he becomes able to think about his own thinking, as noted earlier.

Bowlby (e.g., 1980, 1982, 1988) argued that never-retested expectancies and self-fulfilling prophecies increase the stability of representational models. By definition, avoidant (or defended) working models guard against acknowledging and reexamining painful old beliefs. As a result, they should be especially likely to remain stable over time.

At present, it is hard to say how strong the support for the hypothesis of stability is. That is because the same data are often used both to validate procedures for assessing patterns of attachment after infancy and for demonstrating stability in patterns of attachment (as noted earlier). An illustration may make the problem clear.

■ Longitudinal Research with a Heterogeneous Sample

In a sample of 92 children, Howes and Hamilton (1992b) used Strange Situation assessments at 12 months and reunion behavior after a 2-hour separation at 48 months to assess the pattern of attachment to the mother. During the separation at age 4, the child played with unfamiliar peers in an unfamiliar place. A version of the evolving Cassidy-Marvin system was used for coding reunion behavior from videotapes. At each age, only the A, B, and C categories were used.

Seventy-two percent of the children had the same pattern classification in both assessments. That result initially seems to support two inferences: (1) that, although most children's patterns of attachment are stable, some change over time in a varied sample of families with busy lives, and (2) that the new coding system is valid for 4-year-olds. A closer look at the data, however, reveals a problem. In this study, secure and resistant classifications were significantly more stable than avoidant classifications. Specifically, 89 percent of the secure infants, 73 percent of the resistant infants, and 24 percent of the avoidant infants got the same classification 3 years later. Of the 22 children who were avoidant in infancy, 13 (59 percent) were classified as secure at age 4. According to theory, avoidant or defended children are most likely to block out or misinterpret information that might eventually enable them to modify their representational models. The high rate of change in avoidant attachments in this sample suggests that there may be a need for refining the coding system. However, it is also possible that many of the children who were avoidant in infancy in this particular sample did become secure by age 4. (Day care in this varied sample apparently was not a major influence on changes in the quality of the attachment to the mother.)

When the same data are used to support the validity of a new coding system *and* to demonstrate stability in patterns of attachment, neither inference acquires adequate support. A study like this makes a useful beginning, but research cannot stop there. We need converging support for and evidence of the validity of the coding system from a variety of samples and a variety of theoretically related measures, where possible. If we cannot accumulate persuasive evidence of the validity of the method, then we need to develop a better method for assessing preschoolers' attachments. If, using validated assessment methods, we still cannot accumulate consistent evidence of stability in patterns of attachment, then we must reject the stability hypothesis.

In the same ambitious study, Howes and Hamilton (1992b) also found that the security of attachment to the teacher (or family day care provider), as measured with a 75-item version of the Attachment Q-Set, tended to be stable from infancy to the preschool years. With children up to the age of 30 months, there was no evidence that the working model from the relationship with one teacher was carried into the relationship with a new teacher. After 30 months, however, the qualities of the child's relationships with two different teachers did tend to match. This may imply that the age at which children begin actively transferring working models of relationships with teachers from one relationship to the next is around 30 months.

For the sample as a whole, there was no concordance between the pattern of attachment to the mother at 12 months and the attachment pattern with either the first teacher or the teacher the child had at age 4. (However, the subsample of children enrolled in part-time child care in infancy did show concordant attachments to the mother and the first teacher.) Based on the partially validated methods of assessing attachments in this sample, there was also no concordance between the pattern of attachment to the mother when the child was 4 and the pattern of attachment to the teacher when the child was 4.

■ Longitudinal Research with a Poverty Sample

Both economic circumstances and child-rearing habits varied considerably within the large sample Howes and Hamilton (1992b) accumulated. It may be easier to gauge the validity of the system for classifying preschoolers' attachments using data from a study that controlled for both of those variables.

Cicchetti and Barnett (1991) used a version of the evolving Cassidy-Marvin system to assess patterns of attachment in 125 preschoolers from families of low socioeconomic status. Most of the families were receiving Aid to Families with Dependent Children (AFDC). Approximately half of the children at each age studied—30, 36, and 48 months—were selected for the research because they were maltreated. Most had experienced neglect and/or emotional maltreatment. Some had been physically abused; none were believed to have been sexually abused. Subsamples of the children were assessed at two or more ages, so the study had a longitudinal component as well as a cross-sectional component. As expected, based on assessments of reunion behavior, maltreated children were more likely than adequately reared children to be classified as anxiously attached at each age.

In this study, five categories were used: A, B, C, D, and A-C. In infancy, using the D and A-C categories generally reduces the likelihood of erroneously classifying anxious attachments into group B. Despite the full set of options for classifying insecure attachments, 20 to 30 percent of the maltreated children at each age level were classified into group B. That figure seems too high for this subsample. When the parents neglect and/or abuse the children, how can any of them develop secure attachments? If 2 or 3 of every 10 maltreated children are classified as secure, this may suggest a need for continued refinement of the coding system. However, a possibility we must consider is that some children do develop secure attachments despite some episodes of maltreatment. In addition, some children who are neglected or actively mistreated for a while may become secure if they later experience better care. Their apparent security might, however, be fragile; a new episode of abuse might trigger old insecurities.

The bits of data available from these longitudinal subsamples cannot answer all the questions this study raises about the validity of the assessment system and the stability of attachments. The high percentage of *non*maltreated children who were classified as secure when first seen remained secure at later assessments, as expected. For them, the assessment system seemed valid and the pattern of attachment seemed stable. In contrast, maltreated children who were classified as securely attached at one assessment were *not* likely to be so classified at later assessments. Either one of the assessments was invalid or the security of the maltreated child's attachment changed over a period of 6 to 12 months. To endorse or reject either inference, we will need data from new research.

■ Stability from Infancy to Age 6

For children in the Berkeley sample, Main, Kaplan, and Cassidy (1985) proposed a 3-point scale for translating Strange Situation classifications from infancy into security scores along a continuum. They assigned a score of 3 to infants classified as very secure (subgroup B3), a score of 2 to other securely attached infants (subgroups B1, B2, and B4), and a score of 1 to all types of insecurely attached infants (groups A, C, and D). As explained in Chapter 14, security at age 6 was assigned a score from 1 (very insecure) to 9 (very secure) on the basis of behavior at reunion after a 1-hour separation in the laboratory.

The correlation between security of attachment to the mother at age 1 and at age 6 was very high ($r = .76, p < .001$). Of the 8 children classified as avoidant in infancy, 6 (75 percent) were still avoidant at age 6. The correlation between attachment to the father at 18 months and at age 6 was more modest but still statistically significant ($r = .30, p < .05$).

The Berkeley results were replicated in Regensburg. Wartner (1986) reported that all six subjects who had avoidant attachments to the mother in infancy were again classified as avoidant at age 6. In fact, with the traditional A-B-C classification system, prediction from the pattern in infancy to the pattern at age 6 was accurate for 35 of the 40 children (88 percent). Avoidance showed especially high stability: scores for avoidance during reunions in infancy and at age 6 were highly related.

To date, the Berkeley sample and the Regensburg sample are the only two samples in which attachment patterns have been directly assessed in infancy and at age 6. The Berkeley sample was an upper-middle-class sample; the German sample included families from a range of economic levels. In both samples, most subjects lived in stable family circumstances, and it is likely that patterns of maternal care were consistent over time. Consequently, it is not possible to say whether the observed stability of attachment patterns resulted largely from continuity in care or largely from the effects of self-maintaining representational models.

As noted earlier, we have reason to believe that, in many families, fathers become more involved with their children after infancy and are more likely than mothers to change the ways they interact with their children. Such changes in experience might explain why, in the Berkeley sample, stability of attachment to the father was much lower than stability of attachment to the mother. This explanation would suggest that continuity in the pattern of care did underlie the stability of patterns of attachment to the mother.

What can we infer from these data about continuity and change? At present, we do not have enough validation studies or enough longitudinal studies to say with confidence how stable patterns of attachment are, how early they stabilize, or what circumstances make them or keep them relatively resistant to change. In addition, the assessment methodologies may need refinement and clearly require further validation. Thereafter, we will need several more studies of a variety of samples before we can draw confident conclusions.

SELF-IMAGE

In a study of 52 white, middle-class 6-year-olds, Cassidy found meaningful differences in how secure children and avoidant children completed stories and described themselves to a puppet. She used the Main and Cassidy (1987) system to classify patterns of attachment to the mother at reunion after a one-hour separation in the laboratory. During the period of separation, the children responded to two creative assessments of their self-images. An experimenter gave them beginnings of six stories and asked them to use little dolls to enact a completion of each story. Later, a puppet interviewed the child about how some unspecified "other" viewed him. Responses to the puppet were classified as "perfect" if the child insisted, even when pressed, that he was perfect in every way; "negative" if he made global negative comments about himself; and "open/flexible" if his description of himself was positive but acknowledged some minor flaws. Cassidy found modest but significant associations between attachment classification and self-image. The avoidant children generally claimed that others thought they were perfect. The securely attached children, who showed warm, intimate behavior with their mothers at reunion, saw themselves positively, but most of them admitted that they had normal imperfections. Their doll stories tended to acknowledge the importance of the mother, and the doll mothers in their stories were supportive. This was not the case in the doll stories enacted by avoidant children.

There was one big exception to the pattern of secure children showing positive but not impossibly wonderful attributes: 32 percent of the secure children told the puppet they were perfect, free from any of the little flaws ordinary human beings have. While self-glorification in a play setting is normal in 6-year-olds, its appearance does complicate assessment of defensive idealization of the self. Claims to perfection may in other children reflect an inability to face how low their evaluations of themselves really are. Seven of the 8 avoidant children (88 percent) claimed to be perfect; 14 of the 22 secure children (64 percent) gave open/flexible responses in the puppet interview. The evidence of defensive idealization of the self that Cassidy found is, of course, consistent with the evidence of defensive processes in younger avoidant children, as described in Chapter 7.

BEHAVIOR WITH PARENTS

A British study of fifty-one 2½-year-old children used an early version of the Cassidy-Marvin system to code reunion behavior from both reunions in the Strange Situation

(Achermann et al., 1991). Right after the Strange Situation, the mother was directed to "play naturally" with her child for 10 minutes and then to ask the child to help her clean up the toys. The more secure the child, the more the mother was constructively involved in free play and the more enthusiasm and warmth the mother displayed in asking the child to help clean up. Children with lower security ratings ignored the mother's control statements more and showed more babyish behavior than children with higher security ratings did. As usual, positive interactions were associated with secure attachment, and less-desirable behavior (both from the mother and from the child) was associated with insecure attachment.

There were no significant differences between secure, avoidant, and resistant groups in the frequency of child compliance. Compliance at this age can reflect secure cooperation, the "false self" of a defended child who does not want to provoke the parent's anger, or the coy, disarming half of a coercive child's strategy. Noncompliance at this age may reflect secure assertiveness, the suppressed anger of a defended child, or the open anger of a coercive child. The fact that secure children and insecure children were equally likely to comply with the mother's efforts to get them to help clean up poses no challenge to the theory or to the validity of the coding system. However, concurrent maternal reports of difficult aspects of the child's temperament were associated with low compliance and with other negative behavior.

In Germany, researchers visited most of the families in the Bielefeld sample when the children were 6 years old (Grossmann and Grossmann, 1991). They asked the mother and child to make a building from wooden blocks. As expected, only emotional variables, not intellectual variables or success in completing the task, were related to attachment classifications from infancy. The children with secure histories showed more self-confidence, assertiveness, and involvement but also more open refusal to cooperate and more personal aggression in the play context than those who had avoidant histories showed. The behavior of the children with avoidant histories was more inhibited. Even so, most of the interactive behaviors that ruled the process of building with blocks were related to the socioeconomic status of the family and were *not* related to attachment.

On the same visit, mother, father, and child were asked to stage a little play with hand puppets. In this triadic context, most families let the father control the course of the play. Father-child interactions were more harmonious and positive when they had a history of secure attachment than when they had a history of anxious attachment. The general rating of the emotional climate of the whole session, however, was related to infant-mother attachment quality, not to infant-father attachment quality. In the puppet play, as in the block play, many interactive variables were unrelated to attachment.

Of the 49 Bielefeld families originally studied, Grossmann and Grossmann (1991) relocated 43 when the children were 10 years old. Each child was interviewed in the absence of the parents, so that the child might be free to say things he would be reluctant to have the parent hear. The parents were also interviewed. The children were asked about the nature and amount of support their parents gave them. Contrary to the authors' expectations, perceived support at age 10 was not related to the pattern of attachment to either parent in infancy. Instead, it was estimated from recent, actual events that the children remembered and described clearly, and the parents' behavior in response to the ups and downs of a 10-year-old's everyday life was not related to the child's early attachment history.

The children were also asked about their behavior (1) in everyday problem situations in school, (2) with their parents when negative feelings occurred, and (3) when they were afraid, angry, or sad. It was assumed that all three sorts of situations were somewhat stressful and that effects of representational models based in attachment relationships might arise in all of these stressful situations. The hypothesis was not supported in reports of responses to problems in school or to negative feelings when with the parents. However, strategies for managing fear, anger, and sadness at age 10 were related to infant attachment patterns. Children who had been securely attached to the mother in infancy admitted to having negative feelings more readily than other children did. In addition, they were more likely to say they would use relationship-oriented coping strategies (e.g., going to someone for help or comfort). Children who had been avoidant in infancy reported staying alone and trying to work out the problem by themselves at age 10. This is, of course, exactly the sort of difference that is usually found between secure and avoidant children. What is new here is that the difference could still be found so long after infancy.

BEHAVIOR WITH SIBLINGS

There is some evidence that the relative harmony of the securely attached child's relationship to the parent spills over into the child's interactions with younger siblings. Teti and Ablard (1989) found that children with secure attachments to their mothers were more likely than other children to comfort their younger siblings when the younger ones were distressed. Volling and Belsky (1992) found less conflict during periods of joint play between securely attached children and their younger siblings than between anxiously attached children and their younger siblings. This remained true even after controlling statistically for concurrent and intervening measurements of parent-child relations.

Stewart and Marvin (1984) used games like those described in Chapter 13 to assess social-cognitive perspective-taking skills. Compared to preschoolers who were still cognitively egocentric, preschoolers who were able to take another's perspective were more likely to be asked by the mother to take care of the baby sibling while the mother was, at the experimenter's request, absent from the laboratory playroom. Children who could take another person's conceptual perspective were much more likely than other children to give care and comfort to the baby brother or baby sister during the mother's absence, even if the mother did not ask the child to do so. Perspective-taking ability, not chronological age, predicted which preschoolers would serve as caregivers for their infant siblings. The infants did stay much closer to their preschool siblings during the mother's absence than during prior episodes; they used the siblings as attachment figures.

BEHAVIOR WITH PEERS AND STRANGERS

When the children in the Regensburg sample were 5 years old, Grossmann and Grossmann (1990) located many of them and observed them in their various kindergartens. Those with histories of secure attachment played with more concentration and were less easily disturbed than those with histories of avoidant attachment. More of the secure children showed behavior that was planful and organized and appeared to be relaxed, as judged from their facial and gestural expressions. More of the avoidant children appeared rather erratic, tense, and fidgety. More of them showed a tendency toward frequent conflicts. More of the secure children tended to be friendly, whereas more of the avoidant children were sober and often dissatisfied and in a poor mood during social encounters. The researchers combined a number of variables to define a classification of the 5-year-olds as competent or incompetent. Fourteen of the twenty-one (67 percent) who were securely attached at 12 months were identified as competent in social interactions in preschool 4 years later. Only 3 of the 11 (27 percent) avoidant children were. Among these children from normal families, minor behavior problems such as aggression, hostility, or isolation were much more common in the avoidant children than in the secure children.

The patterns of relationships with peers that the children in the Bielefeld sample reported at age 10 were strongly related to their patterns of attachment to the mother in infancy (Grossmann and Grossmann, 1991). Those who had been securely attached reported that they had one or a few good friends who were trustworthy and reliable. Those who had been anxiously attached either said they had no good friends or claimed that they had very many friends but were unable to name a single one. In addition, the children with anxious attachment histories more often reported problems such as being exploited by their peers, ridiculed by them, or excluded from peer group activities. There was high concordance between what the parents reported about peer relations and what the children reported in separate interviews.

In the same sample, differences between attachment groups also emerged in the subjects' behavior with the interviewer, who did ask some intense and unpleasant questions. Compared to children with secure attachment histories, 10-year-olds with anxious attachment histories were more likely either to ignore the interviewer openly and even rudely or to do the opposite of ignoring—to show overly intimate social behavior, sometimes even seeking close bodily contact with the interviewer. Observable sibling rivalry at age 10 was also more common when the target child had been insecurely attached than when he or she had been securely attached to the mother in infancy.

INTERIM SUMMARY

Few slices of evidence about concurrent correlates of attachment security in the preschool years or about correlates of early attachment patterns in middle childhood are available. Each study breaks new ground and uses measures that have not yet been fully validated. Several of the studies have failed to yield any significant results. Nevertheless, a coherent picture that matches predictions from attachment theory is beginning to emerge. Secure early attachment to the mother generally predicts self-confidence, openness in acknowledging and coping with negative feelings, trust in the parent, willingness to seek help from others, more harmony or less conflict in interactions with siblings, positive relations with peers, and appropriate social behavior with an adult interviewer, all measured 4 to 9 years after infancy. All of these direct effects, indirect effects, or correlated sequelae are associated only with the early pattern of attachment to the mother, not with the early pattern of attachment to the father. In each of the longitudinal samples, the mother was the primary caregiver, so her having a greater or longer-lasting influence is easily understood.

BEHAVIOR PROBLEMS

As described in Chapter 7, children with anxious attachment histories have more difficulties in social interactions with parents and peers than secure children have. Sometimes the conflicts, impulsiveness, noncompliance, and other difficulties are numerous enough or extreme enough to lead to a diagnosis of psychopathology, but often they are just the ordinary sorts of difficulties that emerge as a child learns to manage his own behavior and to get along with others.

■ Subclinical Behavioral Problems

Ninety-six children from the original Minnesota high-risk sample were located at age 4½ to 5 (Erickson, Sroufe, and Egeland, 1985). Their teachers rated their behavior on the Preschool Behavior Questionnaire (Behar and Stringfield, 1974) and on a new behavioral problem scale. The scale included problems that were not serious enough to warrant clinical diagnosis and treatment. As a group, the children with avoidant attachment histories showed more withdrawal than others, more impulsiveness, more hostility, less ability to persist, and higher total behavioral problem scores (Erickson, Sroufe, and Egeland, 1985). Among the children with secure or resistant attachment histories, differences among individuals were great; the average scores of the two groups on the various follow-up measures did not differ significantly.

Of the children who had shown a stable, anxious pattern of attachment to the mother in Strange Situations at 12 and at 18 months, 85% had behavioral problems in preschool. Of those who were classified as secure in one assessment and anxious in the other, 60 percent had behavioral problems. Of those with stable secure attachments in infancy, far fewer—29 percent—had behavioral problems in preschool.

The infant assessments occurred long before the D category was defined. We can only wonder how use of that category might have clarified or modified research results. The available system for classifying attachments indicated that some children who were securely attached to their mothers both at 12 months and at 18 months nevertheless developed behavioral problems in preschool. How could this be? Data from observations and assessments at 24, 30, and 42 months were examined for clues. Evidence of decreasing harmony in the mother-child relationship emerged. Compared to the secure infants who stayed free from behavioral problems, those who developed problems had mothers who were less supportive and less encouraging in observations of the children at 24 and 42 months. At 30 months, these children had fewer play materials and they experienced less maternal involvement. When these children were 42 months old, their mothers were less effective teachers, did not communicate their expectations clearly to their children, and were inconsistent about setting limits. The mothers reported experiencing confusion and disorganized mood states more often than did the mothers of securely attached children who did not develop problems. In the stressful and unstable circumstances of this sample, it is not surprising that some mothers who gave good care in infancy later had difficulties.

Some children with anxious attachments in infancy were not showing behavioral problems at age 4½ or 5. What helped them do better than the children with similar attachment histories who did develop problems? In the data available from assessments at 24 months, no differences were detected. At 30 months, however, these children had more appropriate play materials in their homes and experienced higher maternal involvement. When these children were 42 months old, the mothers of those who did not develop behavioral problems were warmer and more supportive and did a better job of setting limits than the mothers of children who later showed behavioral problems did. In short, for the two groups, those with secure histories and those with anxious attachment histories, similar sets of intervening variables at 30 and 42 months influenced the risk of later behavioral problems.

All this post hoc evidence again suggests that differences in the mother's nurturance, teaching, discipline, and personal coping when the children were 2 and 3 years old contributed to differences in the likelihood of a child's showing a noticeable level of problematic behavior at age 4½ or 5. Certainly, the security of attachment in infancy was not the end of the story for the children in this sample. Both findings are easy to believe and seem likely to be replicated in other studies. The child's representational models are probably still forming and reorganizing through the preschool years; changes in experience should change outcomes. However, the mother's care may not be the only relevant aspect of experience.

In the Minnesota high-risk sample, what the aunts, grandmothers, and male adults in these children's lives may have contributed, after the children's infancy, to the children's representational models, security, self-esteem, and social skills, for better or for worse, directly or indirectly, was not assessed. Furthermore, the maternal care variables that seemed influential in this sample may not match the variables that seem to be influential in other circumstances. It is possible that maternal care that was insufficient to protect children from developing behavioral problems in this high-risk environment would have been sufficient to protect children in less dangerous, more supportive neighborhoods.

Gathering meaningful data about a mother and a child on several separate occasions is hard enough. The fact that research often stops with the dyad, or includes only one other adult (usually the father, hired caregiver, or teacher) is easy to understand. Even so, we need to remember that methodology limits learning. If all of the data we gather focus on the mother and the child, the only parts of the explanation of outcomes we will be able to detect are the influences of the mother's care and the child's characteristics and behavior. What other factors directly or indirectly influence outcomes for the child, how they influence outcomes, and how much they influence outcomes will be lost in the statistical "noise."

■ Childhood Psychopathology

When a child's aggressiveness, noncompliance, tantrums in response to limits, lying, and perhaps even stealing markedly and chronically exceed levels that are normal for that child's age, the child has crossed a boundary into the realm of psychopathology. At this point, parents may seek assistance from a psychotherapist or a child guidance clinic. Clinicians and researchers are likely to classify the child as one who has behavior problems or conduct problems.

Should patterns of attachment in infancy and/or early childhood affect the likelihood that a child will show behavior sufficiently maladaptive to be labeled as behavior problems or a conduct disorder? Greenberg and Speltz (1988) have argued that the same parental behavior that influences attachment behavior in the preschool years also influences the risk of conduct disorders. Parents of children with serious conduct disorders are, they wrote, not good at developing joint goals and plans and are also not good at tolerating their own or others' affective states or communicating about them (Greenberg and Speltz, 1988). Some parents are too rigidly authoritarian, imposing their will on the child. Some are too permissive and fail to set limits and to teach the child self-control. Some vacillate unpredictably between ignoring misbehavior and punishing it harshly. In all three scenarios, the parent fails to help the child learn to communicate with another to develop joint plans. The child does not learn to recognize the perspectives, needs, and feelings of others and to incorporate them into his plans. Behaviors commonly labeled as conduct problems can be viewed as strategies for gaining the approach or attention of caregivers who are often unresponsive to the child's other signals. Healthier means of regulating the relationships with attachment figures or having access to them are not working, so the child exercises negative attention-seeking behaviors.

A few investigators have tested hypotheses about associations between anxious attachment in infancy and behavior problems in preschool, kindergarten, or first grade. Among the first to do so were Lewis, Feiring, McGuffog, and Jaskir (1984). They observed 113 white middle-class children in a separation-reunion procedure at age 1 and asked the mothers to complete the Achenbach (1978) behavior problem checklist when the children were 6 years old. Achenbach's questionnaire is a widely used measure of child behavior problems. From its subscales, clinicians and researchers can calculate a summary score for externalizing (aggressive, destructive) problems, a summary score for internalizing (anxious, withdrawn, etc.) problems, and a behavior problem profile.

Although the interactive scales and the A-B-C classification criteria from the Strange Situation were employed, the separation-reunion procedure Lewis et al. (1984) used was not the Strange Situation. It consisted of a period of free play, one 3-minute separation, and one 3-minute reunion. The episodes with the stranger and the second separation and reunion were omitted. It seems likely that this led to misclassification of some children.

Uncertainty about their validity makes the Lewis et al. (1984) results difficult to interpret. Nonetheless, Lewis et al. (1984) reported that attachment classifications at age 1 helped to predict psychopathology at age 6 in boys, but not in girls. For the sample as a whole, 18 percent of the 56 boys and 15 percent of the 56 girls had psychopathology as defined by the Achenbach behavior problem checklist. Of the 20 anxiously attached boys, 8 (40 percent) developed psychopathology; only 2 of the 36 securely attached boys (6 percent) did. Among boys judged to have anxious attachments, resistant attachments appeared to be a greater risk factor in developing psychopathology than avoidant attachments were. Of the boys classified as resistant, 60 percent showed serious behavioral problems 5 years later; of those classified as avoidant, 33 percent showed serious behavioral problems five years later.

Lewis et al. (1984) compared anxiously attached boys who did develop psychopathology with anxiously attached boys who did not. The more-troubled group had more life stress, fewer friends, and smaller social networks than the boys with no reported behavior problems. They were also more likely than the better-functioning group to be second-born and unplanned.

The results Lewis et al. (1984) obtained were not replicated in follow-up studies of children from the Bloomington sample. Bates, Maslin, and Frankel (1985) tested the hypothesis that anxious attachment in infancy would predict behavior problems in preschool. These children from a low-risk sample of middle- and lower-class families had been assessed in the Strange Situation at the age of 13 months. Both mothers and secondary caregivers (preschool teachers, day care workers, or regular babysitters) completed the Behar Preschool Behavior Questionnaire (Behar, 1977) when the 52 subjects were 3 years old. Neither mothers nor secondary caregivers reported more internalizing or externalizing behavior problems in anxiously attached children than in securely attached children at age 3.

In a later follow-up of some of the children from the Bloomington sample, Bates and Bayles (1988) hypothesized that avoidant children would be especially likely to develop behavior problems involving angry, coercive behavior despite the appearance of being cool and aloof. They would be likely to develop interpersonal strategies of keeping emotionally distant from others and to employ them systematically. Children with resistant attachments would be perceived as angry and would express this anger in disorganized, ambivalent ways. They might show aggression when frustrated, but would not systematically seek to coerce others. As you may have noticed, this is the opposite of the hypothesis Crittenden (e.g., 1992a) later offered; she proposed that infants with resistant attachments would be especially likely to develop coercive behavioral strategies. Bates and Bayles (1988), like Crittenden and others, thought preschoolers with anxious or resistant attachment histories would be likely to show immature dependency.

The mothers and the teachers of the 57 children located for this follow-up completed Achenbach's checklist when the children were 5 or 6 years old. The teachers' reports showed only low correlations with the mothers' reports. Possibly one group was not reporting accurately about the children's behavior. Possibly some children did in fact show more problematic behavior in one setting than in the other. Probably both possibilities help explain the poor match between reports from mothers and reports from teachers.

Contrary to the authors' predictions, there was no association between the child's early attachment pattern and internalizing problems, externalizing problems, or total behavior problems at age 5 or 6 (Bates and Bayles, 1988). Post hoc analyses found some meaningful associations among early measures of mother-child interaction, preschool measures (maternal reports) of difficulties in temperament or behavior, and behavior problems at age 5 or 6.

Bates and Bayles (1988) concluded from their own and others' research that anxious attachment should not be regarded as a clinical problem in itself and may play no direct role in the development of behavior problems in early childhood. I am not sure the risks associated with anxious attachment are so negligible. Because only a minority of anxiously attached children develop psychopathology, we might need a very large sample to test hypotheses about pathological outcomes for children with different attachment histories.

In fact, it would be best to have so many subjects that you could base predictions not on A, B, C, and D groups, but on *sub*groups. For example, it is likely that A1 babies are at considerably greater risk for developing psychopathology than A2 babies are. It also seems likely that the sorts of risks associated with group C subgroups would differ from each other. C1's, being openly angry and demanding, might have frequent conflicts and frustrated outbursts of aggression—externalizing behavior problems. C2's, being passive and helpless, might suffer problems associated with withdrawal and even depression—internalizing behavior problems. These passive, withdrawn children might also be perceived as nice, quiet little children, and frequently overlooked—a bit slow and babyish, perhaps, but not troublesome.

Rutter (1985), reviewing data from samples of children with more-serious disruptions in early attachments, ascribed greater significance to childhood attachment experiences than Bates and Bayles (1988) did. His main point, however, was that, even in the face of dreadful stresses and adversities, fewer than half of all children develop psychopathology. Human beings appear to be very resilient, and the factors that augment resilience or buffer the child from adversity warrant further study. Furthermore, some negative childhood experiences merely make a child more vulnerable to later, severe stressors. In a benign environment, the individual's vulnerability may never show. An example from a study of a different primate species illustrates the point well. Suomi (1983) found that separation from the mother in infancy predisposed monkeys to depression, but the separated monkeys acted just like other monkeys in ordinary circumstances. Only in stressful social situations was their vulnerability apparent.

Recently, Lyons-Ruth, Alpern, and Repacholi (1993) presented data that may contribute much to our ability to chart deviant developmental pathways beginning early in a subject's life. In a longitudinal intervention study of infants and mothers in very poor inner-city families, they found that early attachment classification was the single most powerful predictor of hostile, aggressive behavior toward peers in the classroom at age 5. The other predictors available in their study included maternal depressive symptoms, hostile-intrusive maternal behavior in infancy, degree and quality of maternal involvement, infant mental development, and presence of documented or suspected maltreatment. Furthermore, it was specifically anxious-disorganized attachment, not anxious attachment in general, that predicted hostile-aggressive behavior problems. (Attachment status predicted only hostile-aggressive behavior problems, not anxious or hyperactive behavior problems.) Only 2 of the 24 secure children (9 percent) developed such behavior problems, 3 of the 12 avoidant children (25 percent) did, and 12 of the 27 anxious-disorganized children (44 percent) did. A different way of looking at the same raw totals dramatizes the same conclusion. Of the children who did develop behavior problems, 71 percent had had group D attachments in infancy.

Taken together, these studies make it clear that some 3- to 6-year-olds who were anxiously attached as infants may be quite vulnerable, but are fortunate enough not to encounter challenges that overwhelm their coping skills. Others may learn effective ways of getting along with people and of coping with stresses, despite the anxiety in their early primary attachments. Certainly the literature on other primates (e.g., Harlow and Harlow, 1965) demonstrates that peer relations involve different behaviors and serve different functions from attachments.

Finally, during the childhood years, and in high-risk circumstances, the risk of developing seriously maladaptive behavior is noticeably lower for children with avoidant or resistant attachments than for children with disorganized attachments. (Different sorts and degrees of risk may emerge in adolescence.) The risk for group D children in the buffered circumstances of stable middle-class life may be much lower than it is for group D children in very poor inner-city families.

EGO STRENGTHS

One of Bowlby's (e.g., 1969, 1982, 1988) and Ainsworth's (e.g., 1972, 1983) major propositions about how early attachments affect personality development was that secure attachment lays the foundation for flexible, adaptive behavior and resilience in the face of stressors later in life. The secure personality is not rigid, brittle, or fragile; it has a quality often called "ego-resiliency." Ego-resiliency has been defined as the ability to respond flexibly but also persistently in problem situations. High ego-resiliency should be an opposite of the presence of severe behavioral problems.

This hypothesis has been tested in several studies. In attachment research, the most widely used measure of ego-resiliency is a Q-sort developed by Block and Block (1980). In addition to the above definition of ego-resiliency, Block and Block offered a definition of *ego-control.* Children who have very high levels of ego-control are disposed to repress impulses and emotions. They are rigid and inhibited, they show anxiety in new situations, and they reject unexpected information. Children who have weak ego-control are impulsive and distractible. They cannot concentrate on one task or problem very long. Obviously, children who have a moderate level of ego-control—children who are neither too inhibited nor too impulsive—are likely to have advantages both in solving problems and in getting along with others.

The constructs of ego-resiliency and ego-control have unmistakable psychoanalytic origins, but Block and Block (1980) developed and validated specific observational definitions for these constructs. Their measure, the California Child Q-Sort, or CCQ, consists of 100 behavioral descriptions written on 100 small cards (Block and Block, 1980). A person who knows the child well—usually the child's parent or teacher—sorts the behavior items into nine piles along a continuum from "strikingly absent" in the subject to "strikingly present." Each item is assigned a score that reflects the pile into which it was placed. The score for ego-resiliency is the sum of the scores for the behavior items relevant to that construct. Similarly, the score for ego-control is the sum of the scores for the behavior items relevant to that construct.

The first use of the CCQ in attachment research reached publication before Block and Block's full description of the CCQ did. Arend, Gove, and Sroufe (1979) located 26 five-year-olds who had participated in Strange Situations at the age of 18 months. The children were from stable middle-class families. Both the Q-sorts performed by kindergarten teachers and laboratory observation measures showed the securely attached children to be somewhat more ego-resilient and more curious than the anxiously attached children. There was a small tendency for avoidant subjects to show overly high ego-control, and a small tendency for resistant subjects to show unduly low ego-control, but neither tendency was statistically significant.

In a follow-up study of the Regensburg sample at age 5, researchers found that teachers reported better ego-control and ego-resiliency in children who had had a secure attachment to *either* parent in infancy than in children whose early attachments to *both* parents had been anxious (Grossmann and Grossmann, 1991). The researchers directly observed the children at age 5 in their various preschools. In contrast to children who, in infancy, had had avoidant attachments to their mothers, children who had had secure attachments to their mothers played with more concentration and showed a higher quality of play. Those who had enjoyed secure attachments to their fathers initiated more play activities with other children. Children who had had a secure attachment to either parent were more self-reliant in managing conflict with peers and more successful in resolving the conflicts in ways that were satisfying to both partners. This was a low-risk sample, and severe behavior problems were rare. Behavior problems that were more than minor were associated with histories of anxious attachment to the mother. On any one variable or area of competence in this study, the differences between the secure children and the avoidant children were, in the Grossmanns' words, "not overwhelming" (Grossmann and Grossmann, 1991, p. 101). What gives the findings weight is that every one of the differences the investigators did find favored the securely attached children, as did the teachers' overall evaluations of and sympathy for individual children.

Data about the relation between early attachment patterns and later ego-resiliency in Israel are consistent with results from the United States and Germany. When the children from a kibbutz study of infant attachments to mother, father, and metapelet were 5 years old, Oppenheim, Sagi, and Lamb (1988) located 59 of them. The researchers observed the children unobtrusively during free play in the communal children's houses, where the subjects normally spent most of their time. Then they gave the children some short personality tests and an IQ test. Kindergarten teachers and metaplot completed Q-sorts to describe the children. The children who had been securely attached to their metaplot in infancy (who were different metaplot from those who took care of them at age 5) were more empathic, dominant, purposive, achievement-oriented, and independent than the children who had had resistant attachments to their metaplot in infancy.

How far into childhood do the effects or predictable correlates of infant attachment patterns stretch? Urban, Carlson, Egeland, and Sroufe (1992) observed forty-seven 9- to 11-year-old children from the Minnesota high-risk sample intensively during 4 weeks of day camp. Children with histories of secure attachment differed from children with histories of insecure attachment on measures of social competence and ego-resiliency. Children with insecure attachment histories were rated as more dependent and interacted with adults more than children with secure histories did. Adults initiated contact to offer support or nurturance to children with resistant histories more often than they initiated contact with children with avoidant histories. Camp counselors used a Q-sort procedure to provide overall descriptions of children's personalities. Children with secure histories were more like each other on this measure than they were like other groups, and children with resistant attachment histories resembled each other more than they resembled other groups, but no consistent pattern emerged for children with avoidant histories.

None of the studies reported above found huge differences in ego strengths between groups with different attachment histories measured 4 to 9 years after infancy. Each study did, however, find differences that favored children who had had secure attachments.

■ Puzzles and Sex Differences

In research in Holland, Van IJzendoorn, van der Veer, and van Vliet-Visser (1987) took an unusual approach to analyzing data from Strange Situations and uncovered some puzzling results and some unpredicted sex differences. They failed to replicate the finding that secure attachment in infancy is associated with high ego-resiliency (as perceived by parents and teachers) in kindergartners. Instead, using a Dutch translation of the CCQ, the investigators found that girls showed more ego-resiliency than boys. According to parents (but not teachers), girls also showed more-desirable levels of ego-control than boys did, and no differences in ego-control were associated with attachment classifications.

The sex difference is not overly surprising. Many studies have found that, as a group, boys are more active, more reactive, and harder to socialize than girls are (Maccoby and Jacklin, 1974). But why did attachment security not aid in predicting ego-resiliency and ego-control? One possibility is that the variability among individuals within attachment categories simply was greater than the variability between groups. Another possibility is that the variables were not well-measured.

The measures of ego-resiliency and ego-control seem to have been adequately translated and validated for use in Holland. The classification of attachment patterns is more questionable. Strange Situations were conducted when the children were 24 months old— a little too old for applying the well-established, well-validated original coding criteria. Analyses of the attachment classifications were decidedly unconventional. Instead of comparing secure and anxious groups, the investigators compared four groups: those who were avoidant or resistant (A1, A2, C1, or C2); those who were marginally secure, with some avoidant behavior (B1); those who were secure (B2 or B3); and those who were "anxiously dependent" (B4). Fourteen of the sixty-four children (22 percent) were classified as B4, and that subgroup is traditionally treated as secure or marginally secure, not anxiously dependent, when analyzing results.

Analysis of the teacher ratings of ego-control showed that the pattern of outcomes associated with attachment classification for boys differed from the pattern of associations for girls. To make a good guess about the child's score on ego-control, you had to know both the child's sex and the child's attachment classification. Among girls, groups B2, B3, *and* B4 (marginally secure?, anxiously dependent?) got the best scores, group B1 did worse, and the groups A and C got the worst scores of all. Among boys, groups A and C got the *best* scores for ego-control: Group B1 did worse, and groups B2, B3, and B4 got the worst scores of all. B4's scored only a bit worse than B2's and B3's. These puzzling results will be easier to comprehend if you look at Table 15.1.

Making sense of this complicated pattern of results is not easy. I have included the study principally as a reminder that predictions from infant attachment classifications are not so powerful that they will be supported in *any* study with *any* system of analysis. Psychology is a difficult science, with many factors interacting with each other to produce observed outcomes, and with many variables that are hard to measure. In research on effects and correlates of early attachment patterns, the child's gender should probably be included among the available predictive variables more often than it has been. Outcomes for boys with avoidant or resistant histories could easily differ from outcomes for girls with similar attachment histories.

TABLE 15.1 Teacher's Ratings of Ego-Control for Girls and for Boys with Different Attachment Histories		
Ego-control	Girls	Boys
Optimal	B2, B3; B4	A1, A2, C1, C2
Medium	B1	B1
Poor	A1, A2, C1, C2	B2, B3; B4

Source: Adapted from Van IJzendoorn, van der Veer, and van Vliet-Visser, 1987. Reprinted with permission.

SEX DIFFERENCES

Developmental psychologists routinely test for sex differences if there is any reason to think these differences might exist. In addition, major journals have at times required researchers to test for sex differences even when researchers thought such differences were unlikely to exist. Despite this widespread awareness of the possible existence and impact of sex differences, literally hundreds of studies of infants and toddlers have reported no sex differences in frequencies of insecure attachments or in the determinants of different attachment patterns. It seems safe to say that, except in very high risk samples, secure, resistant, and avoidant attachments are about equally common in boys and in girls in infancy.

In the broad field of developmental psychology, researchers have often found evidence that males are more vulnerable to psychosocial stressors than females are. The few studies that have found sex differences related to attachment in infancy have also found greater vulnerability in boys. For example, as noted in Chapter 6, Egeland and Farber (1984) found that male infants in their Minneapolis high-risk sample were more affected than female infants were by the presence of a husband or boyfriend in the home and by the nature of his relationship to the mother. Similarly, as noted in Chapter 10, two studies suggest that baby boys (but not baby girls) whose mothers are employed may be at risk for anxious attachment to the father.

In their very low socioeconomic status sample, Carlson, Cicchetti, Barnett, and Braunwald (1989b) also found sex differences in patterns of attachment in infancy. As you can see from Table 15.2, boys were significantly more likely than girls to have type D attachments to their mothers (67 percent of the boys versus 36 percent of the girls). Obviously, there was also a main effect for maltreatment: maltreated children were significantly more likely to have type D attachments than children in the comparison group were (82 percent of the maltreated infants versus 19 percent of the other infants). In addition to main effects for maltreatment and for gender, there was a significant interaction between the two factors: maltreatment increased the likelihood of disorganized attachment in boys (91 percent of the maltreated boys versus 40 percent of the comparison group), but it produced a much bigger difference for girls (73 percent of the maltreated girls versus 0 percent of the comparison group).

CHILDHOOD CORRELATES OF ATTACHMENT PATTERNS

TABLE 16.2 Frequencies of D and Non-D Attachments in Boys and Girls with and without Maltreatment				
	Maltreatment Group		**Comparison Group**	
	Boys	Girls	Boys	Girls
D	10	8	4	0
Non-D	1	3	6	11

Source: Adapted from Carlson et al., 1989b. Reprinted with the permission of Cambridge University Press.

Apparently, even in the absence of maltreatment, male infants in families in these difficult, stressful circumstances were at risk for disorganized attachment, but girls were not. In fact, 9 of the 11 girls in the comparison group showed secure attachments.

The frequencies of D attachments in this sample were higher than those reported in any other study. Interpretation of the sex difference must await replication and additional data on associated variables.

Despite these few studies; it seems fairly safe to say that, except when an identifiable risk factor is present, the distribution of avoidant, secure, and resistant attachments in male infants is about the same as the distribution in female infants.

As research moves into the preschool and later years, investigators occasionally do find sex differences in the sequelae of early patterns of attachment. The Dutch study described in the preceding section is a particularly dramatic example (Van IJzendoorn, van der Veer, and van Vliet-Visser, 1987).

In England, Turner (1991) looked for sex differences in the behavior of preschool boys and girls who had had the same pattern of attachment to the mother. The subjects were forty 4-year-olds who were attending five well-equipped preschools near Cambridge. All of the children were second-borns. After a short time alone with the mother in the research laboratory, the child took a picture vocabulary test administered by a female stranger, did a joint task with the mother, was weighed and measured by a male stranger, stayed alone with him for 1 minute, took the projective HSAT (administered by a second female stranger), and then reacted to the mother's return. The Cassidy-Marvin system (1990 version) was used for classifying reunion behavior as secure (24 children), avoidant (5 children), or resistant (11 children). Other insecure categories were not used.

Each child was observed during a period of free play indoors in his or her preschool. Secure boys and secure girls did not differ from each other, but insecure boys and insecure girls did differ from each other. Insecurely attached boys showed more aggressive, disruptive, assertive, controlling, and attention-seeking behavior than securely attached children showed. Compared to secure children, insecure girls showed less assertive and controlling behavior and more dependent behavior, positive expressive behavior, and compliance. If most of the insecure boys had been avoidant and most of the insecure girls had been resistant, or vice versa, an explanation of the sex difference in terms of the particular pattern of insecurity might have been offered. However, that was not the case. Of the 9 insecurely attached girls, 3 were avoidant and 6 were resistant; of the 7 insecurely attached boys, 2 were avoidant and 5 were resistant. Consequently, the sex difference in behavior with peers could not be explained as an effect of the particular pattern of insecure attachment the child showed.

In this study, the associations between insecure attachment and concurrently measured behavior with peers were different for girls than for boys. In the broader developmental literature, it has often been reported that boys tend to be more aggressive, active, and impulsive than girls and that girls tend to be more passive, compliant, and prone to anxiety than boys, although the differences are not huge (Maccoby and Jacklin, 1974). Turner (1991) speculated that gender differences in social behavior may be carried primarily by the subgroup of children who are insecurely attached.

Working with subjects who were 6 years old, Cohn (1990) found effects of attachment status for boys but not for girls. Using the coding system developed by Main and Cassidy (1987), she assessed 89 children's attachment patterns on reunion with the mother after a 1-hour separation in the laboratory. The next fall, when the children were in first grade, both teachers and peers liked securely attached boys better than they liked insecurely attached boys. The peers perceived the insecure boys as more aggressive, and the teachers said they were less competent and had more behavior problems. Neither teachers nor peers reported systematic differences between securely attached girls and insecurely attached girls.

Whenever sex differences have been reported in the attachment literature, boys have been found to be more vulnerable than girls to variables that might underlie anxious attachment or to negative outcomes associated with anxious attachment. That pattern of results is certainly of some importance and does accord with the general body of child development research. However, we should also remember that the overwhelming majority of attachment studies have not found sex differences. Of course, the overwhelming majority of attachment studies have focused on infants and toddlers. As researchers look more and more at older children, they may more often find sex differences either in distributions of attachment patterns or, more likely, in the correlates of attachment patterns.

CHAPTER SUMMARY

The early returns about correlates of attachment after infancy are intriguing. Unfortunately, too little research is available to justify drawing confident conclusions about the questions and hypotheses raised in this chapter. Methods must be validated and results must be replicated before we will know how well these early results stand up. Still, the skepticism science requires need not make the early results any less interesting.

First, it appears that, when family circumstances are stable, the pattern of the child's attachment to the mother shows high stability from infancy to age 6. However, more longitudinal studies are needed before we can be confident about how stable patterns of attachment are, how early they stabilize, or what circumstances make them relatively resistant to change.

Bits of evidence suggest that secure attachment, whether measured in infancy, in the preschool years, or at age 5 or 6, is associated with more-positive or more-desirable interactions with parents, with siblings, with peers, and even with adult interviewers. Some of these correlates of infant attachment patterns have been found in subjects as old as age 10.

Children with anxious attachment histories appear to be more likely than secure children to have minor behavioral problems. Evidence about whether they are also at greater risk for serious behavior problems has been mixed. The best available study, a longitudinal intervention study with a high-risk sample, found that the group D attachment classification in infancy was the strongest of many available predictors of hostile-aggressive behavior problems at age 5. Even so, fewer than half of the group D subjects developed behavior problems (Lyons-Ruth et al., 1993).

A few studies have found that children with secure early attachments show somewhat greater ego-resiliency than is shown by children whose early attachments were anxious. One failure to replicate that result prompted discussions of methodology and of sex differences. There is some evidence that anxious attachment is more of a risk factor for boys than for girls. In addition, the sequelae of avoidant, resistant, or otherwise anxious attachment for girls may differ from the sequelae of such attachments for boys.

4

ADOLESCENCE
AND ADULTHOOD

Most of the theoretical proposi-
tions and research discussed in this unit emerged even more recently
than the ideas and research discussed in Unit 3; no conclusions can be
etched in stone. Despite the fact that no hard proofs about attachments in adolescence and adulthood are available yet, the ideas, methods, and first results are exciting.

Theorists have proposed that falling in love is, like the process of
forming an attachment in infancy, a biologically based social propensity that contributes to the survival of the human species. Sometime
during the years of adolescence or adulthood, a new attachment figure
may replace the parent or parents as the most important attachment
figure in an individual's life. The new attachments that develop after
childhood are often reciprocal. That is, each partner serves as an
attachment figure for the other.

The methods for assessing general representational models of
attachment in adolescents and adults range from a probing clinical
interview to a simple self-report on a single item included on a questionnaire. Two methods for assessing the quality of one specific attachment, not the global attitude toward attachment issues, have also been
developed. Much more work must be done before any of the methods
can be regarded as fully validated.

There is some evidence that adolescents and adults with secure
representational models of attachment enjoy more harmonious, more
satisfying, longer-lasting intimate relationships than other individuals

do. Avoidant attachment is associated with mistrust, emotional distance from others, loneliness, and hostility. Resistant attachment appears to be associated with passion, jealousy, dependency, and unstable relationships. However, some insecure relationships, perhaps usually involving one avoidant partner and one resistant partner, are longlasting. There is some evidence that secure individuals tend to date and marry each other while resistant individuals tend to date and marry avoidant individuals, and vice versa. Interpreting results from students of adolescents' and adults' attachments sometimes requires an awareness of sex role expectations.

Studies of adults' reactions to loss of an attachment figure through death or divorce find responses much like children's responses to long separations from their attachment figures: a period of numbness, a period of protest, anger, yearning, and irrational searching for the lost figure, a period of disorganization and despair, and, eventually, acceptance and reorganization. There is some evidence that adults with insecure attachments have more difficulty resolving grieving than secure adults do.

Even after new attachments form, attachments to parents tend to persist. Late in life, the roles in the attachment relationship may become reversed; the grown child may become the secure base for the aging parent. There is some evidence that having an attachment figure, whether the individual is a grown child or an elderly confidante, increases physical and emotional well-being in senior citizens.

THEORETICAL SPECULATIONS

For many years, the focus of most research and of most theory development in the field of attachment was on infancy. However, Bowlby's associates did explore two topics related to adults' attachments: responses to loss (bereavement) (e.g., Brown and Harris, 1978; Parkes, 1972) and responses to disruptions of attachments (separation and divorce) (e.g., Weiss, 1975). Recently, other theorists have offered specific propositions about normative aspects of forming and maintaining attachments after childhood and hypotheses about individual differences in adult patterns of attachment.

Some of the ideas presented for consideration here may, when more data are available, turn out to be wildly speculative. Perhaps because everything in the field is so new, the forays of attachment theory into the study of attachment in the adult years make exciting reading. Keep in mind, though, that almost every proposition in this chapter is a hypothesis, not a demonstrated fact.

FUNDAMENTAL PROPOSITIONS

What happens to attachments during adolescence and the early years of adulthood? Old ones linger and new ones form. The principal attachments of childhood remain important, but the youth also begins to look for a new partner who may in time replace the parent as his or her principal attachment figure. In addition, if all goes well, sometime in adolescence or in the early adult years, the new attachment relationships that form will have a quality of reciprocity that the asymmetrical attachments of childhood never had. In infancy and early childhood, one partner in the relationship gave care and the other partner received and depended on that care. In the adult years, two partners in an attachment relationship can give care to each other and serve as secure bases for each other. When necessary, each protects the other. Each is an attachment figure for the other.

According to attachment theory, seeking and maintaining attachment bonds is healthy and normal at every stage of human life; doing so is part of our instinctive nature. For adults, as for infants, attachments are a source of security. What is wanted from the attachment figure is much the same at any age: that the figure be accessible when needed, be responsive to communications, and permit close bodily contact in the role of caregiver, not the role of sexual mate, when the attached individual needs such contact (e.g., when there is a perceived threat to the self, to the attachment figure, or to the relationship).

The goal of the attachment system, even for adults, is, in Ainsworth's and Bowlby's opinion, access to the attachment figure (e.g., Ainsworth, 1990; Bowlby, 1982, 1991). For older children and adults, actual physical contact may not often be necessary; cognitive processes become more central.

What relationships or components of relationships in the adult years should be regarded as attachments? Ainsworth (1982, 1991a) recommends several criteria for judging whether an attachment exists. First, the subject, particularly when under stress, wants to be with the attachment figure. Second, he seeks security and comfort in the relationship. Third, he protests when the attachment figure becomes or threatens to become inaccessible and grieves if the attachment figure is lost and cannot be regained. Research with widows and widowers reveals that the protest syndrome in adults is very similar to the protest syndrome in children (Bowlby, 1980). It includes calling and crying, determined and sometimes frantic searching, persistent attention to memories and reminders of the absent figure, restlessness, and, eventually, despair.

By Ainsworth's criteria, most marriages, many lasting sexual relationships, many nonsexual friendships, and many sibling relationships include attachment components as part of the relationship (Ainsworth, 1991). Even in marriages that are full of conflict, each partner's attachment to the other tends to be very persistent, and the relationship provides a more or less stable base from which each spouse can move into the domains of employment, child rearing, and community involvement. Even when the marriage includes much anxiety and anger, each partner may derive some measure of security from it, just as an anxiously attached child, for example, draws some measure of security from the presence of her rejecting or unresponsive father.

Attachment figures are, by definition, the specific individuals you seek out and want to depend on when you need protection and care. In contrast, friends and acquaintances whom you value as companions in work or play, however much they enrich your life, are not attachment figures. If loss of the individual does not lead to grieving, then probably no attachment existed. If involuntary or prolonged separation from a friend or work associate provokes no sadness, anxiety, or anger (each of which may be open or masked), then probably no attachment existed. Involuntary separation from an attachment figure should intensify activation of the attachment system at any age. Even when the separation is voluntary, if it is long-lasting, the attached adult will surely pine for the other person. Securely attached adults can maintain love and trust through long periods of physical separation that result from joint planning. For example, this often occurs when one spouse on active military duty lives away from his or her family for a year or more. It also occurs when one spouse, needing time to make a place for his or her family in a new country and to earn the money to bring them there, emigrates a year or more ahead of the rest of the family. During such separations, the spouses may long for the time when they can be together again. Letters and phone calls cannot take the place of a warm embrace forever.

As Weiss (1991) pointed out, for adults as for children, the attachment is to a *specific* other. Substitutes are insufficient. Each attachment figure has a unique, irreplaceable importance in the subject's life. When a person loses a principal attachment figure, such as a parent or spouse, he grieves and feels lonely. This occurs even if supportive friends are available. A strong, caring network of friends can help in mitigating the individual's grief, but it cannot fill the hole left by the specific other to whom the subject was deeply attached.

Attachments, according to Weiss (1991), seem to persist in the absence of reinforcement and are immune to habituation. In fact, threats elicit attachment behavior more readily in long-established attachments than in more recently formed attachments. Furthermore, the attachment system is in some respects inaccessible to conscious control. Attachments form and persist even when the attachment figure is neglecting or abusive. Separation protest continues even when it is clear that the attachment figure is inaccessible and that adequate substitutes are available. As a long separation continues, pining abates only slowly and imperfectly. Feelings of attachment and efforts to regain the lost figure persist despite knowledge that no earthly reunion is possible, as when the attachment figure has died. If inaccessibility of the figure is fully accepted, the immediate result is not an end to pining but its incorporation into an outlook of despair. Typically, feelings of despair eventually dissipate as grieving is resolved, and the individual reorganizes his life without the attachment figure, but the longing for reunion persists for some time after the loss of any principal attachment figure.

A few words about terminology are necessary here. Social psychologists have at times written about attachment to a supervisor, work group, company, recreation center, neighborhood, or pet. Except in the case of pets, from whom some individuals do derive a sense of comfort and security (Zasloff and Kidd, 1994), what these researchers study is usually only peripherally related to attachment as defined by Bowlby and Ainsworth.

As noted above, two major changes in attachments often occur in adolescence or early in the adult years. One is the development of reciprocal relationships in which each partner serves as an attachment figure for the other. The second change is the replacement of the parent or parents with someone new as the principal attachment figure. Common observation suggests that the first step toward both changes is, ordinarily, forming an attachment to a peer.

FALLING IN LOVE

Prompted by hormonal changes and social norms, the adolescent moves toward a goal-corrected partnership with an age peer. The new relationship, whether heterosexual or homosexual, will involve the sexual mating system and the caregiving system, as well as the attachment system.

Weiss (1987, 1991), Shaver and Hazan (1987), and Shaver, Hazen, and Bradshaw (1987) have expanded the propositions of attachment theory to the arenas of romance and loneliness. They propose that romantic love is, like the instinctive behaviors that tie a baby to her primary caregiver, a biosocial process by which affectional bonds are formed. The biological function of romantic love is to facilitate the formation of an attachment between adult sexual partners. Ainsworth (1991a) has also argued that, over time, each partner in a sexual relationship is likely to build up an attachment to the other. Whether the sexual involvement springs from mutual romantic attraction or results from a marriage arranged by the parents of the husband and wife, there is a good chance that both partners will develop attachment bonds. My own hypothesis is that the practice of resting and sleeping in close proximity to or in physical contact with the partner may contribute to the formation of an attachment more than sexual interaction does, but I know of no relevant research.

When romantic love instincts were evolving, the partners, if heterosexual, were likely to become parents of at least one baby who would need their care and protection for many years. The baby's chances of survival and good health were surely better if the parents were bonded to each other than if they were not, and attachment bonds endure longer than sexual bonds do. Whether the environment is a rain forest with wild animals, a city slum with widespread drug abuse and street crime, or a middle-class neighborhood with cars, concrete stairs, and an occasional copperhead snake, a baby with two (or more) people to protect and nurture him has advantages over a baby with only one caregiver. In addition, the two parents are likely to provide care and protection for each other. Improving each parent's chances of survival and good health indirectly adds to the baby's protection. Probably adults who developed mutual attachments and served as protectors and/or caregivers for each other were more likely to have their offspring survive to reproductive age than adults who did not develop such attachments. (Note that caregiving includes providing food and shelter, not just emotional care.) Consequently, natural selection may have favored an instinctive tendency for sexual partners to become emotionally, lastingly attached to each other.

Speculation about how evolutionary forces affected our species thousands of years ago must, of course, be seasoned with an appropriate level of scientific skepticism. At present, in this society, thousands of parents refuse to contribute to the care and protection of their children after getting divorced from their spouses. These people provide vivid evidence that, if we do have biologically based tendencies to form lasting bonds with sexual partners and to form enduring caregiving bonds to our offspring, these tendencies can be resisted or disconnected. In most times and places in human history, it has not been necessary for one or both of the biological parents to protect and care for their offspring alone. In many cultures, grandparents and other kin are directly involved in the care and protection of infants and young children. In many cultures, other members of the tribe or religious or political group help provide protection for all the parents and children in the group. The adaptive advantage that probably results from the parents becoming attached to each other should not be exaggerated.

If the hypothesized biologically based tendency to form an enduring affective bond to the sexual partner were irresistibly powerful, no other pressure to sustain marriages would be necessary. Apparently external pressure is necessary: most cultures develop marriage laws and customs that encourage relationships between people who are expected to be coparents to endure. One probable result of cultural pressures that encourage such lifelong commitments is an increase in the probability that the young will be adequately cared for. However, the cultural pressures can be explained without invoking the evolutionary advantage. Encouragement of lasting relationships between coparents and discouragement of childbearing outside such relationships make ownership of property and lines of inheritance clear; the risk of conflict between individuals within the tribe is reduced. Most cultures define marriage as a binding economic contract. Whether marriage is expected also to involve emotional or spiritual bonds varies from culture to culture.

Even if the phenomenon of romantic sexual attraction, which appears in the literature and/or visual art of ancient cultures all over the world, is not sufficient to hold partners together without support or pressure from society, it may certainly be a factor in attachment formation. As Shaver, Hazan, and Bradshaw (1987) pointed out, there are some intriguing similarities between adolescent romantic love and infant-to-caregiver attachment. The adolescent's moods may depend heavily on his perceptions of whether the individual who is the object of his longing is responsive or rejecting, just as a baby's feelings of joy and distress depend on his perceptions of his attachment figure's availability and responsiveness. Adolescent romantic love involves many of the specific behaviors that maintain physical and emotional closeness between an infant and her caregiver: holding, touching, caressing, kissing, smiling, making eye contact, and following. Adolescents separated from their romantic partners act much like infants separated from their attachment figures: they become distressed, they strive vigorously to regain contact with the partner, and they become terribly sad if no reunion occurs.

Viewing human beings as systems of behavioral systems, Shaver and Hazan (1987) have conducted research on love and on loneliness. They propose that

> the initial phase of romantic love is fueled by a mixture of sexual attraction and gratification, reduced feelings of loneliness, uncertainty about the security of the developing attachment, and excitement due to the exploration of the novelty of another human being. With time, sexual attraction wanes, attachment anxieties either fade or lead to conflict and withdrawal, novelty gets replaced by familiarity, and lovers either find themselves securely attached and caring deeply about each other or experiencing some form of distress—boredom, disappointment, loneliness, or hostility—and yearning for a more satisfying relationship. . . . When two lovers get beyond being preoccupied with novelty, unpredictability, and urgent sexual attraction, they more readily detect deficiencies in each other's caregiving behavior. (Shaver and Hazan, 1987, pp. 120–121)

From an evolutionary perspective, this integration of hypotheses suffers from its assumption that the partners are in a culture that condones sexual involvement prior to marriage. As a set of propositions about how instinctive tendencies get played out in many modern American lives, however, it provides a rich framework for research.

Obviously, forming romantic attachments in adolescence and adulthood differs in significant ways from forming attachments in infancy. Romantic partners usually hope and expect to have a bidirectional, reciprocal relationship. In a secure adult attachment, the two partners nurture and protect each other; in infancy, the caregiver does not expect a reciprocal exchange. Furthermore, romantic love usually involves sexual attraction, and attachment theorists definitely do not regard infants' attachments to their caregivers as sexual.

What about individual differences in qualities of new attachments? If attachment theory is accurate, the representational models of attachment that a person has developed from earlier relationships will color that individual's behavior in and experience of new romantic relationships. In choosing a partner, forming a new relationship, and participating in building the quality of the new relationship, an individual whose models are both organized and open to new information obviously has an advantage over an individual whose models are multiple, defended, and/or incoherent. A youth with secure representational models would be most likely to communicate openly and honestly, to interpret the partner's emotional behavior appropriately, to reject unsuitable partners, and to select a partner who is both able and willing to participate in a mutually trusting and trustworthy attachment relationship.

Given that representational models are based on earlier experiences, adolescents with any category of anxious attachment to their parents might be expected to have much more difficulty in their new romantic relationships than peers with secure attachment histories. Theory suggests that a youth whose primary model of attachments represented them as resistant or coercive relationships might feel very dependent upon his romantic partners, might respond to small incidences of unresponsive behavior with inappropriately violent anger, and might manipulate the partner with an unconsciously systematic mixture of seductive and coercive behaviors.

A youth with a defended or dismissing representational model of attachment relationships might have difficulty trusting the partner and difficulty acknowledging both her own and her partner's emotional need for an intimate relationship. Bartholomew (1990) proposed that there may be at least two styles of adult avoidance. In one, there is a conscious desire for social contact competing with fear of the dependency associated with attachment. In the other, there is a straightforward denial of the need and desire for all sorts of social bonds, including attachment bonds. In both cases, adult avoidance of intimacy may have its roots in early experiences in which emotional vulnerability was associated with parental rejection.

The period during which a youth or a young adult forms a new attachment is often a time of dramatic change in the individual's life. At such a time, representational models of self, other, and attachment relationships are more likely to be modified and updated than they are at other times. Experiences in the new relationships of adolescence, whether experimental, transitional, or enduring, may eventually modify the individual's representational models of the self. Initially, however, the representational models developed in childhood guide perceptions and interactions with new partners. It seems likely that a history of anxious or disrupted attachments may interfere with communication, problem solving, sexual relations, and mutual caregiving in the relationships of young adults.

These ideas about how early experiences may shape representational models in ways that affect the quality and stability of the new attachments individuals form in adolescence are among the most speculative of the new ideas presented in this chapter. No research relating infant patterns of attachment to the patterns of the intimate relationships the same individuals form in adolescence has been published.

NONSEXUAL NEW ATTACHMENTS

Peers with whom a youth may form sexual pair-bonds are not the only individuals who may become new attachment figures. Although there is hardly any systematic research on the topic, it seems likely that many older children and adolescents form attachments to one or more parent surrogates (e.g., other relatives, teachers, coaches, youth group leaders, religious leaders, and psychotherapists).

In the absence of systematic research, anecdotal and clinical evidence suggests that some of these other figures can play very important roles in a young person's life. The other's role as an attachment figure may be especially important if it is possible for a young person to find in the new relationship the security she could not find in relationships with her parents. The new relationship can give her a basis for revising dysfunctional representational models.

An attachment to one of these secondary or supplementary figures may persist for many years. Even when an adult has been content with very infrequent letters or phone calls and has not sought physical proximity to a certain psychotherapist, college friend, army buddy, or personally valued basketball coach for some years, he may seek comfort from that person in a time of crisis, and news of that figure's death may initiate mourning.

CONTINUATION OF ATTACHMENTS TO PARENTS

As adolescents experiment with life, most continue to derive support and protection from their childhood attachment figures. Theory suggests that those who are unable to derive support from early attachment figures will often persist in seeking it, nonetheless. The clinical literature shows that many adolescents also behave in ways that punish the attachment figures for failing to provide the support and protection the teenage child still needs.

Teenagers in well-functioning families still use the parents as secure bases from which they can go forth to explore the challenging arenas of educational, occupational, and social demands and opportunities. Periodically, they return to "touch base" with their parents before sallying forth again. The intervals between periods of physical proximity often lengthen over time. Early in adolescence, a youth is likely to touch base at least once or twice a day. Later, he may attend a distant school or take a job far from his parents' home, keep in touch by phone or mail, and seek proximity only two or three times a year. Gradually, interactions with the parent affect fewer and fewer aspects of the individual's daily life. Even after marrying, however, young adults ordinarily stay in touch with childhood attachment figures. In times of crisis, adults often do seek care and protection from childhood attachment figures; it is not uncommon for adults who have lived far from their parents for many years to seek proximity to them in a time of crisis.

Ordinarily, the individual's ability to behave independently and to rely on herself, not her parents, increases gradually throughout childhood and adolescence. By the early years of adulthood, most people achieve a sense of autonomy from their parents. However, their attachments to their parents do not disappear. A secure, competent adult is still likely to experience a deep sense of loss when the parent dies, even if the adult is 50 years old and the parent was 75.

Weiss proposed that one process by which adolescents partially wean themselves from their attachments to their parents is by fighting their tendencies to perceive their parents as stronger and wiser than they are. Many Americans believe that a certain amount of

Attachments to parents remain important in the lives of adolescents and young adults.

rebellion against the parents is a normal aspect of adolescence. The extent of this rebellion has not been studied from an attachment perspective. Elsewhere around the planet, it is easy to find cultures in which most individuals move from childhood dependency on their parents (and other kin) into self-reliant adult roles without any stage of adolescent struggling against the parents or the older, wiser leaders of the tribe.

Hypotheses about how patterns of attachment might affect developmental pathways in adolescence suggest themselves readily. In Western cultures, youths with avoidant attachments to their parents might be very likely to have their repressed anger surface violently in adolescence, resulting in high levels of oppositional behavior, rejection of the parents' beliefs and values, and physical distancing from the parents. For youths with resistant attachment histories, frequent, intense arguments and struggles with the parents might be very likely to erupt. The vacillation between dependent, punitive, and coercive behaviors might be very much exaggerated as these youths react to the new freedoms and new pressures of adolescence. Unlike avoidant youths, this group might be likely to stay enmeshed with the family of origin. Youths with secure attachment histories might be expected to explore their new opportunities with more confidence, more competence, and better judgment than their anxiously attached peers would. It seems likely that they would have less need to criticize or fight with their parents as they navigate into adulthood.

The hypothesized attachment-group differences in developmental pathways may affect not only relationships with parents and with peers, but also personality characteristics. Several theorists (Cassidy and Kobak, 1988; Main et al., 1985) have proposed that, as time passes, avoidant children learn not only to deactivate attachment behavior, but also to exclude potentially distressing information from awareness and processing (so that it can't activate attachment behavior) and then to develop views of relationships that minimize or dismiss the importance of such attachment processes as giving and receiving care. In adolescence and adulthood, such individuals would be likely to show the "compulsive self-reliance" Bowlby (1973) described. In severe cases, they might be much like the juvenile thieves Bowlby (1958) described in his first paper on attachment. Prospective research to test these hypotheses is not yet available.

TRANSMITTING PATTERNS FROM ONE GENERATION TO THE NEXT

According to Bowlby (e.g., 1988) some parents are supportive when called upon but also permit and even encourage autonomy. They tend to communicate fairly openly about their own working models of themselves, their children, and others. They also let their children know that working models can be questioned, revised, and updated. Their children generally become relatively stable, self-reliant individuals. Other parents, still carrying anxiety, anger, confusion, defense mechanisms, and multiple representational models from their early attachments, are frequently unresponsive, intrusive, overly restrictive, or otherwise unsupportive. Their children often become anxious, angry, confused, and/or defended, like their parents. In Bowlby's words (1973, p. 323)

> Patterns of interaction are transmitted, more or less faithfully, from one generation to another. Thus the inheritance of mental health and of mental ill health through the medium of family microculture is certainly no less important, and may well be far more important, than is their inheritance through the medium of genes.

Elaborating on Bowlby's conclusions and hypotheses and drawing from later research on cognitive processes, Inge Bretherton (1987, 1991) proposed that when constructing a preliminary model of the self and the baby as partners in an attachment-caregiving relationship, the caregiver uses (1) a general model of the world, (2) a normative model about babies in general, and (3) models of caregiving behavior derived from experiences in childhood. The preliminary model is then corrected in response to feedback from the specific infant. Most parents do not do this consciously and deliberately, of course. However, sensitive responsiveness to an infant depends upon the caregiver's ability to construct, correct, fine-tune, and update a reasonably accurate representational model of the infant. Without such a model, the caregiver could not take the baby's perspective, recognize the baby's goals, and then serve as an effective secure base.

Bowlby, Ainsworth, Main, and other attachment theorists have written strong hypotheses about the impact of the parent's representational model on the parent's behavior and, consequently, on the child's emerging representational model. In adults whose lives have not been disrupted by assault, loss of a major attachment figure, or other traumatic events or major changes in circumstances, attachment theorists expect representational models to be highly stable. Even so, as noted earlier, attachment theory is not overly deterministic, and the parent's model is certainly not regarded as the only factor that influences the child's emerging model. For some children who develop insecure attachments, the major difficulties may lie in the caregiver's circumstances, not in his or her representational models or personality.

When major changes in experiences do occur, what predictions does attachment theory make about transmitting attachment patterns from one generation to the next? Under some circumstances, the adult's internal models are expected to change. For adults with secure models, for example, sudden loss of a partner might take some time to resolve and could produce inconsistent, insensitive, unresponsive behavior in the interim. For adults with dismissing, preoccupied, or unresolved models, on the other hand, psychotherapy or the slower processes of psychological growth in the context of supportive relationships might improve access to and integration of information relevant to attachment, and thus produce sensitively responsive care. Grossmann and Grossmann (1991, p. 110) reported that their interviews with adults offered insights into what helps change an insecure model into a secure one: "psychotherapy, illness, supportive spouses, and emotionally significant others seem to be important." (Because a serious illness makes even an avoidant adult clearly dependent on someone's care, it may sometimes help the individual to discover that loving care is reliably available.)

A hypothetical case study may illustrate how later events can alter the likelihood that an individual who, as a child, enjoyed secure attachments will, as an adult, foster a secure attachment in her baby. Consider Diana. In childhood, she received good care and was securely attached to her mother and to her father. When she was 11, her parents died suddenly in an automobile accident. Afterwards, she went to live with her uncle. He was an overworked, underpaid single parent who liked playing soccer with his sons and Diana. He had always wanted to have a daughter, but he did not know how to act when children got emotional. Diana, who was grieving for her dead parents and adjusting to a new set of rules and habits in a new family in a new neighborhood, often got emotional. Resentful about the attention their busy father gave to her, Diana's two cousins were often mean to her, and there was no other age-peer for her to play with or talk to nearby. Diana missed her parents dreadfully.

When she was 17, Diana fell in love and got married. The honeymoon phase of her marriage lasted for almost a year, but then she and her husband began to quarrel a lot, and his outbursts of temper were at times abusive. He had always been flirtatious with all the women around him, and Diana began to suspect that he was having an affair with one of the sales associates in the department store where he worked. She and her husband began talking about divorce. In the midst of this uncertainty about the quality of her marriage, an unplanned pregnancy began. Neither Diana nor her husband felt ready to have a baby, but they thought arranging an abortion would be wrong, so they decided to stay married and have the baby.

What quality of care will Diana give the child? Her current model of attachment relationships may be disorganized and anxious. Her first two attachment figures died when she was still a child. The only attachment figure available for the next several years had wanted to take good care of her but had had very little time and had not been very understanding. Her new attachment to her husband had become very anxious. The fact that, long ago, she received good care from her mother may or may not be enough to enable her to give good care to her baby.

OLD AGE

Aging eventually brings a number of unwelcome developmental changes. Physical strength, endurance, and sensory abilities decline. Memory and other cognitive abilities may also decline, and health problems often increase. Retirement from employment may bring a welcome sense of freedom, but it can also decrease a person's sense of mastery, control, and status. In general, aging eventually increases the individual's vulnerability and decreases his ability to rely on his own capabilities. The need for care and protection from others increases. The first attachment figures, the parents, are usually dead. Old friends and one or more spouses may also be unavailable because of death or divorce.

To whom do elderly people direct their attachment behavior? Probably a grown child is often selected as an attachment figure; the power and the responsibility in the parent-child relationship shift. The tradition of adults caring for their aging parents is strong in many cultures. In childhood, attachments are ordinarily asymmetrical: the child seeks care and protection, and the adult provides it. There is widespread agreement that reversing these roles is unhealthy when the child is young. If the parent seeks care, support, and security from the child, she places an inappropriate burden on him. When the child becomes an adult, however, the attachment may gradually become symmetrical and reciprocal. When the parent's physical abilities deteriorate because of illness or old age, the roles may be completely reversed.

Attachment theory suggests some likely hypotheses about individual differences in reactions to aging. For example, we might expect senior citizens with secure attachment models to maintain health and happiness longer on the average than people with anxious attachment models do. If, like securely attached children, they usually have more self-confidence, more ego-resilience, and more social competence than peers with anxious attachment models have, we can expect them to need less care and to elicit care more easily than others. We might even expect them to accept death more gracefully when it does come. Senior citizens with feisty, angry attachment models might be expected to keep fighting, using dependent, manipulative, and coercive behavior to get others to care for them. Elderly people with passive-resistant models (analogous to subgroup C2 in infancy) might be likely to give up and get settled into nursing homes relatively early. Senior citizens with avoidant or defended attachment models might be likely to behave in compulsively self-reliant ways, denying themselves access to supportive figures and services that are available. The changes associated with aging might reactivate old anxieties in people who suffered disruptions such as long separations or actual losses early in life. As in the case of adolescence, almost no research has addressed most of these hypotheses.

CHAPTER SUMMARY

This has been a highly speculative chapter. Most elaborations of what attachment theory has to say about normative trends and individual differences in adolescence, adulthood, and old age have come very recently. Hardly any have been well tested in systematic research.

Some intriguing hypotheses about adolescence are now available. For example, it has been proposed that the process of falling in love is, like the process of forming an attachment in infancy, a biologically based social propensity that serves an adaptive function. As the years pass, a new attachment figure may replace the parent or parents as the principal attachment figure. Attachments to parents are likely to persist, but they become less central to the individual's life.

For mentally healthy adolescents and adults, new attachments are likely to be reciprocal, not asymmetrical; the two partners in the relationship give care and protection to each other. According to theory, at every age, individuals with secure representational models of attachments are likely to have more harmonious and more satisfying close relationships than individuals with anxious models are. Specific sorts of difficulties both with parents and with peers may be associated with specific categories of anxious attachment. Teenagers with resistant or coercive models may be likely to have turbulent, enmeshed relationships with their parents and intense, dependent, coercive relationships with new love partners. Teenagers with avoidant or defended models may just distance themselves from their parents and have difficulty forming close bonds to peers. Some of them may experience surges of long-buried hostility toward their parents. Much later in life, as senior citizens cope with the changes age brings, how easily they elicit or accept care from others may reflect their representational models of attachments.

This chapter says little about the longest segment of life, the period between adolescence and old age. Ideas from attachment theory about interactions within marriages, quality of parenting, loneliness, bereavement, and divorce will be discussed, along with relevant data, in Chapter 18.

C H A P T E R

ASSESSING
ADULT ATTACHMENTS

The behavioral clues we can use to infer the pattern or degree of security in a child's attachment are harder to interpret than the clues babies provide. The clues we can use to make inferences about adults' attachments are even more complicated and subtle. What we want to know about is the quality of the enduring emotional bond to a specific individual. However, the affective and cognitive components are not directly observable; they must be inferred. What we *can* observe is behavior, including, in children and adults, speech. What a person says about what he thinks, feels, wants, or intends seems likely to be particularly informative.

Because we must infer the representational organization of the attachment from observable behavior and speech, an adult who wishes to camouflage aspects of her attachments can probably make the clues very hard to read. If defensive processes are well-established, the individual may be unable to report accurately about the qualities of her attachments. How then can we assess patterns of attachments in adults?

THE ADULT ATTACHMENT INTERVIEW (AAI)

The first method developed specifically for assessing adults' attachments was the Adult Attachment Interview (AAI), a structured, 15-question, semiclinical interview that focuses mainly on the subject's early attachment experiences and current thoughts about them (George, Kaplan, and Main, 1985; Main and Goldwyn, 1985).

When using the AAI, a trained interviewer begins by asking the subject to choose five adjectives to describe what the relationship with each parent was like during childhood. She makes no particular effort to put the subject at ease first; the intent is partly to "surprise the unconscious" (Main, 1991, p. 141), to slip past possible defense mechanisms. She then asks the subject for episodic memories that illustrate why each of the adjectives is appropriate. Sometimes the specific memories illustrate the general description well, sometimes they contradict it, and sometimes the subject cannot recall any. Later, the interviewer asks what the subject did in childhood when he was upset, whether he ever felt rejected or threatened by his parents, and, if so, why he now thinks his parents behaved that way. She asks whether the parents ever threatened separation. There are also questions about whether the relationships with the parents have changed since childhood, how the subject feels about his parents now, and how the experiences he has described have influenced his adult personality and functioning. The interviewer memorizes all the questions and follow-up probes in advance so that the interview can flow smoothly.

The coding system relies solely on what the subject says, not on what he does. Even his nonverbal behavior and voice inflections during the interview go uncoded; the coder works with a printed transcript of the interview. Over the years, Main and her colleagues have periodically elaborated and revised the guidelines for coding. Learning to apply them takes considerable time and training.

The coder's task is to assign a single classification for the subject's overall "state of mind with respect to attachment," even when the subject reports different sorts of experiences with different attachment figures (Main, 1991, p. 141). What is being classified is sometimes referred to as the subject's "attitude toward attachment."

In analyzing the interview, the coder examines contradictions and inconsistencies carefully. She rates the interview on a 9-point scale for security with respect to experiences, ideas, and feelings surrounding attachment. Security is defined largely by coherence. The focus is on the adult's representational models of attachments, especially the ability to integrate both factual and affective information from both episodic (specific) and semantic (general) memory. The overall coherence of the subject's presentation of his attachment history is rated on a 9-point scale. Top scores for coherence go to subjects who focus easily on the questions, show few departures from usual forms of narrative or discourse, easily explain what lies behind their responses, and appear to the coders to be truthful. A variety of sorts of incoherence are possible: anomalous changes in wording, intrusions into the topic, slips of the tongue, use of metaphors or rhetoric that is inappropriate to the context of the discourse, inability to focus on the interview questions, and outright self-contradiction. Often, coders who read an incoherent transcript cannot agree with the subject's description of his history and/or with his description of his present attitudes and evaluations. In such a case, the impression is that, in an interview that takes about an hour, the subject seemed to intend to present a single model of his history and attitudes but in fact gave evidence from multiple, incompatible representational models. The subject appeared to have difficulty accessing information related to attachment, keeping the information organized, and/or preventing it from undergoing distortion.

■ Classification of Responses to the AAI

There are four categories for classifying adults' states of mind with respect to attachment, as indicated through their responses to the AAI: secure, dismissing, preoccupied, and unresolved. The optimal pattern has been labeled at different times by different investigators as "secure," "autonomous," or "balanced." Various researchers have at times substituted the terms "detached" or "avoidant" for "dismissing" and "enmeshed," "ambivalent," or "resistant" for "preoccupied."

Adults characterized as secure find it easy to recall and discuss their attachment experiences. Their discussions of their attachment histories and how their early experiences have influenced them are strikingly coherent. These adults value attachment relationships and recognize their importance: they tend to believe attachments and the experiences related to them influence an individual's personality. Secure adults can be objective in describing any particular relationship. They can easily integrate positive with negative aspects of expression and feeling. They tolerate flaws in themselves and others, do not idealize their parents, and generally are able to forgive them for any mistreatment that did occur. Just as securely attached babies keep the attachment system and the exploratory system in an easy balance, secure adults can balance the adult need for an attachment figure with independent interests and activities.

Many subjects who are rated as secure recall favorable childhood experiences, but some report unfavorable experiences, particularly loss or rejection. Those who have had unfavorable experiences appear to have thought about them, perhaps understood the reasons for them, and resolved their feelings about them.

Individuals classified as dismissing report that attachment relationships are of little concern, value, or influence: they dismiss the importance of attachment relationships. Most show one or both of two striking patterns. In one pattern, the subjects report semantic and episodic memories about their parents that contradict each other. They may say their parents were wonderful, almost perfect, but describe specific experiences of rejection or great loneliness. The second pattern is characterized by insistence that they simply cannot remember anything from childhood; the defensive exclusion of attachment history information is extreme. The subjects may say their parents were wonderful, but they are unable to offer any supportive evidence. A few "dismissing" adults do recall their negative childhood experiences. Instead of idealizing their parents, these adults derogate and dismiss them, which may be an equally effective way to keep attachment-relevant memories and wishes at a distance.

The adults characterized as preoccupied appear to be still embroiled with the family of origin, still emotionally dependent on the parents, and still struggling to please them. They can tell many stories of events from their childhoods, but cannot provide organized, coherent descriptions of their early relationships. They often give very long interview responses with unexplained oscillations of viewpoint. They also give a lot of tangential or irrelevant information and occasionally just lose track of the interview question. They often fail to use past tense markers in quoting conversations with their parents. Incoherence permeates their use of language. They often use entangled, confusing, run-on sentences. They often leave sentences unfinished. They often insert many general terms ("that sort of thing," "and this and that") and use nonsense words as sentence endings ("dada-dada-dada").

The fourth category for classifying AAI responses is "unresolved." In research to date, many of the adults so classified have experienced losses, abuse, or other traumatic events (Ainsworth and Eichberg, 1991). They appear to be confused about the loss or trauma, or disoriented and incoherent in describing it or its effects. They oscillate repeatedly between positive and negative viewpoints, give irrational answers, or are unable or unwilling to stay with the topic of the interview or the most recent question.

Some secure, autonomous adults also report histories of rejection, traumatic experiences, and/or loss of an attachment figure. The difference is that the secure adults have resolved their grieving. They can remember information from childhood that is relevant to attachment, and they can organize it coherently. In the adults who have unresolved attitudes toward attachment, it appears that no resolution of grieving has been reached, and the adult remains unable to organize information about attachment coherently.

When responses to the AAI fall into the unresolved category, researchers often specify what the underlying primary attitude or state of mind regarding attachment seems to be: secure, dismissing, or preoccupied. In some studies, researchers have chosen not to use the unresolved category and have forced classifications into one of the other three categories. How much this compromises or enhances the power of a study is not yet clear.

■ AAI and Strange Situation Patterns and Scores

As a first step in validating the AAI, Main et al. (1985) looked for associations between the parent's AAI responses and the child's Strange Situation classification. Why? Following Bowlby's lead, they reasoned that the parent's representational model greatly influences his or her willingness and ability to perceive, interpret, and respond to the baby's signals. The parent's sensitive responsiveness certainly influences the child's attachment pattern. Therefore, the parent's security or attachment pattern should be a good predictor of the infant's security or pattern.

Because other factors also influence an infant's attachment pattern, we should not expect a perfect match between the parent's state of mind with respect to attachment and the infant's attachment pattern. For example, even an adult with secure, open, working representational models of attachments might, in stressful circumstances, lack the time or energy for responding sensitively to a baby's signals. In stable families in safe neighborhoods and in comfortable economic circumstances, however, theory does lead us to expect a high degree of concordance between the parent's representational model and the infant's attachment pattern. It was in such stable, comfortable circumstances that the hypothesis was first tested.

When the children in the Berkeley sample were near their sixth birthdays, they returned to the laboratory with both parents. While the child underwent the series of assessments described in Chapter 14, each parent, in a room apart from the other parent, was asked the questions from the AAI (Main et al., 1985).

From responses to the AAI, each parent's attachment security was rated on a 9-point scale. To create a quasi-interval scale for security in infants, scores were assigned to the Strange Situation patterns. Even though this was only a crude scale for infant security, Main et al. found a high correlation between the mother's AAI security score (when the child was 6) and the security of the baby's attachment to the mother at the age of 12 months ($r = .62$). The correlation between the father's AAI security score and the security of the infant's attachment to the father at age 18 months was also significant, but not as high ($r = .37$).

A correlation does not, of course, prove a causal relationship. In this case, interpreting the correlation as evidence that the parent's model contributed to determining the baby's attachment pattern requires an extra assumption. The AAI was administered $4\frac{1}{2}$ to 5 years *after* the Strange Situation assessment. To argue that the model revealed in the AAI was the one that led the parent to behave in ways that led the baby to form the pattern of attachment observed in the Strange Situation, researchers had to assume that the adult's representational model had been, in most subjects, highly stable over the 5 years between the two assessments. Families that had suffered a death, a divorce, or another disruption of an attachment had been excluded from the follow-up sample. Consequently, the assumption of stability was reasonable. If the parents' internal models were stable over time, then the observed correlation between the parent's model and the infant's attachment pattern may have been a true reflection of the parent's influence on the child, despite the inversion of times of assessment.

As noted in Chapter 15, the children in this sample showed high stability from infancy to age 6 in their attachment patterns. In addition, both the AAI and the reunion assessment of the child's attachment pattern occurred during the same laboratory visit when the child was 6. Consequently, we should expect a strong association between the mother's security score and the 6-year-old child's security score. The reported correlation, $r = .45$, was indeed significant (Main et al., 1985). The analogous correlation for fathers was not reported.

Another way to use the AAI and Strange Situation data to test whether the parent's model affected her interaction with the infant in ways that affected the baby's attachment pattern is to look for matches in *patterns*, not in security scores. Attachment theory predicts that specific types of insecure organizations of attachment-relevant memories, perceptions, affects, and cognitions in the parent should lead to specific types of insensitivities in the parent's responses to his or her infant. The parent-child pairings that, on theoretical grounds, represent matches are secure-secure, dismissing-avoidant, preoccupied-resistant, and unresolved-disorganized.

In Berkeley, Main et al. (1985) reported that the mother's working model very often did match the infant's pattern of attachment. Mothers with secure models generally had babies with secure attachments; mothers with dismissing models generally had babies with avoidant attachments; and mothers with unresolved models generally had babies with anxious-disorganized attachments. Only one child in the follow-up sample had been classified in group C in infancy, so no comment about the association between a "preoccupied" classification for the parent and resistant attachment in the infant was appropriate. Unfortunately, Main et al. (1985) did not report specific rates of concordance.

In Regensburg, Grossmann and Grossmann (e.g., 1991) and their associates made the same assumption about stability over time in parents' working models of attachment relationships. They used the AAI with the parents when the children in their sample were 5 years old.

A question about the cross-cultural validity of the Main and Goldwyn (1985) system for coding responses to the AAI arose. The German research team found that they could not easily transfer the American rating and classification system to their German interviews. The interview questions elicited meaningful responses, but the existing coding system was hard to apply to this sample. Members of the research team therefore created other methods of analysis. The simplest method yielded just two categories: "valuing" or "devaluing" of attachment. With 20 infant-mother dyads, Fremmer-Bombik (cited in Main, 1990) found an 85 percent match between the parent's classification and the child's. "Valuing" went with secure, of course, and "devaluing" went with insecure (avoidant in almost all cases in this small sample).

Working with data from 89 of the Regensburg mother-infant dyads, the German research team also developed a more complex system for analyzing responses to the AAI (Grossmann and Grossmann, 1991). Although they did not follow Main's coding instructions exactly, they focused on highly similar variables. The four parameters they used were (1) the presentation of each parent or other attachment figure as supportive or unsupportive, (2) the ability to focus on the topic of attachment, (3) reflections on the interviewee's own attachment experiences, and (4) defensiveness against discussing the current emotional relationship with the interviewee's parents. Scores on the four parameters led the coders to classify the pattern revealed by the AAI as "positive," "reflexive," "defensive," or "repressive." The first two patterns were strongly associated with having a baby who, 4 or 5 years before the AAI, had been classified as securely attached; the latter two patterns were strongly associated with anxious attachment in the infant. The concordance rate was 78 percent for the sample.

The work in Germany most clearly replicated the Berkeley results in the association between infant avoidance and maternal repression of attachment-relevant information and affect. In Regensburg, as in Berkeley, AAI interview transcripts very often revealed that mothers of avoidant infants idealized their parents, intellectualized, gave inconsistent descriptions of the quality of care they received, and/or insisted that they could not recall anything from their childhoods. In contrast, German mothers who had securely organized representations of attachments talked openly and in detail about their own attachment figures. As in the Berkeley sample, some of them did report having had problematic or unsupportive parents, but they were nevertheless, as adults, open when discussing topics related to attachment. Will the same interview evidence of secure and dismissing representational models in adults be found in non-Western cultures? Relevant data are not yet available.

In the third study to use the AAI with mothers and the Strange Situation with their babies, the two assessments were conducted around the same time; there was no gap of 4 or 5 years. This time, there was no need to make the reasonable but unproven assumption of stability in the parent's representational model. Working with a Charlottesville sample, Eichberg (1987, cited in Main, 1990) found 82 percent concordance between the mother's attachment category and the baby's attachment category (secure-secure, dismissing-avoidant, preoccupied-resistant, or unresolved-disorganized).

In New York City, Levine, Tuber, Slade, and Ward (1991) also found that the mother's AAI classification was a very good predictor of her baby's Strange Situation classification. The association was particularly impressive because the AAI was given during pregnancy and the Strange Situation assessment occurred when the baby was 15 months old. In this study, most of the mothers were younger than any who had previously been given the AAI; the average age at delivery was 16 years. In addition, this study extended use of the AAI to a sample composed largely of people of color: 76 percent of the 42 mothers were African-American, 12 percent were Hispanic, 5 percent were white, and 7 percent were of mixed ethnic origin. For reasons not yet clear, secure attitudes toward attachment were uncommon in this sample of pregnant adolescents: the distribution of AAI categories was 21 percent secure, 48 percent dismissing, 7 percent preoccupied, and 24 percent unresolved. The distribution of Strange Situation classifications was 38 percent secure, 36 percent avoidant, 7 percent resistant, and 19 percent disorganized. There was an exact match between the mother's category and the baby's category in 26 of 42 cases (62 percent).

Grouping all the nonsecure AAI categories together and all the insecure Strange Situation categories together, the researchers found that the mother's category matched the baby's in 35 of the 42 cases (83 percent). All of the young mothers who had secure attitudes toward attachment had babies who developed secure attachments.

In short, four different studies in four different places with four different research teams have found the same predicted result, a strong association between the mother's representational model of attachments and the security or specific pattern of her infant's attachment to her. The fact that the German team used a different system for classifying responses to the AAI is cause for some concern about the validity of the assessment method. Even so, this set of studies does support inferences that (1) the interview itself yields meaningful information about the adult's working model, (2) this information can be systematically evaluated and coded, and (3) the parent's working model is a good predictor of the infant's pattern of attachment. As a first step in validating the AAI for assessing adults' working models of attachments, the results of these first four studies were impressive.

An especially interesting test of predictions from attachment theory becomes possible when a parent who had an insecure or even traumatic childhood is, when assessed as an adult, classified as secure. These parents are coherent in describing, discussing, and evaluating the effects of their painful childhood experiences. If it is childhood experiences that most affect how a parent responds to his or her infant, then the children of these parents should be insecurely attached. If, however, it is the parent's *current* representational model that most affects how he or she responds to the child, then the children of these parents should be securely attached. The number of parent-child dyads available to test these competing predictions is small, and specific statistical analyses have not been attempted. Nevertheless, the preliminary, tentative reports (from Berkeley, Regensburg, and Charlottesville) support the view that the parent's current representational models affect the child more than the parent's early history does.

■ The AAI and Responses to the Infant or Child

The reason the parent's working model of attachments is expected to influence the infant's pattern of attachment is that the parent's model is expected to affect her responses to the infant. If the AAI-based classification of the parent's working model actually predicts how she behaves in response to her infant, that is further evidence that the AAI is a valid assessment method.

In the Regensburg sample, as predicted, the mother's AAI classification when the child was 5 years old did correspond to her sensitive responsiveness during home observations recorded in the child's first year. That is, this sample yielded direct evidence of an association between the mother's working model and the observable behavior that is the mediating variable in the hypothesized chain from the parent's model to the child's attachment pattern (Grossmann and Grossmann, 1990).

Using the AAI in a low-risk sample in the United States, Haft and Slade (1989) also found associations between the mother's representational model and her behavior toward her child. Mothers with secure representational models attuned themselves to their babies' affects, both positive and negative, and responded appropriately to both. Preoccupied mothers tuned in at random moments, both to positive and to negative affective expressions, but failed to attune to the baby's initiatives during play. Dismissing mothers tuned in well to expressions of mastery, autonomy, and separateness but failed to respond or gave misattuned responses to the baby's bids for comfort and reassurance. Unfortunately, the "unresolved" category was not used in this study. The specific, rule-governed dysfunctions that lead to classification into one of the other two insecure AAI categories were associated with behavioral evidence of specific dysfunctional internal rules about when to give attention to the baby and how to respond to the baby's signals. This supports the view that the AAI has validity.

In a study of preschoolers, Crowell and Feldman (1988) also found evidence that the mother's representational model of attachments influences her responses to the child. Of the 64 children in this sample, 20 had behavior problems and were developmentally delayed, 20 had behavior problems but were not developmentally delayed, and 24 were from a matched, nonclinical group. Each mother-child dyad was videotaped through a one-way mirror during 45 to 60 minutes in a laboratory playroom. The dyad began with 10 minutes of free play, then had a 5-minute clean-up period, and then worked together at their own pace on four tasks that were increasingly difficult and were selected according to the individual child's abilities. The child could not complete the third and fourth tasks without assistance from the mother. Then there was a 2-minute separation, and then a reunion. A week later, 73 percent of the clinical group mothers and 92 percent of the comparison group mothers were interviewed using the AAI. Their internal models of attachment relationships were classified as dismissing, preoccupied, or secure. The "unresolved" category was not used. The methodology of the research was further flawed by the fact that the coder who classified AAI responses knew which mothers had children in one of the clinical groups and which mothers had children in the comparison group.

The mother's internal model did predict her behavior in the laboratory session, and the child's behavior was correlated with the mother's. Even when analysis of covariance statistically controlled for the immediate influence of the mother's behavior on the child's, the child's behavior in the observation session and the child's developmental and behavioral status still corresponded to the mother's internal model.

The secure mothers were supportive and gave clear, helpful assistance. Their children were affectionate. The dismissing mothers often seemed controlling, cool, and remote. They focused on getting the task done, not on fostering learning. Their children were cool toward their mothers, but not overtly angry. The preoccupied mothers were not supportive and had difficulty giving directions and suggestions to their children. They gave instructions in ways that left their children confused and sometimes overwhelmed. They were sometimes warm and gentle, but sometimes angry, coercive, or puzzled. Their children were noncompliant, angry, and controlling.

The associations between the mother's AAI classification and the observed behaviors in the dyad were largely unchanged when the effect of the child's problem group (behavior problems plus developmental delays, just behavior problems, or comparison group) was statistically removed. When researchers examined only the children in the comparison group, the same associations between the mother's model and the dyad's behaviors held up. These two bits of evidence suggest that the obvious methodological flaws may not have biased the results much.

■ The AAI and Personality

To people who are not steeped in attachment theory, validating the AAI through its connections to Strange Situation classifications or even through its connections to observed patterns of interaction with the infant or child may seem a roundabout route. Another logical approach to validating the AAI would be to make some theory-based predictions about how classifications of responses to the AAI should be related to other measures of aspects of the adult's current personality functioning and relationships. Results from the first study to attempt this were encouraging. Kobak and Sceery (1988) used the AAI to classify 53 college students' internal models of attachment relationships as secure, preoccupied with attachment issues, or dismissing of the importance of attachments. (As in the Haft and Slade (1989) research, the "unresolved" category was not used.) Several months later, both the subjects themselves and peers who knew them rated the secure group as more ego-resilient, less anxious, and less hostile than the others. On questionnaires, the secure group reported high levels of social support and little distress. That is, by their own and by their peers' reports, the subjects classified as secure on the AAI in the fall were doing well in the spring. They were finding the social support they needed and managing the challenges of a first year in college well.

Peers rated the dismissing group as low on ego-resilience and high on hostility. The dismissing subjects themselves reported more loneliness than other groups and reported low levels of social support from their families. The preoccupied subjects reported high levels of personal distress but viewed their families as more supportive than the families of the dismissing group. Peers described the preoccupied subjects as less ego-resilient and more anxious than other subjects. The results from all three groups matched predictions from attachment theory.

■ Reliability and Discriminant Validity of the AAI

To establish the usefulness of a new assessment procedure, researchers must demonstrate that it is reliable and valid. Bakermans-Kranenburg and Van IJzendoorn (1993) took several steps in that direction. In the Netherlands, 83 white, middle-class mothers from intact families were given the interview once as part of a larger study of mother-child relationships and a second time, by another of the five trained interviewers, two months later. To explain the second administration of the AAI, the second interviewer told the subject that the interview was a new instrument, analogous to a thermometer, and that it had to be applied more than once to test its quality. The subjects accepted the explanation readily.

When AAI classifications were forced into one of the three "main" categories (secure, dismissing, or preoccupied), 65 of the 83 subjects (78 percent) received the same classification at each interview. This is a very respectable level of reliability over time and across interviewers. When the unresolved category was included as an option, test-retest reliability was not as high: only 50 subjects (61 percent) received the same classification both times. A variety of approaches to testing whether one or more of the five interviewers influenced (1) AAI classifications or (2) the likelihood of a change in classifications over time yielded no evidence of such influence.

Bakermans-Kranenburg and Van IJzendoorn (1993) also evaluated the possibilities that AAI classifications might reflect general autobiographical memory abilities (not just *attachment-related* autobiographical memories), intelligence, vocabulary, logical reasoning ability, and/or the tendency to give socially desirable responses. They found no associations between measures of those variables and AAI classifications; this is consistent with the view that the AAI measures something specifically about attachment. Unresolved subjects did report lower levels of education, which raises the unwelcome possibility that increased education may decrease the degree of incoherency in a subject's discussions of loss. The average age of secure subjects in this sample was somewhat higher than the average age of other subjects, but this poses no challenge to the hypothesis that the AAI accurately measures a person's attitude toward attachment. Older subjects have had more life experience and have probably had more time to evaluate their attachment histories objectively.

■ Physiological Evidence of the Impact of the AAI

Dozier and Kobak (1992) argued that adults in the dismissing category use *deactivating* strategies: they often show restricted recall of early attachment-related experiences, and they understate the importance of those experiences. If these codable response tendencies reflect a strategy that requires diverting attention away from attachment issues, then dismissing subjects should experience conflict or inhibition during the AAI, which repeatedly calls their attention to attachment experiences and concerns. Prior research had demonstrated that inhibiting reactions to emotionally charged stimuli produces increases in skin conductance levels. Dozier and Kobak therefore predicted that subjects who used deactivating strategies would show marked increases in skin conductance levels when asked about experiences of separation, rejection, and threats from their parents. In a sample of 50 college students, they did indeed find that increases in skin conductance were associated specifically with a deactivating strategy, not with insecure attachment in general. This psychophysiological evidence supports the view that the AAI captures meaningful differences among states of mind with respect to attachment.

SECTION SUMMARY

We now have several sorts of preliminary evidence that the AAI has validity. First, the mother's AAI security score or pattern classification shows a strong relation to her baby's. Second, the mother's AAI classification predicts her sensitivity to her infant or child. Third, in college students, the AAI classification is associated with personality characteristics in ways theory predicts. Fourth, the AAI appears to be fairly reliable over time and across interviewers. Fifth, it appears to measure something that is specifically about attachment, not about memory, intelligence, or social desirability. Sixth, psychophysiological evidence supports the view that the AAI distinguishes between types of insecure strategies regarding attachment.

Despite this variety of supportive evidence, it is too soon to say with confidence that the validity of the AAI is established. All the types of evidence should be replicated. Interpreting some of the research described above as validation studies is problematical. A few studies did not use the "unresolved" category. Does forcing AAI classifications into one of the three "main" categories make it easier to see associations with other variables, or does it muddy the picture? With the data available so far, we have no way of knowing. A second problem is that the coding system used in the United States was not successfully transported to Germany. Further refinement or even modification of the coding system seems necessary. The decision to have coders work from transcripts, without observing the subject's tone of voice and nonverbal behavior, seems odd. Tone of voice, facial expressions, and body language might reveal much about the secure or incompletely repressed affects associated with descriptions of attachment-relevant beliefs and memories.

Some logical approaches to validating the AAI have not yet been attempted. As noted earlier, attachment theory predicts that personality problems, difficulties in relationships, and actual psychopathology should be more common in adults with insecure representational models of attachments than in secure adults. Specific sorts of difficulties should be associated with the specific types of insecure models. Kobak and Sceery (1988) found some such evidence. Use of well-validated clinical assessment methods along with the AAI should prove informative.

While the AAI is a very promising method for assessing adult attachments, it has some disadvantages. Conducting, transcribing, and scoring the interviews are time-consuming tasks that must be done by well-trained people. In addition, successful use of the method may depend on having subjects who have not been educated about attachment. After reading this chapter, for example, a person might be unable or unwilling to provide valid responses to the AAI. If an equally valid but simpler means of assessment were available, that would delight many researchers. The next method offered for assessing adult attachment patterns was indeed at the opposite extreme on the scale that goes from clinical complexity to objective simplicity.

SELF-CLASSIFICATION

To test their hypotheses about love, romance, and loneliness, Hazan and Shaver (1987) developed a magnificently simple, direct means of assessing adolescents' and adults' attachment patterns: they asked. More specifically, based on attachment theory and the three best-known patterns of attachment in infancy, they wrote three very brief paragraphs, one for each of the three familiar patterns. Then, embedded in a series of other questionnaire items, came the question "Which of the following best describes your feelings?" The three available answers were as follows (Hazan and Shaver, 1987, p. 515):

1. I find it relatively easy to get close to others and am comfortable depending on them and having them depend on me. I don't often worry about being abandoned or about someone getting too close to me.
2. I am somewhat uncomfortable being close to others; I find it difficult to trust them completely, difficult to allow myself to depend on them. I am nervous when anyone gets too close, and often, love partners want me to be more intimate than I feel comfortable being.
3. I find that others are reluctant to get as close as I would like. I often worry that my partner doesn't really love me or won't want to stay with me. I want to merge completely with another person, and this desire sometimes scares people away.

Obviously, answer 1 represents security, answer 2 reflects avoidance, and answer 3 reflects the overt dependency and fear that characterize anxious-resistant attachments. No adult equivalent of anxious-disorganized-disoriented attachment was offered.

Later, Simpson (1990) decomposed Hazan and Shaver's (1987) three descriptions of attachment styles into 13 individual Likert scales ranging from 1 for "strongly disagree" to 7 for "strongly agree." For example, there was a scale for trusting others easily, a scale for wanting to merge completely, a scale for feeling nervous when anyone gets too close, and so on. Working with a similar notion, Collins and Read (1990) translated components of Hazan and Shaver's three descriptions into 18 Likert scales. Both transformations of the trichotomous measure made it possible for a subject to report that one feature of a type characterized him without necessarily reporting agreement with other features of the same type. Preliminary uses of either the set of 13 scales (Simpson, 1990; Simpson, Rholes, and Nelligan, 1992) or the set of 18 scales (Collins and Read, 1990) produced results very similar to those of the single-item measure. Investigators who prefer the psychometric properties of a set of scales to the properties of a one-item trichotomous classification system now have the option available.

Preliminary validation of both self-report methods has rested on patterns of associations with responses to other questionnaire items. The associations have been numerous and meaningful. Details about them are in the next chapter.

Both the AAI and the self-classification measures are designed to assess an adult's overall style or attitude about attachment issues, some generalized representational model. Consequently, the results of the two approaches to classifying an adult's pattern should usually match each other. For example, if many adults who classify themselves as secure are classified as Avoidant or Resistant on the AAI, then at least one of the measures is not doing a good job of measuring what it is intended to measure. No test of concordance between the two measures has been published yet.

BARTHOLOMEW'S ATTACHMENT INTERVIEW

In work that was clearly influenced by the thinking associated with the AAI, Bartholomew (1990) proposed a different model for describing attachment patterns. Specifically, she argued that two largely independent dimensions—the image of the self (positive or negative) and the image of others (positive or negative)—underlie four attachment styles: secure (positive image of self and others), preoccupied (negative image of self, positive image of others), dismissing (positive image of self, negative image of others), and fearful (negative images of self and others). The prototypically *secure* individual values intimate friendships, is able to maintain close relationships without losing personal autonomy, and can discuss relationships coherently and thoughtfully. The prototypically *preoccupied* individual is overinvolved in close relationships, is dependent on others' acceptance for a sense of personal well-being, tends to idealize other people, and discusses relationships incoherently and with exaggerated emotionality. The prototypically *dismissing* individual downplays the importance of close relationships, restricts emotionality, emphasizes independence and self-reliance, and discusses relationships in a way that lacks clarity or credibility. The prototypically *fearful* individual avoids close relationships because of a fear of rejection, a sense of personal insecurity, and a distrust of others. Bartholomew interpreted the dismissing and fearful categories as two different styles of avoidance.

Bartholomew (1990) developed an interview and a system that rates the degree to which an individual expresses secure, dismissing, preoccupied, and fearful characteristics on continuous scale measures of those dimensions. The system also permits classifying attachment styles into the four categories. Bartholomew and Horowitz (1991) found that each style was associated with a distinct profile of interpersonal problems, as reported by young adult subjects (82 college students) and their friends. In a second study reported in the same paper, Bartholomew and Horowitz interviewed 69 college students first about relationships with family members and then, in the same session, about relationships with friends. Each segment of the interview (one about family, one about friends) was used independently to rate the subject according to his or her approximation to each of the four attachment prototypes. As expected, attachment styles with peers were correlated with attachment styles with families.

Batholomew's (1990) interview and classification system soon attracted some interest among other social psychologists. For example, Brennan, Shaver, and Tobey (1991) reported evidence that the same two dimensions underlaid both Bartholomew's four-category typology and Hazan and Shaver's (1987) three-category typology. Consistent with sex role stereotypes, Brennan et al. found that more males than females were classified as dismissing avoidants, and more females than males were classified as fearful avoidants. More research that uses Bartholomew's interview and classification system will be published soon.

MEASURES OF SPECIFIC ADULT ATTACHMENTS

The AAI, the self-classification measures of attachment styles, and Batholomew's interview are all designed to assess the subject's state of mind or style about attachments in general, not the quality of any specific attachment, such as the bond to the subject's spouse, mother, lover, or best friend. However, two methods that are designed to measure the quality of a specific attachment have been developed. Barnas, Pollina, and Cummings (1991) focused each subject's attention on a current relationship. They developed a structured interview that consisted of 11 open-ended questions. Each was designed to tap the provision of security or issues of avoidance or resistance. The focus was on times when the subject needed emotional support or comfort. Responses were scored for evidence of security, avoidance, and resistance.

In research published so far, the interview has been used only with women in West Virginia (Barnas, Pollina, and Cummings, 1991). In the first sample of 50 women 18 to 50 years old, 68 percent of the subjects were classified as having secure attachments to the figures to whom they felt closest and 32 percent as having avoidant attachments. That all 50 attachments could be classified as secure or avoidant—none resistant, incoherent, or unclassifiable—is inconsistent with most other studies of attachment. Nevertheless, attachment patterns were associated with other variables in ways that made sense in the framework of attachment theory. Details are in Chapter 18.

The researchers also gave their interview to 48 elderly white middle-class women (age 65 or older) (Barnas, Pollina, and Cummings, 1991). This time, they asked not about interactions with the figure to whom the subject felt closest, but about interactions with each of the senior citizen's grown children. Based on sums of item scores for security and avoidance, the level of security in the parent's attachment to each child was rated on a

4-point scale. Again, the investigators did not report any systematic way they could interpret evidence suggestive of specific attachments analogous to the general states of mind classified as preoccupied or unresolved on the AAI. There was slight evidence that the senior citizens with anxious attachments to their grown children were having more difficulty than senior citizens who each had at least one secure attachment. However, the average scores on measures of social, psychological, and physical well-being were similar for both sets of women. Further details about this research are in Chapter 18.

The other method for assessing specific attachments in adults that is currently available is the Marital Q-Set developed by Kobak (1989). It has 84 items and assesses marital functioning as well as attachment security. As always in a Q-sort, a predetermined number of items must end up in each pile, and the score assigned to each item depends on the pile it rests in, with appropriate adjustments for negatively worded items. Scores for 14 relevant items are summed to produce a score for "reliance on partner." Relevant items include "avoids disclosing intimate thoughts or feelings," "relies on partner for advice and support," "feels happiest in partner's presence," and "avoids conflicts by 'going along' with partner." Scores for a different subset of items yield a summed score for "psychological availability" to the spouse. The nine items used to define this variable include "is responsive to distress in partner," "spontaneously expresses love for partner," and "receives and gives support with equal ease" (Kobak, 1989).

Each subject sorts the Marital Q-Set once to describe himself or herself and once to describe the spouse. The individual's attachment security score is the result of (1) the score the subject gives himself or herself on the "reliance on partner" scale and (2) the score the subject gives his or her spouse for "psychological availability." That is, individuals who indicate that they rely very much on their partners and that their partners are, psychologically, highly available get the highest scores for security of attachment. Kobak's Marital Q-Set does not classify types of anxious attachment patterns; it merely yields quantitative scores for each of two aspects of security. One study in which it was used is described in Chapter 18.

Both of the above methods for assessing security of specific adult attachments are very new. So far, the only investigators who have published reports about using the interview developed by Barnas, Pollina, and Cummings (1991) or the Marital Q-Set developed by Kobak (1989) are the people who developed them. We will need data from more samples and more investigators before we can say much about the validity of these new methods.

The methods of assessment first used with adults did not include the type of assessment most used with children: observation of behavior at the moment of reunion with the attachment figure after a period of separation. For babies, preschoolers, and 6-year-olds, behavior upon reunion provides very informative clues about the child's representational models, including feelings and expectations about the attachment figure. Examining reunion behavior to assess qualities of attachment between adolescent or adult partners seems an obvious step. Naturalistic observations when one or both spouses get home from their jobs might be very informative. The expressed warmth, gaze aversion, stylized or relaxed physical contact, complaints, critical little verbal digs, or ignoring of each other when the husband and wife reunite each day could reveal much. There are a multitude of ways to say "Hi, Honey, how was your day?" For the psychologist's convenience and the advantages a standardized procedure brings, a reunion after a timed separation in a laboratory could be used. That would avoid the risk of distractions from children or friends. Kobak, Shaver, and Hazan are currently experimenting with coding reunion behavior in a study of young married couples.

For slightly different purposes and with different understandings of the nature and implications of attachments in the adult years, investigators outside the mainstream of attachment research have invented other scales and procedures for assessing aspects of attachments. So far, none of these new methods has been used in enough studies to warrant inclusion in this chapter. Some of them are described along with the associated results in the next chapter.

CHAPTER SUMMARY

The AAI (George, Kaplan, and Main, 1985) is almost certainly here to stay. Methods of analyzing the richness of clinical detail in responses to it are likely to continue to evolve. Research with the AAI does already support the view that mothers who foster secure attachments in their infants can acknowledge ambivalence and conflict in past and current relationships, while mothers who foster avoidance in their infants tend to deny some of the conflicts and hardships of their childhoods and their current relationships.

Like the AAI, Hazan and Shaver's (1987) self-classification measure is probably here to stay. It is so easy to administer and already so well-tied to other questionnaire data that people are likely to keep using it and to keep finding interesting results. Bartholomew's (1990) interview, scales, and classification system are also attracting continuing interest.

All of this work is relatively new, so there is a clear need for convergent and discriminant validation studies of the various measures of attachment for adolescents and adults. We need to find out whether results from the various ways of classifying adults' attachments match each other; whether they correlate as theory predicts with other measures of self-image, personality, and behavior in intimate relationships; and whether they measure something that is specifically about attachment, not something that is generically about overall psychological health and positive functioning.

Behind most of the new measures lies the assumption that the same dimensions and categories that describe how infants organize attachments will continue to characterize how adults organize attachments. This may be an erroneous assumption. It is possible that data about adults' attachments are being artificially forced into categories analogous to the secure, avoidant-defended, resistant-coercive, and disorganized infant attachment categories. To read about one study that yielded direct evidence of continuity between a childhood measure of attachment and a measure of attachment in the same subjects as young adults, see the epilogue to this book.

Two research teams (Barnas, Pollina, and Cummings, 1991, and Kobak and Hazan, 1991) have experimented with ways to assess the quality of an adult's attachment to one *specific* partner, not the quality of the adult's generalized representational model. This area of research is too new to evaluate.

RESEARCH ABOUT ADOLESCENT AND ADULT ATTACHMENTS

Adolescence is a fascinating transitional period, a time of leaving the privileges and constraints of childhood behind and choosing a path into the world of adults. In adolescence, relationships with peers become very important, but the attachments to the parents remain the primary source of security (Greenberg et al., 1983; Kobak and Sceery, 1988). Theory leads us to expect to find correlates of current attachment patterns both in the continuing relationships with parents and in relationships with peers. If relevant research were available, adolescence would warrant a unit of its own in this book. In this early phase of attachment research, however, almost everything we can say about adolescents fits right in with almost everything we can say about adults. The attachment questions that are unique to adolescence have not yet received much research attention. So far, psychologists have not published direct evidence about how an individual's early attachments affect his or her personality or behavior in adolescence.

The research on attachments in adolescence that is available has two major limitations. First, the population of adolescents from which most samples are drawn is college students. Consequently, most of the adolescents studied are 18 or 19, hardly any of them are low in intelligence, many of them are living away from their childhood attachment figures, and most of them come from families that can pay at least part of the cost of college. We have no information about whether the correlates of attachment patterns in these samples match the correlates of attachment patterns in younger or more diverse samples of adolescents.

The second major limitation in existing studies of adolescents is that most of the data come from individuals' responses to questionnaires. Most such studies have included Hazan and Shaver's (1987) assessment of current attachment style in a series of questionnaires and have looked for relationships with other current variables represented in the same set of questionnaires. Only two studies have used the AAI with adolescent samples: Levine et al. (1991, discussed in Chapter 17) and Kobak and Sceery (1988, discussed in this chapter).

According to attachment theory, the aspects of adult life most directly affected by representational models and attachments should be personality and intimate relationships, including marriage. Some relevant research based in attachment theory is now available. In addition, Weiss (1973) proposed the more-focused hypothesis that aspects of personality influenced by attachment experiences should help predict the risk of chronic loneliness, and some research on that topic is available. More recently, Hazan and Shaver (1990) have offered some interesting ideas about how attachment styles may affect employment. Clinical evidence suggests that responses to separation and loss in the adult years are also related to attachment patterns (e.g., Bowlby, 1980; Parkes, 1991). As almost no other attachment data are available for the long years of adulthood, this chapter will conclude with comments on the role attachments play in old age.

Hypotheses that interrelate personality, marriage, loneliness, employment, reactions to death or divorce, and old age are sometimes sketchy. Within this chapter, you will find some abrupt jumps from one topic to another. Researchers have to start somewhere, and much of the available research grew from a hunch that captured someone's curiosity, not from a preexisting body of well-articulated theory and evidence. At present, we have some very intriguing first findings, but no body of compelling, direct evidence that early or current attachment patterns predict adult socioemotional functioning.

PERSONALITY AND RELATIONSHIPS

As noted earlier, attachment theorists expect a person's "state of mind with respect to attachment" to be associated with aspects of interpersonal relationships, especially intimate relationships. Even in more casual social relationships, we might expect secure individuals to be easier to get along with than other youths or adults are. In addition, the individual's representational models of attachment should be associated with variables that are ordinarily regarded as aspects of personality. For example, secure individuals should show more ego-resilience, less chronic anger, and less anxiety than others.

■ College Freshman

Such predictions about the relationship between working models of attachments and personality traits and social relations were tested in the short longitudinal study of college freshmen described in Chapter 17 (Kobak and Sceery, 1988). Students who entered college with secure representational models of attachments were self-confident and relatively free from distress and anxiety. They apparently enjoyed good support from their families and got along easily with their new peers. The group that had dismissing models, which are associated with avoidance, acknowledged feeling lonely and getting little support from their families. Relatively cut off from their families, lacking an attachment to someone who was an effective secure base, and lacking the knowledge of how to find a suitable partner and build such a relationship, these students were less well able to handle the challenges of their work and their new social situations. Peers perceived them as hostile; and anger, either suppressed or redirected, is exactly what we expect in people with a history of avoidant attachments. The students who were preoccupied with attachment issues were the ones most likely to be openly anxious, depressed, and distressed, but not distant from their families.

■ West Virginia Women

As discussed earlier, Barnas, Pollina, and Cummings (1991) asked 50 West Virginia women to think of the person closest to them. Half of the subjects were college undergraduates (aged 18 to 25), and half were 30 to 50 years old. Some of the subjects could not pick one person as the closest figure and so discussed two relationships as most important. Of the 25 undergraduates, 10 chose a parent, 3 chose a grandparent, 5 chose a sibling, 6 chose a friend, and 4 chose a boyfriend. Among the 25 women who were 30 to 50 years old, 10 chose their husbands, 5 chose a boyfriend or fiance, 8 chose a friend, 4 chose a parent, 4 chose one of their children, and 1 chose a sibling.

While the person who is closest to you is not necessarily an attachment figure, it seems likely that most of the subjects were naming their attachment figures. If so, the array of candidates for the role of principal attachment figure is wide. It may be limited, however, to relatives (including adult offspring), friends, and romantic-sexual partners. In this sample, no one identified in the role of teacher, colleague, or counselor made the list. (It is possible, of course, that a colleague, for example, had become a friend, and so was considered in that role as an attachment figure.)

From responses to the Barnas et al. (1991) interview, which asks mainly about times when the subject needed emotional support or comfort, 68 percent of the subjects were classified as having secure attachments and 32 percent as having insecure-avoidant attachments. As noted in Chapter 17, the validity of this new method for assessing patterns of attachment is unknown. Nevertheless, the significant associations between attachment pattern and other variables were consistent with attachment theory.

On a measure of depression, women whose closest relationships were avoidant got scores in the clinical range more often than women whose closest relationships were secure did. The avoidant women also reported more responses in coping with stress than the secure women did. That is, the secure women were more successful in finding ways to manage stress or remove sources of stress; the avoidant women had to keep trying new ways of responding to stress.

Like Kobak and Sceery (1988), Barnas et al. (1991) compared attachment patterns and friends' Q-sort descriptions of the same individuals. In their sample of college males and females, Kobak and Sceery found that friends reported unusually high levels of anxiety in the preoccupied group, but not in the dismissing (avoidant) group, based on AAI classifications. In their female sample, half of whom were 30 to 50 years old, Barnas et al. found that friends reported more anxiety in subjects with avoidant attachments than in subjects with secure attachments. Unlike Kobak and Sceery (1988), they found no significant differences between secure and avoidant subjects on ego undercontrol, ego-resiliency, or hostility.

Each of these multimethod studies broke new ground in designing ways of doing research on attachments and associated variables. In each case, descriptions from friends gave evidence that subjects with secure attachments had more-adaptive or more-desirable personality characteristics and social skills than others possessed. Each study found that subjects with anxious attachments were having more difficulty and more unhappiness than subjects with secure attachments were having. This is what attachment theory predicts. In the details of methodology and of findings about other specific correlates of attachment patterns, however, the two studies differed. We cannot yet know how reliable some of the new methods in these two studies are. Replication studies and refinements in methodology will add much to our understanding.

■ Self-Reported Correlates of Self-Classifications

Results consistent with attachment theory have also emerged from studies that used the simple, trichotomous, self-report attachment assessment developed by Hazan and Shaver (1987). Attachment style was related in predictable and theoretically meaningful ways to how adolescents and adults experienced love, to their representational models of self and of social relationships, and to their experiences with their parents. Hazan and Shaver's first sample had 620 subjects (67 percent female) with a wide age range (mean age = 36 years) (Hazan and Shaver, 1987). Average education was "some college," and 42 percent of the respondents were married at the time of the survey. Their second sample consisted of 108 undergraduates (mean age = 18 years; 65 percent female). Later (Hazan and Shaver, 1990), they gathered another sample of 670 American adults (79 percent female; 49 percent married at the time of the survey). The two large samples were self-selected; they were composed of people who responded to a set of questionnaires published in a newspaper. In Australia, Feeney and Noller (1990) used the attachment item with a sample of 374 Australian undergraduates, almost all of whom were single.

The results for all four samples of adolescents and adults were very consistent. (All of these results are based entirely on responses to questionnaires.) In all four samples, the relative prevalence of the three attachment patterns was fairly similar to the frequency distribution of attachment patterns in infancy in studies that do not use the D category. From 50 to 56 percent of the subjects in each sample classified themselves as secure, from 23 to 30 percent as avoidant, and from 15 to 20 percent as resistant. In each sample, females and males reported highly similar proportions of secure, avoidant, and resistant attachment styles. The absence of sex differences is a bit surprising, as the avoidant self-description accords more with male than with female sex role stereotypes, and the resistant item appears to run counter to male sex-typing.

Secure adolescents and adults described their most important love experiences as especially happy, friendly, and trusting. They were able to accept and support the partner despite the partner's faults. Their relationships tended to endure longer than the relationships of anxious people. They described themselves as easy to get to know and as liked by most people. They thought other people generally had good intentions and were good-hearted. It appeared that they were generally positive and self-assured in their interactions with others. In comparison with insecure subjects, they reported warmer relationships with both of their parents and warmer relationships between their parents.

Avoidant subjects were the most likely to endorse questionnaire items reflecting mistrust of and distance from others. Among adolescents, avoidant subjects were the most likely to report never having been in love or not being currently in love. When their distancing defenses broke down enough to allow an attachment to form, the relationships of avoidant lovers were characterized by fear of intimacy, emotional highs and lows, and jealousy. In adulthood, as in infancy, the seeming independence of people with avoidant defenses may be masking emotional neediness.

The histories that adult avoidant subjects reported helped to explain why they had become avoidant. They tended to describe their mothers as cold and rejecting. This finding is, in the context of evidence from other studies, surprising. Both Kobak and Sceery (1988) and Main et al. (1985) found that "dismissing" (avoidant) subjects tended to idealize their relationships with their parents. They used defensive misperceptions and selective recall to avoid the pain and anger associated with those relationships. On questionnaires, as in interviews, we might therefore expect avoidant subjects to report that their mothers were wonderful. In the studies using the questionnaire item to assess attachment style, adolescent avoidant subjects were more likely than older ones to describe relationships with and between their parents in positive terms. There is a hint here that a significant number of people with avoidant histories eventually learn enough from the relationships they experience or observe in their adult years to become able to recognize and label some of the negative aspects of their early experiences, even though they still describe themselves as "uncomfortable being close to others" and still say they find it difficult to trust others completely and difficult to let themselves depend on others.

The resistant adolescents and adults reported that their experiences of love involved obsession, desire for reciprocation and union, emotional highs and lows, and extreme sexual attraction and jealousy. They showed the most extreme, most passionate, and most neurotic sorts of love. They fell in love easily and had the shortest relationships. They reported self-doubts and felt misunderstood and underappreciated. They got the highest scores of any group on trait and state loneliness. They were the most likely to report a lack of paternal support and often described their fathers as unfair.

In the Australian sample, the occurrence of childhood separation from the mother did predict increased probability of anxious attachment in adolescence (Feeney and Noller, 1990). (Childhood separation from the father did not.) In partial contrast, Hazan and Shaver (1987, 1990) found no significant differences among the three attachment groups in likelihood or duration of separation from either parent during childhood. The parents' separation or divorce during the subject's childhood did not predict insecure attachment in adolescence or adulthood in either study. We certainly have compelling evidence from other research that involuntary separation from a parent triggers considerable anxiety and anger in early childhood and is upsetting throughout childhood and adolescence. If the self-report measures in the American studies of adolescents and adults are valid, then they provide evidence that many people who, as children, experienced their parents' divorce are able to resolve their feelings well and maintain or develop secure representational models.

In the Hazan and Shaver (1987) study, the best predictors of adult attachment type were the subjects' descriptions of the qualities of their relationships with each of their parents and of the parents' relationship with each other. Unlike the AAI, questionnaires about past and present characteristics of the subject's relationships with each of his or her parents provide little or no opportunity for probing for psychological defenses. When two methods so different from each other both find evidence that childhood experiences continue to make a significant contribution toward predicting beliefs and expectations about attachment relationships in the adult years, the argument grows more convincing.

In the Australian sample, questionnaire items about general views of the self and of human relationships discriminated among the three attachment groups much more powerfully than the items specifically about beliefs about romantic love did (Feeney and Noller, 1990). In particular, secure subjects got high scores on self-esteem and low scores on self-conscious anxiety. All of this suggests that the effects of attachment models may be quite pervasive, not focused principally on romantic, sexual relationships. The same comparison was not available in Hazan and Shaver's work.

■ Sex Differences and Multimethod Studies of Attachment Styles

Several more studies that used the Hazan and Shaver (1987) measure or Likert scales derived from it soon supported and added detail to the pictures sketched above about the personalities and relationships of people who report each of the three attachment styles. Some of the research drew from brief laboratory observations or telephone interviews of the subjects, not just from questionnaires. Several bits of evidence began to uncover sex differences in the correlates of the three attachment styles.

In a longitudinal study of 144 heterosexual couples, Simpson (1990) found differences between groups of students with secure and anxious attachment styles. The partners in each dyad had been dating each other for an average of 13.5 months at the outset of the study, and at least one partner of each dyad was a university student. The partners responded separately to a large set of questionnaires that included Simpson's 13-item Likert-scale version of Hazan and Shaver's inquiry about attachments. Their reports indicated that, both for men and for women, secure attachment was associated with greater relationship interdependence, commitment, trust, and satisfaction and fewer negative emotions than resistant or avoidant attachment was.

The statistical association between a subject's attachment style and his or her partner's attachment style was not as great as the association between a subject's attachment style and the same subject's reports of interdependence, commitment, trust, satisfaction, and frequency of positive emotions. Nevertheless, there was a tendency for secure men and secure women to date each other. In addition, an individual's attachment style helped to predict the partner's feelings about that individual. The partners of men and women who got relatively high scores on the index of resistance reported less interdependence and less commitment than other partners reported. Males dating resistant women also reported less satisfaction with their relationships. Partners of both men and women who got relatively high scores on the avoidant index reported less trust and greater insecurity than other partners reported. Partners of the avoidant women also reported less commitment than other men did.

About 6 months after gathering the data described above, interviewers succeeded in contacting both members of 132 of these dyads by telephone. According to independent reports from both partners, 48 couples (36 percent) were no longer dating one another. Over the phone, the interviewers asked those subjects a few simple questions about how much emotional distress they experienced when the couple broke up and how long it lasted. Avoidant men reported less distress than other men reported. The three groups of women did not report differences related to the indices of security, resistance, and avoidance.

Working with a sample of 37 males and 37 females, Feeney and Noller (1991) tape-recorded each subject's verbal description of the partner he or she had been dating for at least a month. Secure subjects showed intermediate levels of idealization of the partner, reported relatively favorable attitudes toward the partner's family, and made more references to positive characteristics in their current dating relationships than other subjects did. Avoidant subjects generally reported low levels of emotional intensity in their dating relationships, and resistant subjects got high (unrealistic) scores for idealization of the partner.

The limitations of data obtained from self-reports on questionnaires and in superficial interviews are obvious. For example, the avoidant males could have been lying about how upset they were right after breaking up with their partners. They may also have been truly relieved, or they may have been unaware of their own symptoms of distress. Despite their limitations, these self-report studies consistently find qualitative differences in the romantic relationships of people with different attachment patterns, and the differences match predictions from attachment theory. Avoidant individuals steer clear of "excessive" intimacy and commitment in relationships. Resistant individuals tend to be very preoccupied with worries about the partner's dependability and trustworthiness.

In a pattern of dyadic interaction often discussed in the clinical literature, one partner, fearful of too much intimacy, distances himself or herself from the other; the other, anxious over the decrease in closeness, responds by increasing dependent behavior; the first responds by distancing himself or herself further; and so on. A self-perpetuating and mutually frustrating cycle evolves and may escalate to the point at which the couple breaks up. Using Hazan and Shaver's one-item measure, Bartholomew (1990) found a positive correlation between ratings of an avoidant style in the self and reports of a highly dependent, ambivalent style in the romantic partner. Individuals who are wary of intimacy may be inclined to perceive their partners as overly dependent and so to activate a self-fulfilling prophecy. Sadly, avoiding intimacy precludes the possibility of building a satisfying, close relationship; the consistently avoidant individual often prevents herself from having the experience that would help her revise her representational model. Unhappy, self-perpetuating representational models may handicap resistant individuals, too. Their confused, needy representational models may make them slow to recognize how lastingly unsatisfying a relationship with an avoidant or resistant partner will be, so they may stay in painful relationships long past the time when secure individuals would have moved on and found more-suitable partners. In addition, their excessively dependent and angrily coercive behaviors probably drive away many partners.

Later research by other investigators confirmed the same pattern of findings. For example, Simpson, Rholes, and Nelligan (1992) unobtrusively videotaped 83 college-age dating couples for 5 minutes in a waiting room while the woman was waiting with the expectation of participating in an activity that was known to make most people anxious. For secure females, seeking comfort and support increased with anxiety; for avoidant women, it decreased with anxiety. As the partner's anxiety increased, highly secure men increased the amount of support they gave, but avoidant men decreased the support they gave to the partner, as measured through observers' ratings of physical contact, supportive comments, and other efforts to give emotional support.

Kirkpatrick and Davis (1994) studied 354 heterosexual couples in serious dating relationships. Most of the subjects had been dating only each other for at least seven months when first contacted. Perhaps because this was a study of people in serious, lasting relationships, it included fewer avoidant or resistant subjects than unselected samples include: over 80 percent of the men and women classified themselves as secure. The first wave of data collection included only questionnaire measures. For the second wave, 7 to 14 months later, and the third wave, 30 to 36 months after the initial contact, data were obtained through telephone interviews.

In the initial set of questionnaires, using scales from 1 to 5, each subject rated how well each of the three descriptions Hazan and Shaver (1987) had written fit the subject. Each subject was assigned to the category to which he or she gave the highest score. Subjects who gave identically high scores to two of the descriptions were labeled unclassifiable and dropped from analyses of associations with the measure. The authors argued that attachment style classifications for the reduced sample (309 women and 275 men) were more reliable than forced classifications into one of the three descriptions would have been.

Results were consistent with the hypothesis that partners select each other on the basis of behavior associated with attachment style: there were *no* cases in which a resistant individual was paired with another resistant individual or an avoidant individual with another avoidant individual! The subject's gender influenced how his or her attachment style related to (1) his or her rating of the current relationship, (2) the partner's rating of the current relationship, and (3) the longevity of the relationship. Relationships of avoidant *men* and of resistant *women* were surprisingly stable over three years, despite the relatively poor ratings both partners gave those relationships in the initial assessment; they lasted at least as long as the relationships of the secure subjects, who initially reported that they were relatively satisfied with their relationships. (Note that these results from prospective research are the opposite of what Feeney and Noller (1990) and Hazan and Shaver (1987) found in retrospective research.) In this prospective research, the resistant *men* and the avoidant *women* had the highest rates of breaking up. Kirkpatrick and Davis argued that this result emerged because, in most heterosexual relationships in this society, maintaining a relationship and ending a relationship fall within the woman's role. Many of the resistant men in relationships that did not last in this study were paired with avoidant women, and avoidant women probably have the poorest skills for maintaining relationships and the greatest inclination to walk away from relationships. In contrast, because of their anxiety about being unloved or abandoned, resistant women may try especially hard to maintain their relationships, even if the relationships are unsatisfying.

In a short longitudinal study based entirely on responses on questionnaires filled out in the laboratory, Keelan, Dion, and Dion (1994) used both the Hazan and Shaver (1987) single-item measure and the 13 Likert scales Simpson (1990) had derived from it. Of the 101 college students who classified themselves both at Time 1 and at Time 2 (4 months later), 80 percent chose the same style both times. Stability over time in self-classification was highest for secure subjects (85 percent), high for avoidant subjects (77 percent), and relatively low for resistant subjects (50 percent). Stability over time on the indices of security, avoidance, and resistance Simpson derived from the Likert scales was also high. Of the 52 subjects who were consistent over time on the Hazan and Shaver measure and were in relationships at Time 1, the secure subjects, including those whose relationships had ended by Time 2, reported higher levels of commitment than the insecure subjects reported, both at Time 1 and at Time 2. At Time 2, subjects whose relationships had ended were asked to describe the characteristics of the relationship just before it ended. For insecure subjects, but not for secure subjects, ending a relationship produced significant drops in reports of commitment, trust, satisfaction, and relationship rewards and a significant increase in reported costs of the relationship.

Collins and Read (1990) decomposed the Hazan and Shaver (1987) single-item measure into 18 Likert scales. Factor analyses of responses to the 18 scales revealed three underlying dimensions: the degree to which the individual (1) felt comfortable with closeness, (2) felt that he or she could depend on others, and (3) felt anxious about being abandoned or unloved. They found that these three dimensions of attachment style were related to questionnaire measures of self-esteem, trust, beliefs about human nature, and styles of loving in ways consistent with attachment theory. In addition, they found that individuals who felt uncomfortable about getting close (avoidant subjects) tended to date partners who were high in fear of abandonment (resistant); while secure subjects tended to date secure partners. Subjects also reported similarity between their dating partners and their parents, especially the opposite sex parent. For women, the extent to which the partner was comfortable with closeness was the best predictor of relationship quality. For men, the extent to which the partner was anxious about being abandoned or unloved was the best predictor of relationship quality.

Three of the studies described here (Collins and Read, 1990; Kirkpatrick and Davis, 1994; and Simpson, 1990) found that avoidant subjects tended to be involved with resistant subjects, and vice versa, not with partners who matched their own attachment style. All of this research was cross-sectional, so it is possible that early experiences in the developing relationships influenced attachment styles, not vice versa. All three studies found that relationships with resistant women were rated by both partners as less satisfying, less viable, and/or more conflicted or ambivalent than relationships with secure or avoidant women. All three studies found that the ratings avoidant men gave their relationships were more negative on almost all dimensions than the ratings secure or resistant men gave their relationships.

MARRIAGE

Very little research on marriage has been done from the viewpoint of attachment theory. However, much well-designed research on marriage has been done, and its results provide findings to which attachment research and theory can be tied. As a review of the literature on marriage is beyond the scope of this book, I rely here primarily on the summary provided by Kobak and Hazan (1991) in their introduction to their own research.

In numerous studies, observers' ratings of the quality of communication during problem-solving discussions are related to other measures of the quality of marital adjustment, such as the ability to regulate emotions. Compared to nondistressed married couples, distressed couples display more dysfunctional negative affect during discussions about solving problems. The partners in a distressed marriage show less support for and validation of each other. Their cycles of dysfunctional expressions and defensive responses probably perpetuate negative expectations about the self and the partner. The quality of emotional communication may mediate between representational models of attachment and marital adjustment. That is, the principal way the working model affects the quality of the marriage may be through its direct effects on emotional communication.

■ Attachment, Problem-Solving, Confiding, and Sex Roles

To test their hypothesis, Kobak and Hazan (1991) gathered a sample of 40 same-race married couples (39 white and 1 black). The spouses had been married to each other for an average of 7 years and had an average family income of $35,000. They ranged in age from 24 to 46. Of the 40 couples, 21 had children, and the children ranged in age from 6 months to 18 years. The selection process for amassing the sample could not be described as random. To be included in the study, the husband and wife had to be willing to come together to the laboratory for two 3-hour sessions that would include some videotaping. People with anxious attachments are probably overrepresented in the group of people who will *not* come with the spouse to be observed by a team of psychologists. In addition, 12 of the 40 couples were recruited through radio advertisements for volunteers for a study of "happily married couples." (The other volunteers had responded to newspaper advertisements.) These recruitment requirements and methods may have biased the sample toward people who had secure attachments to their spouses. They certainly excluded adults whose attachment models were so dysfunctional that they could not sustain a marriage.

The principal measure of security of attachment in this study was neither Main's AAI nor Hazan and Shaver's self-report. Instead, Kobak and Hazan used the Marital Q-Set Kobak (1989) had developed in other research. As described in Chapter 17, the Marital Q-Set yields a score for "reliance on partner" and a score for "psychological availability." Each subject sorted the items once to describe himself or herself and once, a week later, to describe the spouse. Individuals who indicated that they relied very much on their partners and that their partners were, psychologically, highly available got the highest scores for security of attachment. Kobak's Marital Q-Set does not assess the *general* attachment style. It is intended to measure the security of one specific, current attachment.

Marital satisfaction and adjustment were assessed not only through the Marital Q-Set, which has not yet been widely used, but also through the Dyadic Adjustment Scale, (Spanier, 1976), which had been validated in earlier research. In addition to the Q-sort and questionnaire measures, Kobak and Hazan conducted some direct observations of interaction between the two spouses in each dyad. Each couple participated in two videotaped interaction tasks. The first task was one that is standard in research on marriages: a problem-solving discussion. The second interaction assignment was a reciprocal confiding task.

Kobak and Hazan had two Q-sort descriptions of each individual, one provided by the subject and one provided by the spouse. Using all 84 items, correlations between the item scores in the two descriptions provide an index of the degree to which one spouse agreed with or validated the other's working model of the self. For the 40 couples, these correlations ranged from .02 (no relationship at all between the two descriptions) to .77 (very high agreement), with a mean of .55 (substantial agreement). All possible correlations between the level of interspouse agreement in describing the wife, interspouse agreement in describing the husband, the score for marital adjustment from the wife's responses to the Dyadic Adjustment Scale, and the score for marital adjustment from the husband's responses to the Dyadic Adjustment Scale were highly significant. That is, spouses who agreed in separate descriptions of what the wife was like tended also to agree in their separate descriptions of what the husband was like and in their separate ratings of marital adjustment. In fact, agreement between the two spouses' Q-sorts accounted for more than one-third of the variance in marital adjustment. Even after statistically controlling for marital adjustment from the Dyadic Adjustment Scale, the level of agreement between the spouses' Q-sorts helped predict behavior on the problem-solving task. Other ways of analyzing the data also indicated that the agreement index reflected something real about marital adjustment and communication, not just a general tendency for nondistressed couples to say positive things about the self and the partner.

Kobak and Hazan looked for associations between security scores from the Marital Q-Set and behavior in the videotaped interactions. Several of the associations they found lend themselves to interpretations that draw from sex-role expectations as well as attachment theory. When husbands reported low psychological availability of their wives, both spouses displayed more rejection and less support on the problem-solving task. This suggests that these husbands were accurate in saying that their wives were not very available psychologically. The wives' behavior suggests some underlying anger. In showing more rejection and less support than other wives, these women were violating common sex role expectations, which require women to take nurturant, supportive roles, especially in relation to their husbands. Their husbands' behavior also suggests some underlying anger. Nevertheless, the husband's reliance on the wife (assessed through the Marital Q-Set) was unrelated to either spouse's rejecting and supportive behavior during the problem-solving task. In this sample, the husband's reliance on the wife evidently was not much affected by how available she was psychologically or by how rejecting or unsupportive she was behaviorally.

Contrary to the investigators' expectations, neither the wife's reliance on her husband nor her perception of his psychological availability was related to the husband's rejecting or supportive behavior during problem solving. It appeared that the degree of security in the wife's attachment to her husband was unrelated to his observable behavior. (Of course, it is possible that the husbands behaved differently when they were not in front of cameras in a psychologist's laboratory.)

Wives who reported low reliance on or low psychological availability of their husbands (or both) were more rejecting than other wives during the problem-solving discussion. Despite the anger implied by the wife's rejecting behavior, these women were not significantly less supportive of their husbands during the problem-solving task than other wives were. Despite whatever resentment they may have felt, they generally provided the support expected of wives.

On the confiding task, there were hardly any significant correlations between one partner's score for self-disclosure or for listening in an accepting way and either partner's scores on the attachment security scales from the Q-sorts. The exception was that husbands who were good listeners generally had wives who reported greater security. A husband who listens well to his wife is doing more than is automatically required of men. That his willingness and ability to listen increases the degree to which his wife describes him as psychologically available is easy to understand.

The several gender differences in this research fit into a coherent pattern that assumes wives will generally be psychologically available and supportive, while the husband's major contributions to the marriage are assumed to be in other arenas. The husband's security was related to the wife's rejection but not to her listening. For supporting positive marital adjustment, whether the wife was psychologically available to the husband seemed to matter more than whether the husband was psychologically available to the wife. The wife's security was related to the husband's listening well when she confided in him but not to his rejection or support on the problem-solving task.

For both husbands and wives, higher scores for relying on the partner were associated with higher scores for marital adjustment. Both partners' ratings of marital adjustment were related to the husband's perception of the wife's psychological availability. The wife's rating of marital adjustment was also related to her rating of the husband's psychological availability, but the husband's rating of marital adjustment was not.

These gender-related findings from a sample that deliberately included happily married couples match clinical reports of gender differences in goals for spouses in marriage therapy. Distressed wives often ask for more intimacy (higher psychological availability, better listening) with their husbands, while distressed husbands often ask for less conflict with their wives (not more support, but less rejection).

The numerous measures in this study did not all reflect the results predicted from attachment theory, but many of them did, and none contradicted predictions from attachment theory. That is, whenever significant relationships between variables were found, the variables that should be associated with secure attachment (positive marital adjustment, low rejection, high psychological availability, good listening, etc.) were associated with secure attachment. In summarizing their findings, Kobak and Hazan (1991) emphasized the evidence that agreement between the wife's representational models and the husband's was a good predictor of reported marital adjustment and of observed behavior. Agreement between models may index and/or contribute to harmony on any task that requires coordination of the partners' goals and behaviors. Presumably, open, direct communication supports the ability to agree upon and to coordinate goals.

■ Early Security, Marital Status, and Triadic Interaction

I argued above that being married and willing to participate in laboratory research may be associated with secure attachment. As noted earlier, other studies have found some association between being married at all and having a secure attachment style. The latter association may indicate (1) that getting married and staying married contribute toward developing secure representational models or (2) that people who have secure models are more likely than others to date, to marry, and to have their marriages endure. (Note, however, that some insecure marriages do last for decades.)

For example, in a complicated and interesting retrospective study of Australian couples, Kotler and Omedei (1988) found evidence that the quality of early attachment relationships in the family of origin influenced quality of marriage for both men and women in their thirties. This was true even after accounting for socioeconomic status, social support, and experienced stress.

In a direct study of marriage, Cohn, Cowan, Cowan, and Pearson (1992) studied 27 couples, most of whom were white, well-educated, and in their thirties or late twenties. On the basis of the AAI, 20 of the husbands (74 percent) and 14 of the wives (52 percent) were classified as secure. Contrary to expectations, neither husbands' nor wives' marital satisfaction scores on a widely used 15-item self-report measure were related to attachment security. Although the questionnaire did not find evidence of differences in attachment patterns, laboratory observations did. Secure husbands were more likely than insecure husbands to be in dyads that were rated as showing better functioning, more positive behaviors, and fewer conflictual behaviors. The laboratory procedures were unusual for a study of marital interaction: they included the couple's firstborn preschooler. For the first task, an experimenter told the child a story while the parents were not in the room. The parents were then asked to elicit the story from the child. After that, the parents were asked to work with their child to assemble pieces to match a model of a train, a challenging task. Finally, the parents and the child were invited to "build a world" in a sand tray, using a collection of miniature objects.

There was evidence that one secure partner was sufficient to carry the weight of the relationship during the interaction tasks used in this study. Dyads in which both partners were insecure showed more conflict and poorer functioning than other dyads, but insecure-secure dyads and secure-secure dyads did not differ significantly from each other.

■ Matching the Spouse in Attachment Security

As part of a longitudinal study of marriages, Senchak and Leonard (1992) asked both spouses in 322 young, newlywed couples to fill out questionnaire measures of marital intimacy, marital functioning, conflict resolution behaviors, and attachment style (Hazan and Shaver's single-item measure). Because 82 percent of the husbands and 83 percent of the wives reported secure styles, the probability that any given subject would have an insecure spouse was low. Even so, insecure husbands were significantly more likely to be married to insecure wives than secure husbands were (34 percent vs. 14 percent), and insecure wives were significantly more likely to be married to insecure husbands than secure wives were (36 percent vs. 15 percent). Couples in which both partners were secure reported better overall marital adjustment than couples in which one or both partners were insecure reported.

Integrating information from these first studies of marriage from the perspective of attachment theory is not easy. The methods vary greatly from study to study, and most of them require further validation. The hypotheses that have been directly studied also vary greatly from study to study. We certainly have some interesting hypotheses, but few have been directly tested in more than one study. We are barely at the beginning of addressing questions about marriage from the perspective of attachment theory.

LONELINESS

In the extensive research literature on loneliness, results consistent with attachment theory are routinely reported. A few studies of loneliness have been planned and conducted from the focused perspective of attachment theory.

Research on loneliness sometimes distinguishes between *trait loneliness* and *state loneliness*. For example, people who have just moved to a new place are usually lonely. For many of them, this loneliness is a temporary condition that will pass when they have had time to find or make friends in the new place. Just as anxiety and anger serve adaptive functions for many people in many circumstances, transient, situational loneliness might be an adaptive emotion. Feeling lonely prompts healthy people to seek satisfying social relationships.

After conducting extensive interview research with adults who had lost a partner through death or divorce, Weiss (1973) concluded that there are two categories of relationships that make independent and different contributions to well-being. One category is attachment relationships. The second is relationships of community, such as relationships with work colleagues, friends, and kin. Weiss (1973) cited evidence that adequate relationships in each category benefit individuals under stress, and the absence of adequate relationships in either category produces loneliness. The loneliness associated with not having an adequate attachment is distinctly different, he wrote, from the loneliness associated with not having adequate relationships of community (Weiss, 1973). He offered the hypothesis that trait loneliness reflects the absence of secure attachment (Weiss, 1973).

Building on Weiss's work, Shaver and Hazan (1987) noted that insecure individuals reported significantly more loneliness than secure individuals in their two samples of college freshmen. (The measure of security was their self-classification item.)

In one sample, avoidant students reported more loneliness than resistant students. In the other sample, results for avoidant and resistant students were reversed. Both insecure groups reported more trait loneliness than the secure subjects reported. The avoidant students seemed more locked into loneliness than the insecure-resistant students were. They more often said that they had not felt in tune with others, had not been part of a group of friends, and had not felt close to anyone during the past few years. They more often agreed that they would always be lonely and that others thought of them as lonely people. The resistant students were more optimistic and active about seeking attachment partners. Despite histories of loneliness, they were even more likely than secure students to say they were part of a group of friends.

Research undertaken without any special attention to attachment theory very often finds that loneliness is correlated with poor parent-child relationships and with having parents who divorced each other, especially if they did so early in the subject's life (Shaver and Rubenstein, 1980). If the correlations reflect a causal relationship between the variables, early experiences of rejection or loss often have lasting effects on later expectations, feelings, and relationships.

Many investigators have found high negative correlations between loneliness and self-esteem: people with low self-esteem are often lonely (Shaver and Rubenstein, 1980). According to attachment theorists, underlying the low self-esteem and the loneliness might be representational models of past and potential attachment figures as unresponsive and a corresponding model of the self as relatively unlovable and incompetent. Note, however, that all this is inconsistent with some of the findings reported earlier in this chapter.

In a study of students from a different culture (Iran), Hojat (1982) found associations between experiences in childhood and loneliness in the college years similar to the associations Shaver and Rubenstein (1980) found in their U.S. sample. For Hojat's research, over 200 Iranian college students in American universities and over 300 in Iranian universities filled out questionnaires. Those who had not had satisfactory relationships with their parents and those who had not been able to establish meaningful interpersonal relationships with their peers during childhood were more likely than others to experience intense loneliness during their college years.

Except for Weiss's (1973) early work, all of the loneliness research I have reported here depends entirely on subjects' answers on questionnaires. Even so, the results are consistent with attachment theory and have interesting implications. There are indications that an individual's early experiences in attachment relationships affect the likelihood that loneliness will become a chronic condition for him or her. Self-image and social skills in relationships in general, not just in attachment relationships, appear to be affected.

EMPLOYMENT

The world of work is an another arena in which social skills and representational models of social relationships come into play. Do attachment styles influence behavior and affect on the job? Hazan and Shaver (1990) proposed that they may. Specifically, they argued that secure attachments in adulthood may support self-confident, effective involvement in work much as secure attachments in infancy support the infant's self-confident, effective exploration. In addition, they offered hypotheses about how adults with the two types of insecure attachment styles would differ. Avoidant adults might approach their work somewhat compulsively, using it to avoid the difficulties and deficiencies they experience in interpersonal relationships. Resistant adults, being preoccupied with unmet attachment needs, might often allow interpersonal involvements to interfere with their work.

Hazan and Shaver (1990) published their trichotomous self-report measure of attachment style among a large number of questionnaire items about love and work in a Denver newspaper and analyzed the first 670 responses. Unfortunately, 79 percent of the responses were from women; a different pattern of results might emerge in a primarily male sample. The results in this sample supported the hypotheses stated above. Securely attached respondents reported relatively high levels of satisfaction with job security, coworkers, income, and opportunities for challenge and advancement. Of the three groups, they were the least likely to procrastinate or have difficulty completing tasks. They thought they were good workers and were confident that their coworkers thought so, too. They enjoyed their vacations and did not allow their work to jeopardize their relationships or their health. They placed a higher value on relationships than on work and derived more pleasure from their relationships than from their work.

Avoidant subjects were dissatisfied with their coworkers but similar to secure subjects in their self-descriptions of satisfaction with their jobs. However, they gave themselves low ratings on job performance and expected to be given similarly low ratings by their coworkers. They were the most likely to say that work was more important than love and that they would choose success at work over success in love. They were the most likely to say they felt nervous when not working and to say that work interfered with their relationships and their health. They were the least likely to spend their leisure time socializing and the least likely to report gaining new knowledge in their free time. Their vacations were generally pleasureless.

Resistant subjects more often reported feeling insecure about their jobs and unappreciated and unrecognized by their coworkers. For example, they tended to think they were not getting promotions they wanted and deserved. They preferred to work with others, were motivated by approval, and worried that others would find their work unimpressive or would reject them. They were the most likely to say that interpersonal concerns interfered with their work. Their preoccupation with interpersonal needs was apparently costly: they had the lowest average income ($20,000 to $30,000 for them versus $30,000 to $40,000 for each of the other two groups). The lower incomes may have been associated with poorer job performance and/or slower rates of advancement. Another possibility is that preoccupation with relationships led many of the resistant subjects in this mostly female sample into caregiving jobs (e.g., social worker) that are female sex-typed and bring lower salaries than male sex-typed jobs bring. The resistant subjects experienced more pain in relation to love than in relation to work. They were the most likely to report that their leisure activities provided excitement and the most likely to spend their free time shopping.

If optimal mental health includes being able to love, to work, and to keep those two aspects of your life in balance, this self-report evidence supports the view that adults who have secure attachment styles are healthier mentally than avoidant or resistant adults are.

SEPARATION AND LOSS

So far, the research I have discussed in this chapter has focused mostly on individual differences, not on normative phenomena. Now, we return to phenomena that have some significant impact in *any* attachment relationship, regardless of whether the attachment is secure, avoidant-defended, resistant-preoccupied-coercive, or unresolved-disorganized.

■ Long-Term Effects of Childhood Losses

One of the most distressing and potentially damaging events relevant to attachment is loss of a major attachment figure in childhood. We have conclusive evidence that people who experience the divorce of their parents, the death of a parent, or permanent separation from a parent *before the age of 5* have a much increased risk of both psychiatric illness and delinquency as young adults (Rutter, 1985). However, other variables mediate the effects of early childhood losses.

As described earlier, institutional rearing is associated with shallow or anxious emotional bonds in later life. In Rutter's (1985) own study of women raised in institutions, the subjects were twice as likely as a comparison group to react adversely when they found themselves in a discordant marriage and poor living conditions. They were unusually likely to marry for negative reasons and often married men with multiple psychosocial problems from similarly deprived backgrounds. However, when they did have supportive husbands and harmonious marriages, adult outcomes for the institution-reared women were as good as outcomes for the comparison group. The most influential protective factor appeared to be having some sort of success (social, athletic, musical, or, less often, in school). That apparently supported a sense of self-esteem and self-efficacy and increased the chances that the girl would do some planning about marriage and employment. I do not know of an analogous study of men raised in institutions.

Bowlby (e.g., 1988) has summarized evidence from Brown and Harris's (1978) studies of four large, representative samples of the female population in Great Britain. The investigators found four events or conditions to be significantly more common among depressed women than among other women from the same community. Three of the variables were current: a severe adverse event (often a personal loss or disappointment) within a year before the onset of depression, the absence of a confidante (a current attachment figure?), and difficult living conditions, such as extremely bad housing and responsibility for caring for a number of children. The fourth variable was historical: the woman's loss of her mother through death or prolonged separation prior to the age of 11. The greatly increased vulnerability to affective disorders in the presence of the fourth variable was clear in all four studies. Girls who lose their mothers between age 11 and age 17 are also at increased risk for depression in adulthood, but are less vulnerable than those who lose their mothers at an earlier age. The worse the family circumstances before the loss and the poorer the care the girl received after loss of her mother, the more vulnerable to depression she became. Loss of the father during childhood had far less impact on girls than loss of the mother had.

■ Bereavement in Adulthood

As discussed earlier, in the adult years, the spouse or other long-term partner probably replaces the parent as the principal attachment figure. Therefore, the death of the spouse is for most people a major loss. With adult samples, reactions to the death of the spouse have been studied more than reactions to the death of the parent. The death of an elderly parent can be anticipated. The death of the spouse is often untimely. The sudden, unexpected loss of a principal attachment figure is, of course, more disruptive than a loss for which an individual can to some degree prepare himself or herself.

Bowlby (1980) described four phases of the normal mourning process. First comes a period of affective numbness, usually lasting a few hours to a week. Intense bursts of distress and/or anger may interrupt it. Then comes a time of yearning for the lost figure. Seemingly unable to believe the spouse has died, widows and widowers search for the lost mate. This second phase, yearning and searching, commonly lasts for many months and sometimes lasts for years. Then comes a time of disorganization and despair as the individual comes to believe in the reality and permanence of the loss but does not yet know what to do without the lost one. Just managing day-to-day life can be a great struggle. Finally comes a period of more or less reorganization. The analogy to a very young child's responses to prolonged separation from the principal attachment figure should be obvious: a period of protesting and searching, a period of despair, and then a reorganization and resumption of adaptive social behavior, but with long-lasting effects that may become visible if another traumatic event occurs.

Both secure and insecure adults react to major losses with shock, denial, protest, depression, and, if all goes well, eventually, acceptance and reorganization. Even so, evidence from several studies suggests that how an individual responds to loss reflects the quality of that individual's attachment to the deceased figure. People who had secure attachments can resolve their grieving, reorganize their lives, and go on with their lives sooner and more easily than people who had anxious attachments.

This strikes some students as odd. It seems to them that people in secure relationships lose more than people whose attachments were anxious. If the relationship was of poor quality anyway, why hang on to it for an inordinately long time after the spouse or parent has died? The explanation may be that secure individuals do not have to resolve deep conflicts in their feelings about the deceased figure or deal with repressed needs and angers before they can move on. Theory suggests that the representational models of people whose attachments were defended, preoccupied, or unresolved leave them with more guilt, anger, and anxiety to manage, and that they may approach the task with less confidence in their own competence and worth. They have more unfinished business with the deceased and so face a harder task in resolving their ambivalent feelings, expectations, and disappointments.

Normal grieving, despite its pain and irrationality, is not a pathological condition or process. For some people, however, grieving fails to progress normally. Clinicians have often observed three patterns of morbid grief: *delayed grief, chronic grief,* and *conflicted grief.* A few days of emotional numbness are part of the normal reaction to a major loss. If grieving does not begin after a few days, the delay is abnormal. *Chronic grief* is severe and protracted grief. *Conflicted grief* is grief complicated by intense guilt and anger. The onset of conflicted grief is often delayed.

In a recent report on 54 people who sought help from a psychiatrist after the death of a major attachment figure (in most cases, the spouse), Parkes (1991) found that the majority had some prior reason to be regarded as vulnerable. Risk factors included learned fear, learned helplessness, lack of trust in oneself, lack of trust in others, having had an excessively dependent spouse, being compulsively self-reliant, and being elderly and isolated. The only bereaved people who sought help in the absence of such vulnerability factors had suffered sudden and/or multiple losses. Note that almost all of the identified risk factors are the sorts of difficulties associated with a history of anxious attachments. A person who has not had a reliable, accessible secure base is expected to be more fearful, less competent, less self-confident, and less trusting; a subset of this group is at high risk for compulsive self-reliance. The risk factors Parkes (1991) identified may have been reflections of histories of anxious attachment.

Despite the pain of bereavement, 55 percent of the 54 patients used only one or two sessions of psychotherapy interviews, and only 28 percent stayed in treatment for more than five sessions. This is indirect evidence that grieving is in most cases a normal process that requires little or no professional treatment; it is not a pathological condition. For the bereaved patients in this study, the therapist deliberately acted as a surrogate attachment figure, providing warmth, regard, confidence, and support to the bereaved patient. He emphasized the possibility of a positive outcome to grieving, which he labeled a challenge, not an illness or a defeat.

Excessive dependency, which, of course, suggests anxious attachment, is associated with chronic grief. Parkes and Weiss (1983) found that women who had been overly dependent on their husbands often suffered unending, unresolvable grief. It can also be the "strong" partner who develops chronic grief. Parkes (1991) had eight patients who were said to have been unusually dependent on the spouse who died. Only one of them developed chronic grief. There were eight other patients whose spouses were said to have been unusually dependent on them. Four of these patients developed chronic grief after the dependent spouse died. Parkes (1991) also cited a 1962 study in which he found that 19 percent of psychiatric patients (widows and widowers) suffering pathological grief had had dependent spouses, while only 4 percent of the group without pathological grief had had dependent spouses. Parkes suggested that dependency can be a function of a dyad, with the "weak" partner often contributing an important source of role identity and reassurance of strength to the "strong" partner. If so, this suggests that for adults, as for children, even an anxious attachment does provide some amount of security; the spouse is a partially reliable base that supports some adaptive functioning. When either the "weak" or the "strong" partner dies, the other may be left with no secure base at all.

Delayed grief is relatively infrequent. In his study of psychiatric problems after bereavement, Parkes (1991) found that it was diagnosed in 20 percent of the patients. It was, however, disproportionately common among patients classified as compulsively self-reliant or pseudo independent. Unlike the "strong" partners of dependent spouses, the compulsively self-reliant patients appeared to be detached. Following bereavement, they kept up an image of independence and showed little grief. As time passed, it became more and more difficult for them to sustain the pretense that the loss of the spouse did not amount to much. In the language of attachment theory, we would guess that these individuals, with their strong avoidant defenses, were poorly prepared to acknowledge the importance of the lost figure, experience the emotional pain that comes with loss, and gradually resolve their grief.

Clinical findings are always complex. Despite the above classification of types of pathological grieving, Parkes (1991) reported that clinging and avoidance often overlapped, as did dependence and pseudo independence.

In the United States, Sable (1989) found support for some of the hypotheses Parkes and Weiss (1983) had articulated. Among bereaved women, she found that intensification of attachment behavior—a need for the company of others—was a normal response to the death of the husband. Widows who reported that they had supportive and adequate networks of friends and/or relatives adjusted to their losses better than those who lacked such networks. However, social bonds were not interchangeable. That is, friends and family could not make up for the loss of the unique individual to whom a widow had been attached and married for years.

Sable (1989) found that women who described their early attachments to their parents as secure had continuing advantages in recovering from the loss of the husband. Compared to women whose accounts of their childhood experiences reflected anxious attachments, they suffered less distress at the time of the loss and less depression and anxiety after it. Childhood experiences of separation, loss, or threats of abandonment were associated with increased anxiety and depression many years later when the grown woman's husband died. Sable characterized widows who said they had relied on their husbands for "everything" as anxiously attached. They showed more intense sadness and grief than other subjects did.

Much of the research on bereavement relies on nonstandardized clinical interviews, retrospective reports about childhood, and subjective evaluations of progress in resolving grieving. Can researchers develop standardized, objective measures of progress in grieving? So far, most of the adult subjects in studies of responses to loss have been female. Will results from studies of bereaved men match results from studies of bereaved women? The problem of relying on retrospective reports may be the hardest to solve. Prospective longitudinal research that measures (1) attachment patterns in childhood or in the early years of a marriage, (2) relevant intervening experiences, and (3) reactions to the loss of the spouse will take decades.

■ Separation and Divorce

Death is not the only cause of loss of access to an attachment figure. In parts of the modern world, separation and divorce disrupt adult attachment relationships about as often as death does. Despite the biological and cultural factors that encourage marriages to endure, about half of the marriages in the United States now end in divorce.

Attachment theory suggests at least three hypotheses about divorce. The first is that divorce will be more common when one or both partners have insecure representational models of attachments. The second is that loss of the spouse through divorce will be, like loss of the spouse through death, traumatic. The third is that emotional recovery from divorce will be easier and faster for people with secure working models of attachments than for people with anxious working models of attachments.

Let's consider the first hypothesis: people with secure models will be more likely than people with anxious models to form intimate relationships that endure; they will be less likely, once married, to separate and later divorce. For married or unmarried couples in long-term relationships—whether heterosexual, homosexual, or nonsexual—secure models and the open, direct communication associated with them should help partners stay together. The abilities to trust the partner, to communicate needs openly, and to respond caringly to the partner's needs should all contribute to the continuation of a mutually secure, reciprocal attachment.

I do not mean to imply that all marriages between secure partners should last indefinitely or that all marriages between anxious partners are at high risk for divorce. On the contrary, anxious attachments can also be very strong and stable. The fear of being alone can bind unhappy partners together as powerfully as the joy of being connected binds happy partners together. An attachment to a partner who is not really very effective as a secure base can still make a person feel far less anxious than he would feel with no partner at all. Just as anxiously attached people can choose to stay together, people with secure working models can choose to separate and divorce. A couple composed of one secure partner and one anxious partner may break up. Developmental changes in one or both members of a secure dyad can make them no longer suitable for each other. In addition, there is more to marriage than attachment. Factors associated with sex, money, and power may lead to divorce as often as dissatisfaction with the affective relationship does. Such factors can also preclude divorce when emotional dissatisfaction would otherwise make it seem desirable.

What data are available to test the hypothesis that divorce is less common for people with secure working models than it is for people with anxious models of attachments? So far, not many. Prospective studies of divorce are rare. Studies that relate adults' attachment patterns to risk of divorce are also rare. What we do have are the questionnaire data associated with self-classifications of attachment style. As noted earlier, these data indicate that secure people do tend to have longer-lasting relationships than people with avoidant or resistant attachment styles tend to have.

The second hypothesis stated at the beginning of this section was that divorce is, like death, traumatic. The responses to separation and divorce resemble the responses to the death of an attachment figure: initial shock if the failure of the marriage was previously unexpected or unacknowledged, then periods of anger, anxiety, depression, and denial in sequences and durations that vary from person to person.

Because some relatively amicable divorces occur, you may think that calling divorce traumatic overstates the case. Little systematic research is available. Samples for clinical research are seldom randomly selected; the people who seek psychotherapy after separation or divorce are not a representative sample of the people who experience separation and divorce.

Even so, the clinical evidence demonstrates convincingly that, more often than not, the attachment to the ex-spouse endures for months or years after separation, even if the relationship was awful and even in the partner who initiated the separation. However ambivalent or hostile the relationship may have been, and however much both parties will eventually benefit from its termination, the spousal relationship almost always provided some sense of security and some support for each of the partners. One ex-spouse or the other often clings to fantasies of reunion and tries to make the almost impossible reconciliation come true. Because remarriage of the same two people is not entirely impossible, although it is unlikely to be gratifying, the loss of the attachment figure can be very hard to accept.

One of the best-known studies of reactions to divorce was conducted in California by Wallerstein and Kelly (1977). Most of the subjects in their research were from white middle-class families. After counseling 60 families in the early months after divorce, Wallerstein and Kelly (1977) reported high frequencies of guilt, loneliness, depression, and conscious and unconscious fears of being overwhelmed by homosexual, heterosexual, or aggressive impulses. In some subjects, the eruption of impulses was so great that all pretense of rational thinking was abandoned: they attacked the former spouse through burglary, poisoning pets, kidnapping, and brandishing weapons.

A similar intensity of distress and irrationality emerged in another major study of divorce, this one conducted by research psychologists, not clinical psychologists. In a systematic longitudinal study, Hetherington, Cox, and Cox (1977) also found that divorce was indeed traumatic. Each of the 48 families in their research included a child who was 4 years old at the time of the divorce, which occurred about 12 to 18 months after the parents separated. In every case, the mother had custody of the child or children. Shortly after the divorce, 75 percent of the fathers said they were coping less well at work. They complained of not knowing who they were, of being rootless, of having no home or structure to their lives. Nine of the forty-eight also reported increases in sexual dysfunction. For about one-third of the fathers and one-fourth of the mothers, divorce initially brought an ebullient sense of freedom, but the exuberance did not last. A year after the divorce, both mothers and fathers reported much depression, apathy, and anxiety. The mothers, who had custody, were intensely lonely. Many said they felt imprisoned in a child's world. As a group, the divorced women felt helpless, unattractive, and lost. They described themselves as more anxious, depressed, angry, rejected, and incompetent than married mothers typically describe themselves as being. (By the time another year passed, these negative feelings had decreased.)

Just as attachment theory predicts, the attachment to the spouse persisted and in some cases even increased following the escape from daily conflicts. Six of the forty-eight couples in this sample had sexual intercourse with their former spouses in the first 2 months after the divorce. More than half of the subjects (34 of the mothers and 29 of the fathers) said that if a crisis developed, the first person they would call would be the ex-spouse. Seeking help or comfort in a time of crisis certainly sounds like an example of directing attachment behavior to the ex-spouse. One year after the divorce, more than half of the subjects (29 of the fathers and 35 of the mothers) said that they thought the divorce might have been a mistake and that they should have tried harder to resolve their conflicts. Another year later, only 12 of the mothers and 9 of the fathers still thought so. The process of convincing themselves that the separation was real and permanent took much longer than the subjects had expected.

The third hypothesis introduced in this section was that, in recovering from the ending of a relationship, as in recovering from the death of an attachment figure, it is likely that people with secure working models have advantages. If this expectation is correct, secure subjects can more easily acknowledge and resolve their conflicting feelings, seek and use support from relatives and friends, reorganize their lives constructively, and move on. The more anxious the attachment was, the more likely it is that the subsequent mourning will include intense anger and/or self-reproach and depression, and that it will persist for an unusually long time. Clinical and anecdotal evidence shows that some people cling to their rage, their helplessness, and their disrupted attachment to a former spouse for many years. However, systematic prospective research about how people with different attachment models or styles recover from divorce is not yet available.

OLD AGE

Among the elderly, a lack of social support is associated with negative outcomes such as poor physical and mental health, depression, and unwelcome institutionalization. According to Levitt (1991), few investigators have differentiated between close relationships and other relationships in the social network. Close relationships may be attachment relationships. A doctor, a relative who sometimes visits, and the senior citizens who play cards together every Wednesday afternoon may individually and collectively contribute to an elderly person's well-being, but attachment theory suggests that their contribution may be qualitatively different from the contribution of an attachment figure. An attachment figure would be someone to whom the elderly person could go for comfort, care, and protection in times of stress, and probably someone she could confide in. Levitt (1991) cited three studies that have addressed the issue of what types of relationships the social network includes. All three suggest that well-being is related to support from close relationships, not to the support network in general. It appears that the people who provide the most valuable support are the people in the inner circle of the social network.

In her own research, Levitt studied a group of adults who reported having no one in the inner circle. A person who has no close relationships has no functional attachment figure. The affect of people in this group was significantly more negative than the affect of people who had even one close relationship. In affect, the adults who had only one close relationship did not differ significantly from those who had more than one close relationship. These results suggest that having even one close relationship may be sufficient to foster well-being. As in the case of any correlational research, we must be careful about inferring a direction of causality. An alternative interpretation of these data is plausible: having a relatively high level of negative affect may reduce a person's chances of having even one close relationship.

Kalish and Knudtson (1976) cited other research illustrating that it can be enormously important for an elderly person to have someone to talk to and confide in. More than any other single factor, having a confidante differentiated between elderly people who stayed in the community and those who moved into institutions. Losing the confidante resulted in depression. Individuals who maintained a relationship with a confidante could lose other social interactions without suffering changes in their affective well-being. While a confidante may not be a source of protection from physical dangers; it is easy to believe that a person who listens with interest and sympathy as you describe your joys and problems is serving at the affective level as an attachment figure, a secure base.

What little evidence we have, then, lends some support to the view that having an attachment figure remains important for an individual's physical and emotional well-being even in old age.

What about the senior citizen's relationship with adult offspring? How long do most dyads maintain the asymmetrical relationship of early childhood, when the older partner gave care and the young one depended on it? Do roles in attachment-caregiving relationships ordinarily become reciprocal as the child becomes an adult? Do they ordinarily become reversed as the parent ages? What other variables are associated with the security of an aging parent's attachment to his or her child?

To begin studying such questions, Barnas, Pollina, and Cummings (1991) used their structured interview with 48 white middle-class women over age 64. The subject's attachment to each child was rated on a 4-point continuum. A score of 1.0 (secure) indicated that the grown child was an extremely important source of security and served as a stable figure to whom the parent looked for comfort. A score of 2.0 (insecure) indicated that there was clear evidence that the parent had difficulty deriving comfort and security from the child. However, the parent still looked to the child for support, and the child was a relatively predictable figure. A score of 3.5 (very insecure) indicated that there was only slight evidence that the child was ever a source of security. Signs of insecurity were severe and were exhibited in multiple aspects of the relationship. A score of 4.0 (detached) was even worse: there was no evidence of any caring or providing for one another; any contact that occurred was marked by negative interaction.

Over half of the subjects for this study were widows. All lived at home—50 percent alone, 42 percent with a spouse, and 8 percent with a grown child. In these subjects' self-reported hierarchies of close relationships, their children were almost always primary figures. Many of the subjects (38 percent) had no children living nearby and so had to rely on long-distance relationships. Most of the subjects (67 percent) had a secure (1.0 or 1.5) relationship with at least one child. Half of them had an insecure attachment to at least one of their children. Many (31 percent) had a very insecure relationship (3.0 to 4.0) with at least one child.

Ten of the forty-eight subjects (21 percent) had insecure-avoidant attachments with all of their children. Their responses to the interview questions indicated that they were highly avoidant both during stressful situations and during nonstressful ones. Their relationships were more problematic than other women's relationships were. Nineteen women (40 percent) reported mixed patterns. They showed various signs of insecurity across their relationships with their children, but did not consistently avoid or resist interaction with them. Often, they had one or more secure relationships and one or more insecure ones. Nineteen women (40 percent) had secure relationships with all of their children.

Group differences in the qualities of these older women's relations with their grown children were not related to marital status, age, sex of child, number of children, or number of children living in the area. That marital status had no impact is interesting. Compared to women who were still living with their husbands, we might have expected the widows to work harder to develop secure attachments to at least one of their children. A married woman may be able look to her husband when she needs practical assistance, protection, physical care, or emotional support or comfort. A widow must look elsewhere. If, compared to the still-married women, the widows in this sample were working harder to elicit support or comfort from their offspring, they were not attaining more success. This is consistent with the hypothesis that representational models enhance or constrain patterns of interaction and qualities of relationships, regardless of how much the individual needs the relationship to be secure. However, the elderly parents' models clearly were not the sole determinants of qualities of relationships with adult children. Many women (40 percent) had secure attachments to one or more, but not all, of their children.

Contrary to what I would have expected, the average scores on measures of social, psychological, and physical well-being were similar for women with secure attachments to their grown children and women with insecure ones. However, rather extreme negative scores were more common among the women with anxious attachments. They also reported using more strategies for coping with stress. This suggests that the strategies they tried first were not effective, so they had to keep trying something else.

Obviously, attachment research that focuses on senior citizens is in its infancy. Further use and validation of the interview Barnas et al. (1991) developed will be helpful. Using the AAI with this population to assess internal models of attachment and then relating classifications from the AAI to measures of health, independent functioning in the community, and qualities of observed interaction with grown children or with grandchildren would be intriguing. Interaction at the moment of reunion is likely to be highly informative. Long separations and periodic visits between senior citizens and their grown children are routine in many families, so naturalistic observations of reunions might be easy to arrange. The hypothesis that having at least one secure attachment, whether to the spouse, to a grown child, or to a confidante, increases physical and emotional well-being has not been adequately tested. The hypothesis that parents whose children are anxiously attached to them will become senior citizens with anxious attachments to their grown children has not been tested at all.

CHAPTER SUMMARY

The first studies of attachments in the college years and in adults found that secure attachment is associated with high ego-resiliency, high self-confidence, and easy relations with peers. Compared to adults with resistant or avoidant attachment models or styles, secure adults find it easier to build relationships that are happy, friendly, trusting, and long-lasting. They are less likely to report chronic loneliness. Avoidant attachment is associated with mistrust of others, distance from them, loneliness and hostility. Preoccupied or resistant attachment is associated with open anxiety and distress. People with resistant attachment styles tend to have passionate, jealous, short love relationships full of emotional highs and lows.

Results based on questionnaire responses were later supported in studies that also used telephone interviews and/or brief observations in the laboratory, and results based on cross-sectional research were later supported in short longitudinal studies. In addition, these studies yielded some evidence that secure subjects tend to date and marry each other while resistant subjects tend to date and marry avoidant subjects (and vice versa).

The first careful, detailed study of marriage from an attachment perspective (Kobak and Hazan, 1991) yielded a complex array of results. Interpreting the results required some awareness of sex-role expectations as well as attention to attachment models. Both spouses' ratings of marital adjustment were associated with the husband's model of the wife's psychological availability. The wife's rating of the husband's psychological availability contributed to her rating of marital adjustment, but not to his. How well the spouses agreed in independent descriptions of the wife, how well they agreed in independent descriptions of the husband, what score the wife gave them for dyadic adjustment, and what score the husband gave them for dyadic adjustment all clustered together. The level of agreement between the wife's representational models and the husband's, as measured through Kobak's Marital Q-Set, was also a good predictor of harmony in observed behavior.

Using the AAI, Cohn et al. (1992) failed to replicate the association between secure attachment and marital satisfaction. In laboratory observations of husband, wife, and preschool child, however, couples in which both partners were insecure showed more conflict and poorer functioning than couples in which at least one partner was secure.

Loss of a major attachment figure is a blow at any age. Adults normally react with a period of numbness, a period of yearning and irrational searching for the lost attachment figure, a period of disorganization and despair, and then acceptance and reorganization. In some cases, however, grieving does not progress normally. There is some evidence that adults with secure representational models of attachments resolve grieving more easily and more quickly than adults with anxious models do.

Divorce from a spouse, like the death of the spouse, ordinarily constitutes the loss of a major attachment figure. Responses to separation and divorce closely resemble responses to bereavement: sometimes a period of shock, and then anxiety, disbelief, anger, depression, and, if all goes well, eventual acceptance and reorganization.

Preliminary evidence suggests that having at least one attachment figure increases physical and emotional well-being in senior citizens. In some cases, the caregiver/care-receiver attachment between parent and child reverses when the parent grows old; the child becomes the secure base for the aging parent.

Except for the work on separation and loss, most of the research reported in this chapter is quite recent. We will have to wait for further evidence about how reliable and valid the methods were and how consistently these first results can be replicated. Research on characteristics and correlates of attachments in the years of adolescence and adulthood should be an exciting arena in the coming years.

EPILOGUE

This book was in preparation for over three years and then in press for several months. During that time, new research on attachment issues, new elaborations of aspects of attachment theory, and new specifications of relevant hypotheses proliferated faster than they could be integrated into this manuscript.

Although there is too much good new work to incorporate into a short epilogue, mentioning one very recent study seems irresistable. The research was informative in a way that is very difficult to achieve: it involved locating 50 young adults (age 20 to 22) who had been observed in Strange Situations in infancy, using the AAI to assess their representational models of attachments, and testing specific hypotheses about continuity and change in attachment patterns (Waters, Merrick, Albersheim, Treboux, and Crowell, 1995). Assuming that (1) the infant-mother relationship serves as the prototype for later love relationships, (2) quality of care tends to be fairly consistent through childhood in middle-class samples, and (3) representational models, once formed, tend to maintain themselves, the anticipated matches between infant and adult classifications of these white, middle-class subjects were avoidant-dismissing, secure-secure, and resistant-preoccupied. Despite the unavailability of the D category when these subjects were infants and despite the 20-year interval between attachment assessments, classifications matched predictions for 31 of the subjects (62 percent)—an impressive illustration of continuity.

Many of the cases of change in attachment patterns in this sample appeared to reflect intervening experiences that are likely to prompt modifications of representational models: the loss of a parent, parental divorce, life-threatening illness in the parent or the subject, parental psychiatric disorders, and physical or sexual abuse of the subject. Subjects who had not experienced any such events were the most likely to show consistency in attachment patterns from infancy to adulthood. However, even in that group, 9 of the 32 subjects (28 percent) did receive different classifications at the two assessments, suggesting that other, less traumatic experiences can also prompt an individual to update or modify representational models. Problems with the reliability and validity of the measures may account for some mismatches, but experiences after infancy certainly appear to play a role in adult security.

Even as attachment theory and research race forward, huge gaps in the research remain. *One of the top priorities for future research should be a return to ethological observations:* many long visits to the subjects in their natural settings over a period of months or years. Only such research can overcome subjects' tendencies to hide some information from psychological observers and dramatize other information for them. Although such research is expensive and time-consuming, it is the only type of research that can clarify:

- The relative impacts on infants' attachment patterns of (1) the parent's sensitive responsiveness, (2) the baby's temperament, (3) the practical and emotional supports and stresses the parent experiences in her or his social network, including (4) the quality of the parents' marriage, (5) the parent's attachment history, (6) the parent's current representational models of attachment, (7) each parent's role as a primary or secondary caregiver for the infant, and (8) each parent's employment status;
- The ordinary causes of avoidance of the parent or other caregiver;
- What aspects of experience underlie B4 and D behavior in the Strange Situation in infants in low-risk samples;
- Whether infants form lasting emotional bonds to hired caregivers;
- To what degree and in what ways a baby or child carries the expectations and the organization of behavior learned in his or her first love relationship into new social relationships;
- The vicissitudes of primary attachment relationships in the second year, when autonomy and discipline become big issues in many families;
- How the goal-corrected partnership emerges;
- What differences in the everyday behavior of child-parent dyads are associated with the different patterns of behavior three- and four-year-olds show in the Strange Situation;
- How the effects and other sequelae of early attachment patterns differ according to a child's gender and the family's socioeconomic status and racial and cultural background;
- What the real life correlates of patterns of attachment at age 6 are and how valid current methods of assessment are; and
- What the real life correlates of patterns of attachment in adolescents and adults are and how valid current methods of assessment are.

While the importance of repeated, long, ethological observations spaced over many months cannot be overstated, we also need other research approaches. For example, when a specific hypothesis can be tested by conducting a true experiment with random assignment to groups, the contribution to the field is very valuable.

If this book helps to inspire another generation to study attachment issues scientifically, it will have served one of its purposes.

REFERENCES

Achenbach, I. M. (1978). The child behavior profile, 1: Boys aged 6–11. *Journal of Consulting and Clinical Psychology, 46,* 478–488.

Achermann, J., Dinneen, E., & Stevenson-Hinde, J. (1991). Clearing up at 2.5 years. *British Journal of Developmental Psychology, 9,* 365–376.

Ainsworth, M. D. (1967). *Infancy in Uganda.* Baltimore: Johns Hopkins Press.

Ainsworth, M. D. (1972). Attachment and dependency: A comparison. In J. L. Gewirtz (Ed.), *Attachment and dependency.* Washington, DC: V. H. Winston and Sons.

Ainsworth, M. D. (1973). The development of infant-mother attachment. In B. M. Caldwell & H. N. Ricciuti (Eds.), *Review of child development research* (Vol. 3, pp. 1–94). Chicago: University of Chicago Press.

Ainsworth, M. D. (1982). Attachment: Retrospect and prospect. In C. M. Parkes & J. Stevenson-Hinde (Eds.), *The place of attachment in human behavior* (pp. 3–30). London: Tavistock Publications.

Ainsworth, M. D. (1983). Patterns of infant-mother attachment as related to maternal care: Their early history and their contribution to continuity. In D. Magnusson & V. L. Allen (Eds.), *Human development: An interactional perspective* (pp. 35–55). New York: Academic Press.

Ainsworth, M. D. (1989a). Attachments beyond infancy. *American Psychologist, 44,* 709–716.

Ainsworth, M. D. (1990). Some considerations regarding theory and assessment relevant to attachments beyond infancy. In M. Greenberg, D. Cicchetti, and E. M. Cummings (Eds.), *Attachment in the preschool years: Theory, research, and intervention* (pp. 463–488). Chicago: University of Chicago Press.

Ainsworth, M. D. (1991a). Attachments and other affectional bonds across the life cycle. In C. M. Parkes, J. Stevenson-Hinde, & P. Marris (Eds.), *Attachment across the life cycle* (pp. 33–51). London: Routledge.

Ainsworth, M. D., Blehar, M. C., Waters, E., & Wall, S. (1978). *Patterns of attachment: A psychological study of the Strange Situation.* Hillsdale, NJ: Lawrence Erlbaum Associates.

347

348
References

Ainsworth, M. D., & Eichberg, C. (1991). Effects on infant-mother attachment of mother's unresolved loss of an attachment figure, or other traumatic experience. In C. M. Parkes, J. Stevenson-Hinde, & P. Marris (Eds.), *Attachment across the life cycle* (pp. 160–183). London: Routledge.

Ainsworth, M. D., & Wittig, B. A. (1969). Attachment and exploratory behavior of 1-year-olds in a Strange Situation. In B. M. Foss (Ed.), *Determinants of infant behavior* (Vol. 4, pp. 129–173). London: Netheum.

American Psychiatric Association (1994). *Diagnostic and statistical manual of mental disorders: DSM-IV.* Washington, DC: American Psychiatric Association.

Anderson, J. (1972). Attachment behavior out of doors. In N. G. Blurton-Jones (Ed.), *Ethological studies of child behavior.* London: Cambridge University Press.

Andersson, B.-E. (1989). Effects of public day-care: A longitudinal study. *Child Development, 60,* 857–866.

Anisfeld, E., Casper, V., Nozyce, M., & Cunningham, N. (1990). Does infant carrying promote attachment? An experimental study of the effects of increased physical contact on the development of attachment. *Child Development, 61,* 1617–1627.

Arend, R., Gove, F., & Sroufe, L. A. (1979). Continuity of individual adaptation from infancy to kindergarten: A predictive study of ego resiliency and curiosity in preschoolers. *Child Development, 50,* 950–959.

Bakermans-Kranenburg, M. J., & Van IJzendoorn, M. H. (1993). A psychometric study of the Adult Attachment Interview: Reliability and discriminant validity. *Developmental Psychology, 29,* 870–879.

Barnas, M. V., & Cummings, E. M. (1994). Caregiver stability and toddler's attachment-related behavior towards caregivers in day care. *Infant Behavior and Development, 17,* 141–147.

Barnas, M. V., Pollina, L., & Cummings, E. M. (1991). Life-span attachment: Relations between attachment and socioemotional functioning in adult women. *Genetic, Social, and General Psychology Monographs, 117,* 177–202.

Barnett, B., Blignault, I., Holmes, S., Payne, A., & Parker, G. (1987). Quality of attachment in a sample of 1-year-old Australian children. *Journal of the American Academy of Child and Adolescent Psychiatry, 26,* 303–307.

Bartholomew, K. (1990). Avoidance of intimacy: An attachment perspective. *Journal of Social and Personal Relationships, 7,* 147–178.

Bartholomew, K., & Horowitz, L. (1991). Attachment styles among young adults: A test of a four-category model. *Journal of Personality and Social Psychology, 61,* 226–244.

Bartholomew, K., & Perlman, D. (Eds). (1994). *Attachment processes in adulthood: Vol. 5. Advances in personal relationships.* London: Jessica Kingsley Publishers.

Bass, M. L. (1982). *Quality of infant attachment to father as related to amount of father-infant interaction.* Unpublished doctoral dissertation, University of Texas, Dallas.

Bates, J. E., & Bayles, K. (1988). Attachment and the development of behavior problems. In J. Belsky & T. Nezworski (Eds.), *Clinical implications of attachment.* Hillsdale, NJ: Lawrence Erlbaum Associates.

REFERENCES

Bates, J. E., Maslin, C. A., & Frankel, K. A. (1985). Attachment security, mother-child interaction, and temperament as predictors of behavior-problem ratings at age 3 years. In I. Bretherton & E. Waters (Eds.), Growing points of attachment theory and research. *Monographs of the Society for Research in Child Development, 50* (1–2, Serial No. 209), 167–193.

Behar, L. B. (1977). The preschool behavior questionnaire. *Journal of Abnormal Child Psychology, 5,* 265–275.

Behar, L., & Stringfield, S. (1974). A behavior rating scale for the preschool child. *Developmental Psychology, 10,* 601–610.

Bell, R. Q. (1988–89). Neonatal behavior predictors of security of attachment. *Research and Clinical Center for Child Development Annual Report, 12,* 3–13.

Bell, S. M., & Ainsworth, M. D. (1972). Infant crying and maternal responsiveness. *Child Development, 43,* 1171–1190.

Belsky, J. (1988). The "effects" of infant day care reconsidered. *Early Childhood Research Quarterly, 3,* 235–273.

Belsky, J., & Braungart, J. M. (1991). Are insecure-avoidant infants with extensive day-care experience less stressed by and more independent in the Strange Situation? *Child Development, 62,* 567–571.

Belsky, J., & Cassidy, J. (1994). Attachment: Theory and evidence. In M. Rutter, D. Hay, and S. Baron-Cohen (Eds.), *Developmental principles and clinical issues in psychology and psychiatry.* Oxford: Blackwell Science Publishers.

Belsky, J., & Isabella, R. (1988). Maternal, infant, and social-contextual determinants of attachment security. In J. Belsky & T. Nezworski, (Eds)., *Clinical implications of attachment* (pp. 41–94). Hillsdale, NJ: Lawrence Erlbaum Associates.

Belsky, J., & Nezworski, T. (1988). (Eds)., *Clinical implications of attachment.* Hillsdale, NJ: Lawrence Erlbaum Associates.

Belsky, J., & Rovine, M. J. (1987). Temperament and attachment security in the Strange Situation: An empirical rapprochement. *Child Development, 58,* 787–795.

Belsky, J., & Rovine, M. J. (1988). Nonmaternal care in the first year of life and the security of infant-parent attachment. *Child Development, 59,* 157–167.

Belsky, J., & Rovine, M. J. (1990). Q-sort security and first-year nonmaternal care. *New Directions for Child Development: Child Care and Maternal Employment, 49,* 7–22.

Belsky, J., Rovine, M., & Taylor, D. G. (1984). The Pennsylvania infant and family development project, III. The origins of individual differences in infant-mother attachment: Maternal and infant contributions. *Child Development, 55,* 718–728.

Block, J. H., & Block, J. (1980). The role of ego-control and ego-resiliency in the organization of behavior. In A. Collins (Ed)., *Minnesota Symposium of Child Psychology, 13* (pp. 39–101). Hillsdale, NJ: Lawrence Erlbaum Associates.

Bohlin, G., Hagekull, B., Germer, M., Andersson, K., et al. (1989). Avoidant and resistant reunion behaviors as predicted by maternal interactive behavior and infant temperament. *Infant Behavior and Development, 12,* 105–117.

Bornstein, M., & Lamb, M. E. (1992). Development in infancy: An introduction (3rd ed.). New York: McGraw-Hill.

Bowlby, J. (1944). Forty-four juvenile thieves: Their characters and home life. *International Journal of Psychoanalysis, 25,* 19–52, 107–127.

Bowlby, J. (1958). The nature of the child's tie to his mother. *International Journal of Psychoanalysis, 39,* 350–373.

Bowlby, J. ([1969] 1982). *Attachment and loss, Vol. I. Attachment,* (2nd ed.). New York: Basic Books.

Bowlby, J. (1973). *Attachment and loss, Vol. II. Separation: Anxiety and anger.* New York: Basic Books.

Bowlby, J. (1980). *Attachment and loss, Vol III. Loss, sadness, and depression.* New York: Basic Books.

Bowlby, J. (1982). Attachment and loss: Retrospect and prospect. *American Journal of Orthopsychiatry, 52,* 664–678.

Bowlby, J. (1984). Violence in the family as a disorder of the attachment and caregiving systems. *American Journal of Psychoanalysis, 44,* 9–27, 29–31.

Bowlby, J. (1988). Developmental psychiatry comes of age. *American Journal of Psychiatry, 145,* 1–10.

Bowlby, J. (1991). Ethological light on psychoanalytical problems. In P. Bateson (Ed.), *Development and integration of behaviour* (pp. 315–329). Cambridge: Cambridge University Press.

Bradley, R., Caldwell, B., & Rock, S. (1988). Home environment and school performance: A ten-year follow-up and examination of three models of environmental action. *Child Development, 59,* 852–867.

Bradshaw, D. L. (1985–86). Contributions of research on Japanese infants and mothers to the study of attachment. *Research and Clinical Center for Child Development Annual Report, 9,* 19–28.

Braungart, J. M., Plomin, R., DeFries, J. C., & Fulker, D. W. (1992). Genetic influence on tester-related infant temperament as assessed by Bayley's Infant Behavior Record: Nonadoptive and adoptive siblings and twins. *Developmental Psychology, 28,* 40–47.

Braungart, J. M., & Stifter, C. A. (1991). Regulation of negative reactivity during the Strange Situation: Temperament and attachment in 12-month-old infants. *Infant Behavior and Development, 14,* 349–364.

Brazelton, T. B. (1973). *Neonatal Behavioral Assessment Scale.* Philadelphia: J. B. Lippincott.

Brennan, K. A., Shaver, P. R., & Tobey, A. E. (1991). Attachment styles, gender and parental problem drinking. *Journal of Social and Personal Relationships, 8,* 451–466.

Bretherton, I. (1985). Attachment theory: Retrospect and prospect. In I. Bretherton & E. Waters (Eds.), Growing points of attachment theory and research. *Monographs of the Society for Research in Child Development, 50* (1–2, Serial No. 209), 3–35.

Bretherton, I. (1987). New perspectives on attachment relations: Security, communication and internal working models. In J. Osofsky (Ed.), *Handbook of infant development* (2nd ed., pp. 1061–1100). New York: Wiley.

Bretherton, I. (1991). The roots and growing points of attachment theory. In C. M. Parkes, J. Stevenson-Hinde, & P. Marris (Eds.), *Attachment across the life cycle* (pp. 9–32). London: Routledge.

Bretherton, I., Ridgeway, D., & Cassidy, J. (1990). The role of internal working models in the attachment relationship: Theoretical, empirical, and developmental considerations. In M. Greenberg, D. Cicchetti, and E. M. Cummings (Eds.), *Attachment in the preschool years: Theory, research, and intervention* (pp. 273–320). Chicago: University of Chicago Press.

Bridges, L. J., & Connell, J. P. (1991). Consistency and inconsistency in infant emotional and social interactive behavior across contexts and caregivers. *Infant Behavior and Development, 14,* 471–487.

Brinich, E., Drotar, D., & Brinich, P. (1989). Security of attachment and outcome of preschoolers with histories of nonorganic failure to thrive. *Journal of Clinical Child Psychology, 18,* 142–152.

Brown, G. W., & Harris, T. (1978). *The social origins of depression: A study of psychiatric disorder in women.* London: Tavistock Publications.

Bus, A. G., & Van IJzendoorn, M. H. (1988). Mother-child interactions, attachment, and emergent literacy: A cross-sectional study. *Child Development, 59,* 1262–1272.

Caldwell, B. M., & Bradley, R. H. (1979). *Home observation for measurement of the environment.* Little Rock: University of Arkansas Press.

Carey, W. B. (1970). A simplified method for measuring infant temperament. *Journal of Pediatrics, 77,* 188–194.

Carey, W. B., & McDevitt, S. C. (1978). Revision of the infant temperament questionnaire. *Pediatrics, 61,* 735–739.

Carlson, V., Cicchetti, D., Barnett, D., & Braunwald, K. G. (1989a). Disorganized/disoriented attachment relationships in maltreated infants. *Developmental Psychology, 25,* 525–531.

Carlson, V., Cicchetti, D., Barnett, D., & Braunwald, K. G. (1989b). Finding order in disorganization: Lessons from research on maltreated infants' attachments to their caregivers. In D. Cicchetti & V. Carlson (Eds.), *Child maltreatment: Theory and research on the causes and consequences of maltreatment* (pp. 494–528). New York: Cambridge University Press.

Carr, S., Dabbs, J., & Carr, T. (1975). Mother-infant attachment: The importance of mothers' visual field. *Child Development, 46,* 331–338.

Cassidy, J. (1988). Child-mother attachment and the self in 6-year-olds. *Child Development, 59,* 121–134.

Cassidy, J. (1991). *Emotion regulation within attachment relationships.* Unpublished manuscript, Pennsylvania State University, University Park.

Cassidy, J., & Berlin, L. J. (1994). The insecure/ambivalent pattern of attachment: Theory and research. *Child Development, 65,* 971–991.

Cassidy, J., & Kobak, R. R. (1988). Avoidance and its relation to other defensive processes. In J. Belsky & T. Nezworski (Eds.), *Clinical implications of attachment.* Hillsdale, NJ: Lawrence Erlbaum Associates.

Cassidy, J., Marvin, R., and the MacArthur Working Group on Attachment. (1992). *Attachment organization in 3- and 4-year-olds: Guidelines for classification.* Unpublished scoring manual, Pennsylvania State University, University Park.

Chase-Lansdale, P. L., & Owen, M. T. (1987). Maternal employment in a family context: Effects on infant-mother and infant-father attachments. *Child Development, 58,* 1505–1512.

Cicchetti, D. (1987). Developmental psychopathology in infancy: Illustration from the study of maltreated youngsters. *Journal of Consulting and Clinical Psychology, 55,* 837–845.

Cicchetti, D., & Barnett, D. (1991). Attachment organization in maltreated preschoolers. Special issue: Attachment and development psychopathology. *Development and Psychopathology, 3,* 397–411.

Cicchetti, D., Cummings, E. M., Greenberg, M. T., & Marvin, R. S. (1990). An organizational perspective on attachment beyond infancy: Implications for theory, measurement, and research. In M. T. Greenberg, D. Cicchetti, & E. M. Cummings (Eds.), *Attachment in the preschool years: Theory, research, and intervention* (pp. 3–49). Chicago: University of Chicago Press.

Clarke-Stewart, K. A. (1978). And Daddy makes three: The father's impact on mother and young child. *Child Development, 49,* 466–482.

Clarke-Stewart, K. A. (1988). The effects of infant day care reconsidered: Risks for parents, children, and researchers. *Early Childhood Research Quarterly, 3,* 293–318.

Cohen, L. J., & Campos, J. J. (1974). Father, mother and stranger as elicitors of attachment behaviours in infancy. *Developmental Psychology, 10,* 146–154.

Cohn, D. A. (1990). Child-mother attachment of 6-year-olds and social competence at school. *Child Development, 61,* 152–162.

Cohn, D. A., Cowan, P. A., Cowan, C. P., & Pearson, J. (1992). Mothers' and fathers' working models of childhood attachment relationships, parenting styles, and child behavior. *Development and Psychopathology, 4,* 417–431.

Colin, V. (1985). *Hierarchies and patterns of infants' attachments to parents and day caregivers: An exploration.* Unpublished doctoral dissertation, University of Virginia, Charlottesville.

Colin, V. (1987). *Infants' preferences between parents before and after moderate stress activates attachment behavior.* Paper presented at the meeting of the Society for Research in Child Development, Baltimore, MD.

Colin, V. (1991). *Human attachment: What we know now.* Washington DC: U.S. Department of Health and Human Services.

Collins, N. L., & Read, S. J. (1990). Adult attachment, working models, and relationship quality in dating couples. *Journal of Personality and Social Psychology, 58,* 644–663.

Connell, D. B. (1976). *Individual differences in attachment: An investigation into stability, implications, and relationships to structure of early language development.* Unpublished doctoral dissertation, Syracuse University, Syracuse.

Cox, M. J., Owen, M. T., Henderson, V. K., & Margand, N. A. (1992). Prediction of infant-father and infant-mother attachment. *Developmental Psychology, 28,* 474–483.

Crittenden, P. M. (1981). Abusing, neglecting, problematic, and adequate dyads: Differentiating by patterns of interaction. *Merrill-Palmer Quarterly, 27,* 201–218.

Crittenden, P. M. (1983). The effect of mandatory protective daycare on mutual attachment in maltreating mother-infant dyads. *International Journal of Child Abuse and Neglect, 3,* 297–300.

Crittenden, P. M. (1985). Maltreated infants: Vulnerability and resilience. *Journal of Child Psychology and Psychiatry, 26,* 85–96.

Crittenden, P. M. (1988a). Distorted patterns of relationship in maltreating families: The role of internal representational models. *Journal of Reproductive and Infant Psychology, 6,* 183–199.

REFERENCES

Crittenden, P. M. (1988b). Family and dyadic patterns of functioning in maltreating families. In K. Browne, C. Davies, & P. Stratton (Eds.), *Early prediction and prevention of child abuse.* Chichester, England: Wiley.

Crittenden, P. M. (1988c). Relationships at risk. In J. Belsky & T. Nezworski (Eds.), *Clinical implications of attachment.* Hillsdale, NJ: Lawrence Erlbaum Associates.

Crittenden, P. M. (1990). Internal representational models of attachment relationships. *Infant Mental Health Journal, 11,* 259–277.

Crittenden, P. M. (1991). *The Miami Preschool Attachment Classificatory System.* Unpublished coding manual, University of Miami, Miami, FL.

Crittenden, P. M. (1992a). Quality of attachment in the preschool years. *Development and Psychopathology, 4,* 209–241.

Crittenden, P. M. (1992b). Treatment of anxious attachment in infancy and early childhood. *Development and Psychopathology, 4,* 575–602.

Crittenden, P. M. (1993). *Information processing and Ainsworth's patterns of attachment.* Paper presented at *John Bowlby's attachment theory: Historical, clinical, and social significance.* C. M. Hinks Institute, Toronto, Canada.

Crittenden, P. M. (1994). Peering into the black box: An exploratory treatise on the development of self in young children. In D. Cicchetti & S. L. Toth (Eds.), *Rochester Symposium on Developmental Psychopathology: Vol. 5. Disorders and dysfunctions of the self* (pp. 79–148). Rochester, NY: University of Rochester Press.

Crittenden, P. M., & Ainsworth, M. D. (1989). Child maltreatment and attachment theory. In D. Cicchetti & V. Carlson (Eds.), *Child maltreatment: Theory and research on the causes and consequences of child abuse and neglect* (pp. 432–463). New York: Cambridge University Press.

Crockenberg, S. B. (1981). Infant irritability, mother responsiveness, and social support influences on the security of infant-mother attachment. *Child Development, 52,* 857–869.

Crockenberg, S. & McCluskey, K. (1986). Change in maternal behavior during the baby's first year of life. *Child Development, 57,* 746–753.

Crowell, J. A., & Feldman, S. S. (1988). Mothers' internal models of relationships and children's behavioral and developmental status: A study of mother-child interaction. *Child Development, 59,* 1273–1285.

Crowell, J. A., O'Connor, E., Wollmers, G., Sprafkin, J., & Rao, U. (1991). Mothers' conceptualizations of parent-child relationships: Relation to mother-child interaction and child behavior problems. *Development and Psychopathology, 3,* 431–444.

Cummings, E. M. (1980). Caregiver stability and attachment in infant day care. *Developmental Psychology, 16,* 31–37.

Cummings, E. M. (1990). Classification of attachment on a continuum of felt security: Illustrations from the study of children of depressed parents. In M. T. Greenberg, D. Cicchetti, & E. M. Cummings (Eds.), *Attachment in the preschool years: Theory, research, and intervention* (pp. 311–338). Chicago: University of Chicago Press.

D'Angelo, E. J. (1986). Security of attachment in infants with schizophrenic, depressed, and unaffected mothers. *Journal of Genetic Psychology, 147,* 421–422.

DeMulder, E. K., & Radke-Yarrow, M. (1991). Attachment with affectively ill and well mothers: Concurrent behavioral correlates. *Development and Psychopathology, 3,* 227–242.

Donovan, W. L., & Leavitt, L. A. (1989). Maternal self-efficacy and infant attachment: Integrating physiology, perceptions, and behavior. *Child Development, 60,* 460–472.

Dozier, M., & Kobak, R. R. (1992). Psychophysiology in attachment interviews: Converging evidence for deactivating strategies. *Child Development, 63,* 1473–1480.

Easterbrooks, M. A., & Goldberg, W. A. (1987). *Consequences of early family attachment patterns for later social-personality development.* Paper presented at the Society for Research in Child Development, Baltimore, MD.

Egeland, B., & Erickson, M. (1993). Attachment theory and findings: Implications for prevention and intervention. In H. Parens & S. Kramer (Eds)., *Prevention in mental health.* Northvale, NJ: Aronson.

Egeland, B., & Farber, E. A. (1984). Infant-mother attachment: Factors related to its development and changes over time. *Child Development, 55,* 753–771.

Egeland, B., & Sroufe, L. A. (1981). Attachment and early maltreatment. *Child Development, 52,* 44–52.

Eichberg, C. (1987). *Security of attachment in infancy: Contributions of mother's representation of her own experience and child-care attitudes.* Unpublished doctoral dissertation, University of Virginia, Charlottesville.

Erickson, M. F., and Farber, E. A. (1983). *Infancy to preschool: Continuity of adaptation in high-risk children.* Paper presented at the meeting of the Society for Research in Child Development, Detroit.

Erickson, M. F., Korfmacher, J., & Egeland, B. R. (1992). Attachments past and present: Implications for therapeutic intervention with mother-infant dyads. *Development and Psychopathology, 4,* 495–507.

Erickson, M. F., Sroufe, L. A., & Egeland, B. (1985). The relationship between quality of attachment and behavior problems in preschool in a high-risk sample. In I. Bretherton & E. Waters (Eds.), Growing points of attachment theory and research. *Monographs of the Society for Research in Child Development, 50* (1–2, Serial No. 209), 147–166.

Erikson, E. H. (1963). *Childhood and society* (2nd ed.). New York: W. H. Norton.

Escher-Gräub, D., & Grossmann, K. E. (1983). *Bindungsunsicherheit im zweiten Lebensjahr—Die Regensburger Querschnittsuntersuchung* [Insecure attachments in the second year—the Regensburg cross-sectional study]. Unpublished research report, Universität Regensburg, Regensburg, Germany.

Etaugh, C. (1981). Effects of nonmaternal care on children: Research evidence and popular views. *Annual Progress in Child Psychiatry and Child Development,* 392–411.

Fagot, B., & Kavanaugh, K. (1990). The prediction of antisocial behavior from avoidant attachment classifications. *Child Development, 61,* 864–873.

Farran, D. C., & Ramey, C. T. (1977). Infant day care and attachment behavior towards mothers and teachers. *Child Development, 48,* 112–116.

Feeney, J. A., & Noller, P. (1990). Attachment style as a predictor of adult romantic relationships. *Journal of Personality and Social Psychology, 58,* 281–291.

REFERENCES

Feeney, J. A., & Noller, P. (1991). Attachment style and verbal descriptions of romantic partners. *Journal of Social and Personal Relationships, 8,* 187–215.

Feldman, S. S., & Ingham, M. E. (1975). Attachment behavior: A validation study in two age groups. *Child Development, 46,* 319–330.

Field, T. (1987). Interaction and attachment in normal and atypical infants. *Journal of Consulting and Clinical Psychology, 55,* 853–859.

Field, T., Masi, W., Goldstein, S., Perry, S., & Parl, S. (1988). Infant day care facilitates preschool social behavior. *Early Childhood Research Quarterly, 3,* 341–359.

Fonagy, P., Steele, H., & Steele, M. (1991). Maternal representations of attachment during pregnancy predict the organization of infant-mother attachment at 1 year of age. *Child Development, 62,* 891–905.

Fox, N. A. (1992). Frontal brain asymmetry and vulnerability to stress: Individual differences in infant temperament. In T. Field, P. McCabe, & N. Schneiderman (Eds.), *Stress and coping in infancy and childhood* (pp. 83–100). Hillsdale, NJ: Lawrence Erlbaum Associates.

Fox, N. (1977). Attachment of kibbutz infants to mother and metapelet. *Child Development, 48,* 1228–1239.

Fox, N. A., Kimmerly, N. L., & Schafer, W. D. (1991). Attachment to mother/attachment to father: A meta-analysis. *Child Development, 62,* 210–225.

Fraiberg, S. (1982). Pathological defenses in infancy. *Psychoanalytic Quarterly, 51,* 612–634.

Fraiberg, S., Adelson, E., & Shapiro, V. (1975). Ghosts in the nursery. A psychoanalytic approach to the problems of impaired infant-mother relationships. *Journal of the American Academy of Child Psychiatry, 14,* 387–422.

Frankel, K. A., & Bates, J. E. (1990). Mother-toddler problem solving: Antecedents in attachment, home behavior, and temperament. *Child Development, 61,* 810–819.

Frodi, A., Bridges, L., & Grolnick, W. (1985). Correlates of mastery-related behavior: A short-term longitudinal study of infants in their second year. *Child Development, 56,* 1291–1298.

Frodi, A., Bridges, L., & Shonk, S. (1989). Maternal correlates of infant temperament ratings and of infant-mother attachment: A longitudinal study. *Infant Mental Health Journal, 10,* 273–289.

Frodi, A., Lamb, M., Hwang, C., & Frodi, M. (1983). Father-mother-infant interaction in traditional and nontraditional Swedish families: A longitudinal study. *Alternative Lifestyles, 5,* 142–163.

Frodi, A., & Thompson, R. (1985). Infants' affective responses in the Strange Situation: Effects of prematurity and of quality of attachment. *Child Development, 56,* 1280–1290.

Gaensbauer, T. J., and Harmon, R. J. (1982). Attachment behavior in abused/neglected and premature infants: Implications for the concept of attachment. In R. N. Emde & R. J. Harmon (Eds.), *Attachment and affiliative systems: Neurobiological and psychobiological aspects.* New York: Plenum Press.

Gaensbauer, T. J., Harmon, R. J., Culp, A. M., Schultz, L. A., van Doornick, W. J., & Dawson, P. (1985). Relationships between attachment behavior in the laboratory and the caretaking environment. *Infant Behavior and Development, 8,* 355–369.

Gamble, T. J., & Zigler, E. (1986). Effects of infant day care: Another look at the evidence. *American Journal of Orthopsychiatry, 56,* 26–42.

Gardner, W., Lamb, M. E., Thompson, R. A., & Sagi, A. (1986). On individual differences in Strange Situation behavior: Categorical and continuous measurement systems in a cross-cultural data set. *Infant Behavior and Development, 9,* 355–375.

Gelfand, D. M., & Teti, D. M. (1990). The effects of maternal depression on children. *Clinical Psychology Review, 10,* 329–353.

George, C., Kaplan, N., & Main, M. (1985). *The adult attachment interview.* Unpublished manuscript, Department of Psychology, University of California at Berkeley.

Ginsberg, H., & Opper, S. (1969). *Piaget's theory of intellectual development: An introduction.* Englewood Cliffs, NJ: Prentice-Hall.

Goldberg, S. (1990). Attachment in infants at risk: Theory, research, and practice. *Infants and Young Children, 2,* 11–20.

Goldberg, S., Perrotta, M., Minde, K., & Corter, C. (1986). Maternal behavior and attachment in low birthweight twins and singletons. *Child Development, 57,* 34–46.

Goldberg, S., Simmons, R. J., Newman, J., Campbell, K., & Fowler, R. S. (1991). Congenital heart disease, parental stress, and infant-mother relationships. *Journal of Pediatrics, 119,* 661–666.

Goldberg, W. A., & Easterbrooks, M. A. (1984). The role of marital quality in toddler development. *Developmental Psychology, 20,* 504–514.

Goldfarb, W. (1955). Emotional and intellectual consequences of psychological deprivation in infancy: A revaluation. In P. H. Hock & J. Zubin (Eds.), *Psychopathology of childhood.* New York: Grune and Stratton.

Goldsmith, H. H., & Alansky, J. A. (1987). Maternal and infant temperamental predictors of attachment: A meta-analytic review. *Journal of Consulting and Clinical Psychology, 55,* 805–816.

Goldsmith, H. H., Bradshaw, D. L., & Reiser-Danner, L. A. (1986). Temperament as a potential developmental influence on attachment. In J. V. Lerner & R. M. Lerner (Eds.)., *Temperament and social interaction during infancy and childhood* (pp. 5–34). San Francisco: Jossey-Bass.

Goossens, F. A., & Van IJzendoorn, M. H. (1990). Quality of infants' attachments to professional caregivers: Relation to infant-parent attachment and day-care characteristics. *Child Development, 61,* 832–837.

Goossens, F. A., Van IJzendoorn, M. H., Tavecchio, L. W., & Kroonenberg, P. M. (1986). Stability of attachment across time and context in a Dutch sample. *Psychological Reports, 58,* 23–32.

Greenberg, M. T., & Marvin, R. S. (1979). Attachment patterns in profoundly deaf preschool children. *Merrill-Palmer Quarterly, 25,* 265–279.

Greenberg, M. T., Siegel, J. M., & Leitch, C. J. (1983). The nature and importance of attachment relationships to parents and peers during adolescence. *Journal of Youth and Adolescence, 12,* 373–386.

Greenberg, M. T., & Speltz, M. L. (1988). Attachment and the ontogeny of conduct problems. In J. Belsky & T. Nezworski (Eds.), *Clinical implications of attachment* (pp. 177–218). Hillsdale, NJ: Lawrence Erlbaum Associates.

Greenspan, S. I. (1981). *Psychopathology and adaptation in infancy and early childhood: Principles of clinical diagnosis and preventive intervention.* New York: International Universities Press.

Greenspan, S. I., & Lieberman, A. F. (1988). A clinical approach to attachment. In J. Belsky & T. Nezworski (Eds.), *Clinical implications of attachment.* Hillsdale, NJ: Lawrence Erlbaum Associates.

Grossmann, K., Grossman, K. E., Spangler, G., Suess, G., & Unzner, L. (1985). Maternal sensitivity and newborns' orientation responses as related to quality of attachment in northern Germany. In I. Bretherton & E. Waters (Eds.), Growing points of attachment theory and research. *Monographs of the Society for Research in Child Development, 50* (1–2, Serial No. 209), 233–257.

Grossmann, K. E., & Grossmann, K. (1990). The wider concept of attachment in cross-cultural research. *Human Development, 33,* 31–47.

Grossmann, K. E., & Grossmann, K. (1991). Attachment quality as an organizer of emotional and behavioral responses in a longitudinal perspective. In C. M. Parkes, J. Stevenson-Hinde, & P. Marris (Eds.), *Attachment across the life cycle* (pp. 93–114). London: Tavistock/Routledge.

Grossmann, K. E., Grossmann, K., Huber, F., & Wartner, U. (1981). German children's behavior towards their mothers at 12 months and their fathers at 18 months in Ainsworth's Strange Situation. *International Journal of Behavioral Development, 4,* 157–181.

Grossmann, K. E., Grossmann, K., & Schwan, A. (1986). Capturing the wider view of attachment: A reanalysis of Ainsworth's Strange Situation. In C. E. Izard & P. B. Read (Eds.), *Measuring emotions in infants and children 2* (pp. 124–171). New York: Cambridge University Press.

Haft, W. L., & Slade, A. (1989). Affect attunement and maternal attachment: A pilot study. *Infant Mental Health Journal, 10,* 157–172.

Hansburg, H. G. (1972). *Adolescent separation anxiety: A method for the study of adolescent separation problems.* Springfield, IL: Thomas.

Harlow, H. F. (1958). The nature of love. *American Psychologist, 13,* 673–685.

Harlow, H. F., & Harlow, M. K. (1965). The affectional systems. In A. M. Schrier, H. F. Harlow, & F. Stollnitz (Eds.), *Behavior of nonhuman primates,* (Vol. 2). New York: Academic Press.

Harmon, R. J. (1981). Perinatal influences on the family: Some preventive implications. *Journal of Preventive Psychiatry, 1,* 132–139.

Harmon, R. J., Stall, P. J., Emde, R. N., Siegel, C., Kempe, R. S., Margolin, M. H., McGehee, R., & Frederick, S. R. (1990). Unresolved grief: A two-year-old brings her mother for treatment. *Infant Mental Health Journal, 11,* 97–112.

Harmon, R. J., Suwalsky, J. D., & Klein, R. P. (1979). Infants' preferential response for mother versus an unfamiliar adult. *Journal of the Academy of Child Psychiatry, 18,* 437–449.

Harris, E. S., Weston, D. R., & Lieberman, A. F. (1989). Quality of mother-infant attachment and pediatric health care use. *Pediatrics, 84,* 248–254.

Harwood, R. L. (1992). The influence of culturally derived values on Anglo and Puerto Rican mothers' perceptions of attachment behavior. *Child Development, 63,* 822–839.

Hazan, C., & Shaver, P. (1987). Romantic love conceptualized as an attachment process. *Journal of Personality and Social Psychology, 52,* 511–524.

Hazan, C., & Shaver, P. R. (1990). Love and work: An attachment-theoretical perspective. *Journal of Personality and Social Psychology, 59,* 270–280.

Heinicke, C., & Westheimer, I. (1966). *Brief separations.* New York: International Universities Press.

Hetherington, E. M., Cox, M., & Cox, R. (1977). The aftermath of divorce. In J. H. Stevens, Jr., & M. Matthews (Eds)., *Mother-child, father-child relations.* Washington, DC: NAEYC.

Hinde, R. A. (1974). *Biological bases of human social behavior.* New York: McGraw-Hill.

Hinde, R. A. (1982). Attachment: Some conceptual and biological issues. In C. Parkes & J. Stevenson-Hinde (Eds.), *The place of attachment in human behavior.* New York: Basic Books.

Hinde, R. A., & Stevenson-Hinde, J. (1990). Attachment: Biological, cultural and individual desiderata. *Human Development, 33,* 62–72.

Hinde, R. A., & Stevenson-Hinde, J. (1991). Perspectives on attachment. In C. M. Parkes, J. Stevenson-Hinde, & P. Marris (Eds.), *Attachment across the life cycle* (pp. 52–65). London: Routledge.

Hojat, M. (1982). Loneliness as a function of parent-child and peer relations. *Journal of Psychology, 112,* 129–133.

Howes, C. (1990). Can the age of entry into child care and the quality of child care predict adjustment in kindergarten? *Developmental Psychology, 26,* 292–303.

Howes, C., & Hamilton, C. E. (1992a). Children's relationships with caregivers: Mothers and child care teachers. *Child Development, 63,* 859–866.

Howes, C., & Hamilton, C. E. (1992b). Children's relationships with child care teachers: Stability and concordance with parental attachments. *Child Development, 63,* 867–878.

Howes, C. & Rodning, C. (1992). Attachment security and social pretend play negotiation. In C. Howes, O. A. Unger, & C. C. Matheson (Eds.), *The collaborative construction of pretend: Social pretend play functions: SUNY series. Children's play in society.* Albany: State University of New York Press.

Howes, C., Rodning, C., Galluzzo, D. C., & Myers, L. (1988). Attachment and child care: Relationships with mother and caregiver. *Early Childhood Research Quarterly, 3,* 403–416.

Howes, P., & Markman, H. J. (1989). Marital quality and child functioning: A longitudinal investigation. *Child Development, 60,* 1044–1051.

Hubbard, F. O. A., & Van IJzendoorn, M. H. (1987). Maternal unresponsiveness and infant crying. A critical replication of the Bell and Ainsworth study. In L. W. C. Tavecchio & M. H. Van IJzendoorn (Eds.), *Attachment in social networks* (pp. 339–375). Holland: Elsevier Science Publishers B. V.

Isabella, R. A. (1993). Origins of attachment: Maternal interactive behavior across the first year. *Child Development, 64,* 605–621.

Isabella, R. A., & Belsky, J. (1991). Interactional synchrony and the origins of infant-mother attachment: A replication study. *Child Development, 62,* 373–384.

Izard, C. E., Simons, R. F., Haynes, O. M., Hyde, C., Parisi, M., Porges, S. W., & Cohen, B. (1991). Infant cardiac activity: Developmental changes and relations with attachment. *Developmental Psychology, 27,* 432–439.

REFERENCES

Jacobson, J. L., & Wille, D. E. (1986). The influence of attachment pattern on developmental changes in peer interaction from the toddler to the preschool period. *Child Development, 57,* 338–347.

Jacobson, S. W., & Frye, K. F. (1991). Effect of maternal social support on attachment: Experimental evidence. *Child Development, 62,* 572–582.

Jarvis, P. A., & Creasey, G. L. (1991). Parental stress, coping, and attachment in families with an 18-month-old infant. *Infant Behavior and Development, 14,* 383–395.

Jean-Gilles, M., & Crittenden, P. M. (1990). Maltreating families: A look at siblings. *Family Relations, 39,* 323–329.

Joffe, L. (1981, April). *The quality of mother-infant attachment and its relationship to compliance with maternal commands and prohibitions.* Paper presented at the biennial meeting of the Society for Research in Child Development, Boston.

Jolly, A. (1972). *The evolution of primate behavior.* New York: Macmillan.

Kaffman, M., Elizur, E., & Sivan-Sher, A. (1984). Personal choices of kibbutz children in simulated situations of distress and joy. Special issue: Family psychiatry in the kibbutz. *International Journal of Family Therapy, 6,* 284–297.

Kagan, J. (1982). *Psychological research on the human infant: An evaluative summary.* New York: W. T. Grant Foundation.

Kalish, R. A., & Knudtson, F. W. (1976). Attachment versus disengagement: A life-span conceptualization. *Human Development, 19,* 171–181.

Keelan, J. P. R., Dion, K. L., & Dion, K. K. (1994). Attachment style and heterosexual relationships among young adults: A short-term panel study. *Journal of Social and Personal Relationships, 11,* 201–214.

Kermoian, R., & Leiderman, P. H. (1986). Infant attachment to mother and child caretaker in an East African community. *International Journal of Behavioral Development, 9,* 455–469.

Kerns, K. A. (1994). A longitudinal examination of links between mother-child attachment and children's friendships in early childhood. *Journal of Social and Personal Relationships, 11,* 379–381.

Kirkpatrick, L. A., & Davis, K. E. (1994). Attachment style, gender, and relationship stability: A longitudinal analysis. *Journal of Personality and Social Psychology, 66,* 502–512.

Klagsbrun, M., & Bowlby, J. (1976). Responses to separation from parents: A clinical test for young children. *British Journal of Projective Psychology, 21,* 7–21.

Kobak, R. (1989). *The Attachment Interview Q-Set.* Unpublished manuscript, University of Delaware, Newark.

Kobak, R., & Cole, H. (1994). Attachment and meta-monitoring: Implications for adolescent autonomy and psychopathology. In D. Cicchetti & S. L. Toth (Eds.), *Rochester Symposium on Developmental Psychopathology: Vol. 5. Disorders and Dysfunctions of the Self* (pp. 267–297). Rochester, NY: University of Rochester Press.

Kobak, R. R., & Hazen, C. (1991). Attachment in marriage: The effects of security and accuracy of working models. *Journal of Personality and Social Psychology, 60,* 861–869.

Kobak, R. R., & Sceery, A. (1988). Attachment in late adolescence: Working models, affect regulation, and representations of self and others. *Child Development, 59,* 135–146.

Konner, M. J. (1972). Aspects of the developmental ethology of a foraging people. In N. B. Jones (Ed)., *Ethological studies of child behaviour* (pp. 285–304). Cambridge: Cambridge University Press.

Kotelchuck, M. (1972). *The nature of the child's tie to his father.* Unpublished doctoral thesis, Harvard University.

Kotelchuck, M. (1976). The infant's relationship to the father: Experimental evidence. In M. E. Lamb (Ed)., *The role of the father in child development.* New York: Wiley.

Kotler, T., & Omodei, M. (1988). Attachment and emotional health: A life span approach. *Human Relations, 41,* 619–640.

Lamb, M. E. (1978). The father's role in the infant's social world. In J. H. Stevens & M. Matthews (Eds.), *Mother/child, father/child relations.* Washington, DC: National Association for the Education of Young Children.

Lamb, M. E., & Bornstein, M. H. (1987). *Development in infancy: An introduction.* New York: Random House.

Lamb, M. E., Hopps, K., & Elster, A. B. (1987). Strange Situation behavior of infants with adolescent mothers. *Infant Behavior and Development, 10,* 39–48.

Lamb, M. E., Hwang, C., Frodi, A. M., & Frodi, M. (1982). Security of mother- and father-infant attachment and its relation to sociability with strangers in traditional and nontraditional Swedish families. *Infant Behavior and Development, 5,* 355–367.

Lamb, M. E., Sternberg, K., & Prodromidis, M. (1992). Nonmaternal care and the security of infant-mother attachment: A reanalysis of the data. *Infant Behavior and Development, 15,* 71–83.

Lamb, M. E., & Stevenson, M. B. (1978). Father-infant relationships: Their nature and importance. *Youth and Society, 9,* 277–298.

Lamb, M. E., Thompson, R. A., Gardner, W. P., & Charnov, E. L. (Eds.). (1985). *Infant-mother attachment.* Hillsdale, NJ: Lawrence Erlbaum Associates.

Landau, R. (1989). Affect and attachment: Kissing, hugging, and patting as attachment behaviors. *Infant Mental Health Journal, 10,* 59–69.

Lederberg, A. R., & Mobley, C. E. (1990). The effect of hearing impairment on the quality of attachment and mother-toddler interaction. *Child Development, 61,* 1596–1604.

Levine, L. V., Tuber, S. B., Slade, A., & Ward, M. J. (1991). Mothers' mental representations and their relationship to mother-infant attachment. *Bulletin of the Menninger Clinic, 55,* 454–469.

Levine, R. A., & Miller, P. M. (1990). Commentary. *Human Development, 33,* 73–80.

Levitt, M. J. (1991). Attachment and close relationships: A life-span perspective. In J. L. Gewirtz & W. M. Kurtines (Eds.), *Intersections with attachment* (pp. 183–205). Hillsdale, NJ: Lawrence Erlbaum Associates.

Levitt, M. J., Weber, R. A., & Clark, M. C. (1986). Social network relationships as sources of maternal support and well-being. *Developmental Psychology, 22,* 310–316.

Lewis, M., Feiring, C., McGuffog, C., & Jaskir, J. (1984). Predicting psychopathology in 6-year-olds from early social relations. *Child Development, 55,* 123–136.

Lewis, J. M., Owen, M. T., & Cox, M. J. (1988). The transition to parenthood: III. Incorporation of the child into the family. *Family Process, 27,* 411–421.

Lewis, M., & Weinraub, M. (1974). Sex of parent × sex of child: Socioemotional development. In R. Richart, R. Friedman, & R. van de Wiele (Eds.), *Sex differences in behavior.* New York: Wiley.

Lieberman, A. F. (1985). Infant mental health: A model for service delivery. *Journal of Clinical Child Psychology, 14,* 196–201.

Lieberman, A. F. (1990). Culturally sensitive intervention with children and families. *Child and Adolescent Social Work, 7,* 101–120.

Lieberman, A. F. (1991). Attachment theory and infant-parent psychotherapy: Some conceptual, clinical and research considerations. In D. Cicchetti & S. Toth (Eds.), *Rochester Symposium on Development Psychopathology: Vol. 3. Models and integrations* (pp. 261–287). Rochester, NY: University of Rochester Press.

Lieberman, A. F., & Pawl, J. H. (1984). Searching for the best interests of the child: Intervention with an abusive mother and her toddler. *Psychoanalytic Study of the Child, 39,* 527–548.

Lieberman, A. F., & Pawl, J. H. (1988). Clinical applications of attachment theory. In J. Belsky & T. Nezworski (Eds.), *Clinical implications of attachment* (pp. 327–351). Hillsdale, NJ: Lawrence Erlbaum Associates.

Lieberman, A. F., Weston, D. R., & Pawl, J. H. (1991). Preventive intervention and outcome with anxiously attached dyads. *Child Development, 62,* 199–209.

Liederman, P. H., & Liederman, G. T. (1973). Affective and cognitive consequences of polymatric infant care in the East African highlands. In A. D. Pick (Ed.), *Minnesota Symposia on Child Psychology, Vol. 8.* Minneapolis: University of Minnesota Press.

Lipson-Parra, H. (1989). Development and validation of the adult attachment scale: Assessing attachment in elderly adults. *Issues in Mental Health Nursing, 11,* 85–98.

Londerville, S., & Main, M. (1981). Security of attachment, compliance, and maternal training methods in the second year of life. *Developmental Psychology, 17,* 289–299.

Lütkenhaus, P., Grossman, K. E., & Grossman, K. (1985). Infant-mother attachment at 12 months and style of interaction with a stranger at the age of 3 years. *Child Development, 56,* 1538–1542.

Lyons-Ruth, K. (1988, April). *Maternal depression and infant disturbance.* Paper presented at the International Conference on Infant Studies, Washington, DC.

Lyons-Ruth, K. (1991). Rapprochement or approchement: Mahler's theory reconsidered from the vantage point of recent research on early attachment relationships. *Psychoanalytic Psychology, 8,* 1–23.

Lyons-Ruth, K., Alpern, L., & Repacholi, B. (1993). Disorganized infant attachment classification and maternal psychosocial problems as predictors of hostile-aggressive behavior in the preschool classroom. *Child Development, 64,* 572–585.

Lyons-Ruth, K., Connell, D. B., Gruenbaum, H. U., & Botein, S. (1990). Infants at social risk: Maternal depression and family support services as mediators of infant development and security of attachment. *Child Development, 61,* 85–98.

Lyons-Ruth, K., Connell, D. B., Gruenbaum, H., Botein, S., & Zoll, D. (1984). Maternal family history, maternal caretaking, and infant attachment in multiproblem families. *Journal of Preventive Psychiatry, 2,* 403–425.

Lyons-Ruth, K., Connell, D. B., Zoll, D., & Stahl, J. (1987). Infants at social risk: Relations among infant maltreatment, maternal behavior, and infant attachment behavior. *Developmental Psychology, 23,* 223–233.

Maccoby, E., & Jacklin, C. N. (1974). *The psychology of sex differences.* Stanford, CA: Stanford University Press.

Macey, T. J., Harmon, R. J., & Easterbrooks, M. A. (1987). Impact of premature birth on the development of the infant in the family. *Journal of Consulting and Clinical Psychology, 55,* 846–852.

Main, M. (1981). Avoidance in the service of attachment: A working paper. In K. Immelman, G. Barlow, M. Main, & L. Petrinovitch (Eds.), *Behavioral development: The Bielefeld interdisciplinary project* (pp. 651–693). New York: Cambridge University Press.

Main, M. (1990). Cross-cultural studies of attachment organization: Recent studies, changing methodologies, and the concept of conditional strategies. *Human Development, 33,* 48–61.

Main, M. (1991). Metacognitive knowledge, metacognitive monitoring, and singular (coherent) versus multiple (incoherent) models of attachment. Findings and directions for future research. In C. M. Parkes, J. Stevenson-Hinde, & P. Marris (Eds.), *Attachment across the life cycle* (pp. 127–159). London: Routledge.

Main, M., & Cassidy, J. (1987). *Assessment of child-parent attachment at 6 years of age.* Unpublished scoring manual, Department of Psychology, University of California, Berkeley.

Main, M., & Cassidy, J. (1988). Categories of response to reunion with the parent at age 6: Predictable from infant attachment classifications and stable over a 1-month period. *Developmental Psychology, 24,* 415–426.

Main, M., & Goldwyn, R. (1984). Predicting rejection of her infant from mother's representation of her own experiences: A preliminary report. *International Journal of Child Abuse and Neglect, 8,* 203–217.

Main, M., & Goldwyn, R. (1985). *Adult attachment classification and rating system.* Unpublished manuscript, University of California, Berkeley.

Main, M., & Hesse, E. (1990). Lack of resolution of mourning in adulthood and its relationship to infant disorganization: Some speculations regarding causal mechanisms. In M. Greenberg, D. Cicchetti, and E. M. Cummings (Eds.), *Attachment in the preschool years: Theory, research, and intervention.* (pp. 161–184). Chicago: University of Chicago Press.

Main, M., Kaplan, N., & Cassidy, J. (1985). Security in infancy, childhood, and adulthood: A move to the level of representation. In I. Bretherton & E. Waters (Eds.), Growing points in attachment theory and research. *Monographs of the Society for Research in Child Development, 50,* 66–104.

Main, M., & Solomon, J. (1986). Discovery of an insecure-disorganized/disoriented attachment pattern: Procedures, findings and implications for the classification of behavior. In T. B. Brazelton & M. Yogman (Eds.), *Affective development in infancy* (pp. 95–124). Norwood, NJ: Ablex.

REFERENCES

Main, M., & Solomon, J. (1990). Procedures for identifying infants as disorganized/disoriented during the Ainsworth Strange Situation. In M. Greenberg, D. Cicchetti, & M. Cummings (Eds.), *Attachment in the preschool years: Theory, research, and intervention* (pp. 121–160). Chicago: University of Chicago Press.

Main, M., Tomasini, L., & Tolan, W. (1979). Differences among mothers of infants judged to differ in security. *Developmental Psychology, 15,* 472–473.

Main, M., & Weston, D. (1981). The quality of the toddler's relationship to mother and father: Related to conflict behavior and readiness to establish new relationships. *Child Development, 52,* 932–940.

Malatesta, C. Z., Culver, C., Tesman, J. R., & Shepard, B. (1989). The development of emotion expression during the first 2 years of life. *Monographs of the Society for Research in Child Development, 54* (1–2, Serial No. 219).

Mangelsdorf, S., Gunnar, M., Kestenbaum, R., Lang, S., & Andreas, D. (1990). Infant proneness-to-distress temperament, maternal personality, and mother-infant attachment: Associations and goodness of fit. *Child Development, 61,* 820–831.

Marcus, R. F. (1990). The parent/child reunion inventory: A measure of attachment for children beyond the infancy years. *Psychological Reports, 67,* 1329–1330.

Marcus, R. F. (1991). The attachments of children in foster care. *Genetic, Social, and General Psychology Monographs, 117,* 365–394.

Marvin, R. S. (1977). An ethological-cognitive model for the attenuation of mother-child attachment behavior. In T. Alloway, L. Krames, & P. Pliner (Eds.), *Attachment behavior.* New York: Plenum Press.

Marvin, R. S., & Stewart, R. B. (1990). A family systems framework for the study of attachment. In M. Greenberg, D. Cicchetti, & E. M. Cummings (Eds.), *Attachment in the preschool years: Theory, research, and intervention.* Chicago: University of Chicago Press.

Marvin, R. S., VanDevender, T. L., Iwanaga, M. I., LeVine, S., & LeVine, R. A. (1977). Infant-caregiver attachment among the Hausa of Nigeria. In H. M. McGurk (Ed.), *Ecological factors in human development* (pp. 247–260). Amsterdam: North Holland Publishing.

Maslin, C., & Bates, E. (1983). *Precursors of anxious and secure attachments: A multivariate model at age 6 months.* Paper presented at the biennial meeting of the Society for Research in Child Development, Detroit.

Matas, L., Arend, R. A., & Sroufe, L. A. (1978). Continuity of adaptation in the second year: The relationship between quality of attachment and later competence. *Child Development, 49,* 547–556.

McCartney, K., & Galanopoulos, A. (1988). Child care and attachment: A new frontier the second time around. *American Journal of Orthopsychiatry, 58,* 16–24.

Miyake, K., Chen, S., & Campos, J. J. (1985). Infant temperament, mother's mode of interaction, and attachment in Japan: An interim report. In I. Bretherton & E. Waters (Eds.), Growing points of attachment theory and research. *Monographs of the Society for Research in Child Development, 50,* 276–297.

Mizukami, K., Kobayashi, N., Ishii, T., & Iwata, H. (1990). First selective attachment begins in early infancy: A study using telethermography. *Infant Behavior and Development, 13,* 257–271.

Morelli, G. A., Rogoff, B., Oppenheim, D., & Goldsmith, D. (1992). Cultural variation in infants' sleeping arrangements: Questions of independence. *Developmental Psychology, 28,* 604–613.

Morelli, G. A., & Tronick, E. Z. (1991). Efe multiple caretaking and attachment. In J. L. Gewirtz & W. M. Kurtines (Eds.), *Intersections with attachment* (pp. 41–51). Hillsdale, NJ: Lawrence Erlbaum Associates.

Nakagawa, M., Lamb, M. E., & Miyake, K. (1989). Psychological experiences of Japanese infants in the Strange Situation. *Research and Clinical Center for Child Development Annual Report, 11,* 87–88.

Näslund, B., Persson-Blennow, I., McNeil, T. F., Kaij, L., & Malmquist-Larsson, A. (1984). Deviations on exploration, attachment and fear of strangers in high-risk and control infants at 1 year of age. *American Journal of Orthopsychiatry, 54,* 569–577.

Nezworski, T., Tolan, W. J., & Belsky, J. (1988). Intervention in insecure infant attachment. In J. Belsky & T. Nezworski (Eds.), *Clinical implications of attachment* (pp. 352–386). Hillsdale, NJ: Lawrence Erlbaum Associates.

O'Conner, M. J., Sigman, M., & Brill, N. (1987). Disorganization of attachment in relation to maternal alcohol consumption. *Journal of Consulting and Clinical Psychology, 55,* 831–836.

O'Conner, M. J., Sigman, M., & Kasari, C. (1992). Attachment behavior of infants exposed prenatally to alcohol: Mediating effects of infant affect and mother-infant interaction. *Developmental Psychopathology, 4,* 243–256.

Oppenheim, D., Sagi, A., and Lamb, M. E. (1988). Infant-adult attachments on the kibbutz and their relation to socioemotional development 4 years later. *Developmental Psychology, 24,* 427–433.

Owen, M. T., & Chase-Lansdale, L. (1982, April). *Similarity between infant-mother and infant-father attachments.* Paper presented at the biennial meeting of the Southwestern Society for Research in Human Development, Galveston, TX.

Owen, M. T., & Cox, M. J. (1988). Maternal employment and the transition to parenthood. In A. E. Gottfried & A. W. Gottfried (Eds.), *Maternal employment and children's development: Longitudinal research* (pp. 85–119). New York: Plenum Press.

Owen, M. T., Easterbrooks, M. A., Chase-Lansdale, L., & Goldberg, W. A. (1984). The relation between maternal employment status and the stability of attachments to mother and father. *Child Development, 55,* 1894–1901.

Park, K. A., & Waters, E. (1989). Security of attachment and preschool friendships. *Child Development, 60,* 1076–1081.

Parkes, C. M. (1972). *Bereavement: Studies of grief in adult life.* London: Tavistock Publications.

Parkes, C. M. (1991). Attachment, bonding, and psychiatric problems after bereavement in adult life. In C. M. Parkes, J. Stevenson-Hinde, & P. Marris (Eds.), *Attachment across the life cycle* (pp. 268–292). London: Routledge.

Parkes, C. M., & Weiss, R. S. (1983). *Recovery from bereavement.* New York: Basic Books, and London: Harper and Row.

Pastor, D. L. (1981). The quality of mother-infant attachment and its relationship to toddler's initial sociability with peers. *Developmental Psychology, 17,* 326–335.

Patterson, G. R. (1976). The aggressive child: Victim and architect of a coercive system. In L. A. Hamerlynk, L. C. Handy, & E. J. Marsh (Eds)., *Behavior modification and families: Vol. I. Theory and research* (pp. 267–316). New York: Brunner-Mazel.

Patterson, G. R. (1991). Antisocial parents: Unskilled and vulnerable. In P. A. Cowan & E. M. Hetherington (Eds)., *Family transitions. Advances in family research series* (pp. 195–218). Hillsdale, NJ: Lawrence Erlbaum Associates.

Pederson, D. R., & Moran, G. (in press). A categorical description of attachment relationships in the home and its relation to Q-sort measures of infant attachment security and maternal sensitivity. In E. Waters & B. Vaughn (Eds.), *Patterns of secure base behavior: Q-sort perspectives on attachment and caregiving in infancy and childhood.* Hillsdale, NJ: Lawrence Erlbaum Associates.

Pederson, D. R., Moran, G., Sitko, C., Campbell, K., Ghesquire, K., & Acton, H. (1990). Maternal sensitivity and the security of infant-mother attachment: A Q-sort study. *Child Development, 61,* 1974–1983.

Pederson, F. A., & Robson, K. S. (1969). Father participation in infancy. *American Journal of Orthopsychiatry, 39,* 466–472.

Piaget, J. (1952). *The origins of intelligence in children.* New York: International Universities Press.

Piaget, J. (1970). Piaget's theory. In P. H. Mussen (Ed.), *Carmichael's manual of child psychology.* New York: Wiley.

Pianta, R. C., Sroufe, L. A., & Egeland, B. (1989). Continuity and discontinuity in maternal sensitivity at 6, 24, and 42 months in a high-risk sample. *Child Development, 60,* 481–487.

Pierrehumbert, B., Iannotti, R. J., & Cummings, E. M. (1985). Mother-infant attachment, development of social competencies and beliefs of self-responsibility. *Archives de Psychologie, 53,* 365–374.

Pierrehumbert, B., Iannotti, R. J., Cummings, E. M., & Zahn-Waxler, C. (1989). Social functioning with mother and peers at 2 and 5 years: The influence of attachment. *International Journal of Behavioral Development, 12,* 85–100.

Pipp, S., Easterbrooks, M. A., & Harmon, R. J. (1992). The relation between attachment and knowledge of self and mother in 1- to 3-year-old infants. *Child Development, 63,* 738–750.

Plunkett, J. W., Meisels, S. J., Steifel, G. S., Pasick, P. L., & Roloff, D. W. (1986). Patterns of attachment among preterm infants of varying biological risk. *Journal of the American Academy of Child Psychiatry, 25,* 794–800.

Radke-Yarrow, M., Cummings, E. M., Kuczynski, L., & Chapman, M. (1985). Patterns of attachment in 2- and 3-year-olds in normal families and families with parental depression. *Child Development, 56,* 884–893.

Renkin, B., Egeland, B., Marvinney, D., Sroufe, L. A., & Mangelsdorf, S. (1989). Early childhood antecedents of aggression and passive withdrawal in early elementary school. *Journal of Personality, 57,* 257–282.

Rheingold, H., & Eckerman, C. (1970). The infant separates himself from his mother. *Science, 168,* 78–83.

Richters, J. E. (1988). The infant day care controversy: Current status and future directions. *Early Childhood Research Quarterly, 3,* 319–336.

Richters, J. E., Waters, E., & Vaughn, B. E. (1988). Empirical classification of infant-mother relationships from interactive behavior and crying during reunion. *Child Development, 59,* 512–522.

Ricks, M. H. (1985). The social transmission of parental behavior: Attachment across generations. In I. Bretherton & E. Waters (Eds.), Growing points of attachment theory and research. *Monographs of the Society for Research in Child Development, 50* (1–2, Serial No. 209), 211–227.

Robertson, J., & Robertson, J. (1971). Young children in brief separation: A fresh look. *Psychoanalytic Study of the Child, 26,* 264–315.

Rodning, C., Beckwith, L., & Howard, J. (1989). Characteristics of attachment organization and play organization in prenatally drug-exposed toddlers. *Development and Psychopathology, 1,* 277–289.

Rodning, C., Beckwith, L., & Howard, J. (1991). Quality of attachment and home environments in children prenatally exposed to PCP and cocaine. *Development and Psychopathology, 3,* 351–366.

Roe, K. V., Roe, A., Drivas, A., & Bronstein, R. (1990). A curvilinear relationship between maternal vocal stimulation and 3-month-olds' cognitive processing: A cross-cultural phenomenon. *Infant Mental Health Journal, 11,* 175–189.

Roggman, L. A., Langlois, J. H., Hubbs-Tait, L., & Rieser-Danner, L. A. (1994). Infant day-care, attachment, and the "file drawer problem." *Child Development, 65,* 1429–1443.

Rosenblatt, J. S. (1969). The development of maternal responsiveness in the rat. *American Journal of Orthopsychiatry, 39* (1), 36–56.

Rutter, M. (1985). Resilience in the face of adversity: Protective factors and resistance to psychiatric disorder. *British Journal of Psychiatry, 147,* 598–611.

Sable, P. (1989). Attachment, anxiety, and loss of a husband. *American Journal of Orthopsychiatry, 59,* 550–556.

Sagi, A. (1990). Attachment theory and research from a cross-cultural perspective. *Human Development, 33,* 10–22.

Sagi, A., Lamb, M. E., & Gardner, W. (1986). Relations between Strange Situation behavior and stranger sociability among infants on Israeli kibbutzim. *Infant Behavior and Development, 9,* 271–282.

Sagi, A., Lamb, M. E., Lewkowicz, K. S., Shoham, R., Dvir, R., & Estes, D. (1985). Security of infant-mother, -father, and -metapelet attachments among kibbutz-reared Israeli children. In I. Bretherton & E. Waters (Eds.), Growing points of attachment theory and research. *Monographs of the Society for Research in Child Development, 50* (1–2, Serial No. 209), 257–275.

Sagi, A., Van IJzendoorn, M. H., Aviezer, O., Donnell, F., & Mayseless, O. (1994). Sleeping out of home in a kibbutz communal arrangement: It makes a difference for infant-mother attachment. *Child Development, 65,* 992–1004.

Schachere, K. (1990). Attachment between working mothers and their infants: The influences of family processes. *American Journal of Orthopsychiatry, 60,* 19–34.

Schaffer, H. R., & Emerson, P. E. (1964). The development of social attachments in infancy. *Monographs of the Society for Research in Child Development, 29* (3, Serial No. 94).

Schank, R. C. (1982). *Dynamic memory: A theory of reminding and learning in computers and people.* Cambridge: Cambridge University Press.

REFERENCES

Schneider-Rosen, K., Braunwald, K., Carlson, V., & Cicchetti, D. (1985). Current perspectives in attachment theory: Illustration from the study of maltreated infants. In I. Bretherton & E. Waters (Eds.), Growing points in attachment theory and research. *Monographs of the Society for Research in Child Development, 50* (1–2, Serial No. 209), 194–210.

Schneider-Rosen, K., & Cicchetti, D. (1984). The relationship between affect and cognition in maltreated infants: Quality of attachment and the development of visual self-recognition. *Child Development, 55,* 648–658.

Seifer, R., Sameroff, A. J., Barrett, L. C., & Krafchuk, E. (1994). Infant temperament measured by multiple observations and mother report. *Child Development, 65,* 1478–1490.

Senchak, M., & Leonard, K. E. (1992). Attachment styles and marital adjustment among newlywed couples. *Journal of Social and Personal Relationships, 9,* 51–64.

Shaver, P., & Hazan, C. (1987). Being lonely, falling in love: Perspectives from attachment theory. Special issue: Loneliness: Theory, research, and applications. *Journal of Social Behavior and Personality, 2,* 105–124.

Shaver, P., Hazan, C., & Bradshaw, D. (1987). Love as attachment: The integration of three behavioral systems. In R. J. Sternberg & M. Barnes (Eds)., *The psychology of love.* New Haven, CT: Yale University Press.

Shaver, P., & Rubenstein, C. (1980). Childhood attachment experience and adult loneliness. In L. Wheeler (Ed.), *Review of personality and social psychology, 1* (pp. 42–73). Beverly Hills, CA: Sage Publications.

Shouldice, A., & Stevenson-Hinde, J. (1992). Coping with security distress: The separation anxiety test and attachment classification at 4.5 years. *Journal of Child Psychology and Psychiatry, 33,* 331–348.

Simpson, J. A. (1990). Influence of attachment styles on romantic relationships. *Journal of Personality and Social Psychology, 59,* 971–980.

Simpson, J. A., Rholes, W. S., & Nelligan, J. S. (1992). Support seeking and support giving within couples in an anxiety-provoking situation: The role of attachment styles. *Journal of Personality and Social Psychology, 62,* 434–446.

Slade, A. (1987). Quality of attachment and early symbolic play. *Developmental Psychology, 23,* 78–85.

Smith, P. B., & Pederson, D. R. (1988). Maternal sensitivity and patterns of infant-mother attachment. *Child Development, 59,* 1097–1101.

Smith, P. K. (1980). Shared care of young children: Alternative models to monotropism. *Merrill-Palmer Quarterly, 26,* 371–389.

Spangler, G., & Grossman, K. E. (1993). Biobehavioral organization in securely and insecurely attached infants. *Child Development, 64,* 1439–1450.

Spanier, G. B. (1976). Measuring dyadic adjustment: New scales for assessing the quality of marriage and similar dyads. *Journal of Sex and Marital Therapy, 5,* 15–28.

Speltz, M., Greenberg, M. T., & DeKlyn, M. (1990). Attachment in preschoolers with disruptive behavior: A comparison of clinic-referred and nonproblem children. *Development and Psychopathology, 2,* 31–46.

Spencer-Booth, Y., & Hinde, R. A. (1967). The effects of separating rhesus monkey infants from their mothers for 6 days. *Journal of Child Psychology and Psychiatry, 7,* 179–197.

Spencer-Booth, Y. & Hinde, R. A. (1971). The effects of 13 days' maternal separation on infant rhesus monkeys compared with those of shorter and repeated separations. *Animal Behavior, 19,* 595–605.

Spieker, S. J., & Booth, C. L. (1988). Maternal antecedents of attachment quality. In J. Belsky & T. Nezworski (Eds.), *Clinical implications of attachment.* Hillsdale, NJ: Lawrence Erlbaum Associates.

Spitz, R. A. (1945). Hospitalism: An inquiry into the genesis of psychiatric conditions in early childhood. *Psychoanalytic Study of the Child, 1,* 53–74.

Sroufe, L. A. (1979). The coherence of individual development. *American Psychologist, 34,* 834–841.

Sroufe, L. A. (1983). Infant-caregiver attachment and patterns of adaptation in preschool: The roots of maladaptation and competence. In M. Perlmutter (Ed.), *Minnesota Symposium in Child Psychology, 16,* 41–81.

Sroufe, L. A. (1986). Appraisal: Bowlby's contribution to psychoanalytic theory and developmental psychology—attachment, separation, loss. [Special issue: 30th anniversary of the Association for Child Psychology and Psychiatry and Allied Disciplines]. *Journal of Child Psychology and Psychiatry and Allied Disciplines, 27,* 841–849.

Sroufe, L. A. (1988a). A developmental perspective on day care. *Early Childhood Research Quarterly, 3,* 283–291.

Sroufe, L. A. (1988b). The role of infant-caregiver attachment in development. In J. Belsky & T. Nezworski (Eds.), *Clinical implications of attachment.* Hillsdale, NJ: Lawrence Erlbaum Associates.

Sroufe, L. A. (1990, Autumn). The role of training in attachment assessment. *Society for Research in Child Development Newsletter,* 1–2.

Sroufe, L. A., Egeland, B., & Kreutzer, T. (1990). The fate of early experience following developmental change: Longitudinal approaches to individual adaptation in childhood. *Child Development, 61,* 1363–1374.

Sroufe, L. A., Fox, N. E., & Pancake, V. R. (1983). Attachment and dependency in developmental perspective. *Child Development, 54,* 1615–1627.

Sroufe, L. A., & Rutter, M. (1984). The domain of developmental psychopathology. *Child Development, 55,* 17–29.

Sroufe, L. A., & Waters, E. (1977a). Attachment as an organizational construct. *Child Development, 48,* 1184–1199.

Sroufe, L. A., & Waters, E. (1977b). Heart rate as a convergent measure in clinical and developmental research. *Merrill-Palmer Quarterly, 23,* 3–27.

Sroufe, L. A., & Waters, E. (1982). Issues of temperament and attachment. *American Journal of Orthopsychiatry, 52,* 743–746.

Stevenson-Hinde, J. (1991). Temperament and attachment: An eclectic approach. In P. Bateson (Ed.), *The development and integration of behaviour: Essays in honour of Robert Hinde.* Cambridge: Cambridge University Press.

Stewart, R. B., & Marvin, R. S. (1984). Sibling relations: The role of conceptual perspective-taking in the ontogeny of sibling caregiving. *Child Development, 55,* 1322–1332.

Suomi, S. J. (1983). Models of depression in primates. *Psychological Medicine.* 465–468.

Suwalsky, J. T., Klein, R. P., Zaslow, M. J., Rabinovich, B. A., & Gist, N. S. (1987). Dimensions of naturally occurring mother-infant separations during the first year of life. *Infant Mental Health Journal, 8,* 3–18.

Takahashi, K. (1986). Examining the Strange-Situation procedure with Japanese mothers and 12-month-old infants. *Developmental Psychology, 22,* 265–270.

Takahashi, K. (1990). Are the key assumptions of the "Strange Situation" procedure universal? A view from Japanese research. *Human Development, 33,* 23–30.

Teti, D. M., & Ablard, K. E. (1989). Security of attachment and infant-sibling relationships: A laboratory study. *Child Development, 60,* 1519–1528.

Teti, D. M., & Gelfand, D. M. (1991). Behavioral competence among mothers of infants in the first year: The mediational role of maternal self-efficacy. *Child Development, 62,* 918–929.

Teti, D. M., Nakagawa, M., Das, R., & Wirth, O. (1991). Security of attachment between preschoolers and their mothers: Relations among social interaction, parenting stress, and mothers' sorts of the Attachment Q-Set. *Developmental Psychology, 27,* 440–447.

Thompson, R. A. (1988). The effects of infant day care through the prism of attachment theory: A critical appraisal. *Early Childhood Research Quarterly, 3,* 273–282.

Thompson, R. A., & Lamb, M. E. (1983). Security of attachment and stranger sociability in infancy. *Child Development, 19,* 184–191.

Thompson, R. A., Lamb, M. E., & Estes, D. (1982). Stability of infant-mother attachment and its relationship to changing life circumstances in an unselected middle-class sample. *Child Development, 53,* 144–148.

Tizard, B., & Hodges, J. (1978). The effect of early institutional rearing on the development of 8-year-old children. *Journal of Child Psychology and Psychiatry, 19,* 99–118.

Tizard, B., & Rees, J. (1975). The effects of early institutional rearing on the behaviour problems and affectional relationships of 4-year-old children. *Journal of Child Psychology and Psychiatry, 16,* 61–73.

Tronick, E. Z., Morelli, G. A., & Ivey, P. K. (1992). The Efe forager infant and toddler's pattern of social relationships: Multiple and simultaneous. *Developmental Psychology, 28,* 568–577.

Troy, M., & Sroufe, L. A. (1987). Victimization among preschoolers: Role of attachment relationship history. *Journal of American Academy of Child and Adolescent Psychiatry, 26,* 166–172.

Tulving, E. (1972). Episodic and semantic memory. In E. Tulving & W. Donaldson (Eds.)., *Organization of memory* (pp. 382–403). New York: Academic Press.

Tulving, E. (1985). How many memory systems are there? *American Psychologist, 40,* 385–398.

Turner, P. J. (1991). Relations between attachment, gender, and behavior with peers in preschool. *Child Development, 62,* 1475–1488.

Urban, J., Carlson, E., Egeland, B., & Sroufe, L. A. (1992). Patterns of individual adaptation across childhood. *Development and Psychopathology, 3,* 446–460.

Van Dam, M., & Van IJzendoorn, M. H. (1988). Measuring attachment security: Concurrent and predictive validity of the parental attachment Q-set. *Journal of Genetic Psychology, 149,* 447–457.

Van den Boom, D. (1990). Preventive intervention and the quality of mother-infant interaction and infant exploration in irritable infants. In W. Koops, H. J. G. Soppe, J. L. van der Linden, P. C. M. Molenaar, & J. J. F. Schroots (Eds.), *Developmental psychology behind the dikes: An outline of developmental psychological research in the Netherlands.* Delft, Netherlands: Uitgeverij Eburon.

Van den Daele, L. (1986). Homeostasis and attachment: An integration of classical and object relational approaches to the good-enough mother. *American Journal of Psychoanalysis, 46,* 203–218.

Van IJzendoorn, M. H. (1986). The cross-cultural validity of the strange situation from a Vygotskian perspective. *Behavioral and Brain Sciences, 9,* 558–559.

Van IJzendoorn, M. H. (1990). Developments in cross-cultural research on attachment: Some methodological notes. *Human Development, 33,* 3–9.

Van IJzendoorn, M. H., Goldberg, S., Kroonenberg, P. M., & Frenkel, O. J. (1992). The relative effects of maternal and child problems on the quality of attachment: A meta-analysis of attachment in clinical samples. *Child Development, 63,* 840–858.

Van IJzendoorn, M. H., Goossens, F. A., Kroonenberg, P. M., & Tavecchio, L. W. (1985). Dependent attachment: B-4 children in the Strange Situation. *Psychological Reports, 57,* 439–451.

Van IJzendoorn, M. H., & Kroonenberg, P. M. (1988). Cross-cultural patterns of attachment: A meta-analysis of the Strange Situation. *Child Development, 59,* 147–156.

Van IJzendoorn, M. H., & Kroonenberg, P. M. (1990). Cross-cultural consistency of coding the Strange Situation. *Infant Behavior and Development, 13,* 469–485.

Van IJzendoorn, M. H., Sagi, A., & Lambermon, M. W. E. (in press). The multiple caretaker paradox: Some data from Holland and Israel. In R. C. Pianta (Ed.), Relationships between children and non-parental adults. *New directions in child development.* San Francisco: Jossey-Bass.

Van IJzendoorn, M. H., van der Veer, R., & van Vliet-Visser, S. (1987). Attachment 3 years later: Relationships between quality of mother-infant attachment and emotional/cognitive development in kindergarten. In L. W. C. Tavecchio & M. H. Van IJzendoorn (Eds.), *Attachment in social networks* (pp. 185–223). North-Holland: Elsevier Science Publishers B. V.

Van Lawick-Goodall, J. (1968). The behavior of free-living chimpanzees in the Gombe Steam Reserve. *Animal Behavior Monographs, 1,* 161–311.

Vandell, D. L., Owen, M. E., Wilson, K. S., & Henderson, V. K. (1988). Social development in infant twins: Peer and mother-child relationships. *Child Development, 59,* 168–177.

Valenzuela, M. (1990). Attachment in chronically underweight young children. *Child Development, 61,* 1984–1996.

Vaughn, B., Gove, F. L., & Egeland, B. (1980). The relationship between out-of-home care and the quality of infant-mother attachment in an economically disadvantaged population. *Child Development, 51,* 971–975.

Vaughn, B. E., Joffe, L. S., Bradley, C. F., Seifer, R., & Barglow, P. (1987). Maternal characteristics measured prenatally are predictive of ratings of temperamental "difficulty" on the Carey Infant Temperament Questionnaire. *Developmental Psychology, 23,* 152-161.

REFERENCES

Vaughn, B. E., Lefever, G. B., Seifer, R., & Barglow, P. (1989). Attachment behavior, attachment security, and temperament during infancy. *Child Development, 60,* 728–737.

Vaughn, B. E., Stevenson-Hinde, J., Waters, E., Kotsaftis, A., Lefever, G. B., Shouldice, A., Trudel, M., & Belsky, J. (1992). Attachment security and temperament in infancy and early childhood: Some conceptual clarifications. *Developmental Psychology, 28,* 463–473.

Vaughn, B. E., & Waters, E. (1990). Attachment behavior at home and in the laboratory: Q-sort observations and Strange Situation classifications of 1-year-olds. *Child Development, 61,* 1965–1973.

Volling, B. L., & Belsky, J. (1992). The contribution of mother-child and father-child relationships to the quality of sibling interaction: A longitudinal study. *Child Development, 63,* 1209–1222.

Vygotsky, L. S. (1978). *Mind and society.* Cambridge: Harvard University Press.

Wallerstein, J. S., & Kelly, J. B. (1977). Divorce counseling: A community service for families in the midst of divorce. *American Journal of Orthopsychiatry, 47,* 4–22.

Ward, M. J., & Carlson, E. A. (1995). Associations among adult attachment representations, maternal sensitivity, and infant-mother attachment in a sample of adolescent mothers. *Child Development, 66,* 69–79.

Ward, M. J., Vaughn, B. E., & Robb, M. D. (1988). Social-emotional adaptation and infant-mother attachment in siblings: Role of the mother in cross-sibling consistency. *Child Development, 59,* 643–651.

Wartner, V. G. (1986). *Attachment in infancy and at age 6, and children's self-concept: A follow-up of a German longitudinal study.* Unpublished doctoral dissertation, University of Virginia, Charlottesville.

Waters, E. (1978). The reliability and stability of individual differences in infant-mother attachment. *Child Development, 49,* 483–494.

Waters, E., & Deane, K. E. (1985). Defining and assessing individual differences in attachment relationships: Q-methodology and the organization of behavior in infancy and early childhood. In I. Bretherton & E. Waters (Eds.), Growing points of attachment theory and research. *Monographs of the Society for Research in Child Development, 50* (1–2, Serial No. 209), 41–65.

Waters, E., Merrick, S., Albersheim, L., Treboux, & Crowell, J. (1995). Attachment from infancy to early adulthood: A 20-year longitudinal study of relations between infant Strange Situation classifications and attachment representations in adulthood. Paper presented at the biennial meeting of the Society for Research in Child Development, Indianapolis.

Waters, E., & Vaughn, B. (Eds.). (in press). *Patterns of secure base behavior: Q-sort perspectives on attachment and caregiving in infancy and childhood.* Hillsdale, NJ: Lawrence Erlbaum Associates.

Waters, E., Vaughn, B., Posada, G., & Kondo-Ikemura, K. (Eds.). (in press). Caregiving, cultural, and cognitive perspectives on secure base behavior and working models: New growing points in attachment research. *Monographs of the Society for Research in Child Development.*

Waters, E., Wippman, J., & Sroufe, L. A. (1979). Attachment, positive affect, and competence in the peer group: Two studies in construct validation. *Child Development, 50,* 821–829.

Weiss, R. S. (1973). *Loneliness: The experience of social and emotional isolation.* Cambridge: MIT Press.

Weiss, R. S. (1975). *Marital separation.* New York: Basic Books.

Weiss, R. S. (1982). Attachment in adult life. In C. Parkes & J. Stevenson-Hinde (Eds.), *The place of attachment in human behavior* (pp. 171–184). New York: Basic Books.

Weiss, R. S. (1987). Reflections on the present state of loneliness research. In M. Hojat & R. Crandall (Eds)., *Loneliness: Theory, research and applications* (pp. 1–16).

Weiss, R. S. (1991). The attachment bond in childhood and adulthood. In C. M. Parkes, J. Stevenson-Hinde, & P. Marris (Eds.), *Attachment across the life cycle* (pp. 66–76). London: Routledge.

Werner, H. (1940/1980). *Comparative psychology of mental development* (3rd ed.). New York: International Universities Press.

West, M. M., & Konner, M. J. (1976). The role of the father: An anthropological perspective. In M. Lamb (Ed.), *The role of the father in child development.* New York: Wiley.

Wille, D. E. (1991). Relation of preterm birth with quality of infant-mother attachment at 1 year. *Infant Behavior and Development, 14,* 227–240.

Willemsen, E., Flaherty, D., Heaton, C., & Ritchey, G. (1974). Attachment behavior of 1-year-olds as a function of mother versus father, sex of child, session, and toys. *Genetic Psychology Monographs, 90,* 305–324.

Yarrow, L. J. (1964). Separation from parents during early childhood. In M. L. Hoffman & L. W. Hoffman (Eds.), *Review of child development research* (Vol. 1, pp. 89–136). New York: Russell Sage Foundation.

Youngblade, L. M., & Belsky, J. (1992). Parent-child antecedents of 5-year-olds' close friendships: A longitudinal analysis. *Developmental Psychology, 28,* 700–713.

Zasloff, R. L., & Kidd, A. H. (1994). Attachment to feline companions. *Psychological Reports, 74,* 747–752.

Zaslow, M. J., Rabinovich, B. A., Suwalsky, J. T. D., & Klein, R. P. (1988). The role of social context in the prediction of secure and insecure/avoidant infant-mother attachment. *Journal of Applied Developmental Psychology, 9,* 287–299.

Zeanah, C. H., & Zeanah, P. D. (1989). Intergenerational transmission of maltreatment: Insights from attachment theory and research. *Psychiatry, 52,* 177–196.

NAME INDEX

NAME INDEX

SUBJECT INDEX

among children, 261–262
(*See also* Resistant attachment)
Anger, directed, 234, 242
Anxious attachment:
among adolescents, 298
among adults, 18
bereavement and, 336–339
divorce/separation and, 339–341
among elderly adults, 303, 318, 342–343
among infants and children
adaptiveness of, 161–165
alcohol use by caregiver and, 101–102
attachment network and, 197
behavior problems and, 278–283
blaming caregiver for, 122–123
Bloomington study on, 84
cognitive development and, 136–138
correlates/sequelae of, 131–141,
274–283, 286–287
as disorder, 199
drug use during pregnancy and, 101–102
economic status and, 101
family relationships correlated with,
138–141, 275
father-infant, 170, 174, 175, 179
among Ganda in Uganda, 33
hired caregiver-infant, 187–192
intervention with (*see* Intervention)
marital adjustment and, 119–120
maternal employment and, 179–184
mental illness in caregiver and, 97, 100
personality of caregiver and, 100
among premature infants, 115–116
presence of partner of caregiver and, 118,
129
psychopathology correlated to, 22–24,
279–283
representational models and, 220
sensitive responsiveness and, 84, 90–91
story completion classification of, 258
stress on caregiver and, 106, 129
teacher-child interaction and, 131–132
(*See also* Avoidant attachment;
Disorganized-disoriented attachment;
Resistant attachment)
Apprehensive attachment, definition of, 48
Assimilation, and representational models,
20
Attachment, characteristics and definition of,
7
Attachment, development of:
in childhood
defensive exclusion and, 225–226

developmental changes and, 230–237
goal-corrected partnership, 17, 72,
221–224, 233, 266
information processing and, 226–229
memory and, 226–231
among preschool children, 239–244
psychopathological effects on, 224–225,
246–247
among school-age children, 244–246
working models, 239–246
in infancy, 67–75
attachment-in-the-making phase, 69–70
clear-cut-attachment phase, 71–72
disorders of, 74
among Ganda in Uganda, 34, 67
institutionalization and, 73
phases described, 67–72
preattachment phase, 67–69
reflexive behaviors and, 68–69
separation from mother and, 70–71
Attachment behaviors:
activation of, 9–11, 34
attachment hierarchies and, 193–197
biological function of, 8, 161–163
caregiver personality and, 96–100
characteristics summarized, 7–8
definition of, 7
demographic factors and, 100–101
disorders of, 74, 198–199, 211–212
distal attachment, 107, 110, 157–158
drug use during pregnancy and, 101–102
and early experience, 15–16
goal-corrected, 8–9, 17, 18, 71, 72,
221–224, 233, 266
interaction with other behavioral systems,
12–13
motivation for, 11
personality of caregiver and, 96–100
proximal attachment, 107, 110, 157
termination of, 9–11, 34
(*See also* Attachment patterns; Attachment
theory; Correlates and sequelae of
attachment; *specific attachment patterns*)
Attachment figure, definition of, 7, 294–295
Attachment hierarchies, 16–17, 193–197
Attachment-in-the-making phase, 69–70
Attachment network, 196–197
Attachment patterns:
attachment hierarchies and, 193–197
distribution of
among adolescents, 323
in contrasting cultures, 152–156
of father-infant patterns, 170

SUBJECT INDEX